Strategies for Reading Assessment and Instruction

Helping Every Child Succeed

Third Edition

D. Ray Reutzel
Utah State University

Robert B. Cooter, Jr.
University of Memphis

PEARSON
Merrill
Prentice Hall

Upper Saddle River, New Jersey
Columbus, Ohio

KH

Library of Congress Cataloging-in-Publication Data

Reutzel, D. Ray (Douglas Ray),
    Strategies for reading assessment and instruction : helping every child succeed / D. Ray Reutzel, Robert B. Cooter, Jr.—3rd ed.
        p. cm.
    Includes bibliographical references and index.
    ISBN 0-13-172145-3
    1. Reading. 2. Reading—Remedial teaching. 3. Child development. I. Cooter, Robert B. II. Title.

LB1050. R477 2007
372.43—dc22   2006043333

Vice President and Executive Publisher: Jeffery W. Johnston
Senior Editor: Linda Ashe Bishop
Senior Production Editor: Mary M. Irvin
Design Coordinator: Diane C. Lorenzo
Senior Editorial Assistant: Laura Weaver
Text Design and Production Coordination: Carlisle Publishing Services
Cover Designer: Terry Rohrbach
Cover Art: Linda Sorrells Smith
Production Manager: Pamela D. Bennett
Director of Marketing: David Gesell
Marketing Manager: Darey Betts Prybella
Marketing Coordinator: Brian Mounts

This book was set in 10/12 Souvenir by Carlisle Publishing Services and was printed and bound by Hamilton Printing Company. The cover was printed by Coral Graphics.

Photo Credits: Barbara Matthews/Dallas Independent School District, p. 9; Anthony Magnacca/Merrill, p. 91; D. Ray Reutzel, pp. 94, 95; Scott Cunningham/Merrill, p. 166; Robert B. Cooter, Jr., p. 333.

Pearson Education Ltd.   Pearson Education Australia PTY, Limited
Pearson Education Singapore, Pte. Ltd.   Pearson Education North Asia Ltd.
Pearson Education Canada, Ltd.   Pearson Educación de Mexico, S.A. de C.V.
Pearson Education—Japan   Pearson Education Malaysia, Pte. Ltd.

10 9 8 7 6 5 4 3 2 1
ISBN: 0-13-172145-3

8/22/06

For my companion and sweetheart of over 31 years, Pam; my wonderful five children and their spouses; my five grandsons and soon-to-be granddaughter; and my wonderful teacher colleagues; many thanks for making life and learning an everlasting joy!

I am also extremely grateful to the Emma Eccles Jones Foundation for its continuing support of my work in the *Emma Eccles Jones Early Childhood Education Center.*
    —D R R

For Kathy, and in memory of her mom, Therese Spencer.
    —R B C

About the Authors

D. Ray Reutzel

D. Ray Reutzel is currently the Emma Eccles Jones Endowed Chair and Distinguished Professor of Early Childhood Education and Director of the *Emma Eccles Jones Center for Early Childhood Education* at Utah State University. Ray regularly works with teachers and children in local public schools especially those schools that are academic risk. He is a former Provost and Vice President for Academic Affairs at Southern Utah University; Associate Dean of Teacher Education in the David O. McKay School of Education; and former Chair of the Department of Elementary Education at Brigham Young University. While at BYU, he was the recipient of the 1992 Karl G. Maeser Distinguished Research Professor Award. Several years ago, he took a leave from his university faculty position to return to full-time, first-grade classroom teaching in Sage Creek Elementary School to pilot comprehensive balanced reading practices. Ray has taught in Kindergarten, 1st grade, 3rd grade, and 6th grade.

Dr. Reutzel is the author of more than 150 articles, books, book chapters, and monographs. Ray has published in *Reading Research Quarterly, Journal of Reading Behavior, Journal of Literacy Research, Early Childhood Research Quarterly, Journal of Educational Research, Reading Psychology, Reading and Writing Quarterly, Reading Research and Instruction, Language Arts, Journal of Reading,* and *The Reading Teacher, Instructor,* among others. He is the past Editor of *Reading Research and Instruction,* and co-author of the best selling college textbook *Teaching Children to Read: Putting the Pieces Together 4th Edition,* and *Strategies for Reading Assessment and Instruction: Helping Every Child Succeed,* both published by Merrill/Prentice Hall. He has also co-authored the book, *Your Classroom Library,* with Parker C. Fawson published by Scholastic Professional Books. He is or has been a reviewer for *The Reading Teacher, Reading Research Quarterly, Reading Psychology, Reading Research and Instruction, The Journal of Reading Behavior, Journal of Literacy Research,* and *The Elementary School Journal.* He is also an author of Scholastic Incorporated's *Literacy Place* 1996 & 2000® school reading program. Dr. Reutzel received the A.B. Herr Award for Outstanding Research and Published Contributions to Reading Education from the College Reading Association in 1999. Dr. Reutzel is currently with his colleague, Judith P. Mitchell, co-editor of the International Reading Association's elementary section journal—*The Reading Teacher.* He is also Principal Investigator on an *Institute of Education Sciences* research grant (U.S. Department of Education) investigating the relationship of teacher literacy instructional knowledge and children's literacy achievement in grades 1–3.

Robert B. Cooter, Jr.

Dr. Robert B. Cooter, Jr. is Professor of Urban Literacy & Reading Education in the Department of Instruction and Curriculum Leadership at The University of Memphis. His primary research focus pertains to *research-based reading instruction for children living at the poverty level* in grades PK–12. In fall of 2007, Robert Cooter and his colleague J. Helen Perkins become the editors of *The Reading Teacher* for the International Reading Association; *The Reading Teacher* has the largest readership of any literacy journal in the world. Cooter has taught grades 1, 3, 4, 7, 11, and 12 in the public schools, and also served as a Title I reading specialist in Tennessee, Ohio, and Texas.

Prior to coming to Memphis, Professor Cooter served as the first "Reading Czar" (or Associate Superintendent for PK–12 Reading/Language Arts) for the Dallas Independent School District (TX). Robert engineered the district's highly acclaimed *Dallas Reading Plan,* a collaborative project supported by Dallas area business and community enterprises involving the training of approximately 3,000 teachers in "comprehensive literacy instruction" with an annual budget of some $15 million. In March of 1998, Dr. Cooter was recognized as a "Texas State Champion for Reading" by then-Governor George W. Bush and Texas First Lady Laura Bush as a result of the many successes of the Dallas Reading Plan initiative.

More recently, Cooter founded *The Memphis Literacy Academy,* an outreach program with Memphis City Schools dedicated to raising the expertise and effectiveness of hundreds of teachers of reading in kindergarten through third grade and special education, as well as principals serving those schools as "literacy leaders." He is also project director of the *Memphis Content Literacy Academy,* a $16 million middle school research project funded under a major grant by the U.S. Department of Education.

Cooter has authored or co-authored numerous professional books including the best-selling *Teaching Children to Read: Putting the Pieces Together, 4th ed.* (Merrill/Prentice Hall), a scientifically-based reading research (SBRR) text currently used at over 200 universities to prepare elementary teachers; *Perspectives on Rescuing Urban Literacy Education: Spies, Saboteurs, & Saints* (Lawrence Erlbaum Associates), *The Flynt/Cooter Reading Inventory for the Classroom* (Merrill/Prentice-Hall), *The Flynt/Cooter English-Español Reading Inventory* (Merrill/Prentice Hall). *The Comprehensive Reading Inventory* (R. Cooter, E.S. Flynt, & K.S. Cooter), a norm-referenced reading assessment tool, is his latest book from Merrill/Prentice Hall.

Professor Cooter has had over 60 articles on reading education published in such journals as *The Reading Teacher, Journal of Reading, Language Arts,* and the *Journal of Educational Research.* Cooter currently contributes a regular column on Urban Literacy Issues for *The Reading Teacher*, a professional journal of the International Reading Association.

A native of Nashville, Tennessee, Robert lives in Memphis with his wife, Dr. Kathleen Spencer Cooter, a popular Special Education professor and researcher at The University of Memphis, and is owned by their two Golden Retrievers, Mitchell and Spencer.

Preface

Teachers and administrators in today's schools need evidence-based information on how to teach children to read. Ripple effects created by the historic *Report of the National Reading Panel* (2000) and the *No Child Left Behind Act* (2002) leave many teachers searching for a kind of "Reading Instruction Desktop Reference" that can help them select valid and reliable assessment and teaching strategies. As we have continued our work in real-world classrooms, especially in high-poverty schools associated with the *Reading First* federally funded projects across the nation, it has become increasingly apparent that children, and the teaching profession itself, can benefit greatly from an evidence-based compendium of reading assessment tools and instructional strategies. Consequently, we have gone to great lengths to provide you with such a comprehensive collection in our third edition of *Strategies for Reading Assessment and Instruction.*

Strategies for Reading Assessment and Instruction, Third Edition, is a ready reference guide to assist real-world classroom teachers in planning effective instruction for *all* students, including those who struggle, in becoming fluent, strategic, and successful readers. Each chapter is self-contained and, starting with Chapter 5, includes these special segments:

- **Brief research updates** that serve as a kind of "executive summary for teachers."

- **Assessment strategies** and tools for determining each child's reading needs and abilities.

- **An Assessment Information Guide** helps teachers understand the purposes served by each assessment: *screening, diagnostic, progress-monitoring* and *outcomes assessment* for each assessment tool in the chapter. Also provides validity and reliability data for each assessment tool where it was available.

- **An "IF–THEN Chart"** for linking assessments findings for each student to the effective, research-based teaching strategies that can help them grow and succeed as readers. In other words, these charts tells us "IF" we find from our assessment a student needs to learn this specific skill, "THEN" these are the strategies supported by research we should consider using. A powerful tool in the reading teacher's toolbox.

- **Highly effective, evidence-based teaching strategies** from classroom and scientifically based reading research (SBRR) on comprehensive reading instruction in such areas as alphabetics (i.e., phonemic awareness, alphabetic principle, phonics), comprehension, fluency, and much more.

- **Special strategies for English Language Learners** (ELL, ESL, bilingual) are included for this growing population.

- **Accommodations for students with special needs.**

FOR THE PRACTICING EDUCATOR

Classroom reading teachers will also discover that *Strategies for Reading Assessment and Instruction,* Third Edition, provides an extensive selection of research-validated practices and assessment tools to (1) inform your daily instruction, (2) meet the needs of individual learners, and (3) develop an understanding of the essentials of comprehensive reading instruction. For those who teach in special education resource rooms, Title 1 reading programs, and university reading clinics, this volume likewise provides a wide-ranging collection of strategies to assist students with special needs.

ADVANTAGES FOR PRESERVICE TEACHERS

For preservice teachers, this third edition of *Strategies for Reading Assessment and Instruction* offers a practical resource for understanding past and present issues in reading instruction and assessment. It also provides ready-to-use assessment tools and related instructional strategies you can use in your field experiences in reading instruction, clinical experiences and student teaching assignments.

AS A TOOL FOR PROFESSIONAL DEVELOPMENT WORKSHOPS

Strategies for Reading Assessment and Instruction is a proven tool for ongoing professional development in this age of evidence-based reading assessment and instruction. This book contains the latest in research on comprehensive reading instruction and highly effective, reliable, valid, and classroom proven assessments and teaching strategies, and presents this information in an easy-to-use format that makes the implementation of effective reading instruction strategies in the classroom quick and easy. In fact, the second edition of *Strategies for Reading Assessment and Instruction* was used as the primary resource in literally thousands of workshop sessions on evidence-based, comprehensive reading instruction across the United States.

ACKNOWLEDGEMENTS

Our most sincere thanks go out to the reviewers of our manuscript for insightful comments: Denise Fleming, California State University, Hayward; Betty Goerss, Indiana University East; and Pamela Luft, Kent State University.

Thank you, too, for choosing this third edition of *Strategies for Reading Assessment and Instruction*. We trust that it will assist you in your efforts to develop reading instruction plans. Please send us your comments and observations about whether we have achieved our aim.

Best wishes as you work to help every child become a successful reader and a personally fulfilled individual.

D. Ray Reutzel
ray.reutzel@usu.edu

Robert B. Cooter, Jr.
rcooter@memphis.edu

Teacher Preparation Classroom

TEACHER PREP

MERRILL
PRENTICE HALL

See a demo at
www.prenhall.com/teacherprep/demo

Your Class. Their Careers. Our Future. Will your students be prepared?

We invite you to explore our new, innovative and engaging website and all that it has to offer you, your course, and tomorrow's educators! Organized around the major courses pre-service teachers take, the Teacher Preparation site provides media, student/teacher artifacts, strategies, research articles, and other resources to equip your students with the quality tools needed to excel in their courses and prepare them for their first classroom.

This ultimate on-line education resource is available at no cost, when packaged with a Merrill text, and will provide you and your students access to:

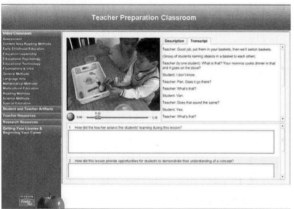

Online Video Library. More than 150 video clips—each tied to a course topic and framed by learning goals and Praxis-type questions—capture real teachers and students working in real classrooms, as well as in-depth interviews with both students and educators.

Student and Teacher Artifacts. More than 200 student and teacher classroom artifacts—each tied to a course topic and framed by learning goals and application questions—provide a wealth of materials and experiences to help make your study to become a professional teacher more concrete and hands-on.

Research Articles. Over 500 articles from ASCD's renowned journal *Educational Leadership*. The site also includes Research Navigator, a searchable database of additional educational journals.

Teaching Strategies. Over 500 strategies and lesson plans for you to use when you become a practicing professional.

Licensure and Career Tools. Resources devoted to helping you pass your licensure exam; learn standards, law, and public policies; plan a teaching portfolio; and succeed in your first year of teaching.

How to ORDER Teacher Prep for you and your students:
For students to receive a *Teacher Prep* Access Code with this text, instructors **must** provide a special value pack ISBN number on their textbook order form. To receive this special ISBN, please email **Merrill.marketing@pearsoned.com** and provide the following information:
* Name and Affiliation
* Author/Title/Edition of Merrill text

Upon ordering *Teacher Prep* for their students, instructors will be given a lifetime *Teacher Prep* Access Code.

Contents

Chapter 8

Phonics and Word Attack Skills   205

Chapter 9

Teaching and Assessing Vocabulary Development   237

Chapter 10

Reading Comprehension: Focus on the Reader   265

Chapter 11

Reading Comprehension: Focus on the Text   313

Chapter 12

Developing Research and Reference Skills   353

Chapter 13

Writing and Reading   379

Chapter 14

Reading Fluency 407

Chapter 15

Engaging in Literature Response 437

SECTION IV GOING BEYOND THE CLASSROOM WALLS

Chapter 16

Getting Families Involved: Helping Parents to Help Their Children 483

Chapter 1

No Child Left Behind: Comprehensive Reading Instruction

Ms. George and Mr. Talango reluctantly seated themselves near the back of the school library. "So, what's on for today?" asked Mr. Talango.

"Oh, I think we're supposed to have a workshop on reading instruction again," replied Ms. George. "I wonder what we'll be told today we've been doing wrong or what we haven't done enough of. Do you know who the presenter will be?"

"I think it's Dr. Reid from the university. She is supposed to really be into this phonemic awareness stuff," Mr. Talango responded. "I've heard her before. I wonder if she's been in a classroom since the Spanish-American War. She always makes it seem as if we have the luxury of focusing on just one thing, mainly reading, to the exclusion of everything else we have to do."

"Yeah, I know how you feel. It seems like when it comes to reading instruction, we are always caught in the middle between what parents want and what the so-called 'experts' tell us we need to be doing."

Ruefully, Ms. George said, "Well, after years of workshops, experts, and fads, I've decided that this too shall pass. So, I guess I'll just keep doing what works for me."

The scenario portrayed in the opening vignette is familiar for many veteran reading teachers. *Strategies for Reading Assessment and Instruction: Helping Every Child Succeed,* third edition, has been developed expressly as a classroom tool for teachers to use who are in need of practical teaching and assessment ideas to complement their existing repertoire of instructional and assessment strategies. It is also for teachers who are weary of the latest and greatest fads and want well-researched and classroom-tested information on how to offer a comprehensive reading program so that all children can succeed.

Beginning in chapter 5, we provide in each chapter a section called "Background Briefing for Teachers," which is a crisp overview of theory and scientific research on the chapter's focus area. Next, we recommend a variety of quick and efficient assessment strategies applicable to that particular area of reading development. For your convenience, we explain how each assessment idea may be used as a *screening, diagnostic, progress-monitoring,* and/or *outcome* assessment according to the *Reading First* and *No Child Left Behind* guidelines.

In this third edition, we have continued our immensely popular "Intervention Strategy Guide," which shows how you can directly link your assessment findings to specific teaching strategies according to each student's need. We call the logic behind our "Intervention

Strategy Guide" *if-then thinking.* In other words, *if* you discover through your assessment strategies that a child is ready to learn a certain reading skill, *then* here are some effective strategies for teaching that skill.

Following the "Intervention Strategy Guide" in each chapter, we offer you a collection of practical teaching strategies that have been validated in research and/or classroom practice. Finally, we explain throughout this book how the strategies offered in each chapter can be adapted to meet the needs of students who struggle with learning to read, as well as students who are English-language learners (ELLs).

It occurs to us that it may be useful for you, our reader, to know what this book is *not* as much as what it is. For instance, this book is not intended to serve as a basic survey or introductory text on comprehensive, evidence-based reading instruction and assessment. Rather, it is a supplemental text for new or experienced teachers who need an extensive collection of classroom-proven assessment and teaching strategies that really work! [*Note:* For those who are just beginning the study of reading/literacy education and require a more complete orientation to the field, we suggest our companion text, *Teaching Children to Read: Putting the Pieces Together,* fourth edition (Reutzel & Cooter, 2004), as a starting point, or one of the other major textbooks used in reading methods courses.] This book is also intended to serve as an advanced professional development resource for practicing teachers providing comprehensive, evidence-based reading assessment and instruction. Finally, this book is also useful as a core text for those preparing to teach reading in school classrooms through alternative licensure or certification routes such as graduate programs that result in the awarding of a teaching credential.

In summary, by using *Strategies for Reading Assessment and Instruction: Helping Every Child Succeed,* third edition, teachers can readily and quickly turn to a chapter that presents current information on ways to assess, teach, and organize for effective and comprehensive reading instruction. Chapters offer practical classroom assessment ideas and a structure for selecting teaching strategies that match student needs. Specifics on teaching oral language, concepts about print, phonemic awareness, phonics, word recognition, fluency, comprehension, vocabulary, and so forth are provided.

In this first chapter, we discuss recent developments in reading education and research that have influenced the direction and nature of contemporary reading instruction. We begin by describing the waning of what has been termed *balanced reading instruction* and why we advocate *comprehensive reading instruction* based on recent research reports on reading instruction. As part of describing the waning of the term *balanced reading instruction,* we briefly discuss the "reading wars" of the late 1990s and early 2000s. Finally, we describe the essential elements of a comprehensive reading program as defined by such documents as *Preventing Reading Difficulties in Young Children* (Snow, Burns, & Griffin, 1998), the *Report of the National Reading Panel* (2000), and *The Voice of Evidence in Reading Research* (McCardle & Chharbra, 2004).

The Reading Wars: A Time of Turmoil in Reading Instruction

In 1994, data from the *National Assessment of Educational Progress* (NAEP) were released showing that fourth-grade students in California and Louisiana were tied for last place among the 50 states in reading achievement. This event led to yet another round of overemphasis on some components of reading instruction at the expense of others (e.g., phonics versus the use of literature books in instruction) (Flippo, 2001; Reutzel & Smith, 2004). Battles between advocates of differing reading instructional approaches, primarily proponents of whole language and skills-based (phonics) approaches, led to what became known as the *reading wars* in the mid-1990s. Don Holdaway (1979), a well-known New Zealand educator, summed up the reading wars in this way:

> America seems to have returned to the crudities of pendulum thinking. Despite the fact that among them are strong voices speaking from a clear vision of what might be, they are stampeded by the recurrent public outcry into a back-to-basics movement without anyone having clarified just what the basics are. (p. 30)

During the mid- to late 1990s, examples of this pendulum thinking could be found almost daily in provocative newspaper headlines, such as "Reading Wars: Endless Squabbles Keep Kids from Getting the Help They Need" (*Chicago Tribune,* Rubin, 1997) and "Lost Generation of Readers Turn to Phonics for Help" (*Atlanta Journal Constitution,* Cumming, 1998). Likewise, some book titles provide evidence of extreme positions taken by some reading educators—see, for example, *Misreading Reading: The Bad Science That Hurts Children* (Coles, 2000); *The Case Against Standardized Testing: Raising the Scores, Ruining the Schools* (Kohn, 2000); and *Why Is Corporate America Bashing Our Public Schools?* (Emery & Ohanian, 2004). Dixie Lee Spiegel (1999) said of the reading wars hyperbole, "Education often appears to be not just a field of dreams, but a field of extremes" (p. 8).

Past reports (see Figure 1.1) indicated stagnating or declining scores in children's reading achievement among specific subgroups (NAEP, 2002). This fact raised frustration levels and concern among parents, politicians, and educators alike. The achievement gap among various subgroups of the childhood population, such as children living at the poverty level in urban centers, seemed to be growing at alarming rates. The widening achievement gap between "the rich and the poor" in reading achievement resulted in yet

 **Figure 1.1** NAEP Chart

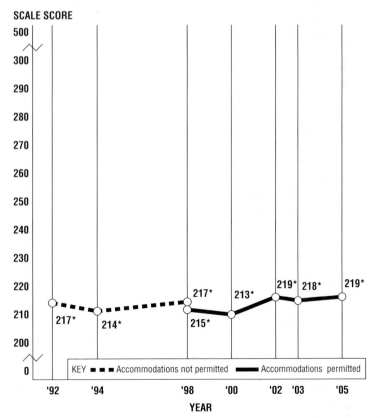

another round of finger pointing and blame placing in the media, political forums, and the education establishment. Making matters worse, the media have often sensationalized the real extent of the reading problem (Berliner & Biddle, 1995; Bracey, 2003); exaggerated the depth of the disagreement among experts (Flippo, 1999, 2001); questioned the competence of teachers, teacher educators, and school administrators; and misrepresented the research.

Former coeditors of *The Reading Teacher*, a journal of the International Reading Association, pronounced the reading wars as an unfruitful exercise that diverted our collective efforts away from the most significant concern: that some children, but most especially large proportions of children living in poverty in urban centers, are failing to read on level by the end of third grade (Rasinski & Padak, 1998). Amid the strident discourse of politicians and reading experts, teachers continue in their steady, unheralded (and, we think, heroic) daily efforts to bring the gift of literacy to increasing numbers of children. But what of the children and teachers who seek genuine support and guidance? Is there no basis for a common understanding of high-quality reading instruction and assessment? Actually, there is.

BALANCED READING INSTRUCTION: ATTEMPTED COMPROMISE, CONFUSED MESSAGE

The balanced reading movement was a much-hoped-for compromise for ending the reading wars. The quest for balanced reading instruction began in 1990 among a small group of educators. They formed an organization to support a moderate, middle-ground position concerning reading instruction and issued a manifesto entitled *Balance: A Manifesto for Balance in the Teaching of Literacy and Language Skills* (Thompson, 1997). Early on, some U.S. schools and districts caught on to the balanced reading movement; but it was not until the results of the 1994 National Assessment of Educational Progress (NAEP) became public in California that the balanced reading movement really took on national momentum.

Bill Honig (1995), then superintendent of public instruction in California, was instrumental in focusing national attention on the deficits of whole language instruction. He contended that whole language instruction was not meeting the needs of diverse students and that what was needed was a more "balanced" instructional approach to reading. Honig's call for "balanced reading" was forcefully captured in the document *Every Child a Reader: Report of the California Reading Task Force*. Other voices of reason and moderation emerged from what became known as the "radical middle" in support of a *balanced reading approach*.

As the national discussion progressed, an important question came into focus: "Balancing what, and by whom?" Some national voices defined *balance* as an approach to reading instruction that brought equilibrium to two opposing views on the teaching of reading: whole language and phonics. What eventually emerged from trying to define *balanced reading instruction* was represented by the image of the "scales of justice." The concept of "balance" then was to *even up* the sides of the scale with equal portions of phonics and whole language on either side, as shown in Figure 1.2 (Baumann, Hoffman, Moon, & Duffy-Hester, 1998; Wharton-McDonald et al., 1997). Soon it became apparent that to define *balanced reading instruction* as an act to even up the sides of the scale invited yet more rounds of this-versus-that thinking.

Others challenged, from a historical viewpoint, that balanced reading instruction was not "new" or in need of redefining at all (Reutzel, 1996a, 1996b, 1999a, 1999b). This

Figure 1.2 Balance As Achieving Instructional Equilibrium

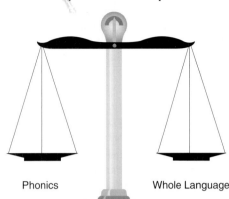

Phonics   Whole Language

opinion held that balanced reading dated back to the popular balanced reading practices of the 1960s in New Zealand, also known as *reading to, with, and by children* (Mooney, 1990; Department of Education, 1985). As far as these reading educators were concerned, *balanced reading* had already been defined and proven effective for many years (Anderson, Hiebert, Scott, & Wilkinson, 1985).

Still others felt that the concept of "balance" represented a philosophy rather than a defined set of practices. Balance was seen as a disciplined form of eclecticism grounded in the judgment and skill of informed teachers (Fitzgerald, 1999; Pearson, 2000; Spiegel, 1999; Strickland, 1998). In some ways this group attempted to describe balance by stating what it was and what it was not. Terms applied to define balanced reading instruction as a philosophy included: *flexible, realistic, decision-making approach, consistency,* and *comprehensive* (Fitzgerald, 1999; Spiegel, 1999).

THE ADVENT OF COMPREHENSIVE READING INSTRUCTION

The difficulty in defining *balanced reading instruction* continued and eventually eroded much of its message and potential. David Pearson, in a presentation made for the Center for the Improvement of Early Reading Achievement (CIERA) in April 2000, stated, "I have stopped using the term 'balanced' because it seems to me that everyone has appropriated it [balance] to describe their highly particular approach. My new term is 'comprehensive.' " This pronouncement was one of many signaling the waning moments of the balanced reading movement. Perhaps the final blow to the balanced reading movement was leveled by Louisa Moats (2000) in a report made to the Fordham Foundation entitled, *Whole Language Lives On: The Illusion of "Balanced" Reading Instruction.* Moats alleged that the term *balance* was nothing more than a cover for continuing the ineffective practices associated with whole language.

We, like others, have abandoned the definitions war associated with the term *balance.* In *Strategies for Reading Assessment and Instruction: Helping Every Child Succeed,* third edition, we describe a comprehensive reading program that is inclusive, is research based, and meets the needs of all learners so that no child is left behind!

WHAT IS A COMPREHENSIVE READING PROGRAM?

To develop a blueprint for a comprehensive reading program, we began our preparation for *Strategies for Reading Assessment and Instruction: Helping Every Child Succeed,* third edition, by conducting a content analysis of the findings and recommendations found in six important national reports and one international report shown in Figure 1.3. After carefully reviewing each of these research reports, we sorted the instructional and programmatic recommendations into seven categories (see Figure 1.4) to help us present to you the elements of a comprehensive reading program.

Comprehensive reading programs are focused on both *programs* and *outcomes.* Comprehensive reading programs are goal driven and results focused. Many reading programs in the past focused so heavily on measuring what goes into a reading program that measuring the results was overlooked or avoided. Reading is a complex human accomplishment and as such is not easily reduced to simplistic measurement. In fact, the extensive contents of this book make clear that reading assessment and instruction are complicated and multifaceted. Comprehensive reading programs:

- Embrace the national goal that 90% of children completing third grade (or 9-year-old children) will read on grade level.

- Recognize the critical role teachers play in helping children achieve their potential as readers.

Figure 1.3   National and International Reading Reports

Flippo, R. F. (2001). *Reading Researchers in Search of Common Ground.* Newark, DE: International Reading Association.

Snow, C. E., Burns, M. S., and Griffin, P. (1998). *Preventing reading difficulties in young children.* Washington, DC: National Academy Press.

Report of the Literacy Taskforce. (1999). Wellington, New Zealand: Ministry of Education.

*Teaching Reading **is** rocket science: What expert teachers of reading should know and be able to do.* (1999). Washington, DC: American Federation of Teachers.

Report of the National Reading Panel: Teaching children to read. (2000). Washington, DC: National Institute of Child Health and Human Development.

Report of the National Education Association's Task Force on Reading 2000. (2000). Washington, DC: National Education Association.

Every Child a Reader. (1998). Ann Arbor, MI: Center for the Improvement of Early Reading Achievement.

McCardle, P., & Chhabra, V. (2004). *The Voice of Evidence in Reading Research,* Baltimore, MD: Paul H. Brookes.

Figure 1.4   Seven Essential Elements of Comprehensive Reading Instruction

Points of Agreement Among National and International Reading Research Reports

Pursuit of a National Goal
School-Home-Community Partnerships
Schoolwide Reforms
Teacher Knowledge
Milestones of Reading Development
Purposeful Assessment
Student Motivation

- Value the role of assessment in informing teachers' instructional choices.
- Support the effective implementation of partnerships among schools, parents, families, communities, corporations, and agencies.
- Identify the best research-based practices associated with comprehensive reading instruction.
- Help students develop reading skills and the love of reading.

When children receive effective, comprehensive reading instruction initially, the educational safety net is spread wide to catch them before they fail. In the pages that follow, we describe in detail the elements of comprehensive reading instruction to help you, the reader, thoughtfully consider how an effective, comprehensive reading program is created and implemented.

PURSUIT OF A NATIONAL GOAL

With shifts in today's employment market away from labor and manufacturing toward service and information jobs, the current importance assigned to literacy skills is amplified. Two presidents, numerous governors and legislators, parents, and educators all agree that a child who does not learn to read and use text-based information has little or no chance to reach his or her potential in society and in the marketplace as an adult. It is rather depressing to note that some states plan for the number of prison beds needed for the future using the numbers of children failing to achieve basic reading proficiency by third grade. Given this grim but realistic predictor, we simply must help all children become fluent, successful readers!

Our national reading goal (Fielding, Kerr, & Rosier, 1998; U.S. Department of Education—Goals 2000) may be stated thus:

> The goal, although seemingly a lofty one, is one worthy of our collective will as a nation. It will take considerable resolve among parents, teachers, administrators, and politicians to see that *no child is left behind* in learning to read competently and successfully—and that *no teacher is left behind* in helping them provide the necessary instruction and learning conditions for achieving this important national goal.

CREATING AND SUSTAINING SCHOOL-HOME-COMMUNITY PARTNERSHIPS

No comprehensive reading program is complete without a school-home-community involvement program that unites our collective efforts to help children succeed in reading. Partnerships with schools, corporations, and government agencies that have coordinated the delivery of reading services to children and their families have increased dramatically in recent years; the *America Reads* school volunteer and tutoring program is a great example. Research on family literacy programs has consistently shown positive results in increasing young children's literacy skills across varying populations (Au, 2000; DeBruin-Parecki & Krol-Sinclair, 2003; Morrow, 1995; Wasik, 2004). In the report, *Beating the Odds in Teaching All Children to Read*, issued by the Center for the Improvement of Early Reading Achievement, Taylor, Pearson, Clark, and Walpole (1999) indicated that one of the chief characteristics associated with the most effective schools "beating the odds" in teaching all children to read was having strong links to parents.

It appears that the media play an increasingly important role in providing support for children's development of reading abilities. For example, Mates and Strommen (1996) described in an article entitled "Why Ernie Can't Read" how the television program *Sesame*

Street failed to help children grasp the "big picture" about reading and learning to read. Ernie, the show's main character, was typically portrayed reading words and identifying letters. He was not shown, however, going to the library or bookstore. Ernie never checked out or purchased a book. He did not read the print in his environment, nor did he read a complete story or text.

On the other hand, Cooter and his colleagues (1999) reported dramatic results in bringing together city and community resources as part of an extensive urban literacy initiative known as the Dallas Reading Plan. Strategies included an annual citywide reading event known as *DEAR Dallas!* (*Deja todo y lee!*), an outreach videotape for parents featuring the PBS wonder dog character *Wishbone*™, and special "reading backpacks" for all K–3 classrooms so that these inner-city students could have books to read at home. Other outreach programs of the Dallas Reading Plan included a summer "food and reading" program cosponsored by area churches (First Lady Laura Bush praised this program as a model for America) and a monthly newsletter for families explaining things they can do at home to support their children as developing readers (called *Refrigerator Reading* because the newsletter could be attached to the family refrigerator). These are just a few of the creative possibilities for bringing together community stakeholders.

In Figure 1.5, we describe several principles for connecting schools and their "communities" in the broadest sense to create collaborative partnerships that serve all children in learning to read successfully (Au, 2000; McGilp & Michael, 1994; Rasinski, 1995; Wasik, Dobbins, & Herrmann, 2001). Observing these principles in creating and sustaining school-home-community partnerships will help to optimize chances for success. All participants must begin with the belief that everyone wants what is best for children.

In chapter 16 of this book, in the section titled "Family and Community Involvement Activities," we provide an expanded look at school-family-community involvement programs including assessment tools, curricula for volunteer training, and effective strategies for creating and sustaining these vitally important partnerships.

Figure 1.5 Principles for Forging Effective School-Home-Community Partnerships for Comprehensive Reading Instruction

Affirm the contributions of all partners to a child's success in learning to read.

Invite partners to make presentations to children on topics in which they have expertise.

Ensure that participation is open to all by providing support for their full access and participation.

Make the programs, training, and discussions enjoyable, efficient, and easy for partners.

Partner involvement needs to be consistent and require commitment.

Time, space, and resources need to be well planned so as not to waste partners' time and efforts.

Provide partners with accessible information about helping children learn to read and write successfully such as "Raising a Reader; Raising a Writer" copublished by the International Reading Association and the National Association for the Education of Young Children or the publication "Starting Out Right" by the National Research Council.

Create a climate of joint ownership or shared venture. People tend to support that which they help to create. Begin with a discussion series with partners to plan the training and program.

Provide effective communication, training, and follow-up between the school and partners. Questions and concerns should be readily addressed and quickly resolved.

Focus on involving partners in real reading and writing with children at home, in the school, through the media, or elsewhere in the community.

Collaborate in the development of a curriculum for training and involvement that is culturally sensitive and respects the multiple literacies found in families of differing backgrounds.

A literacy materials center

SCHOOLWIDE READING PROGRAM REFORMS

Schoolwide practices are important in a comprehensive reading program; they constitute the environment in which teachers teach and children learn. Most reports on school reform call for increasing resources, providing substantial professional development for teachers, and providing committed leadership.

Access to Print

Access to print has been shown to be a critical element influencing children's reading development and achievement (Neuman, 1999; Neuman & Celano, 2001). In the document, *Every Child a Reader: Report of the California Reading Task Force* (Honig, 1995), it was recommended that every classroom have a classroom library of at least 300 books with 1,500 books recommended as the desired collection size. A classroom library collection should contain a wide variety of reading levels and text types. The problem with this recommendation is that most school districts simply do not have the funds to create such libraries in every classroom.

An alternative to establishing classroom libraries is to create well-stocked **literacy materials centers** in each school. These are rooms containing multiple copies of leveled books, big books, and other necessary "tools" of reading instruction set aside solely for teachers to check out for their classroom instruction. Literacy materials centers begin with all reading instruction materials in the school that were purchased with school district resources being collected, sorted, and cataloged. Once this is done, a list of needed books and materials can be created in order to complete the collection. While some teachers may balk at this idea (i.e., those who have collected many books over the years using school district resources), the wisdom of the plan quickly becomes obvious. For example, when teachers discover that they now have, say, nine copies of Shel Silverstein's poetry book *Where the Sidewalk Ends* instead of just the one copy in their classroom for read-aloud experiences on the carpet area, they realize they can now check out as many as they need for small group instruction!

Still, the cost to school districts can be substantial to implement literacy materials centers. Superintendents, curriculum directors, and school principals need to budget for sufficient quantities and types of reading materials if the mission of teaching every child to read is to be accomplished (Neuman & Celano, 2001; Radencich, Beers, & Schumm, 1995; Wepner, Feeley, & Strickland, 2002).

Access to Professional Development

Teachers need continuous and coherent professional development to keep their reading instructional skills honed and to develop new understanding, insights, and skills in teaching reading. Additional resources need to be provided for schools where large numbers of children struggle in learning to read; as much as 1% of the total base district budget is recommended to be reserved for continuing professional development opportunities for teachers in reading (Snow et al., 1998), a paltry amount, really, compared to that spent by corporations (about 30%) to keep their professionals on the leading edge.

Many national policy makers are now realizing that most elementary and early childhood teachers were minimally prepared in their undergraduate teacher education programs to teach reading. Indeed, most teachers had only one or two classes on the assessment and teaching of reading (Strickland, Snow, Griffin, Burns, & McNamara, 2002).

Cooter (2004) found that children make significant gains in reading proficiency when their teachers develop greater expertise through deep training and peer coaching on the fundamental areas of reading instruction. The areas of focus should include phonemic awareness, phonics, reading comprehension, vocabulary development, reading fluency, and writing development. How much training is needed? Cooter concluded that a minimum of 80 classroom hours per year of instruction are needed for teachers coupled with in-classroom coaching by a master reading teacher/coach. Ideally, this **reading academy** course of study is spread over the course of a school year (about 3 hours per week) with peer coaching on a weekly basis.

Informed Leadership

As a group, teachers consistently remark that having strong, informed leadership supportive of quality reading instruction is an indispensable ingredient in the overall success of any reading program (Lipson, Mosenthal, Mekkelsen, & Russ, 2004). In researching the effects of reading academies for teachers on the reading proficiency of urban children in Dallas, Texas, and Memphis, Tennessee, Cooter (2004) found that schools having principals also enrolled in a special reading academy (he calls this the **principals' fellowship**) made the most rapid progress. In this case, the focus of the principals' fellowship was learning about ways to create and sustain schoolwide comprehensive reading programs. Some states now require principals to complete a course in the supervision of school reading programs.

Access to Peer Coaches

Nearly a decade ago, The National Research Council (Snow et al., 1998) recommended that every school have a resident, certified reading specialist available to provide school-level literacy leadership, peer coaching, and demonstrations. Many schools across the nation now have reading coaches in every elementary school to provide these and other services to classroom teachers (Toll, 2005; Walpole & McKenna, 2004).

The practice of giving students who struggle most in learning to read to the least-trained personnel in the school (e.g., Title I aides, volunteers, nonlicensed tutors) must be discontinued. The neediest children deserve access to the best-trained reading teachers and specialists.

Greater Planning Time

A common complaint heard among teachers is that they do not have adequate time during the school day to plan instruction, assess individual student needs, confer with other educational providers in the school, and/or to adapt instruction to meet the special needs of learners. Providing teachers with adequate time to plan and coordinate services with other team members in a school certainly benefits all children, especially those who struggle most (Darling-Hammond, 1997).

Reducing Class Sizes in the Early Years

Reasonable restrictions on class size, especially in the early years, have been recommended in many national reports and professional organizations. One encouraging sign is that some state legislatures have passed laws restricting class size in order to help our nation's teachers succeed and provide our students a greater opportunity to learn (Darling-Hammond,

Figure 1.6   Schoolwide Reforms to Support Comprehensive Reading Programs

> Access to Print
> Access to Professional Development
> Access to Leadership
> Access to Expertise
> Access to Planning Time
> Access to Resources for Reducing Class Size

1997; Goodlad, 1994). A summary of recommendations for schoolwide reforms to support comprehensive reading programs is found in Figure 1.6.

TEACHER KNOWLEDGE IS THE KEY

There was one clear and central theme across all of the national and international reports: *Teachers*—not the method, materials, or approach—make the critical difference as to whether or not students ultimately succeed in learning to read. Linda Darling-Hammond (1996), executive director of the National Commission on Teaching & America's Future, in a report entitled *What Matters Most: Teaching for America's Future*, asserted that "What teachers know and do is the most important influence on what students learn. Competent and caring teaching should be a student right" (p. 6).

The *Becoming a Nation of Readers* report (Anderson et al., 1985) concluded that teacher ability was at least five times more important than adopting a new published or core reading program. An indisputable conclusion of research is that the quality of teaching in the classroom makes a considerable difference in children's learning. Studies indicated that about 15% of the variation among children in reading achievement at the end of the school year was attributable to the skill and effectiveness of the teacher. In contrast, the largest study ever done comparing approaches to beginning reading found that about 3% of the variation in reading achievement at the end of first grade was attributable to the overall approach of the program (Anderson et al., 1985, p. 85).

In the report *Preventing Reading Difficulties in Young Children* (Snow et al., 1998), a similar conclusion was reached about the contribution of teacher competence to children's achievement in reading. Likewise, the *Report of the National Education Association's Task Force on Reading 2000* summarized this critical point succinctly, "The teacher, not the method, makes the real difference in reading success" (p. 7).

Teachers need to understand how children learn, generally, and how children learn to read, in particular, to teach them to read successfully (Smith, 1985; Snow, et al., 2005). Studying the milestones of reading development is an important way for you, the teacher, to understand how children develop reading ability.

THE MILESTONES OF READING DEVELOPMENT: KNOWING WHICH SKILLS TO TEACH AND WHEN

In some areas of study, particularly mathematics, it is possible to say with some assurance which skills must be taught before others can be learned. For example, in order to divide, one must know multiplication and subtraction skills. In reading, like mathematics, there are some skills, concepts, and strategies that must be learned before others can be acquired (e.g., phonemic awareness and alphabet knowledge before phonics, and so on). However, some reading/literacy skills may be learned within a wide span of time in the student's literacy development. Thus, knowing which reading skills, concepts, and strategies are prerequisite and sequential, as well as which are more flexible in terms of instructional timing, can be very important indeed. In this section, we briefly summarize theories pertaining to the general stages of reading development to assist you in observing and assessing students' reading development in the classroom. In later chapters, we describe more precisely the development of reading skills, concepts, and strategies in specific areas (such as phonics, comprehension, phonemic awareness, fluency, and so on based on the National Research Council's *Starting Out Right: A Guide to Promoting Children's Reading Success*, Burns, Griffin, & Snow, 1999).

Some years ago, several teachers had a discussion about what is meant by a "beginning reader." They began to gather classroom data to create a reading development continuum (Cochrane, Cochrane, Scalena, & Buchanan, 1984). Such a continuum would, of course, be extremely helpful to them and their fellow teachers in more accurately assessing student reading development and planning future instruction. [*Note:* For more research on reading development that is quite compatible with Cochrane et al., see also Sulzby (1985).] Cochrane and his colleagues divided the development of reading into two overarching categories: (a) preindependent reading and (b) independent reading. Within each of these super categories, these teachers described three more subdivisions. Within the preindependent reading category, for example, the three subordinate divisions or stages include (a) the magical stage, (b) the self-concepting stage, and (c) the bridging stage. Within the independent reading category, the three subordinate divisions or stages are (a) the take-off stage, (b) the independent reading stage, and (c) the skilled reading stage. Their continuum is shown in Figure 1.7 in checklist form, just as we have adapted it for our own classrooms.

Figure 1.7 Reading Development Continuum

> ## Observation Checklist for Reading Development
>
> Student: _____ Year: _____
> Teacher: _____ School: _____
>
> **Directions:** Write in the date(s) as the child exhibits the behaviors listed below:
>
> **A. PREINDEPENDENT READING STAGES**
>   1. *Magical Stage* [Sulzby's (1985) "Story Not Formed" level occurs about here]
>   _____ Displays an interest in handling books
>   _____ Sees the construction of meaning as magical or exterior to the print and imposed by others
>   _____ Listens to print read to him for extended periods of time
>   _____ Will play with letters or words
>   _____ Begins to notice print in environmental context (signs, labels)
>   _____ Letters may appear in his drawings
>   _____ May mishandle books—observe them upside down; may damage them due to misunderstanding the purpose of books
>   _____ Likes to "name" the pictures in a book, e.g., "lion," "rabbit"
>   2. *Self-Concepting Stage* [Sulzby's (1985) "Story Formed" level begins here]
>   _____ Self-concepts himself as a reader, i.e., engages in readinglike activities
>   _____ Tries to magically impose meaning on new print
>   _____ "Reads" or reconstructs content of familiar storybooks
>   _____ Recognizes his name and some other words in high environmental contexts (signs, labels)
>   _____ His writing may display phonetic influence, i.e., wtbo = Wally, hr = her
>   _____ Can construct story meaning from pictorial clues
>   _____ Cannot pick words out of print consistently

Figure 1.7 Continued

_____ Orally fills in many correct responses in oral cloze reading
_____ Rhymes words
_____ Has increasing control over nonvisual cueing systems
_____ Gives words orally that begin similarly
_____ Displays increasing degree of book handling knowledge
_____ Is able to recall key words
_____ Begins to internalize story grammar, i.e., knows how stories go together: "Once upon a time," "They lived happily ever after"

3. _Bridging Stage_ [Sulzby's (1985) "Story Formed" to "Written Language-Like" level]
_____ Can write and read back his own writing
_____ Can pick out individual words and letters
_____ Can read familiar books or poems that could not be totally repeated without the print
_____ Uses picture clues to supplement the print
_____ Words read in one context may not be read in another
_____ Has increasing control over visual cueing system
_____ Enjoys chants and poems chorally read
_____ Can match or pick out words of poems or chants that have been internalized

B. INDEPENDENT READING STAGES

1. _Take-off Stage_ [Sulzby's (1985) "Print Watched" to "Holistic" level]
_____ Excited about reading
_____ Wants to read to you often
_____ Realizes that print is the base for constructing meaning
_____ Can process (read) words in new (alternate) print situations
_____ Aware of and reads aloud much environmental print (signs, labels, etc.)
_____ Can conserve print from one contextual environment to another
_____ May exhibit temporary tunnel vision (concentrates on words and letters)
_____ Oral reading may be word centered rather than meaning centered
_____ Has increasing control over the Reading Process

2. _Independent Reading Stage_ [Sulzby's (1985) "Holistic" level]
_____ Characterized by comprehension of the author's message by reader
_____ Reader's construction of meaning relies heavily on author's print or implied cues (schema)
_____ Desires to read books to himself for pleasure
_____ Brings his own experiences (schemata) to the print
_____ Reads orally with meaning and expression
_____ May see print as a literal truth—what the print says is right (legalized)
_____ Uses visual and nonvisual cueing systems simultaneously (cyclically)
_____ Has internalized several different print grammars, i.e., fairy tales, general problem-centered stories, simple exposition

3. _Skilled Reading Stage_
_____ Processes material further and further removed from his own experience
_____ Reading content and vocabulary become a part of his experience
_____ Can use a variety of print forms for pleasure
_____ Can discuss several aspects of a story
_____ Can read at varying and appropriate rates
_____ Can make inferences from print
_____ Challenges the validity of print content
_____ Can focus on or utilize the appropriate grammar or structuring of varying forms of print, e.g., stories, science experiments, menus, diagrams, histories

Source: Adapted from Cochrane, Cochrane, Scalena, and Buchanan. (1984). _Reading, Writing, and Caring._ Richard C. Owen Publishers, Inc., New York, New York, and E. Sulzby's (1985) "Children's emergent reading of favorite storybooks: A developmental study." _Reading Research Quarterly 20_(4), 458–481.

The Mystery of Reading: The Magical Stage

Long before children enter school, they begin noticing print in their environment and learn that printed language stands for words they have heard others use or that they have used themselves. Preschool children spontaneously learn to recognize billboards displaying their favorite television channel logo. They can recognize a popular soda brand logo or pick out their favorite cereal at the local supermarket. Although they may not be able to read the print exactly on each of these objects, when asked to tell someone what the soda can says, they may respond with "soda" or "pop."

Children at this stage of reading development love to have books read to them. In quiet moments, these children may crawl up into a large comfortable chair to hold, look at, and tell a story from the pictures in their favorite books. When he was 2 years old, Jeremy enjoyed the naming of each animal in his favorite picture book. After naming each picture, he would enthusiastically make the sounds of each, such as the roaring of a lion or the crowing of a rooster. Parents and teachers of readers who find themselves journeying through the magical stage of reading development may see children who hold books upside down, turn the pages from the back to the front, and even tear out a page unintentionally. Although this may concern parents on one level, children who behave in these ways evidence a need for exposure to and understanding of the purpose of books. Withholding books from these children because they do not know how to handle them or read them at this stage would most certainly prove to be detrimental.

Children in the magical reading developmental stage develop a marked preference for a single or favorite book. Willing adults are often solicited to read this book again and again. Although parents and others may tire rapidly of this book, the affection and familiarity increase with each reading for the child. Favorite books are often repeatedly read to the point at which the child memorizes them. Some parents even try to skip pages or sentences in these books, thinking their child will not notice; they soon learn, however, that their child has internalized these books, and the unsuspecting adult will be caught every time.

The reading of entire contexts such as those found on product logos and in books constitutes evidence to support the fact that young children prefer to process printed language from the whole to the parts. That is, reading the entire context of a sign or label and memorizing an entire book by young children are preferred much before they want or need to focus on the details and parts of printed language.

Look, Mom, I'm Reading: The Self-Concepting Stage

The self-concepting developmental stage describes the child who has come to view himself or herself as a reader. Although this child may not yet be able to read exactly what the print says, he or she is certainly aware of printed language and his or her own progress toward breaking the literacy barrier. Children in this stage will try to read unfamiliar books by telling the story from the pictures and from their own imaginations. Selected words are readily recognized, such as their own name, favorite food labels, and signs on bathroom doors. These readers will try to reconstruct the text of a favorite story from memory and picture clues. These children evidence an increasing awareness of words and sounds. They often ask questions about how words begin and about rhyming words. If given a chance, these children can also complete a sentence when asked to do so. For example, while reading *The Three Little Pigs,* a teacher may say, "And the big bad wolf knocked at the door and said, 'Little Pig, Little Pig . . . .'" Children at this stage will immediately fill in the hanging sentence with "let me come in."

SPANNING THE GAP: THE BRIDGING STAGE

Children at the bridging stage of reading development can pick out familiar words and letters in familiar contexts and books. They often cannot, however, pick these same words out of an unfamiliar book or context when asked to do so. Children in the bridging stage can reconstruct stories from books with greater precision than can children in the previous stage. In fact, children in the bridging stage can no longer reconstruct the story completely without using the print, although they will continue to use picture clues to augment their growing control over the print system.

Children in the bridging stage can also read back what they have written. It has long been a disappointment for us when teachers and parents fail to count these early behaviors as real reading by brushing them aside as cute. Parents or teachers will often remark, "She's not reading. She's got that book memorized." Only by understanding that reading is a developmental process and that memorizing favorite print and books is universal among children will parents and teachers be able to enjoy, recognize, and support the progress their children make toward conventional reading behaviors and skills.

BLAST OFF! THE TAKE-OFF STAGE

Look out for kids at the take-off stage! They are excited about reading and will perform for any reluctantly willing audience. In fact, they want to demonstrate their emerging ability as frequently as others will allow. Children at this stage of reading development have a clear understanding that print forms the basis for reading the story and constructing meaning. Words read in one book or context are now recognized in other books and settings. Signs and environmental print are subjects of intense interest among take-off readers. It seems as if print has a magnetic appeal for these children.

One autumn evening in a parent-teacher conference, while one of the authors was teaching first grade, a parent said that her son, Curt, had requested new breakfast cereals. When his mother asked why, Curt responded, "There's not enough to read on these boxes." His mother then bought him cereal in a box that seemed to display enough print to satisfy his appetite.

Oral reading during the take-off stage may become word or letter centered. Although oral reading before this time may have failed to perfectly represent the print on the page, it was smooth, fluent, and filled with inflection. The fact that words and letters have been discovered at this stage of development may lead to a situation in which children appear to temporarily regress in their reading development. Children in this stage need to focus on print details, which leads to less fluent and inflected oral reading for a time. With sustained opportunities to read and gain control over the reading process and print system, however, fluency and inflection will soon return.

I CAN DO IT BY MYSELF! THE INDEPENDENT READING STAGE

The take-off reader wants an audience, but the independent reader takes great pride in reading books to himself or herself for pleasure. The independent reader has developed control over the entire reading process and cueing systems. Reading is now carried on with simultaneous use of the author's printed clues and the reader's own store of background experiences and knowledge, called *schemata*. Fluency and inflection have returned to oral reading. In fact, chunks or phrases are now read fluently, with no laboring over single words. The independent reader is predicting ahead of the print and using context not just as an aid to decoding but also to construct meaning (Stanovich, 1980). The ability to critically analyze print, however, has not yet been achieved. Thus, these readers may believe everything they read or may exhibit a tendency toward seeing anything in print as literal, truthful, and absolute.

REACHING THE SUMMIT: THE SKILLED READING STAGE

The skilled reader not only understands print but uses print to support and extend thinking. Although this stage is the final stage of reading development, it is not a destination. The process of becoming skilled in reading is a lifelong journey. The journey to skilled reading involves processing print that is farther and farther removed from one's own experiences and knowledge. In other words, print is now used increasingly as a means to acquire new and unfamiliar information. The variety of printed media that skilled readers process increases from narratives and textbooks to magazines, newspapers, television guides, tax forms, and so on. The skilled reader can talk about different types of text organizations, make inferences from print, use print to substantiate opinions, challenge the surface validity of printed materials, and vary his or her reading rate according to the personal purposes for reading, such as by skimming and scanning. Although more research is needed to corroborate the descriptions offered by Cochrane and colleagues (1984) in the reading development continuum, this model provides a useful framework for parents, teachers, and scholars through which they can view the development of a reader with increased understanding and a good deal less anxiety.

In addition to knowing the milestones of reading development, you will need to know the fundamentals of English language structure, grammar, and systems. You need to understand the reciprocal nature of oral and written language. For an in-depth study of these fundamentals, we recommend you read our other text, *Teaching Children to Read: Putting the Pieces Together,* 4th Edition (2004).

In the next section, we take the milestones of reading development in perhaps a more practical direction and look at classroom applications. We answer the question, *What are the key reading benchmark skills that children should accomplish at each grade level to stay on track in their reading development?*

END-OF-YEAR READING BENCHMARK SKILLS

Under the *No Child Left Behind* legislation, as well as with *Reading First* guidelines, teachers are asked to monitor each child's growth in reading development. The previous section gave us one look at how children normally develop reading ability. Now we want to get down to specifics about *minimum* expectations for each grade level. This knowledge can be a tremendously potent tool in your assessment arsenal and help you to plan needed instruction for each child.

Over the past several decades, researchers have pored over the scientific literature to better understand the **reading benchmark skills.** These are the most essential reading skills that must be learned by the end of each grade level for students to stay on track in their development. The research has focused mainly on grades K through 3 because this is the place where most struggling readers seem to first have trouble. Many states (e.g., Texas, Ohio, California, Florida, Tennessee, Michigan, and many more) have now established reading benchmarks based on this type of research.

One of the premier research reports, which includes sections on benchmark "accomplishments," is *Starting Out Right: A Guide to Promoting Children's Reading Success* (Burns et al., 1999). We have summarized its findings in Figure 1.8 to help you better understand the answer to an all-important question, *What should good readers be able to do by the end of each grade level?*

Figure 1.8   Reading Development Sequence

Kindergarten Accomplishments

- Knows the parts of a book and their functions.
- Begins to track print when listening to a familiar text being read or when rereading own writing.
- "Reads" familiar texts emergently, i.e., not necessarily verbatim from the print alone.
- Recognizes and can name all uppercase and lowercase letters.
- Understands that the sequence of letters in a written word represents the sequence of sounds (phonemes) in a spoken word (alphabetic principle).
- Learns many, though not all, one-to-one letter-sound correspondences.
- Recognizes some words by sight, including a few very common ones ("the," "I," "my," "you," "is," "are").
- Uses new vocabulary and grammatical constructions in own speech.
- Makes appropriate switches from oral to written language styles.
- Notices when simple sentences fail to make sense.
- Connects information and events in texts to life and life experiences to text.
- Retells, reenacts, or dramatizes stories or parts of stories.
- Listens attentively to books the teacher reads to class.
- Can name some book titles and authors.
- Demonstrates familiarity with a number of types or genres of text (e.g., storybooks, expository texts, poems, newspapers, and everyday print such as signs, notices, labels).
- Correctly answers questions about stories read aloud.
- Makes predictions based on illustrations or portions of stories.
- Demonstrates understanding that spoken words consist of sequences of phonemes.
- Given spoken sets like "dan, dan, den," can identify the first two as the same and the third as different.
- Given spoken sets like "dak, pat, zen," can identify the first two as sharing one same sound.
- Given spoken segments, can merge them into a meaningful target word.
- Given a spoken word, can produce another word that rhymes with it.
- Independently writes many uppercase and lowercase letters.
- Uses phonemic awareness and letter knowledge to spell independently (invented or creative spelling).
- Writes (unconventionally) to express own meaning.
- Builds a repertoire of some conventionally spelled words.
- Shows awareness of distinction between "kid writing" and conventional orthography.
- Writes own name (first and last) and the first names of some friends or classmates.
- Can write most letters and some words when they are dictated.

First Grade Accomplishments

- Makes a transition from emergent to "real" reading.
- Reads aloud with accuracy and comprehension any text that is appropriately de-signed for the first half of grade one.
- Accurately decodes orthographically regular, one-syllable words and nonsense words (e.g., "sit," "zot"), using print-sound mappings to sound out unknown words.
- Uses letter-sound correspondence knowledge to sound out unknown words when reading text.
- Recognizes common, irregularly spelled words by sight ("have," "said," "where," "two").
- Has a reading vocabulary of 300 to 500 sight words and easily sounded-out words.

continued

Figure 1.8 Continued

- Monitors own reading and self-corrects when an incorrectly identified word does not fit with cues provided by the letters in the word or the context surrounding the word.
- Reads and comprehends both fiction and nonfiction that is appropriately designed for the grade level.
- Shows evidence of expanding language repertoire, including increasing appropriate use of standard, more formal language.
- Creates own written texts for others to read.
- Notices when difficulties are encountered in understanding text.
- Reads and understands simple written instructions.
- Predicts and justifies what will happen next in stories.
- Discusses prior knowledge of topics in expository texts.
- Uses how, why, and what-if questions to discuss nonfiction texts.
- Describes new information gained from texts in own words.
- Distinguishes whether simple sentences are incomplete or fail to make sense; notices when simple texts fail to make sense.
- Can answer simple written comprehension questions based on the material read.
- Can count the number of syllables in a word.
- Can blend or segment the phonemes of most one-syllable words.
- Spells correctly three- and four-letter short vowel words.
- Composes fairly readable first drafts using appropriate parts of the writing process (some attention to planning, drafting, rereading for meaning, and some self-correction).
- Uses invented spelling or phonics-based knowledge to spell independently, when necessary.
- Shows spelling consciousness or sensitivity to conventional spelling.
- Uses basic punctuation and capitalization.
- Produces a variety of types of compositions (e.g., stories, descriptions, journal entries) showing appropriate relationships between printed text, illustrations, and other graphics.
- Engages in a variety of literacy activities voluntarily (e.g., choosing books and stories to read, writing a note to a friend).

Second Grade Accomplishments

- Reads and comprehends both fiction and nonfiction that is appropriately designed for grade level.
- Accurately decodes orthographically regular, multisyllable words and nonsense words (e.g., capital, Kalamazoo).
- Uses knowledge of print-sound mappings to sound out unknown words.
- Accurately reads many irregularly spelled words and such spelling patterns as diphthongs, special vowel spellings, and common word endings.
- Reads and comprehends both fiction and nonfiction that is appropriately designed for the grade.
- Shows evidence of expanding language repertory, including increasing use of more formal language registers.
- Reads voluntarily for interest and own purposes.
- Rereads sentences when meaning is not clear.
- Interprets information from diagrams, charts, and graphs.
- Recalls facts and details of texts.
- Reads nonfiction materials for answers to specific questions or for specific purposes.
- Takes part in creative responses to texts such as dramatizations, oral presentations, fantasy play, and so on.

Figure 1.8 Continued

- Discusses similarities in characters and events across stories.
- Connects and compares information across nonfiction selections.
- Poses possible answers to how, why, and what-if questions.
- Correctly spells previously studied words and spelling patterns in own writing.
- Represents the complete sound of a word when spelling independently.
- Shows sensitivity to using formal language patterns in place of oral language patterns at appropriate spots in own writing (e.g., de-contextualizing sentences, conventions for quoted speech, literary language forms, proper verb forms).
- Makes reasonable judgments about what to include in written products.
- Productively discusses ways to clarify and refine own writing and that of others.
- With assistance, adds use of conferencing, revision, and editing processes to clarify and refine own writing to the steps of the expected parts of the writing process.
- Given organizational help, writes informative, well-structured reports.
- Attends to spelling, mechanics, and presentation for final products.
- Produces a variety of types of compositions (e.g., stories, reports, correspondence).

Third Grade Accomplishments

- Reads aloud with fluency and comprehension any text that is appropriately designed for grade level.
- Uses letter-sound correspondence knowledge and structural analysis to decode words.
- Reads and comprehends both fiction and nonfiction that is appropriately designed for grade level.
- Reads longer fictional selections and chapter books independently.
- Takes part in creative responses to texts such as dramatizations, oral presentations, fantasy play, and so on.
- Can point to or clearly identify specific words or wordings that are causing comprehension difficulties.
- Summarizes major points from fiction and nonfiction texts.
- In interpreting fiction, discusses underlying theme or message.
- Asks how, why, and what-if questions in interpreting nonfiction texts.
- In interpreting nonfiction, distinguishes cause and effect, fact and opinion, main idea and supporting details.
- Uses information and reasoning to examine bases of hypotheses and opinions.
- Infers word meaning from taught roots, prefixes, and suffixes.
- Correctly spells previously studied words and spelling patterns in own writing.
- Begins to incorporate literacy words and language patterns in own writing (e.g., elaborates descriptions; uses figurative wording).
- With some guidance, uses all aspects of the writing process in producing own compositions and reports.
- Combines information from multiple sources in writing reports.
- With assistance, suggests and implements editing and revision to clarify and refine own writing.
- Presents and discusses own writing with other students and responds helpfully to other students' compositions.
- Independently reviews work for spelling, mechanics, and presentation.
- Produces a variety of written work (e.g., literature response, reports, "published" books, semantic maps) in a variety of formats including multimedia forms.

Source: From Burns, M. S., Griffin, P., & Snow, C. E. (Eds.). (1999). *Starting out right: A guide to promoting children's reading success.* Committee on the Prevention of Reading Difficulties In Young Children, Commission on Behavioral and Social Sciences and Education. National Research Council. Washington, DC: National Academy Press. Available online at http://www.nap.edu.

An Invitation . . .

This book is organized into four sections to assist you with planning effective classroom assessment and instruction in reading:

- Section I "Focus on Comprehensive Reading Instruction" (chapters 1–3)
- Section II "Organizing for Instruction" (chapter 4)
- Section III "Assessment and Intervention Strategies" (chapters 5–15)
- Section IV "Going Beyond the Classroom Walls" (chapter 16)

In this first chapter, we introduced you to the elements of comprehensive reading instruction and programs—but this is only the beginning. In chapters 2 and 3, we extend this discussion into the "nuts and bolts" of comprehensive reading instruction.

Section II of the book—"Organizing for Instruction"—describes in detail ways of setting up and maintaining effective comprehensive reading programs for primary through intermediate grades.

Section III—"Assessment and Intervention Strategies"—is the very heart of our book and is intended to serve as a handy desk reference in your professional library. For example, if you have a group of young children who struggle with early decoding skills, then chapters 7 and 8 on phonemic awareness and phonics will help you to assess their specific needs and select appropriate teaching strategies. If you have students who need help reading and comprehending nonfiction/information texts, then ideas found in chapter 11—"Reading Comprehension: Information Texts"—is the place to find help!

Section IV is a special chapter we have included to help you involve parents with the learning process. Online resources are also cited here to help you continue in this vein.

We know that your time is precious and that it is difficult to examine all the books and journals on reading instruction for the "just right" ideas for your students. We, too, have experienced this time crunch dilemma and know how frustrating it can sometimes be when a teacher looks into the eyes of a child who is struggling with reading. Our goal was to fill these pages with current, practical, immediately useful assessment and instructional information for the experienced and the novice teacher. Along the way, we have tried out many of these ideas ourselves with children. As you use this book with your students in the coming years, we hope that you will find that our goal was largely met and, if time permits, you will take time to write us and suggest ways that the next edition can be even better.

Best wishes as you help children in your classroom become readers!

Selected References

Anderson, R. C., Hiebert, E. F., Scott, J. A., & Wilkinson, I. A. G. (1985). *Becoming a nation of readers: The report of the Commission on Reading.* Washington, DC: The National Institute of Education.

Au, K. H. (2000). A multicultural perspective on policies for improving literacy achievement: Equity and excellence. In M. L. Kamil, P. B. Mosenthal, P. D. Pearson, & R. Barr (Eds.), *Handbook of reading research,* (Vol. III, pp. 835–852). Mahwah, NJ: Lawrence Erlbaum Associates.

Baker, L., Dreher, M. J., & Guthrie, J. T. (2000). *Engaging young readers: Promoting achievement and motivation.* New York: Guilford Press.

Baumann, J. F., Hoffman, J. V., Moon, J., & Duffy-Hester, A. M. (1998). Where are teachers' voices in the phonics/whole language debate? Results from a survey of U.S. elementary teachers. *The Reading Teacher, 51,* 636–650.

Berliner, D. C., & Biddle, B. J. (1995). *The manufactured crisis: Myths, fraud, and the attack on America's public schools.* Reading, MA: Addison Wesley.

Blair-Larsen, S. M., & Williams, K. A. (1999). *The balanced reading program: Helping all students achieve success.* Newark, DE: International Reading Association.

Bracey, G. W. (2003). *What you should know about the war against America's public schools.* Boston, MA: Allyn & Bacon.

Burns, M. S., Griffin, P., & Snow, C. E. (Eds.). (1999). *Starting out right: A guide to promoting children's reading success.* Committee on the Prevention of Reading Difficulties in Young Children, Commission on Behavioral and Social Sciences and Education, National Research Council. Washington, DC: National Academy Press.

Calkins, L. M., Montgomery, K., Santman, D., & Falk, B. (1998). *A teacher's guide to standardized reading tests: Knowledge is power.* Portsmouth, NH: Heinemann Educational Book.

Cochrane, O., Cochrane, D., Scalena, D., & Buchanan, E. (1984). *Reading, writing and caring.* New York: Richard C. Owen.

Cohen, M. (1980). *First grade takes a test.* New York: Dell.

Coles, G. (2000). *Misreading reading: The bad science that hurts children.* Portsmouth, NH: Heinemann Educational Books.

Cooter, R. B. (Ed.). (2004). *Perspectives on rescuing urban literacy education: Spies, saboteurs & saints.* Mahwah, NJ: Lawrence Erlbaum Associates.

Cooter, R. B., Mills-House, E., Marrin, P., Mathews, B. A., Campbell, S., & Baker, T. (1999). Family and community involvement: The bedrock of reading success. *The Reading Teacher, 52*(8).

Darling-Hammond, L. (1996). *What matters most: Teaching for America's future.* New York: National Commission on Teaching & America's Future.

Darling-Hammond, L. (1997). *The right to learn: A blueprint for creating schools that work.* San Francisco: Jossey-Bass.

DeBruin-Parecki, A., & Krol-Sinclair, B. (2003). *Family literacy: From theory to practice.* Newark, DE: International Reading Association.

Department of Education. (1985). *Reading in junior classes. Wellington, New Zealand.* New York: Richard C. Owen.

Eckhoff, B. (1983). How reading affects children's writing. *Language Arts, 60*(5), 607–616.

Emery, K., & Ohanian, S. (2004). *Why is corporate America bashing our public schools?* Portsmouth, NH: Heinemann Educational Books.

Fielding, L., Kerr, N., & Rosier, P. (1998). *The 90% reading goal.* Kennewick, WA: New Foundation Press.

Fitzgerald, J. (1999). What is this thing called "balance"? *The Reading Teacher, 53*(2), 100–107.

Flippo, R. F. (1999). *What do the experts say? Helping children learn to read.* Portsmouth, NH: Heinemann Educational Books.

Flippo, R. F. (2001). *Reading researchers in search of common ground.* Newark, DE: International Reading Association.

Goodlad, J. I. (1994). *Educational renewal: Better teachers, better schools.* San Francisco: Jossey-Bass.

Hiebert, E. H., Pearson, P. D., Taylor, B. M., Richardson, V., & Paris, S. G. (1998). *Every child a reader.* Ann Arbor, MI: Center for the Improvement of Early Reading Achievement.

Holdaway, D. (1979). *The foundations of literacy.* New York: Ashton Scholastic.

Honig, B. (1995). *Every child a reader: Report of the California Reading Task Force.* Sacramento, CA: California Department of Education.

Kohn, A. (2000). *The case against standardized testing: Raising the scores,* ruining the schools. Portsmouth, NH: Heinemann Educational Books.

Lipson, M. J., Mosenthal, J. H., Mekkelsen, J., & Russ, B. (2004). Building knowledge and fashioning success one school at a time. *The Reading Teacher, 57*(6), 534–542.

Mates, B. F., & Strommen, L. (1996). Why Ernie can't read: *Sesame Street* and literacy. *The Reading Teacher, 49*(4), 300–306.

McCardle, P., & Chhabra, V. (2004). *The voice of evidence in reading research.* Baltimore, MD: Paul H. Brookes.

McGilp, J., & Michael, M. (1994). *The home-school connection: Guidelines for working with parents.* Portsmouth, NH: Heinemann Educational Books.

McQuillan, J. (1998). *The literacy crises: False claims, real solutions.* Portsmouth, NH: Heinemann Educational Books.

Miesels, S. J., & Piker, R. A. (2001). *An analysis of early literacy assessments used for instruction.* Ann Arbor, MI: Center for the Improvement of Early Reading Achievement.

Moats, L. C. (2000). *Whole language lives on: The illusion of "balanced" reading instruction.* NY: Fordham Foundation. Available online at http://www.edexcellence.net/library/wholelang/moats.htm.

Mooney, M. E. (1990). *Reading to, with, and by children.* Katonah, NY: Richard C. Owen.

Morrow, L. M. (1995). *Family literacy: Connections in schools and communities.* Newark, DE: International Reading Association.

National Assessment of Educational Progress. (2002). Washington, DC: Department of Education.

Neuman, S. B. (1999). Books make a difference: a study of access to literacy. *Reading Research Quarterly, 34*(3), 2–31.

Neuman, S. B., & Celano, D. (2001). Access to print in low-income and middle-income communities: An ecological study of four neighborhoods. *Reading Research Quarterly, 36,* 8–26.

Pearson, P. D. (2000). *What sorts of programs and practices are supported by research? A reading from the radical middle.* Ann Arbor, MI: Center for the Improvement of Early Reading Achievement.

Radencich, M., Beers, P., & Schumm, J. S. (1995). *Handbook for the K–12 reading resource specialist.* New York: Allyn & Bacon.

Rasinski, T. V. (1995). *Parents and teachers: Helping children learn to read and write.* New York: Harcourt Brace.

Rasinski, T., & Padak, N. (1998). The reading wars. *The Reading Teacher, 51,* 630–631.

Report of the National Education Association's Task Force on Reading 2000. (2000). Washington, DC: National Educational Assocaion.

Report of the National Reading Panel: Teaching children to read, (2000). Washington, DC: National Institute of Child Health and Human Development.

Reutzel, D. R. (1996a). A balanced reading approach: Spotlight on theory. In J. Baltas & S. Shafer (Eds.), *Guide to balanced reading: K–2—Making it work for you!* New York: Scholastic.

Reutzel, D. R. (1996b). A balanced reading approach: Spotlight on theory. In J. Baltas & S. Shafer (Eds.), *Guide to balanced reading: 3–6—Making it work for you!* New York: Scholastic.

Reutzel, D. R. (1999a). On balanced reading. *The Reading Teacher, 52*(4), 2–4.

Reutzel, D. R. (1999b). On Welna's sacred cows: Where's the beef? *The Reading Teacher, 53,* 96–99.

Reutzel, D. R. & Cooter, R. B. (2004). *Teaching children to read: Putting the pieces together* (4th ed.). Upper Saddle River, NJ: Merrill/Prentice Hall.

Reutzel, D. R., & Larsen, N. S. (1995). Look what they've done to real children's books in the new basal readers! *Language Arts, 72*(7), 495–507.

Reutzel, D. R., & Smith, J. A. (2004). Accelerating struggling readers' progress: A comparative analysis of "expert opinion" and research recommendations. *Reading and Writing Quarterly: Overcoming Learning Difficulties, 20*(1), 63–89.

Smith, F. (1985). *Reading without nonsense* (2nd ed.). New York: Teachers College Press.

Snow, C. E., Burns, M. S., & Griffin, P. (1998). *Preventing reading difficulties in young children.* Washington, DC: National Academy Press.

Snow, C. E., Griffin, P., & Burns, M. S. (2005). *Knowledge to support the teaching of reading: Preparing teachers for a changing world.* San Francisco, CA: Jossey-Bass.

Spiegel, D. L. (1999). The perspective of the balanced approach. In S. M. Blair-Larsen & K. A. Williams (Eds.), *The balanced reading program: Helping all students achieve success* (pp. 8–23). Newark, DE: International Reading Association.

Stanovich, K. (1980). Toward an interactive-compensatory model of individual differences in the development of reading fluency. *Reading Research Quarterly, 16*(1), 37–71.

Strickland, D. S. (1996, October–November). In search of balance: Restructuring our literacy programs. *Reading Today,* 32.

Strickland, D. S. (1998). Balanced literacy: Teaching the thrills and skills of reading. *Instructor* [Online]. Available online at http://www.scholastic.com/instructor/curriculum/langarts/reading/balance.htm.

Strickland, D., Snow, C., Griffin, P., Burns, M. S., & McNamara, P. (2002). *Preparing our teachers: Opportunities for better reading instruction.* Washington, DC: Joseph Henry Press.

Sulzby, E. (1985). Children's emergent reading of favorite storybooks: A developmental study. *Reading Research Quarterly, 20*(4), 458–481.

Taylor, B. M., Pearson, P. D., Clark, K. F., & Walpole, S. (1999). *Beating the odds in teaching all children to read.* Ann Arbor, MI: Center for the Improvement of Early Reading Achievement.

Thompson, R. (1997). The philosophy of balanced reading instruction. *The Journal of Balanced Reading Instruction, 4*(D1), 28–29.

Toll, C.A. (2005). *The literacy coach's survival guide: Essential questions and practical questions.* Newark, DE: International Reading Association.

Walpole, S., & McKenna, M. C. (2004). *The Literacy Coach's Handbook A Guide to Research-Based Practice.* NY: Guilford Press.

Wasik, B. H. (2004). *Handbook of family literacy.* Mahwah, NJ: Lawrence Erlbaum Associates.

Wasik, B. H., Dobbins, D. R., & Herrmann, S. (2001). Intergenerational family literacy: Concepts, research, and practice. In S. B. Neuman & D. K. Dickinson (Eds.), *Handbook of early literacy research.* New York: Guilford Press.

Wepner, S. B., Feeley, J. T., & Strickland, D. S. (2002). *The administration and supervision of reading programs* (3rd ed.). New York: Teachers College Press.

Wharton-McDonald, R., Pressley, M., Rankin, J., Mistretta, J., Yokoi, L., & Ettenberger, S. (1997). Effective primary-grades literacy instruction = balanced literacy instruction. *The Reading Teacher 50*(6), 518–521.

What matters most: Teaching for America's future. (1996). New York: Teacher's College Columbia University, National Commission on Teaching & America's Future.

Wigfield, A. (1997). Children's motivations for reading and reading engagement. In J. T. Guthrie & A. Wigfield (Eds.), *Reading engagement: Motivating readers through integrated instruction* (pp. 14–33). Newark, DE: International Reading Association.

Wigfield, A., & Guthrie, J. T. (1997). *Reading engagement: Motivating readers through integrated instruction.* Newark, DE: International Reading Association.

Chapter 2

Classroom Reading Assessment

Jason arrived in the classroom of Ms. Catlin Spears in mid-October from a distant state. Unfortunately, his mother was not permitted to bring along his cumulative assessment files from his previous school (they must be mailed by the central office), so Ms. Spears decided she had better gather some preliminary information on his reading, writing, and mathematics abilities. But where to begin?

Catlin was a first-year teacher and felt a bit unsure of herself. And to make the situation a little more dicey, Jason's mom had informed the principal that he had attention-deficit disorder (ADD) and it seemed to affect his learning, especially in reading. With that information in mind, she decided to focus on reading first because it is the most fundamental.

Ms. Spears thought to herself, *Okay, let's stay calm. I know I can pull something together that will let me know where to begin teaching. I'll just pull out that activities book and notes from my college class on reading assessment and go from there.*

After perusing her study notes and readings, the mental haze started to lift along with Catlin's spirits. *I'll just put together a little battery of assessments that will help me find out just where ole Jason is in his reading. For his phonics and decoding, I'll go with a running record. For comprehension, I'll use a retelling form. Ahhh, here's a good observation checklist that'll help me gather some informal data on his reading. Maybe I should also do an interest inventory—that would help me choose some books and other texts that he would enjoy reading. . . .*

Soon Ms. Spears had enough information to begin making some judgments about where Jason was in his development, as well as discovering his "learning frontiers."

Expertise in reading assessment begins with an understanding of the learning fundamentals. The fundamentals—it seems to us, anyway—can be summed up in the answers to two questions, what we refer to as the *how* and *what* questions:

How do children learn?

What should good readers be able to do?

Answer these two questions and you are ready to delve into the principles of effective classroom assessment!

LEARNING FUNDAMENTALS

HOW DO CHILDREN LEARN?

Certainly, volumes can and have been written on the subject of how children learn, so we will necessarily need to limit our conversation here to the bare essentials. For us, there are two primary beliefs as to how children learn that are indispensable in reading instruction: *zone of proximal development* (Vygotsky, 1986, 1990), and *gradual release of responsibility* (Pearson & Gallagher, 1983).

Teaching in the Zone of Proximal Development

Lev Vygotsky (1986, 1990), a Russian psychologist, teacher, and medical doctor, has had a tremendous effect on the field of education since the publication of his works in the West. According to Vygotsky, at any particular point in time, a child has a range in which he or she can learn. Applied to reading, at one end of the range are reading skills the child can do alone and at the other end are reading skills he or she could not do even with assistance. In the middle is what Vygotsky termed the **zone of proximal development.** He is well known for his maxim: *What the child can do in cooperation today he can do alone tomorrow.* Vygotsky (1986) further explained:

> Therefore the only good kind of teaching is that which marches ahead of development and leads it; it must be aimed not so much at the ripe as at the ripening functions . . . Instruction must be oriented toward the future, not the past. (pp. 188–189)

For Vygotsky, therefore, the teacher has a critical role to play in a child's learning. You may think of it this way: A child who has been riding his new bicycle using training wheels for some time asks that they be taken off so he can ride "like a big boy." The attentive parent, after removing the training wheels, runs along with the child with a hand firmly grasping the seat as he pedals his bike. Without the support of the parent, the child would not (in the beginning) have the confidence or skill to ride the bike without training wheels. This is the child's zone of proximal development for bike riding. After more practice that allows his skills to develop, he will one day ride without support. In Vygotskian terms, therefore, the effective reading teacher (a) knows *what* skills one must learn and in what order, (b) is able to figure out *where* a student is in his or her reading development (i.e., via *classroom assessment*), and, (c) knows which skills he or she should learn next (his or her zone of proximal development).

The reason classroom assessment is so important is that it helps the teacher know where the "frontier of learning" is for each student.

The Gradual Release of Responsibility

There is a way of operationalizing Vygotsky's notion of the zone of proximal development called the **gradual release of responsibility** (Pearson & Gallagher, 1983). Once you have correctly identified through classroom assessment the next skill a student is ready to learn, instruction begins with your *modeling* the new skill to be learned for the student. This part of instruction and learning is *all teacher*—the student watches as you model the skill and may ask questions to clarify his or her understanding. When you believe the student understands the new skill you have modeled, you then urge him or her to personally "try out" the skill with your support, much like the parent firmly grasping the child's bicycle seat when he or she first attempts riding without training wheels. This step is known as **guided practice** and comes with massive amounts of practice along with a gradually decreasing amount of teacher support.

Figure 2.1   Gradual Release of Responsibility Mode

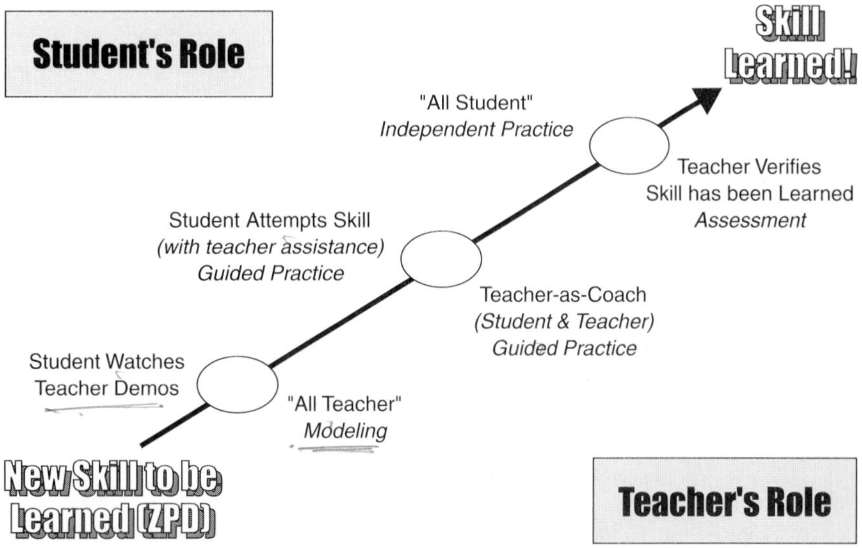

Student's Role

Skill Learned!

"All Student"
Independent Practice

Teacher Verifies
Skill has been Learned
Assessment

Student Attempts Skill
(with teacher assistance)
Guided Practice

Teacher-as-Coach
(Student & Teacher)
Guided Practice

Student Watches
Teacher Demos

"All Teacher"
Modeling

New Skill to be Learned (ZPD)

Teacher's Role

Source: From Pearson, P. D., & Gallagher, M. C. (1983). *The Instruction of Reading Comprehension. Contemporary Educational Psychology, 8* (3), pp. 317–344. Copyright 1983 by Academic Press.

When we believe the student has mastered the skill, we let them try it again without teacher assistance so that we can verify that permanent learning has occurred. We call this last step **independent practice.** The gradual release of responsibility concept of teaching and learning is represented in Figure 2.1. In this figure, you see that teaching a new skill moves from "all teacher" modeling for the student to observe, through guided practice and application activities involving the student with teacher support, and eventually to "all student" individual practice where the skill is finally mastered. Note the three zones of development for modeling, guided practice, and independent practice, indicating that there is a gradual release of responsibility from teacher to student for using the new skill.

Before moving on, let us be clear about what is meant by "teacher" in the gradual release of responsibility concept. It can actually be *anyone* who is more competent than the learner in using the new skill(s) to be learned. Thus, learners can be helped by the teacher, yes, but they can also learn from more competent classmates, family members, or a caring adult (May & Rizzardi, 2002).

WHAT SHOULD GOOD READERS BE ABLE TO DO?

Classroom assessment, more than anything else, is the ongoing process of learning just where a student is in his or her journey to becoming a fluent reader. Gauging where one is in any journey is gauged by considering the starting point and the destination. So, what is our destination for students in their reading at the end of kindergarten, first grade, second grade, and so on? What should they be able to do in reading at each level if they are progressing normally and if they do not have significant learning problems? It stands to reason that if we understand the reading milestone skills students normally learn and in what order, then we can set out to find the best research-proven strategies for measuring each reading milestone skill. (Refer to Figure 1.8 and the discussion of *reading benchmark skills* in chapter 1.)

Principles of Classroom Reading Assessment

There are several basic assumptions that govern good classroom reading assessment. Abiding by these principles helps teachers remain focused, systematic, and purposeful in their teaching.

Principle 1: The Teacher's Goal Is to Find out What Children Can do

The development of reading follows a reasonably certain path with clear markers along the way. Your job as a teacher is to locate where each child is in his or her development so that you can offer appropriate instruction to continue his or her growth. This is done by carefully charting what children *can* do in reading (not what they cannot do) beginning with early reading benchmark skills and moving systematically toward the more complex. This will tell you where each child is in his or her reading development as well as what should come next.

Principle 2: Assessment Informs Instruction

There has been a kind of "chicken versus the egg" debate in past years about which comes first—teaching or assessment. Principle 1 resolves that debate for us; effective teaching cannot possibly begin until we first discover where children are in their reading development. That information helps us know the appropriate "next steps" for students—their *zone of proximal development*—and, conversely, what would be a waste of their time either because they already "own" that particular reading skill or because the skill is too advanced and beyond their grasp at this time.

Reading instruction in many schools and school districts mirrors the state's mandated curriculum and reading tests—sometimes referred to as *high-stakes* tests—because whether or not a child is retained can be decided using these tests. In this scenario, it is clear that reading tests do indeed lead instruction—and not always for the better because it is often the curriculum leading instruction instead of an assessment of the student's needs. Thus, it is important that we make sure that the state tests are measuring appropriate reading skills at each grade level as determined through scientific research. If some of the benchmark skills at your grade level are not being addressed by mandated tests, then we must use supplemental assessments offered in this book to have a complete assessment program.

Principle 3: Be Prepared: Gather Your Assessment "Tools" in Advance

The tools of assessment include such items as leveled books in the language of instruction (i.e., English and/or Spanish in many American classrooms), a cassette recorder and tapes to record student readings, student and class profiling documents (Reutzel & Cooter, 2005), carefully prepared observation checklists, a scope and sequence of reading milestone skills to be learned and charted (see previous section), perhaps an informal reading inventory for quick assessments at the beginning and midpoint of the school year (e.g., *Running Records for Classroom Teachers* [Clay, 2000]; *The Spanish & English Reading Inventory* [Flynt & Cooter, 2003]), and so forth. Chapters 5 through 15 of this book provide you with a veritable arsenal of assessment ideas, strategies, and materials.

Before conducting observations and other assessments on one or more of your students, be certain that you have gathered the necessary tools and references so that the assessments are done in a swift, efficient, and (sometimes) covert way. Being properly prepared will help you to collect valid and reliable assessments.

PRINCIPLE 4: ANALYZE STUDENTS' ASSESSMENT RESULTS USING IF-THEN THINKING

One of the more difficult tasks for many teachers is to *analyze* the assessment data they have gathered on each child, form needs-based small groups for instruction, and choose appropriate teaching strategies for instruction. Put another way, we sometimes get to be pretty good at *gathering* assessment evidence but then have difficulty *analyzing* our findings and converting them into classroom action plans.

Analysis involves what has been termed *if-then thinking*. This is a way of analyzing assessment data and translating them into potent lesson plans. The basic philosophy goes something like this: *If* you know that a child is able to do X in reading, *then* he or she is now ready to learn Y. Put another way, *if* you know the highest level reading skills students can do alone (their *independent* reading level—see Principles 1 and 2), *then* you can accurately predict which reading skill(s) they should learn next with your assistance (their *zone of proximal development*). In each chapter, we provide you with an If-Then Chart in a section titled "Connecting Assessment Data to Teaching" that will help you make instructional decisions based on your assessment data. For example, Figure 2.2 shows an excerpt from chapter 6, "Children's Concepts About Print."

PRINCIPLE 5: DOCUMENT STUDENTS' GROWTH IN READING OVER TIME

Reading assessment is not a one-shot activity done at the beginning of the year but an ongoing and integral part of teaching and learning. Indeed, assessment and good teaching are virtually seamless. It is critical that we carry a veritable arsenal of assessment ideas in our teaching battery to aid us in our daily reading assessments. It is equally critical that we devise ways to document what we learn about each student's reading development to aid us in instructional decisionmaking.

FINDING OUT WHAT KIDS CAN DO: BASIC ASSESSMENT STRATEGIES

In the early development of readers, teachers often focus on two very basic areas in their assessments: **decoding,** or the translation of letters and words into language (also called **word identification**), and **comprehension** of what has been read (comprehension at the word level is also known as **word recognition**). An assessment procedure frequently used to measure decoding skill is the *running record* (Clay, 1997; Wiener & Cohen, 1997). To assess comprehension of story elements, such as setting, characters, problem, and solution, many teachers now prefer to use *retellings* (Tompkins, 2001). In this section, we present the most current methods and ideas regarding the use of running records and retellings as important components in a teacher's reading assessment arsenal.

Figure 2.2 Connecting Assessment Data to Teaching—An *If-Then* Chart

"If" the student is ready to learn ↓ / "Then" try these teaching strategies →	Read Environmental Print	LEA	Voice Point	Frame	Masking Highlighting	Context Transfer	Error Detect	Verbal Punctuation	Shared Reading	Manipulative Letters
Book Handling	−	−	−	−	−	−	−	−	+	−
Directionality	*	*	+	−	−	*	−	−	+	*
Print Carries Message	+	+	+	+	*	+	+	−	+	*
Voice-Print Matching	*	*	+	*	+	+	*	−	+	−
Punctuation	*	+	*	*	+	*	+	+	+	−
Concept of Word/Letter	+	+	*	+	+	*	+	−	+	*
Order—Letters/Words	+	*	*	+	+	*	+	−	+	+
Pragmatic Response to Environmental Print	+	−	*	*	*	+	*	−	−	*
Reader relies on a single strategy to unlock unknown words.	*	*	−	*	*	*	*	−	+	*

Key: + Excellent Strategy
  * Adaptable Strategy
  − Unsuitable Strategy

Informal Reading Inventories (IRI)

RUNNING RECORDS

From the earliest days of formal reading instruction and research, the ability to decode words in print has been viewed as essential. In 1915, for example, William S. Gray published the Standardized Oral Reading Paragraphs for grades 1 through 8, which focused on oral reading errors and reading speed exclusively. In the 1930s and 1940s, Durrell (1940) and Betts (1946) discussed at length the value of studying oral reading errors as a way to inform reading instruction. These and other writings began the development of what we now refer to as informal reading inventories (IRIs), in which oral reading errors are analyzed.

Half a century after Gray's test was published, Marie Clay (1966) began publishing landmark research detailing a systematic analysis of oral reading errors of emergent readers. The examination and interpretation of the relative "value" of oral reading errors (i.e., semantic and syntactic "acceptability") by Clay helped usher in a new age of understanding of decoding processes. A year later, it appears that Y. Goodman (1967) and other researchers mirrored Clay's thinking by employing careful studies of oral reading errors, or *miscue analysis,* to better understand decoding patterns of emergent readers.

In the 1970s, Y. Goodman and Burke (1972), in an assessment manual called the *Reading Miscue Inventory Manual*, and Clay (1972), in her manual called *The Early Detection of Reading Difficulties*, sought to formalize methodology for teachers who wish to focus on decoding assessment. Because of its complexity and impractical nature for classroom use, the Reading Miscue Inventory (RMI) never really gained much acceptance beyond university research settings, although its theoretical base was widely heralded among reading education scholars. Of the two methodologies, Clay's *running records* for analyzing oral reading errors proved to be the more functional for most classroom teachers because of time and other real-world constraints. In the next section, we describe in detail how running records are constructed and used to inform classroom teaching.

Conducting Running Records

Marie Clay (1972, 1985, 1997), a New Zealand educator and a former president of the International Reading Association, described the running record as an informal assessment procedure with high reliability (.90 on error reliabilities) that can inform teachers regarding a student's decoding development. The procedure is not difficult but does require practice. Clay estimates that it takes about 2 hours of practice for teachers to become relatively proficient at running records. In essence, the teacher notes everything the student says or does while reading including all the correct words read orally and all miscues (Wiener & Cohen, 1997). Clay recommends that three running records be obtained for each child on various levels of difficulty for initial reading assessment. Her criteria for oral reading evaluation are based on words correctly read aloud:

Independent level (easy to read)	95%–100% correct
Instructional level (ideal for teaching)	90%–94% correct
Frustration level (too difficult)	80%–89% correct

Running records, with Clay's method, are taken without having to mark a prepared script and may be recorded on a sheet of paper; requiring about 10 minutes to transcribe. Guidelines for administration follow:

1. A sample from the book(s) to be used is needed that is 100–200 words in length. For early readers, the text may fall below 100 words. Allow the student to read the passage one or two times before you take the running record.

2. Sit along side the student while he or she reads so that you can both see the page. It is not really necessary to have your own photocopy of the text; a blank sheet of paper will do. Record all accurate reading by making a check mark on a sheet of blank paper for each word said correctly. Errors or "miscues" should be noted using the notations indicated in Figure 2.3. Figure 2.4 shows an example of a running record taken using the book *Martha Speaks* (Meddaugh, 1992, pp. 1–4) using the marking system. In the figure, the box on the left is a copy of the text the student is reading. The box on the right is the running record taken by the teacher with each of the miscue types noted. Next, we take a look at how you go about analyzing miscues so that you will know what the reader *can* do.

Understanding Miscues: MSV Analysis

Marie Clay (1985) developed a way of interpreting miscues for use in her widely acclaimed reading recovery program. This way of thinking enables you to determine the extent to which the student uses three primary **cuing strategies** when he or she encounters a new word and a miscue occurs: meaning cues (M), syntax cues (S), and visual cues (V). Here is a summary based on the work of Flynt and Cooter (2003).

- *M = Meaning (Semantic—Does it make sense?)*   In reviewing each miscue, consider whether the student is using meaning cues in her attempt to identify the word. Context clues, picture cues, information from the passage are examples of meaning cues used by the reader.

- *S = Syntax (Structure—Does it sound right?)*   A rule system or *grammar*, as with all languages, governs the English language. For example, English is essentially based on a "subject-verb" grammar system. *Syntax* is the application of this subject-verb grammar system in creating sentences. The goal in studying *syntax cues* as part of your miscue analysis is to try and determine the extent to which the student unconsciously uses rules of grammar in attempting to identify unknown words in print. For example, if a word in a passage causing a miscue for the reader is a verb, ask yourself whether the student's miscue was also a verb. Consistent use of the appropriate part of speech in miscues (i.e., a noun for a noun, a verb for a verb, articles for articles, etc.) is an indication that the student has internalized the rule system of English grammar and is applying that knowledge in attacking unknown words.

- *V = Visual (Graphophonic—Does it look right?)*   Sometimes a miscue looks a good bit like the correct word appearing in the text. The miscue may begin with the same letter or letters, for example, saying the *top* for *toy*, or *sit* for *seat*. Another possibility is that the letters of the miscue may look very similar to the word appearing in text (e.g., *introduction* for *introspection*). Use of visual cues is essentially the student's ability (or inability) to apply phonics skills. The extent to which readers use visual cues is an important factor to consider when trying to better understand the skills employed by developing readers when attacking unknown words in print.

Applying MSV thinking is fairly simple once you get the hang of it. In Figure 2.5, we return to the miscues previously noted in Figure 2.4 and conduct an MSV analysis on each. Do you see why each interpretation was made?

The Miscue Grid: An Alternative Running Records Scheme

As useful as the running record can be for teachers in planning instruction, many feel that the time required for administering and analyzing running records can be prohibitive in

Figure 2.3   Notations for a Running Record

Reading Behavior	Notation	Explanation
Accurate Reading	√ √ √ √ √ √	*Notation:* A check is noted for each word pronounced correctly.
Self-Correction	√ √ √ √ Attempt | SC Word in Text |	The child corrects an error himself or herself. This is not counted as a miscue. *Notation: SC* is the notation used for self-corrections.
Omission	————— Word in Text	A word or words are left out during the reading. *Notation:* A dash mark is written over a line above the word(s) from the text that has/have been omitted.
Insertion	Word Inserted —————	The child adds a word that is not in the text. *Notation:* The word inserted by the reader is placed above a line and a dash placed below it.
Student Appeal and Assistance	————— | A Word from Text | T	The child is "stuck" on a word he or she cannot call and asks (verbal or nonverbal) the teacher for help. *Notation: A* is written above a line for "assisted," and the problem word from the text is written below the line.
Repetition	√ √ √ **R** √ √ √	Sometimes children will repeat words or phrases. These repetitions are not scored as errors, but *are* recorded. *Notation:* Write an *R* after the word repeated and draw a line back to the point where the reader returned.
Substitution	Substituted Word Word from Text	The child says a word that is different from the word in the text. *Notation:* The student's substitution word is written above a line under which the correct word from text is written.
Teacher Assistance	————— | Word from Text | T	The student pauses on a word for 5 seconds or more, so the teacher tells him or her the word. *Notation:* The letter *T* is written to the right of a line that follows the word from text. A blank is placed above a cross-line to indicate that the student did not know the word.

Figure 2.4   Running Record Example

Student _____ Paco _____ (Grade 2) _____

Title: **The Pig and the Snake**

Text	Marking
One day Mr. Pig was walking to	✓ ✓ ✓ ✓ ✓ ✓ ✓
town. He saw a big hole in the	✓ ✓ sam|sc / saw ✓ ✓ ✓ ✓
road. A big snake was in the	✓ ✓ −/big ✓ ✓ ✓ ✓
hole. "Help me," said the snake,	✓ ✓ ✓ out/− ✓ ✓ ✓
"and I will be your friend." "No, no,"	✓ ✓ ✓✓ −/friend| A ✓ ✓
said Mr. Pig. "If I help you get	✓ ✓ ✓ ✓ ✓ ✓ ✓ ✓
out you will bite me. You're	✓ ✓ ✓ R ✓ ✓
a snake!" The snake cried and	✓ ✓ ✓ ✓ ✓ ✓
cried. So Mr. Pig pulled the	✓ ✓ ✓ ✓ popped/pulled
snake out of the hole.	✓ ✓ ✓ ✓ ✓
Then the snake said, "Now I am	✓ ✓ ✓ ✓ ✓ ✓ ✓
going to bite you, Mr. Pig."	✓ ✓ ✓ ✓ ✓ ✓
"How can you bite me after	✓ ✓ ✓ ✓ ✓ −/after | T
I helped you out of the hole?"	✓ ✓ ✓ ✓ ✓ ✓ ✓
said Mr. Pig. The snake said,//	✓ ✓ ✓ ✓ ✓ ✓
"You knew I was a snake	✓ ✓ ✓ ✓ ✓ ✓
when you pulled me out!"	✓ ✓ ✓ ✓ ✓

Source: Flynt, E. S., & Cooter, R. B. (2004). *The Flynt/Cooter Reading Inventory for the Classroom* (5th ed). Upper Saddle River, NJ: Merrill/Prentice Hall. Used with permission of the authors.

Figure 2.5   Running Record with MSV Analysis

Student _____ Paco _____ (Grade 2)

Title: **The Pig and the Snake**		E MSV	SC MSV
One day Mr. Pig was walking to	✓ ✓ ✓ ✓ ✓ ✓ ✓		
town. He saw a big hole in the	✓ ✓ sam|sc / saw ✓ ✓ ✓ ✓ ✓		Ⓜ Ⓢ Ⓥ
road. A big snake was in the	✓ ✓ – / big ✓ ✓ ✓ ✓ ✓	M S V	
hole. "Help me," said the snake,	✓ ✓ ✓ out / – ✓ ✓ ✓	Ⓜ Ⓢ V	
"and I will be your friend." "No, no,"	✓ ✓ ✓ ✓ – | A / friend| ✓ ✓	M S V	
said Mr. Pig. "If I help you get	✓ ✓ ✓ ✓ ✓ ✓ ✓ ✓		
out you will bite me. You're	✓ ✓ ✓ R ✓ ✓		Ⓜ Ⓢ Ⓥ
a snake!" The snake cried and	✓ ✓ ✓ ✓ ✓ ✓		
cried. So Mr. Pig pulled the	✓ ✓ ✓ ✓ popped / pulled	Ⓜ Ⓢ Ⓥ	
snake out of the hole.	✓ ✓ ✓ ✓ ✓		
Then the snake said, "Now I am	✓ ✓ ✓ ✓ ✓ ✓ ✓		
going to bite you, Mr. Pig."	✓ ✓ ✓ ✓ ✓ ✓		
"How can you bite me after	✓ ✓ ✓ ✓ ✓ – / after | T	M S V	
I helped you out of the hole?"	✓ ✓ ✓ ✓ ✓ ✓		
said Mr. Pig. The snake said,//	✓ ✓ ✓ ✓ ✓ ✓		
"You knew I was a snake	✓ ✓ ✓ ✓ ✓ ✓		
when you pulled me out!"	✓ ✓ ✓ ✓ ✓		

Source: Flynt, E. S., & Cooter, R. B. (2004). *The Flynt/Cooter Reading Inventory for the Classroom* (5th ed). Upper Saddle River, NJ: Merrill/Prentice Hall. Used with permission of the authors.

public school classes of 25 or more students. To make the process go more quickly and reliably, Flynt and Cooter (2001, 2003) developed a simplified process for completing running records called the **miscue grid** that makes running records more practical for classroom use. In the assessment instrument called *The Comprehensive Reading Inventory* (Cooter, Flynt, & Cooter, in press) teachers learn how to follow along during oral reading, noting miscues on the special miscue grid. Teachers mark the miscue grid according to the kind of miscues the student made. By totaling the number of oral reading errors in each miscue category (i.e., mispronunciations, substitutions, etc.), as well as making an MSV analysis of each miscue, the teacher is then able to quickly determine "miscue patterns" and begin to plan instruction accordingly. Field tested with thousands of teachers, the miscue grid has proven to be an extremely effective classroom tool. Figure 2.6 shows an example of a completed miscue grid for a student named Grace using an excerpt from *Martha Speaks* (Meddaugh, 1992) as the text. In the next section, we show you how a miscue grid can be analyzed using the if-then method described earlier in the chapter.

Analyzing Running Record Findings Using If-Then Thinking

In the example shown in Figure 2.6 we note that the student, Grace, had some difficulty with a text sample from *Martha Speaks*. Notice that for each miscue, a tick mark "|" was recorded under the appropriate column heading, thus classifying each miscue as a mispronunciation, repetition, or other reading error. After all miscues have been studied and their category identified, the tick marks in each column are totaled, which helps the teacher discern where consistent problems are occurring. This process revealed that, at least with this passage, most of Grace's miscues were substitutions (3), repetitions (2), and insertions (2). She also had one teacher assist and a total of six miscues.

When doing an MSV analysis on the six countable errors (repetitions are not analyzed, but use of all three MSV cuing systems is assumed), we conclude that

1. Meaning (M) was used with four out of six miscues.
2. Syntax (S) was also used with four of six miscues.
3. A visual (V) cue such as phonics was only used one out of six times.

With a total of six miscues when reading this 100-word selection (note that we do not count any miscues after the 100th word), simple subtraction tells us that Grace read with 90% accuracy, placing her within the "instructional" reading level with this text sample according to Clay's system mentioned earlier. *Remember:* Conclusions about students' strengths and needs should not be drawn from only one running record—we are doing so here to make a point. As already noted, a minimum of three running records should be taken and comparisons made across all three to determine whether a pattern of reading behavior exists. (Fawson, et al., in press)

Finally, let us summarize what we know about Grace's reading according to this sample running record and a careful study of her miscues. The goal here is to identify what Grace *can* do in reading to help the teacher decide what she should have next in her learning program (see Principle 1 earlier in this chapter).

Grace Is Able to Do the Following in Reading . . .

- Uses *context clues* most of the time to help identify unknown words in print
- Uses *syntax clues* most of the time to help identify unknown words in print
- Uses *beginning sounds* in words as a phonics skill in decoding
- Uses *ending sounds* in words as a phonics skill in decoding

Figure 2.6 Grace's Miscue Grid Analysis Using an Excerpt from *Martha Speaks* (Meddaugh, 1992)

	Error Types							Error Analysis		
	Mis-pronun.	Substitute	Insertions	Tchr. Assist	Omissions	Error Totals	Self-Correct	(M) Meaning	(S) Syntax	(V) Visual
The day Helen gave Martha dog her										
understood / alphabet soup something ~~unusual~~		1				1				1
I . . . let . . . letters (SC) / happened. The ~~letters~~ in the soup went							1			
Brin . . . brain (SC) in / up to Martha's ~~brain~~ instead of down ^			1			1	1	1	1	
to her stomach. That evening, Martha										
Rep. / spoke. "<u>Isn't</u> it time for my dinner?"										
TA / Martha's family had many ~~questions~~ to				1		1				
ask her. Of course, she had a lot to										
Rep. / to tell them. "<u>Have</u> you always understood										
are / what we ~~were~~ saying?" "You bet! Do		1				1		1	1	
Betty / you want to know what ~~Bernie~~ is really		1				1		1	1	
saying?" "Why don't you come when we										
always / call?" "You people are ^ so bossy. Come!			1			1		1	1	
Sit! Stay! You never say please."										
"Do dogs dream?" "Day and (!00)										
night." Last night I dreamed I was chasing										
a giant meatloaf!"										
TOTALS		3	2	1		6	2	4	4	1

Receptions – II (2) MS V is not applicable here.

Source: Based on Flynt, E. S., & Cooter, R. B. (2004). *The Flynt/Cooter Reading Inventory for the Classroom* (5th ed). Upper Saddle River, NJ: Merrill/Prentice Hall. Excerpt from *Martha Speaks* by Susan Meddaugh. Copyright 1992 by Susan Meddaugh. Reprinted by permission of Houghton Mifflin Company. All rights reserved.

- Accurately *decodes one- and two-syllable words*
- Recognizes common, *irregularly spelled words* (e.g., have, questions)
- Uses *print-sound mappings* to sound out unknown words

The next step would be for the teacher to refer to the "What Should Good Readers Be Able to Do?" section earlier in this chapter and use Figure 1.8 to chart Grace's growth. *If*, in Grace's case, she has advanced up through most of the required second grade accomplishments, *then* the teacher may reasonably conclude that some sort of classroom intervention may be needed using grade 3 accomplishments as a guide, as well as tips from our *if-then* charts in relevant chapters. After reviewing grade 3 and higher accomplishments in Figure 1.8, Grace's "zone of proximal development" with regard to (a) phonics/word attack skills and (b) reading fluency seems to include the following:

Grace's "Next Steps" for Reading Instruction

- *Morphemic (structural) analysis* as seen in the miscue "unusual"
- *Syllabication* as seen in the miscues "unusual" and perhaps "Benje"
- *Accuracy of decoding* as seen in the insertion miscues, as well as with the miscues "are" for "were," and "Betty" for "Benje"

The final step in the analysis is to use the *if-then* charts in relevant chapters to decide which teaching strategies found in this book can be used to address Grace's learning needs (i.e., in her "zone of proximal development"). By reviewing the *if-then* charts in chapters 8 and 14, we find that the following teaching strategies may be used to teach the needed skills that our analysis identified:

Skills Needed	Teaching Strategies
Morphemic/Structural Analysis (See Chapter 8)	Explicit Instruction*; Nonsense Words*; Making Words*; Wide Reading*;
Syllabication (See Chapter 8)	Explicit Instruction*; Letter-Sound Cards; Sound Swirl; Tongue Twisters; Nonsense Words*; Making Words*; Wide Reading*;
Accuracy of Decoding (See Chapter 14)	Oral Recitation Lesson; Fluency Development Lesson; Repeated Readings; Assisted Reading

*Note: These strategies aid both morphemic/structural analysis and syllabication.

For the sake of efficiency, most teachers form short-term groups for children having the same needs; in this example, a small group of students would be formed to help students (including Grace) needing help with morphemic/structural analysis, syllabication, and accuracy of decoding.

Running records, when analyzed using the Flynt-Cooter (2003) grid system, can be a most informative addition to one's reading assessment program and make *if-then* analyses go much more quickly.

Implementing Running Records: A Self-Evaluation Rubric

As with most important teaching strategies, becoming an expert in administering running records comes in stages over time; it is a continuum of learning. A team of urban literacy researchers (Cooter, Mathews, Thompson, & Cooter, 2004) developed a rubric for use in

Figure 2.7 Running Records Self-Assessment Rubric

Directions: Using a red marker, draw a vertical line after the description on each row that best describes your current implementation of each aspect of graphic organizers. Using a yellow marker, indicate your end of the year goal for each aspect.

Conventions: Marking System	I have never received training on a universal marking system.	I created my own marking system.	I use markings that can be interpreted by my grade level.	I use markings that can be interpreted by my school. Some markings can be universally read.	I use markings that can be interpreted by district teachers. Most markings can be universally read.	I use markings that can be interpreted universally by teachers.
Scoring • Accuracy Rate • Error Rate • Self-Correction	I do not score running records.	I score for accuracy rate percentage.	I use the conversion chart to score for accuracy rate percentage to group my students.	I use the conversion chart to score for accuracy rate percentage and error rate to group my students.	I use the conversion chart to calculate accuracy rate percentage, error rate, and self-correction rate for grouping.	I use the conversion chart to calculate accuracy, error rate, and self-correction rates daily to inform my instruction.
Analysis: Cuing Systems (MSV) • Meaning • Structure • Visual	I do not analyze my running records.	I sometimes analyze errors on running records.	I analyze all errors on each running record.	I analyze all errors and self-corrections on each running record.	I analyze all errors and self-corrections for meaning, structure, and visual on each running record to guide and inform instruction.	I analyze all errors and self-corrections for meaning, structure, and visual on each running record. In addition, I look for patterns over time to further guide instruction.
Frequency	I do not use running records.	I use running records two times a year, at the beginning and end of school.	I do running records occasionally throughout the year.	I do one running record on my struggling students once per 6 weeks.	I do one running record on all my students once per 6 weeks.	I perform running records daily so that each student is assessed each 6 weeks. My struggling students are done twice each 6 weeks.

Source: Cooter, R. B., Mathews, B., Thompson, S., & Cooter, K. S. (2004). Searching for lessons of mass instruction? Try reading strategy continuums. *The Reading Teacher, 58*(4), 388–393.

coaching teachers who are using running records in their classrooms. It was later published as a self-assessment instrument (see Figure 2.7). In this rubric, running records are divided into conventions (marking system), analysis, and frequency of use. There are six levels of implementation for each category. We recommend that you determine your own levels of implementation monthly as you begin using running records.

Are running records the *only* way to assess decoding skills? Certainly not. In chapter 8, "Phonics and Word Attack Skills," we offer a plethora of ideas for quickly and efficiently assessing decoding skills. In addition, we provide information on one of the most widely used tools in today's classrooms available online known as the *Dynamic Indicators of Basic Early Literacy Skills* (DIBELS®).

Comprehension Assessment Using Retelling

Comprehension is the heart and soul of reading because it involves understanding the author's message. In later chapters, we offer many specialized ways of assessing reading comprehension that you will find quite helpful. In this section, however, we want to share with you one of the most fundamental and versatile ways of assessing reader comprehension with almost any sort of passage, the use of *retelling*.

Retelling is one of the best and most efficient strategies for finding out whether a child understands what he or she has read (Gambrell, Pfeiffer, & Wilson, 1985; Morrow, 1985; Hoyt, 1998; Benson & Cummins, 2000; Flynt & Cooter, 2005), especially when compared to the seemingly endless and tedious question/answer sessions that so often characterize basal readers and their workbook pages (what we sometimes call the *reading inquisition*). Teachers who routinely use retellings for comprehension assessment find that they can monitor student progress effectively and thoroughly and can do so in a fraction of the time required by traditional methods.

Two Phases of Retelling

We recommend two phases in conducting a retelling with students: unaided recall and aided recall. In the first phase, **unaided recall,** students simply retell what they recall from the passage they have just read independently *without* being questioned or prompted by the teacher concerning specific details. While each student retells the passage, the teacher notes important information that has been retold, such as characters, setting, central problem or challenge, conclusion, and theme/moral for story retellings.

It is critical that the teacher keep careful notes in student retellings. Thus, a story grammar retelling record for narrative texts like the one shown in Figure 2.8 can be most helpful to teachers. A teacher is not limited to using a specific format for making notes, but it is essential that careful and thorough notes be made for each retelling.

We have found that after students conclude the unaided recall portion of the retelling, it is often helpful to then ask, "What else can you remember about the passage?" Students will typically offer more information. You can usually use this "What else . . ." strategy each time the student seems to be finished for as many as three times before exhausting the student's ability to recall information in the unaided recall segment.

Once the student has seemingly recalled all the information he or she can without assistance, the assessment progresses to the second phase, **aided recall.** This is the act of questioning students about important elements of the passage that were not remembered during the unaided recall portion of retelling. When using the story grammar retelling record sheet, for example, it is relatively simple for the teacher to quickly survey the sheet for missing information, then use the generic questions provided to draw out additional story memories by the student. For example, if a student retold most of a story during unaided recall but neglected to describe the setting, the teacher may use the first question under "SETTING" (see Figure 2.8) on the Story Grammar Retelling Record, asking "Where did this story take place?" As in the first phase with unaided recall, the teacher records all memories the student has of the story and notes any story elements the student is unable to recall. If it appears that the student is consistently unable to remember certain story elements, then a minilesson should be offered to help him or her learn appropriate comprehension strategies. (*Note:* We talk more about if-then analyses for planning instruction a little later in this chapter.)

Three Levels of Retelling

Retelling has long been recognized as an effective method for assessing reading comprehension of both narrative and expository texts (e.g., Armbruster, Anderson, & Ostertag,

Figure 2.8   Story Grammar Retelling Record Sheet

Student's Name: _____   Date: _____

Story: _____

Source/Book: _____

Category	Prompt Questions (after retelling)	Student's Retelling
SETTING	Where did this story take place? When did this story happen?	
CHARACTERS	Who were the characters in this story? Who was the main character(s) in the story? Describe _____ in the story	
CHALLENGE	What is the main challenge or problem in the story? What were the characters trying to do?	
EVENTS	What were the most important things that happened in the story? What did _____ do in the story?	
SOLUTION	How was the challenge/problem solved? What did _____ do to solve the problem? How did the other characters solve their problems?	
THEME	What was this author trying to tell us? What did _____ learn at the end of the story?	

1987; Rinehart, Stahl, & Erickson, 1986; Taylor, 1982). Benson and Cummins (2000) and Flynt and Cooter (2005) described an effective scheme for assessing and boosting comprehension development to higher levels via a three-level retelling process.

The first retelling level involves **guided oral retelling.** At this level, the goal is for students to retell the text selection using *spoken* language. The term *guided* implies a structure that is first modeled *to* learners by the teacher, then practiced *with* learners, and eventually demonstrated *by* learners.

The second level of retelling is called **graphic organizer retelling** and is based on research showing that graphic organizers can be a powerful tool for improving comprehension in expository materials (e.g., Armbruster, Anderson, & Meyer, 1992; Simmons, Griffin, & Kameenui 1988). This level of retelling builds on the oral retelling process by having students use (a) *written words* and (b) a *graphic organizer*. In this way, students learn to use written words as part of their retelling while also developing an organizational map to connect ideas and concepts. Flynt and Cooter (2005) explained:

> . . . this helps learners move new vocabulary and concept knowledge from short-term memory to permanent learning. Teachers should limit themselves, preferably, to just one or two graphic organizers per semester so that students are *marinated* in their use . . . and can begin using [graphic organizers] automatically in new learning situations. (p. 778)

The highest level is **written retelling.** Here students use their completed graphic organizers as a prewriting tool to construct written summaries of the text selections. Having students construct written summaries of content readings has been shown to boost comprehension and retention of new concepts (Bean & Steenwyk, 1984). As with the prior two levels, extensive teacher modeling is required. It is also recommended that a writing structure be used to help students construct their first drafts. We offer a number of these writing structures in chapter 13, "Writing and Reading."

OBSERVATION AND COLLECTION STRATEGIES

Observation and *collection* are your primary assessment tools for gathering information to understand where students are in their reading development. **Observation** is the part of assessment in which you document students' reading behaviors using indirect methods. We find it best, at least from our own classroom experiences, for teachers to focus on just two or three students daily (without the students' knowledge, if possible) for observation assessments. Here are a few examples of observation tools and processes commonly used by teachers (many more are provided throughout this book beginning in chapter 5):

- *Anecdotal Notes*—Observations taken while observing a student reading. They are very structured and focus on major milestones in the student's reading development and/or reading skills the teacher may be emphasizing or about to emphasize in class. Many teachers like to make their notes on self-adhesive labels such as those used on a computer printer to print addresses. These notes can then be dated and easily attached to the inside of students' reading folders at the end of the day.

- *Reading Logs*—Daily records of student reading habits and interests, usually kept during independent reading periods practice reading times (Cambourne & Turbill, 1990). Students keep these records by completing simple forms held in a reading log folder at students' desks or in other appropriate locations.

- *Observation Checklist*—Teachers often find it helpful to use checklists as a quick reference classroom tool that incorporates what we know about reading development. Some teachers find that checklists that include a kind of Likert scale can be useful in student portfolios, since many reading behaviors become more fluent over time. Diffily (1994), while teaching kindergarten and first grade, developed the checklist shown in Figure 2.9 for use with her students. While the reading behaviors listed in any scale or checklist naturally vary according to the grade level, these formats have proven to be quite helpful.

- *Literature Response Projects*—There are many ways students can demonstrate their reading comprehension. In the past and in many classrooms today, workbook pages and skill sheets have been used in great numbers as a postreading assessment activity. Unfortunately, these kinds of activities are a poor substitute for actual demonstrations of competence (Sizer, 1994). As an alternative, a growing number of classroom teachers are having students complete literature response projects to demonstrate their understanding of what they have read.

  Literature response projects can take many forms and may be completed by individual students or in literature response groups. The idea is for the students to choose a creative way to demonstrate their competence. As we explore many aspects of reading comprehension, you will find numerous literature response ideas described in this book. For example, one group of sixth graders (Cooter & Griffith, 1989), decided to develop a board game in the form of Trivial Pursuit based on their reading of *The*

Figure 2.9   Diffily's Literacy Development Checklist

Literacy Development Checklist

Student's Name: _____   Date: _____

	Seldom				Often
Chooses books for personal enjoyment	1	2	3	4	5
Knows print/picture difference	1	2	3	4	5
Knows print is read from left to right	1	2	3	4	5
Asks to be read to	1	2	3	4	5
Asks that story be read again	1	2	3	4	5
Listens attentively during story time	1	2	3	4	5
Knows what a title is	1	2	3	4	5
Knows what an author is	1	2	3	4	5
Knows what an illustrator is	1	2	3	4	5
In retellings, repeats 2+ details	1	2	3	4	5
Tells beginning, middle, end	1	2	3	4	5
Can read logos	1	2	3	4	5
Uses text in functional ways	1	2	3	4	5
"Reads" familiar books to self/others	1	2	3	4	5
Can read personal words	1	2	3	4	5
Can read sight words from books	1	2	3	4	5
Willing to "write"	1	2	3	4	5
Willing to "read" personal story	1	2	3	4	5
Willing to dictate story to adult	1	2	3	4	5

Source: Gratefully used by the authors with the permission of Deborah Diffily, Ph.D., Southern Methodist University.

Lion, The Witch, and the Wardrobe (Lewis, 1961). In an Ohio classroom, a student working independently decided to create a kind of comic strip that retold the book he had just completed. And a second-grade teacher in south Texas had her class make a "character report card" in which students graded a villain in a book on such character traits as honesty, trustworthiness, and so forth using inference skills and examples from the story to justify their opinions.

- *Writing Samples*—Reading and writing are reciprocal processes (Reutzel & Cooter, 2005); that is, as one skill is developed, it tends to help the student to develop the other. Writing is often a marvelous window for viewing students' understanding of phonics elements, use of context clues, and story elements, for example. Later in this book, we directly address reading and writing connections and ways that writing samples can be used to assess reading development.

   Collection is much more overt than observation strategies and involves direct assessment of student reading abilities, often in small groups or one-on-one situations. Throughout this book, we provide you with collection tools that will assist you in gathering myriad data for charting students' reading development.

- *Interest Inventories*—One of the most important and elusive aspects of reading assessment is affect, which deals with a student's feelings about the reading act

Figure 2.10 Interest Inventory

Interest Inventory

Student's Name: _____

Date: _____

Instructions: Please answer the following questions on a separate sheet of paper.

1. If you could have three wishes, what would they be?
2. What would you do with $50,000?
3. What things in life bother you most?
4. What kind of person would you like to be when you are older?
5. What are your favorite classes at school, and why?
6. Who do you think is the greatest person? Why do you think so?
7. Who is your favorite person? Why?
8. What do you like to do in your free time?
9. Do you read any parts of the newspaper? Which parts?
10. How much TV do you watch each day? What are your favorite shows, and why?
11. What magazines do you like to read?
12. Name three of your favorite movies.
13. What do you like best about your home?
14. What books have you enjoyed reading?
15. What kind of books would you like to read in the future?

(Mathewson, 1994). Attitude, motivation, interest, beliefs, and values are all aspects of affect that have profound effects on reading development. Teachers building balanced literacy programs require information in student portfolios that provides insights not only into reading materials and teaching strategies that may be employed but also into positive affective aspects that drive the reading process. Ultimately, selection of materials and strategies should be based at least in part on affective considerations. A starting point for many teachers is the **interest inventory.** Students are asked to complete or verbally respond to items on a questionnaire such as that shown in Figure 2.10. Responses give teachers a starting point for choosing reading materials that may interest the student and elicit the best reading possible, according to his or her abilities.

- *Teacher-Made Tests*—Though often overused in many classrooms, paper and pencil tests do sometimes serve a purpose. However, we favor **teacher-made tests** that are taken from the books, songs, poetry, and other text forms used in the classroom. Note that the tests should always follow the same format as any other teacher modeling examples presented to the student(s) to ensure transfer of learning. For instance, suppose that a teacher has chosen to use a cloze passage drawn from an old favorite classroom book such as *The Napping House* (Wood, 1984) to teach how context clues may be used to choose appropriate rhyming words. The teacher-made test developed to assess an individual student's understanding of this skill should then be in the form of a cloze passage (as opposed to a multiple-choice test).

- *Family Surveys*—When one is attempting to develop a clear understanding of a student's reading development, his or her reading behavior at home is obviously of great importance. **Family surveys** are brief questionnaires (too long, and they will never be answered!) sent to the student's parents or primary caregivers periodically to provide the teacher with insights into the student's home reading behaviors. Teachers can then combine the family survey response with other assessment evidence from the classroom to develop a reliable profile of the student's reading ability. An example of a family survey is provided in Figure 2.11.

Figure 2.11 Family Survey

September 6, 200_

Dear Adult Family Member:

   As we begin the new school year, I would like to know a little more about your child's reading habits at home. This information will help me provide the best possible learning plan for your child this year. Please take a few minutes to answer the questions below and return this survey in the self-addressed stamped envelope provided. Should you have any questions, feel free to phone me at the school between 3:00 and 5:00 P.M. at 648-7696.

Cordially,

Mrs. Spencer

---

1. **My child likes to read the following at least once a week (check all that apply):**

   comic books _____   sports page _____

   magazines (example: *Highlights*) _____   library books _____

   cereal boxes _____   cooking recipes _____

   TV Guide _____   comics page _____

   others (please name): _____

2. **Have you noticed your child having any reading problems? If so, please explain briefly.**

3. **What are some of your child's favorite books?**

4. **If you would like a conference to discuss your child's reading ability, please indicate which days and times (after school) would be most convenient.**

Figure 2.12   Story Map

Story Map

Name: _____   Date: _____

Title: _____   Author: _____

SETTING (Where and when did this story take place?)

CHARACTERS (Who were the main characters in this story?)

CHALLENGE (What is the main challenge or problem in the story?)

EVENTS (What were the events that happened in the story to solve the problem/challenge?)
　　　Event 1:
　　　Event 2:
　　　Event 3:
(List all the important events that happened.)

SOLUTION (How was the challenge/problem solved or not solved?)

THEME (What was this author trying to tell the reader?)

Source: Adapted from Routman (1988).

- *Story Maps*—**Story maps** (Beck, Omanson, & McKeown, 1982; Routman, 1988) may be used to determine whether a student understands the basic elements of a narrative text or passage: setting, characters, challenge, events, solution, and theme. After reading the story, a student completes a story map. A generic format for the story map, such as the one shown in Figure 2.12, may be applied to almost any narrative text. Reading comprehension assessment and teaching procedures are discussed in detail in chapters 8 and 9 of this book.

- *Audio and Videotapes*—Using audio and/or video taping to record oral reading and retelling and videotapes to record students performing a variety of reading activities is a great way to periodically map reading growth. Recordings made at regular intervals, such as monthly, can be played back for careful analysis by the teacher and during parent-teacher conferences to demonstrate growth over time.

- *Self-Rating Scales*—It is often true that no one knows better how he or she is doing at reading than the reader. In the process of assessment, a teacher should never fail to ask students how they feel about their reading ability. Although this may be best achieved in a one-on-one reading conference, large public school class sizes frequently make this impractical. A good alternative to one-on-one interviews for older elementary children, however, is a student **self-rating scale.** Students complete a questionnaire that is tailored to obtain specific information about the reader—from the reader's point of view.

- *Rubrics (teacher or school-district made)*—As scoring guides or rating systems used in performance-based assessment (Webb & Willoughby, 1993; Farr & Tone, 1997; Reutzel & Cooter, 2005), **rubrics** assist teachers in two ways. First, rubrics make the analysis of student exhibits in the portfolio simpler. Second, rubrics make the rating process more consistent and objective. Because any assessment process is rarely objective, value free, or theoretically neutral (Bintz, 1991), rubrics clearly have an important role. Webb and Willoughby (1993) explain that "the same rubric may be used for many tasks [once established] as long as the tasks require the same skills" (p. 14).

  While there may be any number of ways to establish a rubric, Farr and Tone (1997) suggested a seven-step process of developing rubrics that may be adapted to reading assessment. Reutzel and Cooter (2004) modified the method slightly to conform to reading assessment needs and shortened the process to five relatively easy steps:

Step 1: Identify "anchor papers." Begin by collecting and sorting into several stacks reading exhibits from the portfolio (e.g., reading response activities, student self-analysis papers, content reading responses, etc.) according to quality. These are known as *anchor papers.* Try to analyze objectively why you feel that certain exhibits represent more advanced development in reading than others and also why some exhibits cannot be characterized as belonging in the more "advanced" categories.

Step 2: Choose a scoring scale for the rubric. Usually a three-, four-, or five-point scoring system is used. A three-point scale may be more reliable, meaning that if other teachers were to examine the same reading exhibits, they would be likely to arrive at the same rubric score (1, 2, or 3). However, when multiple criteria are being considered, a five-point scale or greater may be easier to apply. Yet, a major problem with reading rubrics is that they imply a hierarchy of skills that does not really seem to exist in many cases. For example, in the upper grades, is the ability to *skim* text for information a higher- or lower-level skill than *scanning* text for information? Probably neither label applies in this instance.

Step 3: Choose scoring criteria that reflect what you believe about reading development. Two points relative to reading rubrics need to be considered in Step 3: scoring and learning milestones. A rubric is usually scored in a hierarchical fashion. That is, using a five-point scale, if a student fulfills requirements for a 1, 2, and 3 score but not the criteria for a 4, even if he or she may fulfill the criteria for a 5 he or she would be ranked as a 3. In disciplines such as mathematics, certain skills can be ranked hierarchically in a developmental sense. However, many reading skills cannot be ranked so clearly: thus, we recommend a procedure slightly different from that typically used to rank reading skills: If a five-point rubric is being used, survey all five reading skills or strategies identified in the rubric when reviewing exhibits found in the portfolio. If the student has the ability to do four of them, for example, then rank the student as a 4 regardless of where those skills are situated in the rubric. We hasten to add that this modification may not always be appropriate, however, especially with emergent readers for whom clearer developmental milestones are evident.

Step 4: Select sample reading development exhibits for each level of the rubric as exemplars and write descriptive annotations. It is important for teachers to have samples of each performance criterion in mind when attempting to use a rubric. From the Step 1 process in which anchor papers or other kinds of exhibits (e.g., running records, literature response activities, story grammar maps, etc.) were identified, the teacher will have in his or her possession good examples or *exemplars* of each reading skill or strategy being surveyed. After a careful review of these anchor papers, it will be possible to write short descriptive statements, or annotations, that summarize what the teacher is searching for in the assessment for each level of the rubric.

Figure 2.13 shows a sample rubric developed for a fifth-grade class wherein students were to describe (orally and through written response) cause-effect relationships based on in-class readings about water pollution.

Step 5: Modify the rubric criteria as necessary. In any assessment, the teacher should feel free to modify the rubric's criteria as new information emerges.

• *Standardized Test Data*—Standardized test data are usually included in teacher portfolios and are sometimes discussed in parent-teacher conferences. These data do not really inform instruction—a prime motive for classroom assessment—but they do present a limited view of how the student compares to other students nationally who have also taken that particular test. Many times parents or guardians want to know how their child compares to others. Standardized tests are somewhat useful for that purpose. They may also help teachers who work mainly with students with learning problems to maintain perspective. It is sometimes easy to lose sight

Figure 2.13 Sample Rubric for a Fifth-Grade Reading Class

Cause-Effect Relationships: Scale for Oral and Written Response

Level 4: **Student clearly describes a cause and effect of water pollution and provides concrete examples of each.**
Student can provide an example not found in the readings.
"We read about how sometimes toxic wastes are dumped into rivers by factories and most of the fish die. I remember hearing about how there was an oil spill in Alaska that did the same thing to fish and birds living in the area."

Level 3: **Student describes a cause and effect of water pollution found in the readings.**
Student can define *pollution*.
"I remember reading about how factories sometimes dump poisonous chemicals into rivers and all the fish die. *Pollution* means that someone makes a place so dirty that animals can't live there anymore."

Level 2: **Student can provide examples found in the readings of water pollution or effects that pollution had on the environment.**
"I remember reading that having enough clean water to drink is a problem in some places because of garbage being dumped into the rivers."

Level 1: **Student is not able to voluntarily offer information found in the readings about the cause and effects of pollution.**

of what "normal reading development" is when you work only with students having learning problems. While we feel that standardized tests are not useful for making instructional decisions, they may be helpful in the situations we have mentioned.

ONLY THE BEGINNING . . .

The purpose of this book is to provide you with myriad classroom assessment strategies to help you with your daily planning and teaching. This chapter, while providing a few of the mainstays of classroom assessment, only scratches the surface. Chapters 5 and beyond each contain a section on assessment strategies that can help you determine each student's zone of proximal development for each major reading milestone. Each has been carefully researched, and we have used most of them in our own classrooms. So we invite you to keep reading along with us about classroom assessment. This is only the beginning!

SELECTED REFERENCES

Armbruster, B. B., Anderson, T. H., & Meyer, J. L. (1992). Improving content-area reading using instructional graphics. *Reading Research Quarterly, 26*(4), 393–416.

Armbruster, B. B., Anderson, T. H., & Ostertag, J. (1987). Does text structure/summarization instruction facilitate learning from expository text? *Reading Research Quarterly, 22*, 331–346.

Bean, T. W., & Steenwyk, F. L. (1984). The effect of three forms of summarization instruction on sixth graders' summary writing and comprehension. *Journal of Reading Behavior, 16*(4), 297–306.

Beck, I. L., Omanson, R. C., & McKeown, M. G. (1982). An instructional redesign of reading lessons: Effects on comprehension. *Reading Research Quarterly, 17*, 462–481.

Benson, V., & Cummins, C. (2000). *The power of retelling.* New York: The Wright Group.

Betts, E. (1946). *Foundations of reading instruction.* New York: American Book.

Bintz, W. P. (2001). Staying connected—Exploring new functions for assessment. *Contemporary Education, 62*(4), 307–312.

Cambourne, B., & Turbill, J. (1990). Assessment in whole language classrooms: Theory into practice. *Elementary School Journal, 90*, 337–349.

Clay, M. (1966). *Emergent reading behaviour.* Unpublished doctoral dissertation, University of Auckland, New Zealand.

Clay, M. (1972). *The early detection of reading difficulties.* Portsmouth, NH: Heinemann Educational Books.

Clay, M. (1985). *The early detection of reading difficulties* (3rd ed.). Portsmouth, NH: Heinemann Educational Books.

Clay, M. (1997). *An observation survey of early literacy achievement.* Portsmouth, NH: Heinemann Educational Books.

Clay, M. (2000). *Running records for classroom teachers.* Portsmouth, NH: Heinemann Educational Books.

Cooter, R. B., Flynt, E. S., & Cooter, K. S. (in press). *The Comprehensive Reading Inventory.* Upper Saddle River, NJ: Merrill/Prentice Hall.

Cooter, R. B., Mathews, B., Thompson, S., & Cooter, K. S. (2004). Searching for lessons of mass instruction? Try reading strategy continuums. *The Reading Teacher, 58*(4), 388–393.

Cooter, R. B., Jr., & Griffith, R. (1989). Thematic units for middle school: An honorable seduction. *Journal of Reading, 32*(8), 676–681.

Diffily, D. (1994, April). *Portfolio assessment in early literacy settings.* Paper presented in a Professional Development Schools workshop at Texas Christian University, Fort Worth, TX.

Durrell, D. D. (1940). *Improvement of basic reading abilities.* New York: World Book.

Farr, R., & Tone, B. (1997). *Portfolio and performance assessments.* Fort Worth, TX: Harcourt Brace College.

Fawson, P. C., Ludlow, B., Sudweeks, R., Reutzel, D. R. & Smith, J. (in press). Examining the Reliability of Running Records: Attaining Generalizable Results. *Journal of Educational Research.*

Flynt, E. S., & Cooter, R. B. (2001). *The Flynt/Cooter Reading Inventory for the classroom* (4th ed.). Upper Saddle River, NJ: Merrill/Prentice Hall.

Flynt, E. S., & Cooter, R. B. (2003). *The Spanish & English Reading Inventory for the Classroom*. Upper Saddle River, NJ: Merrill/Prentice Hall.

Flynt, E. S., & Cooter, R. B. (2005). Improving middle-grades reading in urban schools: The Memphis Comprehension Framework. *The Reading Teacher, 58*(8), 774–780.

Gambrell, L. B., Pfeiffer, W., & Wilson, R. (1985). The effects of retelling upon reading comprehension and recall of text information. *Journal of Educational Research, 78*, 216–220.

Goodman, Y. M. (1967). *A psycholinguistic description of observed oral reading phenomena in selected young beginning readers*. Unpublished doctoral dissertation, Wayne State University.

Goodman, Y. M., & Burke, C. L. (1972). *Reading miscue inventory manual: Procedures for diagnosis and evaluation*. New York: Macmillan.

Hoyt, L. (1998). *Revisit, reflect, retell*. Portsmouth, NH: Heinemann Educational Books.

Lewis, C. S. (1961). *The lion, the witch, and the wardrobe*. New York: Macmillan.

Mathewson, G. (1994). Toward a comprehensive model of affect in the reading process. In H. Singer & R. B. Ruddell (Eds.), *Theoretical models and processes of reading* (4th ed.). Newark, DE: International Reading Association.

May, F. B., & Rizzardi, L. (2002). *Reading as communication* (6th ed.). Upper Saddle River, NJ: Merrill/Prentice Hall.

Meddaugh, S. (1992). *Martha speaks*. New York: Houghton Mifflin.

Morrow, L. M. (1985). Retelling stories: A strategy for improving children's comprehension, concept of story structure and oral language complexity. *Elementary School Journal, 85*, 647–661.

National Research Council. (1999). *Starting out right: A guide to promoting children's reading success*. Washington, DC: National Academy Press.

Pearson, P. D., & Gallagher, M. C. (1983). The instruction of reading comprehension. *Contemporary Educational Psychology, 8*(3), 317–344.

Reutzel, D. R., & Cooter, R. B. (2005). *The essentials of teaching children to read*. Upper Saddle River, NJ: Merrill/Prentice Hall.

Rinehart, S. D., Stahl, S. A., & Erickson, L. G. (1986). Some effects of summarization training on reading and studying. *Reading Research Quarterly, 21*(4), 422–438.

Routman, R. (1988). *Transitions: From literature to literacy*. Portsmouth, NH: Heinemann Educational Books.

Simmons, D. C., Griffin, C. C., & Kameenui, E. J. (1988). Effects of teacher-constructed pre- and post-graphic organizer instruction on sixth-grade science students' comprehension and recall. *Journal of Educational Research, 82*(1), 15–21.

Sizer, T. (1994). *Reinventing our schools*. Bloomington, IN: Phi Delta Kappa.

Taylor, B. M. (1982). Text structure and children's comprehension and memory for expository material. *Journal of Educational Psychology, 74*(3), 323–340.

Tompkins, G. E. (2001). *Literacy for the 21st century*. Columbus, OH: Merrill, an imprint of Prentice Hall.

Vygotsky, L. S. (1986). *Thought and language*. Cambridge, MA: MIT Press.

Vygotsky, L. S. (1990). *Mind in society*. Boston: Harvard University Press.

Webb, K., & Willoughby, N. (1993). An analytic rubric for scoring graphs. *The Texas School Teacher, 22*(3), 14–15.

Wiener, R. B., & Cohen, J. H. (1997). *Literacy portfolios: Using assessment to guide instruction*. Columbus, OH: Merrill, an imprint of Prentice Hall.

Wood, A. (1984). *The napping house*. New York: Harcourt.

Chapter 3

Understanding Reading Instruction

"You are teaching my child phonics, aren't you?" questioned Mrs. Jenkins, the local PTA president. "I've been hearing that your teachers aren't teaching children to read using phonics."

"Of course we are teaching your child and *all* children phonics as a tool for learning to read," replied Mr. Salinger, the school principal. "But, as I am sure you know, there is more to teaching a child to read than phonics instruction alone. Children need to be read to from good books regularly. They need to talk about those books with others. Children need to see and hear good readers reading. Our teachers are concerned that every child be read to daily at school and at home. They make sure that they teach children phonemic awareness, oral language, print concepts, phonics, vocabulary, comprehension, and fluency strategies as well. They guide the children very carefully in learning to read. They also make sure they get guided and independent reading practice daily. Our teachers not only teach children how to read; they go one step beyond and show them what to do in different reading situations, show them when and how to apply specific strategies, and make sure they understand why they select certain strategies."

"I guess that sounds pretty good, but I just wanted to make sure my child gets phonics instruction as well as books."

"I understand," Mr. Salinger answered soothingly. "We want your child and all children to be successful. That is why our teachers have chosen to use the best, research-validated practices known today. You can have complete confidence that your child will receive a comprehensive reading instructional program in phonics and other critical skills at Dapper Hill Elementary."

READING TO, WITH, AND BY CHILDREN

A teacher's first order of business is to learn and use best practices for effective reading instruction. For over three decades, literacy scholars and practitioners, working first in New Zealand and Australia and later in the United States, have developed and researched a number of "best practices" for providing effective reading instruction compatible with comprehensive reading instruction (Anderson, Hiebert, Scott, & Wilkinson, 1985; Holdaway, 1979; McCardle & Chhabra, 2004; Mooney, 1990; National Institute of Child Health and

Figure 3.1   Reading *to, with,* and *by* Children Instructional Framework

READING TO

- Interactive Read Aloud
- Echoic Choral Reading
- Technology Assists

READING WITH

- Learning About Language Lessons
- Language Experience
- Shared Reading
- Guided Reading

READING BY

- Popcorn Reading
- Read Around the Room
- SSR
- Partner or Buddy Reading

Human Development 2000; Reutzel, 1996a, 1996b; Snow, Burns, & Griffin, 1998; Weaver, 1998; Department of Education, 1985). In this chapter, we offer you a foundation of several research-based "best practices" of reading instruction associated with the "reading *to, with,* and *by* children" instructional framework as found in Figure 3.1 This practical framework will help you to organize effective instruction as you continue through this book.

For reading instruction to be optimally effective, teachers need to teach *systematically* and *explicitly* to properly engage children and ensure learning. The very best reading instruction actively involves both teachers and students in explicit teaching and guided student practice. With younger, emerging readers and writers, teachers often take the major responsibility during reading and writing activities while students listen to and interact with the teacher as he or she reads aloud or models shared writing. As time goes along, teachers release to students the responsibility for the reading and writing until such a time comes when they can read and write independently.

The "best practices" found in the reading *to, with,* and *by* children instructional framework balance the active involvement of children and teachers in reading instruction, as well as gradually releasing from the teacher to children the responsibility for reading the text. In Figure 3.2, we show how several practices within the reading *to, with,* and *by* children instructional framework gradually release responsibility for reading the text or processing the print from the teacher to the children.

READING TO CHILDREN

Reading *to* children is intended as a time for teachers to demonstrate fluent reading for apprentice readers using a variety of text types. Some school administrators and parents truly wonder why a teacher would spend limited instructional time each day reading aloud to children. Although reading aloud to children can be taken to extremes thereby robbing

Figure 3.2   Gradual Release of Responsibility for Reading

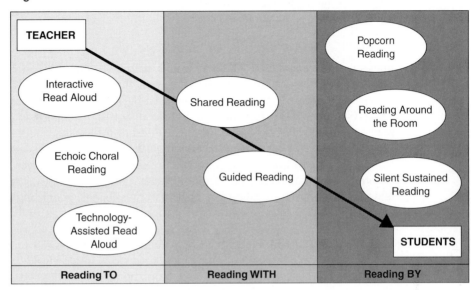

children of the opportunity to practice their reading and teachers of the time to teach, there are nevertheless many good reasons why teachers should read aloud to children for at least 10 to 15 minutes daily. Jim Trelease (2001) offered this insight about the value of reading aloud to children as an important part of high-quality, comprehensive reading instruction:

> [The] reasons are the same reasons you talk to a child: to reassure, to entertain, to inform or explain, to arouse curiosity, and to inspire—and to do it all personally, not impersonally with a machine. All those experiences create or strengthen a positive attitude about reading. (p. 2)

Research by Dolores Durkin (1966) revealed that children who learned to read early without formal instruction often came from homes where parents had read aloud to them regularly. Other researchers have asserted that read-aloud activities help young children develop a sense of how stories and other texts are constructed (Teale & Martinez, 1986; Barrentine, 1996; Beck & McKeown, 2001; Campbell, 2001; Hoffman, Roser, & Battle, 1993; Morrow, 2001; Neuman & Roskos, 1993; Opitz & Rasinski, 1998; Reutzel, 2001; Reutzel & Fawson, 2002). Anderson et al. (1985) further explained in the *Becoming a Nation of Readers* report that the single most important thing that teachers and parents could do to help children get off to a good start in early reading was to read to them and with them regularly.

During **interactive read alouds,** teachers model the reading process (Reutzel, 2001). Children witness firsthand the enjoyment of reading and are exposed to many genres and reading materials (Mooney, 1990; Reutzel, 1996a, 1996b; Reutzel & Cooter, 2004). So, as a teacher you can readily see that interactively reading aloud to children offers them an important exposure to the world of oral and printed language. In addition, interactive read alouds expand children's understanding of the world around them. By listening to stories, books, and texts read aloud along with rich discussion around the selections read aloud, children learn new words, ideas, and concepts *and* vicariously experience events that are within their ability to understand but are well beyond the boundaries of their immediate lives.

The major purpose for reading aloud *to* children is to model how to read for them, what to read, and why reading is important and enjoyable.

Reading Aloud of Trade Books

Interactive reading aloud of trade books with younger children helps them become successful readers as they progress through the early years of learning to read and throughout their years in the elementary school (Bennett, 2001; Campbell, 1992; Labbo, 2001; Neuman, 1999; Rosenhouse, Feitelson, & Kita 1997). Preschool children who are read to and with at home, and who have access to books prior to the time they enter school, become better readers (Neuman, 1999). Wells (1986) found that listening to stories read aloud and taking part in the discussion of stories were strongly related to children's later reading achievement and literacy development. Children learn about books and how they work from being read to by parents, siblings, peers, and teachers (DeTemple, 2001; Dickinson, 2001; Meek, 1984; Strickland & Morrow, 1989; Morrow & Temlock-Fields, 2004).

Heath (1982, 1983) found that not all reading aloud is created equal. To make reading aloud effective, parents and teachers must read aloud interactively; this means that when children or the parents feel a need, they stop and talk about the text and the pictures. It is important for children to be actively involved during read-aloud experiences to make sure they understand what is being read!

Morrow (1988) demonstrated that reading aloud to an entire classroom may not be sufficient to stimulate reading growth for all students. In this study, children were read to in small groups and in one-to-one settings. At the conclusion of the study, children who were carefully selected to be read to in small groups or in one-to-one settings made significantly greater progress over those students who were read to in a whole class setting.

Meyer, Stahl, and Wardrop (1994) conducted a study of reading aloud to children. The study showed that time spent reading traditional-size books aloud to children resulted in lower achievement test scores. For many students, reading achievement is only influenced positively when they actually engage with the print. These researchers did find, however, that students who experienced whole-class read alouds developed new oral language concepts and terms.

Rosenhouse et al. (1997) investigated how reading aloud stories written by the same author compared with reading stories written by different authors on children's reading achievement. It was found that reading stories aloud from the same author in a classroom of children led them to greater increases in decoding, comprehension, and picture storytelling. A "books-aloud" project in inner-city Philadelphia was designed to flood child-care centers with books and to train the staff in these centers on effective read-aloud techniques. This project showed that when adults were trained to read aloud effectively and often to very young children (in addition to having access to books), children's early literacy growth was positively and significantly affected (Neuman, 1999; Neuman & Celano, 2001).

The effectiveness of reading books aloud to children is conditioned by a variety of factors and expectations. Reading aloud has an impact on children's reading achievement. However, simply reading books aloud is insufficient to produce such effects. Teachers and parents must consider the nature of the read-aloud experience. They need to actively involve the child in the reading-aloud experience. They need to talk about the text together (Beck & McKeown, 2001; DeTemple, 2001). They need to consider whether or not it is best to read aloud in whole-class, small-group, or one-to-one settings to engage children in the print and the conversation about books. They need to realize that reading aloud to children is not a reading achievement panacea. It is only a part, albeit an important part, of effective comprehensive reading instruction (Campbell, 2001; Edwards, 1999; Reutzel, 2001). Reading aloud needs to be augmented by efforts to instruct oral language, decoding, comprehension, and fluency. Involving children in print-rich, print-engaging activities with books read aloud coupled with literacy-related play, guidance, and conversation in a variety of social settings will likely produce the optimal outcomes in later reading achievement.

SELECTING READ-ALOUD BOOKS

When selecting books to be read aloud to children, you should look for books, stories, and information books that will challenge children's intellectual development but not exceed their emotional maturity. When the concepts and experiences in books exceed a young child's emotional maturity levels, he or she will not enjoy the experience. For example, children who are read poetry about romance or the symbolic beauties of nature at young ages typically do not enjoy poetry or, even worse, develop contempt for poetry. Instead, wise teachers and parents recognize that 5- and 6-year-olds are not yet emotionally ready for romantic relationships in poetry, so they instead read children humorous poetry by Silverstein or Prelutsky. When teachers observe this simple suggestion, the read-aloud experience becomes a far more engaging experience for young children.

Books selected for read alouds should challenge children's intellectual levels, offering to them new concepts, ideas, and experiences. However, books selected for reading aloud should not be books children could read independently; rather, select books that exceed students' current independent reading abilities. We have created, based on Trelease's (2001) *The New Read-Aloud Handbook*, a listing of the "do's" and "don'ts" of reading aloud (Figure 3.3).

INTERACTIVE READ ALOUDS
IN YOUR CLASSROOM: GETTING STARTED

When teachers read aloud to children, they usually begin with a brief introduction and discussion of the passage to be read aloud (Hahn, 2002). In 1988, Teale and Martinez summarized research in which they sampled journal articles, books, and textbooks on guidelines for reading aloud to children. This study of guidelines revealed that there is no one best way to read aloud to children; but, the general findings of this research did lead to the guidelines summarized in Figure 3.4. As you can see from this list of guidelines for successful teacher read alouds, emphasis was placed on an introduction to the text prior to reading and interacting with students.

In another study of read-aloud practices in classrooms, preservice teachers were surveyed about practices they were observing in classrooms (Hoffman et al., 1993). Results indicated that teachers spent between 10 and 20 minutes per day reading aloud in elementary schools. Of the total time spent on read alouds, only 5 minutes were devoted to interaction between teachers and children or between children and children around the passage read aloud. Interactions between teachers and students about text as it is read aloud are critical to developing children's emerging comprehension abilities and oral language (Beck & McKeown, 2001; Campbell, 2001; Reutzel, 2001; Sipe, 2002; Scully & Roberts, 2002).

Figure 3.3   The Do's and Don'ts of Reading Aloud

Do's

- Do begin reading to children as early in their lives as they can be supported to sit and listen.
- Do use rhymes, raps, songs, chants, poetry, and pictures to stimulate their oral language development, listening, and interaction with others.
- Do read aloud to children at least 10–15 minutes daily, more often if possible.
- Do set aside a time for daily reading aloud in your curriculum schedule.
- Do read picture books to all ages, but also gradually move to reading longer books without pictures as well.
- Do vary the topics and genre of your read-aloud selections.
- Do read aloud books to children that stretch their intellectual and oral language development.
- Do allow plenty of time for interaction before, during, and after the reading.
- Do read aloud with expression and enthusiasm.
- Do add another dimension to your reading sometimes, such as using hand movements, puppets, or dressing up in costume.
- Do carry a book with you at all times to model your love of books and reading.

Don'ts

- Don't read aloud too fast.
- Don't read aloud books children can read independently—give a "book talk" instead!
- Don't read aloud books and stories you don't enjoy yourself.
- Don't read aloud books and stories that exceed the children's emotional development.
- Don't continue reading a book you don't like. Admit it, and choose another.
- Don't impose your interpretations and preferences on children.
- Don't confuse quantity with quality.
- Don't use reading aloud as a reward or punishment.

Source: Based on *The New Read-Aloud Handbook* (pp. 79–85), by J. Trelease, 2001, New York: Penguin.

Figure 3.4   Suggested Reading-Aloud Strategies

- Designate a legitimate time and place in the daily curriculum for reading aloud.
- Select high-quality books.
- Select literature that relates to other literature.
- Prepare by previewing the book.
- Provide the appropriate physical setting.
- Group children to maximize opportunities to respond.
- Provide a brief introduction.
- Read with expression.
- Discuss literature in lively, invitational, thought-provoking ways.
- Encourage children's responses to the book.
- Allow time for discussion and interaction about the book.
- Offer a variety of response and extension opportunities.
- Reread selected stories or books when students indicate a desire.

Source: Based on "Getting on the Right Road to Reading: Bringing Books and Young Children Together in the Classroom" by W. H. Teale and M. G. Martinez, 1988, *Young Children, 44*(1), pp. 10–15; and "Reading Aloud in Classrooms: From the Model to a 'Model'" by J. V. Hoffman, N. Roser, and J. Battle, 1993. *The Reading Teacher, 46*(6), pp: 496–503.

Because reading aloud to children is a critical aspect of any successful literacy program, it is only natural that over time this practice has been improved so as to support the development of reading for enjoyment and new learning (Scully & Roberts, 2002; Smolkin & Donovan, 2003). Although there is no single correct way to read aloud to children, as a profession we have learned the importance of talking about passages with children to improve understanding, sometimes referred to as **interactive read alouds** (Barrentine, 1996).

One potential criticism of interactive read alouds may be that encouraging too much discussion of a passage during reading may undermine the aesthetic flow of the literature and the experience for students. Although we certainly agree that too much analysis and interaction during read alouds can disrupt the pleasure of listening to the story, we also believe that interaction during read alouds draws on student experiences, heightening the relevance of the read-aloud experience. The goal during read alouds is to create a balance between student reactions to the text and ensuring a minimum of distractions and interruptions.

What about the *kinds* of text to be read aloud? It is clear that many children are regularly exposed to the reading of narrative and poetic texts (Pressley, 2002). On the other hand, the reading aloud of expository or information texts is lacking in many elementary classrooms (Duke, 2000a, b; Ivey, 2003; Smolkin & Donovan, 2003). Research has shown that children exposed only to narrative books do not get enough knowledge along with their reading-aloud experiences to grow their understanding of new vocabulary and of their world (Neuman, 2001). We feel strongly that expository passages should be included daily that are drawn from science, history, and the social studies.

Although most reading aloud to children in school takes place with the entire class, Morrow (1988) reminded teachers to take advantage of the benefits associated with reading aloud to smaller groups of young children and individuals. Children whose reading development lags behind that of their peers can be helped a great deal by teachers, volunteers, or older peers who take time to read to them in small-group or one-to-one settings. Recorded read alouds of targeted books can also be done inexpensively by teachers on cassette tapes and placed in listening centers for students to enjoy using headphones. Reading aloud to children who are lagging behind their peers can have added benefits when offered in smaller groups, individually, or in "buddy reading" sessions with a more advanced reader. Our suggestions for conducting interactive read alouds in your classroom are shown in Figure 3.5 and are based on Barrentine (1996).

Echoic Choral Readings

Echoic choral readings involve teachers orally reading a story, poem, or text with students then "echoing" the teacher's voice, just as one hears one's own voice echo in a deserted canyon. The teacher reads, chants, or sings aloud a line of text from a poem, book, or song, then students repeat it back just like an echo. Because the text is first read aloud by the teacher, students experience how fluent reading aloud sounds and feels. And because students and teachers are involved in echoic choral readings together, an active, lively, and participatory experience is had by all. What is more, the support offered to shy or reticent students in a group shields them from potential embarrassment or from feeling singled out for attention while learning to read. Thus, the echoic choral reading experience is a way for teachers to begin sharing the read-aloud responsibility for an information text or story with children.

Figure 3.5　Using Interactive Read Alouds in Classrooms

Carefully select books.

- Books with high quality illustrations, lively characters, rich plots, creative language, predictable patterns, and repeated rhythm encourage student attention to the text. Whereas multiple readings of a text are appropriate for read alouds, introducing new text helps to maintain student interest in this part of the routine. A good place to start is with your favorite books that are also suitable for your students.

Prepare for a successful interactive read aloud.

- Be thoroughly familiar with the book before the read aloud. With picture books this might mean making several readings of the text before the read aloud. With chapter books, it might be necessary to skim the selection you intend to read and familiarize yourself with the structure, plot, problem/resolution, setting, or characters. Be aware of areas of the book that require clarification or enrichment.
- Think about the goals for reading that you have identified for your students and identify what process and strategy are at work in your story. Keep your students in mind as you review the text. What elements in the text need to be expanded on to aid your students in their development as readers? When you think about your students' needs as readers, the read aloud becomes much more relevant in helping each student benefit from the reading.
- Identify where you will encourage students to share predictions about the developing story. Inviting students to make predictions about the story at strategic points in the reading will assist them as they develop an understanding of the text. Allowing class predictions of the story will support the less-able reader in clarifying key information in the story.
- Identify where students' background knowledge may be lacking and needing support. It is important to remember that students' listening comprehension will generally be ahead of their reading comprehension. Some concept or vocabulary development may help students to interact with stories that they otherwise would not be willing or able to handle.
- Give some thought to how you will phrase questions and anticipate student responses. Although it is possible to organize questions you would like to ask before, during, and after the reading, it is not always possible to anticipate student responses to those questions. Remember that your students will probably not grasp elements of the book at the same level that an adult will. Use this as an opportunity to gain a glimpse of their development in understanding the story and use this information to inform your future questioning.
- Be flexible and willing to relinquish your plans. Interactive read alouds are not unidirectional conversations. They are very dynamic and require a great deal of flexibility on the part of the teacher. Student interactions may add insights that you had not considered previously. Be willing to accept these slight detours as rich additions to the conversation.
- Create opportunities for students to explore and extend the book in meaningful ways. It is often appropriate to explore the book in greater detail following the readings. This allows children to achieve greater personalization of the story in their own minds.

Consider the literacy environment.

- It is very important to have a general idea about how you will access books for interactive read alouds and what you will do with the book when you have completed the reading. Will you put all of your books in the classroom library at the beginning of the year or will you hold selected titles back that you will use for interactive read alouds? Will you select books that support an instructional theme that is being presented during the same time frame? How will you arrange the children so that they will all be able to see or hear the text being read?

Figure 3.5   Continued

> ***Where will my read aloud fit into the instructional routine?***
> *   Teachers should negotiate time in their daily literacy routine for reading aloud to stu-
>   dents. If it is not integrated into the schedule where it becomes a part of the plan, then
>   the chances are good that it will not occur. Twenty minutes per day is a general figure
>   for read aloud. Understand, however, that interactive read alouds may take longer
>   depending on the experience of the students.

Source: Based on "Engaging with Reading through Interactive Read-Alouds" by S. B. Barrentine, 1996, *The Reading Teacher, 50*(1), pp. 36–43.

To engage children in an echoic choral reading, begin by selecting a book, poem, or song that can be read one line at a time. To get your feet wet with this activity, try Paul Fleishman's (1988) *A Joyful Noise: Poems for Two Voices*, Maurice Sendak's (1962) *Chicken Soup with Rice*, or favorite song lyrics from *Oh My Aunt Came Back*. Tell children that you are going to read a line from the selected passage and they are to "copy" you. Be sure to first model for students what you expect them to do using several examples so all will understand. For example, say you selected the song lyrics from *Oh My Aunt Came Back* to use for echoic reading. You would begin by singing the first line, *Oh my aunt came back from Timbucktwo,"* and then in a softer voice mimic the "echo." Next, you would repeat the verse, then ask students to sing it back as an echo when you point to them as a group. Then continue singing the next line, *"And she brought with her a wooden shoe,"* then signal the students to echo the verse. You may want to add some body movements to make it more interesting at this point, say by continuously tapping the toe of your right foot. This process continues line by line until you finish the song. We provide our version of the words and actions to this song in Figure 3.6 to get you started. Echoic choral read alouds help children accept limited responsibility for reading the text aloud as well as learning about fluent and expressive reading.

TECHNOLOGY-ASSISTED READ ALOUDS

Technology-assisted read alouds make use of computers, audiocassette tapes, or compact discs. Audiocassettes and compact discs (CD-ROMs) are designed to support readers as they look at the print in a new or relatively unfamiliar book and try to read along with the tape or CD. CD-ROM computer programs are now commercially available for a wide variety of predictable books. When commercially produced audio recordings of books are not available or resources do not allow for their purchase, teachers may record their own versions. These carefully paced, prerecorded read alouds can support children through the reading of a book they cannot yet read on their own.

Audio recordings or CD-ROM computer programs can, for example, be color coded for representing varying levels of text difficulty (e.g., green for emergent, yellow for easy reading, and blue for independent reading) so that children are reading at their instructional or independent levels. Audio recordings may be stored in specially designed storage cases, such as briefcases, or storage shelves for easy retrieval by the teacher and children.

Figure 3.6   Oh My Aunt Came Back

Oh my aunt came back,
From Timbucktwo,
And she brought with her,
A wooden shoe.
(Tap the toe of your right foot.)

Oh my aunt came back,
From old Japan,
And she brought with her,
A waving fan.
(Pretend to be waving a fan with your right hand.)

Oh my aunt came back,
From old Algiers,
And she brought with her,
A pair of shears.
(Pretend with your index and middle finger of your left hand to be cutting something.)

Oh my aunt came back,
From Guadalup,
And she brought with her,
A hulahoop.
(Pretend a hulahoop is around your waist and start swinging your waist.)

Oh my aunt came back,
From the county fair,
And she brought with her,
A rocking chair.
(Pretend to be sitting in a rocker rocking back and forth.)

Oh my aunt came back,
From the city zoo,
And she brought with her,
A nut like you!
(Point to the children who are acting out these motions with you.)

READING WITH CHILDREN

The main purpose of **reading *with* children** is to "coach," support, and encourage children as they try their hand at new reading skills with new texts (daCruz-Payne, 2005; Cooter, 2003). Although some children learn to read from watching teachers model fluent and expressive reading, many children require more intentional, systematic, and explicit guidance to be successful in learning to read. Well-established classroom practices using shared and guided reading provide opportunities for teachers to coach children using a variety of text types and levels to become independent, fluent, and expressive readers.

In reading *with* experiences, the teacher controls the reading typically using an enlarged text. He or she explicitly teaches students how to control print in the text and encourages students to practice new skills in group repeated readings of the text. In *small-group differentiated reading instruction*, which is similar to *guided reading* (Fountas & Pinnell, 1996), students begin to take responsibility for controlling the reading of "leveled" texts (Tyner, 2004). Through well-designed instruction during small-group differentiated reading instruction, students can accelerate their development of reading strategies and fluency. With teacher support, students read "just right" texts selected to match their ability to handle stories and books at their *instructional reading level*.

In the pages that follow, we describe how shared reading and small-group differentiated reading instruction can be used in reading *with* children to gradually release more and more of the responsibility for reading *to* the children. The goal of reading *with* children is to help them develop what Clay (1993b) called *self-extending systems* leading to independence in reading. Developing self-extending systems helps children select and successfully apply an array of reading strategies to become independent readers.

SHARED READING EXPERIENCE

In 1979, Don Holdaway described bedtime story reading as one of the earliest and most significant elements supporting the reading development of young children. **Shared reading,** or what is sometimes called the **shared book experience,** is used with very young readers to model how readers look at, figure out, and understand passages typically using an enlarged text in front of an entire group of children, rather than reading a traditional-size book with an individual child (Slaughter, 1993). To participate in a shared book experience, children and teachers must be able to share the print simultaneously. As noted, this requires that the print be enlarged so that every child can see it and process it together under teacher guidance (Barrett, 1982; daCruz-Payne, 2005).

When selecting books or stories for shared reading experiences, try to find those most loved by children that are available in a **big book** or enlarged print format that the entire group of children can see as easily as if they were sitting on your knee. Shared reading books should have literary merit, engaging content (both fiction and nonfiction), and high interest. Illustrations in shared reading books and stories should augment and expand upon the text. When selecting fiction, pictures should tell or support the reading of the story in proper sequence. Shared reading books are best for young readers if they contain repetition, cumulative sequence, rhyme, and rhythm to entice children into the melody and cadence of language. The very best big books for shared reading experiences "hook" children on the sounds and patterns of language and the multiple purposes of reading.

Books chosen for shared reading should also put reasonable demands on younger readers' capabilities. The number of unknown words in relation to known words in a new book selected for shared reading should not overwhelm them, but there should be some. Big books selected for initial shared reading experiences in fiction should largely carry the story line. Print in these initial shared reading big books may amount to little more than a caption underneath the pictures such as is found in the books *Brown Bear, Brown Bear* or *Polar Bear, Polar Bear* by Martin (1990, 1991).

Conducting a Shared Book Experience

You begin a shared book experience by introducing the book. An introduction is intended to heighten children's desire to read the story and to help them draw on their own experiences and prior knowledge so that they can understand new words in print and more fully enjoy and interpret the story. Once a book is selected for shared reading, begin by inviting children to look at the book cover while reading the title aloud. Talk about the front and back of the book and point out certain features of the cover and title page, such as the author and illustrator names, publisher, and copyright date. Next, say to the students, "Look at the pictures. What do you think the words will tell you?" This typically begins a dialogue and discussion leading to children sharing personal connections and making predictions. Next, read the book with "full dramatic punch, perhaps overdoing a little some of the best parts" (Barrett, 1982, p. 16). While reading the story, invite children to join in reading any repeated or predictable phrases or words. They positively love doing this! At key points during the shared reading, you should pause to encourage children to predict what is coming next in the story and explain their predictions: "That's an interesting prediction. What made you think that?"

After reading, invite children to share their responses to the story. Ask them to talk about their favorite parts and connect the story to their experiences, as well as discuss how well they were able to predict and participate. The shared reading book is reread on subsequent days and will eventually become a part of a selection of "old favorite" stories to be reread. Using hand and body movements, sharing simple props related to the story, and using rhythm instruments are excellent ways we have used to increase student involvement and activity in any rereading of a shared reading book. A sample shared reading lesson is shown in Figure 3.7.

Once a shared reading book has been reread twice, select something from the print in the book to examine in a **close reading** (we sometimes refer to this as a *minilesson*). For example, in the book *The Carrot Seed* (Krauss, 1945), which is also available in big book format, the teacher may decide that students should begin to notice the sight word "the" in the text. To direct students' eyes to the word "the" in the text, the teacher takes "stick 'em" notes from a pad and cuts several to the size necessary to cover or mask the word "the" in the text. As children and teacher engage in a "close reading," they note the

Figure 3.7   Teaching a Shared Reading Lesson

Ms. Harris selects the big book, *Each Peach Pear Plum* (Alhberg, 1978), for shared reading in her first-grade class. She invites her children to come up to the front of the room to be seated on a large carpeted area. As the children quietly but excitedly move to their places, Ms. Harris places the big book on an easel for all to see. "Boys and girls, what do you see here?" she asks. Several children immediately blurt out—A CAT, A COW, FRUIT! "That's right," she affirms. "What do you think the print in the title is telling us?" "It's going to tell us the title of the story," says Megen. "It's going to tell us about the things in the picture," offers Jona. "Well, you've all made some very good predictions. I'll read the title and you watch where I am pointing," instructs Ms. Harris. "EACH PEACH PEAR PLUM," reads Ms. Harris as she points to the words in the title. "Let's turn to the first page. What do you see here?" "A PIE WITH A MOUSE SNIFFING IT," several children respond. "Let's read together what the print tells us about this picture." Ms. Harris reads with a mysterious intonation while pointing to the print, "EACH PEACH PEAR PLUM. In this book, with your little eye, take a look, and play 'I spy.'"

The first reading continues as the children and the teacher read this book together. They interact about the pictures and print until the story is completed. After the reading, the children and teacher discuss other books that are like this, such as "Where is Waldo?" Ms. Harris shows the children several different types of "I Spy" books.

"Shall we read it again?" "YES," the children reply. "O.K. let's think about some hand actions and sounds we can put with our second reading." After a brief discussion it is decided to use their hands shaped like binoculars to look carefully at the pictures as they play "I spy." At the end of the story, they will open their arms to signal "everyone." "Remember boys and girls, you can join in with me any time as we read this book again." The second reading goes smoothly with the students all participating in the hand actions, the sounds, and in the reading.

masked words. The teacher unmasks the first "the" and asks students to look carefully at this word. "What are the letters in the word?" Invite a student to come up and copy the word from the book onto a large card. Each time the word "the" is encountered in the close read, it is unmasked and stressed aloud in the reading. After the close reading for "the," the teacher gives each child a "the" word card. The children are instructed to pick up a pair of scissors from the basket and return to their seats. While at their seats, they cut the card into its three letters and scramble the letters. Each child unscrambles the letters to form the word "the" on his or her desktop. Each child is given a new index card to write the word "the" to keep in his or her own *word bank* collection.

The shared reading experience is the logical setting for teachers to explicitly model, teach, explain, and coach children on a variety of reading and writing concepts and strategies (daCruz-Payne, 2005). Children can, with the guidance of the teacher, examine print concepts, practice letter and word recognition, practice decoding and fluency, discuss vocabulary word meanings, and apply comprehension strategies during shared reading lessons.

Research on the Shared Book Experience

Research by Ribowsky (1985) compared the shared-book-experience approach to a phonics-emphasis approach using the J. B. Lippincott basal reading series and found that the shared book experience resulted in higher end-of-year achievement scores and phonics analysis subtest scores than did the direct-instruction phonics approach used in the Lippincott basal. Reutzel, Hollingsworth, and Eldredge (1994) and Eldredge, Reutzel, and Hollingsworth (1996) showed that the shared book experience resulted in substantial reading progress for second-grade children across measures of word recognition, vocabulary, comprehension, and fluency when compared to other forms of oral reading practice. Thus, schools concerned about making *adequate yearly progress* (AYP) under the *No Child Left Behind* mandates, as well as teachers who simply want to offer the best instruction possible, can be well served by the shared book experience as part of a comprehensive reading program.

GUIDED READING INSTRUCTION

Guided reading instruction (GRI) (Fountas & Pinnell, 1996; Schulman & Payne, 2000; Rog, 2003; Tyner, 2004) is an essential part of reading *with* children in small groups. Guided reading instruction (GRI), in our research-based version, is a structured approach that has teachers using developmentally appropriate books *with* children to help them achieve a high degree of reading fluency. Teachers using this approach work with small, flexible groups of children with similar strengths; group membership changes as students progress to new levels. Teachers using GRI provide only needed support for readers as they attempt new skills through a process called "scaffolding" to develop the habits of independent, lifelong readers (Rog, 2003).

What does reading research tell us about the effectiveness of GRI? In recent research by Menon and Hiebert (2005), instruction using carefully sequenced "little books" was shown to be superior to the use of core or basal reading programs in promoting young children's early reading achievement. Another variation of guided reading called *small-group differentiated reading instruction* (SGDRI) has been shown to be particularly effective with struggling readers (Mathes, et al., 2005). We have incorporated SGDRI in our research-enhanced model of guided reading instruction.

Reading selections for guided reading instruction are carefully chosen according to student ability and needs from a library of *leveled books*. **Leveled books** are books commonly found in school libraries and classrooms that have been classified and grouped according to reading difficulty. In Figure 3.8, we present a chart that describes different leveling systems in use today along with a synopsis of leveling criteria. Because of the popularity of guided reading approaches, there are many other sources available online for identifying leveled books for use in your classroom. We share those a little later in this section on reading *with* children.

Figure 3.8   Selecting Books for Guided Reading Instruction: Reading Level Translations

Reading Levels (Traditional Designations)	Guided Reading (GR) Levels (Extrapolated from Fountas & Pinnell, 1996, 2001)	Common Text Attributes	Exemplar Books & Publishers (Using GR levels)	Approximate Level of Reading Development
Preschool-Kindergarten (Readiness)	A B	Wordless picture books Repeated phrases, text-picture matching, experiences common to readers, short (10–60 words)	**A** = *Dog Day!* (Rigby) **B** = *Fun with Hats* (Mondo)	Emergent
PP (Preprimer)	C D E	Same as above for B, but repeating phrases don't dominate the book, more language variation, by level E, syntax becomes more like regular "book language"	**C** = *Brown Bear, Brown Bear* (Holt) **D** = *The Storm* (Wright Group) **E** = *The Big Toe* (Wright Group)	Emergent → Early
P (Primer)	F G	Longer sentences/less predictable text, new verb forms appear, story grammar elements continue over multiple pages, pictures provide only a little support	**F** = *A Moose Is Loose* (Houghton Mifflin) **G** = *More Spaghetti I Say* (Scholastic)	Early
Grade 2 (Early) Grade 2	J K L	Longer stories with more complicated story grammar elements, varied vocabulary with	**J** = *The Boy Who Cried Wolf* (Scholastic) **K** = *Amelia Bedelia* (Harper & Row)	Transitional → Fluent

Figure 3.8 Continued

Grade 2 (Late)	M	Rich meanings, common to have whole pages of text, more content (nonfiction) selections are in evidence	**L** = *Cam Jansen and the Mystery of the Monster Movie* (Puffin) **M** = *How to Eat Fried Worms* (Dell)	
Grade 3	N–P	Fewer illustrations, more complex nonfiction, complex sentences and challenging vocabulary, higher order thinking begins here	**N** = *Pioneer Cat* (Random House) **O** = *Whipping Boy* (Troll) **P** = *Amelia Earhart* (Dell)	**Fluent (Basic)**
Grade 4	Q–S	Few illustrations, more complex language and concept load, higher order thinking is deepened, appearance of metaphor, topics are farther from student experiences, historical fiction is common, complex ideas are presented	**Q** = *Pony Pals: A Pony for Keeps* (Scholastic) **R** = *Hatchet* (Simon & Schuster) **S** = *Story of Harriet Tubman, Conductor of the Underground Railroad* (Scholastic)	**Fluent →** **Extending to** **Content Texts**

Assessing Children for Placement in Guided Reading Instruction Groups

One of the first tasks to be completed in implementing guided reading instruction (GRI) is to assess children's reading levels using "benchmark" leveled books. With this assessment information, children can be placed into small GRI groups with other children having similar ability for instruction purposes. **Benchmark leveled books** are reserved for assessment purposes only and are not used for instruction or for independent reading in the classroom. Books at different reading levels are selected as benchmark books. During assessment, children are asked to read from progressively increasing levels of benchmark books until they are unable to read a book with at least 90% accuracy.

Before students can be assessed using leveled books, teachers need to have access to leveled books or be able to find leveling information about the books they want to use. This is particularly true when teachers also make use of a core published reading program in which the stories or selections have not yet been leveled (Fawson & Reutzel, 2000). Fountas and Pinnell (1999) and Pinnell and Fountas (2002) describe a text gradient of leveled books from A to Z with approximate grade levels. In order to select leveled reading books to provide the "just right" match for children in each leveled small group, as well as approximate grade level equivalents for guided reading levels A to Z, we provide additional information in Figure 3.8.

Finding Leveled Books

Many current Internet web sites provide information about leveled books using the Fountas and Pinnell (1999) and Pinnell and Fountas (2002) A to Z leveling approach. Some of these are listed here:

> http://www.fountasandpinnellleveledbooks.com/
>
> http://registration.beavton.k12.or.us/lbdb/
>
> http://www.pps.k12.or.us/curriculum/literacy/leveled_books/
>
> http://www.leveledbooks.com/
>
> http://www.readinga-z.com/
>
> http://www.readinglady.com/gr/Leveled_Books/leveled_books.html

We have found the Internet site, http://www.readinga-z.com, to provide many choices, at our last count 1,300 downloadable leveled books, which can be easily used as "benchmark books" for assessment purposes. And in so doing, we have found that teachers do not need to quarantine any of their leveled library books for assessment purposes that were purchased for use in small group GRI instruction.

Assessing Word Knowledge

GRI groups are best formed using assessment information that places children based on both their ability to demonstrate 90% accurate reading of leveled books *and* their word study knowledge levels (Tyner, 2004). Perhaps one of the best known approaches for assessing children's word study knowledge was devised by Bear, Invernizzi, Templeton, and Johnston (2004). Found in *Words Their Way: Word Study for Phonics, Vocabulary, and Spelling Instruction*, these authors provided kindergarten, primary, and intermediate *spelling inventories* for examining children's levels of word structure knowledge from a developmental perspective.

Another excellent tool for assessing student's word study levels is the *Early Reading Screening Instrument* (ERSI) developed by Darrell Morris (1998). The ERSI, when given to end-of-year kindergarten children, has a predictive validity coefficient of .73 with the Woodcock-Johnson comprehension subtest. The ERSI assesses students' alphabet recognition, production, concept of word, phoneme awareness through spelling, word recognition using sight words, and decodable words.

Placing Children in Guided Reading Instruction Groups

Students are placed into guided reading instruction (GRI) groups based upon the highest level benchmark book they can read with 90% accuracy in word recognition, or what are called "just right" books. **"Just right" books** present children with a reasonable level of word recognition challenge but also with a high potential for success because 90% of the words are already recognizable. Books used for guided reading in the early grades should demonstrate a close match of text and pictures and gradual introduction of unfamiliar concepts and words, as well as sufficient repetition of predictable elements to provide support.

In most schools in which GRI is practiced in the primary and intermediate grades, there is a large, centralized collection of leveled reading books, or a **literacy materials center (LMC).** Teachers check out leveled materials from the school's literacy materials center to support guided reading instruction in the classroom, a very cost-effective way of providing teachers with a kind of communal or teacher-shared leveled reading library.

Grouped according to their highest reading level in A to Z leveled books, children are also grouped by their developmental levels in **word study knowledge.** Researchers (Beers & Henderson, 1977; Bear et al., 2004; Tyner, 2004) have identified rather specific developmental levels of word study knowledge, which we have summarized for your use in Figure 3.9.

To summarize, placing children into guided reading instruction (GRI) groups is based on assessment information concerning (a) their 90% accurate reading of leveled books and (b) their word study knowledge development levels.

Figure 3.9   Word Study Knowledge: Developmental Levels for Reading/Writing

Developmental Levels	What Students Can Do (Progressing from Earliest Development to the Latter Part of the Stage)	What Students Confuse (Progressing from Earliest Development to the Latter Part of the Stage)	What Students Are Unable to Do (Progressing from Earliest Behaviors to the Latter Part of the Stage)
Emerging (Prephonemic Understandings; Phonemic Awareness)	• Hold a writing tool • Produce and differentiate between picture drawing and "writing" • Use lines and dots in writing • Produce letter-like marks to symbolize words or phrases • Left-to-right writing (Directionality) • *Phonemic Awareness* is developed	• Drawing & scribbling as writing • Using letters, numbers, and letter-like marks • Left-to-right progression (Directionality) • Letter substitutions that are nearly alike (p/b/d)	• Letter-sound matching (graphophonemics) • Directionality (L–R) • Consistent spacing between words
Letter Naming (*Alphabetic Principle* or Letter-Sound Matching/ Graphophonemics; *Early Phonics*)	• Pre-phonemic Writing such as P = run, B = Sam • *Alphabetic Principle/ Early Phonics*—Begins matching or "mapping" sounds in words to an appropriate letter ("invented" or "temporary" spellings—dg = dog, kt = cat) • Uses many letters of the alphabet • Left-to-right directionality • Consistent letter-sound matching • Consistently uses most beginning and ending consonant letters/ sounds	• Inconsistent sound-letter mapping • Substitute single letters for letter combinations such as "j" for "dr" • Use of some vowels	• Beginning and ending of syllables • Vowels in syllables • Proper spacing between words is missing • Consonant blends and digraphs • Using vowels regularly

continued

Figure 3.9   Continued

Word Patterns, Syllables & Affixes (Phonics, Structural Analysis)	• Beginning & ending consonants • Consonant blends & digraphs • Short & long vowel patterns • Common suffixes such as -ing, -s, -ed • Consonant doubling plus suffix ending such as dropping • Long vowel patterns in accented syllables • Consistent use of onset & rime (e.g., c- plus -at for "cat," st- plus -ack for "stack") • Most common vowel & consonant variations	• Doubling of consonants • Long vowels in accented sentences (e.g., *pertend* for "pretend") • Silent "e" at the end of words (e.g., *cycul* for "cycle") • When to double final consonants before adding a suffix • Some common Latin prefixes (e.g., de-/di-, dis-/dys-, pre-/pro-) • Vowel variations in words (e.g., ie/ei, or/ur, ou/ow)	• Sometimes leaves out middle syllables • May confuse prefixes spellings • May fail to use known root words and/or rimes in spelling or reading new words
Transitional/ Independent (Automaticity)	Students are now progressing toward *Automaticity* both in their word reading and spelling. Some errors may occur, as with most mature readers & writers, but only error "patterns" are of interest for remedial teaching.		

The Nature of Small-Group Guided Reading Instruction

Guided reading instruction is accomplished in small, homogeneous groups of children who reflect a similar range of competencies, experiences, and interests in book reading and word study (Fountas & Pinnell, 1996, 2001; Tyner, 2004). Small-group instruction is intended to focus on teaching children in the **zone of their proximal development** (ZPD) (Vygotsky, 1978) or at that point in their development where they can succeed at a task with some expert help but cannot yet succeed on their own. Therefore, an important consideration in forming small groups for guided reading instruction is matching children in the group with "just right" books and their word study levels.

Small groups for guided reading instruction change as children progress throughout the year. This is a crucial point because failure to modify small-group composition can result in static ability groups like the old "eagles, bluebirds, and buzzards" groups as practiced in previous decades. The static nature of ability groups, particularly for those children in the "lower" developmental groups, caused children to suffer documented self-esteem damage and lowered academic expectations from both the teacher and themselves; the "once a buzzard always a buzzard" mindset.

In GRI lessons, teachers explicitly teach children concepts, skills, and strategies associated with science-based reading and writing strategies such as phonemic awareness, alphabetic principle (letter name knowledge and production), phonics, fluency, vocabulary, comprehension, and writing (National Institute of Child Health and Human Development, 2000; Tyner, 2004). To help children use these concepts, skills, and strategies for successful, fluent reading, you, the teacher, must provide clear, systematic, and explicit instruction.

Systematic instruction implies that you use a school-level curriculum map, a published reading program scope and sequence, district curriculum guide, or a state core curriculum that you follow to make sure that children receive a planned sequence of instruction. **Explicit instruction** means that you provide clear, comprehensive, and careful explanations about how to use strategies, concepts, or skills to read (Duffy, 2003; Hancock, 1999). Explicit instruction is typically recognizable by the following characteristics:

1. The teacher provides an explanation of the concept, skill, or strategies to be learned by specifically addressing: (a) what is to be learned, (b) why it is important to know, and (c) when and where it will be useful (Duffy, 2003).

2. The teacher models *how* to use the concept, strategy, or skill in reading by thinking aloud while demonstrating the application in real texts (Duffy, 2003; Hancock, 1999).

3. The teacher "scaffolds" or carefully structures students' application of the concept, skill, or strategy by gradually releasing responsibility for use from the teacher, to a sharing between the students and the teacher, to independent use by the teacher (Duffy, 2003; Hancock, 1999).

We use an acronym in our work with reading coaches and teachers, **EMS,** to help teachers remember the major parts of explicit reading and writing instruction: *E = explanation, M = model, S = scaffold.* Thus, in our interpretation of small-group guided reading, lesson plans are designed around the systematic and explicit teaching of decoding and comprehension concepts, skills, and strategies that will be coached later during the reading of an appropriately challenging leveled book (Tyner, 2004).

In the earliest stages of small-group guided reading instruction, teachers and children may chorally read books together. Thus, small-group instruction may sometimes look in practice similar to a shared reading experience with a big book. The main differences are the size of the group, the close reading of a regular-size text with individual guidance, and reading a book at the "just right" level of challenge or one that provides the "just right" text features that help the teacher scaffold learning.

Decodable Books

At this point, it is important to note that using only A to Z leveled books leaves unattended the need for children to read in books that use phonic patterns that they are learning, also referred to as **decodable books** (Anderson et al., 1985; Brown, 1999; Hiebert, 1999; Menon & Hiebert, 2005). No school-based leveled reading library is complete without including a substantial collection of texts graded also by decodable patterns. Recent research has shown that scaffolding children's early learning to reading experiences with carefully selected decodable books has significant impact on young children's reading development and progress (Menon & Hiebert, 2005). Many decodable books are available on the Internet or can be had with almost any published core reading program currently available. A listing of these materials is provided in Figure 3.10.

In small groups, children are encouraged to use their fingers to finger-point read in the earliest stages of differentiated reading instruction (Ehri & Sweet, 1991). **Finger-point reading** involves pointing to the words as they are spoken (Reutzel, 1995). During lessons

Figure 3.10 Commercially Available Collections of Decodable and Pattern Readers

Bob Books
Scholastic, Inc.
Available at most major bookstores
http://www.scholastic.com/

Books to Remember
Flyleaf Publishing Co.
P.O. Box 185, Lyme, NH 03768
(603) 795-2875
http://www.flyleafpublishing.com

J and J Readers
Language!
4093 Specialty Place, Longmont,
CO 80504
(303) 651-2829

Reading Sparkers
Children's Research and Development Co.
216 9th Ave, Haddon Heights, NJ 08037
(609) 546-9896

Phonics Readers
Educational Insights
16941 Keegan Ave, Carson, CA 90746
(800) 995-4436
http://www.edin.com

Phonics Readers
Steck-Vaughn (a Harcourt company)
(800) 531-5015
http://www.steck-vaughn.com

The Wright Skills Decodable Books
The Wright Group
19201 120th Ave NE, Bothell, WA 98011
(800) 523-2371
http://www.wrightgroup.com

Phonics Practice Readers
Modern Curriculum Press
P.O. Box 2649, Columbus, OH 43216
(800) 876-5507
http://www.pearsonlearning.com/mcschool/

Open Court
Reading Mastery
SRA, a division of McGraw-Hill
220 E Danieldale Rd, DeSoto,
TX 75115-2490
(888) SRA-4543
http://www.sra4kids.com

High Noon Books
Academic Therapy Publications
20 Commercial Blvd, Novato, CA 94949
(800) 422-7249
http://www.atpub.com

Readers at Work
Readers at Work
P.O. Box 738
Ridgway, CO 81432
http://www.readersatwork.com

with emerging readers, teachers may focus children's attention on print concepts such as directionality (i.e., left to right, top to bottom). With transitional and independent level readers, teachers may focus instruction on processing text using multiple reading strategies such as predicting, sampling, confirming, cross-checking, and self-correcting during small-group instruction. Following the reading of each passage, children are asked to summarize or retell the text again depending on their developmental levels. With time and development, children assume more responsibility for the first reading of the text with the teacher taking a supporting role through echoing, coaching, and helping where needed. This scaffolding of practice condition through gradual release of responsibility generally occurs as children understand basic print concepts, acquire a basic sight word vocabulary, develop automatic decoding, and select and apply appropriate comprehension strategies.

Teaching the Cuing Systems

In small-group guided reading lessons, teachers lead children to understand that there are three important cuing systems that fluent readers use to unlock unfamiliar text: (a) meaning,

(b) structure—sentence organization or *syntax*, and (c) the visual-sound system (Mooney, 1990; Fountas & Pinnell, 1996). As shown in the diagram in Figure 3.11, these three cuing systems are interlinked and interdependent.

To help children use these three cuing systems for fluent reading, you should model their application, then coach children to practice these skills until mastered. This is accomplished by showing children how to select and apply one or more reading strategies: (a) predicting, (b) sampling, (c) confirming, and (d) cross-checking to self-correct. Fountas and Pinnell (1999) give several examples of prompts teachers may use to direct or guide children to select and apply these reading strategies, as shown in Figure 3.12.

Figure 3.11 Interlinked Cuing Systems

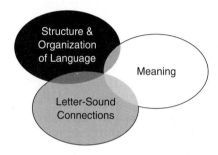

Figure 3.12 Guided Reading Teacher Prompts

Sampling Prompts:
- Read this with your finger.
- Do the words you say match with words on the page?
- Try this word. Would that make sense?
- Try this sound. Does that sound right?
- Can you find the word (or) letter?
- Does that make sense?
- Does this sound right to you? (Repeat what the child said.)
- Do you know a word like that?
- What can you do if you do not know a word?

Confirming Prompts:
- Were there enough words?
- Read that again.
- Try starting the word at the beginning with the first letter and sound.
- What did you notice?
- Does it start that way?
- Does it end with those letters or sounds?
- You almost got it. Can you find what was wrong?

Self-Correction Prompts:
- Why did you stop?
- Check that word again. Does it look right? Sound right?
- Something was not quite right. Try it again.

Figure 3.13 Seven-Part Guided Reading Instruction Lesson

Fluency Practice: Children practice by rereading a book previously read in the small group with a partner.
Word Wall Work: Teachers and children work with sight words displayed on the word wall.
Word Study: Teachers provide explicit instruction and practice with children by working on learning letters, sounds, word patterns, and word parts by sorting or making words using pictures, letter tiles, manipulatives, white boards, gel board, magna doodles, and so on.
Writing: Teacher dictates sight words, high-frequency phrases, or sentences for children to write.
Vocabulary: Teacher provides an activity to help children learn potentially unfamiliar word meanings or expand their known meanings to include others.
Comprehension Strategy: Teacher explicitly teaches comprehension strategies through explanation, modeling, and scaffolding children's use of these during reading of the new and familiar texts.
New Read: Read chorally, orally, in pairs, or silently (depending upon level of development) a new book, chapter, or text segment each day.

From Oral Reading to Silent Reading

As fluency is demonstrated in oral reading situations, teachers gradually help children convert their oral reading to silent reading (Wright, Sherman, & Jones, 2004). As children increase their word decoding and recognition (comprehension) to fluency, teachers broaden guidance and instruction to include an understanding of narrative structure, characterization, and the use of literary devices with narrative (fiction) passages. Similarly, they extend students' understanding of the mechanics and organization of expository (nonfiction) texts.

The stages of independent and critical reading are typically achieved in the intermediate, upper elementary, and middle school years. Once children reach these stages of reading development, teachers broaden their strategies and understandings of text to include studies of various literary genre, reading like a writer (stylistic examinations), text structure, and study/reference skills. A basic lesson pattern employed in our adaptation of guided reading lessons consists of seven phases. These phases are shown in Figure 3.13 and a sample small-group differentiated reading lesson is shown in Figure 3.14.

As children develop increasing fluency and expanding interests in the intermediate years, small-group guided reading instruction experiences change with them. At this level, lessons can include:

- A reading workshop
- A writing workshop
- Working with language

All of the activities associated with guided reading instruction in the intermediate years are intended to sharpen, refine, and hone children's reading fluency and critical thinking with text (Fountas & Pinnell, 2001; Reutzel & Cooter, 1991, 2004; Tyner, 2004). Whether these students are reading the novel *The Hatchet* or reading information text like *The Titanic*, the goal is to read orally with appropriate rate, phrasing, and intonation as well as with the purpose of comprehending the text. The purpose of guided reading with children of this age group is to help them not only understand the text but also develop a deeper understanding of language. Guided reading is aimed at helping independent, intermediate-age students gain insights into how texts are created from a writer's point

~~**Figure 3.14**   Teaching a Guided Reading Instruction Lesson

Mrs. Silva gathers seven children around her U-shaped table where she had laid out a basket of small books read during previous lessons. Children pair up with each other for oral repeated reading fluency practice. The odd student out, number seven, pairs with Mrs. Silva for rereading of a familiar book. During the reading, Mrs. Silva notes strategies used or not by the child with whom she is paired that day for rereading.

Once paired oral reading fluency practice is completed, Mrs. Silva passes out a small 3″ × 5″ slip of paper with five empty blanks and a line for a student name. Children take their pencils from the pencil basket at the table and write their names on the line on this slip of paper. Mrs. Silva begins by saying, "Look at our word wall. This word begins with the letter l, has four letters, only three sounds, and rhymes with book. Write the word in the blank numbered 1." This continues until the children have found and written five words from the word wall.

Next, Mrs. Silva passes out five gel boards and five magnetic stencils. Today's word study lesson is on focused on the rime, "ay." Mrs. Silva begins by giving a brief but explicit lesson on "ay." Next, she involves the students by asking children to write the word, /say/ on their gel boards. Now erase the first letter and write the letters /tr/ in front of /ay/. What is this word? Children raise their hands, and when called upon, Monica says, "tray!" This continues for four more words.

Next, Mrs. Silva asks children to erase their gel boards. She dictates five simple high-frequency phrases using high frequency sight words, such as "I look at it," and asks the children to hold up their gel boards when each dictated element is finished. On a separate clipboard, Mrs. Silva makes notes about how each child responded to the dictated, high-frequency phrases.

After this writing dictation experience, Mrs. Silva distributes copies of the book for today. She places three words and three sentence strip descriptions or definitions of the three words in a scrambled order—*tromp, guarding, disguised*—in a pocket chart in the new book, *Little Mouse, the Red Ripe Strawberry, and the Big Hungry Bear* by Wood and Wood (1989). She asks the children to find each word in the book and point to it. She asks the children to read the sentence with the word in it in the book. They talk about what the meaning might be as they match each word with the definition or description in the pocket chart.

Finally, Mrs. Silva teaches explicitly the comprehension strategy of using story structure to predict. She asks the children to sequence several picture cards taken from the book into a story structure map. After talking about story structure and making predictions using the picture cards placed into the story structure map, the children and teacher read the book aloud together using echoic choral reading. After the reading, they discuss their picture predictions and make any needed adjustments. Each child then turns to a partner and is asked to orally retell the story.

of view. They are introduced to strategies and tools to increase their general enjoyment and satisfaction from reading. We will discuss routines and organizing for small-group reading instruction in the intermediate years in Chapter 4, "Organizing for Effective Comprehensive Reading Instruction."

TEACHING SKILLS AND STRATEGIES EXPLICITLY USING MINILESSONS

Teaching skills and strategies explicitly are well taught via *minilessons* (5 to 10 minutes per session), rather than lengthy lessons of 30 to 45 minutes. **Explicit minilessons** are typically whole-class or small-group lessons used to (a) teach explicitly reading strategies and skills, (b) promote student interaction around what they have read, or (c) teach a necessary procedure (Hagerty, 1992). Because minilessons are brief, it usually takes several

Figure 3.15   Possible Minilesson Topics

Procedural Minilessons	Literary Minilessons	Strategy/Skill Minilessons
Where to sit during reading time	Differences between fiction and nonfiction books	How to choose a book
Giving a book talk		Selecting literature log topics
How to be a good listener in a share session	Learning from dedications	Connecting reading material to your own life
What is an appropriate noise level during reading time	Books that show emotion	Tips for reading aloud
	Books written in the first, second, or third person	Figuring out unknown words
What to do when you finish a book	Author studies	Using context
What kinds of questions to ask during a share session	How authors use quotations	Substituting
	How the story setting fits the story	Using picture clues
Running a small group discussion	Characteristics of different genres	Using the sounds of blends, vowels, contractions, and so on.
Self-evaluation	Development of characters, plot, theme, mood	
Getting ready for a conference		Using Post-its to mark interesting parts
How to have a peer conference	How leads hook us	Monitoring comprehension (Does this make sense and sound right?)
Where to sit during minilessons	How authors use the problem/event/solution pattern	
Taking care of books	Differences between a picture book and a novel	Asking questions while reading
Keeping track of books to read		Making predictions
Rules of the workshop	Titles and their meanings	Emergent strategies
	Characters' points of view	Concept of story
	Examples of similes and metaphors	Concept that print carries meaning
	Examples of foreshadowing	Making sense
	How authors use dialogue	Mapping a story
	Predictable and surprise endings	How to retell a story orally
	Use of descriptive words and phrases	Looking for relationships
	How illustrations enhance the story	Looking for important ideas
	Secrets in books	Making inferences
		Drawing conclusions
		Summarizing a story
		Distinguishing fact from opinion
		Emergent reader skills: directionality, concept of "word," sound/symbol relationships

Note: From *Readers workshop: Real reading* (pp. 113–115), by P. Hagerty, 1992, Ontario, Canada: Scholastic Canada. Copyright 1992 by Patricia Hagerty. Reprinted by permission of Scholastic Canada Ltd.

repetitions of these 5- to 10-minute exercises for most skills or strategies to be fully taught and learned. Explicit minilessons allow teachers to explain briefly, model how to perform the skill or strategy, move efficiently to the application of a skill or strategy, and end a lesson before student attention fades.

Hagerty (1992) described three types of minilessons: (a) procedural, (b) literary, and (c) strategy/skill. A listing of possible minilesson topics is found in Figure 3.15.

A *procedural minilesson*, for example, may involve the teacher and students in learning how to handle new books received for the classroom library corner, as well as how to repair worn books. The teacher may demonstrate how to break in a new book's binding by standing the book on its spine and opening a few pages on either side of the center of the book and carefully pressing them down. Cellophane tape and staplers may be used to demonstrate how to repair tears in a book's pages or cover.

A *literary minilesson* for early readers may involve a child presenting the teacher with a small booklet written at home in the shape of a puppy that retells favorite parts from the book *Taxi Dog* (Barracca & Barracca, 1990). An upper elementary level student may be shown how to assemble a poster resembling the front page of a newspaper in order to depict major events from a novel just read, such as Betsy Byars' *The Summer of the Swans* (1970).

An example of a *strategy/skill minilesson* for early readers may occur during the reading of a big book entitled *Cats and Mice* (Gelman, 1985), in which the teacher makes note of the fact that many of the words in the book end with the participle form of *-ing*. Noticing this regularity in the text, the teacher draws children's attention to the function of *-ing*. For example, while rereading *Cats and Mice* the next day, the teacher may cover each *-ing* ending with a small self-adhesive note, then peel it away while reading to emphasize the word ending. Children are then asked to write several words ending in "ing."

A minilesson for more advanced readers may pertain to text structures used by nonfiction writers to make information books easier to understand (i.e., cause-effect, description, problem-solution, comparisons, and so on). This could involve (a) making a graphic organizer for the patterns used; (b) searching for examples in science, mathematics, and social studies materials; then (c) writing an information essay or report using one of these patterns.

READING BY CHILDREN

Reading *by* children is intended as a time for students to engage in useful, independent practice and application of their emerging skills and strategies during the act of reading a self-selected book. Early in our elementary teaching careers, we, like many other classroom teachers, believed that any successful reading program included allocated time for children to engage in *sustained silent reading* (SSR)—daily, sustained, self-selected, silent reading. It did not take long, however, for us to recognize that simply providing students time to self-select their own books and go off to read did not guarantee that they would actually read! This observation seemed to be particularly true in the early grades in which children's reading is anything but independent, sustained, or silent! In fact, it was not uncommon for several younger children—and older struggling readers—to use books as a prop for *pretend* reading during the allocated independent reading time. In some cases, these non-engaged readers would distract other children in the class who *were* reading. These and other experiences instilled in us concern about the ultimate value and utility of SSR as it has been implemented in our classrooms and many others throughout the nation.

WHY WE NEED STUDENTS TO PRACTICE THEIR READING: RESEARCH EVIDENCE

Though SSR may not be helpful to some children (Shaywitz, 2002), especially struggling readers, research nevertheless *does* indicate that carefully structured independent reading practice *can* improve reading achievement. Indeed, one cannot become a strong reader without practice. Scientifically based reading research (SBRR) confirms that

> Adequate progress in learning to read English (or any alphabetic language) beyond the initial level depends on sufficient practice in reading to achieve fluency with different texts. (Snow et al., 1998, p. 223; National Institute of Child Health and Human Development, 2000, p. 3-1)

Numerous other research studies support teachers providing reading practice time. The much-quoted *Report of the National Reading Panel* (National Institute of Child Health and Human Development, 2000) reviewed a large body of research that revealed a clear and positive relationship between reading time and gains in reading achievement. Anderson, Wilson, and Fielding (1988) showed that time spent reading books and other print materials resulted in consistent reading achievement gains. The highest achievers in fifth grade read up to 200 times as many minutes per day than did the lowest achievers!

In a more recent study titled *NAEP 2004 Trends in Academic Progress Three Decades of Student Performance in Reading and Mathematics* (National Center for Education Statistics, 2005), there was an interesting comparison of how many pages of text were read by students each day versus their reading achievement. Here is a summary of their conclusions:

- At ages 9, 13, and 17, students who indicated that they read five or fewer pages a day had lower reading scores than students in any other category.
- At ages 9 and 13, students who read at least six pages a day had as high reading scores as those who read more than six pages each day.
- At age 17, students who read more than 20 pages a day had higher average reading scores than students who read 11 to 15, 6 to 10, or 5 or fewer pages a day.

Thus, it appears that school experiences that cause students to read six or more pages per day in the early grades and more in later years help students improve in reading proficiency.

Because we know that it is important for students to practice their reading, how can it be done most effectively? Fortunately, there are emerging insights drawn from scientifically based reading research (SBRR) that help us know how to create effective practice reading experiences.

STRUCTURED READING PRACTICE IMPROVES READING ACHIEVEMENT

A **structured reading practice** time offered daily can "improve word recognition, fluency (speed and accuracy of oral reading), and comprehension with most [readers]" (National Institute of Child Health and Human Development, 2000, pp. 3–28).

The most effective structured reading practice experiences for students who are still developing basic reading abilities and fluency typically involve the following:

- Repeated (multiple) oral readings of appropriate ("just right") texts
- Feedback or guidance (i.e., peers, parents, teachers)
- Daily practice sessions that achieve at least 20 minutes per day

Structured reading practice can be done effectively in **dyads** or student pairs (Eldredge, 1990). Benefits of structured oral reading practice reading include improvements to students' knowledge base, language development, comprehension skills, story sequencing, vocabulary, reading fluency, linguistic competence, confidence to move on to more sophisticated and difficult reading, improved spelling and writing quality, and improved use of language mechanics (Caldwell & Gaine, 2000; Cantrell, 1999; Farris & Hancock, 1991; Fredericks, 1992; Krashen, 1989; Taylor, Frye, & Maruyama, 1990).

At this point in time, our recommendation for reading *by* children is twofold. For those students who have not yet achieved word recognition fluency, current research suggests that structured reading practice involving oral repeated readings of the same text with guidance or feedback from a peer, aide, tutor, or teacher is needed (Jenkins, Fuchs, Van den Broek, Espin, & Deno, 2003; Reutzel, Smith, & Fawson (in preparation), Stahl, 2004;

Stanovich, 1980). However, once **automaticity** or rapid and accurate word recognition is achieved, students may derive equal or better fluency development through silent, wide reading (across text types and genres) with systematic monitoring by the teacher that includes feedback, guidance, and accountability (Bryan, Fawson, & Reutzel, 2003; Jenkins et al., 2003; Stahl, 2004; Reutzel, Smith, & Fawson, in preparation).

ACCESS TO BOOKS AND PRINT MAKES INDEPENDENT READING POSSIBLE

Studies over the decades proved time and again that giving students access to books and other print forms improves reading achievement (Allington, 1983; Anderson et al., 1985; Anderson et al., 1988; Duke, 2000a, 2000b; Elley & Mangubhai, 1983; Neuman, 1999; Taylor et al., 1990). In one recent study, for example, Neuman (1999) showed the positive effects of "flooding" local child-care centers in inner-city Philadelphia with books; it improved young children's learning of many early print and reading concepts. Nell Duke (2000a) studied differences in the print environment, access to books, magazines, and displayed language in the rooms provided to children in 20 first-grade classrooms of very low or very high socioeconomic status. Sadly, children in lower socioeconomic classrooms who arguably need even more access to print were by and large exposed to lower amounts, fewer types, and less uses of print. In another study investigating access to information texts (nonfiction) in first grades, Duke (2000b) found a scarcity of informational books in classrooms, particularly the low socioeconomic status schools. The most startling finding was that children in low socioeconomic classrooms only had access to information books about 3.6 minutes per day on average.

Beck and McKeown (2001) support having a wide variety of high-quality books available to young children because "Vivid, delightful pictures are a hallmark of children's trade books, and children are naturally drawn to them" (p. 11). Fader (1976) wrote about the necessity of getting children "hooked on books" and our role as teachers: "If teachers would see themselves first as purveyors of pleasure rather than instructors in skill, they may find that skill will flourish where pleasure has been cultivated" (p. 4). Jim Trelease (2001) summed up well the value of having great books available to children when he wrote,

> Expecting children living in a "print desert" to become competent readers by simply drill and skill, repeatedly teaching the sounds and letters, is the equivalent of expecting children in Israel to become competent skiers with only instruction booklets but no snow. (p. 4)

MOTIVATING STUDENTS TO READ

For 40 years, studies have also shown that students are more motivated to read trade books (a.k.a. "library books") than basal readers or content textbooks (Asher, 1980; Csikszentmihalyi & Csikszentmihalyi, 1988; McQuillan & Conde, 1996; VanSledright, 1995; Wigfield, 1996, 1997; Turner & Paris, 1995; Worthy, Moorman, & Turner, 1999). Asher found in the early 1980s that when students have an high interest for reading materials, this results in greater desires to read and increased reading comprehension.

Unfortunately, what children have an interest in reading is not always available at school. Worthy et al. (1999) reported a study entitled, *"What Johnny Likes to Read Is Hard to Find in School,"* in which they examined the reading preferences and access to a variety of reading materials of sixth-grade students in three large middle schools in the southwestern United States. Comparisons of student preferences for reading were examined by gender, income, reading attitude, and achievement; and the researchers found more similarities than differences. Sixth-grade students enjoyed reading scary books and stories, comics and cartoons, magazines about popular culture, and books and magazines about sports. They were also interested in how students gained access to these preferred readings. The majority of students obtained preferred reading materials from home and stores rather than from schools and libraries. Classrooms ranked a dead last for providing interesting books or magazines even among low-income students! Surely we can do better.

INDEPENDENT READING HELPS STRUGGLING AND SECOND-LANGUAGE LEARNERS

Students learn at different rates; using many learning strategies; and with varying degrees of ability, confidence, and feelings of self-worth. Trade books offer one of the most powerful tools for meeting the needs of a variety of students with special learning needs in schools (Reutzel & DeBoer, 2002). Mangubhai and Elley (1982) declared, "The provision of a rich supply of high-interest storybooks is a much more feasible policy for improving English learning than any pious pronouncements about the urgent need to raise teacher quality" (p. 159). Because trade books offer a wide variety of reading levels, interest, content areas, and cultures, they can be used to meet the needs of a variety of special-needs learners with some amazing results (Flippo, 1999; Hart-Hewins, 1999; Vandergrift, 2001).

Trade books play a major role in helping second-language learners become skilled and fluent readers and speakers of English (Elley, 1991; Laumbach, 1995). Elley (1991) stated, "Those children who are exposed to an extensive range of high-interest illustrated storybooks and encouraged to read and share them are consistently found to learn the target language more quickly" (p. 375). Krashen (1997/1998) wrote, "We must build critically needed reading environments for all our learners—book by book" (p. 21).

Morrow (1992) found in a study of using trade books in a literature-based reading program that minority children from a variety of backgrounds experienced increases in achievement, voluntary reading, and attitudes. Routman (1991) related:

> I started combing local bookstores and buying multiple copies of appealing children's books. These books I used to teach reading. The results with low-ability first graders were impressive. For three years in a row, typically, two of the five children would test out in June [on a standardized test] as high-ability readers, two would be at the average level, and one would remain as a low-ability reader. The results also included students filled with high self-esteem, pride in their accomplishments, and the joy of being competent readers. (p. 10)

It is clear from this brief review of research that reading by students is a powerful ingredient in a comprehensive reading program.

We have found several excellent practices for involving students in independent reading practice: (a) writing what we read around the room, (b) popcorn reading, (c) paired or buddy reading, and (d) silent sustained reading. In writing what we read around the room, the teacher controls the process and students participate. In *popcorn reading*, the responsibility for reading independently is subtly shifted to the students with the teacher exerting less control. In paired or buddy reading, the children assume the full responsibility for reading independently with some feedback and coaching. Finally, students assume the full responsibility for monitoring the quality and success of their own private reading during silent sustained reading. But remember, SSR is the choice for reading practice only when children truly have become independent in recognizing words swiftly and accurately.

Here is more information about some of our preferred ways of providing independent reading practice:

- *Writing What We Read Around the Room.* In writing what we read around the room, the teacher or a student uses a pointer to read words, charts, big books, signs, displays, or other classroom printed materials as a group in unison. Some teachers close the blinds, turn out the lights, and use a flashlight for a pointer to direct students' attention to print in the classroom environment for reading around the room. Students are then asked to write in a "Reading and Writing Around the Room" journal a few things they have read that day. This provides a quick assessment for accountability and engagement.

    Tompkins (1998) described a related approach, called *reading around*, in which students read aloud their favorite sentences or paragraphs one at a time to others. The key to this approach is to allow children time for rehearsal of the text prior to reading aloud. If there is more than one child wanting to read the same passage or text, invite these children to rehearse together a longer piece of text than a sentence or paragraph so that each student gets to read aloud.

- *Popcorn Reading.* Popcorn reading (McCool, 1982) is a very common practice in many elementary classrooms. Children in the whole class or in a small group all have the same book to read. Someone, either the teacher or a child, begins reading aloud. At some point, that person calls out "popcorn" and calls on another person to continue reading. Although this process seems very simple, it does motivate students to pay careful attention and to follow along. A variation on popcorn reading is to stop, say "popcorn," and anyone who wants to start reading jumps in and continues the reading. Many teachers, especially those in the intermediate grades, have found that popcorn reading is a highly motivating form of reading practice.

- *Buddy Reading.* Buddy reading is also a very common practice in many elementary classrooms (Eldredge, 1990; Koskinen & Blum, 1986; Stahl, 2004). In buddy reading, peer-aged students are paired for reading practice. Pairing peer-aged children usually involves placing children together who are not on the same reading level, yet are not so far apart in their reading abilities that one or both will become frustrated by practicing together. Paired reading begins with one child assuming the role of reader and the other child assuming the role of listener, prompter, and responder. The listener has as important a role as the reader. The listener should provide supportive prompts to the reader when needed, feedback on how well the reader read, and encouragement for future growth. It is most helpful if listeners receive a modicum of training about how to prompt and provide feedback from their teacher. Once one child in the pair is finished reading, the roles for each typically reverse.

- *Sustained Silent Reading (SSR).* As discussed earlier, one approach for supporting reading *by* children who are more advanced in their abilities is providing the opportunity to enjoy the reading of self-selected materials within a level of appropriate challenge on a regular basis (Pilgreen, 2000). Sustained silent reading (SSR) is a somewhat structured approach that provides needed reading opportunities and time for students to practice. Hunt (1970) explained that SSR is an allocated time in which children are given regular, fixed time periods for silently reading self-selected materials. Put differently, SSR is an activity in which everyone in the classroom—students, teachers, parents, volunteers—reads silently something they have personally selected for a designated period of time.

    The purposes of SSR are grounded in the belief that anyone—children or adults—gets better at anything they practice regularly: the time-on-task principle. We know that the more children read, the more they will learn about the process of becoming a successful reader. To help children derive greater purpose and understanding from SSR, we offer the following eight factors for SSR success based on Pilgreen's *The SSR Handbook* (2000):

1. Access to books
2. Appeal of books
3. Conducive environment for reading
4. Encouragement and motivation
5. Staff training to involve the school
6. Nonaccountability
7. Follow-up activities
8. Regular time to read

McCracken and McCracken (1978) described several reasons for implementing an SSR program:

1. Reading books is important. Children come to understand what teachers value by taking note of what they are asked to do.
2. Anyone can read a book. Readers with special needs do not feel singled out for attention when they engage in reading or looking at a book during SSR.
3. Children learn that reading is interacting with an author through sustained engagement with a self-selected text.
4. Children develop the ability to remain on task for an extended period of time during SSR.
5. Books were meant to be read in large chunks for extended periods of time. Children may get the wrong idea that reading is done during small segments of time and focus on short texts such as those often found in basal readers.
6. Comprehension is improved through SSR activities (see also Reutzel & Hollingsworth, 1991).
7. Finally, children learn to judge the appropriateness of the materials they select for reading during SSR. (*Note:* Reutzel and Gali [1998] found that for most children the hardest part of learning to read was choosing the right book.)

Implementing an SSR program is a relatively straightforward process. Here is what you do:

1. Designate a specific daily time for reading. Teachers have found that three time slots work well for SSR. The first is as children enter the classroom first thing in the morning. The second is following lunch or recess, and the third is right before children go home for the day. Typically, teachers allocate about 15 to 20 minutes per day for SSR. For younger children, teachers may begin with a 10-minute SSR time and lengthen this time throughout the year as children indicate a desire for more time. We have found that a cooking timer with a bell is a welcome addition for younger children so they do not become worried about watching the clock.
2. Teach a procedural minilesson to describe the rules of SSR. To set the stage for successful experiences with SSR, we suggest that teachers conduct a brief lesson on the rules and expectations associated with SSR time. Begin by

Figure 3.16   The Rules for SSR

Children must select their own books or reading materials.

1. Changing books during the SSR period is discouraged to avoid interruptions.
2. Each individual in the classroom is expected to read silently without interruptions during the fixed period of time for SSR.
3. The teacher and other visitors in the classroom are expected to read silently materials of their own choosing as well.
4. Children are not expected to make reports or answer teacher questions about the books they have been reading during SSR.

stating the purposes of SSR (shown previously). Second, review with children the rules for participation in SSR. We have found that enlarging these rules and placing them on a chart for the class help students take responsibility for their own behavior. Finally, explain how students can ready themselves for this time each day. The rules for SSR are shown in Figure 3.16 in chart form.

3. Extend the experience through sharing. Children can be asked to share their books with other students at the conclusion of SSR through a "say something" or "turn to your neighbor" activity. In addition to these informal share sessions, groups of children may organize a response to a book through art, drama, writing, or musical performances to be shared with others. In any case, beginning an SSR program with young children, even in kindergarten, convinces children of the value of reading and gives them important practice time. Clearly, SSR has the potential to help children develop lifelong reading enjoyment and habits.

As adults, many of the books we choose to read for pleasure are texts that were introduced to us through interactions with others. We have acquired knowledge of various sources we can turn to for suggestions about what we might read such as the "Best Seller" lists that are available. Perhaps we are having an informal conversation with a friend or associate and find ourselves discussing a new or favorite book. Chances are very good that through this recommendation we will seek out the text to read for ourselves. This interaction provides a driving force for us to want to share the text with others and perhaps even seek out additional books to read.

An opportunity for independent reading in most classrooms, which generally allows for student choice and interest, occurs far too infrequently. Many teachers only allow independent reading when students have completed other instructional tasks such as worksheet or workbook activities. Not all teachers make regularly scheduled independent reading time available to students. However, it is an activity that can bring great gains in student reading achievement and interest. We offer one last observation about SSR to increase its success in promoting reading growth and performance. Students experience greater satisfaction from independent reading when they select reading materials of interest from books on their independent reading level. Many teachers provide children "browsing boxes" in which a variety of interesting books are placed at the child's reading level for selection. Children choose from their browsing box or from the classroom library materials to be read during independent reading time.

Finally, we strongly urge teachers during the SSR time to spend their time monitoring the reading of their students rather than engaging in the worn-out and unproven idea that modeling silent personal reading will have a positive impact upon students' reading development and motivation (Stahl, 2004). Bryan et al. (2003) found that randomly scheduled monitoring visits to individual readers to have them read aloud for a moment, answer some questions, and discuss what they were reading had a long-lasting and facilitative effect upon the engagement of the least engaged readers during SSR.

SET UP A LIBRARY CORNER

Books should be displayed in a well-lit and accessible area. The library corner should, where possible, be located out of the traffic flow in the classroom. It is important that this area is relatively quiet so that children are not distracted or disturbed. Bookshelves should be the appropriate size and height so that children can reach the books without standing on a chair or step stool. There should be room enough for children to sit comfortably to read alone or together with another reader. Children should be taught how to care for the books in the library corner, how to keep it clean and well organized, and how to manage a check-out system. If children are to value the time and resources of a classroom library, they must take responsibility for the care of the books and the classroom library space. For additional information on how to create and sustain an effective classroom library, try *Your Classroom Library: New Ways to Give It More Teaching Power* (Reutzel & Fawson, 2002).

IN CONCLUSION

Reading *to, with,* and *by* children provides an instructional framework that helps teachers use best practices of interactive read alouds, choral reading, technology, shared reading, small-group differentiated reading instruction, skill and strategy instruction, read around the room, popcorn reading, buddy reading, and sustained silent reading (SSR) with monitoring to model good reading behaviors; to teach specific reading skills and strategies; and to provide time, resources, and conditions for students to apply their knowledge and skills to reading each and every day. Teachers who have used these practices have consistently provided excellent instruction with equally stellar results (Morrow, Tracey, Woo, & Pressley, 1999; Wharton-McDonald, Pressley, & Rankin, 1997).

SELECTED REFERENCES

Ahlberg, J. (1978). *Each peach pear plum: An "I spy" story*. New York: Viking Press.

Allington, R. L. (1977). If they don't read much, how they ever gonna get good? *Journal of Reading, 21*, 57–61.

Allington, R. L. (1983). The reading instruction provided readers of differing reading abilities. *The Elementary School Journal, 83,* 548–559.

Allington, R. L. (2001). *What really matters for struggling readers: Designing research-based programs.* New York: Addison-Wesley/Longman.

Anderson, R. C., Hiebert, E. F., Scott, J. A., & Wilkinson, I. A. G. (1985). *Becoming a nation of readers: The report of the Commission on Reading.* Washington, DC: The National Institute of Education.

Anderson, R. C., Wilson, P. T., & Fielding, L. G. (1988, Summer). Growth in reading and how children spend their time outside of school. *Reading Research Quarterly, 23,* 285–303.

Asher, S. R. (1980). Topic interest and children's reading comprehension. In R. J. Spiro, B. C. Bruce, & W. F. Brewer (Eds.), *Theoretical issues of reading comprehension* (pp. 525–534). Hillsdale, NJ: Lawrence Erlbaum Associates.

Barracca, D., & Barracca, S. (1990). *Taxi dog.* New York: Dial Books.

Barrentine, S. B. (1996). Engaging with reading through interactive read-alouds. *The Reading Teacher, 50*(1), 36–43.

Barrett, F. L. (1982). *A teacher's guide to shared reading.* Richmond Hill, Ontario, Canada: Scholastic-TAB Publications.

Baumann, J. F., Hoffman, J. V., Duffy-Hester, A. M., & Moon Ro, J. (2000). The first R yesterday and today: U.S. elementary reading instruction practices reported by teachers and administrators. *Reading Research Quarterly, 35,* 338–377.

Baumann, J. F., Hoffman, J. V., Moon, J., & Duffy-Hester, A. M. (1998). Where are the teachers' voices in the phonics/whole language debate? Results from a survey of U.S. elementary classroom teachers. *The Reading Teacher, 51,* 636–650.

Bear, D. R., Invernizzi, M., Templeton, S., & Johnston, F. (2004). *Words their way: Word study for phonics, vocabulary and spelling instruction* (3rd ed.). Upper Saddle River, NJ: Merrill/Prentice Hall.

Beck, I. L., & McKeown, M. G. (2001). Text talk: Capturing the benefits of read-aloud experiences for young children. *The Reading Teacher, 55*(1), 10–20.

Beers, J. W., & Henderson, E. (1977). A study of developing orthographic concepts among first graders. *Research in the Teaching of English, 11,* 133–148.

Bennett, W. J. (2001, April 24). A cure for the illiteracy epidemic. *The Wall Street Journal,* p. A24.

Brown, K. J. (1999). What kind of text—for whom and when? Textual scaffolding for beginning readers. *The Reading Teacher, 53*(4).

Bryan, G., Fawson, P. C., & Reutzel, D. R. (2003). Sustained silent reading: Exploring the value of literature discussion with three non-engaged readers. *Reading Research and Instruction, 43*(1), 47–73.

Byars, B. (1970). *The summer of the swans.* New York: Viking.

Caldwell, K., & Gaine, T. (2000). *"The phantom tollbooth" and how the independent reading of good books improves students' reading performance.* Bloomington, IN: Reading and Communication Skills Clearinghouse. (ERIC Document Reproduction Service No. ED449462).

Campbell, R. (1992). *Reading real books.* Philadelphia: Open University Press.

Campbell, R. (2001). *Read-alouds with young children.* Newark, DE: International Reading Association.

Cantrell, S. C. (1999, Fall). The effects of literacy instruction on primary students' reading and writing achievement. *Reading Research Quarterly, 39*(1), 3–26.

Clay, M. M. (1993a). *An observation survey for early literacy achievement.* Portsmouth, NH: Heinemann Educational Books.

Clay, M. M. (1993b). *Reading recovery: A guidebook for teachers in training.* Portsmouth, NH: Heinemann Educational Books.

Cooter, R. B. (2003). Teacher capacity-building helps urban children succeed in reading. *The Reading Teacher, 57*(2), 198–205.

Csikszentmihalyi, M., & Csikszentmihalyi, I. S. (Eds.). (1988). *Optimal experience: Studies of flow in consciousness.* New York: Cambridge University Press.

daCruz-Payne, C. (2005). *Shared reading for today's classroom.* New York: Scholastic.

Department of Education. (1985). *Reading in junior classes. Wellington, New Zealand.* New York: Richard C. Owen.

DeTemple, J. M. (2001). Parents and children reading books together. In D. K. Dickinson & P. O. Tabors (Eds.), *Beginning literacy with language.* (pp. 31–52). Baltimore, MD: Paul H. Brookes.

Dickinson, D. K. (2001). Book reading in preschool classrooms: Is recommended practice common? In D. K. Dickinson & P. O. Tabors (Eds.), *Beginning literacy with language* (pp. 175–204). Baltimore, MD: Paul H. Brookes.

Duffy, G. G. (2003). *Explaining reading: A resource for teaching concepts, skills, and strategies.* New York: Guilford Press.

Duke, N. K. (2000a). For the rich it's richer: Print experiences and environments offered to children in very low- and very high-socioeconomic status first-grade classrooms. *American Educational Research Journal, 37,* 441–478.

Duke, N. K. (2000b). 3.6 minutes per day: The scarcity of informational texts in first grade. *Reading Research Quarterly, 35*(2), 202–224.

Durkin, D. (1966). *Children who read early: Two longitudinal studies.* New York: Teachers College Press.

Edwards, P. (1999). *A path to follow: Learning to listen to parents.* Portsmouth, NH: Heinemann Educational Books.

Efta, M. (1984). Reading in silence: A chance to read. In A. J. Harris & E. R. Sipay (Eds.), *Readings on reading instruction* (3rd ed., pp. 387–391). New York: Longman.

Ehri, L. C., & Sweet, J. (1991). Finger-point reading of memorized text: What enables beginners to process the print? *Reading Research Quarterly, 26,* 442–462.

Eldredge, J. L. (1990). Increasing the performance of poor readers in the third grade with a group-assisted strategy. *Journal of Educational Research, 84,* 69–77.

Eldredge, J. L., Reutzel, D. R., & Hollingsworth, P. M. (1996, Summer). Comparing the effectiveness of two oral reading practices: Round-robin reading and the shared book experience. *Journal of Literacy Research, 28*(2), 201–225.

Elley, W. B. (1991, September). Acquiring literacy in a second language: The effect of book-based programs. *Language Learning, 41,* 375–411.

Elley, W. B., & Mangubhai, F. (1983, Fall). The impact of reading on second language learning. *Reading Research Quarterly, 19,* 53–67.

Fader, D. N. (1976). *The new hooked on books.* New York: Berkley.

Farris, P. J., & Hancock, M. R. (1991, November–December). The role of literature in reading achievement. *The Clearing House, 65,* 114–117.

Fawson, P. C., & Reutzel, D. R. (2000). But I only have a basal: Implementing guided reading in the early grades. *The Reading Teacher, 54*(1), 84–97.

Fleischman, P. (1988). *Joyful Noise: Poems for two voices.* Harper Trophy Publishers.

Flippo, R. F. (1999). *What do the experts say? Helping children learn to read.* Portsmouth, NH: Heinemann Educational Books.

Fountas, I. C., & Pinnell, G. S. (1996). *Guided reading: Good first teaching for all children.* Portsmouth, NH: Heinemann Educational Books.

Fountas, I. C., & Pinnell, G. S. (1999). *Matching books to readers: Using leveled books in guided reading, K–3.* Portsmouth, NH: Heinemann Educational Books.

Fountas, I. C., & Pinnell, G. S. (2001). *Guiding readers and writers (grades 3–6): Teaching comprehension, genre, and content literacy.* Portsmouth, NH: Heinemann Educational Books.

Fredericks, A. D. (1992). *The integrated curriculum: Book for reluctant readers, grades 2–5.* Englewood, CO: Teacher Ideas Press.

Gambrell, L. B. (1978). Getting started with sustained silent reading and keeping it going. *The Reading Teacher, 32,* 328–331.

Gelman, R. G. (1985). *Cats and mice.* New York: Scholastic.

Grossman, B. (1996). *My little sister ate one hare.* New York: Crown.

Hagerty, P. (1992). *Reader's workshop: Real reading.* Ontario, Canada: Scholastic Canada.

Hahn, M. L. (2002). *Reconsidering read-aloud.* Portland, ME: Stenhouse.

Halpern, H. (1981). An attitude survey of uninterrupted sustained silent reading. *Reading Horizons, 21,* 272–279.

Hancock, J. (1999). *The explicit teaching of reading.* Newark, DE: International Reading Association.

Hart-Hewins, L. (1999). *Better books! Better readers! How to choose, use, and level books for children in the primary grades.* York, ME: Stenhouse.

Heath, S. B. (1982). What no bedtime stories means: Narrative skills at home and school. *Language and Society, 11,* 49–76.

Heath, S. B. (1983). *Ways with words: Language, life and work in communities and classrooms.* Cambridge, UK: Cambridge University Press.

Hiebert, E. H. (1999). Text matters in learning to read. *The Reading Teacher, 52*(6), 552–66.

Hoffman, J. V., Roser, N., & Battle, J. (1993). Reading aloud in classrooms: From the modal to a "model." *The Reading Teacher, 46*(6), 496–503.

Holdaway, D. (1979). *The foundations of literacy.* New York: Ashton Scholastic.

Hunt, L. C. (1970). Effect of self-selection, interest, and motivation upon independent, instructional, and frustrational levels. *The Reading Teacher, 24,* 146–151.

Hunt, L. C., Jr. (1984). Six steps to the individualized reading program (IRP). In A. J. Harris & E. R. Sipay (Eds.), *Readings on reading instruction* (3rd ed., pp. 190–195). New York: Longman.

Ivey, G. (2003). The teacher makes it more explainable and other reasons to read aloud in the intermediate grades. *The Reading Teacher, 56*(8), 812–814.

Jenkins, J. R., Fuchs, L. S., Van den Broek, P., Espin, C., & Deno, S. L. (2003). Accuracy and fluency in list and context reading of skilled and RD groups: Absolute and relative performance levels. *Learning Disabilities Research and Practice, 18*(4), 237–245.

Koskinen, P. S., & Blum, I. H. (1986). Paired repeated reading: A classroom strategy for developing fluent reading. *The Reading Teacher 40*(1), 7–75.

Krashen, S. (1997, December/1998, January). Bridging inequity with books. *Educational Leadership,* 18–22.

Krashen, S. (2002). More smoke and mirrors: A critique of the National Reading Panel on Fluency. In R. L. Allington (Ed.), *Big brother and the national reading curriculum: How ideology trumped evidence* (pp. 112–124). Portsmouth, NH: Heinemann Educational Books.

Krashen, S. D. (1989, Winter). We acquire vocabulary and spelling by reading: Additional evidence for the input hypothesis. *The Modern Language Journal, 73,* 440–464.

Krauss, R. (1945). *The carrot seed.* New York: Scholastic.

Kuhn, M. (2005). Helping students become accurate, expressive readers: Fluency instruction for small groups. *The Reading Teacher, 58*(4), 338–345.

Labbo, L. D. (2001). Supporting children's comprehension of informational text through interactive read alouds. *Literacy and Nonfiction Series, 1*(2), 1–4.

Laumbach, B. (1995, Spring). Reading interests of rural bilingual children. *Rural Educator, 16,* 12–14.

Lee-Daniels, S. L., & Murray, B. A. (2000). DEAR me: What does it take to get my children reading? *The Reading Teacher, 54,* 154–155.

Mangubhai, F., & Elley, W. (1982). The role of reading in promoting ESL. *Language Learning and Communication, 1,* 151–160.

Manning, G. L., & Manning, M. (1984). What models of recreational reading make a difference? *Reading World, 23,* 375–380.

Martin, B. (1990). *Brown bear, brown bear, what do you see?* New York: Henry Holt.

Martin, B. (1991). *Polar bear, polar bear, what do you hear?* New York: Henry Holt.

Mathes, P. G., Denton, C. A., Fletcher, J. M., Anthony, J. L., Francis, D. J., & Schatschneider, C. (2005). The effects of theoretically different instruction and student characteristics on the skills of struggling readers. *Reading Research Quarterly, 40*(2), 148–182.

McCardle, P., & Chhabra, V. (2004). The voice of evidence in reading research. Baltimore, MD: Paul H. Brookes.

McCool, M. (1982). *Reading with a special touch* (Government Documents No. ED220798) Urbana, IL: ERIC Language Arts Center.

McCracken, R. A. (1971). Initiating sustained silent reading. *Journal of Reading, 14,* 521–524, 582–583.

McCracken, R. A., & McCracken, M. J. (1978). Modeling is the key to sustained reading. *The Reading Teacher, 31,* 406–408.

McQuillan, J., & Conde, G. (1996). The conditions of flow in reading: Two studies of optimal experience. *Reading Psychology, 17,* 109–135.

Meek, M. (1984). Forward in J. Trelease (Ed.), *The read aloud handbook.* Harmondsworth, UK: Penguin.

Menon, S., & Hiebert, E. H. (2005). A comparison of first graders' reading with little books or literature-based basal anthologies. *Reading Research Quarterly, 40*(1), 12–38.

Meyer, L. A., Stahl, S. A., & Wardrop, J. L. (1994, November–December). Effects of reading storybooks aloud to children. *The Journal of Educational Research, 88,* 69–85.

Mooney, M. E. (1990). *Reading to, with, and by children.* Katonah, NY: Richard C. Owen.

Moore, J. C., Jones, C. J., & Miller, D. C. (1980). What we know after a decade of sustained silent reading. *The Reading Teacher, 33,* 445–450.

Morris, D. (1998). Assessing printed word knowledge in beginning readers: The Early Reading Screening Instrument (ERSI). *Illinois State Reading Journal, 26*(2), 30–39.

Morrow, L. M. (1988). Young children's responses to one-to-one story reading in school settings. *Reading Research Quarterly, 23,* 89–107.

Morrow, L. M. (1992). The impact of a literature-based program on literacy achievement, use of literature, and attitudes of children from minority backgrounds. *Reading Research Quarterly, 27*(3), 251–275.

Morrow, L. M. (2001). *Literacy development in the early years: Helping children read and write* (4th ed.). Boston, MA: Allyn & Bacon.

Morrow, L. M., & Temlock-Fields, J. (2004). Use of literature in the home and at school. In B. H. Wasik (Ed.), *Handbook of family literacy* (pp. 83–100). Mahwah, NJ: Lawrence Erlbaum Associates.

Morrow, L. M., Tracey, D. H., Woo, D. G., & Pressley, M. (1999). Characteristics of exemplary first-grade literacy instruction. *The Reading Teacher, 52*(5), 462–476.

National Center for Education Statistics. (2005). *NAEP 2004 trends in academic progress three decades of student performance in reading and mathematics* (Publication # NCES 2005464). Washington, DC: U.S. Department of Education.

National Institute of Child Health and Human Development. (2000). *Report of the National Reading Panel: Teaching children to read, an evidence-based assessment of the scientific research literature on reading and its implications for reading instruction (Reports of the Subgroups)* (NIH Publication No. 00-4754). Washington, DC: U.S. Government Printing Office.

Neuman, S. B. (1999). Books make a difference: A study of access to literacy. *Reading Research Quarterly, 34*(3), 2–31.

Neuman, S. B. (2001). The role of knowledge in early literacy. *Reading Research Quarterly, 36*(4), 468–475.

Neuman, S. B., & Celano, D. (2001). Access to print in low-income and middle-income communities. *Reading Research Quarterly, 36*(1), 8–27.

Neuman, S. B., & Roskos, K. A. (1993). *Language and literacy learning in the early years: An integrated approach.* Fort Worth, TX: Harcourt Brace Jovanovich.

Optiz, M. F., & Rasinski, T. V. (1998). *Good-bye round robin: 25 effective oral reading strategies.* Portsmouth, NH: Heinemann Educational Books.

Pilgreen, J. L. (2000). *The SSR handbook: How to organize and manage a silent sustained reading program.* Portsmouth, NH: Heinemann Educational Books.

Pinnell, G. S., & Fountas, I. C. (2002). *Leveled books for readers, grades 3–6.* Portsmouth, NH: Heinemann Educational Books.

Pressley, M. (2002). *Reading instruction that works: The case for balanced teaching* (2nd ed.) New York: The Guilford Press.

Pressley, M., Yokoi, L., & Rankin, J. (2000). A survey of instructional practices of primary teachers nominated as effective in promoting literacy. In R. D. Robinson, M. C. McKenna, & J. M. Wedman (Eds.), *Issues and* trends in literacy education (2nd ed., pp. 10–34). Boston: Allyn & Bacon.

Reutzel, D. R. (1995). Finger-point reading and beyond: Learning about print strategies (LAPS). *Reading Horizons, 35*(4), 310–328.

Reutzel, D. R. (1996a). A balanced reading approach. In J. Baltas & S. Shafer (Eds.), *Scholastic guide to balanced reading: K–2* (pp. 6–12). New York: Scholastic.

Reutzel, D. R. (1996b). A balanced reading approach. In J. Baltas & S. Shafer (Eds.), *Scholastic guide to balanced reading: Grades 3–6* (pp. 7–11). New York: Scholastic.

Reutzel, D. R. (2001, May–June). New research helps you reap the biggest benefits from read aloud. *Scholastic Instructor,* 23–24.

Reutzel, D. R., Smith, J. A., & Fawson, P. C. (in preparation). *Reconsidering silent sustained reading (SSR): A comparative study of modified SSR with oral repeated reading practice.* Logan, UT: Utah State University.

Reutzel, D. R., & Cooter, R. B. (2004). *Teaching children to read: Putting the pieces together* (4th ed.). Upper Saddle River, NJ: Merrill/Prentice Hall.

Reutzel, D. R., & Cooter, R. B., Jr. (1991). Organizing for effective instruction: The reading workshop. *The Reading Teacher, 44*(8), 548–555.

Reutzel, D. R., & DeBoer, B. (2002). *Occasional papers: The importance of reading trade books.* New York: Scholastic.

Reutzel, D. R., & Fawson, P. C. (2002). *Your classroom library: New ways to give it more teaching power.* New York: Scholastic Professional Books.

Reutzel, D. R., & Gali, K. (1998). The art of children's book selection: A labyrinth unexplored. *Reading Psychology, 19*(3), 3–50.

Reutzel, D. R., & Hollingsworth, P. (1991). Reading time in school: Effect on fourth graders' performance on a criterion-referenced comprehension test. *Journal of Educational Research, 84*(3), 170–176.

Reutzel, D. R., Hollingsworth, P. M., & Eldredge, J. L. (1994). Oral reading instruction: The impact on student reading development. *Reading Research Quarterly, 23*(1), 40–62.

Ribowsky, H. (1985). *The effects of a code emphasis approach and a whole language approach upon emergent literacy of kindergarten children* (Report No. CS-008-397). (ERIC Document Reproduction Service No. ED 269 720)

Robertson, C., Keating, I., Shenton, L., & Roberts, I. (1996). Uninterrupted, sustained, silent reading: The rhetoric and the practice. *Journal of Research in Reading, 19*, 25–35.

Rog, L. J. (2003). *Guided reading basics: Organizing, managing, and implementing a balanced literacy program in K–3.* New York: Stenhouse.

Rosenhouse, J., Feitelson, D., & Kita, B. (1997). Interactive reading aloud to Israeli first graders: Its contribution to literacy development. *Reading Research Quarterly, 32,* 168–183.

Routman, R. (1991). *Invitations: Changing as teachers and learners, K–12.* Portsmouth, NH: Heinemann Educational Books.

Scully, P., & Roberts, H. (2002). Phonics, expository writing, and reading aloud: Playful literacy in the primary grades. *Early Childhood Educational Journal, 30*(2), 93–99.

Schulman, M. B., & Payne, C. D. (2000). *Guided reading: Making it work (grades K–3).* New York: Scholastic.

Sendak, M. (1962). *Chicken Soup with Rice.* NY: Harper Collins Publishers.

Shaywitz, S. (Presenter). (2002). *Teaching children to read* (video). Washington, DC: National Institute for Literacy.

Sipe, L. (2002). Talking back and taking over: Young children's expressive engagement during storybook read-alouds. *The Reading Teacher, 55*(5), 476–483.

Slaughter, J. P. (1993). *Beyond storybooks: Young children and the shared book experience.* Newark, DE: International Reading Association.

Smolkin, L. B., & Donovan, C. A. (2003). Supporting comprehension acquisition for emerging and struggling readers: The interactive information book read-aloud. *Exceptionality, 11*(1), 25–38.

Snow, C. E., Burns, M. S., & Griffin, P. (1998). *Preventing reading difficulties in young children* (p. 223). Washington, DC: National Academy Press.

Stahl, S. A. (2004). What do we know about fluency? The findings of the National Reading Panel. In P. McCardle & V. Chhabra (Eds.), *The voice of evidence in reading research* (pp. 187–212). Baltimore, MD: Paul H. Brookes.

Stanovich, K. (1980). Toward an interactive-compensatory model of individual differences in the development of reading fluency. *Reading Research Quarterly, 16*(1), 37–71.

Strickland, D. S., & Morrow, L. M. (1989). Interactive experiences with storybook reading. *The Reading Teacher, 42*(4), 322–323.

Taylor, B. M., Frye, B. J., & Maruyama, G. (1990, Summer). Time spent reading and reading growth. *American Educational Research Journal, 27,* 351–362.

Teale, W. H., & Martinez, M. (1986). Reading in a kindergarten classroom library. *The Reading Teacher, 41*(6), 568–573.

Teale, W. H., & Martinez, M. G. (1988). Getting on the right road to reading: Bringing books and young children together in the classroom. *Young Children, 44*(1), 10–15.

Tompkins, G. (1998). *Fifty literacy strategies step by step.* Upper Saddle River, NJ: Merrill/Prentice Hall.

Trelease, J. (2001a). *Research, trends, essays: 'It's the climate, stupid!' What's new* (pp. 1–6). Retrieved May 9, 2001, from http://www.trelease-on-reading.com/whatsnu_2.html.

Trelease, J. (2001b). *The read-aloud handbook,* 5th ed. New York: Penguin.

Turner, J., & Paris, S. G. (1995). How literacy tasks influence children's motivation for literacy. *The Reading Teacher, 48,* 662–673.

Tyner, B. (2004). *Small-group reading instruction: A differentiated teaching model for beginning and struggling readers.* Newark, DE: International Reading Association.

U.S. Department of Education: Office of Educational Research and Improvement. (2001). *The nation's report card: Fourth-grade reading 2000.* Jessup, MD: National Center for Educational Statistics.

Vandergrift, K. E. (2001). *Linking literature with learning.* Retrieved May 25, 2001, from http://www.scils.rutgers.edu/special/day/linkages.html.

VanSledright, B. A. (1995). *How do multiple text resources influence learning to read American history in fifth grade? NRRC ongoing research* (pp. 4–5). Athens, GA: NRRC News: A Newsletter of the National Reading Research Center. (ERIC Document Reproduction Service No. ED385832)

Vygotsky, L. S. (1978). *Mind in society.* Cambridge, MA: Harvard University Press.

Weaver, C. (1998). *Reconsidering a balanced approach to reading.* Urbana, IL: National Council of Teachers of English.

Wells, C. G. (1986). *The meaning makers: Children learning language and using language to learn.* Portsmouth, NH: Heinemann Educational Books.

Wharton-McDonald, R., Pressley, M., & Rankin, K. (1997). Effective primary-grades literacy instruction = Balanced literacy instruction. *The Reading Teacher, 50*(6), 518–21.

Wigfield, A. (1996). *The nature of children's motivations for reading and their relations to frequency and reading performance* [microform] (Government Documents No. ED1.310/2:398550). Athens, GA: National Reading Research Center.

Wigfield, A. (1997). Children's motivations for reading and reading engagement. In J. T. Guthrie & A. Wigfield (Eds.), *Reading engagement: Motivating readers through integrated instruction* (pp. 14–33). Newark, DE: International Reading Association.

Wood, D., & Wood, A. (1984). *Little mouse, red ripe strawberry, and the big hungry bear.* Wiltshire, England: Children's Play International Publishers.

Worthy, M. J., Moorman, M., & Turner, M. (1999, January–February–March). What Johnny likes to read is hard to find in school. *Reading Research Quarterly, 34*(1), 12–27.

Wright, G., Sherman, R., & Jones, T. B. (2004). Are silent reading behaviors of first graders really silent? *The Reading Teacher, 57*(6), 546–553.

Chapter 4

Organizing for Effective Comprehensive Reading Instruction

Several teachers are talking in the teachers' lounge about the start of school in a few days. Ms. Cella makes a somewhat sarcastic remark about the so-called "super teachers" about whom she is always hearing.

"Yeah, I hear Mrs. Luna over in Washington Elementary has five learning centers in her classroom, teaches several small reading groups daily, conducts individual assessment of each of her students every 3 to 4 weeks, and walks on water too! I've tried for years to organize my teaching for small groups, centers, and individual assessment, but it's just too complex for me. It seems like one big mass of confusion for me and for the students. Every time I've tried to do it, I gave up because I can't manage the students, the materials, the centers, the assessment, and the classroom setup; and on and on it goes!"

Several other teachers nod their heads in agreement. Mrs. Johnson seems to sum up the situation, "We just don't have the time, the resources, and the support to teach like that. And even if we did, I'm just not sure how we would even begin to create and manage the *wonder* classrooms we hear about."

An inviting, print-rich classroom environment is essential for creating and maintaining a classroom context that supports successful readers. Access to print materials, classroom arrangement and management, and time allocation each day determine to a very real degree the effectiveness of classroom reading instruction (Morrow, 2001; Neuman, 1999; Neuman & Roskos, 1990, 1992; Roskos & Neuman, 2001). Teacher decisions about how to supply, create, and manage effective classroom literacy environments typically focus on at least three separate considerations: (a) preparing and organizing the classroom environments, (b) scheduling and managing time and resources, and (c) meeting individual needs through small group differentiated instruction. We discuss each as a way of guiding teachers through the process of organizing for effective reading instruction.

PREPARING AND ORGANIZING AN EFFECTIVE LITERACY ENVIRONMENT IN THE CLASSROOM

Preparing an *effective literacy learning environment* in the classroom begins with "provisioning" or supplying the classroom with a variety of printed materials and instructional tools. Spivak (1973) referred to children who are taught in print-impoverished classrooms as "setting deprived." Access to a wide variety and large quantities of printed materials has been shown to significantly affect children's literacy development and achievement (Allington, 2001; Neuman, 1999; Neuman & Celano, 2001a, 2001b). Once a list of print materials and instructional tools has been acquired, the task of organizing, arranging, and storing these materials for optimal use comes next. Finally, in this next section we discuss how to plan, prepare, and organize classroom space for a variety of instructional and learning activities to engage children with printed materials and literacy instructional tools.

ACCESS TO A VARIETY OF PRINT MATERIALS AND LITERACY INSTRUCTIONAL TOOLS

Access to a rich variety of printed materials and literacy instructional tools is fundamental in preparing a classroom environment to support literacy learning (Allington, 2001; Heald-Taylor, 2001; Hoffman (TEX-IN 3 Study), 2004). In Figure 4.1, we provide a list of printed materials and literacy tools teachers may consider for inclusion in their classroom literacy environments.

The number of books necessary for creating a print-rich literacy environment in the classroom varies with the functions to be served in and out of the classroom such as read

Figure 4.1   Literacy Tools for "Provisioning" a Print-Rich Classroom Environment with Reading Materials

Reading Materials	
Books	Manipulative letters
Textbooks	Business cards
Pamphlets/Brochures	Computer programs
Bumper stickers	Internet access
Magazines	Instructions and directions
Cookbooks	Maps
Newspapers	Calendars
Greeting cards	Schedules
Letters	Application forms
Notes	Reference books
Journals	Comics and cartoons
Message boards	Word puzzles
Pocket charts	Books on tape
Sentence and word strips	Songs on tape
Word cards	Flashlights and pointers
Poetry, rap, and chants	Highlighting tape
Play scripts	Stick 'em notes
Nursery rhymes	Word frames
Telephone books	Easels
Product labels	Costumes and props for drama
Signs	Take-home book bags or backpacks
Posters	Pictures
Charts	Felt story board
Big books	Felt story characters and pictures
Displays	

Figure 4.1 Continued

Writing Materials	
Blank books	Blank sentence strips
Blank comics	Blank word cards
Pattern books	Elkonin boxes
Word books—no illustrations	Chart paper
Illustrated books—no words	Blank calendars, charts, and maps
Application forms	Assorted paper sizes, types, and colors
Recipe cards	Scissors
Handwriting models	Product labels
Manipulative letters	Stapler
Stencils	Hole punch
Stationery	Binding supplies
Envelopes	Markers
Message boards	Crayons
White lap boards	Pens
Rubber stamps	Pencils
Ink pads	Erasers
Blank greeting card stock	Glue
Blank big books	Blank business cards
Index cards	Poetry pattern guides
Clipboards	Editing tape
Writing folders	Old magazines for pictures
Poster paper	Ledger paper
Mural paper	Daily planner sheets
Writing paper	Diary or journals
Construction paper	Blank checks (facsimile)
Wallpaper	Computer programs
Library pockets and cards	Word processing
Blank address books	Illustrations
Notepads	Clip art
Typewriter	Digital camera
Computer and printer	Desktop publishing
Telephone	E-mail
Magnetic letters	Internet access

alouds, shared reading, guided reading, and independent reading. If access to books is needed only to support students' independent reading choices, then about 10 to 12 titles per student in the class are needed as a minimum (Neuman, 2001; Veatch, 1968). This means that if a teacher has 30 children in her classroom, then an adequate book collection for independent reading would be between 300 and 350 book titles. However, if you intend to support cross-curricular studies, take-home reading, guided reading, shared reading, reading aloud, and professional development for the teacher, then the size of the classroom library collection may range from 1,500 to 2,000 titles, including many titles with multiple copies. Figure 4.2 lists recommended size ranges and book types for a minimum classroom library collection of 300 to 350 titles.

Classroom book collections should support and invite students to engage in reading a variety of texts—both narrative and expository (Allington, 2001; Burke, 2000; National Institute of Child Health and Human Development, 2000; Neuman, 2001; Reutzel &

Figure 4.2 Recommended Minimum Classroom Book Collection

Poetry collection books: 3–5 titles
Pattern/Predictable books: 50–60 titles
Leveled books: 120–140 titles
Decodable books: 40–50 titles
Information books: 40–50 titles
Award-winning books: 30–40 titles
Reference books such as dictionaries (5–10), thesaurus (1–2), CD-ROM encyclopedia
   (1–2 disks), atlases (1–2)
Newspapers (1–2), magazines (1–3 subscriptions), recipe books (1–3), catalogs (3–4)
Series books such as *Dear America, Goosebumps, Harry Potter,* etc.: 3–4 series
Play scripts, reader's theater scripts, skits, etc.: 1–3 titles

Figure 4.3 Suggested Text Types for Print-rich Classroom Environment

Textbooks including the classroom reading basal
Computers with bookmarked web pages, National Archives, Library of Congress, etc.
Stories and narrative accounts, i.e., fairy tales, folk tales, biographies, etc.
Picture books that provoke images and display unique uses of artistic talent
Tests, quizzes, and worksheets for "test prep"
Drivers license manuals, auto mechanic guides, maps, telephone books, reports,
   photographs, posters, diaries, letters, etc.
Joke books, comic books, word puzzle books, etc.
Essays, editorials, critiques, etc.

Fawson, 2002). Just as expository texts require that students study, gather, think about, and organize information, so too narrative texts invite students to connect with personal experiences and empathize with the characters in a book. Supporting developing readers requires that every teacher have access to a collection of leveled text materials, both narrative and expository. As noted in chapter 2, many schools are establishing what we term "literacy materials centers," central collections of leveled books (multiple copies) in English and Spanish that are available for teachers to check out for instruction. Sufficient quantities of leveled books need to be available to comply with the "Goldilocks principle" of achieving a "just right" match between the challenges within the text and each student's interests and needs (Ohlhausen & Jepsen, 1992). In Figure 4.3, we suggest several examples of the types and varieties of printed materials that may be included in print-rich literacy environments.

Teachers need to thoughtfully consider whether or not the literacy tools and printed materials selected for inclusion in their classrooms are developmentally appropriate. To determine appropriateness, teachers may ask themselves, "Can children read these print materials successfully and purposefully? Can children use these print materials in age-appropriate ways to communicate and interact?" Next, teachers may determine if reading and print materials selected for inclusion in the classroom are authentic. To decide if reading and other print materials fit this criterion, teachers may ask, "Are these literacy tools and reading materials typically used by people outside the school classroom environment?" We agree with research findings indicating that teachers should teach children to read using far greater numbers of information texts and nonfiction materials than have been typical in the past (Duke, 2000a, 2000b). We say this because the typical adult reads information texts about 86% of the time (Duke, 2000a; Duke, Bennett-Armistead, & Roberts, 2002) and 50% to 85% of test items used to test reading comprehension of children are informational (Calkins, Montgomery, & Santman, 1998). Finally, teachers may ask if reading and print materials are functional. That is, "Do these print materials serve a relevant literacy function valued in society at large?" In the next section, we discuss how teachers can store, arrange, and display this rich collection of print materials to maximize their utility and impact on the reading development of children.

STORING, ARRANGING, AND DISPLAYING PRINT MATERIALS AND LITERACY INSTRUCTIONAL TOOLS

Many researchers (Morrow, 2001; Morrow, Reutzel, & Casey, in press; Morrow & Tracey, 1996; Morrow & Weinstein, 1986; Neuman & Roskos, 1992; Reutzel & Morrow, in press) have determined that the arrangement of literacy materials in a classroom can significantly affect children's literacy-related play, talk, and development. The classroom environment needs to nurture and support the teaching and learning that occur in the classroom. How teachers store, arrange, and display literacy tools and print text materials affects children's access, understanding, and use of those materials. Print text materials and literacy instruction tools are best accessed, used, and replaced by children when they are stored and displayed in well-organized, clearly marked containers in or on shelves. Children cannot use materials as readily if they have to ask teachers to get them. Likewise, teachers will not want to allow children access to print materials and literacy tools if they must clean up, reorganize, and store them after children use them. Rules for and uses of literacy materials should be clearly understood and posted. With the growing availability of digital photography, some teachers have found that creating a photo poster display of children appropriately using literacy tools and print materials helps students to understand how to use literacy materials appropriately (Dragan, 2001). Just as their adult models do, children grow weary of the same old things. They need variety, too! Consequently, literacy tools and print materials should be added, deleted, and rotated on a regular basis—at least monthly if not more often.

Storage areas in the classroom provide much needed organization for classroom literacy learning activities. For example, in a writing storage area, authors' folders, response logs, and learning logs may be neatly filed in corrugated cardboard file boxes inside personal file folders. Children's written drafts can be stored in three-ring binders with the child's name clearly displayed on the spine of the binder for easy retrieval from a bookshelf location. A small

Classroom library arrangement

tablet for recording spelling words can be inserted into the pocket of the writing draft three-ring binder. Rubber tubs can be used to store children's personal or classroom writing materials. The contents of each rubber tub should be clearly labeled with print and a picture for younger children.

Rubber storage tubs may be stored in specially constructed shelves or along coatracks and windowsills. Supplies and materials typically found in a publishing area such as staplers, paper punches, construction paper, and unlined paper need to be arranged for easy accessibility and cleanup. The location of each item in the publishing area needs to be labeled. For younger children, it works well if the teacher traces around the shape of each item in the publishing center and labels the item with the word underneath the object outline. These labeled object outlines can be laminated and taped to the countertop or on the inside of cupboards or bookshelves. Children can easily recognize the object and return it to its place without adult involvement.

It is best if books stored in the reading nook, loft, or classroom library are organized to reflect the functions and activities of the classroom reading program. For example, guided, shared, and independent reading books should be shelved on separate bookshelves and clearly marked. Browsing boxes, multiple copies of single titles, and theme or topic book collections may be stored in separate containers, on bookshelves, or in clearly labeled plastic tubs. Plastic pants hangers with clothespins, extra large pocket charts, or large plastic hanging bags may be used to store or display big books and chart tablets. Bookshelves and countertops can be lined with vinyl rain gutters to display books, covers out.

Reference materials such as dictionaries, atlases, *The Guinness Book of World Records,* encyclopedias, almanacs, and spellers are best if aggregated or placed near an editing area in the classroom. If space for learning centers is limited in the classroom, then writing materials are best stored so that they can be easily transported throughout the classroom to where they are needed. Small plastic tubs or baskets, boxes, cut-down milk containers, and the like can be used for both storage and transporting of crayons, markers, pencils, pens, erasers, and chalk. Organizing and arranging materials in the ways suggested allow children to easily sort and clean up following busy writing output times. In some cases, it works well if small containers are emptied into large-capacity storage bins for storage after transporting to other classroom areas. In so doing, small transport containers can be used for a variety of literacy materials throughout the classroom and then returned, emptied, and used again for other classroom storage and transport needs.

ARRANGING CLASSROOM SPACE FOR INSTRUCTION

Classroom space is more effectively used when broken up into specific learning areas. Just like homes and offices, the space is less useful and functional if built without smaller, purposeful spaces. The work of a kitchen belongs in a space designed expressly for that purpose, and tools and texts for the kitchen are aggregated or placed in or near the kitchen. Likewise, the work and tools associated with a publishing center belong in a space designed expressly for that purpose. Dividing classrooms into functional spaces encourages children to be more cooperative and engaged in literacy learning tasks (Roskos & Neuman, 2001).

One effective and often attractive way of cordoning off specific activity areas in the classroom is to use furnishings (i.e., sofas, chairs, bookcases, and so on). Another way of specifically designating activity areas is through the use of displays, labels, and signs. Although classroom space cannot be specifically designated for every content activity, space can be allocated for specific types of activities across multiple academic subjects. Such spaces may include large gathering areas for the whole class, small learning centers, small-group instruction areas, and so on. In any case, with respect to literacy learning, space planning in the classroom is best organized around the elements of a comprehensive reading program as previously described in chapter 3. Space designed to support a comprehensive reading program would include at a minimum the following areas:

- Print displays
- Whole-group reading instruction
- Small-group differentiated reading instruction
- Literacy and content learning centers
- Independent reading
- Individual reading conference and assessment

We describe how to organize each of these classroom spaces to support the functions and elements of an effective comprehensive reading program.

Print Displays

Print displays are intended to immerse students or, as master teacher Adaliese Harris (May & Rizzardi, 2002) puts it, "marinate children" in an environment of interesting and functional print. Print displays may be located almost anywhere in the classroom from the ceiling to the floor, from the walls to the windows. Displays are most valued by children when they are student generated rather than teacher produced. In our experiences, a morning message board for leaving notes is a wonderful method of communication between teachers and students. A sign-in attendance board encourages even the very youngest children to write their names to begin the school day. Window writing using water-soluble ink pens allows students to transcribe their stories, poems, jokes, riddles, and messages onto the window glass. Children find window writing a fun and novel way to display words, stories, and messages, largely because it seems like a "taboo" activity. Sidewalk chalk is another fun and engaging medium for making displays for outside games, playground science field trips, art, and mapmaking for social studies.

Create an environmental print word wall to show product labels and print that children bring from home. To create an environmental print word wall display, children bring labels from cans, cereal boxes, old packages, bumper stickers, newspaper advertisements, and so on into the classroom. Children are asked to read these print items to the class before they are placed onto the logo language wall. Environmental print items on display are often used by children as writing or reading resources for word study lessons throughout the year. (Be sure to remind children that they must ask if they may remove the label on a can before it is used!) Using environmental print items to teach reading and writing is both fun and instructionally sound. Environmental print has been shown to help even the youngest child to know that he or she can already read and to provide a familiar bridge to the unfamiliar world of decontextualized print (Kuby & Aldridge, 1994).

Another effective classroom display often seen in today's classrooms is the high-frequency or word-family word wall. In this display, high-frequency words or collections of word families (e.g., "-ake" words such as take, make, bake, shake, and so on) help students learn word patterns and remember sight words for reading and writing (Cunningham, 2000). High-frequency and word-family word wall displays become environmental reference points for children when they are reading and come to a word they do not know or when they need to spell a word they do not yet know how to spell conventionally. We talk more about word walls in chapter 9. It is important that word walls not use differing colors for print or background or word shapes because they can draw children's attention away from recognizing the words.

A collection of logo print displayed for children to read

A classroom word wall is a ready reference for young writers and readers

Prominent locations throughout the classroom can be used for posting rules, calendars, lunch menus, television guides, and charts. Informational displays also can be used to exhibit such things as classroom schedules, hints on successful reading and comprehension monitoring, stages of the writing process, steps and media for publishing writing projects, lists of words the class knows, songs the class likes, favorite books, and so on. Other information displays in the classroom can be used to provide children helpful reference information such as numbers, colors, alphabet letters, lunchtime, and classroom helpers.

Scheduling displays may be used for showing the daily flow of classroom events as well as managing appointments with peers and teachers for reading and writing conferences and other individual classroom activities. Labeling objects in the classroom is useful for younger children and for those children learning English as a second language.

Whole-Group Reading Instruction Area

A whole-group reading and writing area is best located near classroom chalkboards or whiteboards and well away from designated quiet areas in the classroom. We suggest using a large piece of well-padded carpet to comfortably seat the entire class or a smaller group of the children in this area. To help with classroom management of student behavior while seated on the carpet together, many teachers divide the carpet into smaller squares for each child to have individual space. Children are reminded that they are not to encroach upon another child's space and to keep their hands, arms, and feet within their own space.

Big books and pocket charts are essentials for a shared reading area

Audiovisual equipment should be easily accessible. Such equipment may include a wall-mounted television; a video player; an overhead projector; a tape or CD player; easels for displaying enlarged print of books, poems, riddles, songs, and group experience charts; and electronic keyboards for music accompaniment. A whole-group reading instruction area should be clear of obstructions and may occupy up to 20% of the total space in the classroom.

Small-Group Differentiated Reading Instruction Area

A small-group differentiated reading instruction area is ideally located in or near the center of the classroom at a kidney- or U-shaped table large enough to seat five to eight students comfortably and within an arm's length of the teacher. Leveled and decodable books used for small-group differentiated reading instruction should be located near the small-group differentiated reading instruction area. A pocket chart display; sentence, word, and letter strips; word and letter frames; highlighting tape; stick-on notes; markers; and a pointer should also be stored in this area of the classroom. Small, dry-erase lapboards, erasers, and markers; Magna Doodles; or gel boards for writing letters or words or making words may also be stored in or near this area of the classroom. Plastic bins with leveled and decodable reading books should be placed here for each group's scheduled use of the small-

A teacher takes a running record while other children re-read a familiar book in the Guided Reading Area

group differentiated reading instruction area (Tyner, 2003). We have found it helpful to have a small file cabinet adjacent to the small-group differentiated reading area to store our student progress monitoring data, including such things as one-minute reading samples, running records, and so on.

Figure 4.5 Book Title and Time Log

Name of Student_____ Week of_____

Monday
Names of Book(s) Read_____
Time Spent Reading_____   One Word Response_____

Tuesday
Names of Book(s) Read_____
Time Spent Reading_____   One Word Response_____

Wednesday
Names of Book(s) Read_____
Time Spent Reading_____   One Word Response_____

Thursday
Names of Book(s) Read_____
Time Spent Reading_____   One Word Response_____

Friday
Names of Book(s) Read_____
Time Spent Reading_____   One Word Response_____

Based on the book *Alexander and the Terrible Horrible No Good Very Bad Day* by Judith Viorst (1972), teachers may establish an "Australia Escape Corner." When things in the classroom or a student's personal life are just too much to handle at the moment, the student may retreat to Australia, just like Alexander, for 10 minutes, no questions asked, once a day. If students need to remain longer than 10 minutes, they should explain their reasons to the teacher privately. Teachers also may retreat on occasion to Australia. This action alone was found to be one of our best classroom discipline techniques!

Individual Reading Conference and Assessment Area

The individual reading conference and assessment area is usually small and quiet. It is typically located near the teacher's desk where student records may be stored and easily accessed. This area is used for conducting reading conferences and assessing each individual student's reading performance. Students are informed of their appointment to meet with the teacher for an individual reading conference. This is accomplished by the teacher putting the child's name on the individual reading conference appointment board, which is shown in Figure 4.6. The teacher and an individual student meet together briefly—about 5 minutes—to read and discuss a selected or assigned trade book or basal reader story passage. As the student reads, the teacher listens, encourages, and assesses performance in a one-minute reading sample (see chapter 14, "Reading Fluency," for more on this).

ASSESSING THE CLASSROOM LITERACY ENVIRONMENT

Roskos and Neuman (2001) recently reviewed the research on classroom environmental influences on children's literacy learning. They found that space allocation and arrangement, complexity and accessibility of materials, and variation and ownership of literacy learning tools influenced children's literacy learning in a variety of ways (see Figures 4.7 and 4.8). Intervention studies (Morrow, 1990; Neuman & Roskos, 1992; Reutzel & Wolfersberger, 1996; Vukelich, 1991, 1994) have shown that creating authentic play

Figure 4.6   Reading Conference Sign-Up Board

(This board works best if produced on a poster board and laminated. Use an overhead water-ink marker for signing up that can be easily erased.)

Monday
Student Name _____
Name of Book or Story _____
Page Number(s) _____
Student Name _____
Name of Book or Story _____
Page Number(s) _____

Tuesday
Student Name _____
Name of Book or Story _____
Page Number(s) _____
Student Name _____
Name of Book or Story _____
Page Number(s) _____

Wednesday
Student Name _____
Name of Book or Story _____
Page Number(s) _____
Student Name _____
Name of Book or Story _____
Page Number(s) _____
ETC.

settings, such as offices, libraries, veterinary centers, flower shops, and so on, positively influenced children's literacy play, talk, and acts. From these studies, it is clear that having a classroom environment rich in literacy tools and reading materials is a key feature of supportive classroom environments. We provide a research-based instrument (Wolfersberger, Reutzel, Sudweeks, and Fawson 2004) the *Classroom Literacy Environmental Profile* (CLEP), for examining the "print richness" of classroom environments in the appendix at the end of the book. In Figure 4.9, we offer another classroom environment checklist that is informal in nature and is relatively easy to use. However, it does not offer the depth of understanding nor reliable outcomes associated with studying the literacy environment of the classroom using the CLEP instrument found in the appendix.

SCHEDULING CLASSROOM READING INSTRUCTION: THE FIVE-BLOCK READING/WRITING ESSENTIALS MODEL

Children develop a sense of security when the events of the school day revolve around a sequence of anticipated activities. Although variety is the spice of life for children, too, they find comfort in familiar instructional routines in a well-organized classroom (Holdaway, 1984). (A tip for beginning teachers or veterans who may experience problems with behavior management: We highly recommend the book *The First Days of School* (Wong & Wong, 1998) as a resource. It is great for helping teachers get the school year off to a good start with very basic routines and expectations. See references at the end of this chapter for ordering information.)

Figure 4.7 Fifth-Grade Classroom Arrangement

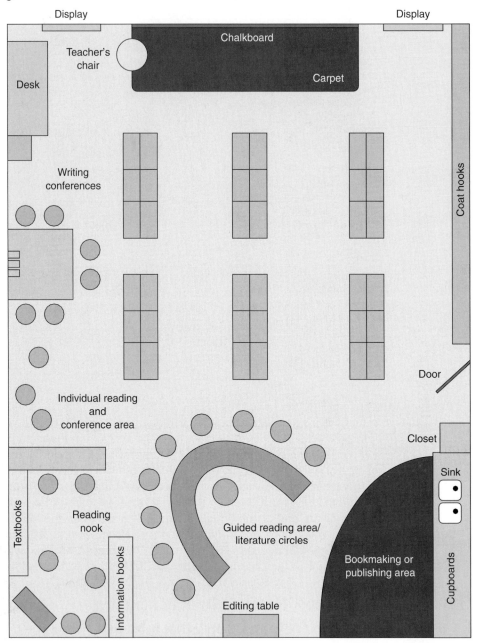

Organizing the activities and scheduling the instruction for each school day can be accomplished in a number of ways. However, it is important that each day children experience a variety of interactive settings in which they are taught the essential components of reading and writing coupled with large amounts of time allocated for reading and writing practice. Children should also experience daily reading and writing instruction in a variety of interactive settings: whole class, small groups, paired, and individual. Groups for reading and writing interactions should be flexible and meet the needs of the students and involve the "best practices" associated with literacy instruction.

Figure 4.8 First-Grade Classroom Arrangement

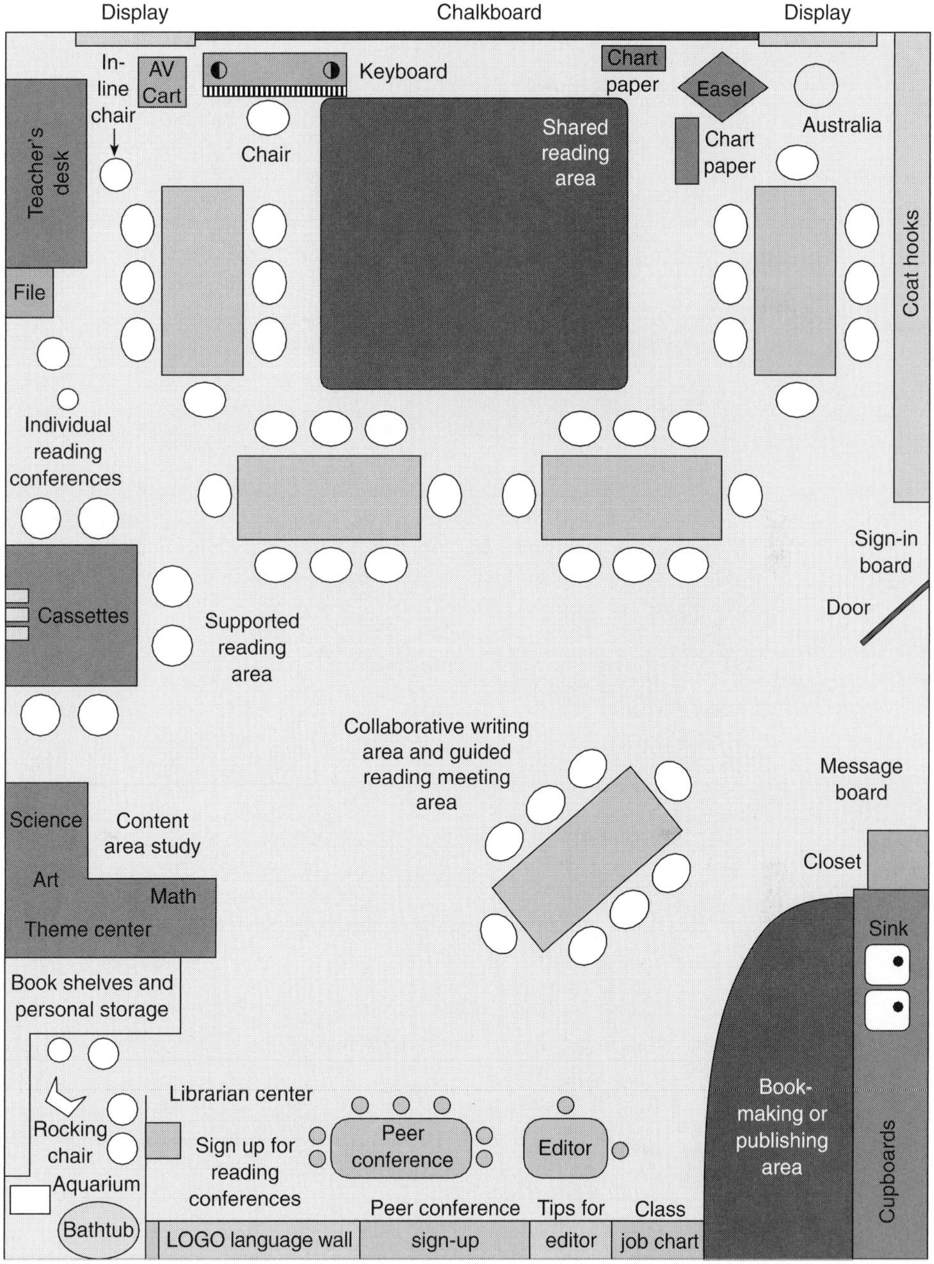

Display   Chalkboard   Display

In-line chair
AV Cart
Keyboard
Chart paper
Easel

Teacher's desk

Chair

Shared reading area

Chart paper

Australia

File

Coat hooks

Individual reading conferences

Cassettes

Supported reading area

Sign-in board

Door

Collaborative writing area and guided reading meeting area

Message board

Closet

Science   Content area study

Art

Math

Theme center

Sink

Book shelves and personal storage

Rocking chair

Librarian center

Book-making or publishing area

Sign up for reading conferences

Peer conference

Editor

Aquarium

Bathtub   LOGO language wall   Peer conference sign-up   Tips for editor   Class job chart

Cupboards

One approach that is increasingly used to organize the school day is the *five-block reading/writing essentials model*. Although this organizational framework was originally proposed for all K–12 students in the public schools of Chicago by Dr. Timothy Shanahan, *we have implemented it successfully in the elementary school (K–6). We have found this organizational framework for reading and writing instruction to be both effective and manageable for many classroom teachers of elementary and middle-school-age children.*

Figure 4.9 Print-Rich Classroom Environmental Survey

Teacher's Name_____   Grade Level of Classroom_____

Directions: *Read each item carefully. Scan the classroom quickly to estimate the level of compliance with each item's description. Score each item as follows: 1 = fails to meet the description, 3 = meets the description, and 5 = exceeds the description.*

1. Literacy tools provided in the classroom contain print (charts, books, displays); are used to produce print (markers, crayons, pencils, paper); and support literacy learning (computers, tape recorders, pointers, pocket charts).
        1   3   5

2. Books and print materials are adequate in number ranging between 300 and 500 individual titles or volumes (Count multiple copies of a single title as one title).
        1   3   5

3. Print materials available in the classroom represent at least five separate genres (fiction, nonfiction, poetry, magazines, newspapers, reference volumes).
        1   3   5

4. Levels of print materials in the classroom span at least three grade levels.
        1   3   5

5. Displays in the classroom represent at least three different purposes and invite student involvement such as information, schedules, sign-in boards, message boards, and labels/directions, etc.
        1   3   5

6. Student and class literacy product displays are mostly student-produced print and prominently displayed in the classroom.
        1   3   5

7. Reference materials are abundant in the classrooms with at least 15 different displays or books.
        1   3   5

8. Writing tools are abundant and represent a wide variety such as pens, pencils, markers, computer processing, sidewalk chalk, overhead markers, stamps, and stencils.
        1   3   5

9. Writing surfaces represent a wide variety of places to write including wall-mounted chalk or marker boards, paper types, stationery, sentence strips, word cards, magnetic letter boards, etc.
        1   3   5

10. Publishing materials include a variety of tools to edit, assemble, and decorate written products.
         1   3   5

11. Furnishings represent a variety of items to divide and make the room comfortable and functional such as tables, chairs, carpets, rocking chairs, beanbag chairs, play centers, author's chair, etc.
         1   3   5

12. Displaying and storing literacy tools is accomplished in a variety of ways including rain gutters, pocket charts, easels, boxes, tubs, shelves, counter tops, etc.
         1   3   5

13. Classroom library has adequate floor space, shelving, and displays to entice students into sustained reading.
         1   3   5

14. Classroom floor space is divided into areas supporting best practices such as read alouds, shared reading, guided reading, independent reading, and learning centers.
         1   3   5

continued

Figure 4.9   Continued

15. Technology resources are abundant including CD players, tape recorders, overhead
projectors, computers and printers, VCR/DVD player, etc.
    1   3   5

Add the total score here for all 15 items _____

Interpret the total scores on classroom print-rich environments as follows:
   15–30 is print poor
   31–55 is print adequate
   56–75 is print rich

Figure 4.10   Five-Block Reading/Writing Essentials Model

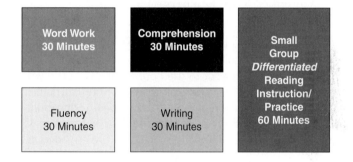

The five-block reading/writing essentials model is a framework for scheduling and fo-cusing daily reading and writing instruction so that all children receive daily instruction in the five essential components of reading: phonemic awareness, phonics, fluency, vocabu-lary, and comprehension strategies + writing. When using the five-block reading/writing essentials model, it is expected that the literacy instructional block will be scheduled for a minimum of 180 minutes (3 hours) in length. It is also best if this time is uninterrupted by outside intrusions as much as possible.

The 180 minutes of allocated literacy instruction time in the five-block reading/writing essentials model is divided into four, 30-minute contiguous blocks of instructional time fol-lowed by a 60-minute block of small-group differentiated reading instruction with the teacher and paired or independent reading and writing practice time. The five-block reading/writing essentials model is shown in Figure 4.10.

Shanahan, a member of the National Reading Panel, reported that installing the five-block reading/writing essentials model of instructional time allocation for reading and writing in-struction in the Chicago Public Schools led to significant improvements in K–12 student read-ing achievement scores in a single year (Shanahan, 2003). In addition to this endorsement of implementation efficacy, many Reading First schools across the nation are now using the five-block reading/writing essentials model as well. To give you insight into how this model works in practice, we describe each of the five components in greater detail.

WORD WORK (30 MINUTES)

During this whole-group instructional time, teachers provide explicit instruction for stu-dents focused on learning to recognize and decode words, learning the structure of words, and learning the meaning of words. This time is devoted to teaching younger children to recognize the alphabet letters (uppercase and lowercase); training children to hear sounds in spoken words (phonological and phonemic awareness); helping children learn to recognize and spell a core of high-frequency sight words; helping them learn to decode and spelling simple consonant–vowel *cv, cvc, cvvc, cvce* words; learning about prefixes, suffixes, word tense, singular and plural, and so on; and studying vocabulary word meanings. In the kindergarten and first-grade years, instruction during the word work time block is focused primarily on learning and writing the alphabet letters, recognizing and spelling sight words, and decoding and spelling simple two- or three-letter words. In the second- and third-grade years, the focus shifts from word recognition and spelling to understanding the structure and meaning of words. In the intermediate and middle-school years, the primary focus of word work is concentrated on acquiring a vast store of word meanings and increasing students' reading vocabularies.

WRITING (30 MINUTES)

During this whole-group instructional time, teachers focus students' attention on the core elements of the elementary school writing curriculum, on a variety of writing products, and on the various phases of the writing process within the learning context of a "writer's workshop." With respect to the core elements of the writing curriculum, teachers explain and model elements of the elementary writing curriculum such as word choice, organization, word and sentence writing fluency, ideas, conventions, voice, and presentation. Teachers also help children understand the various forms of writing such as narrative, poetic, or expository writing. In addition, children are engaged in a variety of writing tasks such as writing letters, reports, recipes, poems, bumper stickers, newspaper headlines, riddles, and so on. All of this occurs within the supportive framework of the writer's workshop (Calkins, 1994), which provides students with teacher-modeled minilessons, drafting, conferencing, revising, editing, and publishing.

FLUENCY (30 MINUTES)

This 30-minute period is divided into two separate sets of activities for teacher and students—explicit fluency instruction with the whole class and small-group or paired fluency practice. During the first 8 to 10 minutes of this block of instruction, the teacher explicitly explains and models various aspects of reading fluency including accuracy, rate, and expression. For an explicit fluency lesson plan, please refer to chapter 14.

During the remaining 20 to 22 minutes, the teacher engages children in whole-class, small-group, and oral repeated reading practice to build automaticity. With very young children in kindergarten and first grade, fluency practice may focus on accurately and quickly recognizing and writing alphabet letters and high-frequency sight words and reading easily decodable words *(cv, cvc)*. This practice can occur through engagement with a variety of fluency practice activities. Choral readings of texts in unison or in echo voices helps students get a sense of how to read with fluency. Encouraging students to re-read a passage helps them read more fluently, thus enabling greater comprehension. One very effective strategy is to engage students in the performance of reader's theater productions. A range of reader's theater scripts can be obtained on the Internet at: http://www.aaronshep. com/rt/RTE.html, http://scriptsforschools.com/, and http://www.geocities.com.

Students who have achieved grade-level automaticity can benefit from individual, wide silent, monitored reading (Stahl, 2004; Reutzel, Smith & Fawson, in preparation). This means that silent reading ranges across a prescribed set of genre types for a given period of time, say a 9-week quarter (fairy tales, biographies, information books, stories, etc.), and each student's silent reading is monitored periodically, often randomly, by the teacher. For the teacher, the bulk of this time is devoted to meeting individually with five to eight students, for 2 minutes each, to hold individual fluency assessment conferences. Students are signed up for a one-minute fluency assessment conference by the teacher. Children read a teacher-selected, grade-level or instructional-level text for one minute; and errors, rate, and expression are assessed and tracked. Information garnered in these fluency assessment conferences is used to set student level fluency goals and inform later fluency instruction.

COMPREHENSION STRATEGY (30 MINUTES)

During this whole-group instructional time, teachers provide explicit comprehension strategy instruction for all students, even for those children in kindergarten and first grade. In these early grades, comprehension strategy instruction may take place through listening rather than reading. But for those children in second grade on up, daily attention to explicit comprehension strategy instruction is a critical part of comprehensive, balanced reading instruction.

Teachers explain which comprehension strategy is to be learned, why it is important to learn, and when and where the strategy can be applied with effectiveness. Next the teacher models how to use the strategy in connection with reading and talking about a text. Very often, this modeling includes the teacher using something called a "think aloud" to help students get a toehold on the often hidden workings of the mind when thinking with and about text using a comprehension strategy. During a "think aloud," the teacher shares his or her inner thinking about how to use a comprehension strategy by talking about his or her thinking out loud. Comprehension strategies include answering questions, generating questions to be answered, understanding narrative structure, using graphic organizers, monitoring one's own comprehension processes, and summarizing. Other strategies include making inferences, visualizing or imagery, predicting, and connecting to one's background experiences. Once the teacher has modeled a comprehension strategy, he or she carefully scaffolds the release of responsibility for using this strategy to the individual student (Pearson & Gallagher, 1983). This is usually accomplished by sharing parts of the mental task for using a comprehension strategy between the teacher and the students. For example, in answering a question, the teacher may give the answer and ask students to find supportive information for the answer in their heads or in the text. Next the teacher may reverse these roles by having the children answer the question and the teacher offers supportive information for the answer from his or her head or from the text. Following this approach, the teacher may have children work in small groups or in pairs sharing the task of answering questions by assigning roles such as the question answerer and the question justifier. Finally, the children practice answering and justifying their answers to questions independently. Daily comprehension strategy instruction should focus on using strategies to understand text, not on learning the strategy per se.

SMALL-GROUP DIFFERENTIATED READING INSTRUCTION/COLLABORATIVE AND INDEPENDENT READING AND WRITING PRACTICE (60 MINUTES)

Recent research by Mathes, Denton, Fletcher, Anthony, Francis, and Schatschneider (2005) has shown that small-group differentiated reading instruction has significant positive effects on young struggling readers' progress and achievement in reading. Small-group differentiated reading instruction ranges from guided reading groups to highly scripted, teacher-directed lessons in small reading groups; the form does not seem to make much of a difference. What seems to make the real difference is the fact that children with similar instructional needs are grouped together into small groups of 5 to 8 students for targeted, focused, and intensive reading instruction under the guidance of a high-quality teacher.

Tyner (2003) describes excellent routines and processes for providing small-group differentiated reading instruction in *Small-Group Reading Instruction: A Differentiated Teaching Model for Beginning and Struggling Readers*. Perhaps the most important thing that can be said about small-group differentiated reading instruction is that teachers monitor students' progress regularly, group membership is changed regularly, and time spent is focused on teaching students the essentials of reading instruction drawn from the science-based reading literature—phonemic awareness, phonics, fluency, vocabulary, and comprehension strategies.

Differentiated reading instruction small groups typically meet daily for 20 minutes. This allows the teacher to have at least three small groups for differentiated instruction. If more than three groups are necessary to meet student needs for a wide range of student abilities, then the more accomplished and independent students' small group may meet every other day.

In order to support the offering of small-group differentiated reading instruction, teachers must also provide for collaborative and independent practice of reading and writing by other students in the classroom who are not in the small group for instruction. The typical approach for providing practice settings for these students involves the establishment of learning centers. An excellent source of information for designing effective literacy centers is found in Morrow's (2002) book, *The Literacy Center: Contexts for Reading and Writing,* second edition. For learning centers to be effective, their use must be carefully trained; the centers must be highly structured with clearly defined rules, directions, and tasks to be completed; and accountability must be built in for students' time and effort. Failure to ensure that these matters are appropriately considered will result in lost and largely useless time. For those teachers whose management skills do not allow for immediately managing multiple learning centers, we recommend that those children not in small-group differentiated reading instruction be paired for 20 minutes of daily fluency and reading practice. Another 20 minutes of time can be devoted to writing, penmanship, or spelling tasks in which children work in pairs who are not in small-group differentiated reading instruction.

Allocating sufficient time to the essential elements of reading and writing instruction are of paramount importance because "time on task" and "academic learning time" have long been shown to be easily influenced but highly effective ways to boost children's reading and writing achievement. On the other hand, allocating more time without an appropriate instructional focus will yield little. Teachers must allocate sufficient time to the important or significant components that cause reading and writing achievement to occur. Thus the five-block reading/writing essentials model helps teachers get the important instructional elements of reading and writing coupled with sufficient amounts of time focused on reading and writing practice to improve student achievement.

SELECTED REFERENCES

Allington, R. L. (2001). *What really matters for struggling readers: Designing research-based programs.* New York: Addison-Wesley/Longman.

Atwell, N. (1987). *In the middle: Writing, reading, and learning with adolescents.* Portsmouth, NH: Heinemann Educational Books.

Burke, J. (2000). *Reading reminders: Tools, tips, and techniques.* Portsmouth, NH: Heinemann Educational Books.

Calkins, L. (1994). *The art of teaching writing* (new ed.). Portsmouth, NH: Heinemann Educational Books.

Calkins, L. M., Montgomery, K., Santman, D., & Falk, B. (1998). A teacher's guide to standardized reading tests: Knowledge is power. Portsmouth, NH: Heinemann Educational Books.

Calkins, L. (2001). *The art of teaching reading.* New York: Addison-Wesley.

Cunningham, P. M. (2000). *Phonics they use: Words for reading and writing* (3rd ed.). New York: Harper-Collins.

Daniels, H. (2002). *Literature circles: Voice and choice in book clubs and reading groups* (2nd ed.). York, ME: Stenhouse.

Dragan, P. B. (2001). *Literacy from day one.* Portsmouth, NH: Heinemann Educational Books.

Duke, N. K. (2000a). For the rich it's richer: Print experiences and environments offered to children in very low- and very high-socioeconomic status first-grade classrooms. *American Educational Research Journal, 37,* 441–478.

Duke, N. K. (2000b). 3.6 minutes per day: The scarcity of informational texts in first grade. *Reading Research Quarterly, 35*(2), 202–224.

Duke, N. K., Bennett-Armistead, S., & Roberts, E. M. (2002). Incorporating informational text in the primary grades. In C. M. Roller (Ed.), Comprehensive reading instruction across the grade levels: A collection of papers from the 2001 Reading Research Conference, 41–54. Newark, DE: International Reading Association.

Fountas, I. C., & Pinnell, G. S. (2001). *Guiding readers and writers (grades 3–6): Teaching comprehension, genre, and content literacy.* Portsmouth, NH: Heinemann Educational Books.

Heald-Taylor, G. (2001). *The beginning reading handbook: Strategies for success.* Portsmouth, NH: Heinemann Educational Books.

Hoffman, J. V., Sailors, M., Duffy, G., & Beretvas, S. N. (2004). The effective classroom literacy environment: Examining the validity of the TEX-IN3 Observation System. *Journal of Literacy Research, 36*(3), 303–334.

Holdaway, D. (1984). *Stability and change in literacy learning.* Portsmouth, NH: Heinemann Educational Books.

Howe, D. (1979). *Bunnicula: A rabbit tale of mystery.* New York: Atheneum.

Kuby, P., & Aldridge, J. (1994). Direct versus indirect environmental print instruction and early reading ability in kindergarten children. *Reading Psychology, 18*(2), 91–104.

Little, E. (1988). *The Trojan horse: How the Greeks won the war.* New York: Random House.

Mathes, P. G., Denton, C. A., Fletcher, J. M., Anthony, J. L., Francis, D. J., & Schatschneider, C. (2005). The effects of theoretically different instruction and student characteristics on the skills of struggling readers. *Reading Research Quarterly, 40*(2), 148–182.

May, F. B., & Rizzardi, L. (2002). *Reading as communication* (6th ed.). Upper Saddle River, NJ: Merrill/Prentice Hall.

McCarrier, A., Pinnell, G. S., & Fountas, I. C. (1999). *Interactive writing: How language & literacy come together, K–2.* Portsmouth, NH: Heinemann Educational Books.

Morrow, L. M. (1990). Preparing the classroom environment to promote literacy during play. *Early Childhood Research Quarterly, 5,* 537–554.

Morrow, L. M. (2001). *Literacy development in the early years: Helping children read and write* (4th ed.). Boston, MA: Allyn & Bacon.

Morrow, L. M. (2002). *The literacy center: Contexts for reading and writing* (2nd ed.). Portland, Maine: Stenhouse Publishers.

Morrow, L. M. Reutzel, D. R., & Casey, H. (in press). Organization and Management of Language Arts Teaching: Classroom Environments, Grouping Practices, and Exemplary Instruction, pp. 559–582. In Evertson, C. (Eds.), *Handbook of Classroom Management.* Mahwah, NJ: Lawrence Erlbaum Associates.

Morrow, L. M., & Tracey, D. H. (1996). Instructional environments for language and learning: Considerations for young children. In J. Flood, S. B. Heath, & D. Lapp (Eds.), *Handbook for literacy educators: Research on teaching the communicative and visual arts.* New York: Macmillan.

Morrow, L. M., & Weinstein, C. S. (1986). Encouraging voluntary reading: The impact of a literature program on children's use of library centers. *Reading Research Quarterly, 21,* 330–346.

National Institute of Child Health and Human Development. (2000). *Report of the National Reading Panel: Teaching children to read, an evidence-based assessment of the scientific research literature on reading and its implications for reading instruction* (NIH Publication. No. 00-4769). Washington, DC: U.S. Government Printing Office.

Neuman, S. B. (1999). Books make a difference: A study of access to literacy. *Reading Research Quarterly, 34,* 286–311.

Neuman, S. B. (2000). *The importance of classroom libraries.* New York: Scholastic.

Newman, S. B. (2001). *The impact of reading trade-books on reading achievement.* New York, Scholastic, Inc.

Neuman, S. B., & Celano, D. (2001a). Access to print in low-income and middle-income communities: An ecological study of four neighborhoods. *Reading Research Quarterly, 36*(1), 8–26.

Neuman, S. B., & Celano, D. (2001b). Books aloud: A campaign to put books in children's hands. *The Reading Teacher, 54*(6), 550–557.

Neuman, S. B., & Roskos, K. (1990). The influence of literacy-enriched play settings on preschoolers' engagement with written language. In J. Zutell & S. McCormick (Eds.), *Literacy theory and research: Analysis from multiple paradigms* (pp. 179–187). 39th yearbook of the National Reading Conference. Chicago, IL: National Reading Conference.

Neuman, S. B., & Roskos, K. (1992). Literacy objects as cultural tools: Effects on children's literacy behaviors in play. *Reading Research Quarterly, 27*(3), 203–225.

Ogle, D. (2001). *Literacy around the world.* Presidential address given at the annual meeting of the Utah Council of the International Reading Association, Salt Lake City, UT.

Ohlhausen, M. M., & Jepsen, M. (1992). Lessons from Goldilocks: "Somebody's been choosing my books but I can make my own choices now!" *New Advocate, 5*(1), 31–46.

Pearson, P. D., & Gallagher, M. C. (1983). The instruction of reading comprehension. *Contemporary Educational Psychology, 8*(3), 317–344.

Pinnell, G. S., & Fountas, I. C. (2002). *Leveled books for readers, grades 3–6: A companion volume to guiding readers and writers.* Portsmouth, NH: Heinemann Educational Books.

Reutzel, D. R., Smith, J. A., & Fawson, P. C. (in preparation). *Reconsidering Silent Sustained Reading (SSR): A Comparative Study of Modified SSR with Oral Repeated Reading Practice.* Logan, UT: Utah State University.

Reutzel, D. R., & Cooter, R. B., Jr. (1991). Organizing for effective instruction: The reading workshop. *The Reading Teacher, 44*(8), 548–555.

Reutzel, D. R., & Fawson, P. C. (2002). *Your classroom library: New ways of giving it more teaching power.* New York, NY: Scholastic, Inc.

Reutzel, D. R., & Morrow, L. M. (in press). Promoting and Assessing Effective Literacy Learning Classroom Environments. In J. R. Paratore and R. L. McCormick (Eds.), *Classroom Literacy Assessment: Making Sense of What Students Know and Do.* New York: Guilford Press.

Reutzel, D. R., & Wolfersberger, M. (1996). An environmental impact statement: Designing supportive literacy classrooms for young children. *Reading Horizons, 36*(3), 266–282.

Richgels, D. J., & Wold, L. S. (1998). Literacy on the road: Backpacking partnerships between school and home. *The Reading Teacher, 52*(1), 18–29.

Robinson, B. (1988). *The best Christmas pageant ever.* New York: HarperCollins.

Roskos, K., & Neuman, S. B. (2001). Environment and its influences for early literacy teaching and learning. In S. B. Neuman & D. K. Dickinson (Eds.), *Handbook of early literacy research* (pp. 281–294). New York: Guilford Press.

Shanahan, T. (2003). *Reporting on the Report of the National Reading Panel: Beyond the Findings to Implementation.* Presentation made at the Utah Reading First Summer Reading Conference, Red Lion Hotel, Salt Lake City, UT.

Snow, C. E., Burns, M. S., & Griffin, P. (1998). *Preventing reading failure in young children.* Washington, DC: National Academy Press.

Tyner, B. (2004). *Small-group reading instruction: A differentiated teaching model for beginning and struggling readers.* Newark, DE: International Reading Association.

Spivak, M. (1973). Archetypal place. *Architectural Forum, 140,* 44–49.

Stahl, S. (2004). What do we know about fluency? In P. McCardle & V. Chhabra (Eds.), *The voice of evidence in reading research,* (pp. 187–211). Baltimore, MD: Brookes.

Veatch, J. (1968). *How to teach reading with children's books.* New York: Richard C. Owen.

Viorst, J. (1972). *Alexander and the terrible horrible no good very bad day* (R. Cruz, Illustrator). New York: Atheneum.

Vukelich, C. (1991). Materials and modeling: Promoting literacy during play. In J. F. Christie (Ed.), *Play and early literacy development* (pp. 215–231). Albany, NY: SUNY Press.

Vukelich, C. (1994). Effect of play intervention on children's reading of environmental print. *Early Childhood Research Quarterly, 9,* 153–170.

Vygotsky, L. S. (1986). *Thought and language.* Cambridge, MA: MIT Press.

Wolfersberger, M., Reutzel, D. R., Sudweeks, R., & Fawson, P. F. (2004). Developing and Validating the Classroom Literacy Environmental Profile (CLEP): A Tool for Examining the "Print Richness" of Elementary Classrooms. *Journal of Literacy Research, 36*(2), 211–272.

Wong, H. K., & Wong, R. T. (1998). *The first days of school: How to be an effective teacher* (2nd ed.). Mountain View, CA: Harry K. Wong Publications. ISBN: 0-9629360-2-2. Online ordering at http://www.effectiveteaching.com.

Chapter 5

Oral Language Assessment and Development

Life is good this year in fifth grade. Janet was able to move into a vacant classroom on the corner with lots of windows, and the students seem eager to learn. So far, so good! The first challenges on Janet's horizon are Molly and Roberto. They both seemed to have limited abilities in speaking English, and for very different reasons.

Molly is one of four children born to a single mother. Molly's mom, Teresa, works hard as a waitress but simply does not earn enough to make ends meet. Molly's family moves around a lot for financial reasons, which has taken its toll on her language learning. When Janet asked Teresa how things were going, her eyes welled up as she explained their situation. Here's the pattern: The rent comes due and Teresa rarely has sufficient resources to pay the bill. After 2 or 3 months of nonpayment, eviction is threatened, so she gathers up her children and moves to another apartment complex running a $99 move-in special. This state of affairs is repeated time and again because Teresa's income remains in the poverty range. In the end, she has very little time to spend with Molly, who stays at home alone tending her younger siblings while her mom works.

Roberto's situation is quite different. His family recently immigrated to the United States from Chile when his father, a civil engineer, was transferred with his company. Roberto studied English at his private Catholic school in Chile and can read and understand the language fairly well. His main problem seems to be oral communication.

It seems obvious that both Molly and Roberto need to build their English vocabulary and develop oral speaking fluency. The questions in Janet's mind are: (a) How can I find out what they already know? and, when I know that, (b) Where should I begin oral language instruction for each of these students?

BACKGROUND BRIEFING FOR TEACHERS

A rich and extensive oral language foundation is critical to the development of reading and writing (Dickinson & Tabors, 2001; Hart & Risley, 1995, 2002). Children must be relatively fluent with their oral language to communicate effectively with the teacher and other students in "learning networks" (Pinnell, 1998). Oral language also paves the way for learning such reading skills as phonemic awareness, alphabetic principles, phonics and decoding abilities, and reading comprehension. In fact, oral language ability is the bedrock foundation upon which all future literacy learning is built. There are essentially four major views of how children acquire oral language: (a) *behaviorist*, (b) *innatist*, (c) *constructivist*, and (d) *social interactionist*. We have found that all of these views help to explain one or more aspects of how children acquire and use oral language.

THE BEHAVIORIST VIEW OF ORAL LANGUAGE DEVELOPMENT

Behaviorists believe that oral language is learned through a process of *conditioning* and *shaping*—a response that involves a stimulus, a reward, or a punishment. Human role models in an infant's social and cultural environment provide the stimuli, rewards, or punishments that shape or condition the acquisition of certain features of oral language. The speech of parents or other caregivers acts as the *stimulus* in the sociocultural speech environment. When a baby imitates the sounds or speech of the adult models, praise and affection are given as *rewards* for the infant's attempts to learn language. Thus, the **behaviorist theory** of language acquisition states that infants learn oral language from other human role models through a process involving stimulation, imitation, rewards, punishment, and practice.

However, behaviorist theories of language development fail to explain a number of important questions associated with children's language acquisition. For example, if a parent is hurried, inattentive, or not present when the child attempts speech, then rewards for the desired speech responses are not always systematically provided. Thus, if a baby's language learning were only motivated by rewards, speech attempts would cease when regular and systematic rewards are absent.

Another problem with the behaviorist theory of oral language acquisition centers on the fact that young children do not simply imitate other human speech. Imitation implies certain behaviors. For example, when mother says, "Baby, say Mama," a baby would imitate or echo the mother by saying, "Baby, say Mama." Anyone who has raised children knows this is not the case. In fact, the baby may not say anything at all! But one thing is clear— children are not mere echo chambers. They are processing language meaning and sorting out the relevant from the irrelevant. Behaviorist language acquisition theories fail to account for this kind of selective or strategic cognitive processing.

Behaviorist language acquisition theories also do not account for speech terms invented by infants. For example, one girl we know used to call a sandwich a *weechie* even though no one in her home called a sandwich by any such name. Another failure of behaviorist theories to fully explain oral language development is the "jargon" language that is often developed between identical twins and no one else. Although behaviorist theories may explain to some extent the role of the social environment and the importance of role models in shaping children's language learning, the explanation seems incomplete. There are several cases against behaviorist language acquisition theories (Piper, 1998):

- Evidence of regression in pronouncing sounds and words previously pronounced correctly
- Evidence of novel forms of language not modeled by others
- Inconsistency of reinforcement or rewards provided
- Learning the use and meaning of abstract words
- Uniformity of language acquisition in humans
- Uniqueness of human language learning

THE INNATIST VIEW OF ORAL LANGUAGE DEVELOPMENT

A second theory about oral language development is called the **innatist theory**. Innatist theorists believe that language learning is natural for human beings. In short, babies enter the world with a biological propensity—an inborn device, as it were—to learn language. Lenneberg (1964) refers to this human built-in device for learning language as the *language acquisition device* (LAD). Thus, the innatist theory explains to some degree how children can generate or invent language they have never heard before.

Chomsky (1965) maintained that children use the LAD to construct an elaborate rule system for generating and inventing complex and interesting speech. Put another way, just as wings allow birds to fly, the LAD allows infant humans to speak. Although the innatist theory provides what appears to be a believable explanation for some aspects of oral language acquisition, researchers have failed to discover supporting evidence. Menyuk (1988) wrote, "Despite the apparent logic of this position, there is still a great deal of mystery that surrounds it" (p. 34). There are several cases against innatist language acquisition theories (Piper, 1998):

- The timing of language learning varies greatly within cultures.
- Feedback from other language users affects language acquisition.
- Environment shapes the language learned and how much language is learned.

THE CONSTRUCTIVIST VIEW OF ORAL LANGUAGE DEVELOPMENT

Constructivist theories of oral language development spring from the work of Jean Piaget (1959). Piaget believed that language development is linked to cognitive development. Even though he believed that cognition and language operate independent of each other, Piaget contended that language development was deeply rooted in the development of cognition or thinking and that concept or cognitive development preceded the development of language ability (Cox, 2002).

Chomsky (1957, 1965, 1997), a leading constructivist scholar, explained that children are constantly forming and testing hypotheses about the way oral language works. Chomsky's generative theory of language contends that each of us has what he termed a *language acquisition device* that helps us interpret and create words, phrases, and sentences we have never heard before. Thus, it is possible for children to understand and/or create an almost infinite number of varied language units.

Cox (2002) offered a summary of the stages of language development using (as was the case with Piaget) her own children as examples. The stages are as follows (with Piaget's cognitive stages noted in parentheses):

- *Preverbal (Sensorimotor) Stage, 0–2 Years.* Preverbal language, from birth to 6 months, is characterized by crying and babbling. Approximation of others' speech also occurs. From 12 to 18 months, you will see repetition of one-syllable sounds typically beginning with consonant phonemes, such as "na-na-na-na." First "words" also begin to appear such as *Da-Da, Ma-Ma,* and *bye-bye.*

- *Vocabulary and True Language (Preoperational) Stage, 2–7 Years.* From 18 months to 2 years of age, students become skillful at naming things in their environment—using one-word utterances called *holophrases* to communicate a complex set of needs or ideas, then two-word sentences called *telegraphic speech*—and grow in their ability to use simple sentences. Children 3 to 4 years of age begin using simple and compound sentences; understand present and past tenses, but over-generalize sometimes (e.g., *goed* for went); understand concepts like *few* and *many, first* and *second*; and may have a speaking vocabulary of up to 1,500 words. Children at this stage are still quite egocentric and do not always use words correctly—like Rob, who after fake-coughing a few moments said, "I have a carburetor stuck in my throat!" From ages 4 to 7 years, sentence length continues to grow both in terms of complexity of concepts and number of words. Children commonly use grammatically correct sentences, learn the rudiments of reading and writing, and expand their speaking vocabularies to between 3,000 and 8,000 words.

- *Logical and Socialized Speech (Concrete Operational) Stage, 7–11 Years.* Speech becomes more adultlike and is essentially mastered, though language skills will continue to grow in complexity. At ages 7 and 8, children use more symbolic language such as concepts (e.g., courage, freedom, time, seasons). From 8 to 10 years, their language becomes more flexible and students are able to engage in abstract discussions, facilitate and nurture less-developed language users, and expand ideas into lengthy discourse. Responses to questions become more logically developed, and children often use language to establish and cement relationships.

- *Abstract Reasoning and Symbolism (Formal Operations) Stage, 11–15 Years— and Beyond.* At this stage, children's speech becomes, at least in function and form, indistinguishable from adult speech. As with abstract thought, some learners seem to never quite reach this level of sophistication, which is why we have inserted the phrase "and beyond" as a caveat.

One of the key points about Piaget's constructivist notions was that children move through the previous stages at fairly predictable times and that external influences, such as schooling, can only minimally affect their evolution. In other words, we progress through these stages according to a biologically linked timetable and external influences (i.e., environment) have very little effect on the pace of growth. This notion is very much at odds with the *social interactionist* perspective.

Social Interactionist View of Oral Language Development

The environment—most importantly, the people in the environment—plays a critical role in the development of language according to **social interactionist** explanations of oral language development. Social interactionist theory assumes that language development is greatly influenced by physical, social, and, of course, linguistic factors (Cox, 2002).

Vygotsky (1986, 1990) demonstrated that adult interactions with children not only could assist in language development but also could affect the pace of language learning (a point Piaget eventually embraced in his later years). In chapter 2, we discussed Vygotsky's *zone of proximal development,* which explains how teachers can help students move from where they are developmentally into new frontiers of learning. This concept is at the heart of the social interactionist view and is the means by which teachers are able to create a kind of *scaffolding* (Bruner, 1978) or temporary structure that helps students construct new language built from what they have previously learned.

In summary, we agree with the constructivists that oral language is strongly connected to cognitive learning. We also agree that children move through very predictable stages of language learning with observable traits. However, we particularly agree with Vygotsky and social interactionists that oral language learning can be positively affected and accelerated by a skillful teacher who scaffolds instruction in the student's zone of proximal development.

Figure 5.1 The Functions of Language

Language Function	Example	Classroom Activities
Instrumental Language to accomplish a task	"May I have a banana?"	Problem solving Describing sequence of activities
Regulatory Language to control persons or circumstances	"I think it's time for us to all sit down."	Following directions Establishing procedures and rules
Interactional Social relationship language	"*We* don't like horror movies."	Group etiquette Discussion (guided)
Personal Language to express one's individuality or personality	"Merry Christmas . . . y'all!"	Sharing feelings Interactive discussion
Heuristic Using language to learn	"What got Benjamin Franklin interested in electricity?"	Questioning strategies Graphic organizers
Imaginative Creative language; exploratory	"Here's what I think it would be like to be the president . . ."	Storytelling Dramatic presentations Raps, rhymes, riddles
Representational Language that explains	"This is a finite amount of fuel for gas-powered engines."	Expounding about a known topic Time sequence (retelling) Explaining cause/effect relationships

Source: Based on *Learning How to Mean: Explorations in the Development of Language,* by M. A. K. Halliday, 1975, London: Edward Arnold.

The Practical Uses of Language

Oral language is an amazingly potent communication tool. Language can be used as an instrument to get things done or to regulate the behavior of others. It can serve as a creative tool at the disposal of a writer or to express our individuality. Children learn to use language quickly when they are able to use it for real purposes rather than as a rote exercise (Pappas, Kiefer, & Levstik, 1999). Halliday (1975) wrote about pragmatics or these functions of language and more, which are summarized in Figure 5.1. As teachers, it is important for us to understand these functions and to weave them into the fabric of our curriculum so that children will become truly fluent users of oral language.

WHAT ARE THE FIVE PHASES OF ORAL LANGUAGE DEVELOPMENT?

Whether you work with slow learners, gifted students who are English-language learners (ELLs), or typical children living in the suburbs, oral language among young children develops along a fairly predictable continuum. These five phases of oral language

Figure 5.2 Phases of Oral Language Development

Phase	Description
Preproduction	This is a short period in which the learner is silent but is actively listening to the more capable language users in his environment.
Early Production	This phase can last up to a year or more. The learner begins using single words and short phrases.
Emergent Speech	Learner is capable of sentences and short narratives.
Developing Fluency	Learner becomes capable of longer narratives/conversations, begins reading and writing, and uses invented spellings in his writing.
Advanced Fluency	Learner uses conventions of speaking, reading, and writing.

development—(a) preproduction, (b) early production, (c) emergent speech, (d) developing fluency, and (e) advanced fluency—are readily observable and can be used by you to help decide just where a student is in his or her development and what he or she is ready for next (i.e., his or her zone of proximal development). The five phases of oral language development are shown in Figure 5.2 and are based on the work of Cox (2002).

Language Deficits and Reading

There is no doubt that language deficits can limit a child's literacy learning in reading and writing (Lyon, 1999; Snow, Scarborough, & Burns, 1999) and are the single most common reason for referrals to special education (Warren, 2001). Research shows that children with weak oral language abilities tend to have (a) small vocabularies characterized by lots of short words that are used frequently, (b) high usage of nonspecific words, and (c) fewer complex sentences and less elaboration (Greenhalgh & Strong, 2001; Paul, 2001; Wiig, Becker-Redding, & Semel, 1983).

Simply put, research confirms that good readers "bring strong vocabularies and good syntactic and grammatical skills to the reading comprehension process" (Lyon, 1999, p. 10). We also know that early intervention with children having language problems can enhance literacy learning (Warren & Yoder, 1997).

Effects of Poverty on Language Development

Poverty, a condition in which an individual or group does without resources (Payne, 1998), is highly correlated with inhibited oral language development. Children of poverty are often denied exposure to many language-related experiences common to children from more affluent families, from a trip to Taco Bell or McDonald's, to participating in youth clubs, to going on summer vacations. Because "working poor" people often have to work several jobs just to make ends meet, parents frequently have little or no time to interact with their children. A common result of poverty for these children is poorly developed oral language. According to the 2002 *National Assessment of Educational Progress, Reading Report Card,* children from poverty score significantly lower in reading proficiency than their more affluent counterparts. These children are often at greatest risk of failing in school and eventually dropping out.

In recent groundbreaking research, Hart and Risley (1995, 2002) recorded every word spoken at home between parents and children in 42 families from various socioeconomic status (SES) backgrounds for $2\frac{1}{2}$ years. These families were categorized according to SES as *professional*, *working-class*, or *welfare* level. When comparing language interactions between professional-level parents and their children versus welfare-level parents and their children, data revealed that

- Professional parents spent more than 40 minutes daily interacting with their young children, while welfare parents spent 15 minutes each day.
- The difference between professional class parents compared to welfare families in verbally responding to their children ranged from 250 times per hour to 50 times per hour respectively.
- Discussion in which parents approved and encouraged children's actions was on average 40 times per hour for professional-level families compared to only 4 times per hour for welfare families.
- Professional families in their interactions usually spoke more than 3,000 words per hour compared to 500 words per hour in welfare homes.
- Access to oral language in both quantity and quality was so consistent within families that the differences in the children's language experience were enormous by age 3.

Results showed that children in professional families would have had experiences with 42 million words, working-class family children would have had experience with 26 million words, and welfare family children would have had experience with 13 million words. In professional families, the extraordinary amount of talk and exposure to many different words—greater richness of nouns, modifiers, and past-tense verbs—suggest a language culture focusing on symbols and analytic problem solving. In the welfare families, the lesser amount of talk was more about teaching socially acceptable behavior—obedience, politeness, and conformity were more likely to be the focus of language.

Factors That Can Positively Affect Oral Language Development

- *Home Environments.* Parents are their children's first teachers, and homes are children's first schools. Parents who read books aloud to their children regularly and provide access to books and other print materials in the home are laying the foundation for developing their children's oral language. Also, parents who talk while playing with their children, use rare (infrequent and mature) vocabulary words while interacting with their children, and take time to engage in rich and extended mealtime conversations provide many of the essential elements for developing oral language (Dickinson & Tabors, 2001; Snow, Scarborough, & Burns, 1999; Watson, 2001).
- *Preschool Experiences.* Like parents, quality literacy experiences in preschool settings have been shown to positively impact young children's oral language development. Teachers who read books aloud to their children regularly and provide access to books and other print materials in the preschool setting are extending children's home-based language learning opportunities. Teachers who integrate literacy experiences with learning and discussing content information, use rare (infrequent and mature) vocabulary words while interacting with their students, and provide opportunities for large- and small-group dramatic and social play time enriched with access to literacy tools offer children rich experiences in which they can extend their development of

oral language facility (Dickinson & Tabors, 2001; Neuman & Roskos, 1992; Snow, Scarborough, & Burns, 1999; Watson, 2001).

Given the significance of oral language development in the early years of a child's life at home and at school, teachers need to know how to assess the extent to which children have acquired a rich oral language base for extending their learning in school. They need to know which features of oral language children yet need to experience through language and print-rich learning experiences.

ASSESSING ORAL LANGUAGE DEVELOPMENT

In this section of the chapter, we examine several ways to assess children's oral language development. The first strategy that may be used to assess oral language development is the *Informal Language Inventory*.

INFORMAL LANGUAGE INVENTORY

Purpose

The *Informal Language Inventory* (ILI) is a simple and quick way to measure students' growth in conversational oral language development. The ILI uses a very traditional approach first described by Melear (1974) and Burns (1980). As an informal inventory or assessment approach, it is up to you, the teacher, to look for patterns in the results and compare these with your own classroom observations before coming to conclusions about a particular student's needs. You may want to refer to Figure 5.2 to help judge each student's progress and needs through the five phases of oral language development.

Materials

You will need to have one or two pictures that have been drawn by the student. He or she may either draw one just before you conduct the interview, or you can have him or her pre-select drawings from past school assignments. Older learners may bring in a photograph of a favorite friend or experience. An audiocassette or digital voice recorder is also recommended.

Procedure

Begin by turning on the recorder and asking the student to tell you about the picture(s). Transcribe the recording; then analyze the student's language as follows:

1. Number of sentences
2. Number of grammatically correct sentences
3. Number of descriptive terms
4. Number of modifying phrases
5. Number of morphemes (these are "meaning-bearing language units" such as prefixes, suffixes, and root words)
6. Number of "mazes" in the student's language (maze, in this context, means confused or tangled groups of words such as uh . . . uh . . . mmm . . . you know . . . like . . .)

We have constructed a coding sheet that you may want to use while administering and analyzing the ILI (see Figure 5.3).

Figure 5.3 Information Language Inventory Worksheet

Transcription of Oral Discussion	# of sentences	# of correct sentences	# of descript. terms	# of mod. phrases	# of morphemes	# of mazes

THE STUDENT ORAL LANGUAGE OBSERVATION MATRIX

Purpose

Teacher judgment is one of the most important and accurate measures of English-language learners' oral language development (Peregoy & Boyle, 2001, p. 131). One observational tool created by the California State Department of Education is the *Student Oral Language Observation Matrix* (SOLOM), which is shown in Figure 5.4. It is designed to be used in everyday classroom activities and is organized as a rubric to focus your attention on general oral language traits. The SOLOM was developed for use in English as a second language (ESL) classrooms but has also been found to be useful with native English speakers evidencing limited oral language development.

Materials

You will need a copy of the SOLOM for each student in a file folder.

Procedure

Conduct your observations of students during normal classroom activities in which a good bit of language is going on, such as small-group work, play, recess, lunch, or other interactive times of the day. Try to make sure that each time you make an observation, the situational context is similar. Limit the length of your observations for each student to about 5 minutes each, but be sure to make multiple observations to ensure greater reliability and generalizabilty of your conclusions.

For each trait, place an *X* in the box that best describes what the student is able to do and note the point value (1 to 5). For example, a student who in the "Comprehension" category understands nearly everything spoken at normal speed would receive a score of 4 for Comprehension. After you have placed an *X* in a box that best describes the student's language use in each trait category, add up the point values to determine his or her stage of development in English proficiency.

A key for scoring your observations is found at the bottom of the SOLOM in Figure 5.4. As an example, say that you have rated Jaime's oral language performance using the SOLOM traits and come up with the following rating:

Comprehension	4
Fluency	4
Vocabulary	4
Pronunciation	3
Grammar	4
Total	19

A score of 19 would indicate that Jaime's oral language development would be Stage III or "Limited English Proficient."

TEACHER RATING OF ORAL LANGUAGE AND LITERACY

Purpose

To be able to read and write effectively, children must develop strong oral language skills. According to Dickinson, McCabe, and Sprague (2003), the *Teacher Rating of Oral Language and Literacy* (TROLL) system measures skills critical to new standards for speaking and listening in today's classrooms. The TROLL can be used to track children's

Figure 5.4   Student Oral Language Observation Matrix

	1	2	3	4	5
COMPREHENSION	Cannot understand simple conversation	Only understands conversational language spoken slowly	Can understand most conversations if the speech is slow and includes repetitions	Understands almost everything at normal speed, but may require some repetitions	Understands class conversations and discussions without difficulty
FLUENCY	Speech is halting and fragmentary; makes it extremely difficult to initiate a conversation	Usually silent or hesitant due to language limitations	Often speech is interrupted while the student searches for the right word or expression	Generally fluent in class discussions, but may lapse sometimes into word searches	Fluent and effortless conversation
VOCABULARY	Very little vocabulary makes conversation nearly impossible	Limited vocabulary and often misuses words	Frequently uses incorrect words, and speech is limited by insufficient vocabulary	Sometimes uses inappropriate terms or must rephrase due to limited vocabulary	Fully capable in using vocabulary and idioms
PRONUNCIATION	Difficult to understand due to severe pronunciation problems	Pronunciation problems make it necessary to repeat himself a great deal	Pronunciation problems cause listeners to have to listen closely; some misunder-standings	Always intelligible, but may have heavy accent or inappropriate intonation patterns	Normal pronunciation and intonation
GRAMMAR	Acute problems with grammar and syntax making speech nearly unintelligible	Grammar and syntax problems often force him to repeat himself and stick to simple/familiar patterns	Frequent errors with grammar and syntax that sometimes alters meanings	Sometimes makes grammar or syntax errors	Appropriate grammar and syntax usage

Stages of Development

Stage I: Score of 5–11 = Not Proficient in English

Stage II: Score of 12–18 = Limited English Proficiency (Emergent)

Stage III: Score of 19–24 = Limited English Proficient (Developing)

Stage IV: Score of 25 = Fully English Proficient

Source: Adapted from an instrument developed by the California State Department of Education.

progress in language and literacy development, to inform curriculum, and to stimulate focused communication between parents and teachers. Oral language skills relevant to later literacy development include the development of the ability to tell stories, use of talk while pretending in play, and varied vocabulary usage (Dickinson & Tabors, 2001). Although oral language skills flourish during the preschool years, they are also very susceptible to stimulation and intervention in the early years of preschool, kindergarten, and primary-grade education.

The TROLL assessment has shown that Cronbach's alpha estimates of internal consistency ranged from .77 to .92 for separate subscales. For the total TROLL scores, alphas exceeded .89 for each age (Dickinson et al., 2003). The TROLL has also been shown to compare favorably to formal assessments such as the well-established Peabody Picture Vocabulary Test (PPVT-III), which is a measure of receptive vocabulary (see discussion later in this section). According to Dickinson et al. (2003), teacher ratings of children's language and literacy development on the TROLL show moderate associations with children's scores on all three areas (oral language, reading, and writing) of those direct assessments. In about 5 minutes, and with no special training on the TROLL, according to Dickinson et al. (2003), teachers themselves can index what trained researchers would spend roughly 25 to 30 minutes per child assessing.

Materials

You will need one copy of the TROLL for each student you observe. (See Figure 5.5.)

Procedure

No formal training is required to use the TROLL instrument, according to its authors. However, the TROLL is most effective if teachers know a bit about language and literacy development. The TROLL requires only 5 to 10 minutes for each child you observe. Use of the TROLL need not disrupt classroom activities.

You can use the information from the TROLL to inform your teaching by identifying children who are displaying evidence of serious oral language developmental delays and who may need formal assessment by speech professionals, or children who are showing high levels of literacy development and may benefit from additional challenges. By completing the TROLL several times over the course of a year, you can track the progress of all your students' oral language development.

Finally, you can combine results for all your students to determine which students need additional oral language experiences and which are in need of more systematic instruction. For example, if all of your students score relatively low on asking questions, you will want to begin providing numerous opportunities to listen to and ask questions during the daily routine in your classroom.

THE DYNAMIC INDICATORS OF BASIC EARLY LITERACY SKILLS WORD USE FLUENCY TEST

Purpose

The *Dynamic Indicators of Basic Early Literacy Skills* (DIBELS®) is a set of several standardized, individually administered measures of early literacy development. The DIBELS® was specifically designed to assess three of the National Reading Panel's (National Institute of Child Health and Human Development, 2000) five essential components of early literacy development: phonological awareness, alphabetic principle, and oral reading fluency (measured as a corrected reading rate) with connected text.

Figure 5.5   Teacher Rating of Oral Language and Literacy (TROLL)

Language Use

1. How would you describe this child's willingness to start a conversation with adults and peers and continue trying to communicate when he or she is not understood on the first attempt? Select the statement that best describes how hard the child works to be understood by others.

1	2	3	4
Child almost never begins a conversation with peers or the teacher and never keeps trying if unsuccessful at first.	Child sometimes begins a conversation with either peers or the teacher. If initial efforts fail, he or she often gives up quickly.	Child begins conversations with both peers and teachers on occasion. If initial efforts fail, he or she will sometimes keep trying.	Child begins conversations with both peers and teachers. If initial efforts fail, he or she will work hard to be understood.

2. How well does the child communicate personal experiences in a clear and logical way? Assign the score that best describes this child when he or she is attempting * tell an adult about events that happened at home or some other place where you were not present.

1	2	3	4
Child is very tentative, only offers a few words, requires you to ask questions, has difficulty responding to questions you ask.	Child offers some information, but information needed to really understand the event is missing (e.g., where or when it happened, who was present, the sequence of what happened).	Child offers information and sometimes includes the necessary information to understand the event fully.	Child freely offers information and tells experiences in a way that is nearly always complete, well sequenced, and comprehensible.

3. How would you describe this child's pattern of asking questions about topics that interest him or her (e.g., why things happen, why people act the way they do)? Assign the score that best describes the child's approach to displaying curiosity by asking adults questions.

1	2	3	4
To your knowledge, the child has never asked an adult a question reflecting curiosity about why things happen or why people do things.	On a few occasions, the child has asked adults some questions. The discussion that resulted was brief and limited in depth.	On several occasions, the child has asked interesting questions. On occasion these have led to an interesting conversation.	Child often asks adults questions reflecting curiosity. These often lead to interesting, extended conversations.

continued

Figure 5.5   Continued

4. How would you describe this child's use of talk while pretending in the house area or when playing with blocks? Consider the child's use of talk with peers to start pretending and to carry it out. Assign the score that best applies.

1	2	3	4
Child rarely or never engages in pretend play or else never talks while pretending.	On occasion the child engages in pretending that includes some talk. Talk is brief, may only be used when starting the play, and is of limited importance to the ongoing play activity.	Child engages in pretending often, and conversations are sometimes important to the play. On occasion child engages in some back-and-forth pretend dialogue with another child.	Child often talks in elaborate ways while pretending. Conversations that are carried out "in role" are common and are an important part of the play. Child sometimes steps out of pretend play to give directions to another.

5. How would you describe the child's ability to recognize and produce rhymes?

1	2	3	4
Child cannot ever say if two words rhyme and cannot produce a rhyme when given examples (e.g., rat, cat).	Child occasionally produces or identifies rhymes when given help.	Child spontaneously produces rhymes and can sometimes tell when word pairs rhyme.	Child spontaneously rhymes words of more than one syllable and always identifies whether words rhyme.

6. How often does child use a varied vocabulary or try out new words (e.g., heard in stories or from teacher)?

1	2	3	4
Never	Rarely	Sometimes	Often

7. When child speaks to adults other than you or the teaching assistant, is he or she understandable?

1	2	3	4
Never	Rarely	Sometimes	Often

8. How often does child express curiosity about how and why things happen?

1	2	3	4
Never	Rarely	Sometimes	Often

Language Use Subtotal ( )

Figure 5.5   Continued

Reading

9. How often does child like to hear books read in the full group?

1 Never	2 Rarely	3 Sometimes	4 Often

10. How often does child attend to stories read in the full group or small groups and react in a way that indicates comprehension?

1 Never	2 Rarely	3 Sometimes	4 Often

11. Is child able to read storybooks on his or her own?

1 Does not pretend to read books	2 Pretends to read	3 Pretends to read and reads some words	4 Reads the written words

12. How often does child remember the story line or characters in books that he or she heard before either at home or in class?

1 Never	2 Rarely	3 Sometimes	4 Often

13. How often does child look at or read books alone or with friends?

1 Never	2 Rarely	3 Sometimes	4 Often

14. Can child recognize letters? (Choose one answer.)

1 None of the letters of the alphabet	2 Some of them (up to 10)	3 Most of them (up to 20)	4 All of them

15. Does child recognize his or her own first name in print?

1 No	2 Yes

16. Does child recognize other names?

1 No	2 One or two	3 A few (up to four or five)	4 Several (six or more)

17. Can child read any other words?

1 No	2 One or two	3 A few (up to four or five)	4 Several (six or more)

continued

Figure 5.5   Continued

18. Does child have a beginning understanding of the relationship between sounds and letters (e.g., the letter *B* makes a "buh" sound)?

1	2	3	4
No	One or two	A few (up to four or five)	Several (six or more)

19. Can child sound out words that he or she has not read before?

1	2	3	4
No	One or two	One-syllable words often	Many words

Reading Subtotal ( )

Writing

20. What does child's writing look like?

1	2	3	4
Only draws or scribbles	Some letterlike marks	Many conventional letters	Conventional letters and words

21. How often does child like to write or pretend to write?

1	2	3	4
Never	Rarely	Sometimes	Often

22. Can child write his or her first name, even if some of the letters are backward?

1	2	3	4
Never	Rarely	Sometimes	Often

23. Does child write other names or real words?

1	2	3	4
No	One or two	A few (up to four or five)	Several (six or more)

24. How often does child write signs or labels?

1	2	3	4
Never	Rarely	Sometimes	Often

25. Does child write stories, songs, poems, or lists?

1	2	3	4
Never	Rarely	Sometimes	Often

Writing Subtotal ( )

Writing Subtotal   ( ) (Out of 24 Possible)
Oral Language Subtotal   ( ) (Out of 32 Possible)
Reading Subtotal   ( ) (Out of 42 Possible)
Total TROLL Score   ( ) (Out of 98 Possible)

Note: Copyright ©1997 Education Development Center, Inc. www.edc.org.

The *Word Use Fluency* (WUF) measure assesses a child's oral language expression ability by asking him or her to use a list of words in sentences. The WUF test begins when children are instructed to listen to a word and use it in a sentence.

A DIBELS® data and reporting service is available on the Internet for a fee of $1 per year per child tested. Using this Internet-based system, teachers can enter assessment data directly into the DIBELS® database on the Web and receive a nearly instantaneous report as often as desired. More recently, DIBELS® measures have become available in Spanish; however, such measures have not yet been validated or proven reliable among Spanish-speaking populations.

Materials

You will need the following:

Stopwatch or timer	Examiner probe
Pencil or pen	Clipboard

Procedure

The Word Use Fluency test directions, examiner probe, and directions are all available over the Internet for free at http://dibels.uoregon.edu/measures/wuf.php or from Sopris West Publishers at http://www.sopriswest.com. (See Figure 5.6.)

GET IT GOT IT GO! INDIVIDUAL GROWTH AND DEVELOPMENT INDICATORS—PICTURE NAMING TEST

Purpose

The *Get it Got it Go!* Individual Growth and Development Indicators are a set of several standardized, individually administered measures of early language and literacy development. The *Get it Got it Go!* Individual Growth and Development Indicators—Picture Naming Test was specifically designed to assess children's language development, ages 3 to 5.

The *Picture Naming* (PN) measure assesses a child's oral language expression ability by asking him or her to look at picture cards drawn from their home, classroom, and community environments such as the one that follows.

Sample Picture Naming Stimulus Card From the Picture Naming Test:
Get it Got it Go!

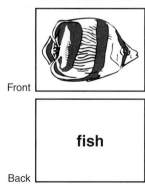

Front

fish

Back

Figure 5.6　Directions for Administration of the Word Use Fluency Test

1. Place the examiner probe on clipboard and position so that student cannot see what you record.

2. Say these specific directions to the student:

Listen to me use a word in a sentence, "green." (Pause) The grass is green. Here is another word, "jump." (Pause) I like to jump rope. Your turn to use a word in a sentence, (pause) "rabbit."

Correct Response:	**Incorrect Response:**
If student uses the word correctly in a phrase, say	If student gives any other response, say,
Very good.	*Listen to me use the word "rabbit" in a sentence.* (Pause) *"The rabbit is eating a carrot." Your turn, "rabbit."*

OK. Here is your first word.

3. Give the student the first word and start your stopwatch. If the student does not begin to use the word after *5 seconds,* give him or her the second word and score the first word as 0.

4. Provide the next word when the student has used the word in a phrase, expression, or utterance or when the student hesitates or pauses for *5 seconds.* As soon as the student is finished using the word, present the next word promptly and clearly.

5. At the end of *1 minute,* stop presenting words and recording further responses. Count the number of words used correctly in phrases, expressions, and sentences, and record at the end of the row. Total these scores and record at the bottom of the scoring sheet.

Source: Copyright 2002 Dynamic Measurement Group, Inc. http://dibels.uoregon.edu/measures/wuf_tutorial.php

Next, children are asked to name the objects in the pictures. The test begins when children are instructed to begin. The PN test; administration guidelines; and stimulus materials, the pictures to be named, are available free on the Internet at http://ggg.umn.edu/.

A *Get it Got it Go!* data and reporting service is available on the Internet for free, but users must enter their own data. By using this Internet-based system, teachers can enter assessment data directly into the *Get it Got it Go!* database on the Web and generate class level reports as often as desired. The Picture Naming test has not yet become available in Spanish. [*Note:* Missal and McConnell (2004) report reliability and validity data for the IGDI Picture Naming test as found in Figure 5.8, "Summary Matrix of Oral Language Assessments."]

Materials

The Picture Naming test directions, picture cards, and scoring forms are all available over the Internet for free at http://ggg.umn.edu/. You will need the following:

- Stopwatch or timer
- Pencil or pen

- Picture naming cards
- Form for recording scores
- Administration instructions
- Clipboard

Procedure

The directions for administration of the Picture Naming test include preparation guidelines and standardized administration directions. The preparation guidelines follow:

- Remember, you need a copy of the instructions to read from while administering tests.
- Be sure to do the *Sample Administration* first, before conducting the *Test Administration*.
- Sit with the child in a quiet area. Finding a distraction-free spot is best.
- Follow the scripted directions *exactly* as they are written.
- Write down the number correct on the recording form *immediately* after completing each test administration. *Do not include* sample responses.

The standardized directions for administering the Picture Naming test follows. They include the *Sample Administration* and the *Test Administration*.

Directions for the Sample Administration of the Picture Naming Test

Remember

- Continue the Picture Naming *Test Administration only* if the child names *all four* sample cards correctly during this *Sample Administration*.
- Follow directions *exactly* as written.
- Read aloud all words in bold.

Procedure

1. Select these four (4) cards from the stack to use as sample items: baby, bear, car, cat. *Do not choose different sample cards, even if you are re-administering the test.*
2. Say, **"I'm going to look at these cards and name these pictures. Watch what I do."**
3. Look at and clearly name the four sample cards while the child observes.
4. Say, **"Now you name these pictures."**
5. Show the four sample cards to the child in the same order as you named them, and give the child an opportunity to name each picture.
6. Praise the child for naming the picture correctly; otherwise, provide the correct picture name. *If the child responds in a different language*, say, **"This is a [picture name]. Call it a [picture name]."**
7. Continue on to *Test Administration only* if the child names *all four* pictures correctly. Write *NA* on the recording form if you do not continue administration.

Directions for the Test Administration of the Picture Naming Test

Remember

- This is a timed, *one-minute* task. Be sure to watch your stopwatch!
- Shuffle cards prior to each administration.

- Separate correctly named pictures into one pile and incorrectly named or skipped pictures into another pile.
- Follow directions *exactly* as written.
- Read aloud all words in bold.

Procedure

1. Say, **"Now we are going to look at some other pictures. This time, name them as fast as you can!"**
2. Start the stopwatch and immediately show the first card to the child.
3. If the child does not respond within 3 seconds, point to the picture and say, **"Do you know what that is?"** or **"What is that?"**
4. If the child still does not respond within an additional 2 seconds, show the next card.
5. As soon as the child names a picture, show the next card.
6. After *one-minute*, stop showing cards to the child. Record the total number of correctly named pictures on the recording form.

THE PEABODY PICTURE VOCABULARY TEST/
RECEPTIVE VOCABULARY TEST

Purpose

The Peabody Picture Vocabulary Test (PPVT)-III was developed primarily to assess younger children's (ages 2 to 6) receptive oral language vocabulary using a series of word prompts and pictures (AGS, 2005). The PPVT-III takes about 10 to 15 minutes to administer to an individual student. It comes in two parallel forms (A and B) for testing and in a new Spanish language version called the *TVIP: Test de Vocabulario en Imagenes Peabody.* Even though the test was developed originally for English-speaking children, more recently the PPVT has found renewed use among teachers who want to assess ELLs' understanding of oral English words as well. The PPVT has also been used in the past as one measure of a young child's verbal intelligence quotient (IQ) to determine discrepancies between current functioning and potential functioning to qualify for federally supported special services and has been approved for use in federally funded Early Reading First and Reading First projects. Norms have been extended in the PPVT-III for ages 2.5 to 90+ years. Test items have increased to 204 for each of the two forms, A and B. There are newer illustrations for better gender and ethnic balance.

Reliability for the PPVT-III is as follows: Internal Alpha range .92 to .98; Split-half: Alternate-form range .86 to .97; Test-Retest range .88 to .96. Validity evidence includes a .91 correlation with verbal ability on the WISC-III VIQ, .89 on the KAIT Crystallized IQ, and .81 with the K-BIT Vocabulary test.

The Expressive Vocabulary Test (EVT) was developed primarily to assess younger children's (ages 2 to 6) expressive oral language vocabulary using a series of word prompts and pictures (AGS, 2005). The EVT takes about 15 minutes to administer to an individual student. The EVT is co-normed with the PPVT-III. For the labeling items (38), the examiner points to a picture or a part of the body and asks the child to respond to a question. On the 152 synonym items, the examiner presents a picture and stimulus word(s) within a phrase. The child responds to each item with a one-word answer. All pictures are in color and balanced for gender and ethnic representation.

The EVT reliability analyses indicate a high degree of internal consistency. Split-half reliabilities range from .83 to .97 with a median of .91. Alphas range from .90 to .98 with a median of .95. Test-retest studies with four separate age samples resulted in reliability coefficients ranging from .77 to .90, indicating a strong degree of test stability.

Materials

Materials needs for administering the PPVT-III or EVT can be purchased by going to the following web site: http://www.agsnet.com/Group.asp?nGroupInfoID=a12010. PPVT-III and EVT materials include:

- PPVT-III/EVT administration manual
- PPVT-III/EVT scoring records
- PPVT-III/EVT picture flip chart
- PPVT-III/EVT scoring software

Procedures

Specific, standardized procedures for administering the PPVT-III/EVT are found in the published administration manuals. A recent addition is a training video/DVD for the *Peabody Picture Vocabulary Test-Third Edition* that can be purchased for training purposes in preparation for administering, scoring, and interpreting the results of the PPVT-III. The PPVT-III and EVT assessments are quick and easy to administer and score. They are excellent screening assessments for examining children's receptive and expressive oral language development.

ORAL LANGUAGE CHECKLIST

Purpose

Many times, teachers are able to learn a great deal by simply making anecdotal records of students they wish to observe, then transferring that information to a checklist. Johnson (1993) developed an oral language checklist based on the research, which is well suited to this type of assessment.

Materials

Duplicate the oral language checklist found in Figure 5.7 for each student whose oral language development you wish to study. A clipboard with a legal pad or peel-off sticky computer labels is also needed for making anecdotal notes during observations.

Procedure

First, carefully review the oral language checklist found in Figure 5.7 for key points to observe. Then, identify one or two children per day whose language development you wish to study. During the school day, keep your clipboard handy and make anecdotal notes on each child according to the criteria represented in the questions on the oral language checklist. At the end of each observation day, transfer your notes to a folder for each child and answer all questions that apply. Observations should be repeated about once every 6 weeks in order to identify growth trends and determine educational (i.e., language development) needs.

In Figure 5.8, we summarize the oral language assessment instruments we have discussed thus far and provide summary information about federally related assessment purposes, such as *screening, diagnosis, progress-monitoring,* or *outcomes assessment*, as well as type of test and psychometric evidence of test scores such as reliability and/or validity evidence.

Figure 5.7 Oral Language Checklist

While interacting with the child you wish to study in your classroom, note any of the following:

1. Was there any indication that the child misperceived words?   Yes   No
   List examples:

2. Did the child have difficulty understanding directions for various tasks?   Yes   No
   Examples:

3. Did the child have difficulty understanding any specific vocabulary?   Yes   No
   Examples:

4. Did the child have difficulty comprehending complex/lengthy sentences?   Yes   No
   Examples:

5. Did the child have difficulty listening to and comprehending extended
   discourse? (e.g., stories)   Yes   No
   Examples:

6. Did the child have difficulty remembering series of instructions?
   How many?   Yes   No
   Give examples:

7. Did the child have difficulty retrieving (recalling) words?
   Under what conditions? Picture naming, spontaneous
   conversation?   Yes   No
   Other:

8. Did the child have difficulty pronouncing multisyllabic words?
   Give examples: Yes   No

9. Did the child make grammatical mistakes when speaking?   Yes   No
   List examples:

10. Could the child convey thoughts clearly when relating an event
    or telling a story?   Yes   No
    Give examples of problems such as sequencing of events, lack
    of transition words, failure to include relevant information.

11. Did the child have good nonverbal communication?   Yes   No
    Give examples: (eye contact, gesture)

12. Did the child have any specific articulation problems?   Yes   No
    Give examples:

13. Were any of the above problems reflected in the child's
    oral reading or reading comprehension?   Yes   No
    Give examples:

14. Were any of the above *oral language* problems reflected
    in the child's written *language?*   Yes   No
    Give examples:

Source: Copyright 1993 by the National Association of School Psychologists, Bethesda, MD. Reprinted with permission of the publisher. www.nasponline.org.

CONNECTING ASSESSMENT FINDINGS TO TEACHING STRATEGIES

Once you have determined who in your class may need further oral language development, as well as the areas of oral language to be developed, then you should select appropriate learning activities. Most oral language development activities tend to fall into certain types: conversations, discussions, description/comparison/evaluation, reporting, storytelling, and creative drama or choral reading. In the *If-Then Strategy Guide for Oral Language Development* we have listed the teaching strategies that appear in the next section and we have linked them to key need areas your oral language assessments are likely to reveal.

TEACHING STRATEGIES FOR DEVELOPING ORAL LANGUAGE

Children's oral language is improved when teachers and family members provide good language models and opportunities to practice oral language in authentic situations and when students receive supportive feedback for their attempts at approximating proficient English usage (Morrow, 1999, 2005). Whether teaching English as a second language or working to shore up the language abilities of native speakers, learning activities selected by teachers should help children improve their receptive (listening/reading) and expressive (speaking/writing) language skills. In this section, we provide a menu of teaching strategies that have served many teachers well in the classroom.

RULE OF FIVE

Purpose

There is a plethora of scientific research showing that helping children increase the length of spoken and added written sentences can have a very positive effect on learning to read (e.g., Dickinson & Tabors, 2001; Tharp & Gallimore, 1988). The **Rule of Five** strategy (Cooter, 2005) is an adaptation of the research findings by Dickinson and Tabors (2001) intended to increase verbal sentence length, also known as *mean length of utterance* (MLU), by simply requiring students (and teachers) to always speak in complete sentences in their conversations using at least *five* words. These researchers concluded that children need opportunities to be part of conversations that use "extended discourse"—talk that requires students to develop complete sentences in explanations, narratives, or even "pretend" talk.

Materials

You will need to produce, copy, and laminate a drawing of a small hand similar to the one shown in Figure 5.9. After laminating The Rule of Five hands, attach a small self-adhesive magnet to each so the children can put them on their refrigerator at home as a reminder to themselves and their parents that our goal is to speak in complete sentences. You should also send home a letter to parents explaining what the Rule of Five is and encourage them to practice this strategy at home in their family interactions.

Procedure

Distribute the Rule of Five hands to each of your students. Explain that it is a fun strategy and easy to do and that both students and teachers must use at least *five* words in all talk.

Figure 5.8 Summary Matrix of Oral Language Assessments

Name of Assessment Tool	Screening Assessment Purpose	Diagnostic Assessment Purpose	Progress-Monitoring Assessment Purpose	Outcomes Assessment Purpose	Norm-Referenced Test	Criterion-Referenced Test	Reliability Evidence	Validity Evidence
Informal Language Inventory (ILI)	+	−	+	−	−	+	Not Available	Not Available
Student Oral Language Observation Matrix (SOLOM)	+	+	+	−	−	+	Not Available	Not Available
Teacher Rating of Oral Language and Literacy (TROLL)	+	−	+	−	−	+	TROLL internal consistency (Cronbach's alpha) ranged from .77 to .92 for three separate subscales. For the total TROLL scores, alphas exceeded .89 for each age.	TROLL shows moderate associations with PPVT-III according to the TROLL's authors.
DIBELS® Word Use Fluency Test (WUF)	+	−	+	−	−	+	As Word Use Fluency is a new DIBELS measure, its technical adequacy has not as of yet been determined.	As Word Use Fluency is a new DIBELS measure, its technical adequacy has not as of yet been determined.

Name of Assessment Tool	Screening Assessment Purpose	Diagnostic Assessment Purpose	Progress-Monitoring Assessment Purpose	Outcomes Assessment Purpose	Norm-Referenced Test	Criterion-Referenced Test	Reliability Evidence	Validity Evidence
Peabody Picture Vocabulary Test/Expressive Vocabulary Test (PPVT/EVT)	+	−	−	+	+	−	PPVT-III: Internal Alpha range .92 to .98; Split-half: Alternate-form range .86 to .97; Test-Retest range .88 to .96.	PPVT-III: .91 correlation with the WISC-III VIQ, .89 with the KAIT Crystallized IQ, and .81 with the K-BIT Vocabulary Test.
Get it Got it Go! Picture Naming Test	+	−	+	−	−	+	Alternate-form range .44 to .78; Test-Retest is .67.	.56 to .75 correlation with the PPVT-III
Oral Language Checklist	−	−	+	−	−	−	Not Available	Not Available

Key: + can be used for
 − not appropriate for

IF-THEN STRATEGY GUIDE FOR ORAL LANGUAGE DEVELOPMENT

"If" the student is ready to learn... / "Then" try these teaching strategies →	Rule of Five	Animal Crackers	One Looks/One Doesn't	Poetry Potpourri: Teacher Modeling	Poetry Potpourri: Unison Reading	Poetry Potpourri: Repeated Lines and Refrains	Poetry Potpourri: Antiphonal Call and Response	Poetry Potpourri: Singing Poems	Poetry Potpourri: Poetry Response	Story-telling	K-W-H-L-S	Critical Dialogues
Comprehensible Expressive Language	+	+	+	+	*	*	–	*	+	+	+	+
Fluent Expressive Language Production	+	–	–	–	+	+	+	+	+	+	–	–
Word Pronunciation	*	–	+	+	+	+	+	+	+	+	+	+
Word Usage	+	+	+	+	+	+	+	+	+	+	+	+
Grammatical Constructions	*	–	+	+	+	+	+	+	+	+	+	+
Comprehends Received Language	–	+	+	*	+	+	+	+	+	+	+	+
Organizes Ideas Logically and Sequentially	*	*	+	+	–	–	–	–	+	+	+	+
Provides Supporting Details	*	–	–	+	–	–	–	–	+	+	*	+
Word Meaning Acquisition	–	+	+	+	*	*	*	*	+	*	+	+

Key: + Excellent strategy
　　　* Adaptable strategy
　　　– Unsuitable strategy

Figure 5.9 A Rule of Five Hand

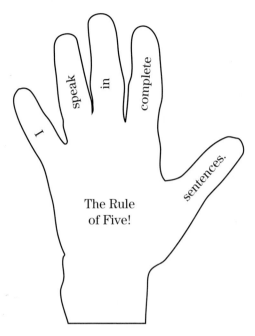

I speak in complete sentences.

The Rule of Five!

As ever, the best way to introduce this activity is with teacher modeling. You may begin by saying, for instance,

> *Girls and boys, instead of me saying something to you like "Line up!" I should say a complete sentence like "Students, it is time for us to line up for lunch."*

You should explain that you expect students to express themselves in at least five or more words. For instance,

> *If I should ask your classmate, Molly, a question like, "How was your weekend, Molly?" I would not accept an answer like "Good." No, the Rule of Five would require Molly to give me a complete sentence of five or more words such as "This weekend I played baseball and I had a great time."*

For best results, introduce the Rule of Five idea to parents at your first open house of the year and ask for their support at home. You will be amazed at the positive results that will occur in reading and writing instruction as a result.

ANIMAL CRACKERS

Purpose

As teachers of language, we must always have a wide range of exercises of varying complexity, interest level, and difficulty available to reach children where they are in their oral language development (Avery & Bryan, 2001). For young learners, this can be as simple and basic as describing familiar things in their environment, such as animal crackers!

Materials

You guessed it! You will need a box of animal crackers from your neighborhood grocery for each group of two or four students (whatever you decide).

Procedure

The idea is to have groups of students (groups of either two or four) sit together and generate words that describe the arrangements of animal crackers. Their descriptions can either be tape recorded or written by a recorder in the group (invented spellings are acceptable for this activity).

Here are some animal cracker themes that can be used for this activity (Brovero, 1996):

- Classify the animals by habitat/environment (graphing could be used here as well).
- Draw each animal and add speech in a cartoonlike bubble.
- Classify animals by their eating habits.
- Have small groups of students invent mathematics word problems involving a variety of animals found in their box of crackers.
- Match animals to the printed word from your word wall (see chapter 9 for a discussion of word walls).

At the end of your activities, students get to eat the animals, of course!

ONE LOOKS, ONE DOESN'T

Purpose

It is important for us to help students expand their oral communications abilities because, as "producers" (speaking) of language, they will also become better "receivers" (reading) of language; these are reciprocal processes. In *One Looks, One Doesn't* (Peregoy & Boyle, 2001), students are able to take turns practicing their oral communications with a peer as they describe a picture or object selected by the teacher.

Materials

You will need stimulus objects for students to describe. These can include interesting pictures from magazines or books, pictures on transparencies shown at the overhead projector for all groups to see and describe, objects that can be held, and so forth. A blindfold for each group (one only for each group) can add a little spice to this activity, too!

Procedure

First, place students in groups of two for this activity (also called *dyads*). If possible, arrange it so that in each twosome you have a more capable speaker of English, such as pairing a native English speaker with an English-language learner (ELL), or perhaps a sixth-grade student paired with a third grader.

If using a transparency of a picture, place the transparency on the overhead projector after explaining that one student will look at the transparency while the other turns away (or wears a blindfold). The student who looks at the picture describes it to his or her partner and the listener attempts to guess what the partner is describing.

A variation is for the listener to try to draw what his or her partner is describing. After about 5 minutes (use an egg timer to keep it fair for all), the one drawing the picture can turn around and compare his or her drawing with what his or her partner was describing.

Areas that could be stressed in teacher-led minilessons for this activity include:

- Expressing ideas clearly and with variety
- Organizing ideas effectively before speaking
- Word usage appropriate for the situation

- Appropriate articulation
- Listening to questions carefully from your partner, and asking for clarification as necessary
- Politely asking the speaker to repeat or explain

Poetry Potpourri

Purpose

Nancy Hadaway and her colleagues (Hadaway, Vardell, & Young, 2001) assembled a wonderful collection of classroom activities that use poetry to stimulate oral language development, particularly for students learning English as a second language. They point out that reading and rereading poetry through read-aloud and choral reading activities promote fluency, develop concept knowledge and vocabulary, and serve as splendid springboards into writing. In this section, we highlight several of the poetry activities that Hadaway et al. recommended.

Materials

You will need a variety of poetry for language-development activities. Here is a listing of the selections cited, many of which are found in school libraries:

Children's poetry books cited by Hadaway et al. (2001)

Ada, A. F., Harris, V., & Hopkins, L. B. (1993). *A chorus of cultures anthology.* Carmel, CA: Hampton Brown.

Fleischman, P. (1985). *I am phoenix.* New York: HarperCollins.

Fleischman, P. (1988). *Joyful noise.* New York: HarperCollins.

Fleischman, P. (2000). *Big talk: Poems for four voices.* Cambridge, MA: Candlewick Press.

Florian, D. (1994). *Bing bang boing.* San Diego, CA: Harcourt Brace.

Greenfield, E. (1978). *Honey, I love.* New York: Harper & Row.

Herrera, J. F. (1998). *Laughing out loud, I fly: Poems in English and Spanish.* New York: HarperCollins.

Holbrook, S. (1996). *The dog ate my homework.* Honesdale, PA: Boyds Mills Press.

Holbrook, S. (1997). *Which way to the dragon!: Poems for the coming-on-strong.* Honesdale, PA: Boyds Mills Press.

Hughes, L. (1932/1994). *The dreamkeeper and other poems.* New York: Knopf.

Johnston, T. (1996). *My Mexico-Mexico mio.* New York: Penguin Putnam.

Kuskin, K. (1975). *Near the window tree.* New York: Harper & Row.

Kuskin, K. (1980). *Dogs and dragons, trees and dreams.* New York: HarperCollins.

Mora, P. (1999). *Confetti: Poems for children.* New York: Lee & Low.

Nye, N. S. (1995). *The tree is older than you are.* New York: Simon & Schuster.

Pappas, T. (1991). *Math talk: Mathematical ideas in poems for two voices.* San Carlos, CA: Wide World/Tetra.

Prelutsky, J. (1984). *The new kid on the block.* New York: Greenwillow.

Shields, C. D. (1995). *Lunch money.* New York: Dutton.

Silverstein, S. (1974). *Where the sidewalk ends.* New York: HarperCollins.

Silverstein, S. (1981). *A light in the attic*. New York: HarperCollins.

Soto, G. (1992). *Neighborhood odes*. San Diego, CA: Harcourt.

Soto, G. (1995). *Canto familiar*. San Diego, CA: Harcourt Brace.

Wong, J. (1996). *A suitcase of seaweed*. New York: Simon & Schuster.

Procedures

Following are brief descriptions of oral language development activities that have been recommended using poetry as the primary catalyst. (Citations in this section are from the preceding "Materials" list.)

- *Teacher Modeling.* It is hard to sell something you do not love yourself, so begin with poems that you particularly like. Introduce key words and phrases at the chalkboard so that students can see as well as hear new vocabulary and concepts. If you need help with this, try "Three Wishes" by Karla Kuskin (1975). All of us "kids" have made wishes and can relate to this poem. For those of us with, shall we say, wacky relatives, Gary Soto's (1992) "Ode to Family Photographs" can be great fun with older students.

- *Unison Reading.* After the previous activity, students will usually be loosened up a bit and ready to take on more of the performance role. Choose shorter poems with repeating lines, and read the poem aloud first yourself to help students get the feel. When we each taught first grade, we found that children could hardly be stopped from joining in on the second reading of a fun poem! "My Monster" (Florian, 1994) is very popular from grades 1 through 4 for example.

- *Repeated Lines and Refrains.* Another great choral activity has students learn about timing and coming in just when their assigned line comes up or as a group when a refrain appears. Sometimes a key word is said extra loud for emphasis, such as with the poem "Louder" by Jack Prelutsky (1984).

- *Antiphonal: Call and Response.* Teachers divide the class into two groups, and one side repeats the lines first spoken by the other. This is a form of antiphonal reading, an ancient tradition begun by monks in monasteries during medieval times. Try out the "call and response" method using "Copycat" by Sara Holbrook (1997).

- *Singing Poems.* Children love to put poetry to song—matching poems and songs having the same meter. It works best when using tunes that are familiar to all such as "Row, Row, Row Your Boat" or "Mary Had a Little Lamb." If you give students a copy of the poem, they will end up reading and singing the poem over and over, providing them with needed repetition of high-frequency words and a chance to develop language fluency. Try "The Dog Ate My Homework" by Sara Holbrook (1996) sung to "On Top of Old Smokey," or the poem "School Cafeteria" (Florian, 1996) sung to the tune of "Ninety-nine Bottles of 'Pop.'"

- *Poetry Response.* A good language-development exercise should elicit a great deal of oral language in an authentic discussion situation for student practice and teacher coaching. Draw students into discussions about interesting poems using such questions as

  What did this poem make you think?

  What did you like about this poem?

  What do you think the poet was trying to say?

  Does this remind you of anything you know about?

  Let's talk about what is going on here . . .

  What is this poem about?

STORYTELLING

Purpose

Many cultures have strong oral traditions to describe their religious beliefs, politics, triumphs, and family stories (McHenry & Heath, 1994). As a tool for language development, story-telling can be powerful (Strickland & Morrow, 1989). As an art form, storytelling has certain aspects that should be respected for the storyteller to be effective in his or her communica-tions. Here we discuss a teacher-directed method for bringing storytelling to the table as a valuable tool in your teaching arsenal.

Materials

It is best, if at all possible, to provide students with what we term *limited choice;* several stories that would be appropriate for retelling from which they can choose one. The story should be easy to read and be in concert with the student's interests and background. You will also need copies of Figure 5.10, "The Storyteller's Planning Guide."

Procedure

Begin with a storytelling experience for the students in which you model telling one of your favorite stories from memory. Next, introduce The Storyteller's Planning Guide (Figure 5.10) and explain each of its key points. Walk through a planning session in which you model how you went about planning to share the story they witnessed you sharing earlier. Be sure to include discussion about any props, voices, and other points that add drama to the telling. Place students into groups of two and have them select one of the stories you have available for them to use in storytelling. Have them account for each step in the planning process using the storyteller's planning guide. When each group of two feels they are ready, have them take turns practicing the storytelling to each other. The final "act" will be for each student to perform his or her favorite part of the story to you (or the entire group, if the student is not too nervous). Follow up the performance with questioning, such as, "Why did you choose that part of the story to tell?" or "Why was that your favorite part of the story?" This draws students into even more dialogue.

K-W-H-L-S CHART

Purpose

This is a teacher-directed activity in which we lead students into discussions about science, mathematics, social studies, and other real-world subjects. The K-W-H-L-S Chart (Baloche, 1998; Cox, 2002) helps students structure new knowledge, build conceptual knowledge, develop questioning skills, and strengthen vocabulary.

Materials

Multiple copies of the K-W-H-L-S Chart (Figure 5.11) will be needed for this activity.

Procedure

The K-W-H-L-S Chart is a super tool for leading a class discussion about a topic of study. The idea is to name a topic from your curriculum that you wish to introduce to the class. Perhaps you will be studying with older students events of the September 11, 2001, terror-ist attack on New York City and Washington, D.C. Discussion that resulted with one group of sixth-grade students a few months after the event occurred are shown in Figure 5.12. Note

Figure 5.10   The Storyteller's Planning Guide

Storyteller _____

Story _____

Source _____

Motivation- *I want to tell this story because . . .*

Props- *What kinds of props ("properties"), if any, would I need to tell this story? (Clothing, sound-making devices, other?)*

Introduction- *How will I begin the story? What are the exact words I should use?*

Setting- *How do I describe the setting? How can I make the listener feel like she is there? Is time and place important to the story?*

Characters- *How can I best describe each character? What makes the main character "tick"? How should I present each character to the audience? Should I use different voices for the different characters? If not, how can I make the audience understand who is talking?*

Sequence of Events- *What are the key events I will describe in my story? What is the correct order for each "scene"?*

Conclusion- *How will I bring my story to a successful end? What are my final words? (Exact words, please) How do I want my audience to feel at the conclusion?*

Rehearsal- *Have I practiced telling my story alone at least three times, and before a friend at least once?*

Figure 5.11   K-W-H-L-S Chart

Topic:

K What I **know**	W What I **want** to learn	H **How** I can learn more about this topic	L What I **learned**	S How I can **share** this new knowledge

Figure 5.12   K-W-H-L-S Chart (Partially Completed on the 9/11 Attack)

Topic:	September 11			
K What I ***know***	**W** What I ***want*** to learn	***How*** I can learn more about this topic	**L** What I ***learned***	**S** How I can ***share*** this new knowledge
Many innocent people were killed that day. Planes were used as flying bombs. Bin Laden was the person behind the attacks. Many of us think he is a coward. President Bush said that this is an act of war. Mayor Giuliani has been called the "Mayor of All America." We all felt afraid when this horrible thing happened. We feel so sad for the families who lost a loved one. Most Islamic people are good and are worried that some Americans will blame them for this horrible event because of bin Laden.	Where is Afghanistan? What are the countries that are on its borders? How far is it from the United States? How are the children in Afghanistan doing? Do they have enough food? What does the religion of Islam teach? What is happening now in the war on terrorism? Did the families of those killed receive help? What is an "act of war" according to the Constitution? Are we safe?	Get a map from the library to locate Afghanistan. Ask an expert about the distances from here to Afghanistan. Look on the Internet for the latest news on Afghan children and the war on terrorism. Go to the American Red Cross web site to find out about aid to surviving families. Interview a law professor from an area university about acts of war as described in the U.S. Constitution. Invite a police officer to speak to the class about our safety and things we can do.		

that this was the first discussion and only the first three columns of the K-W-H-L-S Chart were completed. Remember, in our use of this procedure, the teacher transcribes the discussion offerings onto the chart. This enables him or her to question, clarify, and modify offerings in a "teachable moment" kind of method.

CRITICAL DIALOGUES

Purpose

Critical dialogues are structured conversations between teachers and children around stories, information texts, and other media sources such as DVDs, videos, and computer web sites. Students link their own experiences, feelings, and knowledge to learn content knowledge in science, social studies, mathematics, art, music, and so on. Gentile and McMillan (1992, 1995) based the Critical Dialogue strategy on the work of the Brazilian educator, Paulo Freire, who used dialogues as a method to help free Brazilian peasants from the oppression of illiteracy and poverty. Gentile (2003) claims that using Critical Dialogues helps to create "a threshold level of language proficiency" necessary to build the higher order cognition children need to process information for academic purposes and become literate (p. 38).

Materials

- Critical Dialogue Planning and Lesson Guide (See Figure 5.13)
- One narrative or story text
- One or more short information texts
- One or more media-related resources, for example, videos, web sites, DVDs, CD-ROMS, audio tapes, and so on

Procedure

A Critical Dialogue is planned and executed using a sequential, four-stage approach. In *Stage 1*, the teacher organizes and frames the dialogue. This is accomplished by setting the parameters for a successful conversation, that is, turn taking, active listening, not interrupting a person speaking, participation, and so on. Next, the teacher introduces the topic or theme of the text and media materials—say, for example, "plants"—by assessing, activating, and building students' background knowledge and previous life experiences.

In *Stage 2*, the teacher guides students to identify a significant purpose, set of questions, or "I wonder" brainstorming for listening to, reading, or viewing the texts or media selected on a topic like "plants." Next the teacher highlights new vocabulary, concepts, or information and clearly identifies the main idea, important facts, problems, or story sequence and elements for the students such as *stem, pistol, pollen, ovules, flowering,* and so on. At this point, children view, read, or listen to the story or information texts or the media resources selected by the teacher. After doing so, children are invited to talk about what they were thinking or feeling as they watched, read, or listened.

In *Stage 3*, the teacher develops and expands the dialogue. After their initial conversations about the materials read, listened to, or watched, the teacher asks the children to do two tasks: (a) identify the most important thing they learned; and (b) think of the most important question they could ask about the materials they have viewed, heard, or read. Next, the children and teachers summarize and clarify the major ideas of the selection and their dialogues. Finally, the teacher may model how to pose questions of differing types and how one goes about answering these questions.

Figure 5.13 Critical Dialogue Planning and Lesson Guide for Plants

---

Stage 1: Organizing and Framing the Critical Dialogue

Selected Topic or Theme: **Plants**

Necessary Materials:

Story Text: Krauss, R. (1945). *The Carrot Seed.* New York: Scholastic.
Information Texts: McEvoy, P. (2002). *Plants.* New York: Newbridge.
                    Roberts, C. (2004). *Where Plants Live.* Northborough, MA: Sundance Publishing.
Video/DVD/CD: VHS (2004). *How Do Plants Grow and Change?* Questar, Inc.
Computer/Web Site: *Plants for Kids*—http://www.kathimitchell.com/plants.html

Assessing/Activating Background Knowledge:

- K-W-H-L-S (See later in this section)
- List of Key Vocabulary Concepts

Stage 2: Guiding the Critical Dialogue

Purpose for Learning:

- Ask children what they want to learn about the topic or theme.
- Record their responses in the K-W-H-L-S chart.

Active Processing:

- Read the story text.
- Read the information texts.
- View the media selections.
- Visit the web sites.
- Discuss what was read, viewed, or listened to.

Stage 3: Developing and Expanding the Critical Dialogue

- Ask children what they want to learn about the topic or theme.
- Record their responses in the K-W-H-L-S chart.

Active Processing:

- Read the story text.
- Read the information texts.
- View the media selections.
- Visit the web sites.
- Discuss what was read, viewed, or listened to.

Stage 4: Closing the Dialogue

- Invite children to write a response to several questions posed by the teacher, for example,

  - What is the most important thing you learned about plants from the selections and our dialogues?
  - What is the most important question you have about plants from the selections and our dialogues?
  - What difference does any of this make to you?

Finally, in *Stage 4*, the teacher helps children to close the dialogue. This is accomplished by asking children to write a response to several questions posed by the teacher:

- What is the most important thing you learned from the selections and our dialogues?
- What is the most important question you have about the selections and our dialogues?
- What difference does any of this make to you?

For younger children, the teacher can ask children to respond to these questions orally and write down what the children say on a large chart paper or wall display. This helps to validate the importance of what the children learned and said about what they learned. The questions the children dictate may very well lead to future dialogues, reading, listening, and viewing!

ADAPTING INSTRUCTION FOR THOSE WHO STRUGGLE

How can teachers effectively respond to the variability of children's oral language development and usage in classrooms? Even with the plethora of previously recommended assessments and strategies, we want to offer a few parting suggestions about how oral language instruction can be differentiated to meet the needs of those students who struggle.

- Remember to be a good model of correct English usage.
- You can also help by partnering less capable children with more capable and supportive children.
- Pair pictures and objects with oral language use in the classroom.
- When asking questions or expecting a response, remember to extend the "wait time" before you rephrase or redirect your question or request. When questioning, ask open-ended questions so that children can express themselves more fully than just giving a correct response.
- Provide explicit instruction in oral language vocabulary development, how sentences work, and word pronunciations.
- Encourage language play, extended conversations, and telling and retelling stories with struggling learners. Do not be afraid to use rare words or engage in discussions of a wide range of topics!

SELECTED REFERENCES

Avery, S., & Bryan, C. (2001). Improving spoken and written English: From research to practice. *Teaching in Higher Education, 6*(2), 169–183.

Baloche, L. A. (1998). *The cooperative learning classroom: Empowering learning.* Upper Saddle River, NJ: Prentice Hall.

Brovero, M. (1996). Class menagerie. *Teaching PreK–8, 27*(2), 64.

Bruner, J. (1978). The role of dialog in language acquisition. In A. Sinclair, R. J. Jarvella, & W. M. Levelt (Eds.), *The child's conception of language* (pp. 241–256). New York: Springer-Verlag.

Burns, P. C. (1980). *Assessment and correction of language arts difficulties.* Columbus, OH: Merrill.

Chomsky, N. A. (1957). *Syntactic structures.* The Hague, The Netherlands: Mouton.

Chomsky, N. (1965). *Aspects of the theory of syntax.* Cambridge, MA: MIT Press.

Chomsky, N. (1997). *Perspectives on power.* Montreal, Canada: Black Rose Books.

Cooter, K. S. (2005, February). *The Principals' Fellowship: Strategies for improving oral language and reading abilities.* Paper presented at the meeting of The Principals' Fellowship, Memphis, TN.

Cooter, R. B., & Cooter, K. S. (2002). Challenges to change: Implementing balanced reading instruction in an urban school district. *Balanced Reading Instruction,* No. 1, 8–26.

Cox, C. (2002). *Teaching language arts* (4th ed.). Boston: Allyn & Bacon.

Dickinson, D. K., McCabe, A., & Sprague, K. (2003). Teacher Rating of Oral Language and Literacy (TROLL): Individualizing early literacy instruction with a standards-based rating tool. *The Reading Teacher, 56*(6), 554–564.

Dickinson, D. K., & Tabors, P. O. (2001). *Beginning literacy with language.* Baltimore: Paul H. Brookes.

Dickinson, D. K., Tabors, P. O., & Patton, O. (2002). Fostering language and literacy in classrooms and homes. *Young Children,* No. 2, 10–18.

Dunn, L. M., & Dunn, L. M. (2005). *PPVT-III: Peabody Picture Vocabulary Test*-Third Edition. Retrieved from http://www.agsnet.com/Group.asp?nGroup InfoID=a12010.

Florian, D. (1996). *Bing Bang Boing: Poems and Drawings.* New York: Puffin/Penguin

Gentile, L. M. (2003). *The oracy instructional guide: Linking research and theory to assessment and instruction.* Carlsbad, CA: Dominie Press.

Gentile, L. M., & McMillan, M. (1992). Literacy for students at risk: Developing critical dialogues. *The Journal of Reading, 35*(8), 636–641.

Gentile, L. M., & McMillan, M. (1995). Critical dialogue: A literacy curriculum for students at risk in the middle grades. *Reading and Writing Quarterly, 11,* 123–126.

Greenhalgh, K. S., & Strong, C. J. (2001). Literate language features in spoken narratives of children with typical language and children with language impairments. *Language, Speech, & Hearing Services in Schools, 32*(2), 114–126.

Hadaway, N. L., Vardell, S. M., & Young, T. A. (2001). Scaffolding oral language development through poetry for students learning English. *The Reading Teacher, 54*(8), 796–807.

Halliday, M. A. K. (1975). *Learning how to mean: Explorations in the development of language.* London: Edward Arnold.

Hart, B., & Risley, T. R. (1995). *Meaningful differences in the everyday experience of young American children.* Baltimore, MD: Paul H. Brookes.

Hart, B., & Risley, T. R. (2002). *The social world of children: Learning to talk.* Baltimore, MD: Paul H. Brookes.

Holbrook, S. (1996). *The dog ate my homework.* Honesdale, PA: Boyds Mills Press.

Holbrook, S. (1997). *I never said I wasn't difficult.* Honesdale, PA: Boyds Mills Press.

Huttenlocher, J., Haight, W., Bruk, A., Seltzner, M., & Lyons, T. (1991). Early vocabulary growth: Relation to language input and gender. *Developmental Psychology, 27*(2), 236–248.

Johnson, D. J. (1993). Relationships between oral and written language. *School Psychology Review, 22*(4), 595–610.

Kuskin, K. (1975). *Near the window tree.* New York: Harper & Row.

Lenneberg, E. H. (1964). *New directions in the study of language.* Cambridge, MA: MIT Press.

Lyon, G. R. (1999). Reading development, reading disorders, and reading instruction: Research-based findings. ASHA Special Interest Division I Newsletter. *Language Learning and Education, 6*(1), 8–16.

McHenry, E., & Heath, S. B. (1994). The literate and the literary. *Written Communication, 11*(4), 419–445.

Melear, J. D. (1974). An informal language inventory. *Elementary English, 41,* 508–511.

Menyuk, P. (1988). *Language development knowledge and use.* Glenview, IL: Scott, Foresman/Little, Brown College Division.

Missal, K. N., & McConnell, S. R. (2004). *Technical report: Psychometric characteristics of individual growth and development indicators: Picture naming, rhyming, and alliteration.* Minneapolis: University of Minnesota.

Morrow, L. M. (1999). Where do we go from here in early literacy research and practice? *Issues in ed. 5*(1), 117–125.

Morrow, L. M. (2005). *Literacy development in the early years: Helping children read and write* (5th ed.). Boston: Allyn & Bacon.

National Assessment of Educational Progress. (2000). *The nation's report card: Reading.* Jessup, MD: Education Publications Center (ED Pubs).

National Assessment of Educational Progress, Reading Report Card. (2002). Washington, DC: U.S. Department of Education.

National Institute of Child Health and Human Development. (2000). *Report of the National Reading Panel: Teaching children to read.* Washington, DC.

Neuman, S. B., & Roskos, K. (1992). Literacy objects as cultural tools: Effects on children's literacy behaviors in play. *Reading Research Quarterly, 27,* 202–225.

Pappas, C. C., Kiefer, B. Z., & Levstik, L. S. (1999). *An integrated language perspective in the elementary school* (3rd ed.). New York: Longman.

Paul, R. (2001). *Language disorders from infancy through adolescence* (2nd ed.). St. Louis, MO: Mosby.

Payne, R. K. (1998). *A framework for understanding poverty.* Highlands, TX: RFT.

Peregoy, S. F., & Boyle, O. F. (2001). *Reading, writing, & learning in ESL* (3rd ed.). New York: Longman.

Piaget, J. (1959). *The language and thought of the child* (3rd ed.). London: Routledge & Kegan Paul.

Pinnell, G. S. (1998). *The language foundation of reading recovery.* Keynote address to the Third International Reading Recovery Institute (Third, Cairns, Australia).

Piper, T. (1998). *Language and learning: The home and school years* (2nd ed.). Upper Saddle River, NJ: Merrill/Prentice Hall.

Prelutsky, J. (1984). *The new kid on the block.* New York: Greenwillow/HarperCollins.

Ramey, C.T. (1999). *Right from birth: Building your child's foundation for life, birth to 18.* New York: Goddard Press.

Snow, C. E., Burns, S. M., & Griffin, P. (Eds.). (1998). *Preventing reading difficulties in young children.* Washington, DC: National Academy Press.

Snow, C. E., Scarborough, H. S., & Burns, M. S. (1999). What speech-language pathologists need to know about early reading. *Topics in Language Disorders, 20*(1), 48–58.

Strickland, D. S., & Morrow, L. M. (1989). Oral language development: Children as storytellers (emerging readers and writers). *The Reading Teacher, 43*(3), 260–261.

Tharp, G., & Gallimore, R. (1998). *Rousing minds to life: Teaching, learning, and schooling in social context.* Cambridge, MA: Cambridge University Press.

Vygotsky, L. S. (1986). *Thought and language.* Boston: MIT Press.

Vygotsky, L. S. (1990). *Mind in society.* Boston: Harvard University Press.

Warren, S. F. (2001). The future of early communication and language intervention. *Topics in Early Childhood Special Education, 20*(1), 33–38.

Warren, S. F., & Yoder, P. J. (1997). Emerging model of communication and language intervention. *Mental Retardation and Development Disabilities Research Reviews, 3*, 358–362.

Watson, R. (2001). Literacy and oral language: Implications for early literacy acquisition. In S. B. Neuman & D. K. Dickinson (Eds.), *Handbook of early literacy* (pp. 43–65). New York: Guilford Press.

Wiig, E. H. (2000). Authentic and other assessments of language disabilities: When is fair fair? *Reading & Writing Quarterly, 16*(3), 179–211.

Wiig, E. H., Becker-Redding, U., & Semel, E. M. (1983). A cross-cultural, cross-linguistic comparison of language abilities of 7- to 8- and 12- to 13-year-old children with learning disabilities. *Journal of Learning Disabilities, 16*(10), 576–585.

Chapter 6

Children's Concepts About Print

Ms. Solomon's kindergarten class excitedly gathered around her on the carpet. She had a big book displayed on the easel entitled *On Market Street* (Lobel & Lobel, 1981) and was ready to start reading. As the children settled in, Ms. Solomon pointed to the cover of the book and asked, "What do you see here?"

"A girl carrying a bunch of stuff!"

"Yes, she is. It's quite a stack of things. Where do you suppose she has been to get all that stuff?"

Bobby responded somewhat quizzically, "I guess she's been to a junkyard."

"No, no, she's been shopping!" interrupted Brit.

"Why do you say that, Brit?"

"Because in the picture she is walking away from a town and some buildings."

"Good observation! What do you think the words will tell us about the picture on the cover of this book?"

"It's the title," Jana blurts out confidently.

"Thank you, Jana. That is what the writing on the cover is called. So, let me ask my question another way. What do you think the writing in the title will tell us about the picture on the cover?"

"Oh, I think it will say something about going shopping," answers Brit.

"OK, shall we see? Listen to me read the title and watch as I point to the words with my pointer." Ms. Solomon points to the words one at a time while reading, "ON—MARKET—STREET." Ms. Solomon continues into the book and comes to a picture of a girl covered with clocks.

"What is the letter at the top of this page?"

"C" says Mica.

"Good, by looking at the picture on this page, what do you think the girl is going to buy on Market Street?"

The children cry out as a group, "Clocks."

"Good thinking. Let's look at this word, *clocks.*"

"Does *clocks* start with the letter *c*? Look carefully and compare the first letter in clocks with the letter *c* at the top of the page." The teacher and children interactively share this book noting the pattern in the book—letter at the top of the page, a picture, the letters, and a word on each page that begins with the letter at the top of the page.

After the first reading of the big book *On Market Street,* Ms. Solomon talks with the children about making their own *On Market Street* big book. "Now, let's see if we can make our own big book of what we would buy on Market Street," she says. Ms. Solomon lays out a big pile of labels and print taken from the children's everyday environment. Labels from soda drinks, candy, cereal boxes, and canned goods are all over the floor. "So, we are going to Market Street and we are going to buy something that begins with a *B*. What will we buy?"

One little boy, Jackson, pulls up a candy bar wrapper and says, "Let's buy Butterfinger or Baby Ruth candy bars." They all agree and Ms. Solomon pastes the two candy bar wrappers on the page of the class's innovation on the big book *On Market Street.*

Background Briefing for Teachers

Many children enter school already knowing a great deal about how books work and how to carefully look at printed language, while others do not (Yaden & Templeton, 1986; McGee & Richgels, 2003). Some children know the difference between a word and a letter; others know where a story begins in a book; and others have had little access to books and guided experiences with print (Neuman, 1999; Neuman & Celano, 2001). Concepts associated with printed text, known as **print concepts** (also *concepts about print*), are a critical part of early literacy development and understanding among beginning readers (Hiebert, Pearson, Taylor, Richardson, & Paris, 1998; Clay, 2000a).

Assessing print concepts in the early years is important so that children who come to school without prior learning opportunities, access to books and print, or guided experiences with printed language can be helped to develop these necessary concepts to prevent possible reading problems later on (Clay, 2000a; Snow, Burns, & Griffin, 1998; Durkin, 1989). Wren (2002) noted that teachers can

> . . . observe how the child handles a book, and can assess the child's knowledge about how information is presented in the book . . . [and] determine the child's general knowledge of books. (Does the child know where the cover is? Does the child hold the book right-side up? Does the child turn the pages appropriately? Does the child know the message of the book is contained in the text?) . . . (p. 12)

Research studies have shown that some children require direct, explicit instruction in learning print concepts (Hiebert et al., 1998; Snow et al., 1998). For example, Yaden (1982) found that even after a year of reading instruction some readers' concepts of letters, words, and punctuation marks had not yet developed to a level that was functionally useful. Johns (1980) also learned that first grade students' end-of-first-grade reading achievement could be reliably predicted using students' entering kindergarten knowledge of print concepts. Further, Morrow (1993) found that mastery of certain characteristics, conventions, and details associated with printed language is necessary for successful literacy development. Several other researchers have shown that children's early learning of concepts about print influence language development, initial writing development, phonemic awareness, phonics learning, word reading, and reading development (Lomax & McGee, 1987; Morris, 1993; Roberts, 1992). As a result of these and other findings, Hiebert et al. (1998), in a document disseminated through the Center for the Improvement of Early Reading Achievement (CIERA) called *Every Child a Reader,* have called for teachers, administrators, curriculum developers, and publishers to focus on assessing and developing print concepts among all young learners. You can access *Every Child a Reader* by going to http://www.ciera.org on the Internet. We focus in this next section on defining and explaining print concepts to children.

WHAT ARE THE CONCEPTS ABOUT PRINT?

Concepts about print can be divided into three distinct and different print aspects (Taylor, 1986; Clay, 2000a): (a) the functional aspects of print, (b) the mapping aspects of print, and (c) the technical aspects of print. We discuss each of these separately.

FUNCTIONS OF PRINT

Children learn early that written language is useful for a variety of purposes. Halliday's (1975) landmark research describes how oral and written language functions in our daily lives. The purposes children and adults have for using language can be divided into three parts: (a) *ideational,* or expressing one's thoughts; (b) *interpersonal,* or intimate social language; and (c) *textual,* or informational language. Smith (1977) expanded Halliday's teachings to purposes for which language can be used. Each of the 10 purposes or *functions of language* (p. 640) is detailed here with related examples:

Instrumental. "I want." Language is used as a means of getting things and satisfying material needs.
Examples in written language: Classified advertisements, notes, sign-up sheets, applications, bills, invoices, and so on.

Regulatory. "Do as I tell you." Language is used to control the attitudes, behaviors, and feelings of others.
Examples in written language: Traffic signs, procedures, policies, traffic tickets, prompts, and so on.

Interactional. "Me and you." Language is used as a means of getting along with others and establishing relative status. Also, "Me against you." Language is used for establishing separateness.
Examples in written language: Love notes, invitations, dialogue journals, friendly letters, and so on.

Personal. "Here I come." Language is used to express individuality, awareness of self, and pride.
Examples in written language: Opinion papers, letters to the editor, and so on.

Heuristic. "Tell me why." Language is used to seek and test world knowledge.
Examples in written language: Letters of inquiry, requests, registration forms, and so on.

Imaginative. "Let's pretend." Language is used as a means of creating new worlds and making up stories and poems.
Examples in written language: Stories, tall tales and yarns, and so on.

Representational. "I have something to tell you." Language is used for communicating information, providing descriptions, and expressing propositions.
Examples in written language: Arguments, lists, problem solving, and so on.

Divertive. "Enjoy this." Language is used for humor and fun.
Examples in written language: Puns, jokes, and riddles.

Authoritative/Contractual. "This is how it must be." Language is used to communicate rules.
Examples in written language: Statutes, laws and regulations, and so on.

Perpetuating. "How it was." (Records)
Examples in written language: Personal histories, diaries, journals, scrapbooks, and so on.

Children make varied use of oral language in their own lives, at least in a subconscious way. As you help students become aware of these oral language functions, they will readily apply this knowledge in their written language use as well.

MAPPING SPEECH ONTO PRINT

The ability to match or *map* speech sounds onto the printed symbols (letters) develops rather slowly. Some researchers believe that the ability to map speech sounds onto printed language and knowledge of the sound-symbol code, or phonics knowledge, may develop simultaneously (Lomax & McGee, 1987). Mapping involves several important skills that the student learns. The student

- Understands that speech can be written down and read and that what is written down can be spoken
- Is aware of print in the environment and can read at least some signs and logos
- Understands that the message of the text is constructed from the print more than the pictures
- Knows that written language uses different structures (see Halliday, 1975; and Smith, 1977) from spoken language
- Comprehends that the length of a spoken word is usually related to the length of the written word
- Demonstrates that one written word equals one spoken word
- Identifies some correspondences between spoken sounds and written symbols
- Uses context and other language-related clues to construct meaning and identify words

Mapping speech onto print helps students become successful readers and benefit from further experiences with written language (Reutzel, Oda, & Moore, 1989; Johnston, 1992). For some readers, failing to acquire an understanding of mapping principles can slow their progress in reading and writing development (Ehri & Sweet, 1991; Clay, 2000; Johns, 1980).

TECHNICAL ASPECTS OF PRINT

The phrase *technical aspects of print* refers to the rules or *conventions* that govern written language. Examples include directionality (left-to-right/top-to-bottom progression across the page in reading), spatial orientation, and instructional terms used in classrooms to refer to written language elements. Because many of these technical concepts are commonsense matters for adults, it is little wonder that sometimes teachers and parents mistakenly assume that children already understand them. However, ample evidence exists that this knowledge of the technical aspects of written language develops slowly for many learners (Johns, 1980; Clay, 1979; Day & Day, 1979; Downing & Oliver, 1973; Meltzer & Himse, 1969). A listing of the technical aspects of print follows.

Levels of Language Concepts

Ordinal

- First, second, third, and so on
- Beginning
- Last
- Book
- Paragraph

- Sentence
- Word
- Letter

Visual Clues Embedded in Books and Print

- Cover, spine, pages
- Margins, indentations
- Spacing
- Print size
- Punctuation

Location Concepts

- Top
- Bottom
- Left
- Right
- Beginning (front, start, initial)
- Middle (center, medial, in between)
- End (back, final)

It is very important that teachers assess what young children know about the technical aspects of printed language. In the next section of this chapter, we describe five useful assessment tools for teachers to gain insights into children's understanding of the concepts about print.

ASSESSING CHILDREN'S CONCEPTS ABOUT PRINT

The assessment strategies offered in this section provide you with a comprehensive approach for assessing all three aspects of the concepts about print: (a) the functional aspects of print, (b) the mapping aspects of print, and (c) the technical aspects of print.

CONCEPTS ABOUT PRINT TEST

Purpose

The Concepts About Print (CAP) Test was designed by Marie Clay (1972, 2000a, 2000b) to assess children's mapping and technical aspects of print knowledge such as letter, word, sentence, story, directionality, text versus picture, and punctuation. The CAP test is based upon four small booklets, two published in 1972 and two published in 2000. The two booklets published in 1972 are entitled *Sand* and *Stones*. The two booklets published in 2000 are entitled *New Shoes* and *Follow Me, Moon*. All four of these text booklets are viewed and read by a teacher and an individual student together. One set of booklets may be used as a pretest and posttest in the kindergarten year and the other two may be used as a pretest and a posttest during the first-grade year to measure concepts about print growth.

Instructions for administering the Concepts About Print Test can be found in Clay's (2000a) book entitled *Concepts About Print: What Have Children Learned About the Way We Print Language.* More information about the Concepts About Print test booklets and the manual for administration, scoring, and interpretation can be found on the Internet by going to http://www.heinemann.com.

Materials

You will need the following items, authored by Marie M. Clay (2000a, 2000b) and published by Heinemann Educational Books: *Concepts About Print: What Have Children Learned About the Way We Print Language*; and the four forms of the actual test booklets: *Sand, Stones, New Shoes,* and *Follow Me, Moon.*

Procedures

Procedures for administering, scoring, and interpreting these tests are found in *Concepts About Print: What Have Children Learned About the Way We Print Language* (pp. 8–15). Print concepts tested include: front of book; proper book orientation to begin reading; beginning of book; print rather than pictures carry the message; directional rules of left to right, top to bottom on a page; return sweep to the beginning of a line of print; matching spoken words with written words; concepts of first and last letters in a word; mapping spoken word and letter order onto the print; beginning and ending of a story; punctuation marks; sight words; identifying printed letters, words, and uppercase versus lowercase letters.

In order to adequately test children's print concepts, the *Sand, Stones, New Shoes,* and *Follow Me, Moon* booklets include some rather unusual features. At certain points, the print or pictures are upside down, letter and word order are changed or reversed (*saw* for *was*), and line order is reversed, as well as paragraph indentions removed or inverted.

The CAP test has established a long and excellent record as a valid and reliable screening test to be used as part of a battery of screening tasks for young, inexperienced, or at-risk readers. A major limitation of this test, however, is that it is based on error-detection tasks that require the child to find problems and explain them. Because of the somewhat tedious nature of this test and its tasks, children need to be tested in a calm environment and need to have a trusting relationship with the examiner in order to obtain reliable results.

READING ENVIRONMENTAL PRINT

Purpose

This task is designed to assess students' ability to read commonplace or "highly frequent" print accessible in their local and daily environment, such as signs in the school like STOP, EXIT, or NO SMOKING. Other examples of environmental print include signs on the outside of businesses, stores, and on products commonly available across the nation such as McDonald's, Cheerios, Diet Coke, and so forth.

Environmental print information can be used to assess the access a child has had or the attention given to printed language in the environment (Reutzel et al., 2003). Further, teachers can discover ways that environmental print may be used to help each child develop successful reading and writing behaviors. An added advantage of environmental print is that it encourages beginning readers to develop an "I can read!" attitude. Researchers who have examined the value of teaching children using environmental print have consistently shown it to be useful (Proudfoot, 1992; Neuman & Roskos, 1993; Vukelich, 1994; Kuby & Aldridge, 1997; West & Egley, 1998; Orellana & Hernandez, 1999; Reutzel et al., 2003).

Materials

Materials selected for this task are based upon a survey of children's recognition and access to environmental print completed by Briggs and Richardson (1994). To begin, three sets of 10 plain index cards (30 cards total) are needed to construct this task. The first set of 10 cards is used to display traffic signs or informational logos found on roads and in public buildings. The second set of 10 cards is used to display logos of restaurant chains, television shows, gasoline stations, and national chain stores such as Kmart®. The third set of 10 cards is used to display food product logos such as Pepsi®, Alphabits®, and Butterfinger®.

Procedures

Classification procedures (see Figure 6.1, "Written Language Knowledge Taxonomy") are used to sort student responses to the set of 30 cards into pragmatic response, inclusion of part of the print response, meaning conversion response, and attention to graphic detail response (Harste, Burke, & Woodward, 1981; McGee, LoMax, & Head, 1988). This taxonomy has been used to help reading researchers determine how well children process print in their environment. The environmental print task helps teachers gain insights into students' growing understanding of print concepts using environmental language. Children who show little awareness of print in the environment are also likely to have had few experiences with printed text in other contexts, such as books and writing.

Figure 6.1 Written Language Knowledge Taxonomy

Response Category	Level	Examples
Pragmatic perspective	Attempts to read	
	Maintains communication contract	
	single word or name (with no article),	"potato chips," "bread"
	phrases (not beginning with article "a"),	"trouble with the football team"
	letters, numbers	"A" to telephone (index letter)
	Renegotiates communication contract	"7:30" to TV Guide
	names print object (usually with article)	"a newspaper"
	describes something in picture of print item	"a man"
	describes what can be found on the print item	"words," "telephone numbers,"
	describes what can be done with the print item	"pictures," "take it to the store"
	Refuses to respond	no response or "I don't know"
Inclusion of text from print item	Attempt to read includes text of print item	"State Times" to paper
	Attempt partially includes text of print item (at least one word of response is included in text of print)	"Gulf State" for "State Times" in text
	Attempt does not include text of print item	"gum, candy" not in text of grocery list
Meaning	*Meaningful*	
	Attempt includes print text central in meaning	"eggs" to grocery
	Attempt does not include text but makes sense	"tomato" to grocery list (not in text)
	Nonmeaningful	
	Attempt includes print text not central in meaning	"by," "is" to newspaper
	Attempt does not include text and does not make sense	"redfish" to book (not in text)
	Naming letters embedded in words	"S" "T" to "State" text
Attention to graphic detail	*Evidence of attention to graphic detail*	
	Attempt includes print text for item with no picture	"dog food" to grocery list
	Attempt includes print text when child points to correct text	"potato chips" and points to text "potato chips"
	Attempt practically includes print text (one word plus one letter same)	"Sunday Times" for text "State Times"
	Attempt does not include text, but it's obvious child referred to text	"the" and child points to "to"
	Attempt includes identification of letters in text	"S" "T" to newspaper

Source: Reprinted with permission from the National Reading Conference and Lea McGee, from "Young Children's Written Language Knowledge: What Environmental and Functional Print Reading Reveals" by L. McGee, R. Lomax, & M. Head, 1988, *Journal of Reading Behavior, 20*(2), pg. 105. Copyright 1988 by the National Reading Conference.

Mow Motorcycle Task

Purpose

As children begin to learn to read and write, some discover how spoken words or sounds are mapped onto letters and printed words in books and other written language sources. One concept students need to discover is that the length of the *printed* word is related to the length of the same *spoken* word. The Mow Motorcycle Task (Rozin, Bressman, & Taft, 1974) taps students' awareness of this basic mapping relationship between speech and print.

Materials

Prepare 10 *pairs* of word cards (20 cards total) to be used for this task. Each pair of word cards should contain two words beginning with the same letter and differing in written and spoken length, as shown in OLD Figure 6.2. Print each word card neatly with all upper-case manuscript or printed letters using a computer printer. Use a plain, block, or print style font rather than calligraphic or stylized fonts.

Procedures

Seat the child comfortably next to you at an appropriate-size table or desk. Displaying only one pair of cards at a time, show the child 10 pairs of cards bearing printed words beginning with the same letter. For example, tell the student, "One of these words is *mow* and the other is *motorcycle*. Which one is *mow*?" The child responds by pointing. The total score is the number of correct responses, with 0 to 10 points possible. Items should be varied so that the "target" word (the one you name) and the "foil" (the incorrect choice) are not always in the same position. This helps prevent the possibility that mere guessing on the student's part—always choosing the left-hand word, for example—will result in a high number of false correct responses.

Metalinguistic Interview

Purpose

The Metalinguistic Interview (MI) is a set of questions designed to assess children's understanding of academic or instructional language, that is, language teachers use in instruction as they talk about printed language in books and displayed elsewhere. For example, researchers (Clay, 1966; Downing, 1970, 1971–1972; Reid, 1966; Denny & Weintraub, 1966) interviewed young children and found that they often do not have a clear understanding about many of the common academic or instructional terms used in beginning reading instruction, such as alphabet, letter, word, and sentence. Obviously, knowledge of these terms is most likely linked to how well children understand and respond to early reading and writing instruction.

Figure 6.2   Mow Motorcycle Task

One of these words is *mow* and the other is *motorcycle*. Which one is *mow*?

| MOTORCYCLE | MOW |

Academic or instructional language terms or concepts assessed in the Metalinguistic Interview include the following:

- That the term *alphabet* and/or *ABCs* refers to letters
- That the actual location on a page of a single letter, word, or sentence is an indication of directionality L → R (left to right), T → D (top/down), and so on
- Punctuation
- How to differentiate uppercase and lowercase letters
- Terms such as the *front* and *back* of a book, and an understanding of *page(s)*

Materials

Any children's trade book or literature book containing both pictures and print may be used. For the best early assessment, locate a book that has print on one page and a full-page picture on an adjoining page. A scoring sheet can be easily constructed by duplicating Figure 6.3. For scoring, write a 0 or 1 following each of the 20 questions. Scores on the interview range from a low of 0 to a high of 20. Carefully examine which items were missed to determine areas of future instructional focus.

Procedures

Make a copy of the 20 tasks or questions in Figure 6.3. Seat the child comfortably next to you. Hand the student a picture book such as *The Gingerbread Man* (Schmidt, 1985) or *The Little Red Hen* (McQueen, 1985) upside down, with the spine of the book facing the child. Once the child takes the book, tell him that the two of you are going to read the book together. Then ask him to respond to the 20 tasks listed in Figure 6.3 and mark the responses on the question sheet.

Figure 6.3   The Metalinguistic Interview

1. "What are books for? What do books have in them?"
2. "Show me the front cover. Show me the back cover."
3. "Show me the title of the story."
4. "Show me the author's name."
5. "Open the book to where I should begin reading."
6. "Show me which way my eyes should go when I begin reading."
7. "Show me the last line on the page."
8. Begin reading. At the end of the page ask, "Now where do I go next?"
9. "Show me where to begin reading on this page. Will you point to the words with your finger as I say them?"
10. "Show me a sentence on this page."
11. "Show me the second word in a sentence."
12. "Show me a word."
13. "Show me the first letter in that word."
14. "Show me the last letter in that word."
15. "Show me a period on this page."
16. "Show me a question mark on this page."
17. Show the child a quotation mark and ask, "What is this?"
18. Ask the child to put his fingers around a word.
19. Ask the child to put his fingers around a letter.
20. Ask the child to show you an upper- and lowercase letter.

Correct responses are given a 1 and incorrect responses are scored 0.

THE BURKE READING INTERVIEW

Purpose

The purpose of the Burke Reading Interview (Burke, 1980) is to help you discover what students understand about the reading process and the strategies students use to unlock unknown words and construct meaning. Children are asked to describe how they learned to read, as well as what they can do to become better readers (Burke, 1980; DeFord & Harste, 1982). You can determine whether students recognize that the goal of reading is to understand the author's message, or if they mistakenly think that the only goal of reading is to recode letters into sounds.

Materials

You will need the Burke Reading Interview (Burke, 1980) and a cassette tape recorder to record the child's responses to the interview questions. Interpretation of this instrument is based on the response to each question. A total score is not useful to guide instructional decision making. Each response must be examined to reveal to the teacher the next steps necessary for this child to progress in his or her reading and writing development.

Procedures

Seat the child comfortably near you and the cassette recorder's microphone for effective recording purposes. Visit with the student for a moment to establish rapport. Tell the student that you will be asking him or her a few questions and that you will be recording his or her answers. Then, turn the recorder on and begin by asking the child his or her name. Next ask the questions found in the Burke Reading Interview in Figure 6.4. The tape recording can be used later to analyze student responses.

Figure 6.4   The Burke Reading Interview

Name: _____ Age: _____ Date: _____
Occupation: _____ Educational level: _____
Sex: _____   Interview setting: _____

1. When you are reading and come to something you don't know, what do you do? Do you ever do anything else?
2. Who is a good reader you know?
3. What makes _____ a good reader?
4. Do you think _____ ever comes to something he/she doesn't know?
5. "Yes" When _____ does come to something he/she doesn't know, what do you think he/she does?
   "No" Suppose _____ comes to something he/she doesn't know.
   What do you think he/she would do?
6. If you knew someone was having trouble reading, how would you help that person?
7. What would your teacher do to help that person?
8. How did you learn to read?
9. What would you like to do better as a reader?
10. Do you think you are a good reader? Why?

Source: From *Reading Miscue Inventory: Alternative Procedures* by Y. Goodman, D. Watson, & C. Burke, 1987; New York: Richard C. Owen, Publisher, Inc.

If-Then Thinking: Connecting Assessment Findings to Teaching Strategies

In Figure 6.5 we summarize the tools we have just discussed for assessing factors associated with children's concepts about print. In this *Summary Matrix of Assessments* we provide information about federally related assessment purposes, i.e., *screening diagnosis, progress-monitoring*, or *outcomes* assessment as well as the type of test or procedure (norm referenced test [NRT] or criterion referenced test [CRT]) and psychometric evidence of test or procedure scores including reliability and/or validity evidence, if available. Before discussing intervention strategies, consider the If-then matrix connecting assessment to intervention and/or strategy choices (see Figure 6.5). It is our intention to help you, the teacher, select the most appropriate instructional inventions and strategies to meet students' needs based on assessment data. In the next part of this chapter, we offer strategies for intervention based on the foregoing assessments.

Instructional Interventions and Strategies: Helping Every Student Learn Concepts About Print

After a careful assessment of a student's reading progress, one or more of the following strategies may be appropriately applied. Perhaps the most important thing to remember is that children with poorly developed print concepts must be immersed in a multitude of print-related activities in a "print-rich" classroom environment (Venn & Jahn, 2004). Authentic reading and writing experiences coupled with the informed guidance of a caring teacher or other literate individuals (e.g., parents, peers, and volunteers) can do much to help students learn necessary print concepts.

Environmental Print Reading

Purpose

The purpose of reading environmental print is to give children an experience that allows them to read familiar print drawn from the world around them that they are likely to have seen. Such experiences not only bring the outside world of print closer to the classroom but also build children's confidence in their ultimate ability to learn to read (Reutzel et al., 2003).

Materials

You will need product labels and logos from a variety of items including cans, cups, wrappers, packaging, and so on. Blank books or template books modeled after other children's books can be prepared for children to use in creating their own *I Can Read* environmental print books.

Procedures

Using environmental print commonly found in students' daily lives, teachers and children can learn about important print concepts. One application of using environmental print involves creating *I Can Read* books. Topics for environmental print *I Can Read* books may include *My Favorite Foods, Signs I See, A Trip to the Supermarket, My Favorite Things, My Favorite Toys*, and so on. Children begin by choosing a topic. Next, they can select to use a blank book or a template book. Following their choice of a blank or template book, they select from the environmental print collection of product labels to construct their own

Figure 6.5 Summary Matrix of Assessments to Measure

Name of Assessment Tool	Screening Assessment Purpose	Diagnostic Assessment Purpose	Progress-Monitoring Assessment	Outcomes Assessment	Norm-Referenced Test	Criterion-Referenced Test	Reliability Evidence	Validity Evidence
Concepts about Print Test	+	+	–	+	–	+	+	+
Reading Environmental Print	+	–	–	+	–	+	–	–
Mow Motorcycle Task	+	–	–	+	–	+	–	–
Metalinguistic Interview	+	–	–	+	–	+	–	–
Burke Reading Interview	+	–	–	+	–	+	–	–

Key: + can be used for
     – not appropriate for

IF-THEN STRATEGY GUIDE FOR CONCEPTS ABOUT PRINT (CAP) DEVELOPMENT

"If" the student is ready to learn ↓ / "Then" try these teaching strategies →	Read Environmental Print	Interactive Read Alouds	LEA	Voice Point	Frame	Masking Highlighting	Context Transfer	Error Detect	Verbal Punctuation	Shared Reading	Manipulative Letters
Book Handling	–	+	–	–	–	–	–	–	–	+	–
Directionality	*	+	*	+	–	–	*	–	–	+	*
Print Carries Message	+	+	+	+	+	*	+	+	–	+	*
Voice-Print Matching	*	+	*	+	*	+	+	*	–	+	–
Punctuation	*	+	+	*	*	+	*	+	+	+	–
Concept of Word/Letter	+	+	+	*	+	+	*	+	–	+	*
Order—Letters/Words	+	+	*	*	+	+	*	+	–	+	+
Pragmatic Response to Environmental Print	*	–	–	*	*	*	+	*	–	–	*
Reader relies on a single strategy to unlock unknown words.	*	–	*	–	*	*	*	*	–	+	*
Academic or Instructional Language	–	–	*	*	*	+	*	*	–	+	*

Key: + Excellent Strategy
* Adaptable Strategy
– Unsuitable Strategy

I Can Read books. Using a template book, based on the well-known children's book *On Market Street* (Lobel & Lobel, 1981), students innovate on the contents of the original book by selecting what they would have purchased "on market street" using the product labels to create their own *I Can Read* book. Because students select logos they can already read, they can easily read environmental books while acquiring print concepts. Further, these books become a source of confidence building and enjoyment.

Teachers can create logo language displays in the classroom as well as placing labels on furniture and fixtures in the classroom. Using a pointer or flashlights, teachers and children can "read the room" together by reading the labels in the classroom environment or the logo on the logo language display. By using print familiar to children from their homes and out-of-school world experiences, they very quickly develop an "I can do this . . . I can read!" attitude.

INTERACTIVE READ ALOUDS

Purpose

Interactive read alouds using enlarged text help children develop valuable concepts about print underpinnings needed for later learning in such areas as phonemic awareness, phonics, and comprehension (Venn & Jahn, 2004). Children follow along with the teacher as he or she reads from enlarged text (i.e., big books, rhymes and songs written on large chart paper, etc.) and responds to carefully posed questions. This draws the students' attention to key print concepts.

Materials

Teachers must locate high-quality books and/or enlarged texts diverse in gender and multicultural points of view and from multiple genres, such as nonfiction, storybooks, poetry, songs, and popular rhymes. Following is a sampling of big books and/or books that can be enlarged that we and other teachers have found very useful for interactive read alouds:

Stories

Brown, M. W. (1991). *Good night, moon*. New York: Harper.

Carle, E. (1994). *The very hungry caterpillar*. New York: Scholastic.

Carlstrom, N. (1988). *Better not get wet, Jesse Bear*. New York: Simon & Schuster.

Cowley, J. (1992). *Mrs. Wishy-Washy*. New York: Philomel.

dePaola, T. (1983). *The legend of the bluebonnet*. New York: Putnam.

dePaola, T. (1988). *The legend of the Indian paintbrush*. New York: Putnam.

Guarino, D. (1997). *Is your mama a llama?* New York: Scholastic.

Numeroff, L. (2000). *If you give a mouse a cookie.* New York: HarperCollins.

Westcott, N. (1998). *The lady with the alligator purse.* Boston: Little Brown.

Poetry

Christelow, E. (1998). *Five little monkeys jumping on the bed.* Boston: Houghton Mifflin.

Collins, H. (2003). *Little Miss Muffet.* Toronto: Kids Can Press.

Martin, B. (1983). *Brown bear, brown bear, what do you see?* New York: Henry Holt.

Seuss, Dr. (1960). *Green eggs and ham.* New York: Random House.

Trapani, I. (1994). *Twinkle, twinkle, little star.* Watertown, MA: Charlesbridge.

Wood, A. (1992). *Silly Sally.* New York: Harcourt.

PROCEDURES

During interactive read alouds, children respond to the teacher and their classmates before, during, and after the reading. Careful decisions are made prior to teaching as to which print concepts will be highlighted in the before-, during-, and after-reading experiences that increase the enjoyment and engagement of the learners (Venn & Jahn, 2004).

Enlarged text, such as in big books, enables students to see the teacher modeling such book-handling skills as reading the title, deciding where to start reading, gaining information from pictures, knowing how to proceed through the book, turning pages, and understanding that the message is coming from the text.

Some of the concepts about print that can be taught in an interactive read aloud include:

- Locating the front of the book
- Finding information on the title page
- Learning that print contains the message
- Recognizing one-to-one correspondence of words
- Page turning
- Learning how to handle books properly
- Recognizing picture clues
- Reading from the left page before the right page
- Using a return sweep
- Understanding *first, next,* and *last*

THE LANGUAGE EXPERIENCE APPROACH

Purpose

The **Language Experience Approach** (LEA) uses children's firsthand and/or vicarious experiences to create personalized reading materials. Children learn print conventions and concepts by seeing how their speech looks in printed form. They learn mapping of speech onto print and the technical aspects of print (i.e., directionality, punctuation marks, etc.) from LEA reading materials. Teachers have found that children's dictated LEA stories can be recorded in at least two different forms: (a) The *Group Experience Chart* or (b) the *Individual Language Experience Story.* The latter is tremendously motivating because children have their own story produced in a book format.

THE GROUP EXPERIENCE CHART

Materials

You will need the following materials:

- Large chart paper displayed on an easel. The upper half of each page should be blank for a picture and the lower half of the pages should be one-inch lines for printing the students' dictated story.
- Illustration or drawing supplies for illustrating the stories
- Cut-out pictures or magazines for cutting out pictures to illustrate the stories

Procedures

The Group Experience Chart is a means for recording the experiences of a group of children. In all group LEA activities, it is essential that students have a shared experience about which they can talk and dictate lines, sentences, and stories. The typical steps associated with the creation of a Group Experience Chart are:

- The children participate in a shared experience, such as a field trip, an experiment, or listening to a guest speaker.
- Teachers and children discuss the shared experience.
- Children dictate the story while the teacher transcribes the dictation onto chart paper.
- Teachers and children share in reading the chart story.
- The chart is used to teach about print concepts, words, and other important language concepts.

The selection of an interesting and stimulating experience or topic for children can spell the success or failure of an LEA group activity. Topics and experiences must capture the interest of children in order to provide the motivation necessary for learning. Some examples of previously successful topics and themes follow:

- Our classroom pet had babies last night.
- Let's describe our field trip.
- Writing a new version of a favorite book
- What we want for Christmas
- Planning our Valentine's Day party
- What did Martin Luther King do?
- Scary dreams we've had
- Once I got into trouble for . . . .
- A classmate is ill. Let's make a get well card from the class.

Be sure to discuss the experience or topic carefully. This helps children to self-assess what they know about the topic and to make personal connections. Also, it motivates them to share their knowledge, experiences, and personal connections with others. Be careful not to dominate the discussion, however. Asking too many focused questions can turn what would otherwise be an open and exciting discussion into an interrogation. Questions should invite discussion instead of encouraging short and unelaborated responses. Be careful not to make the mistake of beginning dictation too early in the discussion, as this may lead to a dull, even robotic, recounting of the experience or topic.

After plenty of discussion, ask children to dictate the ideas they wish to contribute to the chart. With learners in the early grades who have special needs, you may want to record each child's dictation in different colored markers to help him or her identify his or her contribution to the chart. Later in the year, write the child's name by his or her dictation rather than using different marker colors. When the chart is complete, read the children's composition aloud in a natural rhythm, pointing to each word as you read. After the first reading, invite students to read along on the second reading. Next, ask volunteers to read aloud portions of the story. Other strategies for reading the composition include the following:

- Read aloud a selected dictation line from the chart and ask a child to come up to the chart and point to the line you just read aloud.
- Copy several lines of the chart onto sentence strips and have children pick a sentence strip and match it to the line in the chart.
- Copy the LEA story onto a duplicating master and make copies to go home with students for individual practice.
- Put copies of favorite words in the chart story onto word cards for word banks and matching activities.

THE INDIVIDUAL LANGUAGE EXPERIENCE STORY

Materials

You will need the following materials:

- Small booklets containing between 8–10 pages of $8^1/2" \times 11"$ paper. The upper half of each page should be blank for a picture, and the lower half of the pages should have $1/2$-inch lines for printing the students' dictated stories.
- Illustration or drawing supplies for illustrating the stories
- Cut-out pictures or magazines for cutting out pictures to illustrate the stories

Procedures

For most young students who are typically in an egocentric stage, no one is more important and exciting to talk or read about than themselves. The Individual Language Experience Story provides an excellent opportunity for learners to talk about their own experiences and to have these events recorded in print to learn about the concepts of print.

Ask the children to tell their stories into a tape recorder and listen to them. Listening and editing on tape can have a very positive transfer value for the writing process. This oral editing encourages children to retell or revise their stories until they are satisfied with the final product. We also suggest, where circumstances permit, that parent volunteers be invited to transcribe students' Individual Language Experience Stories from audiotapes to paper copy.

Next, turn these Individual Language Experience Stories into books. Recognize the value of students' Individual Language Experience Stories by placing a card pocket and library card in each child's book. These books are added to the classroom library for other children to read. A story reader's chair can be established to encourage children to read their Individual Language Experience Stories aloud to peers in their own classroom and in other classrooms in the school.

One variation of Individual Language Experience Stories that children particularly like is shape books. As shown in the photo, the cover and pages of the dictated Individual Language Experience Story are drawn and cut into the shape of the book topic. For example, if a child has just created a story about a recent family trip to Disneyland, the book could be cut into the shape of Mickey Mouse's head; a trip to Texas may be recorded in a book cut into the shape of the state of Texas.

VOICE POINTING

Purpose

Pointing to the print in an enlarged book, on a chart, or on a white board while reading aloud interactively with a group of children draws the eyes of the readers into contact with the print (Clay, 1993). Otherwise, children in the earliest stages of reading acquisition will have a tendency to study the illustrations and listen to the story language without paying a great deal of attention to the print. Voice pointing shows children (a) that the print rather than the picture carries the message of reading; (b) the beginning, ending, and directionality of the print; (c) how the spoken language of the reader is represented or mapped onto print on the page or display; and (d) the technical concepts of print such as word, letter, or punctuation.

Materials

You will need the following materials:

- A pointer ranging from something as simple as an unsharpened pencil to a ruler, from a telescoping pen pointer to a laser pointer
- An enlarged copy of a story, poem, song lyrics, or book

Procedures

Clay (1979) indicates that pointing to the print while reading, or *voice pointing,* is a critical strategy to develop during the early stages of learning to read. To help beginning readers make the connection that the print is guiding the speech of the reader, teachers point to the print as they interactively read aloud.

If the teacher wants to demonstrate the beginning point of print; the flow and directionality of print from top to bottom, left to right, and so on; and where the print ends on the page, then he or she can run the pointer smoothly under the print as he or she reads aloud. However, if the teacher wants to demonstrate how each word read aloud is represented by its corresponding "word" in print, then he or she can move the pointer in a broken, word-by-word method. To draw attention to letters, single words, or punctuation, the teacher should point using a circular motion around the print element to be given attention by the readers.

FRAMING PRINT

Purpose

Some young readers have not yet grasped the idea that a given word is the same *every* time it appears in print. For instance, the word *football* is always *football* whenever and wherever it appears in print, whether it is handwritten text or text appearing in a book. Understanding this basic concept is a major milestone in reading development. *Framing* is one strategy that can help students grasp this important print concept (Holdaway, 1979).

Materials

Several types of framing tools can be constructed using oak tag or poster board materials. A razor knife and a stapler are also needed. A simple frame constructed of white poster board is shown here:

A more complicated shutter frame allows teachers to not only frame words on the page but also expose words to students one letter at a time from left to right to encourage the use of verbal blending of letter sounds in temporal sequence. A shutter frame is shown here that is constructed of white poster board with a white poster board shutter.

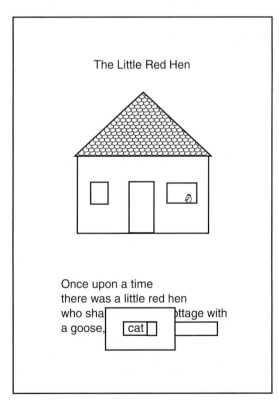

Procedures

Begin by reading aloud an enlarged text several times without interruption or discussion about print features. This can be text from an LEA Group Experience Chart or a big book such as *Brown Bear, Brown Bear* (Martin, 1983). Remember to voice point to the text as you read. Highlight aspects of written language by pointing and framing a word or words using the simple frame. For example, frame the text that asks "Brown Bear, Brown Bear, What do you see?" one word at a time. Frame each highlighted word (e.g., *brown, bear, what, do, you, see*) using the simple frame. After framing several words, ask children to look carefully at a word with only one letter exposed using the shutter frame. Ask children to notice the letters as you expose them. Once all letters are exposed, ask children to look carefully at the word. Talk with them about how words are made up of letters, demonstrating to them the difference between letters and words. Using the shutter frame, teachers can also frame punctuation marks for attention and discussion.

MASKING OR HIGHLIGHTING PRINT

Purpose

Some young readers do not yet know how to look at print or what to look for on the printed page. Helping young children know where to look and what to look for on the printed page is the major purpose for using masking and highlighting techniques. Understanding the basics of how to look at print and knowing what to look at is a critical milestone in the development of young readers before they can profit from instruction about letters, words, and punctuation.

Materials

You will need highlight tapes of differing colors *to highlight* selected print concepts in big books or enlarged print on chart paper. You will need stick-on notes of differing sizes to *mask* selected print concepts in big books or enlarged print on chart paper.

Procedures

Select the print concept to be taught, such as attention to concept of word, concept of letters, punctuation, or figuring out an unknown word. To direct students' visual attention to spaces between words, to letters within words, to specific words, or to punctuation marks, use semitransparent highlighting tape. For example, use light blue highlighting tape to direct students' visual attention to the use of periods in text. Or, use light pink high-lighting tape to direct students' attention to the letter *w* in the big book *Mrs. Wishy-Washy* (Cowley, 1990).

Use stick-on notes to mask from students' view selected concepts about print such as words, letters, and punctuation. Once masked from view, point to the masked print feature and discuss with students what they think would be behind the stick-on note. Once discussion has led to a reasonable prediction, unmask the print feature by removing the stick-on note. Using stick-on notes in this manner to mask print features directs students' attention very specifically to the covered print feature.

Use stick-on notes and enlarged text or big books to also create cloze passages. Masking specific words or masking every fifth word in a pattern creates a cloze passage. Students use the surrounding text and pictures to decide which word(s) would make sense in the place

Figure 6.6   Progressive Cloze Covering the Content, Action, or Descriptive Words

Then he ☐ out,
"Run, ☐
as fast as you ☐
You ☐ catch me.
I'm the gingerbread ☐."

The little ☐ ran after ☐.

Source: From "Fingerpoint Reading and Beyond: Learning About Point Strategies (LAPS)" by D. Ray Reutzel, 1995, *Reading Horizons, 35*(4), pp. 310–328. Copyright 1995 by Western Michigan University.

of the masked word. When students determine the masked word and the stick-on notes are removed, this focus of attention to the masked words brings "closure" to the cloze passage. Masking emphasizes the differences between words and sentences as well as basic concepts about print, while also demonstrating the importance of context clues in understanding the author's message.

Two variations of cloze that can be used to focus young readers' attention on either content or structure words in predictable books are progressive and regressive cloze. In *progressive cloze,* the text is read aloud. Next, several words are masked using stick-on notes, as shown in Figure 6.6, then the text is read aloud again. Each time a deleted word is encountered, children are asked to identify the missing word. When the deleted word is correctly identified, it is uncovered. For example, in the story *The Gingerbread Man* (Schmidt, 1985), the entire text of the book may be read and then several pages used for a progressive cloze procedure.

In *regressive cloze,* the process is also begun by reading the entire text aloud. Next, the text is reduced to only its structure words by covering all content words with stick-on notes. Children are then asked to identify the missing words. As each content word is identified, it is uncovered. By using these cloze variations, children begin to focus on identifying individual words within the context of familiar stories. Teachers can repeat these cloze variations in another context such as on charts, sentence strips, or a chalkboard, as shown in Figure 6.7.

Figure 6.7   Moving the Text to Sentence Strips for Progressive or Regressive Cloze Activities

| Then he____out, |
| "Run,____ |
| as____as you can. |
| ____can't____me. |
| I'm the gingerbread____." |
| The little____ran after him. |

Source: From "Fingerpoint Reading and Beyond: Learning About Point Strategies (LAPS)" by D. Ray Reutzel, 1995, *Reading Horizons, 35*(4), pp. 310–328. Copyright 1995 by Western Michigan University.

PRINT CONTEXT TRANSFER

Purpose

In the earliest stages of reading acquisition, students' recognition of print concepts, words, or letters are context bound—meaning that words read in one context may not be read in another. This means that print concepts, words, or letters encountered and recognized in one print setting are not necessarily transferred from one print setting to another. For children to pay close attention to features of print and transfer their recognition of print elements, text must be removed from the original context to a new context. The purpose of the print context transfer strategy is to help students come to recognize various print concepts, words, and letters in other print settings outside the big book or chart text where they were originally encountered.

Materials

Materials necessary to teach the print context transfer strategy include a pocket chart, sentence strips, and word cards to display sentences or words taken from an original chart text or a big book.

Procedures

Read an enlarged text selection projected onto a screen, in a big book, or on chart paper with the children. For example, sentences can be copied from the big book, *The Napping House* (Wood & Wood, 1984), onto sentence strips and displayed in a wall pocket chart as shown in Figure 6.8.

Demonstrate for students the exact match between the print in the big book or chart text and the print copied onto the sentence strips in the pocket chart. Next, ask children to match the text framed in the original book or chart text with sentence strips or word strips displayed in the wall pocket chart. By observing and participating in this process, young or struggling readers make visual connections between the print in the book and the same print displayed on sentence strips, word cards, or other print displays.

Figure 6.8 Substituting Words to Draw Attention to Print Detail

Original Text	Substitution Text
And on that cat	And on that chicken
there is a mouse,	there is a worm,
a slumbering mouse	a slimy worm,
on a snoozing cat	on a snoozing chicken
on a dozing dog	on a lazy lamb
on a dreaming child	on a dreaming child
on a snoring granny	on a snoring granny
on a cozy bed	on a cozy bed
in a napping house,	in a napping house,
where everyone is sleeping.	where everyone is sleeping.

Source: From "Fingerpoint Reading and Beyond: Learning About Point Strategies (LAPS)" by D. Ray Reutzel, 1995, *Reading Horizons,* 35(4), pp. 310–328. Copyright 1995 by Western Michigan University.

Variations on this print context transfer strategy involve children selecting a sentence strip and placing it directly beneath the matching print in the big book or chart text. After making the direct match, students explain to a peer or classmates how the two sets of print are the same. If children are invited to match words in charts or big books to word cards, it is best if structure or function words such as *the, and, a,* and *there* are not used. Only concrete nouns, action words, and descriptive words that are easy to see in the mind's eye should be highlighted for this type of exercise.

ERROR DETECTION

Purpose

The purpose of the error detection strategy is to cause children to look closely at text to match what is on the page with what is said. Children need to learn to inspect words visually to determine if they "look right" in relation to what is said when the text is read aloud. This type of close reading of the text helps students develop self-correction strategies, because they develop the habit of looking carefully at what they said during reading to make sure it "looks right" and matches the print.

Materials

Materials necessary to teach the error detection strategy include a pocket chart, sentence strips, and word cards to display sentences or words taken from an original chart text or a big book.

Procedures

In the error detection strategy, teachers substitute other words for the words in the original text. These word substitutions, along with the words found in the original text, can be interchanged in a pocket chart display during subsequent rereadings. Exchanging the substitution words with the words found in the original text helps children carefully focus on print details to determine which words have been switched in the text and how such word play can change the author's message.

For example, in the text of the book entitled *Mrs. Wishy-Washy* (Cowley, 1980), the word *mud* can be substituted with the word *dud* on a sentence strip using a white stick-on note or a word card if the words on the sentence strip are cut into individual words in the pocket chart.

> *"Oh, lovely* | *dud* | *," said the pig, and he rolled in it.*

The teacher reminds the children that this text should say, " 'Oh, lovely *mud*,' said the pig, and he rolled in it," but something is wrong here. The teacher then asks, "Can you find what has been changed?" Students are invited to explain what is wrong, how the error was detected, and how the error can be corrected. Once the concept is grasped from this example, other familiar text can be copied to sentence strips. Words on these sentence strips can be substituted using word cards or stick-on notes and presented for students to analyze.

VERBAL PUNCTUATION

Purpose

Drawing students' attention to punctuation is often difficult for both students and teachers. Nonetheless, taking note of punctuation is important for students to achieve reading fluency and comprehension. Students who ignore punctuation often read without proper phrasing, rate, or intonation, which in turn interrupts comprehension. Students who skip or miss punctuation marks often run sentences together, resulting in confused or broken comprehension. The purpose of the verbal punctuation strategy is to help students notice punctuation in a playful and engaging fashion. This strategy was first made famous by the talented comedian Mr. Victor Borge in a nationally acclaimed comedy routine.

Materials

To use verbal punctuation, the students and the teacher must share a common text for reading aloud. This common text can be a big book, chart text, projected overhead transparency, computer projected text, enlarged text on the classroom "black or white" board, or multiple copies of the same text for students at their seats.

Procedures

The verbal punctuation strategy is a process in which each punctuation mark in a piece of text is given a sound. For example, a period may be represented by making the &$*@#) raspberry sound. When a question mark comes up, a rising "uh" sound can be made. This process continues, giving a sound to each punctuation mark found in a text. Once all punctuation marks have been assigned a sound, the teacher may read aloud the first few sentences modeling for students how to make the sounds for each punctuation mark as a part of the rereading. Having modeled the process, students join in the rereading of the text making the sounds of each punctuation mark in the text. Children find this strategy highly engaging and will continue its use spontaneously on later occasions.

SHARED READING

Purpose

It has been known for many years that children can learn to read by having books read with them at bed time or on a loved one's lap (Durkin, 1966; Holdaway, 1979; Taylor, 1983). The practice of *shared reading* in the classroom is intended to help teachers replicate all of the important characteristics of bedtime or lap reading (Holdaway, 1979, 1981) with an entire classroom of children. For teachers and children to share a book together, the print needs to be enlarged so that every child can see it and process it together under the guidance of the teacher (Barrett, 1982). Shared reading, or what is sometimes called the *shared book experience,* is used by teachers with very young readers to model aspects of the reading process for an entire group of children rather than an individual child. In the case of print concepts, the shared reading experience is the perfect instructional context for teachers to guide children's eyes toward significant parts of print to clarify those print-related concepts and academic metalanguage or language used to talk about language.

Materials

To use the shared book or shared reading experience, teachers must enlarge the text so that a text can be seen by an entire group of children in a classroom. As children advance in their reading acquisition, multiple copies of the same text can be used for shared reading as well.

Procedures

Begin a shared book experience by introducing the book. The book introduction is intended to heighten children's desire to read the story and to help them draw on their own experiences and prior knowledge to more fully enjoy and interpret the story. Once a book is selected for shared reading, begin by asking children to look at the book cover while you, the teacher, read the title aloud. Talk about the front and back of the book and point out certain features of the book, such as author and illustrator names, publisher, copyright date, and title page. Next, instruct the students to *"Look at the pictures."* Then ask the children, *"What do you think the words will tell you?"* This request typically opens up a discussion leading to students making personal connections and predictions. Next, read the book with "full dramatic punch, perhaps overdoing a little some of the best parts" (Barrett, 1982, p. 16). During the first reading of the story, invite children to join in on any repeated or predictable phrases or words. At key points during the shared reading, you should pause to encourage children to predict what is coming next in the story.

   After the first reading, invite children to share their responses to the story. Ask them to talk about their favorite parts, connect the story to their experiences, as well as discuss how well they were able to predict and participate. The shared reading book is reread on subsequent days to study the language and print concepts contained in the book as a part of reading instruction.

LETTER MANIPULATIVES

Purpose

One purpose for using letter manipulatives is to help students grasp the concept of letter versus the concept of word or the concept that print rather than pictures carry the author's message. By using manipulative letters, students not only discover that words are made up of smaller discrete elements called *letters* but also learn about the left-to-right directionality of letters within words (Fountas & Pinnell, 1998). Of course, such letter manipulatives can also be used to learn letter names and letter sounds and to learn to build and blend words later on. But for the purposes inherent in this chapter, using manipulative letters to match or copy words in a text allows students to discover the concept of *letter* as compared with the concept of *word* or the concept that print carries the message in a text.

Materials

To use this strategy, magnetic plastic letters are best for a variety of reasons. These letters are easy to pick up, move, and trace for even the youngest of children. To keep these letters together, many teachers have found that a metal cookie sheet is excellent for storage of magnetic letters. Words in pocket charts can also be cut into individual letters for manipulation as well and stored in small, personal letter-size envelopes.

Procedures

Two activities useful for helping students grasp the concept of letters include (a) matching letters to other letters in text or on word cards and (b) sorting multiple sets of manipulative letters into alphabet letter categories. In the first activity, students are given a stack of word cards drawn from the shared reading texts of the class. They are to take a word card and place it in front of them. Next, they match the letters on the word card with plastic magnetic letters from the cookie sheet collection of letters by placing these letters on top of the letters on the word card. In the second activity, students are given a mixed collection of uppercase and lowercase letters to sort into single letter categories underneath the alphabet letters displayed on an oak tag laminated alphabet on a tabletop. Students sort small *a* and capital *A* underneath the alphabet letters until all letters are sorted underneath their alphabet letter category.

ADDITIONAL STRATEGIES FOR ENGLISH-LANGUAGE LEARNERS

CONTEXTUAL DIAGRAMS

Purpose

Pictures and diagrams in which objects in the scene are labeled are of great help to students learning a second or new language. The purpose of labeled pictures and diagrams is to allow students to experience the new language usage in settings other than the school classroom. Associating words and pictures together not only adds to ESL or LEP students' oral language but also serves to help them learn new English words and concepts while learning about words, letters, and print concepts in the new language. Diagrams of the kitchen, bedroom, or bathroom at home can help students begin to learn and associate second-language terms with familiar or even somewhat unfamiliar objects in another setting. Other labeled pictures and diagrams of stores, libraries, mechanic shops, or hospitals can move students' potential for language learning well beyond the physical and social confines of the classroom.

Materials

Enlarged diagrams or photographs of culturally or socially accepted settings such as restaurants, hospitals, stores, homes, or churches are needed to create labeled pictures and diagrams. Objects and actions in each of these may need to be labeled in both the first and second languages. In Figure 6.9, a labeled diagram of a house is shown.

Figure 6.9 Labeled Picture for Language Learning

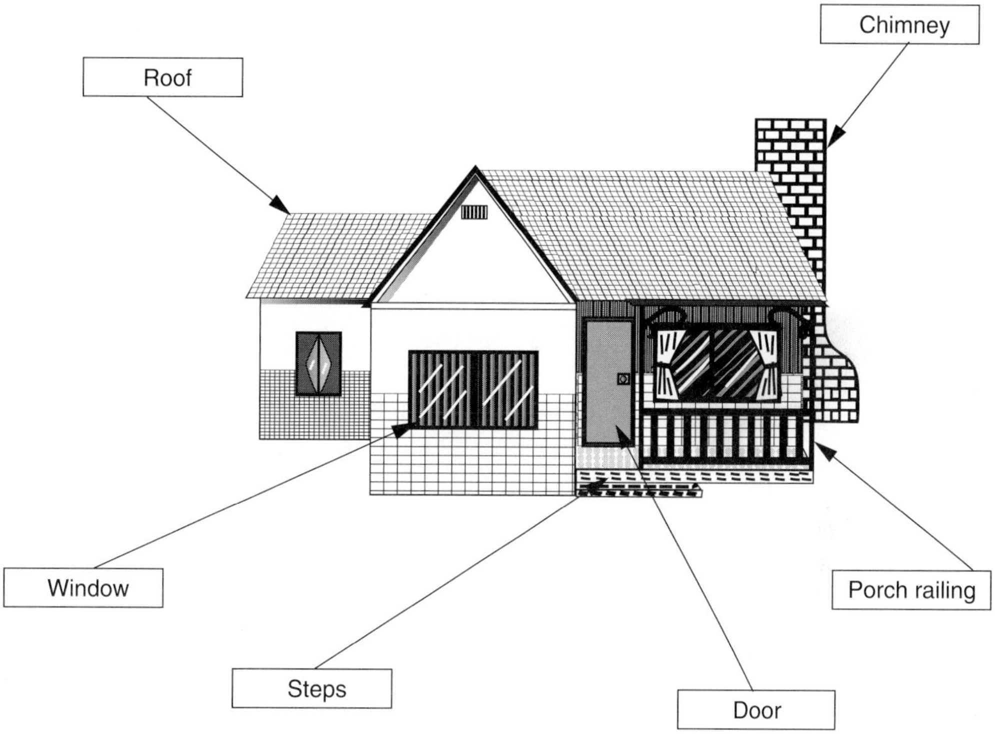

Procedures

Typically, a large piece of butcher paper or poster board can be used to make labeled pictures or diagrams. Teachers with some artistic talent can freehand draw these, although many teachers simply choose to use an enlarged photocopy of a picture or diagram. Label the objects portrayed as shown in Figure 6.9. Enlarged labeled pictures and diagrams can be displayed in the classroom on the walls. Labeled pictures and diagrams that are not poster size can be stored in folders or binders as references for ESL and LEP students.

INCLUDING ALL STUDENTS

DRASTIC STRATEGY

Purpose

In 1980, Patricia Cunningham developed the "drastic strategy" to help students learn to focus carefully on printed words and letters. Although this strategy was intended to be used for teaching and learning function, glue words, or structure words, the strategy can be adapted for a close reading of print to develop struggling readers' attention to the print on the page.

Materials

Word cards, envelopes, markers, scissors, and a classroom chalkboard or dry-erase board are needed to use the "drastic strategy" with struggling readers to develop awareness of the concepts of print.

Procedures

The "drastic strategy" uses a six-step process in which not all steps are necessary. There-fore, teachers should carefully observe the progress of children to determine at which step the strategy has produced the desired behaviors and understandings in the children. The six steps follow.

Step 1:   *Teacher Storytelling.* Select a word, letter, or punctuation mark and enlarge it on a card for each child in the class or group. Tell a story in which the dis-played word, letter, or punctuation mark is used. Before you begin your story, tell the children that you and they are to hold up their cards each time they hear the word, letter, or punctuation mark used in your story. As you tell the story, be sure to pause briefly at the points where the word, letter, or punctu-ation marks are used to "emphasize" the concept of print element to which children should attend.

Step 2:   *Child Storytelling.* Invite children to volunteer to tell a story in which the el-ement displayed on the card is used. Again, the same instructions apply for you and the other children relative to holding up the card each time the print element is used in the child's story. The teacher will need to be an active lis-tener and model for the children during this step.

Step 3:   *Scramble, Sort, and Find.* If the card contains a word, the teacher cuts the word into letters and scrambles these letters on the student's table or desktop. The stu-dent's task is to unscramble the letters to create the word three times. If the card contains a letter, the teacher passes out to the children an alphabet display of ran-dom letters, both uppercase and lowercase. The task for the children is to circle with a pencil each occurrence of the letter on the card in the random alphabet letter display. If the card contains a punctuation mark, the teacher hands out a piece of running text from a big book or chart text the children have been read-ing in shared reading. Students are instructed to find and circle all the instances of the punctuation mark on their card in the text distributed.

Step 4:   *Take a Picture and Write It.* Write the word, letter, or punctuation mark on the board. Ask children to pretend their eyes are the lens and shutter of a cam-era. They are to carefully look at the word, letter, or punctuation mark on the board and close their eyes to take a picture of it in their minds. After this, they should open their eyes to see if they had correctly imaged the item in their minds. This can be repeated three times if necessary. Then, the word, letter, or punctuation mark is erased and the children are to write the word, letter, or punctuation mark on a card at their seats. After all children have written on their cards, the teacher puts the word, letter, or punctuation mark back on the board for checking.

Step 5:   *Fill in the Blank.* Using a pocket chart, place several sentence strips on dis-play containing a blank in the place of the word, letter, or punctuation mark under study. Select sentences from previously read text in a big book or other enlarged text from shared reading. As you read the sentence strips and come to the missing element, be it a word, letter, or punctuation mark, invite a child to come forward and write the missing element on a card or strip and place it in the sentence strip at the correct location.

Step 6:   *New Text Close Reading.* Using a new piece of enlarged text during shared reading, tell children to be on the look out for the word, letter, or punctuation mark under study. When they detect the print element they have studied in the new text, they are to make a signal or sound that the group predetermines before engaging in the shared reading.

SELECTED REFERENCES

Barrett, F. L. (1982). *A teacher's guide to shared reading*. Richmond Hill, Ontario, Canada: Scholastic-TAB Publications.

Briggs, L. D., & Richardson, W. D. (1994). Children's knowledge of environmental print. *Reading Horizons, 33*(3), 225–235.

Burke, C. (1980). The reading interview: 1977. In B. P. Farr & D. J. Strickler (Eds.), *Reading comprehension: Resource guide*. Bloomington, IN: School of Education, Indiana University.

Clay, M. (1966). *Emergent reading behavior*. Unpublished doctoral dissertation, University of Auckland, New Zealand.

Clay, M. (1972). *Sand* and *Stones*. Exeter, NH: Heinemann Educational Books.

Clay, M. (1979). *Reading: The patterning of complex behaviour*. Exeter, NH: Heinemann Educational Books.

Clay, M. (1993). *An observation survey of early literacy achievement*. Portsmouth, NH: Heinemann Educational Books.

Clay, M. (2000a). *Concepts about print: What have children learned about the way we print language*. Portsmouth, NH: Heinemann Educational Books.

Clay, M. (2000b). *New shoes* and *Follow me, moon*. Portsmouth, NH: Heinemann Educational Books.

Clay, M. M. (2000). *Concepts about print: What have children learned about the way we print language?* Portsmouth, NH: Heinemann Educational Books.

Cowley, J. (1990). *Mrs. Wishy-Washy*. San Diego, CA: The Wright Group.

Cunningham, P. (1980). Teaching were, with, what, and other "four-letter" words. *The Reading Teacher, 34*, 160–163.

Darling, S. (2005). Strategies for engaging parents in home support of reading acquisition. *The Reading Teacher, 58*(5), 476–479.

Day, K. C., & Day, H. D. (1979). Development of kindergarten children's understanding of concepts about print and oral language. In M. L. Damil & A. H. Moe (Eds.), *Twenty-eighth yearbook of the National Reading Conference* (pp. 19–22). Clemson, SC: National Reading Conference.

Deford, D. E., & Harste, J.C. (1982). Child language research and curriculum. *Language Arts, 59*(6), 590–601.

Denny, T. P., & Weintraub, S. (1966). First graders' responses to three questions about reading. *Elementary School Journal, 66*, 441–448.

Downing, J. (1970). The development of linguistic concepts in children's thinking. *Research in the Teaching of English, 4*, 5–19.

Downing, J. (1971–1972). Children developing concepts of spoken and written language. *Journal of Reading Behavior, 4*, 1–19.

Downing, J., & Oliver, P. (1973). The child's concept of a word. *Reading Research Quarterly, 9*, 568–582.

Durkin, D. (1966). *Children who read early: Two longitudinal studies*. New York: Teacher's College Press.

Durkin, D. (1989). *Teaching them to read* (5th ed.). New York: Allyn & Bacon.

Ehri, L. C., & Sweet, J. (1991). Fingerpoint-reading of memorized text: What enables beginners to process the print? *Reading Research Quarterly, 26*(4), 442–462.

Fisher, D., McDonald, N., & Strickland, J. (2001). Early literacy development: A sound practice. *General Music Today, 14*(3), 15–20.

Fountas, I. C., & Pinnell, G. S. (1998). *Word matters: Teaching phonics and spelling in the reading/ writing classroom*. Portsmouth, NH: Heinemann Educational Books.

Goodman, Y., Watson, D., & Burke, C. (1987). *Reading miscue inventory: Alternative procedures*. New York: Richard C. Owen.

Halliday, M. A. K. (1975). *Learning how to mean: Explorations in the development of language*. London: Edward Arnold.

Harste, J. C., Burke, C., & Woodward, V. A. (1981). *Children, their language and world: The pragmatics of written language use and learning* (NIE Final Report #NIE-G-80-0121). Bloomington, IN: Indiana University, Language Education Department.

Harste, J. C., & DeFord, D. (1982). Child language research and curriculum. *Language Arts, 59*(6), 590–600.

Hiebert, E. H., Pearson, P. D., Taylor, B., Richardson, V., & Paris, S. G. (1998). *Every child a reader*. Ann Arbor: MI: Center for the Improvement of Early Reading Achievement.

Holdaway, D. (1979). *The foundations of literacy*. Exeter, NH: Heinemann Educational Books.

Holdaway, D. (1981). Shared book experience: Teaching reading using favorite books. *Theory Into Practice, 21*, 293–300.

Johns, J. L. (1980). First graders' concepts about print. *Reading Research Quarterly, 15*, 529–549.

Johnston, P. H. (1992). *Constructive evaluation of literate activity*. New York: Longman.

Kuby, P., & Aldridge, J. (1994). Direct vs. indirect environmental print instruction and early reading ability in kindergarten children. *Reading Psychology 18*(2), 91–104.

Lobel, A., & Lobel, A. (1981). *On Market Street*. New York: Scholastic.

Lomax, R. G., & McGee, L. M. (1987). Young children's concepts about print and reading: Toward a model of word reading acquisition. *Reading Research Quarterly, 22*(2), 237–256.

Martin, B. (1983). *Brown bear, brown bear what do you see?* (Pictures by Eric Carle). New York: Henry Holt.

McGee, L. M., Lomax, R. G., & Head, M. H. (1988). Young children's written language knowledge: What environmental and functional print reading reveals. *Journal of Reading Behavior, 20*(2), 99–118.

McGee, L. M., & Richgels, D. J. (2003). *Designing early literacy programs: Strategies for at-risk preschool and kindergarten children*. New York: Guilford Press.

McQueen, L. (1985). *The little red hen*. New York: Scholastic Books.

Meltzer, N. S., & Himse, R. (1969). The boundaries of written words as seen by first graders. *Journal of Reading Behavior, 1*, 3–13.

Morris, D. (1993). The relationship between children's concept of word in text and phoneme awareness in learning to read: A longitudinal study. *Research in the Teaching of English, 27*(2), 133–154.

Morrow, L. M. (1993). *Literacy development in the early years: Helping children read and write* (2nd ed.). Englewood Cliffs, NJ: Prentice Hall.

Neuman, S. B. (1999). *The importance of classroom libraries: Research monograph*. New York: Scholastic.

Neuman, S. B., & Celano, D. (2001). Access to print in low-income and middle-income communities: An ecological study of four neighborhoods. *Reading Research Quarterly, 36*(1), 8–26.

Neuman, S. B., & Roskos, K. (1993). Access to print for children of poverty: Differential effects of adult mediation and literacy-enriched play settings on environmental and functional print tasks. *American Educational Research Journal, 30*(1), 95–122.

Orellana, M. F., & Hernandez, A. (1999). Talking the walk: Children reading urban environmental print. *The Reading Teacher, 52*(6), 612–619.

Proudfoot, G. (1992). Pssst! There is literacy at the laundromat. *English Quarterly, 24*(1), 10–11.

Reid, J. (1966). Learning to think about reading. *Educational Research, 9*, 56–62.

Reutzel, D. R. (1995). Fingerpoint reading and beyond: Learning about point strategies (LAPS). *Reading Horizons, 35*(4), 310–328.

Reutzel, D. R., Fawson, P., Young, J., & Morrison, T. (2003). Reading environmental print: What is the role of concepts about print in discriminating young readers' responses? *Reading Psychology, 24*(2), 123–162.

Reutzel, D. R., Oda, L. K., & Moore, B. H. (1989). Developing print awareness: The effect of three instructional approaches on kindergartners; print awareness, reading readiness, and word reading. *Journal of Reading Behavior, 21*(3), 197–217.

Roberts, B. (1992). The evolution of the young child's concept of "word" as a unit of spoken and written language. *Reading Research Quarterly, 27*(2), 124–138.

Rozin, P., Bressman, B., & Taft, M. (1974). Do children understand the basic relationship between speech and writing? The mow-motorcycle test? *Journal of Reading Behavior, 6*, 327–334.

Schmidt, K. (1985). *The gingerbread man*. New York: Scholastic Books.

Smith, F. (1977). The uses of language. *Language Arts, 54*(6), 638–644.

Snow, C. E., Burns, M. S., & Griffin, P. (1998). *Preventing reading failure in young children*. Washington, DC: National Academy Press.

Taylor, D. (1983). *Family literacy: Young children learning to read and write*. Portsmouth, NH: Heinemann Educational Books.

Taylor, N. E. (1986). Developing beginning literacy concepts: Content and context. In D. B. Yaden, Jr., & S. Templeton (Eds.), *Metalinguistic awareness and beginning literacy* (pp. 173–184). Portsmouth, NH: Heinemann Educational Books.

Venn, E. C., & Jahn, M. D. (2004). *Teaching and learning in preschool: Using individually appropriate practices in early childhood instruction*. Newark, DE: International Reading Association.

Vukelich, C. (1994). Effects of play interventions on young children's reading of environmental print. *Early Childhood Research Quarterly, 9*(2), 153–170.

West, L. S., & Egley, E. H. (1998). Children get more than a hamburger: Using labels and logos to enhance literacy. *Dimensions of Early Childhood, 26*(3–4), 43–46.

Wood, A., & Wood, D. (1984). *The napping house* (Illustrated by Don Wood). San Diego: Harcourt Brace Jovanovich.

Wren, S. (2002). Methods of assessing cognitive aspects of early reading development. Austin, TX: Southwest Educational Development Lab. Full text copy available online at http://www.sedl.org/reading/topics/assessment.html.

Yaden, D. B., Jr. (1982). A multivariate analysis of first graders' print awareness as related to reading achievement, intelligence, and gender. *Dissertation Abstracts International, 43*, 1912A. (University Microfilms No. 8225520)

Yaden, D. B., Jr., & S. Templeton (Eds.). (1986). *Reading research in metalinguistic awareness: A classification of finding according to focus and methodology* (pp. 41–62). Portsmouth, NH: Heinemann Educational Books.

Chapter 7

Phonemic Awareness and Alphabetic Principle

Mr. Sinclair began his kindergarten class every day with a game. Today's game was a version of the television game, *Concentration*. There was a large poster sign on the board at the front of the room that read, *Start It!* Two dozen picture cards were placed facing away from the children in a pocket chart hung beneath the sign. Excitedly, the children gathered on the carpeted square at the front of the room to start the day. Mr. Sinclair explained that today's game was called *Start It!* as he pointed to the sign above the pocket chart. He told the children that he would choose someone to start the game and each one would have a turn until all the cards were picked. Joshua was picked first. He was told that he could take two picture cards from the pocket chart. If the pictures on the cards began with the same sound, then he could keep the picture cards until the end of the game. Everyone was told to watch carefully and remember where each card was located. The game progressed until all 24 picture cards had been picked and matched by beginning sounds.

After the game, the children who had picture card pairs placed these on the wall underneath the alphabet letter representing the letter that started the words for their picture pair. Following this activity, Mr. Sinclair read the children a new book about the alphabet. Today he read the book *Animalia*. Following read-aloud time, the children sang different alphabet songs together with Mr. Sinclair. Today was a special day for Nigel. Why? Because Nigel had made an important discovery. At the end of the period, he raised his hand and anxiously waited to be called on. In front of all the other children, Nigel shared his new insight. "Mr. Sinclair," he blurted out, "I get it, I get it! The *alphabet* is just like the *ABCs*!"

BACKGROUND BRIEFING FOR TEACHERS

As young children learn to talk, they develop the ability to string together into words, basic speech sounds. When they speak words, their goals are, of course, to make themselves understood to others and to be understood. For students to use reading and writing skills, they must first develop *phonological awareness* (Adams, 2001; Goswami, 2000, 2001), the understanding that spoken language is composed of smaller units such as *phrases, words, syllables, onsets, rimes*, and *phonemes* (sounds). We know that children first become aware of individual words in spoken language. Following word awareness, children develop an awareness of the syllables within words. Next they become aware that syllables are made up of *onsets* (all the sounds in the syllable *before* the vowel) and *rimes* (the vowel and everything following it). Then children become aware of individual sounds, or *phonemes*, in spoken language. Finally, children develop the ability to manipulate individual sounds in language. From these findings, the teacher of reading realizes that children's awareness of spoken language progresses from the whole (ideas shared through speech) to the part (individual words, syllables, onsets, and rimes and then phonemes).

In recent years, a number of researchers and research reports have emphasized the importance of developing phonemic awareness among beginning readers (Adams, 1990, 2001; Adams, Foorman, Lundberg, & Beeler, 1998; Blevins, 1997, 1998; Ericson & Juliebo, 1998; Fox, 2000; Goswami, 2000, 2001; Goswami & Bryant, 1990; Bear, Templeton, Invernizzi, & Johnston, 2003; Lyons, 1998; Moustafa, 1997; National Institute of Child Health and Human Development, 2000; Snow, Burns, & Griffin, 1998; Strickland, 1998; Wilde, 1997; Gately, 2004). It is estimated that roughly 20% of young children lack phonemic awareness (Blevins, 1997). We also know that children from low socioeconomic status circumstances are affected in even more negative ways when phonemic awareness instruction is not addressed (Korat, 2005). Though this *phonemic awareness* factor is not a "magic bullet" for fixing all reading problems (Shanahan, 2003), it is an essential component (Shaywitz & Shaywitz, 2004). So, what is phonemic awareness?

Phonemic awareness is defined both *conceptually* and in terms of *performance*. Phonemic awareness, *conceptually*, is defined as an understanding that spoken language and words are made up of individual sounds. In terms of *performance*, phonemic awareness is defined as the ability to pick out and manipulate sounds in spoken words and language. So, when speaking of phonemic awareness, simple *awareness* is not enough! Children also must be able to perform specified tasks—they must be able to *manipulate* spoken sounds.

Learning that sounds in spoken language and words are represented by symbols or letters, or **graphemes,** is another milestone achievement among beginning readers (Adams, 2001). This milestone occurs after students first become aware of the concept of individual spoken words (Gately, 2004), then individual sounds in spoken words (phonemic awareness). Then they are ready to learn the symbols (letters) used to represent these sounds in spoken words. This latter learning milestone is known as the **alphabetic principle** (Adams, 1990; Anderson, Hiebert, Scott, & Wilkinson, 1985; Harris & Hodges, 1995) and opens the door to learning phonics (Juel, 1991; Adams, 2001). The alphabetic principle is best introduced by explicitly linking or "matching" phonemic awareness (i.e., segmented individual sounds) with alphabet letters (Oudeans, 2003), which is termed *letter-sound matching*.

Recent research by Tivnan and Hemphill (2005), when reviewing the effectiveness of four popular commercial programs for teaching phonemic awareness and phonics, essentially concluded that, in spite of delivering comparable strong outcomes in word reading in high-poverty, first-grade classrooms, the programs failed to achieve grade-level expectations for most children in vocabulary and reading comprehension. For us, this suggests at least two things: (a) that an informed teacher can be successful in teaching phonemic awareness, alphabetic principle, and early phonics without the aid of a commercial program; and (b) that these skills must be a *part* of a comprehensive program that develops comprehension and word meaning simultaneously. Thus said, which skills in phonemic awareness skills should be taught and in about what order?

The ability to perform phonemic awareness tasks develops from least difficult to more difficult tasks as listed here:

1. Development of word concept
2. Rhyming

3. Hearing sounds in words (oddity and same-different judgment tasks)

4. Counting syllables and sounds

5. Isolating beginning, ending, and middle sounds in words

6. Substituting and deleting sounds in words and syllables

7. Blending syllables, onset and rimes, and sounds into words

8. Segmenting words into syllables, onset and rimes, and sounds

9. Representing sounds in language and words with symbols in spelling and writing

In this chapter, we begin with ideas for assessing young children's phonemic awareness and the alphabetic principle. Next, we help you to connect your assessment findings (student needs) to appropriate teaching strategies. Finally, we provide you with details of a number of classroom- and research-proven teaching strategies that assist beginning readers in acquiring phonemic awareness and an understanding of the alphabetic system.

ASSESSING STUDENTS' UNDERSTANDING OF PHONEMIC AWARENESS AND THE ALPHABETIC PRINCIPLE

Developing phonemic awareness is very often accompanied by learning the *concepts about print*, which are covered in detail in chapter 6. Because of the way in which phonological and phonemic awareness develop, we present assessment tools in three categories in this chapter: (a) assessing phonemic awareness, (b) assessing letter knowledge, and (c) assessing knowledge of the alphabetic system.

In the phonemic awareness assessment category, we present assessment tools that follow the levels and types of assessments previously described: rhyming, "oddity tasks," same-different, counting, blending, and segmenting tasks. In the second category of assessment, letter knowledge, we present two assessment tools, letter recognition and a letter production task. In the final category, understanding the alphabetic principle, we present the alphabet awareness task and a dictation task.

ASSESSMENT CATEGORY 1: ASSESSING PHONEMIC AWARENESS

RECOGNIZING RHYMING WORDS: DO THESE RHYME?

Purpose

Students are asked to recognize whether or not pairs of words rhyme to assess levels of basic phonemic awareness. According to Adams (1990, 2001) and Adams et al. (1998), the ability to determine rhyme is the easiest of all phonemic awareness tasks.

Materials

You will need a list of 20 word pairs. At least 50% of the word pairs should rhyme.

Procedures

Model the concept of rhyming by giving several examples and non-examples. Explain that rhyming words end with the same sound(s). Then, using the word pairs shown in Figure 7.1, read aloud each pair of words asking the child if they rhyme. Note their responses to

Figure 7.1 Rhyming Word Pair Task List

plate	dog
fat	cat
book	hook
desk	shelf
fish	swish
shoe	ball
tree	grass
flower	power
key	lock
pen	tape
swing	thing
sat	rat
box	clock
bark	smart
berry	hairy
cow	milk
brick	thick
malt	halt
wall	call
toy	love

each pair. According to Yopp (1988), kindergarten children usually achieve a mean score of 75% correct or 15 out of the 20 target word pairs identified correctly. If students score poorly on this task, teachers should provide contextual reading and writing experiences to hear sounds in words with a particular emphasis upon rhyming texts.

ODDITY TASK: WHICH ONE DOES NOT BELONG?

Purpose

Bradley and Bryant (1983) designed the oddity task to measure children's development of onset and rime awareness versus phoneme awareness. Oddity tasks require that students spot the "odd word out" of a list of spoken words. Typically, children listen to (or say from pictures) a group of spoken words and then select the word that has a different sound from the others. Oddity tasks can focus on rhyming words and/or beginning, ending, and middle sounds in words.

Materials

A list of 10 word sets of three words each or a collection of 10 picture sets of three pictures each. The word set in Figure 7.2 demonstrates a beginning consonant oddity task. Children pick the "odd word out" from the list or picture collections with at least 70% accuracy.

Procedures

Seat the child across from you at a table. Place the list in your lap so that you can see the words. Using a puppet, demonstrate how the puppet listens and picks out the odd word. For example, say, "Kermit the Frog is going to listen to three words I will say or will look at three pictures I put on the table." Next, say the three words—*pan, pig,* and *kite.* Then let

Figure 7.2   Beginning Consonant Oddity Task List

soap	six	dog
car	man	mop
duck	dog	five
pig	pack	fan
fish	fan	leaf
nest	nut	wheel
cat	cake	nine
sun	tree	tie
clock	bee	bat
sock	feet	fish

the puppet figure—in this case, Kermit the Frog—select which of the three words is the odd word out. Demonstrate this again with the words *coat, bus,* and *ball* if necessary.

Have a puppet figure pronounce the words in Figure 7.2 very slowly and clearly. Ask the child to tell the puppet which word is the odd word out. Make a record of how well the child does directly on a copy of the word list. This word list task can be modified to include oddity tasks related to rhyming words and ending and middle sounds as well.

SYLLABLE AND SOUND COUNTING TASK

Purpose

The counting task is a variation of the tapping task developed by Liberman, and others (1977). The counting task is designed to measure children's development of syllable and phoneme awareness. Counting tasks require that students count the number of syllables or sounds in a word or shown in a picture. Typically, children listen to (or say from a picture) a word and then they count the number of syllables or sounds. Counting tasks can focus on beginning, ending, and middle syllables and sounds of words.

Materials

A list of 10 word pairs or a collection of 10 picture pairs is needed for the counting task. The picture set found in Figure 7.3 demonstrates a sound counting task. Children should be able to accurately count the number of sounds or syllables within the words or pictures with at least 50% accuracy.

Procedures

Seat the child next to you at a table. Place the pictures in Figure 7.3 on the tabletop so that you and the child can see the words. Demonstrate how to count the sounds in samples A and B. For example say, "I am looking at this picture [point]." Next, say the word aloud and count the sounds you hear with your fingers. Tell the child the number of sounds in Sample A is four—f-r-o-g. Demonstrate this again with the picture in Sample B if necessary.

Have the child look at picture number one in Figure 7.3 very carefully. Ask the child to say what the picture is and count the sounds with his or her fingers. Then ask the child to tell you the number of sounds in the word. Make a record of how well the child does on a word list. This counting can be modified to include pictures related to ending and middle syllables and sounds as well.

Figure 7.3   Picture Sound Counting Task

Initial Consonant Sounds Test

Purpose

The Initial Consonant Sounds Test (ICST) (Cooter, Flynt, & Cooter, in press) measures whether children have developed the awareness of beginning sounds in spoken words. This type of test requires that students identify the odd beginning sound out of a list of spoken words. (*Note:* The beginning consonant sound in a one-syllable word is also known as the *onset,* and the remainder of the word is known as the *rime.*)

Materials

Reproduce a copy of the Initial Consonant Sounds Test as shown in Figure 7.4 for each student to be assessed. The directions for administration follow in the "Procedures" section.

Procedure

1. Seat the child across from you at a table.
2. Say, "We are going to play a word game, and I will show you how it is played. I am going to say three words slowly. Then, I will figure out which word has a different sound at the beginning."
3. Next, say the words "*pan, pig, kite*" slowly, emphasizing the beginning sound of each word just a little more than other sounds in the word. Say, "I will say the words one more time to see if I can tell which word has a different sound at the beginning—*pan, pig, kite.*"
4. Say, "The words *pan* and *pig* sound the same at the beginning, but *kite* has a different beginning sound."

Figure 7.4 Initial Consonant Sounds Test

soap	six	dog
car	man	mop
duck	dog	five
pig	pack	fan
fish	fan	leaf
nest	nut	wheel
cat	cake	nine
sun	tree	tie
clock	bee	bat
sock	feet	fish

Mastery Criterion: The student should be able to identify 8 out of 10 odd words out correctly.

5. Say, "Let me do one more for you—*coat, bus, ball*. Did you notice that *coat* has a different sound at the beginning than *bus* and *ball*? Now you try it."

6. Ask the child now to decide which word is the odd word out. Say, "*Run, rope, call*. Which word had a different sound at the beginning?" If the child has difficulty, you may repeat the words. *Note:* You may say each row of words twice for the student.

SAME-DIFFERENT WORD PAIR TASK

Purpose

Treiman and Zukowski (1991) designed the same-different task to measure children's development of syllable, onset and rime, and phoneme awareness. Same-different tasks require that students say whether a pair of words or a pair of pictures share the same beginning, ending, or middle syllable or sounds. Typically, children listen to (or say from pictures) a pair of spoken words and then say if the word pair is the same or different. Same-different tasks can focus on rhyming words and beginning, ending, and middle syllables and sounds in words.

Materials

A list of 10 word pairs or a collection of 10 picture pairs is needed for the same-different task. The word set found in Figure 7.5 demonstrates a beginning syllable same-different task. Children should be able to respond if the word or picture pairs have the same syllable or sound with at least 50% accuracy.

Figure 7.5   Beginning Syllable Same-Different Task List

hammer	hammock
little	local
window	winner
single	sickle
maple	motor
donkey	dinky
camera	camshaft
twinkle	twinkie
belly	balloon
fabric	furnish

Procedures

Seat the child across from you at a table. Place the list in your lap so that you can see the words. Using a puppet, demonstrate how the puppet listens and says whether the word pair is the same or different. For example say, "Peter the Bunny is going to listen to two words I will say or will look at two pictures I put on the table." Next, say the word pair, *partly* and *partition*. Then let the puppet figure—in this case, Peter the Bunny—say whether the two words are the same or different. Demonstrate this again with the words *dandy* and *dislike,* if necessary.

Have a puppet figure pronounce the words in Figure 7.5 very slowly and clearly. Ask the child to tell the puppet if the word pairs are the same or different. Make a record of how well the child does directly on a copy of the word list. This word list task can be modified to include same-different tasks related to ending and middle syllables and sounds as well.

AUDITORY SOUND BLENDING TASK

Purpose

Students are asked to recognize words by blending the sounds in words that teachers stretch out into segmented units, for example, *m-an* or *sh-i-p* (we call this "word rubber banding"). According to Griffith and Olson (1992), the ability to guess what the word is from its blended form demonstrates a slightly higher level of phonemic awareness than recognizing rhyming sounds.

Materials

Prepare a list of 30 words divided into three sets of 10 each (as shown in Figure 7.6).

- The first 10 words should be two-phoneme words
- The second set of 10 words should be three- or four-phoneme words that are divided before the vowel, demonstrating the onset and rime, for example, *c* (onset) *ap* (rime).
- The third set of 10 words should be three- or four-phoneme words that are segmented completely, for example, *ch-i-p*.

Procedures

Tell the child that you will be stretching words out like a rubber band saying each sound. Model several of these stretched words for the child as well as telling them the word you have stretched. For example, stretch the word *s-i-t*. Then say the word *sit*. Do this several

Figure 7.6 Word Lists for Blending

at	l-ap	l-o-ck
two	t-ip	s-t-e-m
in	m-an	b-ea-k
if	st-ate	h-i-de
be	b-ox	c-a-sh
as	sc-ab	m-i-c-e
sea	r-ug	sh-ee-t
now	m-ind	f-r-o-g
go	th-ink	j-u-m-p
sew	p-ig	t-ur-key

times. Next, stretch a word and ask the child to tell you the word. Once this has been accomplished, tell the child you are going to play a game in which you say a word stretched out and they are to answer the question, What am I saying? According to Yopp's (1988) research, kindergarten children achieve a mean score of 66% correct or 20 out of the 30 target words identified correctly. If students score poorly on this task, teachers should provide reading and writing experiences that help children hear sounds in words. Creating invented spellings for writing new words, and using word rubber banding to sound out new words found in trade books, are just two examples.

SEGMENTING SOUNDS

Purpose

Students are asked to listen to and isolate sounds in the initial, medial, and final positions in a word. A child's ability to isolate sounds in words is an excellent indication of whether he or she can profit from decoding instruction.

Materials

Construct a list of 15 words consisting of three phonemes each. Target sounds in the beginning, middle, and end of the words like the ones shown in Figure 7.7.

Procedures

Model how phonemes can be pronounced by showing how *sit* starts with the /s/ sound, *hike* has the /i/ sound in the middle, and *look* ends with the /k/ sound. Next, tell the child you are going to play a quick game together. You will say a word, then you will ask him or

Figure 7.7 Word List for Segmenting Sounds

d ime	yar*d*
hu*sh*	k *i* ss
fi *v* e	g *e* t
clo*ck*	raf*t*
cu t	*b* ike
f ool	mu *g*
l *oo* p	
r ode	
h ome	

her to tell you the sound he or she hears in a specific place in the word, such as beginning, middle, or end. For example you may say: "*Slam.* Say the sound at the end of the word *slam.*" The child responds correctly by articulating the sound /m/. Now, begin the list of words shown in Figure 7.7. Record each response.

According to Yopp's (1988) research study, kindergarten children achieve a mean score of 9% correct or one to two correct responses out of 15 target words. If students score poorly on this task, teachers should provide reading and writing experiences focusing on hearing sounds in specific locations within words.

ASSESSMENT CATEGORY II: ASSESSING LETTER KNOWLEDGE

LETTER IDENTIFICATION

Purpose

Similar to the activity just described, this task, based on the work of Marie Clay (1993), determines whether readers with special learning needs can identify letters of the alphabet.

Materials

Reproduce the randomized alphabet letter display (shown in Figure 7.8) on a sheet of paper or chart paper for use in this exercise.

Procedures

Invite the student to be seated next to you and explain that you would like to find out which letters of the alphabet he or she can name as you point to them on a chart. Begin pointing at the top of the alphabet letter display working line by line and left to right to

Figure 7.8 Alphabet Letter Display

```
              E

            P  v

          r  D  f  o

        A  m  l  X  T

          i  Y  w  K

            u  C

              J
```

Figure 7.9   Random Letter Production Task

1. b	2. m	3. e	4. f	5. t
6. i	7. p	8. o	9. s	10. h

the bottom of the display keeping letters below your line of focus covered. Using a photocopy of the display, mark which of the letters were correctly named. Next, ask the child to point to the letter you name in the display. Record this information. Most children, even readers with special learning needs, will be able to identify at least 50% of the letters requested. However, students who have little familiarity with letters may perform poorly.

LETTER PRODUCTION TASK

Purpose

This task is designed to determine whether or not students know and can write letters of the alphabet. Unlike simple letter identification, this task requires that students be able to produce letters from memory. Letter knowledge is an indication of how well students have sorted out sound and symbol processes but is not logically necessary for successful reading. It does, however, make learning to read easier (Venezky, 1975). Letter naming and production can be likened to a bridge that helps children cross the river of early reading and writing.

Materials

Create a list of 10 letters drawn randomly from the alphabet. Be sure to include at least three vowel letters in the selection, as shown in Figure 7.9. Provide the child with a pencil and a blank piece of paper.

Procedures

Ask the student if he or she knows any letters. Next, ask the student to write down any letters he or she may know and name them. Following this exercise, invite the student to write the letters you name from the random letter list you created. Most students in first grade will score at least 70% on this task. However, students who have little familiarity with letters may perform poorly. This should be interpreted as a need to engage in strategies and activities outlined later in this chapter.

ASSESSMENT CATEGORY III: ASSESSING ALPHABETIC PRINCIPLE KNOWLEDGE

ALPHABET AWARENESS TASK

Purpose

The purpose of this task is to determine whether or not children can in some way identify the concept of an alphabet in written and spoken language. Walsh, Price, and Gillingham (1988) found that letter naming was strongly related to early reading achievement for

Figure 7.10 Alphabet Awareness Task

1. Have you ever heard of the alphabet or ABC's? Yes _____ No _____

2. Can you tell me what this is? Answer _____
   A B C D E F G H I J K L M N O P Q R S T U V W X Y Z

3. Can you tell me any alphabet letters you know?

4. Do you know any songs, poems, books, or rhymes about the alphabet?
   Yes _____ No _____
   Give me an example

5. Can you tell me the order of the alphabet letters beginning with the letter *A*?
   Yes _____ No _____

   Answer _____

kindergarten children. Simple awareness that an alphabet exists is necessary for understanding any alphabetic language system.

Materials

You will need one copy of the "Alphabet Awareness Task" form shown in Figure 7.10.

Procedures

Begin this task by seating the child next to you. Ask each question on the Alphabet Awareness Task form. On Question 3, if another alphabet display is available in the immediate area (such as those typically displayed over chalkboards), point to this display and ask the same question. Results of this task should give teachers a sense of alphabet awareness. Teachers should view these results as a means to inform and direct their selection of alphabet and phonemic awareness activities discussed later in this chapter.

DICTATION

Purpose

Students are asked to listen to several words stretched out or "rubber banded." Next, students are asked to rubber band the word(s) as the teacher dictates them and write the sounds heard in each word. Calkins (1986) relates how word rubber banding is used in her Teacher's College Writing Project to help children learn how to listen for sounds. Carnine, Silbert, and Kameenui (1990) refer to a similar approach for stretching words called *auditory telescoping*. Yopp (1992) indicates that the ability to speak the phonemes within a word is a very difficult level of phonemic awareness to achieve. The ability to both speak and write phonemes in words indicates an advanced level of phonemic awareness that can be used effectively in reading and writing instruction.

Materials

Compile a list of 22 words of two or three phonemes each in length. Be sure to include a variety of words with varying consonant and vowel patterns (i.e., some that begin with consonants, others that begin with vowel sounds). An example list is shown in Figure 7.11.

Figure 7.11   Dictation Word List

page	me	my	now
live	can	this	but
big	get	have	come
sat	on	some	tile
men	at	back	
no	did	say	

Procedures

Demonstrate how several words can be stretched or rubber banded into sounds—both orally and in writing. Invite the child to rubber band and write the words in your list as you did. This task assesses whether or not children have developed an ability to hear and "map" sounds through writing and using invented spellings. Yopp (1988) found that the response rate for kindergartners to this task was 12 out of 22 or about 55% correct. Griffith and Olson (1992) indicate that the word rubber-banding task has been shown to be a highly reliable, authentic measure of phonemic awareness and a good indication as to whether a child is ready for decoding instruction.

In Figure 7.12 we summarize the procedures and instruments we have just discussed for assessing factors associated with phonemic awareness and alphabetic principle. In this *Summary Matrix of Assessments* we provide information about federally related assessment purposes, i.e., *screening, diagnosis, progress-monitoring,* or *outcomes* assessment as well as the type of test or procedure (norm referenced test [NRT] or criterion referenced test [CRT] and psychometric evidence of test or procedure scores including reliability and/or validity evidence, if available.

CONNECTING ASSESSMENT FINDINGS TO TEACHING STRATEGIES

Before discussing phonemic awareness and alphabetic principle intervention strategies, we have constructed a matrix connecting assessment to intervention and/or strategy choices. It is our intention to help you, the teacher, select the most appropriate instructional interventions and strategies to meet your students' needs based on assessment data. In the next part of this chapter, we offer phonemic awareness and alphabetic principle strategies for intervention based on the foregoing assessments.

DEVELOPING PHONEMIC AWARENESS AND THE ALPHABETIC PRINCIPLE

Several effective strategies for helping readers with special learning needs in the areas of simple alphabet knowledge, the alphabetic principle, and phonemic awareness are described in this section of the chapter.

INTERVENTION CATEGORY I: STRATEGIES FOR TEACHING PHONEMIC AWARENESS

PLAYING WITH RHYMES AND ALLITERATION

Purpose

As teachers get to know their students' phonemic and alphabet needs, they often search for opportunities to teach these concepts in books, songs, or poems. When the teacher consciously searches for and locates books, songs, poems, or other print opportunities to

Figure 7.12   Summary Matrix of Assessments to Measure Phonemic Awareness and Alphabetic Principle

Name of Assessment Tool	Screening Assessment	Diagnostic Assessment	Progress-Monitoring Assessment	Outcomes Assessment	Norm-Referenced Test	Criterion-Referenced Test	Reliability Evidence	Validity Evidence
Recognizing Rhyming Word	+	+	+	+	−	+	−	+
Oddity Task	+	+	+	+	−	+	−	+
Syllable and Sound Counting Task	+	+	+	+	−	+	−	+
Initial Consonant Sound Test (from Comprehensive Reading Inventory [CRI]	+	+	+	+	−	+	+	+
Same-Different Word Pair Task	+	+	+	+	−	+	−	+
Auditory Sound Blending Task	+	+	+	+	−	+	−	+
Segmenting Sounds	+	+	+	+	−	+	−	+
Letter Identification	+	+	+	+	−	+	−	+
Letter Production Task	+	+	−	−	−	+	−	+
Alphabet Awareness Task	+	+	−	−	−	+	−	−
Dictation	+	+	−	−	−	+	−	−

Key: + can be used for
         − not applicable for

teach language concepts like rhyming and alliteration, this act is called *language watching* (Reutzel, 1992). Books, songs, and poems typically contain many examples of rhyming and alliterative words that may be used to teach the concepts of rhyming and alliteration.

Materials

Texts, stories, or poems may be used to highlight rhyming and alliterative sounds in words.

Procedures

Option 1.   Select a poem, for instance, "Sister for Sale" (Silverstein, 1976), for a shared reading experience. After reading, analyze this poem. It provides an excellent opportunity to demonstrate the alliterative beginning sound associated with the letter *s*—"Sister for Sale."

Option 2.   Select a poem or song, for example, the song "Do Your Ears Hang Low." After singing, analyze this song for pairs of rhyming words. Then, invite the children to think of other words that rhyme with pairs of rhyming

IF-THEN STRATEGY GUIDE FOR PHONEMIC AWARENESS AND ALPHABETIC PRINCIPLE

"If" the student is ready to learn ↓ / "Then" try these teaching strategies →	Playing With Rhymes and Alliteration	Grab the Odd One Out	Picture Box Sound Counting (Elkonin Boxes)	Children's Names	Add/ Take a Sound	Sing It Out	Word Rubber Banding	Environ-mental Print	Playing With the Alphabet	Alphabet Books	Song, Chant, and Poetry	The Sounds Rhythm Band
Rhyming Words	+	*	–	+	–	*	–	*	*		+	–
Oddity Task (Same/Different Sounds)	*	+	–	+	*	*	–	*	–		*	*
Syllables/Sound Counting	–	–	+	*	–	–	*	–	*		*	+
Initial Consonant Sounds												
Same/Different Word Pairs												
Auditory Blending	–	–	–	+	*	+	*	*	–		*	*
Segmenting Sounds	–	–	–	*	*	–	+	*	–		*	*
Letter Production	–	–	–	+	–	–	–	+	+		–	–
Alphabet Awareness	*	*	–	+	*	–	*	*	+		*	–
Dictation	*	*	–	–	*	–	*	*	–		–	*

Key: + Excellent Strategy
* Adaptable Strategy
– Unsuitable Strategy

words found in the song. Make a Rhyming Word Wall from the songs, poems, and stories read in the classroom during shared reading or singing experiences.

GRAB THE ODD ONE OUT

Purpose

The purpose of the Grab the Odd One Out game is to help children develop phonemic awareness through a playful "oddity task" activity. The ability to determine which spoken word does not fit among three choices relates to the oddity task described in the assessment section of this chapter. This game may focus children's attention on beginning, ending, or middle sounds in words. Once a list of beginning syllable words is created, then a list of ending sounds, and then medial sounds should be created for this game as well.

Materials

You will need the following materials for this task:

- One paper sack
- A list of 10 sets of three words (i.e., *hen, hammer,* and *pencil*)
- Objects for the "odd word out"

Procedures

This game is played by comfortably seating a group of children on the floor or at a table. Begin by saying that you have a "grab bag" filled with objects while showing children the bag. Next, tell the children you will be saying three words and that they are to listen carefully for the word that does not fit. If they know the word, they are to raise their hand but not call it out. A child is selected to reach into the "grab bag" without looking and feel around to find the object. When he or she finds it, the child can say the word and show the object to the group. This process continues until all the objects in the "grab bag" have been used. When an object has been used, it is to be returned to the "grab bag" for use with the next set of words.

PICTURE BOX SOUND COUNTING ("ELKONIN BOXES")

Purpose

Learning to hear sounds in words requires that students hear syllables and sounds (phonemes). Students need to develop the ability to hear syllables and sounds in words in proper sequence. Counting the number of syllables and sounds in words helps children attend more carefully to the sounds and syllables in words (Yopp & Troyer, 1992). A version of this activity (Elkonin, 1963) has been used successfully for a number of years in successful intervention programs such as Reading Recovery.

Materials

Prepare 5 to 10 cards with pictures using words already familiar to the student, as shown in Figure 7.13.

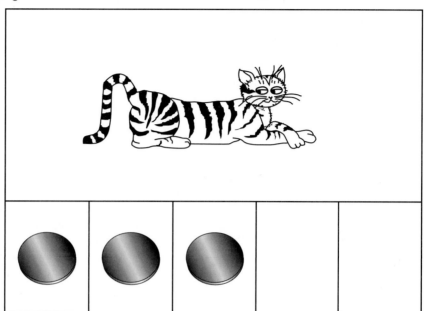

~~Figure 7.13~~   Elkonin Box for Sound Counting in Words

Procedure

This activity uses a word card with a picture, such as the one shown in Figure 7.13 for the word *cat*. The teacher begins by pronouncing the word very slowly while placing a chip into a box below for each letter or sound heard, progressing sound by sound (CCCCC—AAAAAAA—TTTTTT). After an initial demonstration, the child is encouraged to join in the activity by saying the next word for the picture on the card while the teacher places a chip into a box below each letter or sound.

The teacher gradually releases responsibility to the child by exchanging roles. For example, the teacher can pronounce the word and the child can place chips into the boxes below each letter or sound. Finally, the child both says the word and places a chip into a box below each letter or sound entirely on his or her own. Eventually, children should be able to count the number of sounds in a word and be able to answer questions about the order of sounds in words (Griffith & Olson, 1992).

BEGINNING WITH CHILDREN'S NAMES

Purpose

Children's names can be used to teach many phonemic awareness tasks (Kirk & Clark, 2005). By using children's (and classmates') own names, an inherently motivational activity, teachers can draw students' attention to specific sounds in words they wish to emphasize.

Materials

The only real tool needed for this activity is your student roster of first names.

Procedure

Decide which phonemic awareness segmenting or blending task you should emphasize with a particular small group, or with the whole class, based on your prior assessments. This activity is appropriate for any of the phonemic awareness tasks. Follow your usual procedures—teacher modeling using selected student names, extensive guided practice with teacher coaching, and, when students are ready, students working independently. Picture sound boxes as previously described can be a great tool in this activity. Once students understand the phonemic awareness concept demonstrated using student names, *bridge* this new knowledge to other common words (nouns work best) that students know such as locomotion words (e.g., *truck, car, airplane, jeep*).

ADD A SOUND/TAKE A SOUND

Purpose

Adding or substituting sounds in words in familiar songs, stories, or rhymes may help readers with special needs and younger readers attend to the sounds in their speech. The ability to add or substitute sounds in words in familiar language is easier than segmenting sounds and benefits students in many of the same ways.

Materials

Any song, rhyme, chant, or song will be useful.

Procedure

Two strategies add enjoyment to developing awareness of phonemes and the alphabetic principle. The first of these is *consonant substitution*. When using this strategy, initial, final, or medial consonants in words found in a phrase or sentence can be exchanged. For example, in the Shel Silverstein (1976) poem "Jimmie Jet and His TV Set," change the consonants from /j/ to /n/ or /b/ to produce:

"Nimmie Net and His TV Set"
"Bimmie Bet and His TV Set"

Another approach is to delete the sound /j/ as follows:

"Jimmie Jet and His TV Set"
"immie et and His TV Set"

Young children find the nonsensical result to be both humorous and helpful in understanding how consonants work in connected text. Other consonants may be exchanged in the future to vary the number of consonants exchanged and the position of the consonants in the words.

A second strategy is *vowel substitution*. When using a vowel substitution strategy, a single vowel (and sound) is selected and substituted in key words in the text. For example in the poem, "Mary Had a Little Lamb," the vowel sounds can be changed to produce a completely nonsensical version with *Miry hid a little limb* by substituting the /i/ short vowel sound in place of the vowels in the original poem.

Children find that adding, changing, or substituting sounds in this way turns learning about letters and sounds into a game. One first-grade, Chapter 1 student who had been working with his teacher late one afternoon using these strategies remarked on his way out the door to catch his bus, "Teacher, can we play some more games tomorrow?"

This statement sums up the enthusiasm these two strategies generate among young children as they learn to focus their attention on phonemic awareness.

SING IT OUT

Purpose

The purpose of *sounding it out* when one reads is to blend spoken sounds together to form words. Blending is a critical skill for learning to read successfully. Hearing individual sounds and then putting these together quickly to hear a word that is already known orally are the result of an instructional command often used by teachers when they say, "Sound it out!" Listening to spoken sounds and saying these sounds quickly to blend them together into words are what most teachers mean when they say to sound it out.

Materials

You will need one copy of the song "When You're Happy and You Know It."

Procedures

Teacher modeling is needed in the beginning to help children understand the process. Sing the song "When You're Happy and You Know It" several times so that children learn the song and the words. Change the words at the end of the song from "clap your hands" to "say this word." Then give the letters of a word you want the children to blend together. For example, the sounds b/rrr/d are spoken slowly for the children. When you clap, they are to say the word—*bird*! The song can go on for as long as you wish engaging children in auditory blending of the spoken sounds you offer to make words. By singing and saying words phoneme, by phoneme, students blend these sounds together to discover words.

WORD RUBBER BANDING

Purpose

Segmenting refers to isolating individual sounds in a spoken word. Segmenting can be one of the more difficult phonemic awareness tasks for students. It is, however, an important skill for children to develop if they are to profit from implicit or indirect instruction related to letter names, sounds, and the connections between the two. Segmenting sounds in words can be done by rubber banding or stretching a word into its sounds like a rubber band as described in the following "Procedures."

Materials

Any song, poem, rhyme, chant, or story may be used.

Procedures

Begin by singing a favorite song such as "Old MacDonald Had a Farm." Next, ask the children to repeat the first sounds of selected words as follows: "Old m-m-m-MacDonald had a f-f-f-farm, e i e i o, and on this f-f-f-farm he had a c-c-c-cow, e i e i o. With a m-m-m-moo here and a m-m-m-moo there, here a moo there a moo everywhere a moo moo. . . ." Children's names can be used in this fashion such as J-J-J-JASON, or K-K-K-KATE. Still another variation involves drawing a sound out or exaggerating the sound, for example, MMMMMaaaaarrrryyyy had a little lllllllaaaaammmmm. Beyond this iterative technique, children can be asked to segment entire words. Yopp (1992) recommends a song set to the tune of "Twinkle, Twinkle Little Star" for this purpose.

> Listen, Listen
> To my word
> Tell me all the sounds you heard: *race* [pronounce this word slowly]
> /r/ is one sound
> /a/ is two
> /s/ is last in *race*
> It's true.

When working with the segmentation of entire words, it is best to use words of no more than three to four sounds because of the difficulty of these tasks for younger learners or learners with special needs. Children seem to enjoy these tasks and with careful guidance can enjoy high levels of success as they develop phonemic awareness through segmentation tasks.

Intervention Category II: Strategy for Learning About Letters

Using Environmental Print

Purpose

The purpose of this strategy is to use familiar examples of writing from the students' environment (such as cereal boxes, signs, bumper stickers, and candy wrappers) to help them begin to understand how sounds and letters go together (the alphabetic principle). Hiebert and Ham (1981) have found in their research that children who were taught using environmental print learned significantly more letter names and sounds than did children who learned alphabet letters without using environmental print. Familiar print in the environment can be used in interesting ways to give children confidence in reading and writing and to help them understand how print works.

Materials

The only materials needed for this strategy are collectibles from home and school. Can labels, empty cereal boxes, bumper stickers, advertisements from the local papers, and other old boxes or containers are usually available in large quantities.

Procedures

Begin by setting aside a classroom display area, bulletin board, or wall that is designated as an *Environmental Print* wall. Children may be asked to bring environmental print or product logos from home to put on this display wall in random order. Next, environmental print can be taken down and rearranged in an alphabet display with 26 blocks or areas reserved for each alphabet letter, as shown in Figure 7.14. For example, specific print items such as *Butterfinger, Baby Ruth,* and *Batman* can be placed in a block for the letter *B*.

In some cases, children can be asked to bring environmental print to school for a specific letter name or sound. After discussing and displaying letter-specific environmental print, teachers and children can cut and paste environmental print items onto 5″ × 7″ plain index cards. These letter-specific environmental print collections are often bound together to be read in small groups or by individuals in an alphabet and letter play center.

Figure 7.14 Environmental Print Chart

Alphabet Wall		Aa	Bb Butterfinger	Cc Coca-Cola	Dd	Ee
Ff	Gg	Hh	Ii	Jj	Kk	Ll
Mm	Nn	Oo	Pp	Qq	Rr	Ss
Tt	Uu	Vv	Ww	Xx	Yy	Zz

Selected letters can be taught from known environmental print items such as *C* in the example shown in Figure 7.15. Environmental print logos can be collected and bound together to represent the selected letter, such as Snicker, Sprite, and Sugar. Other possibilities for using environmental print to produce letter knowledge include cutting up environmental print to compose or make new words or making letter collages for an art activity.

Figure 7.15 Environmental Print Ring

Intervention Category III: Teaching the Alphabetic System

Playing with the Alphabet

Purpose

Morrow (2001) has suggested that children can learn the alphabetic principle by enjoying playful activities centering on letter naming, letter sounds, and the connection between letter names and sounds. Providing relaxed and gamelike learning opportunities can often spark the desire to learn the letters and sounds.

Materials

Alphabet puzzles, magnetic letters, sandpaper letters, alphabet games, letter stencils, letter flash cards, alphabet charts, dry-erase boards, clay trays, paper, pencils, markers, painting easels, alphabet logos, cereals and foods, and commercially published alphabet books all may be used in constructing alphabet play games.

Procedures

An alphabet station or center stocked with alphabet puzzles, magnetic letters, sandpaper letters, alphabet games, stencils, flash cards, and alphabet charts can be a part of every kindergarten or first-grade classroom station or learning center. Children are invited to write, trace, or copy alphabet letters. Individual-size chalkboards, dry-erase boards, clay trays, tracing paper, and painting easels naturally draw children into copying, tracing, and experimenting with letters.

Delicious possibilities can be periodically added to this rich alphabet activity menu. Samples of alphabet soup, animal crackers, and Alphabits® cereal may be provided. Children may be encouraged to sort the letters or animals into alphabet letter categories prior to eating. Children can be encouraged to eat in pairs or small groups and talk about which letter they are eating. This playful interaction increases children's awareness of letters, sounds, and alphabetical order. Other playful experiences may be used as well. To emphasize specific letter sounds found in the course of language watching, activities involving a sip of Sprite, a bite of a Snickers candy bar, a long spaghetti noodle to munch on, and a handful of Skittles to taste may be used successfully to emphasize /s/. Art experiences can be designed in which children create pictures using an *S* as the beginning point. Collages of things that begin with /s/, such as a sack, screw, safety pin, salt, silver, or sand can be created and displayed.

Environmental print logos can be used to make *I Can Read Alphabet* pattern books. These books are often patterned after well-known alphabet books such as *The Z Was Zapped* (Van Allsburg, 1987) and *On Market Street* (Lobel, 1981). Children select a product label to represent the /c/ sound from a group of alphabetized logos such as Coca-Cola®, Coco Puffs®, Captain Crunch®, and so on. Other alphabetized product labels are selected to represent the remaining letters of the alphabet in child-produced *I Can Read Alphabet* pattern books. Because children select product logos they can already read, every child easily reads these pattern books. They become a source of confidence building and enjoyment.

Reading Published Alphabet Books

Purpose

The purpose of using alphabet books is to assist young readers and readers with special needs to discover the order and elements of the alphabet, both names and sounds. To do this, teachers may wish to acquire collections of quality alphabet trade books. *On Market*

Street (Lobel, 1981), *Animalia* (Base, 1986), and *The Z Was Zapped* (Van Allsburg, 1987) are just a few of the many delightful books that can be used to teach children the alphabet.

Materials

You will need commercially published alphabet books.

Procedures

After multiple readings of commercially produced alphabet books, teachers and children can construct their own highly predictable *alphabet books* using the commercial books as patterns. In an established writing center, young students can create both *reproductions* and *innovations* of commercial alphabet books shared in class. A *reproduction* is a student-made copy of an original commercially produced alphabet book. Children copy the text of each page exactly and draw their own illustrations for a reproduction. *Innovations* borrow the basic pattern of commercially produced alphabet books but change the selected words. For instance, one group of first-grade students made innovations on the book *The Z Was Zapped* (Van Allsburg, 1987). Each child chose a letter and made a new illustration as an innovation. One child, Kevin, picked the letter *D* and drew a picture of the letter *D* in the shape of a doughnut being dunked into a cup of hot chocolate. The caption underneath the picture read, THE "D" WAS DUNKED. Reproductions and innovations of alphabet books help students take ownership of familiar text and encourage them to learn about the alphabetic principle through experimentation. Reproductions and innovations of alphabet books also help children sense that they can learn to read successfully.

ADDITIONAL STRATEGIES FOR ENGLISH-LANGUAGE LEARNERS

SONG, CHANT, AND POETRY

Purpose

The purpose of using songs, chants, and poetry is to explore and discover how letter sounds combine to create words, word parts, and, when combined, written and oral language. Weaver (1988, 1990) suggested that many teachers use songs, poetry, raps, and chants to convey the alphabetic principle as an alternative to the more tedious direct teaching and drill of phonic generalizations and letter sounds.

Materials

You will need suggested songs, chants, and poems organized by alphabet letter themes.

Procedures

When using poetry, songs, and chants, teachers can watch for specific letters that are repeated in texts to be used as examples for learning the alphabetic principle and developing phonemic awareness. For example, to emphasize the letter *s* for a day or so, teachers may select and enlarge onto chart paper the text of the chants "Sally go round the sun" or "Squid Sauce" to be read aloud by the group. Songs such as "See Saw, Margery Daw" or "Sandy Land" may be selected and the lyrics enlarged onto charts for practice and group singing. Shel Silverstein's (1976) "Sister for Sale" or Jack Prelutsky's (1984) "Sneaky Sue" poems could be likewise enlarged and used to emphasize the name and sound of the letter *S* through repeated group readings.

THE SOUNDS RHYTHM BAND

Purpose

The tapping task developed by Liberman et al. (1974) is the basis for the Sounds Rhythm Band activity. Using this activity, children learn to hear sounds in words in sequence. This is a critical prerequisite for blending sounds together to make words in reading and for segmenting words into sounds for writing and spelling words.

Materials

Prepare a list of 5 to 10 words containing two, three, and four sounds.

Procedures

This activity uses different rhythm band instruments to "tap out" the number of sounds in spoken words. Rhythm band instruments include sticks, bells, tambourines, metal triangles, and so on that can be used to make a noise for each sound heard in a word. Begin by modeling a word very slowly while striking the rhythm band instrument for each letter or sound, progressing sound by sound—(C—AAAAAAA—T). After an initial demonstration, the children are encouraged to join in the activity by saying the next word with the teacher while striking their instruments for each sound they hear.

The teacher gradually releases responsibility to the children by exchanging roles. For example, the teacher can pronounce the word and the children strike the number of sounds they hear on their instruments. Or conversely, the children say the word slowly and the teacher strikes the number of sounds she hears on her instrument. Finally, the children both say the word slowly and strike their instruments for each sound they hear in the word. We suggest this activity begin as a choral activity with all the children participating together and progress to a point where individual children are asked to "solo" the saying of a word and striking the sounds he or she hears in a word. Eventually, children should be able to count the number of sounds in a word and be able to answer questions about the order of sounds in words (Griffith & Olson, 1992).

SELECTED REFERENCES

Adams, M. J. (1990). *Beginning to read: Thinking and learning about print.* Cambridge, MA: M.I.T. Press.

Adams, M. J. (2001). Alphabetic anxiety and explicit, systematic phonics instruction: A cognitive science perspective. In S. B. Neuman & D. K. Dickinson (Eds.), *Handbook of early literacy research.* New York: Guilford Press.

Adams, M. J., Foorman, B. R., Lundberg, I., & Beeler, T. (1998). *Phonemic awareness in young children: A classroom curriculum.* Baltimore, MD: Paul H. Brookes.

Anderson, R. C., Hiebert, E. F., Scott, J. A., & Wilkinson, I. A. G. (1985). *Becoming a nation of readers: The report of the Commission on Reading.* Washington, DC: The National Institute of Education.

Base, G. (1986). *Animalia.* New York: Harry N. Abrams.

Bear, D. R., Invernizzi, M., Templeton, S., & Johnston, F. (2000). *Words their way: Word study for phonics, vocabulary, and spelling instruction.* Upper Saddle River, NJ: Merrill/Prentice Hall.

Bear, D., Templeton, S., Invernizzi, M., & Johnston, F. (2003). *Words their way: Word study for phonics, vocabulary, and spelling instruction.* Upper Saddle River, NJ: Merrill/Prentice Hall.

Blevins, W. (1997). *Phonemic awareness activities for early reading success: Easy, playful activities that prepare children for phonics instruction.* New York: Scholastic Inc.

Blevins, W. (1998). *Phonics from A to Z: A practical guide.* New York: Scholastic Professional Books.

Bradley, L., & Bryant, P. E. (1983). Categorising sounds and learning to read: A causal connection. *Nature, 310*, 419–421.

Byrne, B., & Fielding-Barnsley, R. (1989). Phonemic awareness and letter knowledge in the child's acquisition of the alphabetic principle. *Journal of Educational Psychology, 81*, 313–321.

Byrne, B., & Fielding-Barnsley, R. (1993). Evaluation of a program to teach phonemic awareness to young children: A 1-year follow-up. *Journal of Educational Psychology, 85*(1), 104–111.

Calkins, L. (1986). *The art of teaching writing.* Portsmouth, NH: Heinemann Educational Books.

Carnine, D., Silbert, J. & Kameenui, E. (1990). *Direct instruction reading* (2nd ed.). Columbus, OH: Merrill.

Castle, J. M., Riach, J., & Nicholson, T. (1994). Getting off to a better start in reading and spelling: The effects of phonemic awareness instruction within a whole language program. *Journal of Educational Psychology, 86*(3), 350–359.

Chall, J. S. (1996). *Stages of reading development.* Fort Worth, TX: Harcourt Brace.

Clay, M. M. (1993). *An observation survey of early literacy achievement.* Portsmouth, NH: Heinemann Educational Books.

Cooter, R. B., Flynt, E. S., & Cooter, K. S. (in press). *The comprehensive reading inventory.* Upper Saddle River, NJ: Merrill/Prentice Hall.

Cunningham, A. E. (1990). Explicit versus implicit instruction in phonemic awareness. *Journal of Experimental Child Psychology, 50*, 429–444.

Degen, B. (1983). *Jamberry.* New York: Harper & Row.

Elkonin, D. B. (1963). The psychology of mastering the elements of reading. In B. Simon & J. Simon (Eds.), *Educational psychology in the U.S.S.R* (pp. 165–179). London: Routledge & Kegan Paul.

Ericson, L., & Juliebo, M. F. (1998). *The phonological awareness handbook for kindergarten and primary teachers.* Newark, DE: International Reading Association.

Fox, B. J. (2000). *Word identification strategies: Phonics from a new perspective* (2nd ed.). Upper Saddle River, NJ: Merrill/Prentice Hall.

Gately, S. E. (2004). Developing concept of word. *Teaching Exceptional Children, 36*(6), 16–22.

Goodman, K. S. (1986). *What's whole in whole language?* Ontario, Canada: Scholastic.

Goswami, U. (2000). Phonological and lexical processes. In M. L. Kamil, P. B. Mosenthal, P. D. Pearson, & R. Barr (Eds.), *Handbook of reading research, Vol. III.* Mahwah, NJ: Lawrence Erlbaum Associates.

Goswami, U. (2001). Early phonological development and the acquisition of literacy. In S. B. Neuman &

D. K. Dickinson (Eds.), *Handbook of early literacy research.* New York: Guilford Press.

Goswami, U., & Bryant, P. (1990) *Phonological skills and learning to read.* East Sussex, UK: Lawrence Earlbaum Associates.

Griffith, P. L., & Olson, M. W. (1992). Phonemic awareness helps beginning readers break the code. *The Reading Teacher, 45*, 516–523.

Harris, T. L., & Hodges, R. E. (1995). *The literacy dictionary: The vocabulary of reading and writing.* Newark, DE: International Reading Association.

Hiebert, E., & Ham, D. (1981). *Young children and environmental print.* Paper presented at the annual meeting of the National Reading Conference, Dallas, TX.

Holdaway, D. (1979). *The foundations of literacy.* New York: Ashton Scholastic.

Juel, C. (1991). Beginning reading. In R. Barr, M. Kamil, P. Mosenthal, & P. D. Pearson (Eds.), *Handbook of reading research: Volume 2.* New York: Longman.

Kirk, E. W., & Clark, P. (2005). Beginning with names to facilitate early literacy learning. *Childhood Education, 81*(3), 139–144.

Korat, O. (2005). Contextual and noncontextual knowledge in emergent literacy development: A comparison between children from low SES and middle SES communities. *Early Childhood Research Quarterly, 20*(2), 220–238.

Liberman, I., Shankweiler, D., Liberman, A., Fowler, C., & Fuscher, F. (1977). Phonetic Segmentation and decoding in the beginning reader. In A. S. Reber & D. L. Scarborough (Eds.), *Toward a psychology of reading* (pp. 207–225). Hillsdale, NJ: Erlbaum.

Liberman, I. Y., Shankweiter, D., Fischer, F. W., & Carter, B. (1974). Explicit syllable and phoneme segmentation in the young child. *Journal of Experimental Child Psychology, 18*, 201–212.

Lobel, A. (1981). *On Market Street* (Pictures by Anita Lobel; words by Arnold Lobel). New York: Scholastic.

Lomax, R. G., & McGee, L. M. (1987). Young children's concepts about print and reading: Toward a model of word reading acquisition. *Reading Research Quarterly, 22*(2), 237–256.

Lyon, G. R. (1998). Why reading is not a natural process. *Educational Leadership, 55*(6), 14–18.

Mason, J. M. (1980). When do children begin to read: An exploration of four-year-old children's letter and word reading competencies. *Reading Research Quarterly, 15*, 203–227.

Morrow, L. M. (1993). *Literacy development in the early years: Helping children read and write.* Boston, MA: Allyn & Bacon.

Morrow, L. M. (2001). *Literacy development in the early years. Helping children read and write* (4th ed.). Needham Heights, MA: Allyn & Bacon.

Moustafa, M. (1997). *Beyond traditional phonics: Research discoveries and reading instruction.* Portsmouth, NH: Heinemann Educational Books.

National Institute of Child Health and Human Development. (2000). *Report of the National Reading Panel: Teaching children to read.* Washington, DC: U.S. Government Printing Office.

Oudeans, M. K. (2003). Integration of letter-sound correspondences and phonemic awareness skills of blending and segmenting: A pilot study examining the effects of instructional sequence on word reading for kindergarten children with low phonological awareness. *Learning Disability Quarterly, 26*(4), 258–280.

Prelutsky, J. (1984). *The new kid on the block.* New York: Greenwillow Books.

Reutzel, D. R. (1992). Breaking the letter a week tradition: Conveying the alphabetic principle to young children. *Childhood Education, 69*(1), 20–24.

Richgels, D. J., Poremba, K. J., & McGee, L. M. (1996). Kindergarteners talk about print: Phonemic awareness in meaningful contexts. *The Reading Teacher, 49*(8), 632–642.

Shanahan, T. (2003). Research-based reading instruction: Myths about the National Reading Panel report. *The Reading Teacher, 56*(7), 646–655.

Shaywitz, S. E., & Shaywitz, B. A. (2004). The new science of reading and its implications for the classroom. *Education Canada, 44*(1), 20–23.

Silverstein, S. (1976). *A light in the attic.* New York: Harper & Row.

Snow, C. E., Burns, M. N., & Griffin, P. (1998). *Preventing reading difficulties in young children.* Washington, DC: National Academy Press.

Stahl, S. A., & Murray, B. A. (1994). Defining phonological awareness and its relationship to early reading. *Journal of Educational Psychology, 86*(2), 221–234.

Stevens, J. (1985). *The house that Jack built.* New York: Holiday House.

Strickland, D. S. (1998). *Teaching Phonics today: A primer for educators.* Newark, DE: International Reading Association.

Tivnan, T., & Hemphill, L. (2005). Comparing four literacy reform models in high-poverty schools: Patterns of first-grade achievement. *The Elementary School Journal, 105*(5), 419–441.

Treiman, R. & Zukowski, A. (1991). Levels of phonological awareness. In S. Brady & D. Shankweiler (Eds.), *Phonological processes in literacy* (pp. 67–83). Hillsdale, NJ: Lawrence Erlbaum Associates.

Van Allsburg, C. (1987). *The Z was zapped.* Boston: Houghton Mifflin.

Venezky, R. L. (1975). The curious role of letter names in reading instruction. *Visible Language, 9*, 7–23.

Walsh, D. J., Price, G. G., & Gillingham, M. G. (1988). The critical but transitory importance of letter naming. *Reading Research Quarterly, 23*, 108–122.

Weaver, C. (1988). *Reading process and practice: From socio-psycholinguistics to whole language.* Portsmouth, NH: Heinemann Educational Books.

Weaver, C. (1990). *Understanding whole language: From principles to practices.* Portsmouth, NH: Heinemann Educational Books.

Wilde, S. (1997). *What's schwa sound anyway? A holistic guide to phonetics, phonics, and spelling.* Portsmouth, NH: Heinemann Educational Books.

Yopp, H. K. (1988). The validity and reliability of phonemic awareness tests. *Reading Research Quarterly, 23*, 159–177.

Yopp, H. K. (1992). Developing phonemic awareness in young children. *The Reading Teacher, 45*, 696–703.

Yopp, H. K., & Troyer, S. (1992). *Training phonemic awareness in young children.* Unpublished manuscript.

Chapter 8

Phonics and Word Attack Skills

George is seated next to his teacher, Ms. Abrams, reading from that wonderful classic, *Elmer,* by David McKee (1968). The first sentence in the book reads, *There was once a herd of elephants.*

Ms. Abrams says, "George, I'm so happy you've chosen one of my favorite read-aloud books to read for *me* today. Let's start at the very beginning."

Excited and pleased, George begins, "Th-th-there w-was o-o-only . . ."

Wanting to help, Ms. Abrams offers, "That word is 'once,' George."

George repeats, "There was once a h-h-hard . . ."

Ms. Abrams: "*Herd.*"

George, with beads of perspiration now forming on his brow, reads, "Herd! There was once a *herd* of elephants."

Ms. Abrams responds, "*Great,* George! Let's continue," all the while thinking to herself, *Hmmmm. Not so great. I need to take a closer look at George's phonics knowledge. He's really struggling with what I thought would surely be an independent reading book for him. . . .*

BACKGROUND BRIEFING FOR TEACHERS

Phonics refers to teaching practices that emphasize how spellings are related to speech sounds in systematic ways (letter-sound relationships) and to the reader's use of this knowledge to decode unknown words (Rasinski & Padak, 1996; National Research Council, 1999). Phonics is an extremely important element of reading instruction. In the context of great literature and varied language experiences, children can learn to read with the aid of a strong phonics program and a caring and skillful teacher (Blevins, 1996).

Phonics instruction is an essential part of comprehensive reading programs in the early grades and is one component of a larger constellation of word analysis students learn known as *word attack*. Other word attack skills (besides phonics) include structural analysis, onset and rime, and use of sight words. Each is discussed in this chapter. A comprehensive approach to reading instruction emphasizes both meaning and word attack cues and provides numerous opportunities to practice these cuing systems.

In this chapter we summarize some of the more recent research on word attack skills, particularly phonics, and suggest activities we have found useful in assessing and developing this important area.

RESEARCH ON PHONICS

Surveys conducted by The International Reading Association (IRA) indicated that phonics is one of the most talked about subjects in the field of reading education (second only to the topic of balanced reading). In reviewing the literature, we have concluded that there are two essential areas for you to know about: *which* phonics skills and generalizations are important for students to learn, and *how* you might teach these skills in your classroom.

Because teachers should be *the* phonics expert in the classroom, you may want to begin your study of phonics with a little self-assessment. We have included a *Phonics Quick Test* in Figure 8.1 so that you can determine just how much you already know. (The results may surprise you!) Please complete the exercise before reading on.

Figure 8.1 Phonics Quick Test

1. The word *charkle* is divided between _____ and _____ . The *a* has an

   _____ - controlled sound, and the *e* is _____ .

2. In the word *small, sm-* is known as the *onset* and *-all* is known as the _____ .

3. *Ch* in the word *chair* is known as a _____ .

4. The letter *c* in the word *city* has a _____ sound; in the word *cow,* the letter *c* has

   a _____ sound.

5. The letters *bl* in the word *blue* are referred to as a consonant _____ .

6. The underlined vowels in the words *author*, *spread*, and *blue* are known as vowel

   _____ .

7. The words *tag, run, cot,* and *get* have which vowel pattern? _____

8. The words *glide, take,* and *use* have the _____ vowel pattern.

9. The single most powerful phonics skill we can teach to emergent readers for decoding

   unfamiliar words in print is _____ sounds in words. We introduce this skill using

   (*consonants* or *vowels*—choose one) _____ sounds first because they are the

   most _____ .

10. The word part *work* in the word *working* is known as a _____ .

11. The word part *-ing* in the word *working* is known as a _____ .

12. Cues to the meaning and pronunciation of unfamiliar words in print are often found in

    the print surrounding the unfamiliar, also known as the _____ .

THE NEED FOR EXPLICIT AND SYSTEMATIC PHONICS INSTRUCTION

Research confirms that systematic and explicit phonics instruction is more effective than nonsystematic instruction or programs that ignore phonics (Stahl, 1992; National Institute of Child Health and Human Development, 2000; Carnine, Silbert, Kameenui, Tarver, & Jongjohann, 2006). When delivered as part of a comprehensive reading program—one that includes expansive vocabulary instruction, comprehension development, reading fluency practice in great books, and writing development, all delivered by a skillful teacher, phonics instruction can help children become enthusiastic lifelong readers. Similarly, if offered in isolation, it can stifle children's reading growth and create a dislike for reading, especially for children living at the poverty level (Kozol, 2005).

Marilyn Jager Adams (1990), in her exhaustive review of phonics and other factors essential to word identification entitled *Beginning to Read: Thinking and Learning About Print,* found that approaches in which systematic code instruction was included with the reading of meaningful connected text resulted in superior reading achievement overall, for both low-readiness and better-prepared students (p. 125). Adams also noted that these conclusions seem to hold true regardless of the instructional approach through which reading is taught.

APPROACHES TO PHONICS INSTRUCTION

Several approaches to phonics instruction have found support in the research (National Institute of Child Health and Human Development, 2000; Armbruster & Osborn, 2001; Reutzel & Cooter, 2005). These approaches are sometimes modified or combined in reading programs.

Synthetic phonics instruction. Traditional phonics instruction in which students learn how to change letters or letter combinations into speech sounds, then blend them together to form known words (*sounding out*).

Embedded phonics instruction. Teaching students phonics by embedding phonics instruction in text reading, a more implicit approach that relies to some extent on incidental learning (National Institute of Child Health and Human Development, 2000, p. 8).

Analogy-based phonics. A variation of onset and rime instruction that has students use their knowledge of word families to identify new words that have that same word part. For example, students learn to pronounce *light* by using their prior knowledge of the *-ight* rime from three words they already know: *right, might,* and *night.*

Analytic phonics instruction. In this variation of the previous two approaches, students study previously learned whole words to discover letter-sound relationships. For example, *Stan, steam,* and *story* all include the *st* word element (*st* is known as a *consonant blend*).

Phonics through spelling. Students segment spoken words into phonemes and write letters that represent those sounds to create the word in print. For example, *rat* can be sounded out and written phonetically. This approach is often used as part of a *process writing* program.

The question in building a comprehensive reading program is not whether one should teach phonics strategies. Rather, we need to ask, *Which phonics skills should be taught and how should we teach them?* The next section partially answers the "which phonics skills" question.

PHONICS THEY WILL USE

We have compiled a little phonics *primer* for you that summarizes the main content of instruction, beginning with the most simple, individual sound-symbol relationships and proceeding to the more complex.

Letter Sounds

Though the English alphabet has only 26 letters, there are actually some 44 speech sounds. These 44 sounds can be represented in about 350 different ways; hence, English can become a formidable challenge for children when they try to "crack the code." Fortunately, there is a high degree of regularity in English that teachers can focus on to introduce phonics rules and relationships.

The place to begin is at the beginning: individual letter sounds. In Figure 8.2, we have compiled a list of the 44 speech sounds and the most common way they are represented by various alphabet letters. Note that in many cases we have listed the percentage of the time each sound is represented by a specific letter. For instance, speech sound /b/ (pronounced *buh* as in the beginning sound heard in *basket* and *bunk*) is represented by the letter *b* 97% of the time in written English.

Common Rules Governing Letter Sounds

There are several rules governing letter sounds that have a high degree of reliability and are certainly worth teaching. Here they are!

The C Rule. The letter *c* is an irregular consonant letter that has no phoneme of its own. Instead, it assumes two other phonemes found in different words: /k/ and /s/. In general, when the letter *c* is followed by *a, o,* or *u,* it will represent the sound /k/ we usually associate with the letter *k,* also known as the "hard *c* sound." Some examples are the words *cake, cosmic,* and *cute.* On the other hand, the letter *c* can sometimes represent the sound /s/ commonly associated with the letter *s.* This is referred to as the "soft *c* sound." The soft *c* sound is usually produced when *c* is followed by *e, i,* or *y.* Examples of the soft *c* sound are in the words *celebrate, circus,* and *cycle.*

The G Rule. *G* is the key symbol for the phoneme /g/ we hear in the word *get* (Hull, 1989). It is also irregular, having a soft *g* and a hard *g* sound. The rules remain the same as they are for the letter *c.* When *g* is followed by the letters *e, i,* or *y,* it represents a soft *g* or /j/ sound, as in the words *gently, giraffe,* and *gym.* If *g* is followed by the letters *a, o,* or *u,* then it usually represents the hard (or regular) sound, as in the words *garden, go,* and *sugar.*

The CVC Generalization. When a vowel comes between two consonants, it usually has a short vowel sound. Examples of words following the *CVC* pattern include *sat, ran, let, pen, win, fit, hot, mop, sun,* and *cut.*

Vowel Digraphs. When two vowels come together in a word, usually the first vowel is long and the second vowel is silent. This occurs especially often with the *oa, ee,* and *ay* combinations. Some examples are *toad, fleet,* and *day.* A common slogan used by teachers, which helps children remember this generalization, is "when two vowels go walking, the first one does the talking."

The VCE Final E Generalization. When two vowels appear in a word separated by a consonant *and* the final one is an *e* at the end of the word, the first vowel is generally long and the final *e* is silent. Examples include *cape, rope,* and *kite.*

The CV Generalization. When a consonant is followed by a vowel, the vowel usually produces a long sound. This is especially easy to see in two-letter words such as *be, go,* and *so.*

Figure 8.2   The 44 Sounds of English and Their Most Common Spellings*

Sound	Spellings	Examples
1. /b/	b (97%), bb	ball
2. /d/	d (98%), dd, ed	dot
3. /f/	f (78%), ff, ph, lf	fun
4. /g/	g (88%), gg, gh	goat
5. /h/	h (98%), wh	hall
6. /j/	g (66%), j (22%), dg	jug
7. /k/	c (73%), cc, k (13%), ck, lk, q	kite
8. /l/	l (91%), ll	leap
9. /m/	m (94%), mm	moat
10. /n/	n (97%), nn, kn, gn	no
11. /p/	p (96%), pp	pit
12. /r/	r (97%), rr, wr	rubber
13. /s/	s (73%), c (17%), ss	sat
14. /t/	t (97%), tt, ed	tap
15. /v/	v (99.5%), f	vast; of
16. /w/	w (92%)	wood
17. /y/	i (55%), y (44%)	onion; yell
18. /z/	z (23%), zz, s (64%)	zip
19. /ch/	ch (55%), t (31%)	chair
20. /sh/	ti (53%), sh (26%), ssi, si, sci	shorts
21. /zh/	si (49%), s, ss, z	Asia; azure
22. /th/	th (100%)	(voiceless sound) bath
23. /th/	th (100%)	(voiced) than, together
24. /hw/	wh (100%)	what, wheat
25. /ng/	ng (59%), n (41%)	rung, sing
26. /ā/	ā (45%), ā_e (35%), āi, āy, eā	A; bāke
27. /ē/	ē (70%), y, eā (10%), ēē (10%), iē	frēē
28. /ī/	ī_e (37%), ī (37%), y (14%)	fīvē
29. /ō/	ō (73%), ō_e (14%), ōw, ōā, ōē	gō

continued

*Adapted from Blevins (1998).

Figure 8.2   Continued

Sound	Spellings	Examples
30. /yōō/	u (69%), u_ē (22%), ēw, uē	cubē
31. /ă/	ă (96%)	căb
32. /ē/	ē (91%), ē_ē (15%)	bēst
33. /ĭ/	ĭ (66%), y (23%)	brĭck
34. /ŏ/	ŏ (79%)	hŏt
35. /u/	u (86%), ō, ōu	bug
36. /ə/ (schwā)	ā (24%), ē (13%), ī (22%), ō (27%), u	Amērĭcā
37. /â/	ā (29%), -ārē (23%), -āīr (21%)	dārē
38. /û/	-ēr (40%), -īr (13%), -ur (26%)	bīrd
39. /ä/	ā (89%)	bär
40. /ô/	ō, ā, āu, āw, ōugh, āugh	fōr
41. /ōī/	ōι (62%), ōy (32%)	bōīl, bōy
42. /ōu/	ōu (56%), ōw (29%)	trōut
43. /ōō/	ōō (38%), u (21%), ō, ōu, u_ē	bōōm
44. /oo/	oo (31%), u (54%), o (8%), ould, ou, o	cook

R-Controlled Vowels. Vowels that appear before the letter *r* are usually neither long nor short but tend to be overpowered or "swallowed up" by the /r/ sound. Examples include *person, player, neighborhood,* and *herself.*

Special Consonant Rules

Single Consonants. Single consonants nearly always make the same sound. We recommend that they be taught in the following order due to their frequency in our language: *T, N, R, M, D, S* (*sat*), *L, C* (*cat*), *P, S, F, V, G* (*got*), *H, W, K, J, Z, Y.*

Consonant Digraphs. This is defined as two consonants together in a word that produce only one speech sound (*th, sh, ng*).

Initial Consonant Blends or "Clusters." Two or more consonants coming together in which the speech sounds of all the consonants may be heard are called *consonant blends* (*bl, fr, sk, spl*). Consonant blends that come at the beginning of words are the most consistent in the sounds they make. It is recommended that they be taught in the following order due to their frequency in English:

Group 1	Group 2	Group 3	Group 4
st	pl	sc	sm
pr	sp	bl	gl
tr	cr	fl	sn
gr	cl	sk	tw
br	dr	sl	
	fr	sw	

Double Consonants. When two consonants come together in a word, they typically make the sound of a single consonant (e.g., *all, apple, arrow, attic*, etc.).

PH and the /f/ Sound. *Ph* is always pronounced as /f/ (e.g., *phone, phoneme, philosophy, phobia, phenomenon*, etc.).

Special Vowel Rules

Schwa /ə/ A vowel letter that produces the "uh" sound (*A* in *America*) is known as a *schwa*. The schwa is represented by the upside-down *e* symbol (/ə/).

Diphthongs. A *diphthong* consists of two vowels together in a word that produce a single, glided sound (*oi* in *oil*, *oy* in *boy*).

Y Rules. When the letter *y* comes at the end of a long word (or a word having at least one other vowel), it will have the sound of long *e* (/ē/) as in *baby*. When *y* comes at the end of a short word or in the middle of a word, it will make the sound of long *i* (/i/) as in *cry* and *cycle*.

RESEARCH ON OTHER WORD ATTACK SKILLS

Onset and Rime: "Word Families"

We need to keep in mind that knowing letter names is not all there is in learning to decode. Learning to analyze a printed word into component sounds followed by blending of those sounds requires knowledge of other reliable letter-sound associations (Pressley, 1998). Significant research in recent years confirms that certain word elements known as *onset* and *rime* are extremely reliable sound-symbol patterns and can be very helpful to new decoders. Simply put, a **rime** is the vowel at the beginning of a syllable and the **onset** is the consonant or consonants that come just before the vowel. For example, in the word *tack, t* is the onset and *-ack* is the rime; in the word *snow, sn* is the onset and *-ow* is the rime. In Figure 8.3, we have provided a comprehensive list of rimes for your use. The rimes in bold should be taught first and, when combined with various onsets (i.e., beginning consonants, consonant blends, or consonant digraphs), produce some 500 primary level words (Adams, 1990).

Syllabication

The ability to segment words into syllables is yet another form of "phonic awareness" that can be useful when encountering unknown words. The research has been very inconclusive indeed as to whether teaching syllabication actually helps students with identifying unknown words in print. Nevertheless, we include in Figures 8.4 and 8.5 the syllabication rules that seem to be the most reliable for (a) dividing words and (b) pronouncing words (Manzo & Manzo, 1993). (*Note:* We tend to favor teaching students to use common onset and rime knowledge whenever possible to segment words in print.)

Structural Analysis

Structural analysis refers to the study of words to identify their individual meaning elements (called *morphemes*). Words are made up of two classes or morphemes—free and bound. *Free morphemes* are word parts (words, really) that sometimes stand alone. They are also known as "root words." For example, in the word *working, work* is the root word (free morpheme). In contrast, *bound morphemes* must be attached to a root word to carry meaning. Prefixes and suffixes (together referred to as *affixes*) are bound morphemes. Common prefixes, which come *before* a root word, include *intro-, pro-, post-, sub-,* and

Figure 8.3 Rimes* (Word Families**)

-ab	-ang	-ear (short e)	**-ice**	**-ir**	-out
-ace	**-ank**	**-eat**	**-ick**	-it	-ow (snow)
-ack	**-ap**	-ed	-id	-ob	-ow (sow)
-ad	-ar	-ee	**-ide**	**-ock**	-ub
-ade	-are	-eed	-ies	-od	**-uck**
-ag	-ark	-eek	-ig	-og	-uff
-ail	**-ash**	-eep	**-ight**	**-oke**	**-ug**
-ain	**-at**	-eet	-ile	-old	-um
-ake	**-ate**	**-ell**	**-ill**	-one	**-ump**
-ale	-ave	-ell	-im	-ong	-ung
-all	**-aw**	-end	-ime	-oop	**-unk**
-am	**-ay**	-ent	**-in**	**-op**	-ush
-ame	-aze	-ess	**-ine**	-ope	-ust
-amp	-eak	**-est**	**-ing**	**-or**	-ut
-an	-eal	-et	**-ink**	**-ore**	-y
-ane	-eam	-ew	**-ip**	-ot	

*Adapted from Adams (1990), Fry, Kress, and Fountoukidis (1993), and Pressley (1998).
**_Note:_ Rimes in bold type have some of the most reliable sounds and, when adding an onset (consonant, consonant blends, or digraphs), create some 500 primary-level words.

Figure 8.4 Syllabication Rules for Dividing Words

1. When two identical consonants come together, they are divided to form two syllables. Examples: _ap / ple, but / ter, lit / tle._
2. The number of vowel sounds that occur in a word usually indicate how many syllables there will be in the word. Examples: _slave_ (one vowel sound/one syllable); _caboose_ (four vowels, but only two vowel sounds, hence, two syllables—_ca / boose_).
3. Two unlike consonants are also usually divided to form syllables, unless they form a consonant digraph. Example: _car / pet._
4. Small words within a compound word are syllables (as with onset/rimes). Examples: _book / store, fire / fly._

Source: From _Literary Disorders: Holistic Diagnosis and Remediation,_ 1st ed. by MANZO/MANZO, 1993. Reprinted with permission of Wadsworth, a division of Thomson Learning: www.thomsonrights.com.

Figure 8.5 Syllabication Rules for Pronouncing Words

> 1. *le* is pronounced as *ul* when it appears at the end of a word. Examples: *shuttle, little, remarkable.*
> 2. Syllables that end with a vowel usually have a long vowel sound. Examples: *bi / lingual, re / read.*
> 3. When a vowel does not come at the end of a syllable, and it is followed by two consonants, it will usually have a short sound. Examples: *let / ter, all, attic.*

Source: From *Literacy Disorders: Holistic Diagnosis and Remediation,* 1st ed. by MANZO/MANZO, 1993. Reprinted with permission of Wadsworth, a division of Thomson Learning: www.thomsonrights.com.

dis-. Some of the more common suffixes, which come *after* a root word, include *-ant, -ist, -ence, -ism, -s,* and *-ed.*

Sight Words

Many reading experts and researchers feel that the learning of high-frequency vocabulary or **sight words** is an important component of word attack for beginning readers. These are words that occur frequently in print and are usually best learned through memorization; words like *is, are, the, was, this,* and so on. We agree that sight words are an element of word attack, but because sight words are also "vocabulary," we have chosen to include this information in chapter 9, "Teaching and Assessing Vocabulary Development." So stay tuned for that information in our next chapter.

WHEN TO TEACH SPECIFIC PHONICS AND OTHER WORD ATTACK SKILLS: THE SCOPE OF INSTRUCTION

When should word attack skills be taught? Does research suggest a specific order? As with so many things in life, the answer is not entirely clear. For instance, there is no set rule about how quickly or how slowly to introduce sound-letter relations (Chard & Osborne, 1999), but there is adequate scientific research data for us to set down a comprehensive listing of important skills.

In Figure 8.6, we suggest a scope and sequence of word attack instruction based on some of the most credible research (e.g., Bear, Templeton, Invernizzi, & Johnston, 1996; Eldredge, 1995; Moustafa, 1997; Blevins, 1997; Pressley, 1998; National Research Council, 1999). Instead of trying to enumerate each minute skill, in most cases we simply recommend major categories in sequence and leave decisions about the fine points to you. This knowledge of *what* and *when* to teach can be extremely helpful in (a) assessing phonics knowledge in students and (b) planning instruction and grouping effectively to meet their needs.

WHAT DOES A GOOD PHONICS AND WORD ATTACK PROGRAM LOOK LIKE?

Three main accomplishments characterize good readers: they understand the alphabetic system of English to identify printed words; they have and use background knowledge and strategies to obtain meaning from print; and they read fluently (National Research

Figure 8.6　Recommended Scope and Sequence of Instruction

Kindergarten

- Sound structure of spoken words
- Recognition and production of letters
- Basic print concepts
- Familiarity with the basic purposes and mechanisms of reading and writing
- Phonemic awareness
- Alphabet recognition
- Sense of story
- Vocabulary development (oral, some high-frequency words)

First Grade

- Explicit instruction on phonemic awareness (if not previously developed in kindergarten)
- Letter-sound correspondences and common spelling conventions and uses in identifying printed words

1. Consonants in beginning, ending, and medial positions as part of a decoding strategy. Letters pronounced the same regardless of context: d, f, l, n, r, v, z
2. Short vowels: a, e, i, o, and u
3. Consonant-vowel-consonant (cvc) pattern. Use simple words that begin with consistent sounds to introduce simple blending such as *fan, lad, ran.*
4. Vowel-consonant-e (vce) pattern
5. Long vowel digraphs (ai, ay, ea, ee, oa, ow)
6. Consonant blends (tr, br, bl, cl, st, etc.)
7. Early structural analysis such as suffixes

- Sight recognition of frequent words
- Use of context clues
- Independent reading including reading aloud (A wide variety of well-written and engaging texts that are below the children's frustration level should be provided)

Second Grade and Above

- Sound out and identify visually unfamiliar words.
- Recognize words primarily through attention to letter-sound relationships.
- Context and pictures should be used only to monitor word recognition.
- Accuracy in word recognition and fluency should be assessed regularly.

Council, 1999, p. 6). Similarly, successful phonics instruction has a number of common qualities (Stahl, 1992). First of all, it builds on children's knowledge about how print functions. In the early stages, phonics and word attack instruction also builds on students' phonological awareness when the alphabet is introduced.

We also know that exemplary instruction is clear and direct (explicit). Phonics is integrated into a comprehensive reading program and focuses, ultimately, on reading words, not memorizing rules. Research confirms that effective programs include onset and rime instruction. It is also woven into writing instruction (for instance, using "temporary" or *phonemic* spellings). A prime objective of exemplary phonics instruction is to develop independent word-recognition strategies, focusing attention on the internal structure of words (structural analysis). All effective instruction is preceded by an assessment of student knowledge, our next topic.

ASSESSING PHONICS AND WORD ATTACK KNOWLEDGE

The goal of phonics and word attack assessment is to discover what students understand about sound-symbol relationships. Knowing what a student can and cannot do makes it clear what your course of action should be in the classroom. There are a number of basic strategies that one can use to discover which skills have been learned and which need attention. In general, assessment should proceed developmentally according to the sequence in which skills are learned: phonemic awareness, to alphabetic principle knowledge, to phonics and other word attack skills.

Assessment of phonics and word attack knowledge often begins with a running record. Using words in context, running records permit teachers to observe how well a student's phonics skills are developing while reading real text. In chapter 2, we discussed how to conduct running records, so we do not duplicate that information in this chapter; just know that we see running records as *the* way to assess phonics and decoding in context.

Another assessment procedure we recommend is The Starpoint Phonics Assessment (Williams, Cooter, & Cooter, 2003). It uses nonsense words read in a list (without context). A similar test of phonics knowledge included in this section is the Reutzel/Cooter Word Attack Survey, which focuses on common vowel and consonant generalizations discussed earlier. Together with running records, you will learn a great deal about students' phonics and word attack knowledge using these two assessment tools. [*Note:* We have included a Student Phonics Knowledge Checklist in Figure 8.10 later in the chapter to help you tally up areas of strength and need based on your assessments and observations.]

THE STARPOINT PHONICS ASSESSMENT

Purpose

For many years, nonsense words ("made-up words" having common phonics patterns) have been used in reading assessment to determine students' knowledge of English spelling patterns. These nonsense words are usually read in a list and the teacher records any miscues. Critics say that nonsense words, because they are not real words, do not permit students to use their prior knowledge—a primary reading tool used in decoding unfamiliar words in print. Advocates counter that nonsense words, because they deny the student the ability to use background knowledge, force the student to use only those phonics skills that he or she has internalized. We support the limited use of nonsense words as simply one tool in a teacher's toolbox of assessment ideas that may shed some light on a student's phonics skills development.

The Starpoint Phonics Assessment (SPA) (Williams, Cooter, & Cooter, 2003) was designed to provide a beginning-of-the-year phonics assessment for children attending the Starpoint Laboratory School at Texas Christian University. The SPA is also included as a subtest in *The Spanish & English Reading Inventory for the Classroom,* second edition (Flynt & Cooter, 2003). Areas of special focus include initial consonant sounds (onsets), correct pronunciation of common rimes, syllabication, affixes (prefixes/suffixes), and r-controlled vowels. These phonics areas are embedded within nonsense words that students are asked to read (see Figure 8.7). Analysis of children's phonics abilities focus on these five areas.

Figure 8.7   Starpoint Phonics Assessment Nonsense Words

1. runk	mip	bor
2. pight	caw	jor
3. wunk	lemmock	zatting
4. nash	soug	zad
5. battump	dapping	yod
6. mur	hote	seg
7. lattum	yinter	poat
8. telbin	vike	leak
9. dar	mur	foat
10. pice	gar	whesp
11. dop	femmit	yadder
12. gapple	sheal	telbis
13. lome	ridnip	hade
14. tade	chogging	vappel
15. minzif	kosh	waig
16. tain	demsug	nater
17. festrip	bowunk	thiping
18. wapir	polide	wabor
19. polide	siler	jiper
20. atur	niping	quen

Materials

Reproduce each row of nonsense words from Figure 8.7 on cardstock as flash cards (example: Row 1 words on one card—*runk, mip, bor*). You will also need a copy of the SPA Analysis Grid Form (Figure 8.8) for each student to be assessed. Finally, it is important to record students as they read each group of words so that you can check your analysis, so appropriate equipment will be needed.

Procedure

Seat the student at a table directly across from where you are sitting. Turn on your cassette tape player and say the student's name aloud and the date to mark the record, then continue. Beginning with the first flash card you have prepared from Figure 8.7, say to the student, "Please read the words on each card as I hold it up. The words are all *nonsense* words. That means they are not real words. Just pronounce them the way you think they would sound. For instance, this first word is *runk*. Go ahead and try to say the other words for me as I hold them up."

Figure 8.8 Starpoint Phonics Assessment Analysis Grid Form

			Initial Sound	Rimes	Syllab.	Affixes	R-contr.
1. runk	mip	bor					
2. pight	caw	jor					
3. wunk	lemmock	zatting					
4. nashed	soug	zads					
5. battump	dapping	yod					
6. mur	hote	seg					
7. lattum	yinter	poat					
8. telbin	advike	leak					
9. dar	mur	foat					
10. pice	subgar	whesp					
11. dop	femmit	yadder					
12. gapple	sheal	telbis					
13. lome	ridnip	hade					
14. tade	chogging	vappel					
15. minzif	koshes	waig					
16. tain	demsug	disnater					
17. festrip	bowunks	thiping					
18. wapir	polide	wabor					
19. polide	siler	jiper					
20. atur	niping	quen					
Totals							

Examiner's Notes:

As the student reads each word, make a notation to the right of each grouping of words on the SPA Analysis Grid Form (Figure 8.8) indicating whether the child said the word correctly. Words pronounced correctly should be noted with a checkmark (✓). Incorrect pronunciations should be written phonetically. For example, if a student pronounced the nonsense word *wabor* (line 18), it may be written as "*way-bee*" to the right of the word cluster on line 18 reflecting the way the student said it. Continue having the student read each cluster of words marking any *miscues* (a mispronounced word) in the blank area to the right of each word cluster.

ANALYZING THE MISCUES

The Starpoint Phonics Assessment (SPA) is quick and easy to analyze. Analysis begins after the student has read all of the words from Figure 8.7 and has returned to his or her normal school activities.

First, replay the cassette recording to be sure that any miscues have been correctly recorded. Next, for each miscue noted, simply place a hash mark "|" in the box to the right indicating which phonics skill(s) the student seems to be lacking when trying to decode that particular nonsense word: beginning sounds (onset), rimes, syllabication, affixes (common prefixes and suffixes), and/or *r*-controlled vowels. You should have at least one box marked for each miscue. If none of the phonics categories seems to be appropriate, which is possible, then make a note of the miscue at the bottom of the sheet in the area marked "Examiner's Notes" along with your interpretation of what the student may need to learn (e.g., *CVC* rule, hard *g* sound, vowel digraphs, etc.). If this happens, be sure to administer the Reutzel/Cooter Word Attack Survey discussed in the next section.

Finally, add up the number of miscues in each column and record that number in the appropriate "Totals" box. In instances in which the student has had two or more miscues in that category (i.e., beginning sounds/onset, rimes, syllabication, affixes, or *r*-controlled vowels), you should consider developing explicit instruction plans to teach that skill.

THE REUTZEL/COOTER WORD ATTACK SURVEY

Purpose

The Reutzel/Cooter Word Attack Survey (WAS), like the Starpoint Phonics Assessment (SPA), uses nonsense words to help you diagnose students' needs and abilities in phonics. The primary focus in the WAS is on vowel and consonant generalizations.

Materials

You will need to reproduce the word cards provided at the end of this chapter for the students to read. Also, make copies of the Word Attack Survey Form (see Figure 8.9) for use in noting student responses.

Procedure

Directions for administering The Reutzel/Cooter Word Attack Survey follow.

1. Seat the student across from you at a small table.
2. Begin by showing him or her the examples provided using the pre-made flash cards (see word cards at the end of the chapter). Say, "I would like for you to read aloud some words on these flash cards. These are not real words but are make-believe words, so they may sound kind of funny to you. Just try to say them the way you think they should be pronounced. For example, this first word (*sim*) is pronounced *sim*."

Figure 8.9   The Reutzel/Cooter Word Attack Survey Form

Student name: _____   Date: _____

Part 1: Vowel Generalizations

Sample Item:	sim	cip	sar

A. CVC/Beginning Consonant Sounds
  1. tat   _____
  2. nan   _____
  3. rin   _____
  4. mup   _____
  5. det   _____
  6. sim   _____
  7. loj   _____
  8. cal   _____
  9. pif   _____
  10. fek   _____

B. Vowel Digraphs
  11. geem   _____
  12. hoad   _____
  13. kait   _____
  14. weam   _____

C. VCE Pattern
  15. jape   _____
  16. zote   _____

  17. gipe   _____
  18. tope   _____

D. CV Pattern
  19. bo   _____
  20. ka   _____
  21. fi   _____
  22. tu   _____

E. R-Controlled Vowels
  23. sar   _____
  24. wir   _____
  25. der   _____
  26. nur   _____

F. Schwa Sound
  27. ahurla   _____
  28. thup   _____
  29. cremon   _____
  30. laken   _____

Part 2: Consonant Generalizations

G. Hard and Soft *C*
  31. cale   _____
  32. cose   _____
  33. cimmy   _____
  34. cyler   _____

H. Hard and Soft *G*
  35. gare   _____
  36. gob   _____
  37. gime   _____
  38. genry   _____

I. Consonant Digraphs
  39. chur   _____
  40. thim   _____
  41. shar   _____
  42. whilly   _____
  43. thar   _____

J. Double Consonants
  44. nally   _____
  45. ipple   _____
  46. attawap   _____
  47. urrit   _____

K. Ph (f sound)
  48. phur   _____
  49. phattle   _____
  50. phenoblab _____

L. Single Consonants*

M. Syllabication Rule**
  51. lappo   _____
  52. pabute   _____
  53. larpin   _____
  54. witnit   _____

*See section A
**Besides Items 51–54, there are many other syllabication examples throughout the *R/CWAS*.

Comments:

(Note: The teacher pronounces the word for the student). "Now I would like for you to pronounce the next word for me." (Show the word *cip*.) Praise the child for saying the word correctly (or explain again the instructions, if necessary). After asking the student to do the third example word (*sar*), go ahead to the next step.

3. Say, "Now I would like for you to say each word as I show it to you. These are also make-believe words, so they will not sound much like any word you know. Just say them the way you think they should be pronounced." Then, work your way through the words and note any mispronunciations on the Word Attack Survey Form (Figure 8.9).

4. Once the student has completed reading through the word cards, praise him or her for his or her hard work and allow him or her to go on to other activities. Tally up any miscues using the Word Attack Survey Form (Figure 8.9).

5. Determine areas of phonics knowledge the student may be having difficulty with based on repeated miscues. We recommend that your instructional decisions be based on a pattern of errors repeated over time. Thus, you will need to hear the child read more than once before deciding which areas must be addressed in phonics minilessons.

One of the challenges for busy classroom teachers is organizing assessment information so that you can make enlightened teaching decisions and group effectively for instruction. To help you in this process, we offer a Student Phonics Knowledge Checklist in Figure 8.10.

Figure 8.10   Student Phonics Knowledge Checklist

Student Phonics Knowledge Checklist

Student's name: _____

Skill(s)	**Date Observed**

Level 1: Phonemic Awareness
1. Rhyming   _____
2. Alliteration   _____
3. Oddity tasks   _____
4. Oral blending: syllables, onset/rime, phoneme by phoneme   _____
5. Oral segmentation: syllables, onset/rime, phoneme by phoneme   _____
6. Phonemic manipulation: substitution *(i, f, v)*; deletion *(s, i, f)*   _____

Level 2: Alphabetic Principle
7. Making the connection between sounds and symbols   _____

Level 3: Explicit Phonics Instruction
8. Specific letter sounds/Specific letter names
   a. Onset/consonants and rimes   _____
   b. Continuous consonants   _____
   c. Short vowel sounds   _____
   d. Continue teaching both vowels and consonants   _____
   e. Consonant digraphs: *wh, ch, th, sh,* etc.   _____
   f. Vowel dipthongs: *oi, oy, ou*   _____
   g. Vowel digraphs: *ee, ea, ai, ay,* etc.   _____
9. Word play with onset and rime blending   _____
10. L → R blending of letter-sounds in words   _____
11. Segmentation of sounds in words, and writing segmented sounds   _____

Source: From *Phonemic Awareness for Early Reading Success,* by W. Blevins, 1997. Reprinted by permission of Scholastic, Inc.

Figure 8.11   Summary Matrix of Assessments to Measure Phonics and Word Attack Skills

Name of Assessment Tool	Screening Assessment	Diagnostic Assessment	Progress-Monitoring Assessment	Outcomes Assessment	Norm-Referenced Test	Criterion-Referenced Test	Reliability Evidence	Validity Evidence
Starpoint Phonics Assessment	+	+	+	+	+	+	−	+
Reutzel/Cooter Word Attack Survey	+	+	+	+	−	+	−	+
Running Records	+	+	+	+	−	+	*	+

Key: + can be used for   − not appropriate for

*Note: Reliability evidence is not usually available for running records since it is an "informal" procedure used by teachers with passages they select. However, the new *Comprehensive Reading Inventory (CRI)* by R. Cooter, E.S. Flynt, and K.S. Cooter (Merrill/Prentice Hall Publishers) does provide realibility and validity data for all of its running records.

Assessing Via Running Records

OK, we just could not resist putting in one last reminder that you should use running records as your primary assessment tool for analyzing student decoding ability. Chapter 2 gives you the full picture on using this valuable diagnostic procedure.

In Figure 8.11 we summarize the procedures and instruments we have just discussed for assessing factors associated with phonics and word attack skills. In this *Summary Matrix of Assessments* we provide information about federally related assessment purposes, i.e., *screening, diagnosis, progress-monitoring*, or *outcomes* assessment as well as the type of test or procedure (norm referenced test [NRT] or criterion referenced test [CRT]) and psychometric evidence of test or procedure scores including reliability and/or validity evidence, if available.

Connecting Assessment Findings to Teaching Strategies

Before discussing phonics and word attack teaching strategies, we have constructed an *if-then* chart connecting assessment findings to intervention and/or strategy choices. It is our intention to help you select the most appropriate instructional interventions and strategies to meet your students' needs based on assessment data. In the next part of this chapter, we offer instruction strategies for interventions based on the foregoing assessments.

Teaching Strategies: Helping Students Increase Phonics and Word Attack Knowledge

Tips on Teaching Phonics

Research over the past decade or so has taught us much about the best ways to teach phonics (Stahl, 1992; Blevins, 1998; National Institute of Child Health and Human Development, 2000; Carnine et al., 2006; Cooter, 2001). Here is our advice about what you should (and should not) do to establish solid phonics instruction.

Ten Things to Do

1. *Sequence your instruction*—Earlier in the chapter, we provided you with a scope and sequence of instruction (see Figure 8.6)

"If" the student is ready to learn → / "Then" try these strategies ↑	Explicit Phonics Instruction	Letter Sound Cards	Phonics Fish	Sound Swirl	Button Sounds	Stomping, Clapping, Tapping, Snapping Sounds	Tongue Twisters	Nonsense Words	Making Words	Wide Reading	Word Boxes	Word Detectives
Letter sounds	+	+	*	+	+	−	+	+	+	+	+	+
C rule	+	+	*	*	−	−	−	+	+	+	+	+
G rule	+	+	*	*	−	−	−	+	+	+	+	+
CVC Generalization	+	+	+	−	−	−	−	+	+	+	−	+
Vowel Digraphs	+	+	+	−	−	−	−	+	+	+	−	+
VCE (Final E) Generalization	+	+	+	−	−	−	−	+	+	+	−	+
CV Generalization	+	+	+	−	−	−	−	+	+	+	−	+
R-Controlled Vowels	+	+	+	−	−	−	−	+	+	+	−	+
Single Consonant Sounds	+	+	+	−	+	−	−	+	+	+	+	+
Consonant Digraphs	+	+	*	−	+	−	−	+	+	+	*	+
Consonant Blends	+	+	*	−	+	−	−	+	+	+	*	+
Double Consonants	+	+	*	−	*	−	−	+	+	+	*	+
Onset and Rime	+	+	+	+	*	+	+	+	+	+	+	+
Syllabication	+	+	−	−	−	+	*	+	+	+	−	+
Sight Words	+	−	−	−	+	−	−	+	+	+	−	+
Structural Analysis	+	*	*	*	−	−	−	+	+	+	*	+

Key: + Excellent Strategy   * Adaptable Strategy   − Unsuitable Strategy

2. *Be very direct (explicit and implicit) in your teaching*—Model each new skill thoroughly, offer students a good bit of practice under your guidance, and then assess to make sure they have it.

3. *Have daily lessons and review sessions*—Phonics instruction should be an everyday occurrence in the early grades (K–2) and include a great deal of repetition. Teachers sometimes forget that even our best students need as much as 30 days of repetition for a new phonics skill to become their own (Cooter, 2001). According to the National Research Council (1999),

> . . . [Children] need sufficient practice with a variety of texts to achieve fluency, so that both word recognition and reading comprehension become increasingly fast, accurate, and well-coordinated. (p. 6)

4. *Focus on one skill at a time*—All too often, we try to do too much in introducing new skills and, consequently, teach few skills well. Phonics lessons should keep a tight focus and work on the target skill until the student becomes proficient.

5. *Keep lessons brief*—If, in fact, you are teaching within the student's "frontier of learning," then you must limit instruction sessions to 10 to 15 minutes. Otherwise, the student's attention wanders and your teaching is ineffective.

6. *When practicing a new phonics skill, use easy reading materials*—Many times, the very best way to introduce new phonics skills is through the use of great books, poems, songs, chants, or raps. Be sure that reading materials are predominantly at students' independent reading level with the "target" words (i.e., words unknown to the students in print that you will use to introduce a new phonics skill) woven into the text. That way, students can use what they already know, as well as some context information, to aid them in practicing the new skill.

7. *Help kids become "wordsmiths"*—We have noticed that great readers and writers are also word watchers; they seem to always notice new and interesting words in their text encounters. We must do whatever we can each day to model the attitude of fascination with words and how they are put together. This makes word study far more interesting to students—"A spoonful of sugar helps the medicine go down."

8. *Adjust the pace of instruction to meet the individual needs of students*—This can only be done consistently in small-group instruction in which students come together based on a common need to know.

9. *Link phonics instruction to spelling*—Enough said on this one?!

10. *Make clear what you want kids to do*—Be sure to say in clear terms (i.e, the words of a 7-year-old instead of college-level jargon) what the skill is, why it is worth knowing, and what you will expect students to do as a result of this lesson.

What Not to Do

1. *Avoid round-robin teaching*—Do not have kids waiting continually for their turn. Small-group instruction usually makes this problem go away.

2. *Try not to direct students too quickly*—Let kids have an opportunity to self-correct before intervening.

3. *Avoid drill-and-kill teaching*—There is no question that phonics knowledge is important. However, we need to avoid militaristic teaching that drums information into young readers' heads at the cost of killing their interest in reading. Some things must be learned by rote, but be sure to include ample practice in rich and interesting texts.

In this section, we recommend several activities that may be used with many of the phonics skills enumerated earlier. Therefore, please note that if we recommend an activity that is useful in teaching, say, consonant sounds, it may be just as useful in teaching consonant digraphs, rimes, or vowel generalizations.

A FORMAT FOR EXPLICIT PHONICS INSTRUCTION

Purpose

Glazer (1998) has developed a step-by-step procedure for teaching phonics skills. Try it as one way to provide explicit instruction for your students.

Materials

Tongue twisters, riddles, jokes, songs, poems, or stories specially selected for the phonics pattern you wish to teach are needed for this procedure.

Procedure

Step 1:   ***Bombard students with correct models.*** New phonics knowledge is heavily dependent on students having already internalized in their listening and speaking vocabularies correct pronunciations and usages of thousands of words. After deciding which phonics element you wish to teach, select reading materials that use the element. Read, retell, organize simple plays or raps involving students, or use other means to build in many encounters with the words you want to emphasize. As you use the target words in your readings or retellings, write the words on your easel chart paper or highlight them when using a big book. Say, "Read these words with me as I say them." Then, ask "What is the same about these words we just read?" to guide them to the phonics element you want to emphasize. Always provide the correct answer if the students are in doubt.

Step 2:   ***Provide structured practice.*** With students gathered in a small group, write the letter(s) being emphasized at the top of your easel chart. If, for instance, we are emphasizing the consonant digraph *ch*, then the following words can be written and said aloud slowly by the teacher: *cheese, church, cherry*. Then, students are encouraged to contribute others having that same beginning sound (perhaps *chain, change, charm, child*).

Step 3:   ***Assess learning using this phonics game.*** The object of this game is to assess student learning by matching the letter or letter combination being emphasized with pictures beginning with that sound. Here is how to do it:

  • Create cards for each student having the letter or sound being studied.

  • Collect several pictures of objects or creatures from magazines whose names begin with that letter or sound.

  • Cut a sheet of tagboard into several pieces about flash card size.

  • Place students into pairs. Then, demonstrate to students how to cut and paste pictures from magazines onto tagboard that have the beginning sound you are emphasizing. Repeat the exercise; only this time students are doing the task with you in their groups of two (i.e., finding pictures of objects or creatures whose names begin with that sound).

- Check the products from each group with the students. Ask them to name the picture that begins with that sound.

Step 4: ***Sharing what they have learned.*** Children love to share (and brag about) their accomplishments. Help them create word banks, pocket dictionaries, or word charts showing off how many words they could find containing the phonics element you have been studying together. These may include the names of animals, food, toys, friends, family members, and objects from their environment having the target letter-sound combination. Have students share their accomplishments in small groups or with the whole class in a kind of author's chair format. They will love showing off their new knowledge!

LETTER-SOUND CARDS

Purpose

Letter-sound cards are intended as prompts to help students remember individual and combination (i.e., digraphs and blends) letter sounds that have been introduced during mini-lessons or other teachable moments.

Materials

You will need to have a word bank for each child (children's shoe boxes, recipe boxes, or other small containers in which index cards can be filed), alphabetic divider cards to separate words in the word bank, index cards, and colored markers.

Procedure

This is essentially the same idea as the word bank activity shown in chapter 9 on vocabulary instruction. The idea is to provide students with their own word cards on which you (or they) have written a key letter sound or sounds on one side and a word that uses that sound on the other. Whenever possible, it is best to use nouns or other words that can be depicted with a picture, so that, for emergent readers, a drawing can be added to the side having the word (as needed). Two examples are shown in Figure 8.12.

PHONICS FISH (OR FONIKS PHISH?) CARD GAME

Purpose

Remember the age-old children's card game "Fish" (sometimes called "Go Fish")? This review activity helps students use their growing visual awareness of phonics sounds and patterns to construct word families (i.e., groups of words having the same phonetic pattern). It can be played in small groups, at a learning center with two to four children, or during reading groups with the teacher.

Materials

You will need a deck of word cards. The words can be selected from the students' word banks or chosen by the teacher or parent/teaching assistant from among those familiar to all students. The word cards should contain ample examples of at least three or four phonetic patterns that you wish to review (e.g., beginning consonant sounds, *r*-controlled vowels, clusters, digraphs, rime families, etc.).

Figure 8.12 Letter-Sound Card Examples

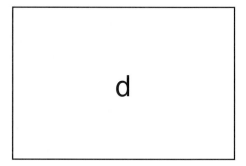

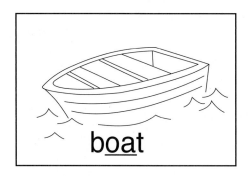

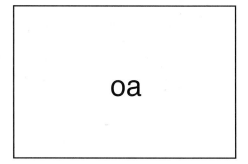

Procedure

Before beginning the game, explain which word families or sound patterns are to be used in this game of "Phonics Fish." Next, explain the rules of the game:

1. Each child will be dealt five cards.
2. The remaining cards (deck of about 50) are placed face down in the middle of the group.
3. Taking turns in a round-robin fashion, each child can ask any other if he or she is holding a word having a particular sound or pattern. For example, if one of the patterns included is the /sh/ sound, then the first student may say something like, "Juanita, do you have any words with the /sh/ sound?" If the student being asked does not have any word cards with that pattern, he or she can say "Go Fish!" The student asking the question then draws a card from the deck.
4. Cards having matching patterns (two or more) are placed face up in front of the student asking the question.
5. The first student to get rid of all his or her cards wins the game.

Sound Swirl

Purpose

Sound Swirl is a simple activity that is used (a) to help students think of "words in their head" that have a certain sound element and (b) then to use invented or "temporary" spellings to construct the words they have recalled. This helps students learn to sound out words and to notice particular word sounds as their phonics awareness grows. This activity is usually best applied as a Guided Practice or for review.

Materials

You will need some chart paper and markers in different colors.

Procedure

Gather a group of children around you with whom you wish to review a phonics sound pattern (for our example here, we will use the beginning sound represented by the letters /ch/ as in *church*). Write the letters representing the sound you wish to emphasize (/ch/ in our example) on the chart paper using a colorful marker. Say, "Boys and girls, I want us to see just how many words we can think of that begin with the sound made by the letters *ch*, which make the /ch/ sound. So, get your mouth ready to make the /ch/ sound, swirl around all the letters in your head (*Note:* Here, the teacher makes a grand gesture of a swirling motion above his or her head), and say the first words that come to your mind, right now!!!" At this point, the students will call out such words as *church, chump, change, child, chirp,* and so on. Select a few of the words they called out and, in whole-group fashion (using volunteers), have them sound out the written words (beginning each time with *ch* in a different color from the rest of the word) so they can recognize visually how words can be sounded out and written.

"BUTTON" SOUNDS

Purpose

Children often enjoy wearing buttons that are unique. Similarly, many schools have button-making machines that can inexpensively produce buttons for special projects. "Button sounds," as we call them, take advantage of children's attraction to buttons to help cement their understanding of introductory sounds in words. (*Note:* This is recommended only as an adjunct to other more comprehensive minilessons.)

Materials

You will need access to a button-making machine and materials or a local vendor who can make the buttons for you inexpensively.

Procedure

Identify the phonics sounds or symbols you wish to emphasize. For example, we first used this activity with first-grade students to help them learn alphabet letters as initial sounds in words (e.g., *Bb* together with a picture of a butterfly, *Cc* with a picture of a cat, *Gg* with a picture of a goat, etc.). However, any sound or symbol relationship can be used that can be illustrated with a picture. Once you have introduced the "sound for the day" and linked it to a key illustration (e.g., a witch for the letters *Ww* or a ship for the digraph *sh*), distribute the buttons to all students in the group or class. You should instruct the children that whenever they are asked by anyone about their button, they should respond with a statement such as "This is my *sh* and *ship* button." An example of a button is shown in Figure 8.13.

Figure 8.13   Button From "Button Sounds" Activity

wh

wheelchair

STOMPING, CLAPPING, TAPPING, AND SNAPPING SOUNDS

Purposes

Helping children hear syllables in words enables them to segment sounds. This knowledge can be used in myriad ways to improve writing and spelling, increase awareness of letter combinations used to produce speech sounds, and apply knowledge of onsets and rimes. All these skills and more enable students to sound out words in print more effectively. For ages, teachers have found success in helping children hear syllables by clapping them out when reading nursery rhymes, such as "Mar-y had a lit-tle lamb, lit-tle lamb, lit-tle lamb. . . ."

Materials

We prefer to use rhyming poetry, songs, chants, or raps for these syllabication activities. Use an enlarged version produced for an overhead projector, use a big book version, or simply rewrite the text on large chart paper using a colored ink marker.

Procedures

First, model reading the enlarged text aloud in a normal cadence for your students. Reread the selection at a normal cadence, inviting students to join in as they wish. Next, explain that you will reread the selection but that this time you will clap (or snap, or stomp, etc.) the syllables in the words. (*Note:* If you have not already explained the concept of syllables, you will need to do so at this point.) Finally, invite students to clap (or make whatever gesture or sound that you have chosen), as you reread the passage.

TONGUE TWISTERS

Purpose

Many students enjoy word play. Tongue twisters can be a wonderful way of reviewing consonants (Cunningham, 1995) in a way that is fun for students. We have found that tongue twister activities can combine reading and creative writing processes to help children deepen their understanding of phonics elements.

Materials

There are many traditional tongue twisters in published children's literature that may be used. However, we find that children enjoy creating their own tongue twisters perhaps even more. All you need to do is decide which sounds or letter pattern families are to be used.

Procedure

Cunningham (1995) suggests that you begin by simply reciting some tongue twisters aloud and inviting students to join in. We recommend that you produce two or three examples on chart paper and post them on the wall as you introduce the concept of tongue twisters. For example, you may use the following:

> Silly Sally sat in strawberries.

> Peter Piper picked a peck of pickled peppers.
> If Peter Piper picked a peck of pickled peppers,
> Then how many peppers did Peter Piper pick?
> Peter Piper panhandles pepperoni pizza,
> With his pint-sized pick-up he packs a peck of pepperoni pizzas,
> For Patti his portly patron.

> Simple Simon met a pieman going to the fair,
> Said Simple Simon to the pieman,
> "Let me taste your wares!"
> Said the pieman to Simple Simon,
> "Show me first your penny!"
> Said Simple Simon to the pieman,
> "I'm afraid I haven't any."

Children especially love it when teachers create tongue twisters using names of children in the class, such as the following example:

> Pretty Pam picked pink peonies for Patty's party.

Last, challenge students to create their own tongue twisters to "stump the class." It may be fun to award students coupons that can be used to purchase take-home books for coming up with clever tongue twisters.

CREATING NONSENSE WORDS

Purpose

Many of the most popular poets, such as Shel Silverstein and Jack Prelutsky, have tapped into children's fascination with word play in their very creative poetry. For instance, when Silverstein (1974) speaks of "gloppy glumps of cold oatmeal," we all understand what he means, even though *gloppy* and *glumps* are really nonsense words. Getting students to create nonsense words and apply them to popular poetry is a motivating way to help students practice phonics patterns.

Materials

First decide which phonics sound or letter pattern families you wish to emphasize. For instance, it may be appropriate to review the letter or sound families represented by *-ack, -ide, -ing,* and *-ore.* Also needed are books of poetry or songs with rhyming phrases, chart paper or overhead transparencies, and markers.

Procedure

As with all activities, begin by modeling what you expect students to do. On a large sheet of chart paper or at the overhead projector, write the word family parts that you wish to emphasize (for this example, we used *-ack, -ide, -ing,* and *-ore*). Illustrate how you can convert the word parts into nonsense words by adding a consonant, consonant blend, or consonant digraph before each one, such as shown by the following:

-ack	-ide	-ing	-ore
gack	spide	gacking	zore
clack	mide	zwing	glore
chack	plide	kaching	jore

In the next phase of the demonstration, select a poem or song that rhymes and review it with students (use enlarged text for all of your modeling). Next, show students a revised copy of the song or poem in which you have substituted nonsense words. Here is one example we have used with the song "I Know an Old Lady Who Swallowed a Fly." We show only the first verse here, but you could use the entire song, substituting a nonsense word in each stanza. The original version follows:

> I know an old lady who swallowed a fly,
> I don't know why,
> she swallowed the fly,
> I guess she'll die.

Here is the nonsense word version:

> I know an old lady who swallowed a **zwing,**
> I don't know why,
> she swallowed the **zwing,**
> I guess she'll die.

MAKING WORDS

Cunningham and Cunningham (1992) describe making words as a hands-on manipulative activity in which students look for patterns in words. Students also learn how new words can be created by simply changing one letter or letter combination. Making words can be useful for either vocabulary building or for developing phonetic understanding. For a complete explanation of making words, please see the discussion of this activity in chapter 9.

Wide Reading

John J. Pikulski (1998), a recent president of the International Reading Association, has noted the importance of massive amounts of reading in high-quality texts as a tool for developing decoding fluency. Specifically, he points out that children can benefit from three main types of practice: wide reading, independent level reading, and multiple re-readings of texts.

Wide reading simply refers to the notion of encouraging children to read in a variety of topics and genre. Teachers can encourage wide reading by regularly conducting "book talks." With book talks, the teacher reads aloud a particularly interesting portion of a great book or other text form but leaves the students "hanging" at a particularly suspenseful point in the narrative. This often makes students mad with desire to finish reading the selection!

Independent level reading refers to helping children find many and varied books of interest that are easy for them to read. In this case, "easy" reading refers to books in which students will be able to read about 98% or more of the words without difficulty. In addition to improving phonics fluency, research shows that independent level reading for at least 20 minutes each day also greatly improves reading rate.

Multiple re-readings of texts means just what the words imply—re-reading favorite books, poems, or other text forms. Multiple re-readings will essentially provide the same benefits as independent level reading.

To make wide reading, independent level reading, and multiple re-readings happen every day, we recommend that you institute *DEAR* time (*Drop Everything And Read*) in your classroom. For about 20 to 30 minutes each day, have students stop at a designated time and read a book of their choosing. DEAR can be broken into two shorter time segments just as effectively, if you wish. The teacher may participate and read a book for fun or work with a small group of struggling readers re-reading familiar texts in choral fashion. You will love the results.

WORD BOXES

Purpose

Word boxes (Clay, 1993) are "designed to help children make letter-sound correspondences and note letter-sound sequence patterns in words (Devault & Joseph, 2004, p. 22). This technique consists of a drawn rectangle divided into sections according to the number of sounds in a word. Magnetic or tile letters are placed below the divided boxes, and the children slide the letters into the respective sections of the rectangle as each sound is articulated. This technique has been found to be effective for helping first graders and elementary children with disabilities achieve phonemic awareness, word identification, and spelling skills, as well as for high-school students with severe reading difficulties.

Materials

You will need word boxes like the one shown in Figure 8.14 for each focus word and individual letters that can be slid into and from each box. Magnetic letters, letter tiles from a "Scrabble" game, or laminated cutout letters may be used.

Figure 8.14   Word Box (for the Word "Snake")

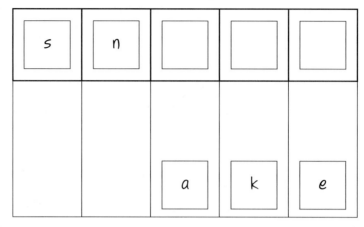

Procedure

Repeated readings coupled with word boxes can be practiced, depending on the student's age and attention span, for 5 to 10 minutes for approximately 5 days per week. Begin (in small groups of four or so) with a modeling exercise involving a read aloud of a favorite book at the group's instructional (i.e., zone of proximal development) reading level. Using a preselected target word displayed below a large word box with letters on index cards, say each sound represented by each letter while sliding letters into the divided sections of the word box.

After modeling this activity to the point of overlearning for students, have students begin trying it themselves; provide feedback and correction as needed. At the completion of each word boxes lesson, present the same level passage and provide students with appropriate time to read it orally. During the following session, a different passage should be presented using the same procedures as previously described.

WORD DETECTIVES

Purpose

Word detectives (Gaskins, 2004) is an approach to phonics awareness that asks students to segment words in print into sounds, compare sounds to the letters they see, and decide which letter or letters match each sound. The job of a "word detective" is to discover letter-sound matches.

Materials

This activity requires a book(s) on the student's instructional level and paper and pencil or a small white board and markers.

Procedure

We believe strongly in lessons that proceed from whole text, to text elements (words), to reapplication of the new skill learned in a new text. We also believe that direct instruction should progress from teacher modeling, to guided practice with teacher input as needed, to independent practice, to conclusion with reapplication of the new knowledge in other texts. Thus, you should begin with a read aloud with an interesting book on the student's instructional level, then model repeatedly word detective examples drawn from the text just read.

In modeling, begin by choosing a word from the text you wish to target for learning. Instruct the students to use "word rubber banding" to stretch the word, and then model this

A Phonics Quick Test (Answer Key)

1. The word *charkle* is divided between _r_ and _k_. The *a* has an *r-* controlled sound, and the *e* is _silent_.
2. In the word *small, sm-* is known as the *onset* and *-all* is known as the *rime*. (See chapter 8 for a full explanation.)
3. *Ch* in the word *chair* is known as a _consonant digraph_.
4. The letter *c* in the word *city* is a _soft_ sound; in the word *cow*, the letter *c* is a _hard_ sound.
5. The letters *bl* in the word *blue* are referred to as a consonant _blend_.
6. The underlined vowels in the words _author_, _spread_, and _blue_ are known as vowel _digraphs_.
7. The words *tag, run, cot,* and *get* have which vowel pattern? _consonant - vowel - consonant (CVC)_
8. The words *glide, take,* and *use* have the _vowel - consonant - "e"_ vowel pattern.
9. The single most powerful phonics skill we can teach to emergent readers for decoding unfamiliar words in print is _beginning_ sounds in words. We introduce this skill using _consonant_ sounds first because they are the most _constant (or "dependable" or "reliable")_.
10. The word part *work* in the word *working* is known as a _root (or "base" or "unbound morpheme")_ word.
11. The word part *-ing* in the word *working* is known as a _suffix (or "bound morpheme")_.
12. Cues to the meaning and pronunciation of unfamiliar words in print are often found in the print surrounding the unfamiliar, also known as the _context_.

Grading Key for Teachers

Number Correct	Evaluation
12	Wow, you're good! (You must have had no social life in college.)
10–11	Not too bad, but you may need a brushup. (Read this chapter.)
7–9	Emergency! Take a refresher course, quick! (Read this chapter.)
0–6	Have you ever considered a career in telemarketing?! (Just kidding, but read this chapter . . . right away!)

step for them holding up a finger for each sound you say. Ask students to repeat the word rubber-banding technique in unison with the target word and holding up a finger for each sound they hear as it is spoken. Next, using a *word box* and letter cards (as described in the previous activity), ask students to tell you which letter should go in each box to represent the sounds of the target word. In this way, you can help students proceed from decoding letter-sound relationships to blending these same sounds to again create whole words as well as focus on unusual spellings. This procedure has been shown to be very effective in a longitudinal study by Gaskins (2004).

SELECTED REFERENCES

Adams, M. J. (1990). *Beginning to read: Thinking and learning about print*. Cambridge, MA: MIT Press.

Armbruster, B. B., & Osborn, J. (2001). *Put reading first: The research building blocks for teaching children to read*. Washington, DC: National Institute for Literacy. Available free online at http://www.nifl.gov.

Bear, D. R., Templeton, S., Invernizzi, M., & Johnston, F. (1996). *Words their way: Word study for phonics, vocabulary, and spelling instruction*. Columbus, OH: Merrill/Prentice Hall.

Blevins, W. (1996). *Phonics: Quick-and-easy learning games*. New York: Scholastic Professional Books.

Blevins, W. (1997). *Phonemic awareness activities for early reading success*. New York: Scholastic Professional Books.

Blevins, W. (1998). *Phonics from A to Z: A practical guide*. New York: Scholastic Professional Books.

Carnine, D. W., Silbert, J., Kameenui, E. J., Tarver, S. G., & Jongjohann, K. (2006). *Teaching struggling and at-risk readers: A direct instruction approach*. Upper Saddle River, NJ: Prentice Hall.

Chall, J. S. (1967). *Learning to read: The great debate.* New York: McGraw-Hill.

Chard, D. J., & Osborn, J. (1999). Phonics and word recognition instruction in early reading programs: Guidelines for accessibility. *Learning Disabilities Research & Practice, 14*(2), 107–125.

Clay, M. M. (1993). *An observation survey for early literacy achievement.* Portsmouth, NH: Heinemann Educational Books.

Cooter, K. S. (2001, November). *Teaching phonics skills to urban student populations.* Unpublished manuscript, Texas Christian University, Fort Worth, TX.

Cooter, R. B., & Cooter, K. S. (1998, March). *Using classroom assessment to inform teaching: Focus on K–3.* Texas State Reading Association Annual Conference, El Paso.

Cooter, R. B., Flynt, E. S., & Cooter, K. S. (in press for fall 2006). *The Comprehensive Reading Inventory (CRI): Measuring Reading Development in Regular and Special Education Classrooms* (English and Spanish Forms). Upper Saddle River, NJ: Merrill/Prentice Hall.

Cunningham, P. M. (1995). *Phonics they use* (2nd ed.). New York: HarperCollins.

Cunningham, P. M., & Cunningham, J. W. (1992). Making words: Enhancing the invented spelling-decoding connection. *The Reading Teacher, 46,* 106–107.

Devault, R., & Joseph, L. M. (2004). Repeated readings combined with word boxes phonics technique increases fluency levels of high school students with severe reading delays. *Preventing School Failure, 49*(1), 22–27.

Ehri, L., & Stahl, S. A. (2001). Beyond the smoke and mirrors: Putting out the fire. *Phi Delta Kappan, 83*(1), 17–26.

Eldredge, J. L. (1995). *Teaching decoding in holistic classrooms.* Columbus, OH: Merrill/Prentice Hall.

Flynt, E. S., & Cooter, R. B. (2003). *The Spanish & English Reading Inventory for the Classroom* (2nd ed.). Upper Saddle River, NJ: Merrill/Prentice Hall.

Foorman, B. R., Fletcher, J. M., & Francis, D. J. (1998). Strategic phonics: Research-based phonics strategies bolster your reading program. *Instructor-Primary, 108*(2), 102–109.

Foorman, B. R., Francis, D. J., Fletcher, J. M., & Schatschneider, C. (1998). The role of instruction in learning to read: Preventing reading failure in at-risk children. *Journal of Educational Psychology, 90*(1), 37–55.

Fry, E. B., Kress, J. E., & Fountoukidis, D. L. (1993). *The reading teacher's book of lists* (3rd ed.). Paramus, NJ: Prentice Hall.

Gaskins, I. W. (2004). Word detectives. *Educational Leadership, 61*(6), 70–73.

Glazer, S. M. (1998). A format for explicit phonics instruction. *Teaching PreK–8, 28*(4), 102–105.

Hull, M. A. (1989). *Phonics for the teacher of reading.* Upper Saddle River, NJ: Merrill/Prentice Hall.

Kozol, J. (2005). *The shame of the nation: The restoration of apartheid schooling in America.* New York: Crown.

Manzo, A. V., & Manzo, U. C. (1993). *Literacy disorders: Holistic diagnosis and remediation.* Fort Worth, TX: Harcourt Brace Jovanovich College Publishers.

McKee, D. (1968). *Elmer.* New York: McGraw-Hill.

Moustafa, M. (1997). *Beyond traditional phonics: Research discoveries and reading instruction.* Portsmouth, NH: Heinemann Educational Books.

National Institute of Child Health and Human Development. (2000). *Report of the National Reading Panel: Teaching children to read* (NIH Pub. No. 00-4769). Washington, DC: U.S. Government Printing Office.

National Research Council. (1998). *Preventing reading difficulties in young children.* Washington, DC: National Academy Press.

National Research Council. (1999). *Starting out right: A guide for promoting children's reading success.* Washington, DC: National Academy Press.

Pikulski, J. J. (1998, February). *Improving reading achievement: Major instructional considerations for the primary grades.* Commissioner's Reading Day Statewide Conference, Austin, TX.

Pressley, M. (1998). *Reading instruction that works: The case for balanced teaching.* New York: Guilford Press.

Rasinski, T., & Padak, N. (1996). *Holistic reading strategies: Teaching children who find reading difficult.* Columbus, OH: Merrill/Prentice Hall.

Reutzel, D. R., & Cooter, R. B. (2005). *The essentials of teaching children to read.* Upper Saddle River, NJ: Merrill/Prentice Hall.

Routman, R. (1996). *Literacy at the crossroads.* Portsmouth, NH: Heinemann Educational Books.

Silverstein, S. (1974). *Where the sidewalk ends.* New York: HarperCollins.

Stahl, S. (1992). Saying the "p" word: Nine guidelines for exemplary phonics instruction. *The Reading Teacher, 45*(8).

Williams, S. G., Cooter, K. S., & Cooter, R. B. (2003). The Starpoint Phonics Quick Test. Unpublished manuscript.

Wilson, R. M., & Hall, M. (1997). *Programmed word attack for teachers* (6th ed.). Columbus, OH: Merrill/Prentice Hall.

Wyse, D. (2000). Phonics—The whole story? A critical review of empirical evidence. *Educational Studies, 26*(3), 355–366.

Word Cards for The Reutzel/Cooter Word Attack Survey

tat
nan
rin
mup

det
sim
loj
cal
pif

fek
geem
hoad
kait

weam
jape
zote
gipe
tope

bo
ka
fi
tu

sar
wir
der
nur
ahurla

Continued

mup
cremon
laken
cale

cose
cimmy
cyler
gare
gob

gime
genry
chur
thim

shar
whilly
thar
nally
ipple

attawap
urrit
phur
phattle

phenoblab
lappo
pabute
larpin
witnit

Chapter 9

Teaching and Assessing Vocabulary Development

The sun was streaming into the classroom on a crisp October morning as Mr. Roberts sat with a group of fifth-grade students. They were about to begin learning about the rainforests of the Amazon. Tomorrow they would begin an interactive exploration via the Internet on a site called passporttoknowledge.com, so Mr. Roberts thought a little vocabulary lesson would help the kiddos get the most out of the experience. Because they lived in an urban setting in a desert region of the West, he knew there would be some fairly alien notions for his students.

Mr. Roberts wrote the following words on the easel chart—*Amazon River, South America, biodiversity, canopy, Brazil, photosynthesis, species,* then said, "As I mentioned this morning, we're going to begin an exciting unit of study on the rainforests of the Amazon. These are a few of the words from the lesson guide that will be coming up in our Internet experiences, so I thought we should talk about them a little. Let's begin with the basics—who can tell me where South America is?"

James eagerly responded, "I think it's near Orlando."

LaJean retorted, "I don't think so. It's where Chile is, isn't it."

Mr. Roberts said, "Very good, LaJean. Let's all take a look at the map and see exactly where South America is." He then proceeded with a short geography lesson using the global map. Roberts then returned to the vocabulary words he had written on the easel chart.

"Okay, then, can anyone tell me something about the word *biodiversity?* I'll give you a hint: if you break away the first part of the word, *bio,* which means 'life,' that leaves you with a pretty familiar word—*diversity.* What does *diversity* mean?"

After a long silence and blank stares, Mr. Roberts tried another tack.

"OK, forget that one for now. What about the word *canopy?*"

Again, no takers.

Finally, Julio took a chance, "Isn't *canopy* the stuff they make tents out of?"

Clearly, these students did not have the slightest notion what these words meant, so some serious vocabulary development was in order. Fortunately, Mr. Roberts had prepared for this possibility.

"Good try, Julio! I think you're referring to *canvas,* which looks a lot like *canopy,* but its meaning is very different. Well, not to worry—I have a few games we can play [teacher talk for "learning activities"] that will get us ready to explore the rainforests. So let's go."

BACKGROUND BRIEFING FOR TEACHERS

Words are the symbols we use to express ideas—*captions*, you may say, that describe our life experiences. Vocabulary development is a process that goes on throughout life and can be enhanced in the classroom through enticing learning experiences. Except for children who are economically deprived or handicapped, most acquire a vocabulary of over 10,000 words during the first 5 years of their lives (Smith, 1987). Most school-children will learn between 2,000 and 3,600 words per year, though estimates vary from 1,500 to more than 8,000 (Nagy, Herman, & Anderson, 1985; Clark, 1993; Johnson, 2001).

Clearly, vocabulary development is a critical aspect of successful reading (Rupley, Logan, & Nichols, 1999). There seems to be a cyclical effect between vocabulary knowledge and reading. As Johnson and Rasmussen (1998) have stated: "Word knowledge affects reading comprehension, which in turn helps students expand their knowledge bases, which in turn facilitates vocabulary growth and reading comprehension" (p. 204). As students progress in their schooling, vocabulary becomes even more important in content area instruction because it constitutes both information students must learn and concepts they need to understand to function within the subject (Rekrut, 1996).

Since the latter part of the 19th century in America, there has been a great deal of research and debate about the role of vocabulary knowledge in learning to read. James M. Cattell in 1885 argued that children should learn entire words as a method of beginning reading. Though learning "sight words" alone is no longer recommended as an effective beginning reading approach, most teachers and researchers still believe that the acquisition of a large number of sight words should be part of every child's beginning reading program.

There are actually several different "vocabularies" housed in one's mind and usable for language transactions. The largest of these is known as the **listening vocabulary.** These are words you are able to hear and understand but not necessarily use in your own speech. For example, when the famous Hale-Bopp Comet visited our solar system in 1997, most children in the middle and upper elementary grades were quite capable of watching news that was telecast about the comet and understanding most of what was reported. However, if you were to ask many of these same children to explain what they had just learned, many of the technical words and factual bits of information would not be included in their description. It is not that the children somehow forgot everything they had just learned; rather, they did not "own" the words for speech purposes quite yet—they were only able to hear and understand the technical words.

Words that students can hear, understand, *and* use in their speech are known as their **speaking vocabulary.** It is a subset of the listening vocabulary and, thus, is smaller. The gap between peoples' listening and speaking vocabularies is greatest in youth. The gap tends to narrow as adulthood approaches, though the two vocabularies are never equal. The next largest vocabulary is the **reading vocabulary.** As you may guess, it is a subset of one's listening and speaking vocabularies and consists of words one can read and understand. The smallest vocabulary that one acquires is the **writing vocabulary**—words that one can understand when listening, speaking, and reading, *and* can reproduce when writing.

Cooter and Flynt (1996) group listening and reading vocabularies into a collective category known as the *receptive vocabulary,* and they group writing and speaking vocabularies into a category known as the *expressive vocabulary.* These descriptors reflect the broader language functions of these vocabularies for the student as either information receiver or spoken or written language producer.

For students to be able to read and understand a word, they must have first acquired it at the listening and speaking levels. Teachers, then, must somehow find out which words are already "owned" by their students as listening and speaking vocabulary and teach the unknown words that may be critical in their assigned reading. Without this kind of knowledge, adequate context for word identification will be missing and can threaten further reading development and, of course, damage comprehension.

RESEARCH FINDINGS ON VOCABULARY LEARNING

To determine how vocabulary can best be taught and related to the reading comprehension process, the National Reading Panel (National Institute of Child Health and Human Development, 2000) examined more than 20,000 research citations identified through electronic and manual literature searches. From this set, citations were removed if they did not meet predetermined scientific criteria. Fifty studies dating from 1979 to 2000 were reviewed in detail. In the next sections, we briefly summarize key research-supported findings by the National Reading Panel, as well as other important research.

There Are Levels of Vocabulary Learning

The truth is, words are *not* either "known" or "unknown." As with most new learning, new vocabulary words and concepts are learned by degree. The Partnership for Reading (2001), in summarizing conclusions drawn by the National Reading Panel, described three levels of vocabulary learning: *unknown, acquainted,* and *established.* Definitions for each of these three levels are presented in Figure 9.1. Bear in mind that these levels or "degrees" of learning apply to each of the four vocabulary types—listening, speaking, reading, and writing, so helping children build strong reading and writing vocabularies can sometimes be a formidable task indeed.

Sometimes we learn new meanings to words that are already known to us. The word *race,* for example, has many different meanings (a running competition, a classification of human beings, etc.). One of the most challenging tasks for students can be learning the meaning of a new word representing an unknown concept. According to the research,

> Much of learning in the content areas involves this type of word learning. As students learn about *deserts, hurricanes,* and *immigrants,* they may be learning both new concepts and new words. Learning words and concepts in science, social studies, and mathematics is even more challenging because each major concept often is associated with many other new concepts. For example, the concept *deserts* is often associated with other concepts that may be unfamiliar, such as *cactus, plateau,* and *mesa.* (Partnership for Reading, 2001, p. 43)

Figure 9.1   Levels of Vocabulary Learning

Level of Word Knowledge	Definition
Unknown	The word is completely unfamiliar and its meaning is unknown.
Acquainted	The word is somewhat familiar; the student has some idea of its basic meaning.
Established	The word is very familiar; the student can immediately recognize its meaning and use the word correctly.

Source: Partnership for Reading (2001).

What Research Tells Us About Teaching Vocabulary

Most vocabulary is learned indirectly, but some vocabulary *must* be taught directly. The following conclusions about indirect vocabulary learning and direct vocabulary instruction are of particular interest and value to classroom teachers (National Institute of Child Health and Human Development, 2000):

- *Children learn the meanings of most words indirectly through everyday experiences with oral and written language.* There are typically three ways children learn vocabulary indirectly. First, they participate in oral language every day. Children learn word meanings through conversations with other people; and, as they participate in conversations, they often hear words repeated several times. The more conversations children have, the more words they learn!

  Another indirect way children learn words is by being read to. Reading aloud is especially powerful when the reader pauses during reading to define an unfamiliar word and, after reading, engages the child in a conversation about the book. Conversations about books help children to learn new words and concepts and to relate them to their prior knowledge and experience (Partnership for Reading, 2001).

  The third way children learn new words indirectly is through their own reading. This is one of many reasons why many teachers feel that daily independent reading practice of 10 to 20 minutes is so critical (Krashen, 1993). Put simply, the more children read, the more words they will learn! There is a caveat to mention on this point, however. Struggling readers are often incapable of sitting and reading on their own for extended periods of time. For best results, many readers will get much more from their practice reading when working with a "buddy" who has greater ability.

  From the *evidenced-based* reading research, we can conclude that students learn vocabulary indirectly when they hear and see words used in many different contexts. Conversations, read-aloud experiences, and independent reading are essential.

- *Students learn vocabulary when they are taught individual words and word-learning strategies through direct instruction.* Direct instruction helps students learn difficult words (Johnson, 2001), such as words that represent complex concepts that are not part of students' everyday experiences (National Institute of Child Health and Human Development, 2000). We also know that when a teacher *preteaches* new words that are associated with a text the students are about to read, better reading comprehension results (Wixson, 1986; Brett, Rothlein, & Hurley, 1996). As mentioned earlier, direct vocabulary instruction should include specific word learning, as well as teaching students word-learning strategies they can use on their own.

- *Developing "word consciousness" can boost vocabulary learning.* Word consciousness learning activities stimulate an awareness and interest in words, their meanings, and their *power*. Word-conscious students enjoy words and are zealous about learning them. In addition, they have been taught how to learn new and interesting words.

  The key to capitalizing on word consciousness is through wide reading and use of the writing process. When reading a new book aloud to students, call their attention to the way the author chooses his or her words to convey particular meanings. Imagine the fun you can have discussing some of the intense words used by Gary Paulsen (1987) in his book *Hatchet,* Shel Silverstein's (1974) clever use of rhyming words in his book of poetry *Where the Sidewalk Ends,* or the downright "magical" word selection employed by J. K. Rowling (1997) in *Harry Potter and the Sorcerer's*

Stone. Encourage your students to play with words, such as with puns or self-created raps. Help them research a word's history and search for examples of a word's usage in their everyday lives.

MEETING THE NEEDS OF ENGLISH-LANGUAGE LEARNERS: ESL CONNECTIONS

A growing percentage of students in our schools are learning to read in a second language—English. According to the National Center for Educational Statistics (1999), about 17 percent of all students are classified as Hispanic (14%) or Asian/Pacific Islander (3%). Many of these students speak a language other than English as their native tongue. As it was in the earliest days of our country for most newcomers, learning to read and write in English can be a formidable challenge, but one that must be successfully addressed if these students are to reach their potential in our society. *Literacy is in so many ways the gateway to social equity.*

One of the common needs of English-language learners (ELLs) is assistance with unfamiliar vocabulary they encounter while reading. Peregoy and Boyle (2001), in their book *Reading, Writing, & Learning in ESL,* recommend some guidelines for vocabulary development. First, select words to emphasize that you consider important to comprehending the assigned passage. Next, create several sentences loaded with context using these target words. This will give students an opportunity to use context to predict the meaning of the target words. Teacher modeling of prediction strategies using context is a must for students to grasp this strategy. Follow these modeling and guided practice sessions with discussion using excerpts from the text they will be assigned in which the target words appear.

Two vocabulary-development activities that appear later in this chapter are highly recommended for ELL students (Peregoy & Boyle, 2001; May & Rizzardi, 2002): the Vocabulary Cluster and the Semantic Map. Certainly, any of the strategies found in this chapter are appropriate for ELL students as long as you are direct and explicit in your teaching. Direct instruction helps ELL students create mental scaffolding for support of new vocabulary and concepts.

JOHNSON'S VOCABULARY INSTRUCTION GUIDELINES

Dale Johnson, a well-known reading researcher having a particular interest in vocabulary instruction, suggests guidelines for instruction in his book entitled *Vocabulary in the Elementary and Middle School* (2001, pp. 41–48). They are based on his extensive review of the research and are very congruent indeed with the philosophy of comprehensive instruction. Following is a summary of Johnson's vocabulary instruction guidelines.

- *Word knowledge is essential for reading comprehension.* Vocabulary instruction should utilize activities like the ones found in this chapter that link word learning to concept and schema development.

- *Wide reading should be encouraged and made possible in the classroom.* Literally thousands of words are learned through regular and sustained reading. Time should be set aside each day for this crucial learning activity. As an example, Johnson advocates the use of a program called "Read a Million Minutes," which was designed to foster wide reading throughout Iowa. All students set their own in-school and out-of-school reading goal, which contributes to the school's goal.

- *Use direct instruction to teach words that are necessary for passage comprehension.* Considering how critical some words are for comprehending a new passage, teachers should not leave vocabulary learning to incidental encounters but, rather, should plan regular direct instruction lessons to make sure that essential words are learned.

- *Active learning activities yield the best results.* According to research conducted by Stahl (1986), vocabulary instruction that provided only definitional information (i.e., dictionary activities) failed to significantly improve comprehension. Active learning opportunities—such as creation of word webs, playing word games, and discussing new words in reading groups or literature circles—are far more effective in cementing new knowledge and improving comprehension.

- *Students require a good bit of repetition to learn new words and integrate them into existing knowledge (schemas).* In some cases, students may require as many as 40 encounters to fully learn new vocabulary. To know a word well means knowing what it means, how to pronounce it, and how its meaning changes in different contexts. Repeated exposure to the word in different contexts is the key to successful learning.

- *Students should be helped to develop their own strategies for word learning from written and oral contexts.* This includes the use of context clues, structural analysis (root words, prefixes, suffixes), and research skills (use of the dictionary, thesaurus, etc.).

ASSESSING VOCABULARY KNOWLEDGE

Most vocabulary assessment done by master teachers is through careful classroom observations of student reading behaviors. As teachers work with their pupils each day in needs-based group instruction, they discover high-utility words that seem to cause trouble for one or more students. Teachers can work these words into vocabulary-instruction activities like those featured later in this chapter. But this is not to suggest that more cannot be done early in the school year to discover which words most of your students need to learn. Following are a few classroom-proven ideas to help with that process.

ORAL READING ASSESSMENT

Purpose

Oral reading assessment is a method by which problem vocabulary words in print can be distinguished by the teacher in a quick and efficient manner. It is drawn from the running record style of assessment frequently used to note reading miscues.

Materials

You will need photocopies (two copies each) of three or four passages for the student to read that you believe to be at the *instructional* or *frustration* reading level. The passages should be drawn from reading materials commonly used in your classroom curriculum. Ideally, the passages should be sufficiently challenging so that students will have trouble with about 5% to 10% of the words. It will be necessary for you to do a quick word count to determine if the passages are appropriate once the student has read them. It is also essential that you have a range of passages, in terms of difficulty, to account for the vast differences between students' reading ability. (*Note:* If the student calls less than 10% of the words correctly, he or she may not be getting enough context from the passages for adequate comprehension.)

Procedure

Give the student a copy of the first passage you want him or her to read and keep one for yourself. Ask the student to read the passage aloud. While the student reads, note any words that he or she either does not know or mispronounces. Repeat the procedure until the student has read all of the passages. We recommend that you discontinue a passage if the student consistently has trouble with more than one or two words in any one sentence. After the student has finished, tally the number of miscalled words and determine if the passage is acceptable for analysis (no more than about 10% miscalled or unknown words). List any words that seem to be problematic for the student.

Repeat this procedure with all of your students during the first week or so of the new school year; (a) create a master list of words that seem to be problematic, and (b) determine the number or percentage of the class who seem to find each word difficult or unknown. Use the more frequent problem words as part of your vocabulary instruction program.

CLOZE PASSAGES

Cloze passages are short (250 words) passages drawn from typical reading materials found in your instructional program. These passages have key words deleted and replaced with a blank line (Johnson, 2001). Students are asked to read the cloze passage(s) and see if they can fill in the missing words based on what they believe makes sense using context clues. Cloze tests cause students to use their "schema knowledge" of a subject, understanding of basic syntax (word order relationships), and/or word and sentence meaning (semantics) knowledge to guess what a missing or familiar word in print may be. We encourage teachers to administer cloze passages to the whole class at once as a starting point to determine vocabulary needs.

VOCABULARY FLASH CARDS

Purpose

One of the most traditional ways to do a quick assessment of a student's vocabulary knowledge is the flash card technique. High-frequency words and those appearing most in print, as well as other high-utility words for specific grade levels, are printed individually on flash cards and shown to students for them to identify. Though some reading researchers argue that flash cards are not a valid assessment tool because the words are presented in isolation instead of in complete sentences and paragraphs, flash cards continue to be used by many master teachers as one way to determine the direction of classroom instruction.

Materials

Obtain a list of high-frequency sight words (*Note:* We provide a copy of the Fry [1980] word list later in the chapter in Figure 9.10). Copy each word, one word each, onto index cards using a bold marker. An alternative is to type the words into a classroom computer and print them in a large font size onto heavy paper stock. Then, cut the words into a uniform flash card size. For recording purposes, you will also need a photocopy/master list of the words for each student in your class.

Figure 9.2 Summary Matrix of Assessments to Measure Vocabulary Development

Name of Assessment Tool	Screening Assessment	Diagnostic Assessment	Progress-Monitoring Assessment	Outcomes Assessment Test	Norm-Referenced Test	Criterion-Referenced	Reliability Evidence	Validity Evidence
Oral Reading Assessment	+	−	−	+	−	+	−	−
Cloze Passages	+	+	+	+	−	+	−	+
Vocabulary Flash Cards	+	−	+	+	−	+	−	−

Key: + can be used for   − not appropriate for

Procedure

"Flash" each card to the student one at a time and ask him or her to name the word. Allow about 5 seconds for the student to identify each word. Circle any unknown or mispronounced words on a copy of the master sheet you are using for that student (simply note the student's name at the top of the photocopy along with the date of testing). After you have shown the flashcards to all students, compile a master list of troublesome words for whole-class or small-group instruction. We highly recommend the "Word Banks" activity found later in this chapter as one way to use this information. The flash cards can be reused periodically to determine if students have learned the words being taught.

In Figure 9.2 we summarize the procedures and instruments we have just discussed for assessing factors associated with vocabulary development. In this *Summary Matrix of Assessments* we provide information about federally related assessment purposes, i.e., *screening, diagnosis, progress-monitoring*, or *outcomes* assessment as well as the type of test or procedure (norm referenced test (NRT) or criterion referenced test (CRT) and psychometric evidence of test or procedure scores including reliability and/or validity evidence, if available.

CONNECTING ASSESSMENT FINDINGS TO TEACHING STRATEGIES

Before discussing phonics and word attack teaching strategies, we have constructed an if-then chart connecting assessment findings to intervention and/or strategy choices. It is our intention to help you select the most appropriate instructional interventions and strategies to meet your students' needs based on assessment data. Teaching strategies described in the next section are listed across the top of the grid in the figure. Areas of vocabulary instruction are listed vertically in the left-hand column. Here is a brief description of each vocabulary instruction area found in the *if-then strategy guide*.

- *Reading vocabulary.* Word is in the student's listening and speaking vocabularies but is not yet recognized in print.
- *Writing vocabulary.* Word is in the student's listening, speaking, and reading vocabularies but is not yet known well enough to be used when writing compositions.
- *Concept/schema.* The student does not comprehend the new word because of a lack of conceptual knowledge related to the word.
- *Technical Vocabulary.* The new word is unknown to the student and is directly related to a content area (i.e., science, social studies, mathematics, etc.).

If-Then Strategy Guide for Vocabulary Instruction

"Then" try these teaching strategies → / "If" the student is ready to learn ↑	Word Walls	Morph Analk	Five-Step	Frayer	Cubing	Vocab Bingo!	SAVOR	Peer Teach	Pers. Word List	Semantic Maps	Making Words	Word Banks	Comp. Grid	Vocab. Cluster	Content Redef.
Reading Vocabulary	+	+	+	–	+	+	*	*	+	+	+	+	–	+	+
Writing Vocabulary	+	+	+	*	–	+	*	+	+	+	+	+	*	+	+
Concept/Schema	–	–	–	+	*	*	+	+	–	+	*	–	+	+	+
Technical Vocabulary	*	+	*	+	*	*	+	+	+	+	–	+	+	+	+
Context	–	*	–	*	–	*	+	*	–	–	–	–	–	+	+
Morphemic Analysis	+	+	–	*	*	–	–	+	*	–	*	*	–	–	–
Sight Words	+	–	+	–	–	+	–	*	+	–	*	+	–	–	–

Key: + Excellent Strategy
  * Adaptable Strategy
  – Unsuitable Strategy

- *Context.* The student has trouble using context clues to figure out the meaning of an unknown word.
- *Morphemic Analysis.* Student lacks sufficient knowledge about word parts such as prefixes, suffixes, and root words—also known as *structural analysis*.
- *Sight Words.* Some common words in print are unknown.

In the next part of this chapter, we offer vocabulary instruction strategies for intervention based on the foregoing assessments.

TEACHING STRATEGIES: HELPING STUDENTS INCREASE THEIR READING VOCABULARIES

Susan Watts (1995) described five attributes of effective vocabulary instruction. You will discover that we have selected teaching activities that fulfill these criteria in this chapter.

- Students should be provided with (a) multiple exposures to new words (b) in a variety of contexts (c) over time. This will help you move new vocabulary from short-term to long-term (permanent) memory.
- Words should be taught within the context of a content area unit or topic, theme, or story. This helps the new vocabulary to find the right "schema home."
- Teachers should help students activate prior knowledge when learning new words.
- Relationships should be emphasized in your lesson between *known* words and concepts and the *new* vocabulary you are introducing. This provides the all-important *scaffolding* for learning.
- Students should be taught to use context clues and reference tools in their reading and writing (i.e., dictionary, thesaurus) for building word knowledge.

WORD WALLS

Purpose

Pat Cunningham (2000) provides us with a wonderful description of a *word wall*: a place where teachers can direct students' attention to high-frequency words, important words in a content unit of study, or useful words for books they are reading. There are many possible types of word walls. In essence, you simply post important words on a section of wall, usually on butcher paper or a pocket chart, and categorize them according to your purpose.

Materials

Most word walls are made from large sheets of butcher paper, or pocket charts, or bulletin boards. They need not be fancy.

Procedure

Begin by making a blank word wall with a section for each letter of the alphabet. Then, introduce two or three words every few days or week. As you introduce them, draw their attention to common word parts, inflectional endings, meanings, and so forth. Be sure to write the words clearly using a dark marker, and make letters large enough for everyone to see. An example is shown in Figure 9.3.

Figure 9.3 **Word Wall** (A Portion of High-Frequency and Other Common Words)

G	H	I	J	K	L
get	him	if	Judy	keep	left
go	his	it	jam		like
girl	he	is	jingle		
	high				

MORPHEMIC ANALYSIS (STRUCTURAL ANALYSIS)

Purpose

Morphemic analysis, also referred to as *structural analysis,* is the process of using one's knowledge of word parts to deduce meanings of unknown words. A *morpheme* is the smallest unit of meaning in a word. There are two types of morphemes: free and bound. A *free morpheme* is a freestanding root or base of any word that cannot be further divided and still have meaning. In the word *farmer, farm* is the root word or free morpheme. The *-er* portion of the word *farmer* is considered to be a bound morpheme. *Bound morphemes* carry meaning but only when attached to a free morpheme. The most common bound morphemes are *prefixes (in-, pre-, mono-), suffixes (-er, -ous, -ology),* and *inflectional endings (-s, -es, -ing, -ed, -est).*

There are several ways that teachers commonly introduce morphemic analysis to students as a way of learning the meaning of new words. Sometimes we use students' knowledge of morphemes to analyze the meaning of a new word by showing a list of similar words having the same morpheme (e.g., words ending in the morpheme *-phobia* or *-er* to decipher meaning). Other times, teachers simply tell students the meanings of new morphemes and let them figure out meanings on their own or in small groups.

Materials

The essential activity for teachers is to research the meanings of morphemes and, in the case of activities involving word family lists, examples of other words having the morphemes to be used. A resource we have found helpful in planning many vocabulary activities is *The Reading Teacher's Book of Lists* (Fry, Kress, & Fountoukidis, 2000).

Procedures

Preselect words to be learned from the reading selection, then do the necessary background research and planning about the morphemes found in the new words. One activity is to construct *word family lists* that help students determine morpheme meanings. For example, a middle-school teacher may decide to focus on the word *claustrophobia*. Her research into the morpheme *-phobia* may lead to the construction of the following list:

claustrophobia

cardiophobia

olfactophobia

telephonophobia

verbaphobia

This activity causes students to use *compare-and-contrast methods* of morphemic analysis. That is, they must look at the unfamiliar word and use their prior knowledge of other words that look like parts of the unfamiliar word to figure out what each word probably means. For example, *cardio-* probably reminds you of *cardiac,* which deals with the heart, and *-phobia* means "fear of." Therefore, *cardiophobia* must mean a fear of heart disease. To use this compare-and-contrast technique with students, first select words that have morphemes that can be compared to other words students are likely to know, then present both the new word and other words that begin or end like the unfamiliar word. Look at the following example from Cooter and Flynt (1996):

Because of my expansive vocabulary, my teacher called me a verbivore.

verbi-	vore
verbal	carnivore
verbose	herbivore
verbalize	omnivore

The teacher would write the sentence on the chalkboard and list below it examples of words that begin and end like the unfamiliar word. Then, through questioning, the teacher would lead students to specify the word's meaning by comparing and contrasting the known words to the unfamiliar one, thus concluding: A verbivore is a person who loves (eats) words.

Another way of using morphemic analysis to help students deduce meaning is to present unfamiliar terms along with explanations of the morphemes that make up the unfamiliar terms. The following procedure may be used as part of an introduction to a new text containing the words listed.

Step 1: Identify the terms that need preteaching.

pro-life

illegal

pro-choice

rearrest

unable

forewarn

Step 2: Along with these terms, write on the board a list of appropriate morphemes and their meanings.

pro = in favor of

il = not

fore = earlier

re = to do again

un = not

Step 3: Engage students in a discussion of what each term means and how the terms are interrelated. When there is confusion or disagreement, direct students to the terms in the text and/or the glossary for verification.

As useful as morphemic analysis can be, Cooter and Flynt (1996) offer a word of caution concerning morphemic analysis:

> Although we encourage the teaching of how to use context and morphemic analysis, we in no way advocate the overuse of these two techniques nor the memorization of lists of morphemes or types of context clues. Teachers who make students memorize common prefixes and suffixes run the risk of having students view the task as an end and not a means to help them become better readers. The story is told of a student who memorized the prefix *trans-* as meaning *across*. Later the same week, the student was reading a science text and was asked what the word *transparent* meant. He replied confidently "a cross mother or father." The point being that all vocabulary instruction in the upper grades should be meaning-oriented, connected to text, functional, and capable of being used in the future. (p. 154)

FIVE-STEP METHOD

Purpose

Smith and Johnson (1980) suggested a five-step direct method of teaching new vocabulary for instant recognition. It uses multiple modalities to help students bring new words into the four vocabularies: listening, speaking, reading, and writing.

Materials

A variety of materials may be used in the five-step method, including a dry-erase board or chalkboard, an overhead projector, flash cards, and different color markers.

Procedure

1.	Seeing	The new vocabulary word is shown on the overhead projector, chalkboard, or dry-erase board in the context of a sentence or (better) a short paragraph.
2.	Listening	The teacher next discusses the word with students and verifies that they understand its meaning.
3.	Discussing	Students are asked to create their own sentences using the new word or, perhaps, to think of a synonym or antonym for the word. This is done orally.
4.	Defining	Students try to create their own definitions for the new word. This is often much more difficult than using it in a sentence and may not even be possible for some words (i.e., *is, the, if,* etc.). Sometimes it is helpful to ask students questions such as "What does this word mean?" or "What does this word do in the sentence?"
5.	Writing	We advocate using word banks or similar strategies in grades K–3. Students, sometimes requiring help, add each new word to their word bank and file it in alphabetical order. List the word in isolation on one side of an index card and in the context of a sentence on the reverse side. Emergent readers may want to draw a picture clue on the word bank card to remind them of the word's meaning.

FRAYER MODEL

Purpose

The Frayer Model (Frayer, Frederick, & Klausmeir, 1969) is a classic strategy that helps students understand new vocabulary and concepts in relation to what is already known. Frayer is especially useful for nonfiction terms—especially in the sciences—because it presents essential and nonessential information related to the term, as well as examples and nonexamples.

Materials

You will need a blank Frayer Model form on a transparency and an overhead projector for demonstration purposes. Students will need paper and pencils for notetaking.

Procedure

The teacher presents or helps students determine essential and nonessential information about a concept, find examples and nonexamples of the concept, and recognize coordinate and subordinate relationships of the concept. This classification procedure can be done as a group, in dyads, or individually. Figure 9.4 is an example for the concept of mammals.

CUBING: THE DIE IS CAST!

Purpose

Cubing (Cowan & Cowan, 1980) is a postreading activity requiring students to analyze, discuss, and write about important new terms. By so doing, they activate prior knowledge or schemata that relate to the new term, which in turn helps the new information to become part of their long-term memory.

Materials

You will need a large foam or wooden cube covered with Con-Tact® paper. On each side of the cube is written a different direction or question. Here are some examples that may be used for the term wheelchair:

1. Describe what it looks like.
2. What is it similar to or different from?

Figure 9.4 Frayer Model: Mammals

Concept: MAMMALS

Essential Information or Attributes:	**Examples:**
1. higher-order vertebrates	1. dogs
2. nourish young with milk from mammary glands	2. humans
3. warm blooded	3. monkeys
4. have skin covered with hair	4. whales
Nonessential Information or Attributes:	**Nonexamples:**
1. size of the mammal	1. spiders
2. number of young born	2. fish
3. where the mammal lives (i.e., water, land, etc.)	3. reptiles

3. What else does it make you think of?
4. What is it made of?
5. How can it be used?
6. Where are you likely to find one?

Once the cube is rolled and the direction facing the class or group is seen, each student is given a set number of minutes to record his or her answer. All six sides of the cube can be used in the activity or, if you prefer, only a few. Once the cubing has ended, students can share their responses with the class or in small groups.

VOCABULARY BINGO!

Purpose

Vocabulary Bingo! (Spencer, 1997) is a whole-group word review activity in the format of the popular game "Bingo." This activity is an especially useful review for students learning English as a second language (ESL) and students in language enrichment programs, as well as for students whose first language is English.

Materials

For all students, make *Vocabulary Bingo!* boards on which you have printed new words learned in reading and writing activities during the year. The *Vocabulary Bingo!* cards can all be the same or can differ from one another, depending on the size of the group and the abilities of the learners. These words can be chosen from a classroom word bank, if one is being kept. For each word found on the cards, you will also need definitions written on slips of paper for the "caller" to read aloud during the game.

Procedure

Unlike traditional "Bingo" games in which participants cover spaces on their boards when a number such as *B23* is called, students playing *Vocabulary Bingo!* cover board spaces upon which are printed review vocabulary words matching the definitions that are read aloud by a caller. When all spaces in a row are covered, they call out "Bingo!" An example of a *Vocabulary Bingo!* card is shown in Figure 9.5.

Figure 9.5 Vocabulary Bingo! Card

VOCABULARY BINGO!				
silo	desert	umpire	dromedary	elevator
aviatrix	conifer	photography	precious	caravan
financier	meteoric	flank	declaration	cleats
maladjusted	payee	odoriferous	seizure	oasis
biannual	proceed	semicircle	humorous	proverb

SUBJECT AREA VOCABULARY REINFORCEMENT ACTIVITY

Purpose

The Subject Area Vocabulary Reinforcement Activity (SAVOR) (Stieglitz & Stieglitz, 1981) is an excellent postreading vocabulary learning procedure. As its name implies, SAVOR is intended for use with factual readings. Students combine research and rereading skills to identify similarities and differences between new terms.

Materials

Construct a SAVOR grid on a bulletin board or worksheet to be photocopied. Base it on a topic being studied in science, social studies, mathematics, health, history, or another content area. Make a content analysis of the unit of study and select new terms, to be listed in the left-hand column of the SAVOR grid, and characteristics related to the terms, to be listed across the top row. An example is shown in Figure 9.6.

Procedure

SAVOR is intended to be used as a postreading activity to reinforce learning of new vocabulary. After students have completed their initial reading of the subject matter text, introduce the SAVOR grid bulletin board or photocopied worksheet. Discuss how to complete each grid space with either a plus (+) or minus (−), based on whether the term has the trait listed across the top of the grid. As with all minilessons, the teacher should first model the thinking process he or she is using to determine whether to put a plus or minus in the space provided. In Figure 9.6, we show an example of a SAVOR grid that was completed by children in a school in southern Texas as they studied the solar system.

PEER TEACHING

Purpose

An activity that has been proven to be effective with ESL students is called peer teaching (Johnson & Steele, 1996). It is considered to be a *generative strategy,* or one that is student-initiated and monitored and can be used in different situations. Peer teaching has

Figure 9.6 SAVOR Grid: Solar System

Planets	Inner planet	Outer planet	Made up of gas	Has more than one moon	Longer revolution than Earth's 365 days	Has rings	Has been visited by a space probe	Stronger gravity than Earth's
Venus	+	−	−	−	−	−	+	−
Neptune	−	+	+	+	+	?	+	+
Saturn	−	+	+	+	+	+	+	+
Mercury	+	−	−	−	−	−	+	−

individual students choosing from the reading selection a word that they feel is new and important. Next, one child teaches his or her term to another student, then vice versa.

Materials

Materials needed include only a reading selection to be shared with the whole group and the kind of supplies usually found in a writing center for students to use as they wish. It is also helpful to list several ways of teaching new vocabulary words to others, like those techniques found in this chapter that you commonly use with the students in your class.

Procedure

First, conduct a one- or two-session minilesson in which you model how you may choose a word from the reading selection that seems to be important to understanding what the author is saying. As an example, in Betsy Byars's Newberry Award–winning book *The Summer of the Swans* (1970), the main character, Sara, has a "grudging tolerance" of her Aunt Willie. Because this is important to understanding Sara and her feelings, you may select "grudging tolerance" as a term to teach someone reading the book. Next, model how you would choose one of the common strategies you use in class (on a list you post for all to see) and demonstrate how you would plan to teach your term to another. Finally, ask someone to role-play with you as you teach "grudging tolerance."

PERSONAL WORD LISTS

Purpose

Most words are learned through repeated encounters in a meaningful context in spoken and written forms. All too often, however, when students come to a word they do not know, they simply run to the dictionary or to someone else for a quick definition instead of using sentence or passage context to figure out for themselves the word's meaning. While, certainly, we want students to develop dictionary skills, the first line of attack for gaining word meaning should be sentence or passage context. Personal word lists, as described in this section, have been around elementary and secondary classrooms for a very long time and have recently found success with ESL learners (Johnson & Steele, 1996). A personal word list is a structured way of helping students develop the habit of using context to determine vocabulary meaning and to permanently fix the vocabulary in long-term memory.

Materials

You will need multiple blank copies of the personal word list, as shown in Figure 9.7, and a transparency version for demonstrations on the classroom overhead projector.

Procedure

Distribute blank copies of the personal word list sheet for students to review as you explain its function. Using a passage read recently by the class, model two or three examples of how you would complete the form for words you found in the passage that seemed important. Next, do a guided practice exercise with the whole group in which you provide several more words from the passage. Ask students to complete the form for each word, and have volunteers share what they found with the class. Once students seem secure with the personal word list form, ask them to make several new entries with words of their own choosing in the next reading assignment. This will serve as a kind of individual practice exercise. Further use of the personal word list will depend on your class needs and how well you feel it works with your students. An example of a personal word list for the book *Lincoln* (Donald, 1995) is shown in Figure 9.7.

Figure 9.7   Personal Word List: *Lincoln* (Donald, 1995)

New Word	What I think it means . . .	Clues from the book or passage . . .	Dictionary definition (only when I needed to look)
1. abolitionists	people against slavery	John Brown was called one and was the leader of the Harper's Ferry raid.	
2. Republican	the party that Lincoln joined and ran for President	Lincoln went to the first meeting in 1855 (page 187) and later became its candidate in 1860.	
3. dispatches	a telegraph	Lincoln and Lee sent dispatches to people during the Civil War.	a message sent with speed

SEMANTIC MAPS

Purpose

Semantic maps are useful in tying together new vocabulary with prior knowledge and related terms (Johnson & Pearson, 1984; Monroe, 1998). Semantic maps are essentially a kind of "schema blueprint" in which students map what is stored in their brain about a topic and related concepts. Semantic maps help students relate new information to schemata already in the brain, integrate new information, and restructure existing information for greater clarity (Yopp & Yopp, 1996). Further, for students having learning problems, using semantic maps prior to reading a selection has also proven to promote better story recall than traditional methods (Sinatra, Stahl-Gemake, & Berg, 1984).

Materials

Writing materials are the only supplies needed.

Procedure

There are many ways to introduce semantic mapping to students, but the first time around you will likely want to use a structured approach. One way is to introduce semantic maps through something we call "wacky webbing." The idea is to take a topic familiar to all, such as the name of one's home state, and portray it in the center of the web, inside an oval. Major categories related to the theme are connected to the central concept using either bold lines or double lines. Details that relate to the major categories are connected using single lines. Figure 9.8 shows a semantic web for the topic "Tennessee."

Semantic webs can also be constructed that relate to a story or chapter book the students are reading. In Figure 9.9, we share one example of a semantic web from a story in the book *Golden Tales: Myths, Legends, and Folktales From Latin America* (Delacre, 1996).

MAKING WORDS

Purpose

Making Words (Cunningham & Cunningham, 1992) is a word-learning strategy that may fit just as well in our chapter on phonics. It is a strategy that helps children improve their

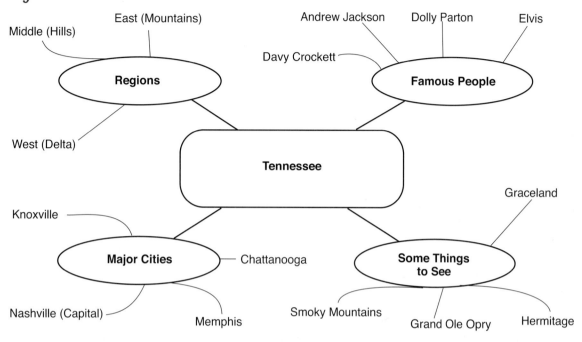

Figure 9.8 Tennessee Semantic Web

Middle (Hills)

East (Mountains)

Regions

West (Delta)

Andrew Jackson   Dolly Parton   Elvis

Davy Crockett

Famous People

Tennessee

Knoxville

Major Cities

Chattanooga

Nashville (Capital)

Memphis

Graceland

Some Things to See

Smoky Mountains

Grand Ole Opry   Hermitage

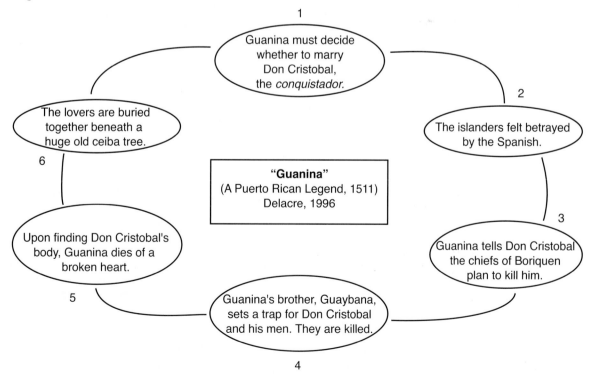

Figure 9.9 Semantic Web: "Guanina"

1
Guanina must decide whether to marry Don Cristobal, the *conquistador*.

The lovers are buried together beneath a huge old ceiba tree.

6

"Guanina"
(A Puerto Rican Legend, 1511)
Delacre, 1996

Upon finding Don Cristobal's body, Guanina dies of a broken heart.

5

Guanina's brother, Guaybana, sets a trap for Don Cristobal and his men. They are killed.

4

2
The islanders felt betrayed by the Spanish.

3
Guanina tells Don Cristobal the chiefs of Boriquen plan to kill him.

255

phonetic understanding of words through invented or "temporary" spellings (Reutzel & Cooter, 2000) while also increasing their repertoire of vocabulary words they can recognize in print. Making Words will be a familiar strategy for anyone who has ever played the crossword board game "Scrabble."

Materials

You will need a pocket chart, large index cards, and markers.

Procedure

In the Making Words activity, students are given a number of letters with which to make words. They begin by making two- or three-letter words using the letters during a set amount of time, then progress to making words having more letters until they finally arrive at the teacher's target word that uses all of the letters. This final word can be the main word to be taught for the day, but the other words discovered during the activity may also be new for some students. By manipulating the letters to make words of two, three, four, and more letters using temporary spellings, students have an opportunity to practice their phonemic awareness skills. Making words is recommended as a 15-minute activity when used with first and second graders. In figures 9.10 and 9.11, we summarize and adapt the steps in

Figure 9.10   Planning a "Making Words" Lesson

1. Choose the final word to be emphasized in the lesson. It should be a key word from a reading selection, fiction or nonfiction, to be read by the class, or it may be of particular interest to the group. Be sure to select a word that has enough vowels and/or one that fits letter-sound patterns useful for most children at their developmental stage in reading and writing. For illustrative purposes, in these instructions we will use the word *thunder* that was suggested by Cunningham and Cunningham (1992).
2. Make a list of shorter words that can be spelled using the main word to be learned. For the word *thunder,* one could derive the following words: *red, Ted, Ned/den/end* (Note: these all use the same letters), *her, hut, herd, turn, hunt, hurt, under, hunted, turned, thunder.*

   From the You Were Able To list, select 12–15 words that include such aspects of written language as a) words that can be used to emphasize a certain kind of pattern, b) big and little words, c) words that can be made with the same letters in different positions (as with *Ned, end, den*), d) a proper noun, if possible, to remind students about using capital letters, and especially e) words that students already have in their listening vocabularies.
3. Write all of these words on large index cards and order them from the smallest to the largest words. Also, write each of the individual letters found in the key word for the day on large index cards (make two sets of these).
4. Reorder the words one more time to group them according to letter patterns and/or to demonstrate how shifting around letters can form new words. Store the two sets of large single-letter cards in two envelopes—one for the teacher, and one for children participating during the modeling activity.
5. Store the word stacks in envelopes and note on the outside of each the words/patterns to be emphasized during the lesson. Also, note definitions you can use with the children to help them discover the words you desire. For example, spell *Den* is a three-letter word that is the name of the room in some people's homes where they like to watch television. "See if you can spell *den.*"

Source: Based on "Making Words: Enhancing the Invented Spelling-Decoding Connection" by P. M. Cunningham and J. Cunningham, 1992, *The Reading Teacher, 46*(2), 106–115. Used with permission of the International Reading Association.

Figure 9.11 Teaching a "Making Words" Lesson

1. Place the large single letters from the key word in the pocket chart or along the chalkboard ledge.
2. For modeling purposes, the first time you use Making Words, select one of the students to be the "passer" and ask that child to pass the large single letters to other designated children.
3. Hold up and name each of the letter cards and have students selected to participate in the modeling exercise respond by holding up their matching card.
4. Write the numeral 2 (or 3, if there are no two-letter words in this lesson) on the board. Next, tell the student "volunteers" the desired word and its definition. Then, tell the student volunteers to put together two (or three) of their letters to form the desired word.
5. Continue directing the students to make more words using the letter cards until you have helped them discover all but the final key word (the one that uses all the letters). Ask the student volunteers if they can guess the key word. If not, ask the remainder of the class if anyone can guess it. If no one is able to do so, offer students a meaning clue (e.g., "I am thinking of a word with _____ letters that means . . .").
6. As a guided practice activity, repeat these steps the next day with the whole group using a new word.

Source: Based on "Making Words: Enhancing the Invented Spelling-Decoding Connection" by P. M. Cunningham and J. Cunningham, 1992, *The Reading Teacher, 46*(2), 106–115. Used with permission of the International Reading Association.

Figure 9.12 Making Words: Additional Examples

Lesson Using One Vowel:

Letter cards: u k n r s t

Words to make: us, nut, rut, sun, sunk, runs, ruts/rust, tusk, stun, stunk, trunk, *trunks* (the key word)

You can sort for . . . rhymes, "s" pairs (run, runs; rut, ruts; trunk, trunks)

Lesson Using Big Words:

Letter cards: a a a e i b c h l l p t

Words to make: itch, able, cable, table, batch, patch, pitch, petal, label, chapel, capital, capable, alphabet, *alphabetical* (the key word)

You can sort for . . . el, le, al, -itch, -atch

Source: Based on "Making Words: Enhancing the Invented Spelling-Decoding Connection" by P. M. Cunningham and J. Cunningham, 1992, *The Reading Teacher, 46*(2), 106–115. Used with permission of the International Reading Association.

planning and teaching a Making Words lesson as suggested by Cunningham and Cunningham (1992). Figure 9.12 provides details necessary for making two more Making Words lessons suggested by Cunningham and Cunningham (1992) that may be useful for helping students learn the procedure.

WORD BANKS

Purpose

It is important for students to learn to recognize a number of words on sight to facilitate the decoding process. Many words carry little meaning (*the, of*, and *a*) but provide the "glue" of language that helps us represent thoughts. One question for teachers is how to go about helping students increase the numbers of words they can recognize immediately on sight. *Word banks* are used to help students collect and review these "sight words." Word banks also can be used as personal dictionaries. A word bank is simply a student-constructed box, file, or notebook in which newly discovered words are stored and reviewed.

Materials

In the early grades, teachers often collect small shoe boxes from local stores to serve as word banks. The children are asked at the beginning of the year to decorate the boxes in order to make them their own. In the upper grades, more formal-looking word banks are used. Notebooks or recipe boxes are generally selected. Alphabetic dividers can also be used at all levels to facilitate the quick location of word bank words. In addition, use of alphabetic dividers in the early grades helps students rehearse and reinforce knowledge of alphabetical order. Figure 9.13 shows an example of a word bank.

Figure 9.13 A Word Bank

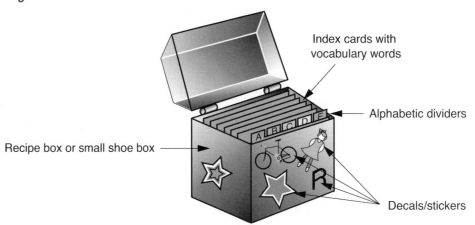

Index cards with vocabulary words

Alphabetic dividers

Recipe box or small shoe box

Decals/stickers

A word bank is a box in which children keep/file new words they are learning. The words are usually written in isolation on one side of the card, and in a sentence on the back of the card (usually with a picture clue).

Example:

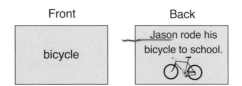

Front — bicycle

Back — Jason rode his bicycle to school.

Source: From *Teaching Children to Read: Putting the Pieces Together,* 4th ed., by D. Ray Reutzel, and Robert B. Cooter, Jr., 2004, Upper Saddle River, NJ: Merrill/Prentice Hall.

Procedure

Once students have constructed word banks, the next issue for the teacher is helping students decide which words should be included and from what sources. At least four sources can be considered for sight word selection and inclusion in word banks (Reutzel & Cooter, 2000): basal reader sight word lists; "key vocabulary" words that students have self-selected for learning (Ashton-Warner, 1963); "discovery" words (i.e., words that are discovered during class discussions); and "function words" (words that supply structure to sentences but carry little or no meaning, such as *with, were, what, is, of*). A list of high-frequency sight words is supplied in Figure 9.14.

COMPARISON GRIDS FOR CONTENT AREA VOCABULARY

Purpose

In content area instruction, it is important to try and create conceptual bridges between new vocabulary and their meanings and their relationships to other concepts (Harmon, Hedrick, & Fox, 2000). Comparison grids can create a kind of two-dimensional framework for students that greatly simplifies abstract thinking.

Materials

All you will need is a simple grid that has one set of terms along the left-hand column and the vocabulary you want students to compare and contrast along the top row. See Figure 9.15 for an example adapted from Harmon et al. (2000) for the new vocabulary terms *executive, legislative,* and *judicial*.

VOCABULARY CLUSTER

Purpose

It is especially important that students who struggle with reading use the context of a passage with vocabulary they know, to understand new words in print. English-language learners (ELLs) and students who have language deficiencies due to poverty are two large groups of students who benefit from direct instruction of this kind (Peregoy & Boyle, 2001). With the "vocabulary cluster" strategy, students are helped to read a passage, gather context clues, and then predict the meaning of a new word targeted by you, the teacher, for learning.

Materials

You will need multiple copies of a text students are to read, an overhead transparency and projector, and erasable marking pens for transparencies.

Procedure

First, select vocabulary you want to teach from a text the students will be reading. This could be a poem, a song, a novel, a nonfiction textbook, or other appropriate reading. Next, gather the students around the overhead projector and draw their attention to the transparency you have prepared. The transparency should contain an excerpt from the text with sufficient context to help students predict what the unknown word may be. The target word should have been deleted and replaced with a blank line, much the same as with a cloze passage (discussed earlier in this chapter). In Figure 9.16 you will see a passage prepared in this way along with a vocabulary cluster supporting the new

Figure 9.14 Instant Words

Teach these words any way you can. Teaching suggestions might include: 1. Flashcards for flashing and sorting. 2. World Walls. 3. Pocket charts for short sentences or stories using Instant Words. 4. Teacher written cooperative stories written on the chalk board. 5. Spelling lessons. 6. Games such as Bingo or board games. 7. Lots of easy reading. 8. Give a copy of this sheet to the student for home study.

Test these words by asking the students to read them instantly. If they can cross to the word. Test each student beginning, mid-ear, and end-year.

First Hundred				Second Hundred				Third Hundred			
1-25	26-50	51-75	76-100	101-125	126-150	151-175	176-200	201-225	226-250	251-275	276-300
the	or	will	number	over	say	set	try	high	saw	important	miss
of	one	up	no	new	great	put	kind	every	left	until	idea
and	had	other	way	sound	where	end	hand	near	don't	children	enough
a	by	about	could	take	help	does	picture	add	few	side	eat
to	words	out	people	only	through	another	again	food	while	feet	face
in	but	many	my	little	much	well	change	between	along	car	watch
is	not	then	than	work	before	large	off	own	might	mile	far
you	what	them	first	know	line	must	play	below	close	night	Indian
that	all	these	water	place	right	big	spell	country	something	walk	really
it	were	so	been	year	too	even	air	plant	seem	white	almost
he	we	some	call	live	mean	such	away	last	next	sea	let
was	when	her	who	me	old	because	animal	school	hard	began	above
for	your	would	am	back	any	turn	house	father	open	grow	girl
on	can	make	its	give	same	here	point	keep	example	took	sometimes
are	said	like	now	most	tell	why	page	tree	begin	river	mountain
as	there	him	find	very	boy	ask	letter	never	life	four	cut
with	use	into	long	after	follow	went	mother	start	always	carry	young
his	an	time	down	thing	came	men	answer	city	those	state	talk
they	each	has	day	our	want	read	found	earth	both	once	soon
I	which	look	did	just	show	need	study	eye	paper	book	list
at	she	two	get	name	also	land	still	light	together	hear	song
be	do	more	come	good	around	different	learn	thought	got	stop	being
this	how	write	made	sentence	farm	home	should	head	group	without	leave
have	their	go	may	man	three	us	America	under	often	second	family
from	if	see	part	think	small	move	world	story	run	later	it's

Source: Copyright 1999 by Edward Fry.

260

Figure 9.15 Comparison Grid: Branches of Government

Directions: Decide which of the words or phrases in the left-hand column can be used to describe each of the three branches of government. Write "yes" or "no" in each block, and be prepared to share your ideas with a partner.

	Executive	Legislative	Judicial
Elected			
Veto power			
President			
Judges			
Representatives			
Senators			
Commander-in-chief			
Constitutional authority			
Checks and balances			
Amendment			
Declares war			
Protects and defends the Constitution			

word to be learned. This example is based on the book *Honey Baby Sugar Child* by Alice Faye Duncan (2005) written as a read aloud book for young children. Through discussion, you will lead students into predicting what the unknown word may be. If the word is not already in students' listening vocabulary, as with ELL students or those with otherwise limited vocabularies, then you will be able to introduce the new word quite well using the context and synonyms provided in the vocabulary cluster.

CONTEXTUAL REDEFINITION FOR TECHNICAL VOCABULARY

Purpose

While there has been some debate over the years about the extent to which context should be emphasized, it is clear that learning from context is a very important component of vocabulary acquisition (Adams, 1990, p. 150). An excellent method of introducing terminology in context, such as that found in informational readings, as well as demonstrating to students why they should use context whenever possible to figure out unfamiliar words, is a strategy called *contextual redefinition* (Cunningham, Cunningham, & Arthur, 1981).

Materials

This is an activity that can be conducted mainly at the chalkboard, overhead projector, and/or by using teacher-constructed activity sheets.

Figure 9.16 Vocabulary Cluster based on *Honey Baby Sugar Child* (Duncan, 2005).: Target word "twirl"

You make me laugh.

We jump and _____.

We run in the green, green grass.

And when the clouds rush in twirl

on a rainy day,

yo smile is my sunshine. (Duncan, 2005, p. 7–8)

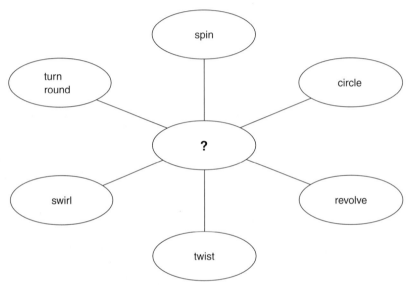

Source: *Honey Baby Sugar Child* by A.F. Duncan and illustrated by S. Keeter, 2005, New York, Simon & Schuster Children's Publishing. Used with permission.

Procedure

The steps in this procedure, as adapted by Cooter and Flynt (1996), follow:

Step 1: Select five or six terms that are unfamiliar or probably known by only a few students in the class. Introduce the topic and display the new terms on the chalkboard or overhead. Ask each student or pair of students to predict a brief definition for each term. Encourage students to guess at word meanings, reminding them that the goal is to try to come up with logical ideas and not to worry about being "right." After the students have had an opportunity to discuss probable definitions, call for individuals to share their ideas and write them on the chalkboard or overhead projector transparency. Briefly discuss why the students were unable to do much more than guess at the word's meanings.

Step 2: Next, tell the students that you have these same words written in sentences or short paragraphs and that you want them to read each passage to see if they want to revise their original guesses. Be sure to present each word in a contextually rich sentence. During the ensuing discussion, encourage students to explain why they think the word means what they now think it means. Record varying responses next to each term as they occur.

Step 3:   Finally, if there are differences, have students find the word in either the text or the glossary and read its definition. Then have students copy the finalized sentences in their notebooks or journals.

Contextual redefinition provides students with opportunities to share their skills in using context and can be helpful in promoting independent use of context clues. Teachers find it an invigorating means for preteaching terms and showing that the glossary is not the first tool readers can use in figuring out the meaning of new words: context usually is.

Selected References

Adams, M. J. (1990a). *Beginning to read: Thinking and learning about print.* Cambridge MA: MIT Press.

Ashton-Warner, S. (1963). *Teacher.* New York: Simon & Schuster.

Beck, I. L., McCaslin, E. S., & McKeown, M. G. (1980). *The rationale and design of a program to teach vocabulary to fourth grade students* (LRDC No. 1980-25). Pittsburgh: University of Pittsburgh, Learning Research and Development Center.

Bradley, C. A. (1988, April). *The relationship between mathematics language facility and mathematics achievement among junior high school students.* Paper presented at the Annual Meeting of the American Educational Research Association, New Orleans, LA. (Educational Resources Information Center No. ED 293 727)

Brett, A., Rothlein, L., & Hurley, M. (1996). Vocabulary acquisition from listening to stories and explanations of target words. *Elementary School Journal, 96*(4), 415–422.

Byars, B. (1970). *The summer of the swans.* New York: Puffin Books.

Cattell, J. M. (1885). Veber die zeit der erkennung und bennenung von schriftzeichen, bildem und farben. *Philosophische Studien, 2,* 635–650.

Clark, E. (1993). *The lexicon in acquisition.* Cambridge, United Kingdom: Cambridge University Press.

Cooter, R. B., & Flynt, E. S. (1996). *Teaching reading in the content areas: Developing content literacy for all students.* Columbus, OH: Merrill, an imprint of Prentice Hall.

Cowan, E., & Cowan, G. (1980). *Writing.* New York: John Wiley & Sons.

Cox, C., & Boyd-Batstone, P. (1997). *Crossroads: Literature and language in culturally and linguistically diverse classrooms.* Columbus, OH: Merrill/Prentice Hall.

Cunningham, J., Cunningham, P., & Arthur, S. V. (1981). *Middle and secondary school reading.* New York: Longman.

Cunningham, P. M. (2000). *Phonics they use* (3rd ed.). New York: Addison-Wesley.

Cunningham, P. M., & Cunningham, J. (1992). Making words: Enhancing the invented spelling-decoding connection. *Reading Teacher, 46*(2), 106–115.

Delacre, L. (1996). *Golden tales: Myths, legends, and folktales from Latin America.* New York: Scholastic.

Donald, D. H. (1995). *Lincoln.* New York: Simon & Schuster.

Flynt, E. S., & Cooter, R. B., Jr. (2001). *The Flynt/Cooter Reading Inventory for the Classroom* (4th ed.). Columbus, OH: Merrill/Prentice Hall.

Frayer, D., Frederick, W. C., & Klausmeir, H. J. (1969). *A schema for testing the level of concept mastery* (Working Paper No. 16). Madison: University of Wisconsin, Wisconsin Research and Development Center for Cognitive Learning.

Fry, E. B. (1980). The new instant word list. *The Reading Teacher, 34,* 284–289.

Fry, E. B., Kress, J. E., & Fountoukidis, D .L. (2000). *The reading teacher's book of lists* (4th ed.). San Francisco Jossey-Bass.

Harmon, J. M., Hedrick, W. B., & Fox, E. A. (2000). A content analysis of vocabulary instruction in social studies textbooks for grades K–8. *The Elementary School Journal, 100*(3), 253–271.

Irwin, J. L. (1990). *Vocabulary knowledge: Guidelines for instruction. What research says to the teacher.* Washington, DC: National Education Association. (ERIC Document Reproduction Service No. ED 319 001)

Jenkins, J. R., Matlock, B., & Slocum, T. A. (1989). Two approaches to vocabulary instruction: The teaching of individual word meanings and practice in deriving word meaning from context. *Reading Research Quarterly, 24*(2), 215–235.

Johnson, A. P., & Rasmussen, J. B. (1998). Classifying and super word web: Two strategies to improve productive vocabulary. *Journal of Adolescent & Adult Literacy, 42*(3), 204–209.

Johnson, D. D. (2001). *Vocabulary in the elementary and middle school.* Boston, MA: Allyn & Bacon.

Johnson, D. D., & Pearson, P. D. (1984). *Teaching reading vocabulary.* New York: Holt, Rinehart & Winston.

Johnson, D., & Steele, V. (1996). So many words, so little time: Helping college ESL learners acquire vocabulary strategies. *Journal of Adolescent & Adult Literacy, 39*(5), 348–357.

Krashen, S. (1993). *The power of reading: Insights from the research.* Englewood, CO: Libraries Unlimited.

May, F. B., & Rizzardi, L. (2002). *Reading as communication* (6th ed.). Upper Saddle River, NJ: Merrill/Prentice Hall.

Meddaugh, S. (1992). *Martha speaks.* Boston: Houghton Mifflin.

Monroe, E. E. (1998). Using graphic organizers to teach vocabulary: Does available research inform mathematics instruction? *Education, 118*(4), 538–542.

Nagy, W. E., & Herman, P. A. (1984). *Limitations of vocabulary instruction* (Technical Report No. 326). Champaign: University of Illinois Center for the Study of Reading.

Nagy, W. E., Herman, P. A., & Anderson, R. C. (1985). Learning words from context. *Reading Research Quarterly, 20*(2), 233–253.

National Center for Educational Statistics. (1999, September). *NAEP 1998: Writing report card for the nation and the states.* Washington, DC: U.S. Department of Education.

National Institute of Child Health and Human Development. (2000). *The Report of the National Reading Panel: Teaching children to read: An evidence-based assessment of the scientific research literature on reading and its implications for reading instruction: Reports of the subgroups.* Washington, DC: U.S. Government Printing Office.

Partnership for Reading. (2001). *Put reading first: Helping your child learn to read.* Washington, DC: The Partnership for Reading.

Paulsen, G. (1987). *Hatchet.* New York: Bradbury Press.

Peregoy, S. F., & Boyle, O. F. (2001). *Reading, writing, & learning in ESL.* New York: Longman.

Rekrut, M. D. (1996). Effective vocabulary instruction. *High School Journal, 80*(1), 66–78.

Reutzel, D. R., & Cooter, R. B., Jr. (2004). *Teaching children to read: Putting the pieces together* (4th ed.). Upper Saddle River, NJ: Merrill/Prentice Hall.

Rowling, J. K. (1997). *Harry Potter and the sorcerer's stone.* New York: Scholastic.

Rupley, W. H., Logan, J. W., & Nichols, W. D. (1999). Vocabulary instruction in a balanced reading program. *The Reading Teacher, 52*(4), 336–347.

Ryder, R. J., & Graves, M. F. (1994). *Reading and learning in content areas.* Columbus, OH: Merrill.

Silverstein, S. (1974). *Where the sidewalk ends.* New York: HarperCollins.

Sinatra, R., Stahl-Gemake, J., & Berg, D. (1984). Improving reading comprehension of disabled readers through semantic mapping. *The Reading Teacher, 38,* 22–29.

Smith, F. (1987). *Insult to intelligence.* Portsmouth, NH: Heinemann Educational Books.

Smith, R. J., & Johnson, D. D. (1980). *Teaching children to read.* Reading, MA: Addison-Wesley.

Spencer, K. M. (1997). Vocabulary Bingo!: A language review activity. Unpublished manuscript, Texas Christian University.

Stahl, S. (1986). Three principles of effective vocabulary instruction. *Journal of Reading, 29*(7), 662–668.

Stieglitz, E. L., & Stieglitz, V. S. (1981). SAVOR the word to reinforce vocabulary in the content areas. *Journal of Reading, 25,* 46–51.

Watts, S. (1995). Vocabulary instruction during reading lessons in six classrooms. *Journal of Reading Behavior, 27,* 399–424.

Wixson, K. K. (1986). Vocabulary instruction and children's comprehension of basal stories. *Reading Research Quarterly, 21*(3), 317–329.

Yopp, H. K., & Yopp, R. H. (1996). *Literature-based reading activities.* Boston: Allyn & Bacon.

Chapter 10

Reading Comprehension: Focus on the *Reader*

"Gather around, boys and girls." Mrs. Jensen spoke gently, "I have a new book to read to you today. How many of you know the story of *Peter Cottontail*?"

"Teacher, I know what a cottontail is, it's a tiny bunny with a tail that looks like a cotton ball," exclaims Julianna.

"Very good thinking, Julianna, but this story isn't really about a bunny. It is a story about something that all little boys and girls need to learn. Have any of you ever disobeyed your parents? Can you share with us what it was you did and what happened when you disobeyed?"

"Oh, once my Mom told me not to ride my scooter off jumps or I would wreck and hurt myself. I didn't listen and did it anyway. One day I made a big jump off a wooden ramp at Georgio's house and landed sideways and fell over. I put my hand out to stop from falling and broke my wrist real bad. It had to be in a cast for 6 weeks," explained José.

"Well that is a very good example, José. Our story today tells us about a little rabbit named Peter, who always liked to stop in the best garden in the country for a snack on the way home from school: Mr. McGregor's garden. And Mr. McGregor didn't like having bunnies in his garden patch eating his prize vegetables. Peter's mom bought him some nice new clothes and reminded him *not* to go into Mr. McGregor's garden. What do you think might have happened?"

"Before we read, boys and girls," intones Mrs. Jensen, "let's think of some questions we might ask about Peter's adventure in Mr. McGregor's garden. Turn to your neighbor on the rug and talk about one question you might want to have answered as we read the story of *Peter Cottontail*. I will give you 2 minutes to think of a question. Then, when you are ready, fold your arms so that I know you have a question to ask. When everyone is ready, I will call on one person in your pair to tell me your question. I will write the questions on this large piece of chart paper. I'll leave a space for filling in the answers as we read," Mrs. Jensen.

Mrs. Jensen skillfully introduced this age-old tale, helping children connect to experiences they or others have had when disobeying their parents' instructions. By asking the right questions, Mrs. Jensen helped her students activate the appropriate prior knowledge related to the message of the story, disobedience, rather than activating knowledge related to the topic, rabbits, to help guide their comprehension of the text. To motivate children to read with a purpose, Mrs. Jensen invited the children through collaboration with a partner to choose questions they would like to have answered by reading the story. As they read, they will discuss the answers to the questions that are displayed on the chart paper.

This is an excellent way to help children begin to monitor their understanding of a text. They soon realize that reading should result in getting answers to their own questions and that they should monitor whether they are getting the answers to their questions as they go along in reading. Mrs. Jensen is one of those rare primary grade teachers who help students understand from the outset of reading instruction that comprehension is the ultimate goal!

Background Briefing for Teachers

Reading comprehension has recently been defined by two major national review panels: (a) *The National Reading Panel* (National Institute of Child Health and Human Development, 2000) and (b) *The RAND Reading Study Group* (2001). The National Reading Panel defined reading comprehension as follows: "Comprehension is a complex process . . . often viewed as 'the essence of reading.' Reading comprehension is . . . intentional thinking during which meaning is constructed through interactions between text and reader. Meaning resides in the intentional, problem-solving, thinking processes of the reader that occur during an interchange with a text. The content of meaning is influenced by the text and by the reader's prior knowledge and experience that are brought to bear on it. Reading comprehension is the construction of the meaning of a written text through a reciprocal interchange of ideas between the reader and the message in a particular text" (pp. 4–5).

By way of comparison, the RAND Reading Study Group (2001) defined reading comprehension (Sweet & Snow, 2003, p. 1) "as the process of simultaneously extracting and constructing meaning." Within this definition, the dual challenges of "figuring out how print represents words (the text)" and "how to integrate new meanings with old information (prior and new knowledge)" are acknowledged. The act of comprehending entails four essential elements: (a) the reader, (b) the text, (c) the activity, and (d) the sociocultural context. The first three essential elements of reading comprehension occur within the fourth essential element of reading comprehension—the sociocultural context of the school classroom, the home, and other social and cultural situations.

Because reading comprehension is a complex process and because it is also the ultimate goal of reading instruction, we devote two full chapters in this revision of our strategies book to the study of reading comprehension. In chapter 10, we discuss the first essential element of reading comprehension—the reader or the one doing the comprehending. In chapter 11, we discuss the second essential element of reading comprehension—the text or the object to be comprehended. Within the discussion of *the reader* and *the text* in these two chapters, we simultaneously discuss cognitive comprehension strategies and sociocultural contexts that are supported by scientific research evidence for improving children's reading comprehension of texts.

The Reader

The first essential element of reading comprehension in the Rand Reading Study Group's (2001) definition of reading comprehension is *the reader*. In 1978–1979, Durkin made what was at the time a startling discovery—U.S. elementary schoolchildren were not receiving much instruction on how to comprehend what they read. The National Reading Panel (National Institute of Child Health and Human Development, 2000), in its extensive review of research on teaching reading comprehension, found a paucity of research focused on comprehension instruction in the early grades (K–2). Taylor, Pearson, Clark, and

Walpole (1999) reported that only 16% of teachers emphasized comprehension as a part of primary grade reading instruction. Neuman similarly observed in 2001 that there is "little" comprehension instruction occurring in early childhood classrooms (K–3) across the nation. Pearson and Duke in 2002 commented that the terms *comprehension instruction* and *primary grades* do not often appear in the same sentence. In fact, many primary grade educators do not consider comprehension instruction to be an important part of primary grade education (Pearson & Duke, 2002). From this long line of research, we can conclude that children are not getting sufficient instruction in reading comprehension nor is the little comprehension instruction children do receive appropriately focused on effective tasks, strategies, and so on, and promoted with effective instructional and classroom contexts. Consequently, there is considerable variation among young children's abilities to comprehend what they read.

Why do children differ in their ability to comprehend what they read? The RAND Reading Study Group (2002) describes four factors that explain the variability we often see among students with differing abilities in reading comprehension: (a) oral language development; (b) word recognition fluency; (c) world and domain knowledge and experiences; and (d) motivation, purposes, goals, and strategies. Because we have previously discussed oral language development in chapter 5 and fluency development in chapter 14, we focus our attention in this chapter on understanding how the *reader's* background knowledge and the *reader's* motivations, purposes, goals, and strategies influence reading comprehension.

The Influence of Readers' Prior Knowledge and Experience on Reading Comprehension

Research in the past 25 to 30 years has contributed greatly to our collective understanding of the cognitive or thinking processes involved in reading comprehension. Reading comprehension instruction has been profoundly influenced in the past by **schema theory,** a theory that explained how information we have stored in our minds and what we already know help us gain new knowledge. A **schema** (plural is *schemata* or *schemas*) can be thought of as a kind of file cabinet of information in our brains containing related (a) concepts (chairs, birds, ships), (b) events (weddings, birthdays, school experiences), (c) emotions (anger, frustration, joy, pleasure), and (d) roles (parent, judge, teacher) drawn from our life experiences (Rumelhart, 1981).

Researchers have represented the total collection of our schemata as neural networks of connected associated meanings (Collins & Quillian, 1969; Lindsay & Norman, 1977). Each schema is connected to other related schemata, forming our own, unique, vast, interconnected network of knowledge and experiences. The size and content of each schema are influenced by past opportunities to learn. Thus, younger children typically possess fewer, less well developed schemata than do mature adults.

One of the most important findings from the past two to three decades of comprehension research, from our point of view, is that readers can remember a text without learning from it and they can learn from a text without remembering much about it (Kintsch, 1998). When readers successfully comprehend what they read, the levels of meaning constructed are interrelated to form a coherent, integrated representation of meaning in memory that readers draw on in other circumstances to help themselves understand and learn from new experiences and from reading other texts.

Kintsch (1998) developed construction-integration theory to explain the complex cognitive processes employed by readers to comprehend a text. Let us briefly illustrate how this construction-integration process works using the example of the story, *The Frog Prince Continued,* by Jon Scieszka (1991).* We begin by reading a familiar series of statements in the text:

> The Princess kissed the frog.
> He turned into a prince.
> And they lived happily ever after . . .

To understand these three lines, we draw from our previous experiences reading or having been read to from the fairy tale genre in general. The familiar ending in fairy tales is that everyone lives happily ever after. We also call up our specific situational recollections for this particular fairy tale; the princess kissed a frog, and the frog turned into a prince. This, of course, would make sense since princesses and princes living together happily makes more sense than frogs living with princesses. Next we read:

> Well, let's just say they lived sort of happily for a long time.

At this point, we focus in on the meaning of "sort of," which means not really, not so, and so forth. This alerts our curiosity and motivates us to keep reading because we are now alerted to something that is not normally the case. Next we read:

> Okay, so they weren't so happy.
> In fact, they were miserable.

These two clauses lead us to the conclusion that this fairy tale is going to be different than most. Our motivation is engaged to find out why, in this fairy tale, the traditional "happily ever after" situation does not apply.

The surface code or written text as shown in the preceding excerpts preserves for an extremely short period of time the exact letters, words, and grammatical organization or syntax of the text in our iconic memory. This memory is like the image you see quickly fading in your eyes after turning off your television set in a dark room. Once the surface information is moved from iconic memory and processed through short-term or working memory, it is transformed into a text base that preserves the meaning of the text and represents details in the text. This may include connective inferences, for example, the inference that a kiss from a princess has a transformative effect on frogs (the microstructure). This also includes important or "gist" ideas such as the fact that princesses and princes always live happily ever after (the macrostructure). Once the text base is placed into long-term memory, it is usually retained for several hours but may also be forgotten in a few days. As the text base is formed and placed into long-term memory, these same memory processes integrate the details of the text base to form what is called a *situation model*. The situation model, according to Kintsch (1998) is what the text is about: ideas, people, objects, processes, or world events; and it is the situation model that is remembered longest—lasting days, months, or even years. Processing of a text by a reader occurs in cycles, usually clause by clause, just as we discussed in the story of the frog prince, and it involves multiple, simultaneous cognitive processes. The cognitive processes involved in creating a situation model are influenced by (a) the reader's knowledge about the topic or message; (b) the reader's goals, motivations, and strategy selection and use; (c) the reader's ability to function in the sociocultural context (group, classroom) in which the text is processed; (d) the genre, type, and difficulty of the text; and (e) the processing constraints of the reader's memory (Kintsch, 1998; van Dijk, 1999).

---

* From *The Frog Prince Continued* by Jon Scieszka, copyright 1991 by John Scieszka. Used by permission of Viking Penguin, A Division of Penguin Young Readers Group. A member of Penguin Group (USA) Inc., 345 Hudson Street, New York, NY 10014. All rights reserved.

Two phases of processing occur for each clause the reader encounters: (a) a construction phase and (b) an integration phase. In the construction phase, lower-level processes, such as activating prior knowledge and experiences, retrieving word meanings, examining the surface and grammatical structure of the printed text, and analyzing each clause into idea units called *propositions* occur. Propositions include text elements, connecting inferences, and generalizations, which are formed into a coherent network of connected meanings. For example, a sentence like "The student placed a tack on the teacher's chair" would be reduced in memory to a generalization that the student played a "prank" on his teacher (Zwann, 1999). In the *construction phase* of processing, other closely associated ideas also are activated, including irrelevant and even contradictory ideas. If, for example, a reader encounters the phrase " 'Stop sticking your tongue out like that,' nagged the Princess" in the story *The Frog Prince Continued* (Scieszka, 1991), this particular clause may activate associated concepts such as frogs, eating, and inappropriate facial expressions. All of these activated elements are initially part of the coherence network of meaning under construction.

During the second phase of processing meaning, the *integration phase,* the ideas from the text that are strongly interconnected with our prior knowledge are strengthened; those associated concepts that do not fit with the meaning context of the story or text are deactivated and deleted from the network. From this two-phase process, one first constructs meaning from text and then integrates it with prior knowledge to make what Kintsch (1998) calls the *situational model* that is stored in and retrieved from long-term memory. In the case of Scieszka's (1991) *The Frog Prince Continued,* the situational model categorizes this story as a "fractured fairy tale" and stores this particular instance with other such instances in long-term memory.

As important as prior knowledge is, it only partly explains how readers comprehend texts and create a situational memory model for later recall and use. Motivation, social situation, selection, and orchestration of cognitive comprehension strategies also influence readers' ability to comprehend what they read.

THE INFLUENCE OF READERS' MOTIVATIONS, SOCIOCULTURAL CONTEXTS, AND STRATEGIES ON READING COMPREHENSION

Researchers in the past decade have added substantially to our understanding of how reading comprehension is considerably influenced by readers' motivations to engage a text and to take intentional control of their thinking processes while reading a text. Wigfield (1997) describes various facets of motivation that influence children's engagement in reading:

- *Efficacy.* The sense that "I can do this"
- *Challenge.* Easy and more difficult tasks
- *Curiosity.* The desire to know or find out
- *Involvement.* Active, intentional control of one's thinking
- *Importance.* Personal value or worth
- *Recognition.* Praise, certificates, awards, and so on.
- *Grades.* A specific form of recognition in schools
- *Social.* Working cooperatively with others
- *Competition.* Working to win or be the best
- *Compliance.* Working to avoid punishment or negative recognition
- *Work Avoidance.* Seeking the pleasurable and avoiding the difficult

Other researchers, Turner and Paris (1995), have reduced the foregoing complex web of motivations to six *C*s: (a) choice, (b) challenge, (c) control, (d) collaboration, (e) constructing meaning, and (f) consequences. We briefly discuss each of these six motivational factors that influence readers' comprehension of text.

Choice is the first of these. Choice, of course, does not mean that students are free to choose to comprehend any text in the world or to choose to remember what is in the text or make up what they have read. Choices are never unlimited; instead, they are bounded or limited. To offer choice may mean choosing to read from two different information books on rocks and rock formations. To offer students choice also means to encourage them to make connections between the text and their own knowledge and experiences. It does not mean they should just say words and make up what they have read when discussing it with others or when answering questions you have posed. But when children have some sense that they can make *some* choices, they are more willing to persist and remain intellectually engaged while reading.

Challenge is the second way in which we can encourage increased reading motivation and engagement to increase reading comprehension. Turner and Paris (1995) suggested that the common wisdom that children like "easy" reading texts and tasks more than more difficult or challenging reading texts or tasks is not supported in research. In fact, children enjoy a sense of being challenged. Of course, here again, the level of challenge associated with the text or task must not become excessive to the point of frustration. But giving children appropriately challenging texts and tasks has been shown to positively impact upon readers' motivations to read for comprehension.

Control is the third motivational factor associated with increasing students' reading comprehension. Sharing the control of texts and tasks in the classroom with the teacher or other students is associated with greater engagement while reading. Children need to feel and sense that they have an integral role to play while reading a text in order to take sufficient control of their own thinking processes to be successful in reading for comprehension.

Collaboration has been shown to be one of eight comprehension strategies for which there is sufficient scientific evidence that the National Reading Panel (National Institute of Child Health and Human Development, 2000) recommended this as ready for immediate implementation into classroom practice to improve students' reading comprehension. This requires that students discuss, interact, and work together with each other and their teachers to construct the meaning of texts to improve reading comprehension. Collaboration results in students obtaining greater insights into the thinking processes of others around a text. Collaborative discussions and interactions also elaborate the outcomes of the reading comprehension process by adding to one another's memories for and meanings constructed from the reading of a text.

Constructing meaning is the very essence of reading comprehension instruction. This requires the conscious selection, control, and use of various cognitive comprehension strategies while engaged in reading a text. Again, the National Reading Panel (National Institute of Child Health and Human Development, 2000) found that there was sufficient scientific evidence to warrant the immediate implementation of six cognitive comprehension strategies in classrooms to aid in the construction of meaning from text: (a) using graphic organizers, (b) monitoring comprehension, (c) answering questions, (d) self-posing of questions, (e) story or text structure, and (f) summarizing. When these are used as a group or as a set, comprehension strategies have even more power to impact on students' abilities to construct meaning (National Institute of Child Health and Human Development, 2000; Reutzel, Smith, & Fawson, in preparation).

Consequences represent the final factor that leads students to increased motivation and reading comprehension. This concept refers to the nature of the outcomes expected when comprehending. If the outcome expected is completing or participating in an open- rather than a closed-end task, such as contributing to a discussion rather than getting the "right" answers to questions on a worksheet, then students interpret their failures in comprehension differently. When seeking correct or "right" answers, they often feel that they just do not have enough ability (Turner & Paris, 1995). On the other hand, if through discussion they detect that they failed to pick up on some element in the text, they often view this failure as the result of insufficiently or improperly selecting or applying effective comprehension strategies rather than just that they are not "smart enough" or "do not have the ability."

In conclusion, when preparing to teach reading comprehension, teachers must carefully prepare the *reader*, the one who is doing the reading, by assessing, activating, building, or modifying prior knowledge in relation to the theme (narratives) or topic (expository) of the text. Also, teachers need to consider how they can increase students' motivation to actively engage in and take control of their own thinking processes while reading texts such as using the six Cs we have discussed: choice, challenge, control, collaboration, constructing meaning, and consequences.

ASSESSING FACTORS WITHIN THE READER THAT INFLUENCE READING COMPREHENSION

How can students' background knowledge, strategy selection and use, and motivations be assessed? How can students be helped to activate their background knowledge, appropriately select strategies, and be motivated to increase their reading enjoyment and comprehension? Teachers need to have a repertoire of successful and proven assessment and instructional alternatives available to assist children in activating their prior knowledge, select effective comprehension strategies, and increase their engagement and motivation. The assessment strategies outlined in this section provide you with the means to assess these factors that influence children's comprehension.

ASSESSING READERS' PRIOR KNOWLEDGE

LANGER'S BACKGROUND KNOWLEDGE ASSESSMENT PROCEDURE

Purpose

Children's background information and experiences are among the most important contributors or inhibitors of comprehension. Researchers have determined that students who possess a great deal of background information about a subject tend to recall greater amounts of information more accurately from reading than do students with little or no background knowledge (Carr & Thompson, 1996; Pearson, Hansen, & Gordon, 1979; Pressley, 2000). It is also a well-known fact that well-developed background information can inhibit the comprehension of new information that conflicts with or refutes prior knowledge and assumptions about a specific topic. Thus, knowing how much knowledge a reader has about a concept or topic can help teachers better prepare students to read and comprehend successfully. One way that teachers can assess background knowledge and experience is to use a procedure developed by Langer (1982) for assessing the amount and content of students' background knowledge about selected topics, themes, concepts, and events.

Figure 10.1   Checklist of Levels of Prior Knowledge

Phrase 1	What comes to mind when. . . ?
Phrase 2	What made you think of. . . ?
Phrase 3	Have you any new ideas about. . . ?

Stimulus used to elicit student background knowledge _____

(Picture, word, or phrase, etc.)

	Much - (3)	Some - (2)	Little - (1)
	category labels	examples	personal associations
	definitions	attributes	morphemes
	analogies	defining characteristics	sound alikes
	relationships		personal experiences

Student name	Much - (3)	Some - (2)	Little - (1)
Maria	_____	__X__	_____
Jawan	__X__	_____	_____
_____	_____	_____	_____
_____	_____	_____	_____
_____	_____	_____	_____

Materials

Use the checklist and materials represented in Figure 10.1.

Procedure

Select a story for children to read. Construct a list of specific vocabulary terms or story concepts related to the topic, message, theme, or events to be experienced in reading the story. For example, students may read the story *Stone Fox* by John R. Gardiner (1980) about a boy named Willy who saves his grandfather's farm from the tax collector. Construct a list of 5 to 10 specific vocabulary terms or concepts related to the story. Use this list to probe background knowledge and experiences of the students about the story's message and plot. Such a list may include the following:

1. Broke
2. Taxes
3. Tax collector
4. Dogsled race
5. Samoyeds

Students are asked to respond to each of these terms in writing or through discussion. This is accomplished by using one of several stem statements, as shown in Figure 10.1, such as, "What comes to mind when you think of paying bills and you hear the term 'broke'?"

Students then respond. Once students have responded to each of the specific terms, the teacher can score the responses using the information in Figure 10.1 to survey the class or individual's knowledge and experience. Awarding the number of points that most closely represents the level of prior knowledge in the response is used to score each item. Divide the total score by the number of terms or concepts in the list (five in our example) to determine the average knowledge level of individual students. These average scores are compared against the Checklist of Levels of Prior Knowledge in Figure 10.1 for each student. By scanning the x's in the checklist, a teacher can get a sense of the entire class's overall level of prior knowledge. Information thus gathered can be used to inform both the content and nature of whole-group comprehension instruction.

ASSESSING READERS' USE OF COMPREHENSION STRATEGIES

A CLASSROOM MODIFIED VERSION OF THE READING STRATEGY USE SCALE

Purpose

Metacognition refers to two important concepts related to reading comprehension: (a) a reader's knowledge of the status of his or her own thinking and the appropriate strategies to facilitate ongoing comprehension; and (b) the executive control one has over one's own thinking, including the use of comprehension strategies to facilitate or repair failing comprehension as he or she reads (Paris, Wasik, & Turner, 1991). For many readers, problems in comprehension result from failures related to one or both of these two important concepts. The purpose of metacognitive assessment is to gain insight into how students select strategies to use in comprehending text and how well they regulate the status of their own comprehension as they read. We have modified the Reading Strategy Use (RSU) scale developed by Pereira-Laird and Deane (1997) for classroom application. Scores obtained from administering the Classroom Modified Reading Strategy Use (CMRSU) scale provide insights into how well students select, apply, and regulate their use of comprehension strategies.

Materials

The Classroom Modified Reading Strategy Use scale shown in Figure 10.2 can be used with most text selections.

Procedure

The CMRSU scale is group administered. Tell students that the CMRSU scale is not a test and there are no right or wrong answers. Ask students to fill in the personal information at the top of the CMRSU scale. Read the directions aloud and ask children if they have any questions about the nature of the responses to be given to each statement. Once you, the teacher, are sure that the students understand, instruct them to read each item and circle the number under the response that best represents their behavior in relation to each statement. When children finish the CMRSU scale, ask them to remain in their seats. They should quietly take out a book, write, or draw so as not to disturb others who are still completing the scale.

Scoring is accomplished by summing the response numbers circled and dividing by the total of the 15 items in the CMRSU scale:

Sum of individual responses/15 items = the mean score.

Figure 10.2   A Classroom Modified Version of the Reading Strategy Use Scale

Name _____   Grade _____

Teacher_____   School _____

Directions: Read each item and the number of the word that best describes how often you do what is stated. Let's do number 1 together to make sure you understand how you are to respond to each item.

1. I read quickly through the story to get the general idea before I read the story closely.

   | Always | Sometimes | Never |
   | 3 | 2 | 1 |

2. When I come to a part of the story that is hard to read, I slow my reading down.

   | Always | Sometimes | Never |
   | 3 | 2 | 1 |

3. I am able to tell the difference between important story parts and less important details.

   | Always | Sometimes | Never |
   | 3 | 2 | 1 |

4. When I read, I stop once in a while to go over in my head what I have been reading to see if it is making sense.

   | Always | Sometimes | Never |
   | 3 | 2 | 1 |

5. I adjust the speed of my reading by deciding how difficult the story is to read.

   | Always | Sometimes | Never |
   | 3 | 2 | 1 |

6. I stop once in a while and ask myself questions about the story to see how well I understand what I am reading.

   | Always | Sometimes | Never |
   | 3 | 2 | 1 |

7. After reading a story, I sit and think about it for a while to check my memory of the story parts and the order of the story parts.

   | Always | Sometimes | Never |
   | 3 | 2 | 1 |

8. When I get lost while reading, I go back to the place in the story where I first had trouble and reread.

   | Always | Sometimes | Never |
   | 3 | 2 | 1 |

9. When I find I do not understand something when reading, I read it again and try to figure it out.

   | Always | Sometimes | Never |
   | 3 | 2 | 1 |

10. When reading, I check how well I understand the meaning of the story by asking myself whether the ideas fit with the other information in the story.

    | Always | Sometimes | Never |
    | 3 | 2 | 1 |

11. I find it hard to pay attention when I read.

    | Always | Sometimes | Never |
    | 3 | 2 | 1 |

12. To help me remember what I read, I sometimes draw a map or outline the story.

    | Always | Sometimes | Never |
    | 3 | 2 | 1 |

13. To help me understand what I have read in a story, I try to retell it in my own words.

    | Always | Sometimes | Never |
    | 3 | 2 | 1 |

14. I learn new words by trying to make a picture of the words in my mind.

    | Always | Sometimes | Never |
    | 3 | 2 | 1 |

15. When reading about something, I try to relate it to my own experiences.

    | Always | Sometimes | Never |
    | 3 | 2 | 1 |

A mean score near 3 indicates strong selection, use, and self-regulation of comprehension monitoring strategies. A mean score near 2 indicates occasional selection and use of comprehension monitoring strategies. The pattern of responses should be carefully studied to see which of the comprehension monitoring strategies are in use and which are not to inform instructional planning for the future. A mean score near 1 indicates poorly developed selection, use, and self-regulation of comprehension monitoring strategies. These students need explicit teacher explanation of (a) comprehension monitoring strategies; (b) how, when, and why to use comprehension monitoring strategies; (c) teacher modeling of comprehension monitoring strategy use; and (d) guided practice applying selected comprehension monitoring strategies during the reading and discussion of stories in the classroom.

METACOMPREHENSION STRATEGY INDEX

Purpose

The Metacomprehension Strategy Index (MSI) developed by M. C. Schmitt (1988, 1990, 2005), is a valuable tool for assessing students' awareness of a variety of reading comprehension strategies that are appropriate for use before, during, and after the reading of a text. The individual items in the MSI are correlated with six categories of reading comprehension strategies: (a) predicting and verifying, (b) previewing, (c) purpose setting, (d) self-questioning, (e) drawing from prior knowledge, and (f) summarizing and using fix-up strategies. Schmitt (2005) asserts that the MSI is "a valid means for measuring learners' metacognition or metacomprehension for the purpose of designing instructional programs [interventions]" (Schmitt, 2005, p. 106). She has also shown that the MSI correlates with other measures of strategy use and metacognition such as the Index of Reading Awareness (Paris & Jacobs, 1984).

Materials

The MSI scale shown in Figure 10.3 can be used with most text selections.

Procedures

The MSI can be given to students as a group if they are able to read it without undo difficulty. If there is any doubt, the MSI should be read aloud to the students during administration. To begin, children are instructed to "Think about what kinds of things you can do to help you understand a story [text] better before, during, and after you read it." Next, you, the teacher, read each item in the MSI aloud. Tell children that they are to be thinking about which of the four responses underneath each item they believe would "help them the most." Children are also told that there are no right or wrong answers. Then children are told to circle one of the four responses underneath each of the 25 total MSI items.

Schmitt (2005) indicates that the scores on the MSI can be used to assess students' individual weaknesses in strategy selection and use or the MSI can be used to determine general patterns of strengths and weaknesses in an entire class's selection and use of comprehension strategies. Schmitt recommends that teachers begin by examining the performance of the entire class. To help with the analysis process, she recommends contemplating the following three questions:

1. Which strategies were the most well known?

2. Were there differences among the before, during, and after stages that might signal specific areas of concern?

3. Were there patterns indicating difficulty with understanding the items on the MSI? The class selects a distracter underneath an item that makes no sense.

Figure 10.3   Metacomprehension Strategy Index

Directions

Think about what kinds of things you can do to help you understand a story better before, during, and after you read it. Read each of the lists of four statements and decide which one of them would help *you* the most. *There are no right or wrong answers*. It is just what *you* think would help the most. Circle the letter of the statement you choose.

Questionnaire Items

In each set of four, choose the one statement that tells a good thing to do to help you understand a story better *before you read it*.

1. *Before* I begin reading, it is a good idea to
   A. see how many pages are in the story.
   B. look up all of the big words in the dictionary.
   C. make some guesses about what I think will happen in the story.
   D. think about what has happened so far in the story.

2. *Before* I begin reading, it is a good idea to
   A. look at the pictures to see what the story is about.
   B. decide how long it will take me to read the story.
   C. sound out the words I do not know.
   D. check to see if the story is making sense.

3. *Before* I begin reading, it's a good idea to
   A. ask someone to read the story to me.
   B. read the title to see what the story is about.
   C. check to see if most of the words have long or short vowels in them.
   D. check to see if the pictures are in order and make sense.

4. *Before* I begin reading, it is a good idea to
   A. check to see that no pages are missing.
   B. make a list of the words I am not sure about.
   C. use the title and pictures to help me make guesses about what will happen in the story.
   D. read the last sentence so I will know how the story ends.

5. *Before* I begin reading, it is a good idea to
   A. decide on why I am going to read the story.
   B. use the difficult words to help me make guesses about what will happen in the story.
   C. reread some parts to see if I can figure out what is happening if things are not making sense.
   D. ask for help with the difficult words.

6. *Before* I begin reading, it is a good idea to
   A. retell all of the main points that have happened so far.
   B. ask myself questions that I will like to have answered in the story.
   C. think about the meanings of the words that have more than one meaning.
   D. look through the story to find all of the words with three or more syllables.

7. *Before* I begin reading, it is a good idea to
   A. check to see if I have read this story *before*.
   B. use my questions and guesses as a reason for reading the story.
   C. make sure I can pronounce all of the words *before* I start.
   D. think of a better title for the story.

~~Figure 10.3   Continued

8. *Before* I begin reading, it is a good idea to
   A. think of what I already know about the things I see in the pictures.
   B. see how may pages are in the story.
   C. choose the best part of the story to read again.
   D. read the story aloud to someone.

9. *Before* I begin reading, it is a good idea to
   A. practice reading the story aloud.
   B. retell all of the main points to make sure I can remember the story.
   C. think of what the people in the story might be like.
   D. decide if I have enough time to read the story.

10. *Before* I begin reading, it is a good idea to
    A. check to see if I am understanding the story so far.
    B. check to see if the words have more than one meaning.
    C. think about where the story might be taking place.
    D. list all of the important details.

In each set of four, choose the one statement that tells a good thing to do to help you understand a story better *while you are reading it.*

11. *While* I am reading, it is a good idea to
    A. read the story very slowly so that I will not miss any important parts.
    B. read the title to see what the story is about.
    C. check to see if the pictures have anything missing.
    D. check to see if the story is making sense by seeing if I can tell what has happened so far.

12. *While* I am reading, it is a good idea to
    A. stop to retell the main points to see if I am understanding what has happened so far.
    B. read the story quickly so that I can find out what happened.
    C. read only the beginning and the end of the story to find out what it is about.
    D. skip the parts that are too difficult for me.

13. *While* I am reading, it is a good idea to
    A. look all of the big words up in the dictionary.
    B. put the book away and find another one if things are not making sense.
    C. keep thinking about the title and the pictures to help me decide what is going to happen next.
    D. keep track of how many pages I have left to read.

14. *While* I am reading, it is a good idea to
    A. keep track of how long it is taking me to read the story.
    B. check to see if I can answer any of the questions I asked *before* I started reading.
    C. read the title to see what the story is going to be about.
    D. add the missing details to the pictures.

15. *While* I am reading, it is a good idea to
    A. have someone read the story aloud to me.
    B. keep track of how many pages I have read.
    C. list the story's main characters.
    D. check to see if my guesses are right or wrong.

16. *While* I am reading, it is a good idea to
    A. check to see that the characters are real.
    B. make a lot of guesses about what is going to happen next.
    C. not look at the pictures because they might confuse me.
    D. read the story aloud to someone.

continued

Figure 10.3   Continued

17. *While* I am reading, it is a good idea to
    A. try to answer the questions I asked myself.
    B. try not to confuse what I already know with what I am reading about.
    C. read the story silently.
    D. check to see if I am saying the new vocabulary words correctly.

18. *While* I am reading, it is a good idea to
    A. try to see if my guesses are going to be right or wrong.
    B. reread to be sure I have not missed any of the words.
    C. decide on why I am reading the story.
    D. list what happened first, second, third, and so on.

19. *While* I am reading, it is a good idea to
    A. see if I can recognize the new vocabulary words.
    B. be careful not to skip any parts of the story.
    C. check to see how many of the words I already know.
    D. keep thinking of what I already know about the things and ideas in the story to help me decide what is going to happen.

20. *While* I am reading, it is a good idea to
    A. reread some parts or read ahead to see if I can figure out what is happening if things are not making sense.
    B. take my time reading so that I can be sure I understand what is happening.
    C. change the ending so that it makes sense.
    D. check to see if there are enough pictures to help make the story ideas clear.

In each set of four, choose the one statement that tells a good thing to do to help you understand the story better *after you have read it.*

21. *After* I have read a story, it is a good idea to
    A. count how many pages I read with no mistakes.
    B. check to see if there were enough pictures to go with the story to make it interesting.
    C. check to see if I met my purpose for reading the story.
    D. underline the causes and effects.

22. *After* I have read a story, it is a good idea to
    A. underline the main idea.
    B. retell the main points of the whole story so that I can check to see if I understood it.
    C. read the story again to be sure I said all of the words right.
    D. practice reading the story aloud.

23. *After* I have read a story, it is a good idea to
    A. read the title and look over the story to see what it is about.
    B. check to see if I skipped any of the vocabulary words.
    C. think about what made me make good or bad predictions.
    D. make a guess about what will happen next in the story.

24. *After* I have read a story, it is a good idea to
    A. look up all of the big words in the dictionary.
    B. read the best parts aloud.
    C. have someone read the story aloud to me.
    D. think about how the story was like things I already knew about *before* I started reading.

25. *After* I have read a story, it is a good idea to
    A. think about how I would have acted if I were the main character in the story.
    B. practice reading the story silently for practice of good reading.
    C. look over the story title and picture to see what will happen.
    D. make a list of the things I understood the most.

Assessing Readers' Social Collaborations in Reading Comprehension

Social Collaboration Performance Outcome Evaluation

Purpose

Although process is important during cooperative and collaborative learning activities, a quality process should frequently result in a quality product. Assessment of the collaborative performance outcome is necessary to ensure that a spirit of accountability and consequence is maintained. As discussed previously, an essential element of quality cooperative learning groups is to ensure an element of accountability and consequence for task completion whether it is an open- or closed-end test. The Collaboration Performance Outcome Evaluation tool is a means of helping teachers assess the products of collaboration and discussion around texts to promote reading comprehension.

Materials

An example of a Performance Outcome Evaluation form is shown in Figure 10.4. Though much of this sort of assessment is preferably ungraded, you will note that a column is provided for grading if that is required.

Procedures

Teachers collect student or group projects, papers, or other products for evaluation. We suggest that students be provided the form shown in Figure 10.4 as a guide for their own understanding of teacher expectations. Upon completed evaluation, the form should accompany feedback to the group or team about the quality of the team's product.

Self-Assessment of Collaboration: Individual and Group Accountability

Purpose

The purpose of self-assessment centers on developing each student's ability to judge the quality of his or her own contributions to a cooperative team effort (Johnson & Johnson, 1991; Ellis & Whalen, 1990). Students of any age and ability can engage in self-assessment. This is important to cooperative learning because it helps students take responsibility for their own behavior and learning.

Materials

Examples of group and individual assessment forms are shown in Figure 10.5 and Figure 10.6. These or modified forms can be duplicated and distributed to teams or individuals to be completed at the conclusion of daily cooperative group activities.

Procedures

For group assessment, students can fill out the form shown in Figure 10.5 individually. Then, students can be encouraged to share their responses with the group and compare

Figure 10.4   Performance Outcome Team Evaluation Form

Team Name_____	Date_____
Teacher's Name_____	Class_____

Outcomes	Points	Grade
Completes assigned tasks (assignments, quizzes, reports, work units, homework)		
Applies skills taught in task completion (work units, use in problem-solving situations, homework)		
Understands concepts and principles (team scores, reports, homework, observations)		

Communication
  1. Communicates ideas and feelings effectively (observations, direct discussion)
  2. Participates actively in problem-solving groups		

Writing work (homework, reports)		
Cooperation (observations, team products)		
Competitive ability (observations, performances in competitions)		
Independent work (observations, performances in individualized activities)		
Affective learning		
Appreciation of subject areas		
Appreciates learning (receives enjoyment and satisfaction from learning)		
Aware of and appreciates own abilities, achievements, talents, and resources		
When appropriate, helps others, shares resources, etc.		
Accepts and appreciates cultural, ethnic, linguistic, and individual differences		
Values free and open inquiry into all problems		
Total		

how they perceived the group functioning with their teammates. At the conclusion of the discussion, the group fills out a single form representing the consensus of the group. Dissenting opinions should be given space at the bottom of the form to express their differences from the group.

For individual assessment, students simply fill out the form shown in Figure 10.6 independently and turn these in to the teacher by placing them in a self-assessment file. Teachers can create a file on each child to keep a running account of how each child rates his or her own learning and involvement.

Figure 10.5   Group Self-Assessment

Group:_____   **Date:** _____

Today:

1. **We offered our ideas to each other.**
   Usually _____ Sometimes _____ Seldom _____

2. **We listened carefully to each other.**
   Usually _____ Sometimes _____ Seldom _____

3. **We offered encouragement to each other.**
   Usually _____ Sometimes _____ Seldom _____

4. **We helped each other with building ideas or solving problems.**
   Usually _____ Sometimes _____ Seldom _____

5. **We completed the assigned tasks well.**
   Usually _____ Sometimes _____ Seldom _____

Signatures

_____   _____

_____   _____

_____   _____

Figure 10.6   Individual Self-Assessment

Name:_____   **Date:**_____

Today:

1. **I offered my ideas.**
   Usually _____ Sometimes _____ Seldom _____

2. **I listened carefully to others.**
   Usually _____ Sometimes _____ Seldom _____

3. **I offered encouragement to others.**
   Usually _____ Sometimes _____ Seldom _____

4. **I helped others with building ideas or solving problems.**
   Usually _____ Sometimes _____ Seldom _____

5. **I completed the assigned tasks well.**
   Usually _____ Sometimes _____ Seldom _____

Signatures

_____   _____

_____   _____

_____   _____

ASSESSING STUDENT MOTIVATION FOR READING

MOTIVATION FOR READING QUESTIONNAIRE, REVISED VERSION

Purpose

The Motivation for Reading Questionnaire (MRQ), Revised Version, was designed to assess eight different possible dimensions of reading motivations (Wigfield, Guthrie, & McGough, 1996): (a) curiosity, (b) involvement, (c) preference for challenge, (d) recognition, (e) grades, (f) social, (g) competition, and (h) compliance. These eight dimensions of reading motivations tap into both extrinsic and intrinsic motivational factors. The MRQ has been used as a measure of the reading motivation in many reported and published research studies in recent years because of the extensive validation and reliability work surrounding the development and use of this easy-to-use instrument. Changing the classroom environment and the dimensions of classroom literacy instructional practices can only occur when teachers have access to data that help them to understand how their practices, programs, and environments are affecting the development of students' reading motivations. Promoting lifelong engagement in reading is a primary goal for all literacy educators; and, as such, the MRQ instrument allows teachers to measure the efficacy and effects of their in-school and out-of-school literacy programs on children's ongoing literacy motivation and engagement (Wigfield, 1997).

Materials

You will need the following materials:

- Multiple copies of the Motivation for Reading Questionnaire, Revised Version, for recording individual student responses (Figure 10.7)
- One paper copy for recording categories of class responses

Procedures

Distribute sufficient individual paper copies of the MRQ, Revised Version, for individual students within your classroom. Have the children put their name in the upper right-hand corner of the first page of the MRQ, Revised Version. If the children are capable of reading the items on the MRQ, Revised Version, independently, then they may do so. Otherwise, each item is read aloud by the teacher and each student is asked to mark independently his or her response on the 4-point scale beneath the item. Once all 44 items have been read aloud by the teacher and responded to by the students, the MRQs are picked up.

A class copy of the MRQ can then be used to tally the number of responses underneath each item for the four points of the scale. Once the tally is complete, the teacher should carefully note which students have low motivation across or within motivational categories. Also, the teacher can make note of which reading motivation dimensions are low in the whole class of students. By doing this, the teacher has a way to screen for problems in an individual child's reading motivations as well as to monitor the reading motivation of the whole class. Furthermore, the MRQ, Revised Version, can be used to individually diagnose areas of motivation that are strengths and weaknesses in individual student reading motivations. As a result, the teacher can select individual or small-group reading motivation strategies to address these measured weaknesses. The teacher can also measure the motivation of the whole class and determine interventions that may be used to promote increased motivation at the whole-class level.

Figure 10.7   The Motivation for Reading Questionnaire, Revised Version

Curiosity

1. I like to read because I always feel happy when I read things that are of interest to me.

1	2	3	4
Very different from me	*A little different from me*	*A little like me*	*A lot like me*

2. If the teacher discusses something interesting, I might read more about it.

1	2	3	4
Very different from me	*A little different from me*	*A little like me*	*A lot like me*

3. I have favorite subjects that I like to read about.

1	2	3	4
Very different from me	*A little different from me*	*A little like me*	*A lot like me*

4. I read to learn new information about topics that interest me.

1	2	3	4
Very different from me	*A little different from me*	*A little like me*	*A lot like me*

5. I read about my hobbies to learn more about them.

1	2	3	4
Very different from me	*A little different from me*	*A little like me*	*A lot like me*

6. I like to read about new things.

1	2	3	4
Very different from me	*A little different from me*	*A little like me*	*A lot like me*

7. I enjoy reading books about people in different countries.

1	2	3	4
Very different from me	*A little different from me*	*A little like me*	*A lot like me*

Involvement

8. If I am reading about an interesting topic, I sometimes lose track of time.

1	2	3	4
Very different from me	*A little different from me*	*A little like me*	*A lot like me*

9. I read stories about fantasy and make believe.

1	2	3	4
Very different from me	*A little different from me*	*A little like me*	*A lot like me*

10. I like mysteries.

1	2	3	4
Very different from me	*A little different from me*	*A little like me*	*A lot like me*

11. I make pictures in my mind when I read.

1	2	3	4
Very different from me	*A little different from me*	*A little like me*	*A lot like me*

12. I feel like I made friends with people in good books.

1	2	3	4
Very different from me	*A little different from me*	*A little like me*	*A lot like me*

13. I like to read a lot of adventure stories.

1	2	3	4
Very different from me	*A little different from me*	*A little like me*	*A lot like me*

14. I enjoy a long, involved story or fiction book.

1	2	3	4
Very different from me	*A little different from me*	*A little like me*	*A lot like me*

continued

Figure 10.7   Continued

Preference for Challenge

15. I like hard, challenging books.

1	2	3	4
Very different from me	*A little different from me*	*A little like me*	*A lot like me*

16. If the project is interesting, I can read difficult material.

1	2	3	4
Very different from me	*A little different from me*	*A little like me*	*A lot like me*

17. I like it when the questions in books make me think.

1	2	3	4
Very different from me	*A little different from me*	*A little like me*	*A lot like me*

18. I usually learn difficult things by reading.

1	2	3	4
Very different from me	*A little different from me*	*A little like me*	*A lot like me*

19. If a book is interesting, I do not care how hard it is to read.

1	2	3	4
Very different from me	*A little different from me*	*A little like me*	*A lot like me*

Recognition

20. I like having the teacher say I read well.

1	2	3	4
Very different from me	*A little different from me*	*A little like me*	*A lot like me*

21. I like having my friends sometimes tell me I am a good reader.

1	2	3	4
Very different from me	*A little different from me*	*A little like me*	*A lot like me*

22. I like to get compliments for my reading.

1	2	3	4
Very different from me	*A little different from me*	*A little like me*	*A lot like me*

23. I am happy when someone recognizes my reading.

1	2	3	4
Very different from me	*A little different from me*	*A little like me*	*A lot like me*

24. I like having my parents often tell me what a good job I am doing in reading.

1	2	3	4
Very different from me	*A little different from me*	*A little like me*	*A lot like me*

Grades

25. Grades are a good way to see how well you are doing in reading.

1	2	3	4
Very different from me	*A little different from me*	*A little like me*	*A lot like me*

26. I look forward to finding out my grade in reading on my report card.

1	2	3	4
Very different from me	*A little different from me*	*A little like me*	*A lot like me*

27. I like to read to improve my grades.

1	2	3	4
Very different from me	*A little different from me*	*A little like me*	*A lot like me*

Figure 10.7   Continued

28. I like my parents to ask me about my reading grade.

1	2	3	4
Very different from me	*A little different from me*	*A little like me*	*A lot like me*

Social

29. I like to visit the library often with my family.

1	2	3	4
Very different from me	*A little different from me*	*A little like me*	*A lot like me*

30. I often like to read to my brother or sister.

1	2	3	4
Very different from me	*A little different from me*	*A little like me*	*A lot like me*

31. My friends and I like to trade things to read.

1	2	3	4
Very different from me	*A little different from me*	*A little like me*	*A lot like me*

32. I sometimes read to my parents.

1	2	3	4
Very different from me	*A little different from me*	*A little like me*	*A lot like me*

33. I like to talk to my friends about what I am reading.

1	2	3	4
Very different from me	*A little different from me*	*A little like me*	*A lot like me*

34. I like to help my friends with their schoolwork in reading.

1	2	3	4
Very different from me	*A little different from me*	*A little like me*	*A lot like me*

35. I like to tell my family about what I am reading.

1	2	3	4
Very different from me	*A little different from me*	*A little like me*	*A lot like me*

Competition

36. I try to get more answers right than my friends.

1	2	3	4
Very different from me	*A little different from me*	*A little like me*	*A lot like me*

37. I like being the best at reading.

1	2	3	4
Very different from me	*A little different from me*	*A little like me*	*A lot like me*

38. I like to finish my reading before other students.

1	2	3	4
Very different from me	*A little different from me*	*A little like me*	*A lot like me*

39. I like being the only one who knows an answer in something we read.

1	2	3	4
Very different from me	*A little different from me*	*A little like me*	*A lot like me*

40. I am willing to work hard to read better than my friends.

1	2	3	4
Very different from me	*A little different from me*	*A little like me*	*A lot like me*

continued

Figure 10.7   Continued

Compliance

41. I always do my reading work exactly as the teacher wants it.

1	2	3	4
Very different from me	*A little different from me*	*A little like me*	*A lot like me*

42. Finishing every reading assignment is very important to me.

1	2	3	4
Very different from me	*A little different from me*	*A little like me*	*A lot like me*

43. I read because I have to read.

1	2	3	4
Very different from me	*A little different from me*	*A little like me*	*A lot like me*

44. I always try to finish my reading on time.

1	2	3	4
Very different from me	*A little different from me*	*A little like me*	*A lot like me*

THE READER SELF-PERCEPTION SCALE

Purpose

A sense of personal or self-efficacy in learning and using comprehension strategies plays a key role in every reader's development of competence and confidence. Self-efficacy denotes one's beliefs about his or her own capabilities to learn or to perform a given task at specified or designated levels of proficiency (Bandura, 1986; Paris & Winograd, 2001; Schunk & Zimmerman, 1997). Previous research has clearly demonstrated a strong link between learners' sense of self-efficacy, motivation, and self-regulatory processes (Schunk, 1996). Self-efficacy has been shown to influence task choice, effort, persistence, and ultimate achievement. Effective comprehension strategy instruction requires that students develop a sense of self-efficacy as well as self-regulating behaviors and dispositions. Henk and Melnick (1995) developed an instrument for measuring how children feel about themselves as readers, an indicator of self-efficacy, called the Reader Self-Perception Scale (RSPS). (See a description of the scale and instructions for use in Figure 10.8.)

Materials

You will need the following materials:

- One copy for each student of the Reader Self-Perception Scale (RSPS) shown in Figure 10.9
- One copy for each student of the RSPS scoring sheet shown in Figure 10.10

Procedure

The RSPS assessment tool is group rather than individually administered. In order to obtain valid results, it is imperative that students clearly understand the nature of the task and be given sufficient time to thoughtfully and honestly respond to each item. Children are to be told that this is not a test and that there are no right or wrong answers. Responses will be kept strictly confidential. Ask children to fill in the personal information at the top of the RSPS. Read the directions aloud to the group and guide them through the completion

Figure 10.8   Directions for Administration, Scoring, and Interpretation of the Reader Self-Perception Scale

---

The Reader Self-Perception Scale (RSPS) is intended to provide an assessment of how children feel about themselves as readers. The scale consists of 33 items that assess self-perceptions along four dimensions of self-efficacy (Progress, Observational Comparison, Social Feedback, and Physiological States). Children are asked to indicate how strongly they agree or disagree with each statement on a 5-point scale (5 = Strongly Agree, 1 = Strongly Disagree). The information gained from this scale can be used to devise ways to enhance children's self-esteem in reading and, ideally, to increase their motivation to read. The following directions explain specifically what you are to do.

Administration
For the results to be of any use, the children must: (a) understand exactly what they are to do, (b) have sufficient time to complete all items, and (c) respond honestly and thoughtfully. Briefly explain to the children that they are being asked to complete a questionnaire about reading. Emphasize that this is not a *test* and that there are no *right* answers. Tell them that they should be as honest as possible because their responses will be confidential. Ask the children to fill in their names, grade levels, and classrooms as appropriate. Read the directions aloud and work through the example with the students as a group. Discuss the response options and make sure that all children understand the rating scale before moving on. It is important that children know that they may raise their hands to ask questions about any words or ideas they do not understand.

The children should then read each item and circle their response for the item. They should work at their own pace. Remind the children that they should be sure to respond to all items. When all items are completed, the children should stop, put their pencils down, and wait for further instructions. Care should be taken that children who work more slowly are not disturbed by children who have already finished.

Scoring
To score the RSPS, enter the following point values for each response on the RSPS scoring sheet (Strongly Agree = 5, Agree = 4, Undecided = 3, Disagree = 2, Strongly Disagree = 1) for each item number under the appropriate scale. Sum each column to obtain a raw score for each of the four specific scales.

Interpretation
Each scale is interpreted in relation to its total possible score. For example, because the RSPS uses a 5-point scale and the Progress scale consists of 9 items, the highest total score for Progress is 45 (9 × 5 = 45). Therefore, a score that would fall approximately in the middle of the range (22–23) would indicate a child's somewhat indifferent perception of herself or himself as a reader with respect to Progress. Note that each scale has a different possible total raw score (Progress = 45, Observational Comparison = 30, Social Feedback = 45, and Physiological States = 40) and should be interpreted accordingly.

---

of the example item. Make sure children understand the response categories and understand the task. Then have them complete their response for each item of the RSPS. When children finish the RSPS, ask them to quietly take out a book, write, or draw at their seats so as not to disturb others who are still completing the scale.

Scoring is accomplished by using the RSPS scoring sheet. Sum the numerical rating for each RSPS item within the categories listed on the RSPS scoring sheet. Interpretation of the scores obtained for the RSPS are found at the bottom of the scoring sheet.

Figure 10.9   The Reader Self-Perception Scale

Listed below are statements about reading. Please read each statement carefully. Then circle the letters that show how much you agree or disagree with the statement. Use the following:

SA = Strongly Agree
A = Agree
U = Undecided
D = Disagree
SD = Strongly Disagree

Example: **I think pizza with pepperoni is the best.**   SA   A   U   D   SD

If you are *really positive* that pepperoni pizza is best, circle SA (Strongly Agree).
If you *think* that it is good but maybe not great, circle A (Agree).
If you *can't decide* whether or not it is best, circle U (undecided).
If you *think* that pepperoni pizza is not all that good, circle D (Disagree).
If you are *really positive* that pepperoni pizza is not very good, circle SD (Strongly Disagree).

	1. I think I am a good reader.	SA	A	U	D	SD
[SF]	2. I can tell that my teacher likes to listen to me read.	SA	A	U	D	SD
[SF]	3. My teacher thinks that my reading is fine.	SA	A	U	D	SD
[OC]	4. I read faster than other kids.	SA	A	U	D	SD
[PS]	5. I like to read aloud.	SA	A	U	D	SD
[OC]	6. When I read, I can figure out words better than other kids.	SA	A	U	D	SD
[SF]	7. My classmates like to listen to me read.	SA	A	U	D	SD
[PS]	8. I feel good inside when I read.	SA	A	U	D	SD
[SF]	9. My classmates think that I read pretty well.	SA	A	U	D	SD
[PR]	10. When I read, I don't have to try as hard as I used to.	SA	A	U	D	SD
[OC]	11. I seem to know more words than other kids when I read.	SA	A	U	D	SD
[SF]	12. People in my family think I am a good reader.	SA	A	U	D	SD
[PR]	13. I am getting better at reading.	SA	A	U	D	SD
[OC]	14. I understand what I read as well as other kids do.	SA	A	U	D	SD
[PR]	15. When I read, I need less help than I used to.	SA	A	U	D	SD
[PS]	16. Reading makes me feel happy inside.	SA	A	U	D	SD
[SF]	17. My teacher thinks I am a good reader.	SA	A	U	D	SD
[PR]	18. Reading is easier for me than it used to be.	SA	A	U	D	SD
[PR]	19. I read faster than I could before.	SA	A	U	D	SD
[OC]	20. I read better than other kids in my class.	SA	A	U	D	SD
[PS]	21. I feel calm when I read.	SA	A	U	D	SD
[OC]	22. I read more than other kids.	SA	A	U	D	SD
[PR]	23. I understand what I read better than I could before.	SA	A	U	D	SD
[PR]	24. I can figure out words better than I could before.	SA	A	U	D	SD
[PS]	25. I feel comfortable when I read.	SA	A	U	D	SD
[PS]	26. I think reading is relaxing.	SA	A	U	D	SD
[PR]	27. I read better now than I could before.	SA	A	U	D	SD
[PR]	28. When I read, I recognize more words than I used to.	SA	A	U	D	SD
[PS]	29. Reading makes me feel good.	SA	A	U	D	SD
[SF]	30. Other kids think I'm a good reader.	SA	A	U	D	SD
[SF]	31. People in my family think I read pretty well.	SA	A	U	D	SD
[PS]	32. I enjoy reading.	SA	A	U	D	SD
[SF]	33. People in my family like to listen to me read.	SA	A	U	D	SD

Figure 10.10   The Reader Self-Perception Scale Scoring Sheet

Student name _____

Teacher _____

Grade _____ Date _____

Scoring key: 5 = Strongly Agree (SA)
                    4 = Agree (A)
                    3 = Undecided (U)
                    2 = Disagree (D)
                    1 = Strongly Disagree (SD)

Scales

General Perception	Progress	Observational Comparison	Social Feedback	Physiological States
1. _____	10. _____	4. _____	2. _____	5. _____
	13. _____	6. _____	3. _____	8. _____
	15. _____	11. _____	7. _____	16. _____
	18. _____	14. _____	9. _____	21. _____
	19. _____	20. _____	12. _____	25. _____
	23. _____	22. _____	17. _____	26. _____
	24. _____		30. _____	29. _____
	27. _____		31. _____	32. _____
	28. _____		33. _____	
Raw score	_____ of 45	_____ of 30	_____ of 45	_____ of 40

Score interpretation				
High	44+	26+	38+	37+
Average	39	21	33	31
Low	34	16	27	25

STUDENT READING INTEREST SURVEY

Purpose

For many years, researchers have found that reading comprehension is positively affected when children are interested in the reading materials (Asher, 1980; Corno & Randi, 1997). This is so much the case that interest in reading materials has been shown also to compensate for children's lack of strategy, use, and ability in comprehension specifically and reading generally (Sweet, 1997). Knowing how important student interests are in shaping and influencing students' reading comprehension, the Student Reading Interest Survey (SRIS) (see Figure 10.11) provides teachers with an efficient and effective tool to gain insights into student interests.

Figure 10.11   Student Reading Interest Survey

In-School Interests

What is the title of your favorite book that you have read?

Do you have a favorite book title that someone has read to you?

What kinds of books do you like to read on your own?

Do you have favorite books, magazines, or comic books at home?

Do you ever read the newspaper at home? If so, what parts of the newspaper do you read?

What is your favorite school subject (other than recess and lunch)?

Have you ever done a special research project? What was the topic?

Out-of-School Interests

What do you do for fun on weekends or after school?

Do you have a hobby? If so, what?

What is your favorite TV show?

What is your favorite movie?

Do you play sports? If so, what?

Do you like animals or have a pet?

Do you have favorite video or computer games?

If you surf the Internet, what do you generally look for as you surf?

Have you ever collected something like coins, stamps, and so on? If you have, what?

Materials

You will need the following materials:

- One laminated copy of the questions found in the Student Reading Interest Survey
- One paper copy for recording individual student responses
- One paper copy for recording categories of class responses

Procedure

Once the necessary materials are in place, schedule a time during the day to meet with students individually. Using the laminated copy of the SRIS, seat the child comfortably next to you at a table in a quiet corner of the classroom. (This survey may also be given by an aide or volunteer so long as he or she has been trained to completely record answers.) Ask children each question and record the answers given. After each response, be sure to tell each child that if he or she remembers anything else to tell you, that child is welcome to share it at a later time.

After the entire class has been surveyed, compile the individual responses into a class survey response profile (see Figure 10.12). Record abbreviated answers to each question for each student in the class response profile. Look over the responses to each

Figure 10.12   Class Student Reading Interest Survey Profile Recording Table

Student Names	Q1	Q2							

question by all of the children for categories of interests to be observed in your teaching and reading materials acquisition plan.

During the year, particularly if children's writing skills are well developed, distribute the SRIS to the entire group of children. Ask them to write their answers to the SRIS questions on their own copy and turn it in. Make any changes you discover throughout the year on the class profile sheet. This updated information about your students' reading interests will help you adjust your selection of topics and reading materials as the year progresses.

In Figure 10.13, we summarize the procedures and instruments we have just discussed for assessing factors associated with the *reader* that affect reading comprehension. In this

Figure 10.13   Summary Matrix of Assessments to Measure Comprehension Factors Associated With the Reader

Name of Assessment Tool	Screening Assessment Purpose	Diagnostic Assessment Purpose	Progress-Monitoring Assessment Purpose	Outcomes Assessment Purpose	Norm-Referenced Test	Criterion-Referenced Test	Reliability Evidence	Validity Evidence
Langer's Background Knowledge Assessment Procedure	−	−	+	−	−	+	Not Available	Not Available
A Classroom Modified Version of the Reading Strategy Use Scale	+	−	−	+	−	+	Cronbach's Alpha for Subscales Ranged From .70–.72	Factor Analysis Intercor-relation Ranged From .65–.78 With the Three-Factor Model at .97

continued

Figure 10.13   Continued

Name of Assessment Tool	Screening Assessment Purpose	Diagnostic Assessment Purpose	Progress-Monitoring Assessment Purpose	Outcomes Assessment Purpose	Norm-Referenced Test	Criterion-Referenced Test	Reliability Evidence	Validity Evidence
Metacompre-hension Strategy Index (MSI)	+	−	−	+	−	+	Kuder Richardson Formula 20–.87 Coefficient	Concurrent Validity With Index of Reading Awareness .48; .49 With Cloze Task; .50 With Error Detection Task
Social Collabora-tion Performance Outcome Evaluation	−	−	+	+		+	Not Available	Not Available
Self-Assessment of Collaboration: Group Accountability	+	−	−	+	−	+	Not Available	Not Available
Self-Assessment of Collaboration: Individual Accountability	+	−	−	+	−	+	Not Available	Not Available
Motivation for Reading Questionnaire (MRQ), Revised Version	+	+	+	+	−	+	Cronbach's Alpha Reliability on Eight Subscales of .43–.83	Principal Components Factor Analysis All But Two Items Loaded at Greater Than .40 on Primary Factor Motivation
The Reader Self-Perception Scale (RSPS)	+	−	+	+	−	+	Cronbach's Alpha Ranges: .81–.84	Construct Validity Drawn From Theoretical Literature on Self-Efficacy
Student Reading Interest Survey	+	−	+	−	−	+	Not Available	Not Available

Key: + can be used for   − not appropriate for

Summary Matrix of Assessments to Measure Comprehension Factors Associated With the Reader, we provide information about federally related assessment purposes, for example, *screening, diagnosis, progress monitoring,* or *outcomes assessment,* as well as the type of test or procedure (norm referenced or criterion referenced) and psychometric evidence of test or procedure scores including reliability and/or validity evidence.

CONNECTING ASSESSMENT FINDINGS TO TEACHING STRATEGIES

Before discussing intervention strategies, we have constructed a guide connecting assessment to intervention and/or strategy choices. It is our intention to help you, the teacher, select the most appropriate instructional interventions and strategies to meet students' needs based on assessment data. In the next part of this chapter, we offer strategies for intervention based on the foregoing assessments.

INSTRUCTIONAL INTERVENTIONS AND STRATEGIES: HELPING THE READER IMPROVE READING COMPREHENSION

After a careful assessment of a student's comprehension, one or more of the following strategies may be appropriately applied. Perhaps the most important thing to remember is that children with a poor background knowledge, motivation, and strategy selection or use can be helped to improve their comprehension by teachers who are sensitive to the need to assess these components of reading comprehension and take affirmative steps to address student needs. If students lack background, then teachers need to build it. If they have incorrect or incomplete background knowledge, then teachers need to activate this knowledge and add to it or modify or correct it. If students lack motivation, then teachers need to know what is lacking and why. Then they can select strategies that socially involve students actively in comprehension to increase motivation. Finally, if students lack strategies, then teachers can take steps to teach these cognitive comprehension strategies explicitly and scaffold their use to student independence. Our first comprehension instructional strategy—interactive read aloud—is valuable for activating and building students' prior or background knowledge, teaching comprehension strategies, and motivating students to comprehend what they read. Following the discussion of this general strategy, we present strategies in three groupings: (a) activating and building students' prior or background knowledge, (b) increasing students' motivation to comprehend what they read, and (c) explicitly teaching cognitive comprehension strategies.

INTERACTIVE READ ALOUD

Purpose

Reading aloud to children has long been supported as the most important means to motivate and demonstrate for children the strategies and motivations for reading. "*The single most important activity for building the knowledge for eventual success in reading is reading aloud to children. This is especially so in the preschool years. The benefits are the greatest when the child is an active participant, engaging in discussions about*

If-Then Strategy Guide for Improving Readers' Comprehension

"If" the student is ready to learn ↓ / "Then" try these teaching strategies →	Interactive Read Aloud	K-W-L	Semantic Clues Webbing	Numbered Heads Together	Think-Pair-Share	Teaching Comprehension Strategies Explicitly	Click or Clunk and Fix-Up	Comprehension Strategy Framework	QAR	Elaborative Interrogation	RT
Cognitive Strategies	+	−	−	−	−	+	+	*	+	+	+
Background Knowledge	*	+	+	−	−	*	−	*	*	−	*
Choice	*	−	−	*	*	−	−	*	−	−	−
Challenge	*	*	*	*	*	*	*	*	*	*	*
Consequences	*	*	*	*	*	+	+	*	+	+	+
Control	*	+	*	−	*	−	+	*	+	*	*
Collaboration	+	+	+	+	+	*	*	*	*	*	*

Key: + Excellent Strategy
     * Adaptable Strategy
     − Unsuitable Strategy

294

stories, learning to identify letters and words, and talking about meanings of words" (Anderson, Hiebert, Scott, & Wilkinson, 1985, p. 23). More recently, reading books aloud to students has been viewed as an effective vehicle for transporting students into the world of learning how to select and apply cognitive reading strategies (Sweeney, 2004).

Interactive read aloud is a strategy that can help you, the teacher, explicitly teach the selection and use of cognitive comprehension strategies (see "Cognitive Comprehension Strategies . . ." later in this section) to younger or older children through thinking aloud and interacting with them over multiple texts (Campbell, 2001; Martens, 1996; Martin & Reutzel, 1999; Schikendanz, 1990). Using differing grouping structures that encourage greater student involvement and interaction help to motivate students to comprehend what they read (National Institute of Child Health and Human Development, 2000). Most read alouds in school take place with an entire class or group of children, but Morrow (1988, 2005) reminds us not to overlook the motivational benefits and social importance of reading aloud to smaller groups and individuals. Children whose reading development is lagging behind their peers can be helped a great deal by teachers and parents who take time to read to them in small-group or individual settings and talk through the text with children. During interactive read alouds (Campbell, 2001), it is expected that teachers and children will stop to ask questions, make comments, or respond to each other and the text. Morrow (2005) suggests that, when possible, individual or small-group readings be recorded and analyzed to provide diagnostic information to inform instruction.

Finally, interactive read alouds using simple children's picture books are a wonderful way to convey complex ideas, topics, and processes in a more simplistic form to build background knowledge. By reading, discussing, and carefully examining the pictures, diagrams, or other visual aids in these books, children who have little background knowledge can improve their reading comprehension (Giorgis & Johnson, 2002; Ebbers, 2002).

Materials

No special materials are needed other than books correctly matched to students' interests and strategy learning needs. It is best if you select texts that are of high interest and have some familiarity to students but contain some challenging new ideas and concepts, as well as texts in which there are multiple opportunities to model the comprehension strategy you have selected to teach to the children.

Procedure

Graham and Kelly (1997) and Campbell (2001) described how to get an Interactive Read Aloud started in the classroom. Campbell (2001) suggested that teachers need to (a) prepare for effective interactive read alouds, (b) read the book aloud as a performance, and (c) ensure that children take part. Preparations for an interactive read aloud can be divided into four sequential steps: (a) select, (b) plan, (c) practice, and (d) deliver (Graham & Kelly, 1997). Books selected should match the intellectual, social, and emotional levels of the children to sustain interest and motivation (Trelease, 2001). In planning for an effective interactive read aloud, decide on the strategy or strategies to be modeled, scaffolded, and released to the students; determine any resources or props that may be needed; decide how much of the book will be read aloud in one sitting; decide how to introduce the book; determine points to be raised for discussion; decide how to end the session if the book is not read in its entirety; and decide how to involve the children in the reading. Campbell (2001) suggested that the book be first presented as a performance; this means that teachers should read the text aloud with enthusiasm and expression. Following the reading, demonstrate for children a quality retelling that contains all of the important elements of the text in the correct order. When you feel that the students are ready to begin producing their own oral retellings, let them know before you read aloud that you will want them to give retelling a try (Morrow, 2005). We have also found that it is best that students be encouraged to try out their retellings with peers prior to sharing it with the teacher or the group.

STRATEGIES TO ACTIVATE AND BUILD STUDENTS' PRIOR OR BACKGROUND KNOWLEDGE

K-W-L

Purpose

Activating students' background knowledge in preparation for reading is significant for promoting reading comprehension. In fact, many teachers' guides and editions contain a section entitled "Activating Prior Knowledge" or "Building Background Knowledge." One strategy called *K-W-L* is widely used and commonly known by many classroom teachers, although research has yet to validate its effectiveness (Stahl, 2004). Ogle (1986), the originator of K-W-L, asserts that this strategy is best suited for use with information texts but it can be adapted for use with story texts by asking children about the theme or message of the story rather than the topic of the story; for example, disobedience is the theme or message of the tale of *Peter Rabbit,* but the topic would be rabbits. We argue that to understand the story, prior knowledge about the consequences of disobedience rather than knowledge about rabbits needs to be activated.

Materials

You will need the following materials:

- An information or narrative book or selection
- A chart or white board on which to display a chart as shown in Figure 10.14
- Markers for recording student contributions

Procedures

Step K: What I Know

This first step of K-W-L strategy lessons is composed of two levels of accessing prior knowledge: (a) brainstorming and (b) categorizing information. Ask children to brainstorm about

Figure 10.14 K-W-L Chart

Know	What I Want to Learn	Learned

a particular topic (in the case of a narrative, brainstorm a particular theme or message). For instance, you may ask children what they know about bats. A list of associations is formed through brainstorming. When students make a contribution, Ogle (1986) suggests asking them where or how they got their information to challenge them to use higher levels of thinking.

Next, ask students to look for ways in which the brainstorming list can be reorganized into categories of information. For example, you may notice that the brainstorming list shows three related pieces of information about how bats navigate. These can be reorganized into a "navigation" category. Encourage children to look at the list and think about other categories represented in the brainstorming list.

Step W: What Do I Want to Learn?

During Step W, students recognize gaps, inaccuracies, and disagreements in their prior knowledge to decide what they want to learn. You, the teacher, can play a central role in pointing out these problems and helping students frame questions for which they would like to have answers. Questions can be framed by using the stem "I wonder." After children generate a series of questions to be answered from the reading, they are to write down personal questions for which they would like answers. These are often selected from those questions generated by the group.

Step L: What I Learned

After reading, ask students to write down what they learned. This can take the form of answers to specific questions they asked or a concise written summary of their learning. These questions and answers may be discussed as a group or shared between pairs of students. In this way, other children benefit from the learning of their peers as well as from their own learning. In summary, K-W-L has been shown to be effective in improving reading comprehension by causing students to activate, think about, and organize their prior knowledge as an aid to reading comprehension (DeWitz & Carr, 1987).

SEMANTIC CLUES WEBBING

Purpose

Semantic clues webbing is an adaptation of the well-known and somewhat well-worn semantic webbing strategy (Johnson & Pearson, 1984; Johnson, Toms-Bronkowski, & Pittleman, 1982; Nagy, 1988), in which students are given a target concept or word and are encouraged to brainstorm their associations. Semantic clues webbing reverses this process by beginning with a series of clues that actively lead participants to activate their prior knowledge to determine the target word or concept. We especially like this strategy for engaging students around a topic, theme, or concept for which the teacher is relatively certain at least some children in the group have knowledge and experience they can draw upon and contribute during the process.

Materials

Start with stories that contain familiar beginning and ending phrases, such as *once upon a time* and *they lived happily ever after*. After choosing a story, determine the target knowledge to be activated, such as *Cinderella*. Prepare a listing of clues that will be revealed one at a time until the children locate the target concept of *Cinderella* in their prior knowledge.

Procedure

To begin the lesson, place an incomplete semantic web with one clue on the overhead, computer projector, or white board as shown in Figure 10.15.

Let children talk with each other and you about what they are thinking after reading the first clue. Record these ideas as shown under Clue 1 in the semantic clues web. Continue with Clue 2 through Clue 7, repeating this cycle. After the last clue has been read and discussed, ask the class to indicate what should be the target concept or word (i.e., *Cinderella*) that belongs in the middle of the semantic web. As you create your clue list, begin with very general clues associated with the target concept. Present clues that are increasingly more closely associated with the target concept. Children are very much engaged in activating and talking about their background knowledge using the semantic clues webbing process. Very often, a child figures out the target concept with only one or two clues, but do not stop if this happens. Write down that student's response on the web, and keep on giving clues. This allows more children to work with their prior knowledge and take advantage of the thinking of their peers through rich and collaborative conversations and thinking aloud. We also encourage you to get children in collaborative groups using, for example, "turn to your neighbor," numbered heads together, or think-pair-share strategies to discuss these clues as discussed in the next section of this chapter.

Figure 10.15 Incomplete Semantic Clues Web for Activating Background Knowledge

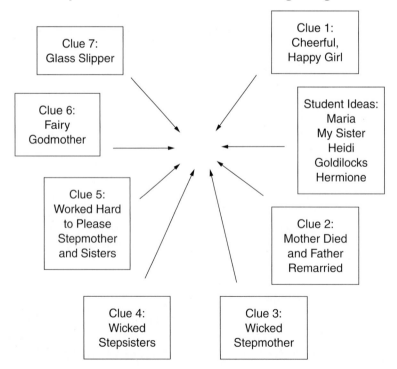

COOPERATIVE OR COLLABORATIVE STRATEGIES TO INCREASE STUDENT INTERACTION AND MOTIVATION

NUMBERED HEADS TOGETHER: "READERS COLLABORATE TO COMPREHEND"

Purpose

This approach to collaboration is effective in helping students understand and comprehend knowledge or comprehension strategy–based activities as well as to provide structured practice and increased student interaction during text discussions and interactions (Kagan, 1990; Johnson & Johnson, 1998). In this collaborative comprehension strategy, all students feel motivated to be actively involved in comprehending the text because they could easily be called upon to represent their group at any time.

Materials

A poster that describes the expectations and process of the numbered heads together strategy such as the one shown in Figure 10.16 may be helpful for younger and older students. This poster should be displayed in a prominent location in the classroom.

Procedures

Numbered heads together is a simple collaboration strategy made up of four major steps. The first step is, *Students number off.* Each student numbers off from 1 to 5. The second

Figure 10.16   Numbered Heads Together Poster

Numbered Heads Together

1. Students Number Off.

2. Teacher Asks a Question.

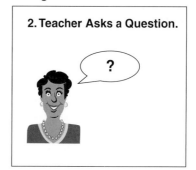

3. Heads Together.

Discuss

4. A Number From 1 to 5 is Called at Random by the Teacher. Student With That Number Answers.

1

Answer

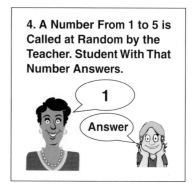

step is, *Teacher asks a question* and sets a time limit for the group to discuss. The next step is, *Heads together,* in which students literally put their heads together and make sure the others in the group know the answer to the question or problem posed by the teacher. One student may be appointed group checker to quickly review with the group that each member has and understands the answer. The final step is, *Teacher calls a number.* At this point in the strategy, the teacher calls out a number at random from 1 to 5. Students in each group with that number raise their hands to answer the question. Finally, the teacher calls upon one of the group members to answer the teacher's question.

THINK-PAIR-SHARE: "READERS COLLABORATE TO COMPREHEND"

Purpose

Teachers often want children to share their ideas and feelings with one another. A typical way of accomplishing this end is for the teacher to ask students to volunteer to share ideas one at a time with the group. For teachers who want to increase motivation and collaborative opportunities for their students to respond, share, think, and problem solve with others around a text, Lyman and McTighe's (1988) think-pair-share strategy provides a successful "across the curriculum" method (Slavin, 1995), especially when reading information texts but also with narrative texts (Wood & Jones, 1994).

Materials

A poster that describes the expectations and processes of the think-pair-share strategy is shown in Figure 10.17.

Figure 10.17 Think-Pair-Share Poster

Think-Pair-Share

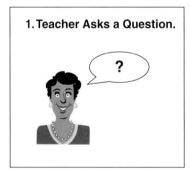

1. Teacher Asks a Question.

2. Students Think.

3. Pair.

Discuss

4. Share With the Whole Group.

Share

Procedures

The process is begun by the teacher instructing students to listen to a question or problem. Students are given time to think of a response to the question or problem. Next, students are told to share their responses with a neighboring peer. Finally, students are encouraged to share their responses with the whole group. A time limit is typically set for each segment of the think-pair-share strategy.

COGNITIVE COMPREHENSION STRATEGIES TO INCREASE STUDENTS' READING COMPREHENSION

EXPLICIT COGNITIVE COMPREHENSION STRATEGY INSTRUCTION

Purpose

The primary purpose of explicit cognitive comprehension strategy instruction is twofold: (a) to teach students to clearly understand what is meant by "comprehension monitoring"; and (b) to teach students how to self-monitor, evaluate, self-regulate, and otherwise "fix up" their own comprehension problems over time. "Some students struggle with reading because they lack information about what they are trying to do and how to do it. They look around at their fellow students who are learning to read [fluently and well] and say to themselves, 'How are they doing that?' In short they are mystified about how to do what other students seem to do with ease" (Duffy, 2004, p. 9).

It is typically very difficult for teachers to provide explicit cognitive comprehension strategy explanations for how to monitor one's own construction of meaning from a text. To do so, they must become aware of the processes they use to monitor their own reading comprehension processes. However, because teachers are already readers who comprehend what they read, they do not think deeply or systematically about the processes they use to do so (Duffy, 2004).

Materials

Materials for explicit cognitive comprehension strategy instruction should be selected from among several text sources that represent at least the genres of information and story. Texts selected for providing explicit cognitive comprehension strategy should be complete books that can be read and discussed in a single sitting.

Procedure

To teach an explicit cognitive comprehension strategy lesson, a framework lesson plan template is needed. Reutzel has developed an explicit lesson framework based on Duffy (2004) called **EMS—E**xplanation, **M**odel, **S**caffold. Explanations include what is to be learned, where and when it is to be used, and why it is important. Modeling requires teachers to demonstrate, often through think alouds with a text, how an aspect of comprehension monitoring, like using fix ups, is to be done. Finally, teachers gradually release through a series of guided practice experiences the reading of a text to individual application through a process we call *You* (teacher model)—*You and Me* (teacher and student share the monitoring task reading with the whole class or with partners)—*and Me* (student monitors reading comprehension independently). A template explicit cognitive comprehension strategy lesson on comprehension monitoring is found in Figure 10.18 to demonstrate each of the parts of the EMS explicit cognitive comprehension strategy lesson.

Figure 10.18   Explicit Comprehension Monitoring Strategy Lesson Plan Template

Objective: *Children will monitor their own comprehension processes and use fix-up strategies to repair broken comprehension processes when necessary.*
Supplies:
- Excellent story or information text

Explain:
What
- Today boys and girls, we are going to be learning about how to monitor or check our understanding or comprehension as we read. The first step in learning to monitor our understanding or comprehension as we read is to learn to stop periodically and ask ourselves a few simple questions like: Is this making sense? Am I getting it? or Do I understand what this is about?

Why
- We need to monitor our comprehension or understanding when we read because what we read should make sense to us. If it does not make sense, there is no point in continuing to read. Monitoring our comprehension while reading helps us to be aware of whether or not we are understanding or making sense of what we read so we can just keep on reading if we understand or stop and do something to help us understand if the text is making sense to us.

When/Where
- Whenever we read, we should monitor or think about whether or not we are understanding or comprehending what we are reading.

Model:
- I am going to read aloud the first two pages of our story, *Thunder Cake,* (Polacco, 1990). After reading the first two pages, I am going to stop and monitor my comprehension. I will think out loud about the questions I should ask when I stop to monitor my comprehension: Is this making sense? Am I getting it? or Do I understand what this is about? I have written these monitoring steps (stop and question) on a poster to help me remember. I have also written the three comprehension monitoring questions on the poster to help me remember. After thinking about these questions for a minute, I will answer the question, yes or no. If *yes*, I will continue to read. If my answer is *no*, I will have to stop for now because I do not yet know what I should do when it does not make sense to me. See, I have also put *yes* and *no* on our poster to help me know what to do when I answer *yes* or *no* to the three comprehension monitoring questions. OK, here I go:

Thunder Cake
On a sultry summer days at my grandma's farm in Michigan, the air get damp and heavy. Storm clouds drift low over the fields. Birds fly close to the ground. The clouds glow for an instant with a sharp, crackling light, and then a roaring, low, tumbling sound of thunder makes the window shudder in their panes. The sound used to scare me when I was little.
(Stop!)

Am I getting it? Is it making sense? Do I understand what this is about? *Yes,* I think I do. This story is about going to Grandma's farm and hearing the sound of thunder. So, if it makes sense and I answer *yes,* I just keep on reading. After I read a few more pages, I should *stop* to monitor my comprehension again. . . .
(Repeat this cycle with a few more pages and one or two more stopping points for modeling.)

Scaffolding (Me, You and Me, You):
Whole Group (Me and You)
- Now that I have shown you how I *stop* and monitor my comprehension, I want to share this task with you. So, let us read three more pages. At the end of the page, I want you to call out, *Stop!* After I stop, I want you to ask me the three monitoring questions on our

Figure 10.18   Continued

poster: Is this making sense? Am I getting it? and Do I understand what this is about? I will answer *yes* or *no*. If I answer *yes*, tell me what to do. If I answer *no*, then tell me I will have to quit reading until we learn what to do tomorrow. OK, ready.

> Grandma looked at the horizon, drew a deep breath and said, "This is Thunder Cake baking weather, all right. Looks like a storm coming to me."
>
> *(Stop!)*

Small Group/Partners/Teams (Me and You)

☐   Now that we have shared the process of *stopping* and monitoring our comprehension as a group when we read, I want you to share this monitoring process with a partner. I am going to give you a number 1 or 2. Remember your number. (Count heads by one and two.) We are going to read three more pages in our story. At the end of the three pages, I want the partner with the number 1 to call out, *Stop!* Then, I want partner number 2 to ask partner number 1 the three monitoring questions on our poster: Is this making sense? Am I getting it? and Do I understand what this is about? Then, partner number 1 will answer the questions asked by partner number 2 with a *yes* or *no*. If partner number 1 answers *yes*, partner number 2 tells him or her to keep on reading. If partner number 1 answers *no*, then partner number 2 tells him or her to quit reading until we learn what to do tomorrow. OK, ready.

> Her eyes surveyed the black clouds a way off in the distance. Then she strode into the kitchen. Her worn hands pulled a thick book from the shelf above the woodstove. "Let's find that recipe, child, " she crowed as she lovingly fingered the grease-stained pages to a creased spot. "Here it is . . . Thunder Cake!"
>
> *(Stop)*

Individual (You)

☐   Finally, today we have learned that when we read we should *stop* every few pages and monitor our comprehension or understanding by asking ourselves three questions. During the day today during small-group reading or in paired reading, I would like for you to practice monitoring comprehension with a friend and/or by yourself as you read. *Stop* every few pages and ask yourself the three questions on our poster and then decide if you should keep on reading or quit reading and wait until tomorrow when we will learn about what to do when what you read is not making sense.

Assess:

■   Pass out a bookmark that reminds students to stop every few pages while reading and ask the three questions. Put the three questions on the bookmark to remind students!

Reflect:

■   What went well in the lesson?
■   How would you change the lesson?

Source: From *Thunder Cake* by Patricia Polacco, 1990. Used by permission of Philomes Books. A Division of Penguin Young Readers Group. A member of Penguin Group (USA) Inc., 345 Hudson Street, New York, NY 10014. All rights reserved.

Remember, as unpopular as what we are about to say is with many teachers, to begin the process of becoming an explicit comprehension strategy teacher one must write down a lesson plan! In fact, this is the *only* way for you to become an explicit comprehension strategy teacher! Doing so helps you in at least three different ways. Writing down a lesson plan helps you to (a) think through what to say and how to say it, (b) internalize the lesson template for explicit instruction, and (c) internalize the language necessary for explicit instruction.

CLICK OR CLUNK AND FIX-UP STRATEGIES

Purpose

The act of monitoring one's unfolding comprehension of text and taking steps to "fix" comprehension when it is not occurring is referred to as *metacognition* or, sometimes, as *metacomprehension*. The click or clunk strategy was designed to help students recognize when and where their comprehension breaks down during reading. Coupling the click or clunk strategy with instruction on comprehension "fix-up" strategies, students can come to know what to do to detect and correct comprehension breakdowns. If readers fail to detect comprehension breakdowns, they will take no action to correct misinterpretations of the text. If students fail to correct misinterpretations of a text, then their comprehension of texts will likely be both inaccurate and incomplete.

Materials

You will need the following materials:

- One book or story that children have read collectively or individually
- A poster display of the repair strategies shown in Figure 10.19

Procedure

To help students develop the ability to monitor their own comprehension processes, Carr (1985) suggested a strategy called *click or clunk*. This strategy urges readers to reflect at the end of each sentence, paragraph, or section of reading by stopping and asking themselves if the meaning or message "clicks" for them or goes "clunk." If it clunks, what is wrong? What can be done to make sense of it? Once a comprehension breakdown has been detected, it is important to know which strategies to select in repairing broken comprehension, as well as when to use these strategies. In fact, students may know that they need to take steps to repair comprehension but they may not know which steps to take or when to take them. As a consequence, children should be introduced to several well-known repair options for repairing broken comprehension.

To demonstrate the use of a "fix-up" poster, model for students using a "think-aloud" process to help them develop a sense for when to select certain repair strategies for failing comprehension. Read part of a text aloud and, as you proceed, comment on your thinking. Reveal to students your thinking, the hypotheses you have formed for the text, and anything that strikes you as difficult or unclear. By doing so, you demonstrate for students the processes that successful readers use to comprehend a text. Next, remind them of the click or clunk strategy. Gradually release the responsibility for modeling metacognitive strategies to the children during follow-up lessons on

Figure 10.19 Metacomprehension "Fix Up" Strategies

Broken Comprehension Fix Up Strategies

- **Read on.**
- **Reread** the sentence.
- **Go back** and reread the paragraph.
- **Seek** information from glossary or reference materials.
- **Ask** someone near you who may be able to help, such as one of your peers.

Source: Adapted from Babbs (1994).

metacognitive monitoring. Display the repair strategies in a prominent place in your classroom. Be sure to draw your students' attention to these strategies throughout the year.

COMPREHENSION STRATEGY FRAMEWORK

Purpose

The purpose of the *comprehension strategy framework* (CSF) (Dowhower, 1999) is twofold: (a) to provide students with small pieces of text to comprehend and (b) to provide an instructional framework for teaching cognitive comprehension strategies. The rationale for the structure of the CSF is found in five important principles of effective comprehension strategy instruction. First, the text is chunked into cycles of instruction either using the parts of a story—setting, problem, events, resolution—or using the subheadings within an information text to break the text into smaller chunks. Second, a purpose is set for reading to guide and provide a purpose for students' reading. Third, students are encouraged to read silently. Silent reading has been shown to be better than oral reading for facilitating comprehension processes because oral reading diverts attention to an accurate and lively performance of the text rather than to comprehension. Fourth, instruction is embedded in the discussion of a text. Finally, the discussion is focused around a theme or topic because themes or topics help students move beyond literal processes and toward constructing their own interpretations and understandings of texts.

Learning and orchestrating a repertoire of flexible comprehension strategies within a comprehension instructional framework are critically important for all students but especially for ELL students. These students need to experience comprehension strategy instruction within a consistent, reliable, and cohesive framework to learn the unique demands of comprehending text in another language.

Materials

You will need the following materials:

- One well-formed story or storybook
- One copy of the Comprehension Strategy Framework (CSF) Overview shown in Figure 10.20
- One copy of a lesson plan for using the CSF with the story selected

Procedure

Select a well-formed story or information text for reading together as a class or small group. Chunk the text into segments to provide several cycles of practice using purpose setting, silent reading, and discussion. Remember to select a large enough text chunk for prereading to allow students to activate and relate the text to their prior knowledge, as well as to provide an example of using a selected comprehension strategy for instruction such as constructing visual images. At the conclusion of the cycles of practice using text segments from the text, students are encouraged to engage in independent follow-up activities. These may include a number of response activities, such as those outlined in chapter 15, or the completion of graphic organizers (chapter 11), or answering questions.

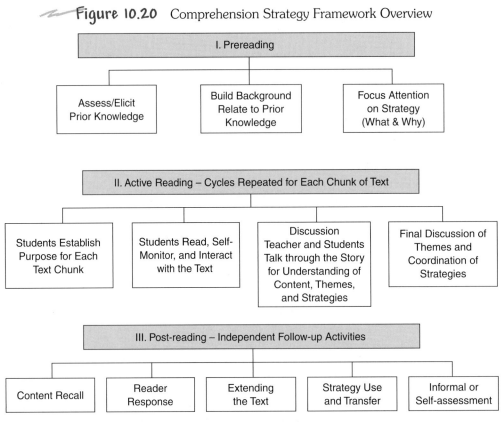

Figure 10.20 Comprehension Strategy Framework Overview

Source: Based on "Supporting a Strategic Stance in the Classroom: A Comprehension Framework for Helping Teachers Help Students to Be Strategic," by S. Dowhower, 1999, *The Reading Teacher, 52*(7), 672–683.

ELABORATIVE INTERROGATION

Purpose

Elaborative interrogation is a questioning intervention that uses student-generated "why" questions to promote active processing of factual reading materials (Wood, Pressley, & Winne, 1990). Students are encouraged in elaborative interrogation to activate their prior knowledge and experiences and use these to pose their own "why" questions using statements in the text to link facts together from text. Facts linked together into a network of relationships improve students' understanding and memory for text information. It is important that the "why" questions generated require students to activate their prior knowledge supporting the facts they need to learn; otherwise, such questions will not enhance comprehension and memory for text.

Menke and Pressley (1994) assert, "*Answering why questions is as good as constructing images to boost memory for facts, providing the questions are well focused*" (p. 644). The elaborative interrogation strategy has been validated to improve readers' comprehension of factual material among students ranging from elementary school ages to adult. It is recommended that teachers use elaborative interrogation when they train struggling students to access relevant prior knowledge in situations in which they typically do not do so spontaneously.

Materials

You will need the following materials:

- An information or narrative book at the appropriate grade or reading level of your students
- A written lesson plan as shown in Figure 10.21.
- A graphic organizer containing the *why* questions generated from the statements found in the book

Procedures

We describe the *elaborative interrogation* strategy using a trade book entitled *My Picture Book of the Planets* (Krulik, 1991), in a model lesson shown in Figure 10.21.

- Read the pages again looking for an answer. Read on to another page to look for the answer.
- If you can, write an answer to your *why* question.
- If you cannot write an answer to your *why* question, save it for our group discussion after reading.

Figure 10.21   Example Lesson Using Elaborative Interrogation Question Posing Strategy

---

Purpose for Learning the Strategy: This strategy will help you relate your own experiences and knowledge to the facts you read in books and other texts. By using this strategy, you will improve your understanding of and memory for the text.

Objective: Rephrase statements in text as if they were stated as *why* questions.

Teacher Explanation and Modeling: This strategy begins by reading a section of text. For example, in the book *My Book of the Planets,* I begin by reading the title. I may ask myself, "Why would someone write a book about the planets?" My answer may include such ideas as the author wanted to teach others and me about planets as compared with stars, or I may wonder if other planets can support life like on Earth, and so on. Next, I read about the first planet, Mercury, in the book. "Mercury is the planet closest to the sun. It is very hot and dry" (Krulik, 1991). I may ask myself the *why* question, "Why is Mercury so hot?" I read on, "Because it is so close to the sun, Mercury takes the shortest amount of time of any of the planets to circle the sun." I ask myself, "Why is closeness to the sun related to a shorter time needed to circle the sun?"

Guided Application: Now let us try this strategy together. Mariann, come read this statement aloud for the class. After she has read this statement, I will make a *why* question from the statement. OK, read this statement. Mariann reads, "Mercury is gray and covered with craters." My question is, "Why would Mercury be gray and covered with craters?" Students are invited to use their knowledge and background to answer this *why* question.

   Now let us reverse the roles. I will read aloud the next statement and you make this statement into a *why* question. Teacher reads aloud, "Some of Mercury's craters are bigger than the whole state of Texas!" Children raise their hands. Benji is called upon. He asks, "Why are the craters on Mercury so big?" A discussion ensues to potentially answer these *why* questions.

---

continued

Figure 10.21   Continued

Individual Application: Now I want you to read the rest of this book. When you get to the end of each page, pick one statement to write a *why* question in your notebooks. Next, see if you can answer the question from your own knowledge or experiences. If not, try using the book to answer your question. If neither source can answer your question, save it for our discussion of the book when we are all finished reading. Now, go ahead and read. If you forget what I want you to do, look at this poster for step-by-step directions. The teacher displays the following poster at the front of the room on the board.

Using the Elaborative Interrogation Strategy

- Read each page carefully.
- Stop at the end of each page and pick a statement.
- Write a "why" question for the statement you pick in your reading notebooks.
- Think about an answer to the "why" question using your own knowledge and experiences.
- If you can, write an answer to your "why" question.
- Read the pages again looking for an answer. Read on to another page to look for the answer.
- If you can, write an answer to your "why" question.
- If you can't write an answer to your "why" question save it for our group discussion after reading.

Source: From Reutzel, D.R., Campbell, K., & Smith, J.A., "Hitting the Wall: Helping Struggling Readers Comprehend" in Gambrell, B., Collins-Block, C., and Pressley, M. (Eds). *Improving Comprehension Instruction: Rethinking Research, Theory, and Classroom Practice* (Jossey Bass Education Series). Copyright 2002 by John Wiley & Sons.

Assessment: After the children read, hold a discussion in which children are asked to share their *why* questions and answers. Ask children to hand in reading notebooks with their *why* questions and answers. Examine these notebooks to determine the success of using this strategy. Unanswered *why* questions can be placed into a *question* web for further reading and research. The web may look something like the one shown here.

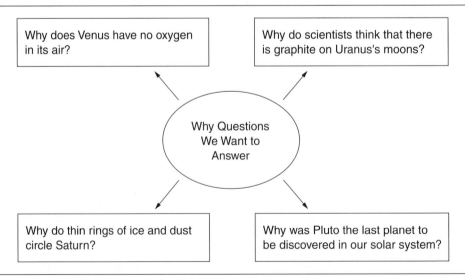

Why does Venus have no oxygen in its air?

Why do scientists think that there is graphite on Uranus's moons?

Why Questions We Want to Answer

Why do thin rings of ice and dust circle Saturn?

Why was Pluto the last planet to be discovered in our solar system?

Other trade books, reference books, and textbooks may be used to answer the questions in this *why* question web.

Planned Review: In about one week, plan to review the use of the elaborative interrogation strategy by using trade books or textbooks with other curricular subjects such as health or social studies or with mathematics word problems.

ADAPTING STRATEGY INSTRUCTION FOR THOSE WHO STRUGGLE

RECIPROCAL TEACHING

Purpose

Palincsar and Brown (1985) designed and evaluated an approach for improving the reading comprehension and comprehension monitoring of special needs students who scored 2 years below grade level on standardized tests of reading comprehension. Their results suggested a teaching strategy called *reciprocal teaching* that is useful for helping students who have difficulties with comprehension and comprehension monitoring, as well as those who are learning English (Casanave, 1988; Johnson-Glenberg, 2000; Rosenshine & Meister, 1994). Although reciprocal teaching was originally intended for use with expository text, we can see no reason why this intervention strategy cannot be used with narrative texts by focusing discussion and reading on the major elements of stories.

Material

You will need the following materials:

- A trade book, basal reader, or textbook selection
- A poster displaying the four comprehension strategies and what they mean: predicting, questioning, summarizing, and clarifying

Procedure

Essentially, this multiple-strategy lesson requires that teachers and students exchange roles, which is intended to increase student involvement in the lesson. The reciprocal teaching lesson comprises four phases or steps (Oczkus, 2004):

- *Prediction.* Students predict from the title and pictures the possible content of the text. The teacher records the predictions.
- *Question Generation.* Students generate purpose questions after reading a predetermined segment of the text, such as a paragraph, page, and so on.
- *Summarizing.* Students write a brief summary (see chapter 11) for the text by starting with "This paragraph was about. . . ." Summarizing helps students capture the gist of the text.
- *Clarifying.* Students and teacher discuss various reasons a text may be hard or confusing, such as difficult vocabulary, poor text organization, unfamiliar content, or lack of cohesion. Students are then instructed in a variety of comprehension fix-up or repair strategies.

When teachers have modeled this process with several segments of text, the teacher assigns one of the students (preferably a good student) to assume the role of teacher for the next segment of text. The teacher may also, while acting in the student role, provide appropriate prompts and feedback when necessary. When the next segment of text is completed, the student assigned as teacher assigns another student to assume that role.

Teachers who use reciprocal teaching to help students with comprehension difficulties should follow four simple guidelines suggested by Palincsar and Brown (1985). First, assess student difficulties and provide reading materials appropriate to students' decoding abilities. Second, use reciprocal teaching for at least 30 minutes a day for 15 to 20 consecutive days. Third, model frequently and provide corrective feedback. Finally, monitor student progress regularly and individually to determine whether the instruction is having the intended effect. Palincsar and Brown reported positive results for this intervention procedure by demonstrating dramatic changes in students' ineffective reading behaviors. Other research has demonstrated the effectiveness of reciprocal teaching with a variety of students (Casanave, 1988; Johnson-Glenberg, 2000; Kelly, Moore, & Tuck, 1994; King & Parent-Johnson, 1999; Pressley & Wharton-McDonald, 1997; Rosenshine & Meister, 1994).

SELECTED REFERENCES

Anderson, R. C., Hiebert, E. F., Scott, J. A., & Wilkinson, I. A. G. (1985). *Becoming a nation of readers: The report of the Commission on Reading.* Washington, DC: The National Institute of Education.

Asher, S. R. (1980). Topic interest and children's reading comprehension. In R. J. Spiro, B. C. Bruce, & W. F. Brewer (Eds.), *Theoretical issues in reading comprehension* (pp. 525–534). Hillsdale, NJ: Erlbaum.

Babbs, P. (1994). Monitoring cards help improve comprehension. *The Reading Teacher, 38*(3), 200–204.

Bandura, A. (1986*). Social foundations of thought and action: A social cognitive theory.* Englewood Cliffs, NJ: Prentice Hall.

Campbell, R. (2001). *Read-alouds with young children.* Newark, DE: International Reading Association.

Carr, E. (1985). The vocabulary overview guide: A metacognitive strategy to improve vocabulary comprehension and retention. *Journal of Reading, 28*(8), 684–689.

Carr, S., & Thompson, B. (1996). The effects of prior knowledge and schema activation strategies on the inferential reading comprehension of children with and without learning disabilities. *Learning Disabilities Quarterly, 19*(2), 48–61.

Casanave, C. P. (1988). Comprehension monitoring in ESL reading: A neglected essential. *TESOL Quarterly, 22*(2), 283–302.

Collins, A. M., & Quillian, M. R. (1969). Retrieval time from semantic memory. *Journal of Verbal Learning and Verbal Behavior, 8,* 240–247.

Corno, L., & Randi, J. (1997). Motivation, volition, and collaborative innovation in classroom literacy. In J. T. Guthrie & A. Wigfield (Eds.), *Reading engagement: Motivating readers through integrated instruction* (pp. 51–67). Newark, DE: International Reading Association.

Dewitz, P., & Carr, E. M. (1987, December). Teaching comprehension as a student directed process. In P. Dewitz (Chair), *Teaching reading comprehension, summarizing and writing in content area.* Symposium conducted at the National Reading Conference, Florida.

Dowhower, S. L. (1999). Supporting a strategic stance in the classroom: A comprehension framework for helping teachers help students to be strategic. *The Reading Teacher, 52*(7), 672–688.

Duffy, G. G. (2004). *Explaining reading: A resource for teaching concepts, skills, and strategies.* New York: Guilford Press.

Durkin, D. (1978–1979). What classroom observations reveal about reading comprehension instruction. *Reading Research Quarterly, 12,* 481–538.

Ebbers, M. (2002). Science text sets: Using various genres to promote literacy and inquiry. *Language Arts, 80*(1), 40–50.

Ellis, S. S., & Whalen, S. F. (1990). *Cooperative learning: Getting started.* New York: Scholastic.

Gardiner, J. R. (1980). *Stone fox.* New York: Scholastic.

Giorgis, C., & Johnson, N. J. (2002). Text sets. *The Reading Teacher 56*(2), 200–208.

Graham, J., & Kelly, A. (1997). *Reading under control: Teaching reading in the primary school.* London: David Fulton.

Henk, W. A., & Melnick, S. A. (1995). The Reader Self-Perception Scale (RSPS): A new tool for measuring how children feel about themselves as readers. *The Reading Teacher, 48*(6), 470–482.

Johnson, D. D., & Pearson, P. D. (1984). *Teaching reading vocabulary* (2nd ed.). New York: Holt, Rinehart, & Winston.

Johnson, D. D., Toms-Bronowski, S., & Pittleman, S. (1982). *An investigation of the effectiveness of semantic mapping and semantic feature analysis with intermediate grade level children* (Program Report 83-3). Madison: Center for Educational Research, University of Wisconsin.

Johnson, D. W., & Johnson, R. T. (1991). *Learning together and alone: Cooperative, competitive, and individualistic learning.* Boston, MA: Allyn & Bacon.

Johnson, D. W., & Johnson, R. T. (1998). Learning *together and alone: Cooperative, competitive, and individualistic learning* (5th ed.). Boston, MA: Allyn & Bacon.

Johnson-Glenberg, M. C. (2000). Training reading comprehension in adequate decoders/poor comprehenders verbal versus visual strategies. *Journal of Educational Psychology, 92*(4), 772–782.

Kagan, S. (1990). *Cooperative learning.* San Juan Capistrano, CA: Resources for Teachers.

Kelly, M., Moore, D. W., & Tuck, B. F. (1994). Reciprocal teaching in a regular primary school classroom. *Journal of Educational Research, 88*(1), 53–61.

King, C. M., & Parent-Johnson, L. M. (1999). Constructing meaning via reciprocal teaching. *Reading Research and Instruction, 38*(3), 169–186.

Kintsch, W. (1998). *Comprehension: A paradigm for cognition.* Cambridge: Cambridge University Press.

Krulik, N. E. (1991). *My picture book of the planets.* New York: Scholastic.

Langer, J. A. (1982). Facilitating text processing: The elaboration of prior knowledge. In J. A. Langer & M. Smith-Burke (Eds.), *Reader meets author: Bridging the gap* (pp. 149–162). Newark, DE: International Reading Association.

Lindsay, P. H., & Norman, D. A. (1977). *Human information processing: An introduction to psychology.* New York: Academic Press.

Lyman, F. T., & McTighe, J. (1988). Cueing thinking in the classroom: The promise of theory-embedded tools. *Educational Leadership, 45,* 18–24.

Martens, P. (1996). *I already know how to read: A child's view of literacy.* Portsmouth, NH: Heinemann Educational Books.

Martin, L., & Reutzel, D. R. (1999). Sharing books: Examining how and why mothers deviate from the print. *Reading Research and Instruction, 39*(1), 39–70.

Menke, D. J., & Pressley, M. (1994). Elaborative interrogation: Using "why" questions to enhance learning from text. *Journal of Reading, 37*(8), 642–645.

Morrow, L. M. (1988). Young children's responses to one-to-one story reading in school settings. *The Reading Teacher, 23*(1), 89–107.

Morrow, L. M. (2005). *Literacy development in the early years: Helping children read and write* (5th ed.). New York: Allyn & Bacon.

Nagy, W. E. (1988). *Teaching vocabulary to improve reading comprehension.* Newark, DE: International Reading Association.

National Institute of Child Health and Human Development. (2000). *Report of the National Reading Panel: Teaching children to read, an evidence-based assessment of the scientific research literature on reading and its implications for reading instruction.* Washington, DC: U.S. Government Printing Office.

Neuman, S. B. (2001). The role of knowledge in early literacy. *Reading Research Quarterly, 36*(4), 468–475.

Oczkus, L. D. (2004). *Reciprocal teaching at work: Strategies for improving reading comprehension.* Newark, DE: International Reading Association.

Ogle, D. M. (1986). K-W-L: A teaching model that develops active reading of expository text. *The Reading Teacher, 39*(6), 564–570.

Palincsar, A., & Brown, A. (1985). Reciprocal teaching: A means to a meaningful end. In J. Osborn, P. T. Wilson, & R. C. Anderson (Eds.), *Reading education: Foundations for a literate America* (pp. 299–310). Lexington, MA: D. C. Heath and Company.

Paris, S. G., & Jacobs, J. E. (1984). The benefits of informed instruction for children's reading awareness and comprehension skills. *Child Development, 55,* 2083–2093.

Paris, S. G., Wasik, B., & Turner, J. C. (1991). The development of strategic readers. In R. Barr, M. L. Kamil, P. Mosenthal, & P. D. Pearson (Eds.), *Handbook of reading research, Vol. II* (pp. 641–668). New York: Longman.

Paris, S. G., & Winograd, P. (2001). *The role of self-regulated learning in contextual teaching: Principles and practices for teacher preparation.* Ann Arbor, MI: Center for the Improvement of Early Reading Achievement.

Pearson, P. D., & Duke, N. K. (2002). Comprehension instruction in the primary grades. In C. Collins-Block & M. Pressley (Eds.), *Comprehension instruction: Research-based best practices* (pp. 247–258). New York: Guilford Press.

Pearson, P. D., Hansen, J., & Gordon, C. (1979). The effect of background knowledge on children's comprehension of implicit and explicit information. *Journal of Reading Behavior, 11*(3), 201–209.

Pereira-Laird, J. A., & Deane, F. P. (1997). Development and validation of a self-report measure of reading strategy use. *Reading Psychology, 18*(3), 185–235.

Polacco, P. (1990). *Thunder cake.* New York: Philomel Books.

Potter, B. (1987). *The tale of Peter Rabbit.* Harmondsworth, Middlesex, England; New York: F. Warne Publishers.

Pressley, M. (2000). What should comprehension instruction be the instruction of? In M. L. Kamil, P. B. Mosenthal, P. D. Pearson, & R. Barr (Eds.), *Handbook of reading research, Vol. 3* (pp. 545–561). Mahwah, NJ: Erlbaum.

Pressley, M., & Wharton-McDonald, R. (1997). Skilled comprehension and its development through instruction. *School Psychology Review, 26*(3), 448–466.

RAND Reading Study Group. (2002). *Reading for understanding: Toward an R&D program in reading comprehension.* Santa Monica, CA: Science and Technology Policy Institute, RAND Education.

Reutzel, D. R., Smith, J. A., & Fawson, P.C. (in preparation) *Reconsidering Silent Sustained Reading (SSR): A Comparative Study of Modified SSR with Oral Repeated Reading Practice.* Logan, UT: Utah State University.

Rosenshine, B., & Meister, C. (1994). Reciprocal teaching: A review of the research. *Review of Educational Research, 64*(4), 479–530.

Rumelhart, D. E. (1981). Schemata: The building blocks of cognition. In J. T. Guthrie (Ed.), *Comprehension and teaching: Research reviews* (pp. 3–26). Newark, DE: International Reading Association.

Schikendanz, J. A. (1990*). Adam's righting revolutions.* Portsmouth, NH: Heinemann Educational Books.

Schmitt, M. C. (1988). The effect of an elaborated directed reading activity on the metacomprehension skills of third graders. In J. E. Readence & R. S. Baldwin (Eds.), *Dialogues in literacy research* (pp. 167–189). Chicago: National Reading Conference.

Schmitt, M. C. (1990). A questionnaire to measure children's awareness of strategic reading processes. *The Reading Teacher, 43,* 454–461.

Schmitt, M. C. (2005). Measuring students' awareness and control of strategic processes. In S. E. Israel, C. C. Block, K. L. Bauserman, & K. Kinnucan-Welsch (Eds.), *Metacognition in literacy learning: Theory, assessment, instruction, and professional development* (pp. 101–119). Mahwah, NJ: Lawrence Erlbaum Associates.

Schunk, D. H. (1996). Goal and self-evaluative influences during children's cognitive skill learning. *American Educational Research Journal, 33,* 359–382.

Schunk, D. H., & Zimmerman, B. J. (1997). Developing self-efficacious readers and writers: The role of social and self-regulatory processes. In J. T. Guthrie & A. Wigfield (Eds.), *Reading engagement: Motivating readers through integrated instruction* (pp. 34–50). Newark, DE: International Reading Association.

Scieszka, J. (1991). *The frog prince continued.* New York: Viking Penguin.

Slavin, R. E. (1995). *Cooperative learning: Theory, research, and practice.* Needham Heights, MA: Allyn & Bacon.

Stahl, K. A. D. (2004). Proof, practice, and promise: Comprehension strategy instruction in the primary grades. *The Reading Teacher, 57*(7), 598–609.

Sweeney, A. (2004). *Teaching the essentials of reading with picture books: 15 lessons that use favorite picture books to teach phonemic awareness, phonics, fluency, comprehension, and vocabulary.* New York: Scholastic.

Sweet, A. P. (1997). Teacher perceptions of student motivation and their relation to literacy learning. In J. T. Guthrie & A. Wigfield (Eds.), *Reading engagement: Motivating readers through integrated instruction* (pp. 86–101). Newark, DE: International Reading Association.

Sweet, A. P & Snow, C. E. (2003). Rethinking reading comprehension. New York: Guilford Press.

Taylor, B. M., Pearson, P. D., Clark, K. F., & Walpole, S. (1999). *Beating the odds in teaching all children to read* (CIERA Report No. 2-006). Ann Arbor, MI: Center for the Improvement of Early Reading Achievement.

Trelease, J. (2001). *The read aloud handbook* (5th ed.). New York: Penguin.

Turner, J., & Paris, S. (1995). How literacy tasks influence children's motivation for literacy. *The Reading Teacher, 48*(8), 662–673.

van Dijk, T. A. (1999). Context models in discourse processing. In H. van Oostendorp & S. R. Goldman (Eds.), *Construction of mental representations during reading* (pp. 123–148). Mahwah, NJ: Lawrence Erlbaum Associates.

Wigfield, A. (1997). Children's motivations for reading and reading engagement. In J. T. Guthrie & A. Wigfield (Eds.), *Reading engagement: Motivating readers through integrated instruction* (pp. 14–33). Newark, DE: International Reading Association.

Wigfield, A., Guthrie, J. T., & McGough, K. (1996). *A questionnaire measure of children's motivations for reading* (Instructional Resource No. 22). Athens, GA: National Reading Research Center.

Wood, E., Pressley, M., & Winne, P. H. (1990). Elaborative interrogation effects on children's learning of factual content. *Journal of Educational Psychology, 82,* 741–748.

Wood, K. D., & Jones, J. P. (1994). Integrating collaborative learning across the curriculum. *Middle School Journal, 20,* 19–23.

Zwann, R. A. (1999). Embodied cognition, perceptual symbols, and situation models. *Discourse Processes, 28*(1), 81–88.

Chapter 11

Reading Comprehension: Focus on the *Text*

Millie is a fourth-grade student in Ms. Franklin's class. Millie is one of those kids that simply blasted their way through their first several years of school reading well above grade level. When it came to reading in story and chapter books, poetry, and about everything else encountered in the basal reader, Millie was by all accounts through the second grade a very good student in reading.

When Millie reached the last half of third grade and the reading selections and general curriculum took a decided swing toward informational texts and content area learning, her reading performance began to falter. Especially in science, Millie seemed to be having some serious difficulties with comprehension and vocabulary, and, worse yet, her motivation and excitement about school in general and reading in particular were beginning to fade. At a recent teacher-parent conference, Millie's father expressed some concerns about her not wanting to come to school on Monday mornings—what he called "Mondaynucleosis." It was a humorous label but, nonetheless, a disturbing outcome. Worse yet, Millie's father noted that Millie's voracious reading habits were disappearing and in their place a hardened resistance to reading was developing.

Ms. Franklin had seen this development in children before and knew just what to do. She knew that Millie, like so many other intermediate grade children, struggled with transferring her previously acquired and well-practiced reading skills in one type of text, like narrative or poetry, into another type of text, like informational or expository text. Knowing this fact, that comprehension skills development is genre or text type specific was critical for Ms. Franklin. She was not panicked at all and set out to peruse the "Summary Matrix of Text-Based Comprehension Assessments" in this chapter, searching for just the right text-based comprehension teaching strategies for Millie and the other children in her class experiencing similar needs. "A piece of cake!" mused Ms. Franklin to herself as she planned lessons that would help her young readers tackle the challenges of differing text types. "They're going to positively love learning how to use these text-based comprehension strategies to read differing text structures!" she whispered to herself.

BACKGROUND BRIEFING FOR TEACHERS

Does this scenario sound familiar? Remember from chapter 10 that the RAND Reading Study Group (2002) asserted that the act of comprehending entails four essential elements: (a) the reader, (b) the text, (c) the activity, and (d) the sociocultural context. The first three essential elements of reading comprehension occur within the fourth essential element of reading comprehension—the sociocultural context of the school classroom, the home, and other social and cultural situations. In chapter 11, we discuss the second essential element of reading comprehension—the text or the object to be comprehended. Within the discussion of the *text* as part of the comprehension process, we simultaneously discuss cognitive comprehension strategies and sociocultural contexts that are supported by scientific research evidence for improving children's reading comprehension of texts.

Many elementary, intermediate, and secondary teachers find out sooner or later that their students struggle to read texts that convey information rather than those that tell a story. Some teachers conclude either that some texts are too hard for their students to read or that their students are not putting forth enough effort to read differing text types. But the conclusions of many classroom teachers regarding children's text-based reading difficulties are not always the case. For many children in primary-grade elementary classrooms, access to and experience with text that conveys information have been shown to be quite limited (Duke, 2000; Moss & Newton, 2002). Without exposure to and experience with expository texts, elementary children often bring their ideas about stories or narratives to help them process expository texts.

Content classrooms (such as social studies, science, mathematics, and so on) are heavily populated with students for whom reading expository texts is a particular challenge (Romine, McKenna, & Robinson, 1996). These students, who may have been good readers in early grades highly focused on narrative, story, or poetry text, must sometimes think to themselves, "What has happened? Why am I such a lousy reader now when I used to be so good?!"

The answer is relatively simple; differing texts types use very different organizational structures and techniques to convey ideas. One of the most important tasks teachers have is to help students learn to strategically organize and construct new knowledge from differing text types (Farnan, 1996; Simpson, 1996). Even though a number of effective strategies have been identified for use in elementary- and intermediate-grade classrooms to help students succeed (see, for example, Alvermann & Moore, 1991; Guthrie, Van Meter, McCann, Wigfield, Bennett, Poundstone, et al., 1996; Swafford & Bryan, 2000), startlingly few teachers actually use them (Irvin & Connors, 1989; Romine et al., 1996; Stahl, 2004).

When readers approach differing text types—such as narrative or story text, poetry, or informational texts—without the proper frame of reference, they typically experience exertion, frustration, and eventual comprehension failure. Successful comprehension of narrative and expository texts requires that teachers and children understand through substantial experience with both types of texts how these text types differ in the way they are structured or organized.

For nearly three decades, it has been well documented that children are not receiving sustained—explicit, or coherent reading comprehension instruction (Durkin, 1978–1979; National Institute of Child Health and Human Development, 2000; Pressley, 2002; Taylor, Pearson, Clark, & Walpole, 1999; Sweet & Snow, 2003). Although there is little research that specifically examines the quality and extent of reading comprehension text structure instruction in classrooms, one can safely assume that such instruction would most likely be less commonplace than general classroom reading comprehension instruction. This is truly unfortunate.

Research has consistently shown that increasing children's awareness of differing text structures has positive effects on their comprehension of a variety of text types and structures (Armbruster, Anderson, & Ostertag, 1987; Dickson, Simmons, & Kameenui, 1998b; Donovan & Smolkin, 2002). Research on text structure can be examined in any number of ways. In what follows, we examine text structure research from two separate perspectives: (a) What are the explicit, physical features of text that affect readers' awareness of text structure? and (b) How does awareness of implicit text structure affect readers' text comprehension?

EXPLICIT TEXT FEATURES: PHYSICAL AND OBSERVABLE TEXT CHARACTERISTICS

How do the physical, observable, explicit, or surface features found in narrative and expository texts help readers understand the importance of ideas as well as the relationship among ideas within a text? Research has consistently shown that placing macropropositions, gist statements, or main ideas in the first sentence of a paragraph helps readers to better identify and remember important text ideas and information (Seidenberg, 1989). A separate body of research shows that explicit main idea statements are better understood by most readers than are poorly stated, hinted, or implicit statements of the main ideas (Dickson et al., 1998b).

Well-crafted topic sentences and appropriately placed signal words positively affect readers' awareness of the structure of a variety of text types. The use of headings and subheadings (including tables of contents), typographic cues, and line and word spacing helps young, adolescent, and adult readers understand main ideas and relate these to other ideas contained within a text (Dickson et al., 1998b). Headings and subheadings are often signaled through the selective use of typographic cues such as font size and font styles, as well as line, letter, and word spacing.

The physical use of spacing cues within lines of text has been shown also to help younger and older readers recognize important information in text leading to improved comprehension of main ideas (Casteel, 1990). When important ideas are signaled by a process known as *chunking,* in which main ideas are separated by four spaces rather than a single space between phrases or clauses in text, struggling readers are significantly helped to recognize and remember main ideas.

The use of insets or adjunct aids in text such as photographs, diagrams, charts, graphs, captions, questions, or **marginal gloss** has been shown to help some children, distract or confuse others, or be ignored altogether (Dickson et al., 1998a). The use of insets or adjunct aids tends to be far more pronounced in expository texts than in narratives. These additional layers of information found in expository texts tend to be viewed by many teachers as adding to the complexity of teaching children to comprehend expository texts.

In summary, well-presented texts provide several types of layered explicit features that reveal text structure and the interrelationship of ideas within a text. Ideas organized within a text using a predictable pattern of main ideas followed by supporting details also help facilitate identification of text structure and subsequent comprehension of a variety of text types. The use of signal words, headings, typographic features, and spacing, as well as insets and adjunct visual aids, provides additional ways of helping readers discern the structure and flow of text. When readers can determine text organization and structure, they are more apt to comprehend, remember, and use what they read.

IMPLICIT TEXT FEATURES: TACIT ORGANIZATIONAL PATTERNS AND TEXT STRUCTURE

There is convincing empirical evidence that readers' awareness of and use of deep or implicit text structure or organization positively affect reading comprehension. *Implicit text structure* refers to the way in which authors organize text without necessarily telling the reader how they have done so. Research on implicit text structure has generally focused on two types of texts that children encounter in the elementary grades—narrative and expository (Dickson et al., 1998b). As a consequence, we discuss each major text type separately, then together, in the following sections.

Narrative Text Structure

Narrative texts are most often described as texts that tell a story, such as *Jack and the Beanstalk* or *Summer of the Monkeys*. Some obvious exceptions to story texts are those found in mathematics story problems that are called "stories" but do not follow a traditional story structure or a paragraph structure in which the topic sentence appears first (Reutzel, 1983). Narrative or story structure, the prototypical or traditional way in which authors organize their text to convey a story, is the most common text structure encountered in elementary school classrooms and is the most researched (Graesser, Golding, & Long, 1991). Narrative or story structure is found in a variety of story genres such as fables, tall tales, folktales, novels, short stories, comedy, fables, epics, mysteries, and myths. Understanding the way in which authors organize and structure their ideas in texts is key to effective reading comprehension (Simmons & Kameenui, 1998; Pearson & Duke, 2002; Pressley, 2000).

The major elements of story structure have been captured in a system of rules called **story grammars** (Thorndyke, 1977; Mandler & Johnson, 1977; Stein & Glenn, 1979). Story grammars are the rules or descriptions of the necessary elements to make a story and the expected sequence for these elements. Researchers generally agree on the following elements and sequence in a story grammar: *setting, problem, goal, events,* and *resolution.*

Developing a sense of how stories are written and organized helps readers predict what is coming next with greater proficiency, store information in schemas more efficiently, and recall story elements with increased accuracy and completeness (National Institute of Child Health and Human Development, 2000). Graesser et al. (1991) showed that there is strong research support showing that most students are more sensitive to narrative than to expository text structure. However, at-risk or learning disabled children struggle to remember narrative texts because, as some researchers suggest, they have not completely internalized story structure (Montague, Maddux & Dereshiwsky, 1990).

Expository Text Structures

Expository texts (Duke & Bennett-Armistead, 2003) include a range of text types or "genres" that include information texts, reference texts, information texts, biographies, and so on. Nearly 85% of all adult reading has as its purpose to obtain information (Duke, Bennett-Armistead, & Roberts, 2002). Expository texts contain facts, details, descriptions, and procedures that are necessary for understanding concepts and events in the world around us. Children's information books are only one example of many other expository texts, such as biographies, essays, photographic essays, instruction or *how-to* books, encyclopedias, reference books, activity/experiment books, scientific reports, newspaper articles, and so on.

Authors organize expository texts using several well-known text patterns or structures. Armbruster and Anderson (1981) and Meyer (1975) researched the text structures most used by authors of expository texts. These included time order (putting information into a chronological sequence), cause and effect (showing how something occurs because of another event), problem and solution (presenting a problem along with a solution to the problem), comparison (examining similarities and differences among concepts and events), simple listing (registering in list form a group of facts, concepts, or events); and descriptions.

Readers who understand an author's expository organizational pattern or expository text structure recall more from reading information texts than readers who do not (Bartlett, 1978; Meyer, Brandt, & Bluth, 1980; Dickson et al., 1998b). This same research has also shown that poor or struggling readers are less likely to be able to identify and use an author's organization of text to recall information. Thus, teachers need to teach struggling students how to identify the author's implicit organizational pattern or text structure and how to use this knowledge to help them remember, organize, retrieve, and apply what they read.

Hybrid or Dual-Purpose Texts: Easier to Access or More Confusing?

Researchers have for over a decade been discussing a type of text in which authors combine the explicit and implicit features of narrative-story and nonnarrative informational texts (Donovan & Smolkin, 2002; Leal, 1993; Pappas, Keifer, & Levstik, 1999; Skurzynski, 1992). Donovan and Smolkin (2002) have called these types of texts *dual-purpose texts,* while we have referred to them in our work as *hybrid* texts. Hybrid or dual-purpose texts are intended to present facts about a particular topic or body of content knowledge embedded within the overall implicit text structure of a story or narrative. Very often, the physical format or features of these types of texts combine those features found in both, namely, a predictable story line laying out facts in a temporal order along with graphs, diagrams, photos, and charts. Hybrid or dual-purpose texts ostensibly allow readers to access them either as a story or as a text that contains facts about everyday things. Thus, a reader may enter the book at the beginning and follow the story through to its resolution or a reader may enter the book at any point and find information about the topic on virtually any page.

Research on dual-purpose or hybrid texts and students' comprehension has provided rather mixed results. Leal (1992) found that after a hybrid book was read aloud to elementary-school-age children, the children retained more information and had better story discussions than they did when either a story or an information book was read to them. On the other hand, Jetton (1994) and Maria and Junge (1994) found that embedding information within a story structure actually impeded access to and remembrance of information. Consequently, little is known about how teachers can help students to access dual-purpose or hybrid texts successfully.

In summary, research clearly demonstrates that teachers can help children comprehend text better when they are guided by a knowledgeable teacher to study closely, identify, and use an author's organization or structure across differing text types. However, before teaching children to identify and use text structure or text organization to improve reading comprehension, the wise teacher assesses what children know about text structure in order to determine which of many available instructional interventions will be most effective.

ASSESSING STUDENTS' KNOWLEDGE OF TEXT FEATURES AND STRUCTURE: NARRATIVE AND EXPOSITORY TEXT

The key to effective text-based comprehension instruction lies in the accurate identification of the types of text structures students are able to read effectively, as well as the genres or text structures that are difficult for them to comprehend. We have found several forms of text-structure assessments that not only are text-structure specific but also are easily adaptable to differing text types, narrative and expository, and can help teachers plan effective instruction. Offered in this chapter are some examples of each for your consideration.

ORAL STORY RETELLINGS: NARRATIVE TEXT STRUCTURE

Purpose

One of the most effective processes for finding out if a child understands narrative or story text structure is to use oral story retellings (Brown & Cambourne, 1987; Gambrell, Pfeiffer, & Wilson, 1985; Morrow, 1985; Morrow, Gambrell, Kapinus, Koskinen, Marshall, & Mitchell, 1986). Asking children to retell a story involves reconstructing the entire story structure including the story sequence, recalling important elements of the plot, making inferences, and noticing relevant details. Thus, oral story retellings assess story comprehension and narrative or story structure knowledge in a holistic, sequenced, and organized way.

Materials

For an oral retelling, you will need the following materials:

- Blank audiotape
- Portable audiocassette recorder with internal microphone
- Brief story
- "Parsing" of the story (see "Procedure")
- Scoring sheet

Procedure

Select a brief story for students to listen to or read. For example, *The Carrot Seed* by Ruth Krauss (1945)* could be selected. Next, type the text of the story onto a separate piece of paper for parsing. Parsing, in this instance, refers to dividing a story into four major and somewhat simplified story grammar categories: setting, problem, events, and resolution, as shown here.

STORY GRAMMAR PARSING OF "THE CARROT SEED"

Setting

A little boy planted a carrot seed.

Problem (Getting the Seed to Grow)

His mother said, "I'm afraid it won't come up."
His father said, "I'm afraid it won't come up."
And his big brother said, "It won't come up."

Events

Every day the little boy pulled up the weeds around the seed and sprinkled the ground with water.
But nothing came up.
And nothing came up.

---

* Text copyright 1945 by Ruth Krauss. Used by permission of HarperCollins Publishers.

Everyone kept saying it wouldn't come up.
But he still pulled up the weeds around it every day and sprinkled the ground
   with water.

Resolution

And then, one day, a carrot came up just as the little boy had known it would.

Oral story retellings may be elicited from children in a number of ways. One way involves the use of pictures or verbal prompts from the story. As pictures in the story are flashed sequentially, the child is asked to retell the story as remembered from listening or reading. Morrow (2005) suggested that teachers prompt children to begin story retellings with a statement such as: "A little while ago, we read a story called [Name the story]. Retell the story as if you were telling it to a friend who has never heard it before." Other prompts during the oral story retelling may be framed as questions:

- "How does the story begin?" or "Once upon a time. . . ."
- "What happens next?"
- "What happened to [the main character] when . . .?"
- "Where did the story take place?"
- "When did the story take place?"
- "How did the main character solve the problem in the story?"
- "How did the story end?"

Morrow (2005) recommends that teachers offer only general prompts such as those listed previously rather than asking about specific details, ideas, or a sequence of events in the story. Remember, when asking questions such as those previously listed, you are moving from free recall of text to a form of assisted recall of text information. Coincidentally, you should know that assisted recall of story text information is especially useful with struggling readers.

A second way to elicit oral story retellings from students is to use unaided recall, in which students retell the story without pictures or verbal prompts. Asking the child to tell the story "as if he or she were telling it to someone who had never heard or read the story before" begins an unaided oral story retelling. To record critical elements of the story structure included in the child's oral story retelling, use an audiotape recording and oral story retelling coding sheet like the one shown in Figure 11.1. The information gleaned from an oral story retelling may be used to help you, the teacher, focus future instruction on enhancing students' understanding of narrative or story text structure.

ORAL RETELLINGS: EXPOSITORY STRUCTURE

Purpose

McGee (1982) found that children in the elementary grades are aware of expository text structures although good readers in fifth grade are more aware than are poor readers in fifth grade or good readers in third grade. One of the most effective ways to find out if a child understands expository text is to use oral retellings (Duke & Bennett-Armistead, 2003). An oral retelling is an oral recounting of a text that has been read either silently or orally. Asking children to retell an expository text involves reconstructing the contents of the expository text including the major, main, or superordinate ideas; the minor or subordinate details; and the underlying organization of the ideas in the text such as

Figure 11.1 Oral Story Retelling Coding Form

Student's name: _____   Grade: _____
Title of story: _____   Date: _____

General directions: Give 1 point for each element included, as well as for "gist." Give 1 point for each character named, as well as for such words as *boy, girl,* or *dog.* Credit plurals (*friends,* for instance) with 2 points under characters.

Setting
   a. Begins with an introduction   _____
   b. Indicates main character   _____
   c. Other characters named   _____
   d. Includes statement about time or place   _____

Objective
   a. Refers to main character's goal or problem to be solved   _____

Events
   a. Number of events recalled   _____
   b. Number of events in story   _____
   c. Score for "events" (a/b)   _____

Resolution
   a. Tells how main character resolves the story problem   _____

Sequence
Summarizes story in order: setting, objective, episodes, and resolution. (Score 2 for correct order, 1 for partial order, 0 for no sequence.)   _____

Possible score: _____   **Student's score:** _____

compare/contrast, cause effect, description, list, enumeration, and so on. Thus, oral expository text retellings assess content comprehension and text structure knowledge in holistic, sequenced, and organized ways.

Materials

For an oral retelling, you will need the following materials:

- Blank audiotape
- Portable audiocassette recorder with internal microphone
- A full or partial expository text such as an information book or textbook chapter
- A main idea/detail "parsing" of the text
- Scoring sheet

Procedure

Select a brief information trade book or textbook chapter for students to listen to or read either aloud or silently depending on the grade level and development of the child. We recommend that children listen to the text read aloud in K–1, read the text aloud in grades 2–3, and silent read the text in grade 4 and beyond. For example, *Is It a Fish?* by Cutting and Cutting (2002) from the Wright Group Science Collection could be selected. Next, type the text of the book onto a separate piece of paper for parsing. Parsing, in this instance,

Figure 11.2   Oral Expository Text Retelling Coding Form

Put a checkmark by everything the child retells from his or her reading of the text.

_____**Big Idea: A fish is an animal.**

_____Detail: It has a backbone (skeleton inside).

_____Detail: Most fish have scales.

_____Detail: It is cold-blooded.

_____**Big Idea: All fish live in water.**

_____Detail: Some live in saltwater.

_____Detail: Some live in freshwater.

_____Detail: Salmon and eels live in saltwater and freshwater.

_____Detail: Salmon leave the sea to lay eggs in the river.

_____**Big Idea: All fish breathe with gills.**

_____Detail: All animals breathe oxygen.

_____Detail: Some get oxygen from the air.

_____Detail: Fish get oxygen from the water.

_____Detail: A shark is a fish.

_____Detail: Gills look like slits.

_____Detail: A ray's gills are on the underside of its body.

_____Detail: A ray breathes through holes on top of its head when it rests.

_____**Big Idea: Most fish have fins to help them swim.**

_____Detail: A sailfish has a huge fin that looks like a sail on its back.

_____Detail: A (sting) ray waves its pectoral fin up and down.

Scoring:

Please tally the marks for the big ideas and details. Place the total number in the blanks shown below.

Big Ideas _____/4   Details: _____/16   Number of Prompts _____

Sequentially Retold (Circle One):   Yes   No

Other Ideas Recalled Including Inferences: _____

refers to dividing a text into main ideas or superordinate ideas and details or subordinate ideas as shown in Figure 11.2.

Expository text oral retellings may be elicited from children in a number of ways. One way involves the use of pictures or verbal prompts from the text. As pictures in the text are flashed sequentially, the children are asked to retell what they remember from listening or reading about this picture. This approach is modeled after the work of Beaver (1997) in the *Developmental Reading Assessment* and the work of Leslie and Caldwell (2001) in the *Qualitative Reading Inventory—3*. Morrow (1985, 2005) suggested that teachers prompt children to begin oral retellings with a statement such as: "A little while ago, we read a book or text called [Name the text or book]. Retell the text or book as if you were telling it to a friend who has never heard about it before." Other prompts during the recall may include the following:

- "Tell me more about . . . ."
- "You said _____. Is there anything else you can tell me about . . . . "
- "Tell me about gills."
- "Tell me about fins."
- "Tell me how fish move, look, or breathe."

Asking students to retell what they remember using these types of prompts is a form of assisted recall and may be especially useful with struggling readers.

A second way to elicit expository text oral retellings from students is to use unaided recall, in which students retell the contents and order of the content in a book or text without pictures or verbal prompts. Asking the child to retell the information read "as if he or she were telling it to someone who had never heard or read the content of the book or text before" is used to begin an unaided expository text oral retelling. To record critical elements of the expository text oral retelling included in the child's oral retelling, use an audiotape recording. To make judgments about the quality of an unaided expository text oral retelling, you may use a rating guide sheet like the one shown in Figure 11.3 based on the work of Moss (1997).

As you develop the ability to listen to expository text oral retellings, you may no longer require the use of an audio recording and may just make notes on the scoring sheet as to the features you heard the child include in his or her oral retelling. The information gleaned from an expository text oral retelling may be used to help teachers focus their future instruction on enhancing students' understanding of expository text structures, developing sensitivity to main ideas and details, improving sequencing ability, and summarizing information.

Figure 11.3 A Qualitative Assessment of Student Expository Text Oral Retellings

Rating Level	Criteria for Establishing a Level
5	Student includes all main ideas and supporting details, sequences properly, infers beyond the text, relates text to own life, understands text organization, summarizes, gives opinion and justifies it, may ask additional questions —very cohesive and complete retelling.
4	Student includes most main ideas and supporting details, sequences properly, relates text to own life, understands text organization, summarizes, gives opinion—fairly complete retelling.
3	Student includes some main ideas and details, sequences most material, understands text organization, gives opinion—fairly complete retelling.
2	Student includes a few main ideas and details, has some difficulty sequencing, may give irrelevant information, gives opinion—fairly incomplete retelling.
1	Student gives details only, has poor sequencing, gives irrelevant information—very incomplete retelling.

Source: Moss, B. (1997). A qualitative assessment of first graders' retelling of expository text. *Reading Research and Instruction, 37*(1), 1–13.

SCRAMBLED SCHEMA STORY TASK

Purpose

A scrambled schema story task assesses how well readers can reconstruct the order of a story based on their innate understanding of story structure. In this task, a story or major portions of a story are divided into its components—such as setting, problem, events, and resolution—and then scrambled. Students are asked to read each element of the story and then organize the story elements in order on a story board. Results from this analysis can be used to help teachers know whether to increase interactions about story parts during teacher interactive reading aloud and/or to provide explicit instruction in story parts to help readers build a better internal sense of story structure.

Materials

You will need to select a short story or storybook.

1. A simple story board made of laminated poster board
2. Parts of the story typed onto regular $8 1/2'' \times 11''$ white paper and cut into story part strips
3. One white legal-size envelope for storing the typed story part strips
4. An oral retelling story scoring sheet based on the design of the story board to score each student's response

Procedure

Choose a simple story for this activity. Parse or divide the story selected into story grammar elements, as shown for the story of *The Carrot Seed* in the "Oral Story Retellings" assessment activity. After parsing the story, transcribe the entire story text if it is a simple story—a story with no more than two lines of text per page. If not, transcribe only a few sentences from the story that provide the reader sufficient clues about where the story parts were in the sequence and structure of the story. Type the transcribed text onto plain white paper and, with scissors, cut the text into the parts of the story. Scramble the pieces and place them into a plain white legal-size envelope. Hand the child the envelope and ask him or her to read each part of the story. You may want to assist the child with any decoding problems. Next, ask the child to put the pieces of the scrambled story in order on the story board. Ask him or her to reread the story strips on the storyboard to check that his or her ordering of the story makes sense. Record the child's responses to this task on the form shown in Figure 11.1.

Poor performance on this task is typically due to limited exposure to hearing stories read aloud and discussing these with others. As a consequence, daily interactive teacher read alouds along with explicit story structure instruction (National Institute of Child Health and Human Development, 2000) are logical means for helping children who perform poorly on this task to develop an improved sense of story.

CONTENT-AREA READING INVENTORY

Purpose

The Content-Area Reading Inventory (CARI) (Farr, Tulley, & Pritchard, 1989; Readence, Bean, & Baldwin, 1992) is an informal reading inventory assessing whether students have learned sufficient reading and study strategies to succeed with content materials. The CARI can be administered to groups of students and typically includes three major sections (Farr et al., 1989) that assess (a) student knowledge of and ability to use common textbook components (i.e., table of contents, glossary, index) and supplemental research aids (card catalog, reference books, periodicals); (b) student knowledge of important vocabulary and skills, such as context clues; and (c) comprehension skills important to understanding expository texts. For the last two sections of the CARI assessment, students are asked to read a selection from the adopted text.

Materials

Readence et al. (1992) suggested contents for a CARI, which are described (and slightly adapted) here:

PART I: TEXTUAL READING AND STUDY AIDS

- A. Internal aids
    1. Table of contents
    2. Index
    3. Glossary
    4. Chapter introduction/summaries
    5. Information from pictures
    6. Other aids included in the text
- B. Supplemental research aids
    1. Card catalog
    2. Periodicals
    3. Encyclopedias
    4. Other relevant aids for the content area

PART II: VOCABULARY KNOWLEDGE

- A. Knowledge and recall of relevant vocabulary
- B. Use of context clues

PART III: COMPREHENSION SKILLS AND STRATEGIES

- A. Text-explicit (literal) information
- B. Text-implicit (inferred) information
- C. Knowledge of text structures and related strategies

Procedure

To develop a CARI, follow this process:

Step 1: Choose a passage of at least three to four pages from the textbook(s) to be used. The passage selected should represent the typical writing style of the author.

Step 2: Construct about 20 questions related to the text. Readence et al. (1992) recommended 8 to 10 questions for Part I, 4 to 6 questions for Part II, and 7 to 9 questions for Part III. We urge the use of questions based on writing patterns used in the sample selection; they should reflect the facts, concepts, and generalizations in the selection.

Step 3: Explain to students that the CARI is not used for grading purposes but is useful for planning teaching activities that will help them succeed. Using a minilesson kind of format, walk students through the different sections of the CARI and model responses.

Step 4:   Administer Part I first, then Parts II and III on separate day(s). It may take several sessions to work through the CARI. We recommend devoting only about 20 minutes per day to administering parts of the CARI, so that other class needs are not ignored during the assessment phase.

Readence et al. (1992) suggested the following criteria for assessing the CARI:

Percentage Correct	Text Difficulty
86%–100%	Easy reading
64%–85%	Adequate for instruction
63% or below	Too difficult

From careful analysis of this assessment, teachers can plan specific lessons to help students cope with difficult expository readings and internalize important information. Students may be grouped according to need for these lessons while practicing strategies that lead to increased comprehension.

STORY GRAMMAR QUESTIONING

Purpose

Questions are an integral part of life in and out of school. From birth, we learn about our world by asking questions and questioning our answers against the confines of reality. Beck and McKeown (1981) and Sadow (1982) suggested that teachers follow a logical model of questioning to probe those areas of comprehension that may not be freely offered in an oral retelling of a text (Rathvon, 2004). Research (Mandler & Johnson, 1977) indicates that story grammars provide just such a model for asking questions about stories. These same researchers have found that developing questions for stories using a story grammar framework produced improved reading comprehension among children as measured by the ability to correctly and completely answer comprehension questions about stories (Beck, Omanson, & McKeown, 1982). Other evidence from research on story grammar questioning suggests that good readers have well-developed understanding of story structure, whereas poor readers do not (Whaley, 1981). Therefore, using a story grammar to guide teacher questioning and self-questioning can help teachers and students to better assess understanding of story structure.

Materials

You will need the following materials:

- One simple story to be read aloud or individually and silently
- One copy of an empty or blank story grammar map (see Figure 11.4)
- One set of questions dealing with each element shown in blank or empty boxes on the story map (see Figure 11.5) (*Hint:* It is best if questions are sequenced in the order of the story map.)
- One story grammar questioning summary scoring sheet

Procedure

Select a simple story like *Jack and the Beanstalk*. Construct a story grammar map for the story as shown in Figure 11.4 for the story of *Jack and the Beanstalk*.

Figure 11.4 Story Grammar Map of *Jack and the Beanstalk*

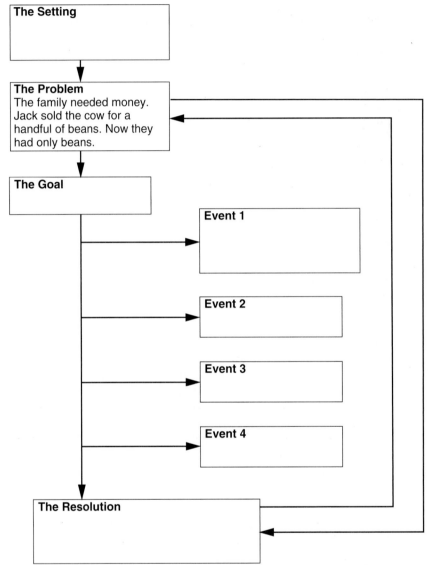

Figure 11.5 Story Grammar Questioning for *Jack and the Beanstalk*

Setting:	In the beginning of the story, why did Jack's mother want him to sell the cow?
Problem:	When Jack traded the cow for a handful of beans, what kind of a problem did this decision create for Jack and his mother?
Events:	When Jack climbed the beanstalk the first time, relate what happened to him. Why did Jack climb the beanstalk a second time?
Resolution:	At the end of the story, what had happened to Jack and his mother to solve the problem of trading the cow for a handful of beans?

Next, write one question for selected major elements in the story grammar map, as shown in the example questions in Figure 11.5.

Students can be asked, depending on their level of writing development, to answer the questions orally or in written form. Answers to each question are evaluated for accuracy and completeness. Story elements missed in the story grammar questioning should be stressed in future story discussions and/or in future explicit story structure instruction.

EXPOSITORY TEXT FRAMES

Purpose

Expository text frames are useful in identifying types of expository text patterns that may be troublesome for students. Based on the "story frames" concept (Fowler, 1982; Nichols, 1980), expository text frames are completed by the student after reading an expository passage. Expository text frames can be used to probe students' comprehension of text-based information that is not given in an expository text oral retelling.

Materials

You will need a textbook or information book, a computer and word processing program, and a means by which to copy the expository text frames for students. Abbreviated examples of expository text frames for several of the common expository text patterns are shown in Figure 11.6 through Figure 11.10.

Figure 11.6 Expository Text Frames: Description

Decimals are another way to write fractions when _____
_____
_____
_____

Figure 11.7 Expository Text Frames: Collection

Water Habitats

Freshwater habitats are found in _____, _____, _____, and rivers. Each freshwater habitat has special kinds of _____ and _____ that live there. Some plants and animals live in waters that are very _____. Others live in waters that are _____. Some plants and animals adapt to waters that flow _____.

Figure 11.8 Expository Text Frames: Causation

America Enters the War

On Sunday, December 7, 1941, World War II came to the United States. The entry of the United States into World War II was triggered by _____. Roosevelt said that it was a day that would "live in Infamy." *Infamy* (IN · fuh · mee) means remembered for being evil.

Figure 11.9   Expository Text Frames: Problem/Solution

Agreement by Compromise
Events that led to the Civil War

For a while there were an equal number of Southern and Northern states. That meant that there were just as many senators in Congress from slave states as from free states. Neither had more votes in the Senate, so they usually reached agreement on new laws by compromise. One way that the balance of power was maintained in Congress was _____ _____.

Figure 11.10   Expository Text Frames: Comparison

Segregation

Many people said that the segregation laws were unfair. But in 1896, the Supreme Court ruled segregation legal if _____ _____. "Separate but equal" became the law in many parts of the country.

But separate was not equal. One of the most serious problems was education. Black parents felt _____ _____. Sometimes the segregated schools had teachers who were not _____ as teachers in the white schools. Textbooks were often _____, if they had any books at all. But in many of the white schools the books were _____. Without a good education, the blacks argued, their children would not be able to get good jobs as adults.

Procedure

Before reading the selection, list the major vocabulary and concepts. Discuss what students already know about the topic and display it on the chalkboard or on chart paper. Next, have students read an expository selection similar to the one you will ask them to read in class. Once the passage has been read, model the process for completing expository text frames using mock examples. Now have them read the actual selection for the unit of study. Finally, have students complete the expository text frame(s) you have prepared for this passage. For students who have trouble with any of the frames, conduct a one-on-one reading conference to determine the thinking processes going on as the student completed the expository text frame.

In Figure 11.11, we summarize the procedures and instruments we have discussed previously for assessing factors associated with the text that affect reading comprehension. In this "Summary Matrix of Text-Based Comprehension Assessments," we provide information about federally related assessment purposes such as *screening, diagnosis, progress monitoring,* or *outcomes* assessment, as well as the type of test or procedure (norm referenced or criterion referenced) and psychometric evidence of test or procedure scores including reliability and/or validity evidence. It is noteworthy that there are few classroom-based, informal comprehension assessments that report reliability or validity evidence. To obtain valid and reliable comprehension scores on individual students, one must typically turn to the subtests of norm-referenced reading achievement batteries, for example, the *Stanford 10* or the *Iowa Test of Basic Skills.*

Figure 11.11 Summary Matrix of Text-Based Comprehension Assessments

Name of Assessment Tool	Screening Assessment Purpose	Diagnostic Assessment Purpose	Progress-Monitoring Assessment Purpose	Outcomes Assessment Purpose	Norm-Referenced Test	Criterion-Referenced Test	Reliability Evidence	Validity Evidence
Oral Retellings: Narrative Text Structure	+	–	+	–	–	+	NA	NA
Oral Retellings: Expository Structure	+	–	+	–	–	+	NA	NA
Scrambled Schema Story Task	+	–	+	–	–	+	NA	NA
Content-Area Reading Inventory (CARI)	+	–	+	–	–	+	NA	NA
Story Grammar Questioning	+	–	+	–	–	+	NA	NA
Expository Text Frames	+	–	+	–	–	+	NA	NA

Key: + can be used for   – not appropriate for

CONNECTING ASSESSMENT FINDINGS TO TEACHING STRATEGIES

Before discussing text-based comprehension teaching strategies, we have constructed a guide connecting assessments outcomes on those assessments previously described to intervention and/or strategy choices for improving students' text-based reading comprehension. It is our intention in creating this matrix to help you, the teacher, select the most appropriate instructional interventions and strategies to meet students' text-based comprehension needs based on text-based comprehension assessment data. In the following section, we offer comprehension teaching strategies that have been shown to be effective in improving students' text-based reading comprehension.

TEXT COMPREHENSION INSTRUCTIONAL STRATEGIES: A FOCUS ON NARRATIVE TEXT

STORY GRAMMAR INSTRUCTION: LEARNING ABOUT STORY STRUCTURE

Purpose

Developing a sense of how stories are formed through story grammar instruction helps students who are having reading problems predict with greater facility, store information more efficiently, and recall story elements with increased accuracy and completeness. The National Institute of Child Health and Human Development (2000) has recommended the

If-Then Strategy Guide for Improving Text Comprehension

"If" the student is ready to learn → / "Then" try these teaching strategies →	Story Grammar Instruction	Graphic Organizers for Stories	Schema Stories	Question Answer Relationships (QARS)	Graphic Organizers for Expository Texts	Summary Writing	Concept-Oriented Reading Instruction (CORI)	Internet Search and "I" Charts
Recall Main Ideas	+	+	+	*	+	+	*	*
Recall Details	–	+	–	*	+	–	*	+
Recall Text Events in Order	+	+	+	*	+	+	*	+
Use the Author's Text/Story Structure(s)	+	+	+	*	+	+	+	+
Answering Questions Correctly	*	*	*	+	*	–	*	*
Summarize a Text	*	+	*	–	+	+	*	+

Key: + Excellent Strategy
  * Adaptable Strategy
  – Unsuitable Strategy

teaching of story structure as a comprehension strategy for which there is abundant scientific evidence of effectiveness.

Materials

Well-formed stories and a visual organizer to guide the introduction of story grammar concepts are the materials needed for this activity. We suggest making a blank, poster-size, laminated story grammar map like that shown in Figure 11.4. This blank map can then be used repeatedly by you, the teacher, and the children when modeling how one goes about rendering a complete and properly sequenced story oral retelling.

Procedure

A number of reading researchers have described instructional procedures for developing readers' story schemas or story grammar awareness. Gordon and Braun (1983) recommended several guidelines for teaching story grammar. We have adapted these recommendations as follows:

1. Story grammar instruction should use well-formed stories such as *Jack and the Beanstalk.*

   A visual organizer can be used to guide the introduction of the concept of story grammar. For the first story used in story grammar instruction, read the story aloud, stop at key points in the story, and discuss the information needed to fill in the diagram. For stories read after introducing the concept of story grammar, use the visual organizer to introduce the story and make predictions about the story prior to reading. During and after reading, a visual organizer can be used to guide a discussion.

2. Set the purposes for reading by asking questions related to the structure of the story.

   Questioning developed to follow the structure of the story will focus students' attention on major story elements.

3. After questioning and discussing story structure, specific questions about the story content can be asked.

4. For continued instruction, gradually introduce less well-formed stories so that students will learn that not all stories are "ideal" in organization.

5. Extend instruction by encouraging children to ask their own questions using story structure and to apply this understanding in writing their own stories.

GRAPHIC ORGANIZERS FOR STORIES: SEEING THE STRUCTURE OF STORIES

Purpose

Graphic organizers are visual representations of key story elements and the interrelationships among these parts. Several researchers over the years have demonstrated the efficacy of using graphic organizers to teach children how stories are constructed to improve their comprehension of stories (Beck & McKeown, 1981; Reutzel, 1985, 1986). The National Reading Panel (National Institute of Child Health and Human Development, 2000) has recommended the use of graphic organizers as a comprehension strategy for which there is abundant scientific evidence of effectiveness. Graphic organizers, like story maps or webs, have been used to effectively increase children's comprehension of stories (Boyle, 1996; Bromley, 1993; Reutzel, 1985, 1986).

Reutzel and Fawson (1989; 1991) designed a successful strategy lesson to be used with young readers' predictable storybooks for building children's understanding of story structure. A literature web is constructed from the major story elements in a predictable book by selecting sentences from a book that tell about each major element of the story (i.e., setting, problem, events, and resolution).

To cement or correct comprehension of text after reading, you may want to conduct a class discussion. Most class discussions tend to center around the teacher and a few vocal

Figure 11.12 Random-Order Literature Web

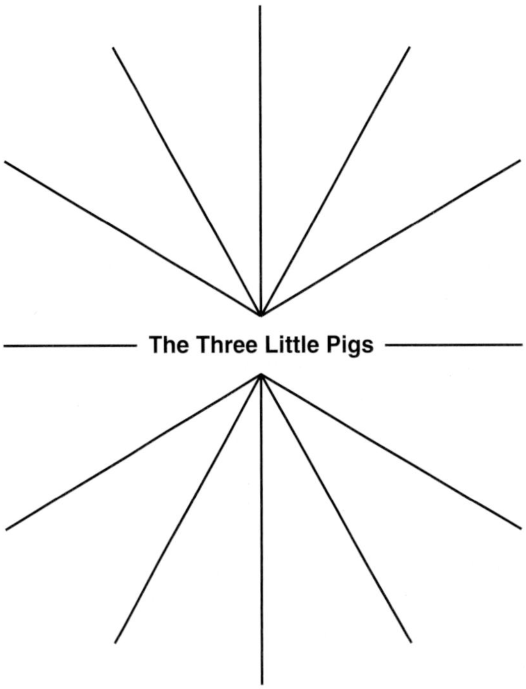

One pig met a man carrying a bundle of sticks. "May I have those sticks to build myself a house?" asked the pig. "You may," answered the man.

And the three little pigs lived happily ever after in a brick house built for three.

One day the wolf came knocking at the door of the brick house. "Little pig, little pig, let me come in." "Not by the hair of my chinny chin chin," said the pig. "Then I'll huff and I'll puff and I'll blow your house in." But the house would not fall down.

The wolf fell, kersplot, into a kettle of hot water. He jumped out with a start and ran out the door and never came back again.

One day the wolf came knocking at the door of the straw house. "Little pig, little pig, let me come in." "Not by the hair of my chinny chin chin," said the pig. "Then I'll huff and I'll puff and I'll blow your house in." And he blew the house down.

Once upon a time, three little pigs set out to make their fortune.

The Three Little Pigs

The wolf got so angry that he climbed to the top of the house and jumped down the chimney.

One pig met a man with a load of bricks. "May I have those bricks to build myself a house?" asked the pig. "You may," answered the man.

One pig met a man carrying a bundle of straw. "May I have that straw to build myself a house?" asked the pig. "You may," answered the man.

One day the wolf came knocking at the door of the stick house. "Little pig, little pig, let me come in." "Not by the hair of my chinny chin chin," said the pig. "Then I'll huff and I'll puff and I'll blow your house in." And he blew the house down.

children, with the rest of the class passively listening, or worse, completely inattentive. A discussion web (Alvermann, 1991) is a practical technique for enhancing student participation and thought during class discussions after reading.

Materials

The following materials are needed for constructing a graphic organizer for stories:

- One well-formed story
- Sentence strips
- Hand-drawn or copied pictures from the selected story
- A chalkboard or other display area for posting the literature web
- A felt pen or marker for drawing lines of relationships

Procedure

Sentences from the story are copied onto strips. The title of the story is copied onto a sentence strip. The sentence strip with the title is placed in the center of the board or display area. The remaining sentence strips are placed in random order on the chalk tray or some other display area (see Figure 11.12 for an example).

Prior to reading the story—whether reading it aloud in a shared-book experience or encouraging students to read it in a guided reading small group, the class or group reads the sentences aloud with the teacher. In the early part of the school year, the sentences selected for the literature web sentence strips are usually heavily augmented with hand-drawn or computer-scanned pictures from the book.

Organize children into small groups and give each group one of the picture and sentence cards from the board. The children are asked which group thinks it has the first part of the story. After discussion and group agreement is reached, the first sentence and picture card is placed at the one o'clock position on the literature web graphic organizer. The remainder of the groups are asked which sentence and picture combination comes next, and the sentence strips and pictures are placed around the graphic organizer in clockwise order. Figure 11.13 shows how one group of students arranged a graphic organizer to represent their predictions.

Next, the story is read aloud or silently from a traditional-size trade book or from a big book in a shared reading. Children listen attentively to confirm or correct their graphic organizer predictions. After the reading, predictions are revised in the graphic organizer as necessary (see Figure 11.14).

Children respond to the story, and these responses are recorded near the end of the graphic organizer. Other books similar to the one read may be discussed and comments recorded on the web. Finally, the children and teacher brainstorm together some ideas about how to extend the

Dr. Robert Cooter (co-author) using a big book

Figure 11.13 Literature Web Predictions

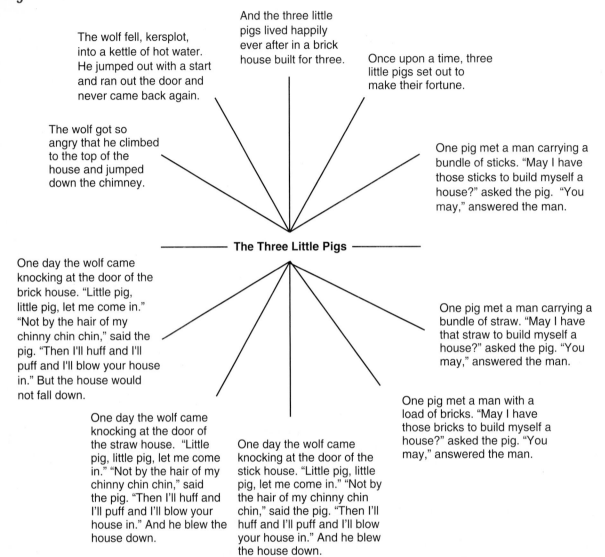

The wolf fell, kersplot, into a kettle of hot water. He jumped out with a start and ran out the door and never came back again.

And the three little pigs lived happily ever after in a brick house built for three.

Once upon a time, three little pigs set out to make their fortune.

The wolf got so angry that he climbed to the top of the house and jumped down the chimney.

One pig met a man carrying a bundle of sticks. "May I have those sticks to build myself a house?" asked the pig. "You may," answered the man.

The Three Little Pigs

One day the wolf came knocking at the door of the brick house. "Little pig, little pig, let me come in." "Not by the hair of my chinny chin chin," said the pig. "Then I'll huff and I'll puff and I'll blow your house in." But the house would not fall down.

One pig met a man carrying a bundle of straw. "May I have that straw to build myself a house?" asked the pig. "You may," answered the man.

One day the wolf came knocking at the door of the straw house. "Little pig, little pig, let me come in." "Not by the hair of my chinny chin chin," said the pig. "Then I'll huff and I'll puff and I'll blow your house in." And he blew the house down.

One day the wolf came knocking at the door of the stick house. "Little pig, little pig, let me come in." "Not by the hair of my chinny chin chin," said the pig. "Then I'll huff and I'll puff and I'll blow your house in." And he blew the house down.

One pig met a man with a load of bricks. "May I have those bricks to build myself a house?" asked the pig. "You may," answered the man.

reading of the book into the other language arts while recording these ideas on the graphic organizer.

Reutzel and Fawson (1991) also demonstrated that children having reading problems who participate in using a graphic organizer of a predictable storybook learn to read these books with fewer oral reading miscues, fewer miscues that distort comprehension, and greater recall. They attribute this to the fact that children must impose an organization onto their predictions when using graphic organizers rather than simply making random predictions from story titles and pictures.

To use a discussion web graphic organizer after reading a story, begin by preparing students to read a text selection or book as you normally would (see Figure 11.15.). Help them think of related background experiences, and invite them to set a purpose for reading the story. You may want to ask an open-end question about the story. For example, using *The*

Figure 11.14   Completed Literature Web

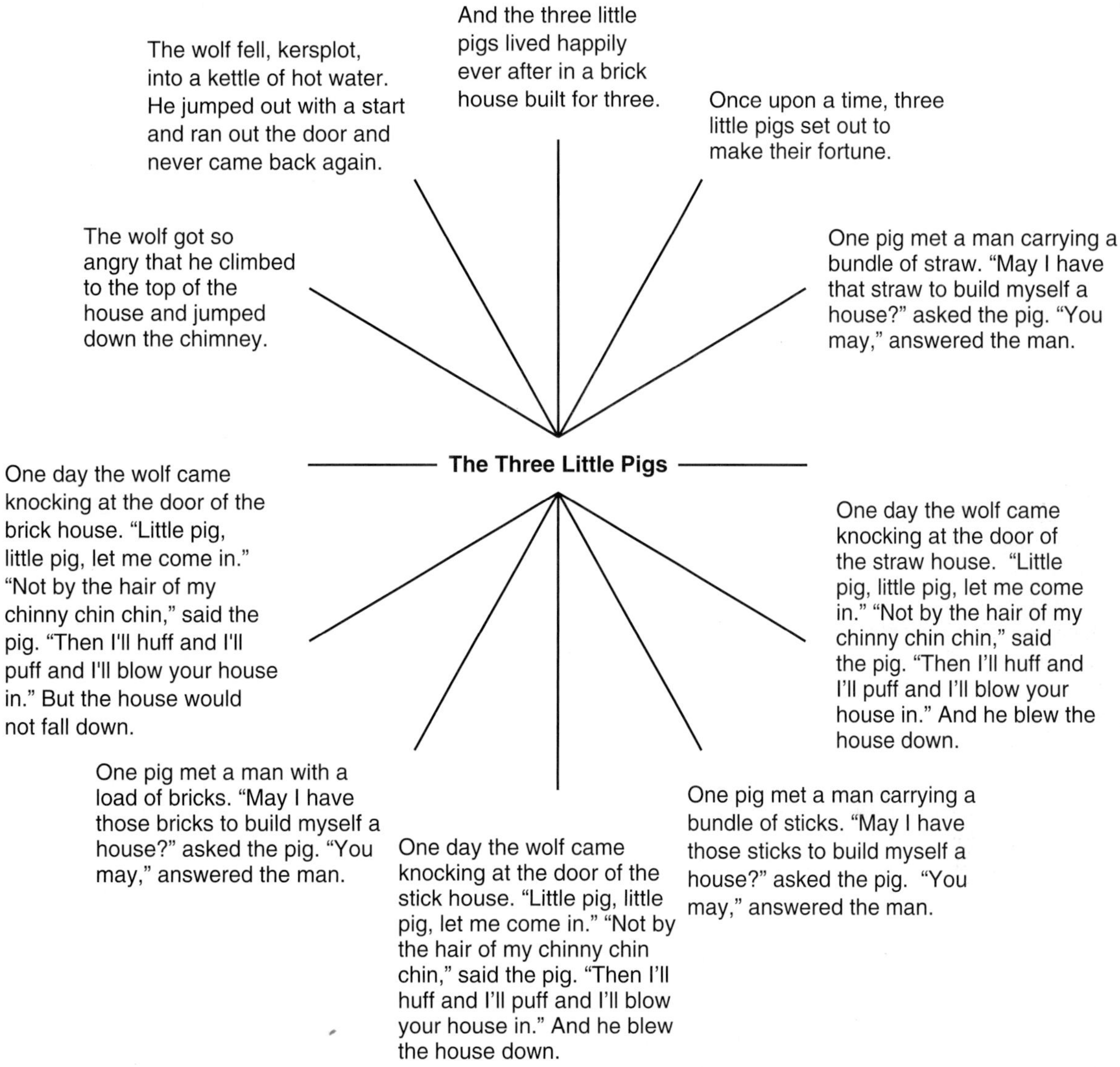

The wolf fell, kersplot, into a kettle of hot water. He jumped out with a start and ran out the door and never came back again.

And the three little pigs lived happily ever after in a brick house built for three.

Once upon a time, three little pigs set out to make their fortune.

The wolf got so angry that he climbed to the top of the house and jumped down the chimney.

One pig met a man carrying a bundle of straw. "May I have that straw to build myself a house?" asked the pig. "You may," answered the man.

The Three Little Pigs

One day the wolf came knocking at the door of the brick house. "Little pig, little pig, let me come in." "Not by the hair of my chinny chin chin," said the pig. "Then I'll huff and I'll puff and I'll blow your house in." But the house would not fall down.

One day the wolf came knocking at the door of the straw house. "Little pig, little pig, let me come in." "Not by the hair of my chinny chin chin," said the pig. "Then I'll huff and I'll puff and I'll blow your house in." And he blew the house down.

One pig met a man with a load of bricks. "May I have those bricks to build myself a house?" asked the pig. "You may," answered the man.

One day the wolf came knocking at the door of the stick house. "Little pig, little pig, let me come in." "Not by the hair of my chinny chin chin," said the pig. "Then I'll huff and I'll puff and I'll blow your house in." And he blew the house down.

One pig met a man carrying a bundle of sticks. "May I have those sticks to build myself a house?" asked the pig. "You may," answered the man.

Widow's Broom by Chris Van Allsburg (1992), you may ask, "Do you think the widow Minna Shaw should have tricked her neighbors?" Group students in pairs and ask them to answer the question according to their own feelings and the facts they remember from the story. Help them focus on why a certain answer could be true. Ask students to think also of some reasons the opposite answer could be true.

For example, one student may say, "Yes, they were trying to take her magic broom away."

A partner may add, "Yes, those rotten Spivey kids were the ones who needed to be taken away." In this example, these students have voiced two *yes* answers. Next, the teacher should ask the students to think of some *no* answers, as well.

After students have discussed their ideas in pairs, you may want to ask them to share their thinking with another pair of students. Ask each pair to choose its best answer to the

Figure 11.15   Discussion Web

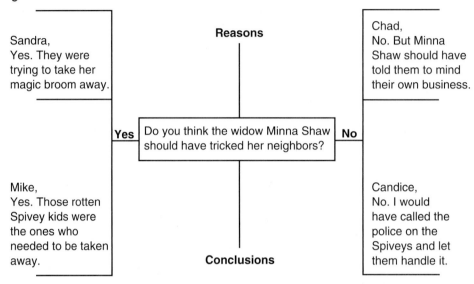

question, as well as the strongest reason supporting the student's thinking. Then, bring the children together and ask one student from each pair to report the pair's best answer and the reason supporting that answer. As each student speaks, include the reason in the diagram. After each pair reports, invite others to suggest additional ideas for the discussion web. You may want to reach a class conclusion, or you may want to stop just before a conclusion is reached to avoid a "right" or "wrong" feeling for the answers. (*Note:* Some teachers of very young students use the discussion web strategy in a whole-class setting rather than grouping students in pairs. Vary the approach according to your teaching style and class needs.)

Merkley and Jeffries (2001) encouraged teachers to use the following guidelines in teaching with graphic organizers to help students improve their comprehension:

- Talk about the links or relationships among the concepts or events expressed in the visual.
- Provide opportunity for student input in shaping the content and order of the visual.
- Connect the new learning to past learning and to other stories to demonstrate relationships.
- Reference an upcoming story that will be read soon.
- Use the text in the visual of a graphic organizer to reinforce decoding and other word study skills.
- Although the graphic organizer may be distributed as a worksheet, the secret to success is to use graphic organizers to organize discussion, text talk, and thinking.

SCHEMA STORIES: USING STORY STRUCTURE KNOWLEDGE TO GUIDE TEXT COMPREHENSION

Purpose

Watson and Crowley (1988), originators of this strategy lesson, described schema stories as a reading strategy lesson that helps readers "reconstruct the order of a text based on meaning and story grammar" (p. 263). This strategy helps students learn to anticipate such elements as setting, problem to be addressed by the characters, key events in the story, and resolution of the story (Simmons & Kameenui, 1998).

Materials

Start with stories that contain familiar beginning and ending phrases, such as *Once upon a time* and *They lived happily ever after*. After choosing an interesting story, prepare the schema story strategy lesson by making a photocopy of the text and physically cutting the photocopy into sections or parts that are long enough to contain at least one main idea. Usually, one or two paragraphs will be a sufficient length to accomplish this purpose.

Procedure

To begin the lesson, distribute a section or part of the story to each small group of students (four to eight students in each group is about right). Typically, one student is selected in each group to read the text aloud for his or her group. Once each group has read its story part, ask if any group believes it was given the section of the story that comes at the beginning of the story. Students who believe they have the beginning of the story are to raise their hands to respond. Those who raise their hands must state why they believe they have the beginning of the story. After the majority of the students agree as to which section or story part is first, the group proceeds to the next segment of the story. This process continues as described until all of the segments have been placed in a predicted order.

Schema story lessons make excellent small-group or individual activities that can be located at a classroom center or station devoted to developing a sense of story. All of the segments of a text can be placed into an envelope and filed in the center. Small groups of children or individuals can come to the center and select an envelope, then work individually or collectively on reconstructing a story. A "key" for self-checking can be included in the envelope, as well, to reduce the amount of teacher supervision necessary in the center. As children work through a schema story strategy lesson, they talk about how language works, ways authors construct texts, and how meaning can be used to make sense out of the scrambled elements of a text or story.

QUESTION-ANSWER RELATIONSHIPS: ANSWERING QUESTIONS ABOUT TEXT

Purpose

The National Reading Panel (National Institute of Child Health and Human Development, 2000) has identified answering and posing questions about texts as comprehension strategies for which there is abundant scientific evidence of effectiveness. Raphael (1982, 1986) identified four question-answer relationships (QARs) to help children identify the connection between the type of questions asked of them by teachers and textbooks and the information sources necessary and available to them for answering questions: (a) right there, (b) think and search, (c) author and you, and (d) on my own. Research by Raphael and Pearson (1982) provided evidence that training students to recognize question-answer relationships (QARs) results in improved comprehension and question-answering behavior. In addition, using the QARs question-answering training strategy is useful for another purpose: helping teachers examine their own questioning with respect to the types of questions and the information sources that students need to use to answer their questions. By using QARs to monitor their own questioning behaviors, some teachers may find that they are asking only "right there" types of questions. This discovery very often leads teachers to ask other questions that require the use of additional or seldom-used information sources.

Materials

The materials needed include a variety of texts for asking and answering questions, a poster displaying the information in the classroom to heighten childrens' and teachers' awareness of the types of questions asked, and the information sources available for answering those questions. Figure 11.16 provides examples of each of the four types of question-answer relationships (QARs).

Procedure

Instruction using QARs begins by explaining to students that when they answer questions about reading, there are basically two places they can look to get information: in

Figure 11.16   Illustrations to Explain Question-Answer-Relationships to Students

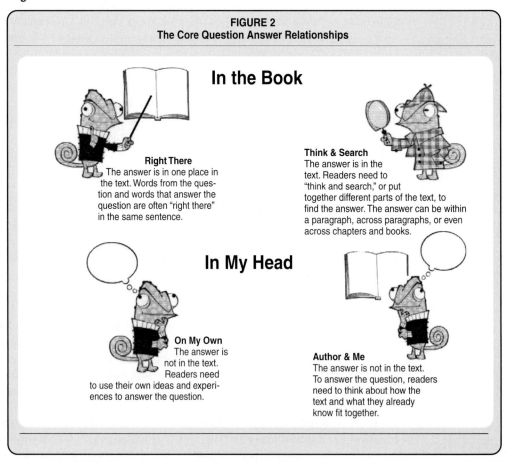

FIGURE 2
The Core Question Answer Relationships

In the Book

Right There
The answer is in one place in the text. Words from the question and words that answer the question are often "right there" in the same sentence.

Think & Search
The answer is in the text. Readers need to "think and search," or put together different parts of the text, to find the answer. The answer can be within a paragraph, across paragraphs, or even across chapters and books.

In My Head

On My Own
The answer is not in the text. Readers need to use their own ideas and experiences to answer the question.

Author & Me
The answer is not in the text. To answer the question, readers need to think about how the text and what they already know fit together.

Source: From "QAR: Enhancing comprehension and test taking across grades and content areas" by T. E. Raphael and K. H. Au. *The Reading Teacher,* 59(3), pp. 206–221.

the book and in my head. This concept should be practiced with the students by reading aloud a text, asking questions, and having the students explain or show where they found their answers. Once students understand the two-category approach, expand the in-the-book category to include right there and putting it together. The distinction between these two categories should be practiced by reading and discussing several texts. For older students, Raphael (1986) suggested that students be shown specific strategies for locating the answers to right-there questions. These include looking in a single sentence or looking in two sentences connected by a pronoun. For putting-it-together questions, students can be asked to focus their attention on the structure of the text, such as cause effect, problem solution, listing example, compare contrast, and explanation.

Next, instruction should be directed toward two subcategories within the in-my-head category: "author and me" and "on my own." Here again, these categories can be practiced as a group by reading a text aloud, answering the questions, and discussing the sources of information. To expand this training, students can be asked to identify the types of questions asked in their basal readers, workbooks, content-area texts, and tests; in addition, they can determine the sources of information needed to answer these questions. Students may be informed that certain types of questions are asked before and after reading a text. For example, questions asked before reading typically invite students to activate their own knowledge. Therefore, questions asked before reading will usually be on-my-own questions. However, questions asked after reading will make use of information found in the text. Thus, questions asked after reading will typically focus on the right-there, putting-it-together, and author-and-me types of questions. As a culminating training activity for QARs, children are asked to write their own questions for each of the QAR categories.

TEXT COMPREHENSION INSTRUCTIONAL STRATEGIES: A FOCUS ON EXPOSITORY TEXT

GRAPHIC ORGANIZERS FOR EXPOSITORY TEXTS: VISUAL REPRESENTATION

Purpose

Authors of expository texts typically organize their writing using several well-known text patterns or structures. Armbruster and Anderson (1981) and Meyer (1975) researched the text structures most used by authors of expository texts. These included: *time order* (putting information into a chronological sequence), *cause and effect* (showing how something occurs because of another event), *problem and solution* (presenting a problem along with a solution to the problem), *comparison* (examining similarities and differences among concepts and events), *simple listing* (registering in list form a group of facts, concepts, or events), and *descriptions*.

Readers who understand the organizational pattern(s) or text structure(s) an author has used in producing an expository text recall more from their reading than readers who do not (Bartlett, 1978; Meyer et al., 1980; Dickson et al., 1998b). The National Reading Panel (National Institute of Child Health and Human Development, 2000) has strongly recommended the use of graphic organizers as a comprehension strategy for which there is abundant scientific evidence of effectiveness.

Materials

The following materials are needed for constructing a graphic organizer for working with expository texts:

- One well-formed expository text using a single organizational pattern or text structure selected from among the common structures previously discussed: *time order*, *cause and effect*, *problem and solution*, *comparison*, *simple listing*, and *descriptions*
- Commercially produced sentence strips
- Hand-drawn or copied pictures from the selected text, especially but not exclusively for working with expository texts with younger children
- A white board or other display area for displaying the graphic organizer
- A felt pen or dry-erase marker for drawing lines of relationships

Procedures

Begin by selecting an excellent information text that employs a single organizational pattern or text structure. This means finding an expository text that exemplifies the clear and simple use of one of the six expository text structures such as problem and solution or question and answer. As we considered these characteristics and you, our reader, we decided to select a simple information text, *Name That Shape!* (Stafford, 2004), as our example. *Name That Shape!* uses a typical expository text structure—question and answer or problem and solution. Each page begins with a question about a particular shape. Answers are then offered and reinforced by the use of photographs showing an object that exemplifies that particular geometric shape. For younger children, a simple graphic organizer using icons or pictures to accompany the print can be helpful. For older students, a more complex graphic organizer may include student-generated questions for which they will seek and retrieve answers to their questions through reading across a variety of other information texts on the topic of geometric shapes. An example of a question-and-answer graphic organizer for the book *Name That Shape!* is shown in Figure 11.17.

It is very important to scaffold graphic organizer instruction effectively in the classroom. *Scaffolding* refers to gradually releasing the control and responsibility for selecting a graphic organizer design and using it to guide comprehension. Children need to learn to recognize

Figure 11.17   Question-and-Answer Graphic Organizer for the Book *Name That Shape!*

?	
What is round and does not have corners?	It is a circle. Do you see the circles in the picture?
What has four sides that are the same length and four corners?	It is a square. Do you see the squares in the picture?

the organizational pattern(s) or text structure(s) the author has used to produce a text. An easy place to begin this process is in the "Table of Contents" of the book or textbook. Very often, the way the author titles each section in the "Table of Contents" and the order of the sections may give away the structure or organization of the text. Next, children need to be helped to select the appropriate graphic organizer to re-represent the organization of and information in the text. In Figure 11.18, we show several different graphic organizers.

We have labeled each graphic organizer type with the text structure or organizational pattern that each is intended to represent. It is important that you, the teacher, understand that the power in using graphic organizers is in selecting the appropriate one to represent the underlying organization or text structure used by the author. Teaching children to recognize text structure and select the appropriate type of graphic organizer will require multiple lessons such as the one just described with *Name That Shape!*, using a variety of expository books that use question-and-answer text structure such as *Bridges* (Ring, 2003), *How Do Spiders Live?* (F. Biddulph & J. Biddulph, 1992), and others.

In the first lesson, the teacher explains and thinks aloud how she figured out that the author was using a question-and-answer structure in the graphic organizer. Next, the teacher selects the appropriate graphic organizer from those in Figure 11.19. Finally, she models reading the text aloud and filling in the question on the one side and the answer on the other side of the question-and-answer graphic organizer until the text reading is complete. In the second and third lessons, the teacher perhaps shares the explaining of question-and-answer expository text structure, thinking aloud, selecting of the appropriate graphic organizer, and representing the elements of question-and-answer expository text structure in the graphic organizer with the children. Finally, in the fourth lesson, the students do most of the explaining, thinking aloud, selecting, and representing the elements of question-and-answer expository text structure and in the graphic organizer. This teaches children the process of determining and using text structure and finding an appropriate graphic organizer to represent the text structure and provides a structure for organizing and remembering important information from reading expository texts.

Summary Writing: Focusing on the Significant in Text

Purpose

The purpose of writing a summary is to extract main or important ideas from a reading selection. Good readers are constantly stopping themselves during reading to monitor or think about their comprehension and to take corrective action when necessary. Summaries are important because they help form memory structures that readers can use to select and store relevant main ideas and details from their reading. Some readers do not spontaneously summarize their reading and, as a result, have poor understanding and recall of what they read (Brown, Day, & Jones, 1983).

Materials

An expository trade book, basal selection, or content-area textbook selection is needed, along with a chart displaying the rules for summary writing. An example based on the work of Hare and Borchordt (1984) is shown in Figure 11.19.

Procedure

Begin by distributing copies of the expository trade book or basal or textbook selections to be read by the group. Have the students silently read the first few passages. Next, on an overhead transparency, model for the children how you would use the five summary rules in Figure 11.19 to write a summary. After modeling how you would write a summary, instruct the

Figure 11.18 Different Expository Test Structure Graphic Organizers

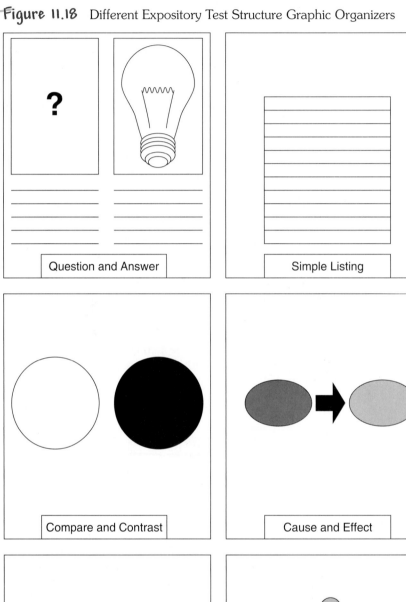

Question and Answer

Simple Listing

Compare and Contrast

Cause and Effect

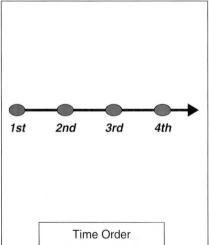

1st   2nd   3rd   4th

Time Order

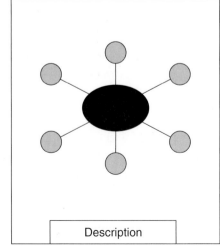

Description

Figure 11.19   Five Rules for Writing a Summary

1. *Collapse lists.* If there is a list of things, supply a word or phrase for the whole list. For example, if you saw *swimming, sailing, fishing,* and *surfing,* you could substitute *water sports.*
2. *Use topic sentences.* Sometimes authors write a sentence that summarizes the whole paragraph. If so, use that sentence in your summary. If not, you'll have to make up your own topic sentences.
3. *Get rid of unnecessary detail.* Sometimes information is repeated or is stated in several different ways. Some information may be trivial and unnecessary. Get rid of repetitive or trivial information. Summaries should be short.
4. *Collapse paragraphs.* Often, paragraphs are related to each other. For example, some paragraphs simply explain or expand on other paragraphs in a selection. Some paragraphs are more important than others. Join the paragraphs that are related. Important paragraphs should stand alone.
5. *Polish the summary.* When you collapse a lot of information from many paragraphs into one or two paragraphs, the resulting summary sometimes sounds awkward and unnatural. There are several ways to remedy this: add connecting words such as *like* or *because,* or write introductory or closing statements. Another method is to paraphrase the material; this will improve your ability to remember what you read and enable you to avoid plagiarism—using the exact words of the author.

Source: From "Direct Instruction of Summarization Skills" by V. C. Hare & K. M. Borchordt, 1984. *Reading Research Quarterly, 20*(1), pp. 62–78. Copyright 1984 by the International Reading Association.

children to finish reading the entire chapter or passage. Divide the chalkboard into four sections relating to the topic. For example, if you are learning about an animal (say, alligators), your subcategories may be "Description," "Food," "Home," and "Interesting Facts." As the groups read, students can write facts on the chalkboard under the different category headings.

Next, organize students into cooperative-learning groups, or teams of five, to work on writing a summary together. Each student is assigned to take charge of one of the five summary writing rules shown in Figure 11.19. Move about the classroom to assist the groups as needed. After reading the selection and working in their groups, the students in each group with the topic statement rule should read their topic statement aloud. Next, the students can discuss the facts they have listed at the board, erase any duplicates, and write the remaining main ideas and detail facts in complete sentences. You may want to have students use different-color transparency pens for each of the five summary rules to record their work. For example, green may be used for lists, red for eliminating unnecessary details, and so on. Share each group's summary writing processes and products with the entire class on the overhead projector. Be sure to provide additional practice on summary writing throughout the year with other books, moving toward asking individual children to perform all of the summary writing processes.

Some students encounter difficulties initially using the five rules in Figure 11.19. We have found the following procedure by Noyce and Christie (1989) to be easier for most students who struggle with summary writing. (Naturally, you, the teacher, will need to model this process and then guide students as they work in groups discussing how to do it.) It is built on these four easy steps:

Step 1:   Write a topic sentence, that is, one that summarizes in general terms what the content is about. You need to either select one that the author has written or write your own.

Step 2:   Delete all unnecessary or irrelevant sentences, words, and other information from the entire passage.

Step 3: After sorting all terms into categories, think of a collective term(s) for those things that fall into the same category.

Step 4: Collapse paragraphs on the same subject down to one when they are largely redundant.

Concept-Oriented Reading Instruction

Purpose

Guthrie et al. (1996) researched a teaching framework called concept-oriented reading instruction (CORI), designed to improve students' learning in science. Easily applied to other content areas, CORI helps students become deeply engaged in new content, helps students crystallize and connect new knowledge to what is already known, and shows students how to demonstrate their learning in some interesting ways. The direct-instruction components of CORI have also been shown to be effective with low-achieving students in elementary grades 3 and 5 (Guthrie et al.; Swafford & Bryan, 2000). CORI provides a sound basic platform for teaching and learning in the concept areas that can be modified to suit your instructional goals.

Materials

Frankly, it is a little difficult to generalize a specific list of materials for CORI, as that depends heavily on the subject area, content to be studied, and available texts for instruction. You will see what we mean as we move through our description; but, typically, the materials will include subject-linked textbooks, materials for the writing process, access to the World Wide Web and Internet search engines, and other research tools usually available in the school library or media center.

Procedure

The CORI framework includes the following: real-world observations, conceptual themes, self-directed learning, explicit instruction on strategies, peer collaboration, and self-expression of learning. The four parts of this instructional model are described next.

Part I: Observe and Personalize. Students are led through hands-on experiences designed to activate their prior knowledge that is relevant to the new topic and to motivate them to want to know more. After the hands-on experiences, the teacher leads students through a discussion about what they observed and helps them to form theories and generate questions for further study. The teacher-led discussion can help students move from concrete-only thinking into the more sophisticated forms of abstract thinking.

Part II: Search and Retrieve. In this stage, the teacher introduces search strategies for finding answers to students' questions. For each search strategy, the teacher provides a clear description, models using the strategy, and has practice sessions (guided practice) and collaborative group work. Strategies to be learned include goal setting (what they want to learn), categorizing (learning how information is organized and presented in books and learning how to find information in the library or on the Internet), extracting (taking notes, summarizing, and paraphrasing information), and abstracting (forming generalizations).

Part III: Comprehend and Integrate. The goal here is to help students better understand the new information they have gathered in Part II. Teacher modeling and students' discussions about the following strategies usually occur: comprehension monitoring (metacognition), developing images or graphics, rereading to clarify, and modifying reading rate to match purpose and varying text types. Identification of central ideas and supporting details is also a priority in this stage of instruction. Guthrie et al. (1996) recommended the use of *idea circles* (student-led small-group discussions) and group self-monitoring as ways to transfer learning responsibility to students, leading to more productive discussions. This is especially useful when they discover information that is conflicting or when it contradicts their earlier hypotheses.

Part IV: Communication. The communication phase of CORI focuses on students sharing what they have learned. They often communicate their new understandings through debates, discussions, or written reports. Some students prefer more creative expressions such as Microsoft PowerPoint presentations, poetry, dramas, raps, songs, or graphic illustrations. As with the other phases of CORI, teacher support and modeling are critical in helping students develop effective communication skills to present their new knowledge and strengthen their social development (Swafford & Bryan, 2000). The elements of content-oriented reading instruction (CORI) are summarized in Figure 11.20.

Figure 11.20   Concept Oriented Reading Instruction

Part I: Observe and Personalize

1. Hands-on experiences
2. Relate hands-on experience to prior experiences
3. Teacher-led discussion
4. Form theories
5. Generate questions for further study

Part II: Search and Retrieve

Teacher introduces search strategies for finding answers to their questions . . .

1. *Goal setting* (what they want to learn)
2. *Categorizing* (learning how information is organized and presented in books and how to find information in the library or on the Internet)
3. *Extracting* (taking notes, summarizing, and paraphrasing information)
4. *Abstracting* (forming generalizations)

Part III: Comprehend and Integrate

Teacher modeling and students discussions about . . .

1. Comprehension monitoring (metacognition)
2. Developing images or graphics
3. Rereading to clarify
4. Modifying reading rate to match purpose and varying text types
5. Identification of central ideas and supporting details

Part IV: Communication

Communication of new knowledge through such media as . . .

Debates
Discussions
Written reports
Technology (e.g., Microsoft PowerPoint presentations)
Poetry
Dramas
Raps or songs
Graphic illustrations

Expository Texts on the Internet: Using I-Charts

Purpose

One of the most common assignments in classrooms today is a research project, even as early as kindergarten (Chard, 1998). Nearly 85% of all adult reading has as its purpose to obtain information (Duke et al., 2002). Children's information books are only one example of many other expository texts, such as biographies, essays, photographic essays, instruction or *how-to* books, encyclopedias, reference books, activity/experiment books, scientific reports, newspaper articles, hypertext, and so on. In fact, in today's classroom world, children are perhaps more at home surfing the Internet for information than they are searching for information in libraries and books. As a result, an obvious and easily accessible approach for developing children's comprehension of expository texts is to teach them how to search, evaluate, and comprehend information text found on the Internet!

Kletzien and Dreher (2004); Hiede and Stilborne (1999); and Wepner, Valmont, and Thurlow (2000) encourage teaching even young children how to seek answers to their questions using the Internet. To begin this process, select topics and questions ahead of time. You should model for children how you go about determining which words to select as Internet "search terms." Also, remember to show children the results of using different search terms and how the selection of these terms are critical in finding the information you want and need.

Next, show children how you sort through web sites to find relevant information on the topic you are researching. You may then want to demonstrate how you can take information from a web site and organize this information on your own home page or web site using a free service like Backflip (http://www.backflip.com/login.ihtml). Once you have located and organized Internet information in a web page or home page context, then you will need to help children read and comprehend this Internet expository text information successfully. It is no secret that many students have a great deal of difficulty going about these search, gather, organize, and summary activities in a logical, orderly, and sequential manner. As a result, their efforts to process information in expository texts often lead to much frustration and confusion. Information charts, or I-charts (Hoffman, 1992; Randall, 1996), provide a workable initial structure to help teachers guide students through these explorations and later on provide a continuing structure students can use to conduct independent explorations of Internet text information.

The version we share here was adapted by Randall (1996, p. 537) for use in her eighth-grade language arts classes. It involves three components: preparing the charts, research and note taking using the charts, and the completion of the final product using the charts.

Materials

You will need access to reference materials, 10 copies of an I-chart such as that shown in Figure 11.21, and multiple enlarged copies of the I-chart on poster board.

Procedure

Planning for your research

1. *Topic identification and necessary skills*—Students first explore topics related to the new unit of study, brainstorming subjects of interest to them, and deciding what their individual topics may be. The teacher also offers a lesson on needed research-related skills such as Internet searching skills, skimming, scanning, para-

Figure 11.21   I-Chart

Student: _____   Topic/Subject: _____
Subtopic: _____
What I already know . . . _____
Bibliography #:

Other related information: _____
Important words: _____
New questions to learn about . . .

phrasing, interviewing techniques, library skills, and knowing how to record bibliographic entries.

2. *Writing topic proposals*—Students write their topic proposals for the teacher, including an explanation of their interest in their proposed topics. Also included is a tentative strategy for finding needed information. The teacher is then able to confer with students and/or make written suggestions to help guide them in shaping their topic proposals.

3. *Brainstorming questions*—Students generate specific questions to be answered. This is a great activity for cooperative learning groups. These questions should then be turned into subtopics to help students fine-tune their research efforts.

4. *Setting up I-charts*—Provide students with about 10 copies of the I-chart. Students should write one subtopic or question at the top of each I-chart, then complete the section titled "What I already know . . ." for each subtopic. Sometimes students may know a good deal about a topic, while at other times they may simply write, "Nothing." Their I-charts should be kept in a looseleaf notebook for easy access during this process.

5. *Modeling*—As with all new learning experiences, it is important that students be able to see someone with expertise (the teacher, usually) modeling the task. Using the large poster board copies of the I-chart, lead a class simulation pertaining to topics related to the unit of study. Complete each step on the I-chart with the help of student volunteers.

Research and note taking

1. *Finding resources*—Randall (1996) advocated spending about a class period each day for a week in the school library. Make "house calls" (Reutzel & Cooter, 2004) on the students to make sure that each is using the I-charts to guide his or her searches for information and to provide coaching as needed. Also, as homework, students should be encouraged to continue their quest for information at local public libraries, through governmental agencies that have relevant print information, and in interviews with experts.

2. *Answering research questions*—Students should have their I-chart notebooks in front of them as they skim new information sources, pulling relevant I-chart subtopics as they discover information that may be pertinent to their research (Randall, 1996, p. 539). The corresponding I-chart should be pulled out of the notebook as new information is discovered, then numbered and summarized on the I-chart in the bibliography section. A line should be drawn between bibliographic entries and corresponding information to keep things straight.

3. *Making bibliographic entries*—For each bibliographic entry made on the various I-chart forms, the student should make one complete bibliographic entry on a sheet labeled "References" at the end of the notebook. This will save him or her from having to make the same reference repeatedly on the different I-chart forms when a reference is used more than once.

4. *Completing the I-chart*—As students come across "Other related information" that is of interest but is not really pertinent to the subtopic or question, they can note it in the appropriate space. Sometimes this information can be included in a research report to make the report more interesting—like adding color to a black-and-white photograph. Likewise, "Important words" related to the subject—especially unusual words previously unknown to the student—should be noted in the space provided. Sometimes these words will require further research for clarity. Finally, "New questions to learn about . . ." that have arisen as a result of the research should be noted and answered before moving on to the final product stage.

5. *Critically evaluating research findings*—Sometimes students are not able to locate authoritative sources to complete their I-charts. If they cannot locate print information or an expert to interview, then that particular I-chart should be abandoned (Randall, 1996). Students should constantly evaluate whether they have accumulated enough information to consider a given I-chart complete before moving on.

Completion of final products

- *Writing research papers.* I-charts create a natural bridge from research to outlining. They should be used (after considerable modeling by the teacher) to construct webs, traditional outlines, or structured overviews of the information. Time lines, maps, flowcharts, bar graphs, lists, and other graphic aids can also be constructed as prewriting tools to aid students in organizing facts, concepts, and generalizations. Each subtopic or I-chart naturally becomes a category under the primary topic or generalization, with information noted in the "Bibliography" and "Important words" sections becoming concepts and facts in subordinate categories. Once an outline of the information is completed, students can begin their first drafts of their research papers.

Remember, readers who understand an author's organizational pattern or text structure recall more from reading information texts than readers who do not (Bartlett, 1978; Meyer et al., 1980; Dickson et al., 1998b). Poor or struggling readers are even less likely to be able to identify and use an author's organization of text to recall information. Thus, teachers need to teach struggling readers how to identify the author's implicit organizational pattern or text structure and how to use this knowledge to help them remember, organize, retrieve, and apply what they read.

SELECTED REFERENCES

Alvermann, D. E. (1991). The discussion web: A graphic aide for learning across the curriculum. *The Reading Teacher, 45,* 92–99.

Alvermann, D. E., & Moore, D. W. (1991). Secondary school reading. In R. Barr, M. L. Kamil, P. B. Mosenthal, & P. D. Pearson (Eds.), *Handbook of reading research, Vol. 2* (pp. 951–983). White Plains, NY: Longman.

Armbruster, B., & Anderson, T. (1981). *Content area textbooks* (Reading Education Report No. 23). Urbana–Champaign: University of Illinois, Center for the Study of Reading.

Armbruster, B. B., Anderson, T. H., & Ostertag, J. (1987). Does text structure/summarization instruction facilitate learning from expository text? *Reading Research Quarterly, 22*(3), 331–346.

Bartlett, B. J. (1978). *Top-level structure as an organizational strategy for recall of classroom text.* Unpublished doctoral dissertation, Arizona State University, Tempe.

Beaver, J. (1997). *Developmental Reading Assessment* (DRA). New York: Pearson Learning Group.

Beck, I. L., & McKeown, M. G. (1981). Developing questions that promote comprehension: The story map. *Language Arts, 58,* 913–918.

Beck, I. L., Omanson, R. C., & McKeown, M. G. (1982). An instructional redesign of reading lessons: Effects on comprehension. *Reading Research Quarterly, 17,* 462–481.

Biddulph, F., & Biddulph, J. (1992). *How do spiders live?* Bothell, WA: The Wright Group.

Boyle, J. R. (1996). The effects of cognitive mapping strategy on the literal and inferential comprehension of students with mild disabilities. *Learning Disability Quarterly, 19*(3); 86–98.

Bromley, K. (1993). *Webbing with literature: Creating story maps with children's books* (2nd ed.). Boston: Allyn & Bacon.

Brown, A. L., Day, J. D., & Jones, R. S. (1983). The development of plans for summarzing texts. *Child Development, 54,* 968–979.

Brown, H., & Cambourne, B. (1987). *Read and retell.* Portsmouth, NH: Heinemann Educational Books.

Casteel, C. A. (1990). Effects of chunked text materials on reading comprehension of high and low ability readers. *Reading Improvement, 27,* 269–275.

Chard, S. (1998). *The project approach: Making curriculum come alive.* New York: Scholastic.

Cutting, B., & Cutting, J. (2002). *Is it a fish?—Sunshine Science Series.* Bothell, WA: Wright Group/McGraw-Hill.

Dickson, S. V., Simmons, D. C., & Kameenui, E. J. (1998a). Text organization: Instructional and curricular basics and implications. In D. C. Simmons & E. J. Kameenui (Eds.), *What reading research tells us about children with diverse learning needs: Bases and basics.* Mahwah, NJ: Lawrence Erlbaum Associates.

Dickson, S. V., Simmons, D. C., & Kameenui, E. J. (1998b). Text organization: Research bases. In D. C. Simmons & E. J. Kameenui (Eds.), *What reading research tells us about children with diverse learning needs* (pp. 239–278). Mahwah, NJ: Erlbaum.

Donovan, C. A., & Smolkin, L. B. (2002). Considering genre, context, and visual features in the selection of trade books for science instruction. *The Reading Teacher, 55*(6), 502–520.

Duke, N. K. (2000). 3.6 minutes per day: The scarcity of informational texts in first grade. *Reading Research Quarterly, 35*(2), 202–224.

Duke, N. K., & Bennett-Armistead, S. (2003). *Reading and writing informational text in the primary grades: Research-based practices.* New York: Scholastic.

Duke, N. K., Bennett-Armistead, S., & Roberts, E. M. (2002). Incorporating informational text in the primary grades. In C. M. Roller (Ed.), *Comprehensive reading instruction across the grade levels: A collection of papers from the 2001 Reading Research Conference* (pp. 41–54). Newark, DE: International Reading Association.

Durkin, D. (1978–1979). What classroom observations reveal about reading comprehension instruction. *Reading Research Quarterly, 12,* 481–538.

Farnan, N. (1996). Connecting adolescents and reading: Goals at the middle level. *Journal of Adolescent & Adult Literacy, 39*(6), 436–445.

Farr, R., Tulley, M. A., & Pritchard, R. (1989). Assessment instruments and techniques used by the content area teacher. In D. Lapp, J. Flood, & N. Farnan (Eds.), *Content area reading and learning* (pp. 346–356). Englewood Cliffs, NJ: Prentice Hall.

Fowler, G. L. (1982). Developing comprehension skills in primary students through the use of story frames. *The Reading Teacher, 36*(2), 176–179.

Gambrell, L. B., Pfeiffer, W., & Wilson, R. (1985). The effects of retelling upon reading comprehension and recall of text information. *Journal of Educational Research, 78,* 216–220.

Gordon, C. J., & Braun, C. (1983). Using story schema as an aid to reading and writing. *The Reading Teacher, 37*(2), 116–121.

Graesser, A., Golding, J. M., & Long, D. L. (1991). Narrative representation and comprehension. In R. Barr, M. L. Kamil, P. Mosenthal, & P. D. Pearson (Eds.), *Handbook of reading research, Vol. 2.* (pp. 171–204). White Plains, NY: Longman.

Guthrie, J. T., Van Meter, P., McCann, A. D., Wigfield, A., Bennett, L., Poundstone, C., et al. (1996). Growth of literacy engagement: Changes in motivations and strategies during concept-oriented reading instruction. *Reading Research Quarterly, 31*(3), 306–332.

Hare, V. C., & Borchordt, K. M. (1984). Direct instruction of summarization skills. *Reading Research Quarterly, 20*(1), 62–78.

Hiede, A., & Stilborne, L. (1999). *The teacher's complete and easy guide to the Internet.* New York: Teacher's College Press.

Hoffman, J. V. (1992). Critical reading/thinking across the curriculum: Using I-charts to support learning. *Language Arts, 69,* 121–127.

Irvin, J. L., & Connors, N. A. (1989). Reading instruction in middle level schools: Results of a U.S. survey. *Journal of Reading, 32,* 306–311.

Jetton, T. L. (1994). Information-driven versus story-driven: What children remember when they are read informational stories. *Reading Psychology, 15,* 109–130.

Kletzien, S. B., & Dreher, M. J. (2004). *Informational text in K–3 classrooms: Helping children read and write.* Newark, DE: International Reading Association.

Krauss, R. (1945). *The carrot seed.* HarperCollins Publishers. New York: Scholastic.

Leal, D. J. (1992). The nature of talk about three types of text during peer group discussions. *Journal of Reading Behavior, 24,* 313–338.

Leal, D. J. (1993). Storybooks, information books, and informational storybooks: An explication of the ambiguous grey genre. *The New Advocate, 6,* 61–70.

Leslie, L., & Caldwell, J. (2001). *Qualitative reading inventory—3.* New York: Longman.

Mandler, J. M., & Johnson, N. S. (1977). Remembrance of things parsed: Story structure and recall. *Cognitive Psychology, 9,* 111–151.

Maria, K., & Junge, K. (1994). A comparison of fifth graders' comprehension and retention of scientific information using a science textbook and an information storybook. In C. K. Kinzer & D. J. Leu (Eds.), *Multidimensional aspects of literacy research, theory, and practice. 43rd Yearbook of the National Reading Conference* (pp. 146–152). Chicago: National Reading Conference.

McGee, L. M. (1982). Awareness of text structure: Effects on children's recall of expository text. *Reading Research Quarterly, 17*(4), 581–590.

Merkley, D. M., & Jeffries, D. (2001). Guidelines for implementing a graphic organizer. *The Reading Teacher, 54*(4), 350–357.

Meyer, B. J. F. (1975). *The organization of prose and its effects on memory.* Amsterdam: North-Holland.

Meyer, B. J. F., Brandt, D. M., & Bluth, G. J. (1980). Use of top-level structure in text: Key for reading comprehension of ninth-grade students. *Reading Research Quarterly, 16,* 72–103.

Montague, M., Maddux, C. D., & Dereshiwsky, M. I. (1990). Story grammar and comprehension and production of narrative prose by students with learning disabilities. *Journal of Learning Disabilities, 23,* 190–197.

Morrow, L. M. (1985). Retelling stories: A strategy for improving children's comprehension, concept of story structure and oral language complexity. *Elementary School Journal, 85,* 647–661.

Morrow, L. M. (2005). *Literacy development in the early years: Helping children read and write* (5th ed.). New York: Allyn & Bacon.

Morrow, L. M., Gambrell, L. B., Kapinus, B., Koskinen, P. S., Marshall, N., & Mitchell, J. N. (1986). Retelling: A strategy for reading instruction and assessment. In J. A. Niles & R. V. Lalik (Eds.), *Solving problems in literacy: Learners, teachers and researchers: Thirty-fifth yearbook of the National Reading Conference* (pp. 73–80). Rochester, NY: National Reading Conference.

Moss, B. (1997). A qualitative assessment of first graders' retelling of expository text. *Reading Research and Instruction, 37*(1), 1–13.

Moss, B., & Newton, E. (2002). An examination of the informational text genre in basal readers. *Reading Psychology: An International Quarterly, 23*(1), 1–14.

National Institute of Child Health and Human Development. (2000). *Report of the National Reading Panel: Teaching children to read, an evidence-based assessment of the scientific research literature on reading and its implications for reading instruction.* Washington, DC: U.S. Government Printing Office.

Nichols, J. (1980). Using paragraph frames to help remedial high school students with written assignments. *Journal of Reading, 24,* 228–231.

Noyce, R. M., & Christie, J. F. (1989). *Integrating reading and writing instruction.* Boston: Allyn & Bacon.

Pappas, C. C., Keifer, B. Z., & Levstik, L. S. (1999). *An integrated language perspective in the elementary school: An action approach* (3rd ed.). White Plains, NY: Longman.

Pearson, P. D., & Duke, N. K. (2002). Comprehension instruction in the primary grades. In C. Collins-Block & M. Pressley (Eds.), *Comprehension instruction: Research-based best practices,* (pp. 247–258). New York: Guilford Press.

Pressley, M. (2000). What should comprehension instruction be the instruction of? In M. L. Kamil, P. B. Mosenthal, P. D. Pearson, & R. Barr (Eds.), *Handbook of reading research,* Vol. 3, (pp. 545–561). Mahwah, NJ: Erlbaum.

Pressley, M. (2002a). Comprehension strategies instruction: A turn-of-the-century status report. In C. Collins-Block & M. Pressley (Eds.), Comprehension Instruction: Research-Based Best Practices, 11–27. New York: Guilford Press.

RAND Reading Study Group. (2002). *Reading for understanding: Toward an R&D program in reading comprehension.* Santa Monica, CA: Science and Technology Policy Institute, RAND Education.

Randall, S. N. (1996). Information charts: A strategy for organizing student research. *Journal of Adolescent & Adult Literacy, 39*(7), 536–542.

Raphael, T. E. (1982). Question-answering strategies for children. *The Reading Teacher, 36,* 186–191.

Raphael, T. E. (1986). Teaching question answer relationships, revisited. *The Reading Teacher, 39*(6), 516–523.

Raphael, T. E., & Pearson, P. D. (1982). *The effect of metacognitive training on children's question answering behaviors.* Urbana, Il: Center for the Study of Reading. (ERIC Document Reproduction Service No. ED215315)

Rathvon, N. (2004). *Early reading assessment: A practitioner's handbook.* New York: Guilford Press.

Readence, J. E., Bean, T. W., & Baldwin, R. S. (1992). *Content area reading: An integrated approach* (4th ed.). Dubuque, IA: Kendall/Hunt.

Reutzel, D. R. (1983). C^6: A model for teaching arithmetic story problem solving. *The Reading Teacher, 37*(1), 38–43.

Reutzel, D. R. (1985). Story maps improve comprehension. *The Reading Teacher, 38*(4), 400–405.

Reutzel, D. R. (1986). Clozing in on comprehension: The cloze story map. *The Reading Teacher, 39*(6), 524–529.

Reutzel, D. R., & Cooter, R. B. (2004). *Teaching children to read: Putting the pieces together* (4th ed.). Upper Saddle River, NJ: Merrill/Prentice Hall.

Reutzel, D. R., & Fawson, P.C. (1989). Using a Literature Webbing Strategy Lesson with Predictable Books. *The Reading Teacher, 43,* 208–215.

Reutzel, D. R., & Fawson, P. C. (1991). Literature webbing predictable books: A prediction strategy that helps below-average, first-grade readers. *Reading Research and Instruction, 30*(4), 20–30.

Ring, S. (2003). *Bridges.* Boston, MA: Newbridge.

Romine, B. G., McKenna, M. C., & Robinson, R. D. (1996). Reading coursework requirements for middle and high school content area teachers: A U.S. survey.

Journal of Adolescent & Adult Literacy, 40(3), 194–198.

Sadow, M. W. (1982). The use of story grammar in the design of questions. *The Reading Teacher, 35,* 518–523.

Seidenberg, P. L. (1989). Relating text-processing research to reading and writing instruction for learning disabled students. *Learning Disabilities Focus, 5*(1), 4–12.

Simmons, D., & Kameenui, E. (1998). What reading research tells us about children with diverse learning needs (pp. 239–278). Mahwah, NJ: Erlbaum.

Simpson, M. (1996). Conducting reality checks to improve students' strategic learning. *Journal of Adolescent & Adult Literacy, 40*(2), 102–109.

Skurzynski, G. (1992). Up for discussion: Blended books. *School Library Journal, 38*(10), 46–47.

Stafford, J. (2004). *Name that shape!—Reading Power Works series.* Northborough, MA: Sundance.

Stahl, K. A. D. (2004). Proof, practice, and promise: Comprehension strategy instruction in the primary grades. *The Reading Teacher, 57*(7), 598–609.

Stein, N. L., & Glenn, C. G. (1979). An analysis of story comprehension in elementary schoolchildren. In R. O. Freedle (Ed.), *New directions in discourse processing* (pp. 53–120). Hillsdale, NJ: Lawrence Erlbaum Associates.

Swafford, J., & Bryan, J. K. (2000). Instructional strategies for promoting conceptual change: Supporting middle school students. *Reading & Writing Quarterly, 16*(2), 139–161.

Sweet, A. P., & Snow, C. E. (2003). *Rethinking reading comprehension.* New York: Guilford Press.

Taylor, B. M., Pearson, P. D., Clark, K. F., & Walpole, S. (1999). *Beating the odds in teaching all children to read* (CIERA Report No. 2-006). Ann Arbor, MI: Center for the Improvement of Early Reading Achievement.

Thorndyke, P. N. (1977). Cognitive structure in comprehension and memory of narrative discourse. *Cognitive Psychology, 9*(1), 77–110.

Van Allsburg, C. (1992). *The widow's broom.* Boston: Houghton Mifflin.

Watson, D., & Crowley, P. (1988). How can we implement a whole-language approach? In C. Weaver (Ed.), *Reading process and practice* (pp. 232–279). Portsmouth, NH: Heinemann Educational Books.

Wepner, S. B., Valmont, W. J., & Thurlow, R. (2000). *Linking literacy and technology: A guide for K–8 classrooms.* Newark, DE: International Reading Association.

Whaley, J. F. (1981). Readers' expectations for story structures. *Reading Research Quarterly, 17,* 90–114.

Chapter 12

Developing Research and Reference Skills

James McLeary is the great-grandfather of Jon McLeary in my sixth-grade class and came to share his experiences in the early 20th century as an immigrant. He came to the United States an ocean of time ago from his homeland of Ireland at the age of 17. Mr. McLeary told us about seeing the Statue of Liberty for the first time and his landing at Ellis Island with a clarity that made you feel you were there with him. Later, Mr. McLeary spoke of his trek to Chicago, his first jobs as a roofer and craftsman, and later as a policeman in the checkered cap. Tears appeared in his eyes when he spoke of first meeting his future wife of 53 years, Kathleen. The room was mesmerized.

The next day, I said to my class, "Mr. McLeary's story was a wonderful beginning to our study of world history this year. His testimony was what is called a 'primary source.' That is information that comes to us firsthand, and we can witness it for ourselves. Over the next several weeks, we will learn many interesting and important things about Ireland. We'll learn something about Ireland's history, its people today, and its conflicts. We will also take a close look at the influences Irish Americans have on the United States. Perhaps the most important thing we will learn about Ireland is how the story of Irish immigrants is so much like the stories of immigrants from other countries in South America, Africa, Asia, and Europe.

"Folks, we are also going to learn some very cool ways to gather information about our world, what I call 'research tools.' These are tools that will save you a lot of time and make learning much easier. In fact, these are the tools you will need for the rest of your lives—in high school, college, and in your adult career. Best of all, these research tools are downright fun! Let's get started."

As students develop as fluent readers, they are challenged to apply their skills to learn more about the world in which they live. In chapter 11, we reviewed various ways students can apply their skills to read and comprehend expository texts. In this chapter, we describe ways students can be helped to acquire research and reference skills, the logical next step in conquering expository texts. These practical skills help students discover and draw upon various resources commonly found in libraries or media centers as they pursue knowledge in specific areas of interest.

BACKGROUND BRIEFING FOR TEACHERS

Readence, Bean, and Baldwin (2000) stated that the teaching of study strategies, which include research and reference skills, is crucial in helping students achieve independent learning. Research and reference skills include such diverse areas as note taking, mapping known and unknown information areas, choosing sources for obtaining information (e.g., Internet search engines, reference materials, expert interviews, etc.), and searching card catalogs electronically and manually. Some of the key strategies offered in this chapter help students to choose areas to research, to organize new information, and to learn efficient ways to locate facts.

Much of what is contained in this chapter relates directly to *metacognition*—helping students to determine what they know or do not know about a topic. In addition, many of these activities help students understand *how* they know what they know and recognize which research and reference skills they have already partially internalized.

Another major component of this chapter is the presentation of tools that can help readers categorize known information, identify gaps in their knowledge, and self-select appropriate sources to fill those blank areas with pertinent facts.

We begin by suggesting ways that teachers can assess student knowledge of research and reference skills. In the latter part of the chapter, we suggest strategies for research and reference skill improvement that can easily be modeled for students to improve their skills.

Assessing Student Knowledge of Research and Reference Skills

Investigations conducted by researchers to help teachers determine what research and reference skills students possess are few. There are some informal strategies, however, that can help teachers determine what students know about a topic of study or survey the kinds of materials that students may be using in their research. We have included in this section the strategies that have been most helpful in our classrooms. When used as teaching activities, these strategies help students to recognize their own needs—an important motivational teaching practice.

Research Logs

Purpose

An effective activity for determining the kinds of research methods and materials students are using is the research log. Research logs are a simple listing of materials used over time in the content classroom to complete research projects. By periodically reviewing research logs, teachers can survey patterns of reading or study behavior in their classrooms and plan instruction to help fill in gaps in students' knowledge about research resources.

Materials

Students will benefit from a structured research log form. A simple format for research logs is presented in Figure 12.1.

Procedure

First, develop a brief minilesson modeling how you would use a research log while completing a class assignment. Using a recent assignment as the context will save time in your minilesson and will lead students to contribute to the conversation. Once you have modeled how to record information on the log form, distribute copies of the research log to the students. If possible, introduce the research log just prior to beginning a new unit of study and provide a folder in which the logs may be kept. Check the logs at the midpoint of the unit of study to determine which research materials are being used, then offer research

Figure 12.1   Research Log

Date	Assignment/ Topic	Materials Selected	Pages/ Programs Used	Notes

Name: _____

Subject: _____   Period: _____   Homeroom: _____

skills minilessons as needed. Review the logs again at the conclusion of the unit to determine student progress and for future lesson planning.

SELF-RATING SCALES

Purpose

It is often true that no one knows better how he or she is doing in reading than the reader him- or herself. This is especially true when it comes to the reader's ability to use research and reference materials in the library stacks. A teacher carrying out an assessment agenda should never overlook the obvious—ask the student what he or she is good at doing! Although this may be best achieved in a one-on-one discussion setting, large class sizes frequently make this impractical. A good alternative to one-on-one interviews for older elementary children is a student self-rating scale. In applying this strategy, students complete a questionnaire that is custom tailored to obtain specific information about the reader and his or her skills with research and reference tools—from the reader's point of view.

Materials

You will need to construct a self-rating scale that conforms to the research and reference skills you want each of your students to possess. Figure 12.2 shows an example of a self-rating scale.

Figure 12.2　Self-Rating Scale

Self-Rating Scale: Researching the "Evolution of Surgery"

Name: _____　　Date: _____

Directions: Answer the following questions as they pertain to how you will find out more about the ways surgery has improved in the United States in the last 100 years.

The first three things I will do to find out more about how surgery has improved in the United States when I enter the library is:

1.
2.
3.

Three things I know about entries (cards) in the card catalog in the library are:

1.
2.
3.

Three sources of information I can use in this study of surgery are:

1.
2.
3.

I can organize the information and data I find by . . .

I feel I could use some help in understanding how to use library resources or research skills in these areas (check all that apply):

_____ using the card catalog
_____ taking notes
_____ finding periodicals from a particular time period or topic
_____ finding books that relate to our unit on surgery
_____ using the Internet to find information
_____ organizing information to write a report
_____ interviewing experts
_____ knowing where to begin my research
_____ locating information quickly in a book

Procedures

We prefer to use self-rating scales within the context of an actual unit of study about to commence or with a unit just completed. For example, let us assume that you are about to begin a new unit of study pertaining to "The Evolution of Surgery" in this country from 1900 to the present. After having a brief warm-up conversation with the students about the field of medicine and surgery, distribute the self-rating scale you have developed. Once the students have completed their self-rating scales, collect and analyze the scales to determine in a cursory way the skills the students feel that they possess. (*Note:* This is only a survey of student perceptions. You will also need to collect further observations as the students begin to actually use library resources to complete assignments.)

PREREADING PLAN

Purpose

This three-stage strategy by Langer (1981) helps teachers assess and activate the prior knowledge of students about a topic of study. This assessment and instruction activity may be used with a whole class or small groups. The first step uses a question to determine any associations students may have with a topic, concept, or term to be studied. The second step asks students to review and interpret their first impressions. The final step has students work with the teacher to identify existing gaps in their knowledge to help guide their research into the topic.

Materials

There are no materials required to do the Prereading Plan (PreP) activity beyond the usual paper, pencils, and chalkboards normally found in classrooms. However, large pictures or other artifacts that relate to the topic of study may help jog students' memories in the first activity.

Procedure

As already noted, the first step is to ask students what they know about the topic to be studied. These initial associations provide insights into how much prior knowledge exists in the class and helps students to begin building concept-related associations about the topic (Cooter & Flynt, 1996). For example, in teaching a lesson about the Civil Rights movement of the 1960s, you may start off by asking your class, "What do you think of when you hear the words 'civil rights'?" Showing pictures from the 1950s and 1960s of lunch counter sit-ins; the Little Rock, Arkansas, school desegregation incident; or of Rosa Parks and Dr. Martin Luther King, Jr., could be quite helpful in stimulating initial discussion. After recording students' first associations, the next step is to have students think about or reflect on their initial associations. During this reflection stage, your goal is to have students discuss and explain why the associations they had about the topic came to mind—"What made you think of . . . ?" This interactive stage further taps prior knowledge, builds a common network of ideas about the topic, and facilitates a student-centered discussion.

The last stage of PreP is called *reformulation of knowledge*. Your goal is to have students recognize and define what they know about the topic before they begin research to learn more about it. We find that creating an outline or concept web about the topic helps many students see graphically what they already know, create categories for known information, and provoke questions about what must still be learned through the research process.

SEMANTIC MAPS

Purpose

Another useful strategy that can be used to activate students' prior knowledge of a topic and lead them to preview text material via student-centered discussion is the *semantic map*. Based on schema theory, semantic maps are essentially "road maps" of what is known by students with clusters of related information noted. Semantic maps can help students better understand metacognitively what is known and not known, as well as the research sources that can be employed to help find information. Because semantic maps depict known information in precisely the same way the brain stores information, they are inherently logical for students and can provide valuable insights for teachers.

Materials

You will need a large chart or tablet on an easel and colored markers to illustrate the semantic map. An alternative is to use an overhead projector, blank transparencies, and markers.

Procedure

The procedure starts with the teacher writing the topic on the chart or transparency. Similar to the PreP procedure discussed earlier, students are then asked to volunteer any information they associate with the identified topic. As the students offer them, the teacher lists their associations on the chart or transparency. Next, the teacher asks students to examine all headings, subheadings, and visuals in a textbook selection to be used as part of the introduction to gather more information. Students may do this work independently or with a partner. The new information is then added to the semantic map. At this time, students are asked to read the textbook selection carefully to provoke more discussion and to find more relevant information that can be added to the semantic map. A postreading discussion centers on the various questions that remain to be answered more completely and research sources that could be used in answering the questions. In Figure 12.3, we illustrate a typical semantic map that was created by students with teacher assistance regarding the Civil Rights movement topic mentioned earlier in the chapter. Note that a product that grew out of the semantic map's construction was a listing of research sources available for locating needed information.

In other chapters we offered a *Summary Matrix of Assessments* for procedures and instruments presented for a particular area of reading instruction. Because the topic of this chapter does not, strictly speaking, align with federally mandated areas of reading instruction, nor do the types of assessments presented lend themselves to rigorous reliability or validity studies, we have elected not to include a *Summary Matrix of Assessments* for this chapter.

Connecting Assessment Findings to Teaching Strategies

Before moving on to specific research strategies, we have constructed an if-then chart connecting assessment findings to intervention and/or strategy choices. Teaching strategies described in the next section are listed across the top of the *if-then chart,* and potential instructional areas are listed vertically in the left-hand column.

Teaching Students Research and Reference Skills

Teaching students how to become effective researchers of knowledge is paramount if they are to become independent learners in later years. Thus, we better be good at setting up these kinds of learning experiences! Susan De la Paz (1999; Swanson & De la Paz, 1998) developed an effective process for teaching students the kinds of research and reference skills we discuss in the remainder of this chapter. We think you will see a familiar Vygotskian thread to this process she calls the **Self-Regulated Strategy Development Model** (SRSD) and highly recommend SRSD as the framework for introducing and practicing research strategies. Here is the gist of her recommendations.

1. *Describe the Strategy.* Explicitly describe the strategy steps and discuss why and when the strategy can be useful and what it accomplishes.

If-Then Strategy Guide for Study Skills

"If" the student is ready to learn ↓ / "Then" try these teaching strategies →	Graphic Organizers	Note Taking	SQ3R	Venn Hula Hoops	K-W-L-S	K-W-W-L
Organizational Skills	+	–	+	+	+	+
Test Performance	+	–	+	–	+	+
Problem Solving	*	*	*	+	*	*
Research Skills	*	+	*	–	+	+
Retaining Information	+	+	+	+	+	+

Key: + Excellent Strategy   * Adaptable Strategy   – Unsuitable Strategy

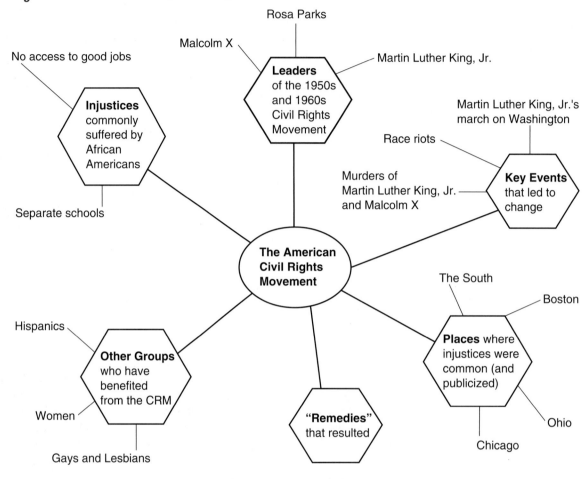

Figure 12.3 Semantic Map: Civil Rights Movement

Rosa Parks

Malcolm X

Leaders of the 1950s and 1960s Civil Rights Movement

Martin Luther King, Jr.

No access to good jobs

Injustices commonly suffered by African Americans

Separate schools

Martin Luther King, Jr.'s march on Washington

Race riots

Murders of Martin Luther King, Jr. and Malcolm X

Key Events that led to change

The American Civil Rights Movement

The South

Boston

Hispanics

Other Groups who have benefited from the CRM

Women

Gays and Lesbians

"Remedies" that resulted

Places where injustices were common (and publicized)

Ohio

Chicago

Questions to Answer

1. What are some of the greatest injustices suffered by African Americans that led to the Civil Rights Movement (CRM)?

2. Who were the Americans who seemed to have helped the CRM to be successful?

3. What were the key events that seemed to trigger the CRM?

4. Where were changes needed most in the United States?

5. What changes or remedies resulted?

Research Sources Available

History books, periodicals from that era, interviews with people who lived in the 1950s and 1960s, Internet searches, M.L. King Center in Atlanta, historians, card catalog entries, NAACP literature.

2. *Activate Prior Knowledge.* Review information the students may have already learned that may be useful in learning the new strategy.

3. *Review Students' Current Level of Functioning.* Provide information to students about their current performance levels and how this strategy can help them achieve a higher level of performance.

4. *Model the Strategy.* Show the student how to use the strategy using multiple examples. Allow for student input and feedback.

5. *Provide Collaborative Practice.* Provide numerous opportunities for students to practice the new strategy in whole group, small groups, pairs, and/or individually, depending on what you believe will be most effective. Teacher support will be faded out over time.

6. *Include Independent Practice.* Students should have ample opportunities to practice the strategy alone. They should have teacher or peer support available at first; but, ultimately, they should demonstrate proficiency in using the strategy alone.

7. *Generalize the Strategy.* After learning has taken place, be sure to use the strategy routinely in future teaching and learning experiences. If the strategy is worth teaching, it is worth using and allowing it to become, as they say in the military, "SOP" (standard operating procedure).

GRAPHIC ORGANIZERS

Purpose

The purpose of research conducted by students is to gain and understand new knowledge about a topic. Many students struggle with this process and often seem to find disparate bits of information that they are unable to assimilate into what they already know. Without assimilation, no new learning is likely to result. *Graphic organizers* (GOs) can be used to help students comprehend new information, assimilate new information into what they already know, and recall that information later on when needed. Donna Merkley and Debra Jeffries (2001) have developed guidelines for constructing and implementing GOs effectively in the classroom.

Materials

The teacher will first identify a fairly short (5 to 15 pages) expository text selection that is germane to the content curriculum. Next, follow the steps in the "Procedures" section and analyze the selection identifying important key terms, descriptions, and concepts. Select a simple GO format and construct examples for classroom demonstrations or modeling with the GO in varying degrees of completion. We like to use overhead transparencies and an overhead projector for this kind of modeling.

Procedures

Merkley and Jeffries (2001) have summarized ways of (a) creating graphic organizers (GOs), and (b) implementing GOs in the classroom. We have adapted and combined these steps so that you can present them as a process tool to students. As always, extensive description and modeling on your part are essential. The goal is to have students internalize these processes so that they begin using GOs as a tool in their research activities.

Step 1: Show students ways of analyzing new information for important key words, descriptions, and global concepts. Verbalize relationships between concepts and key words. Provide opportunities for student questions and input.

Step 2: Arrange key words, descriptive phrases, and concepts into an illustration to show interrelationships and patterns of organization. As you construct a graphic organizer (GO), verbalize for students how their earlier work in Step 1 flows in a natural way into the selection of an appropriate GO design (see examples shown in Figure 12.8-12.13.). Demonstrate how new knowledge can connect to students' prior knowledge.

Step 3: Review and evaluate the relationships in the GO for clarity, simplicity, and visual effectiveness. Demonstrate how the need for more information in some areas can help students formulate research questions leading to further reading and a search for missing links.

To summarize, the key elements to teaching students about GOs are (Merkley & Jeffries, 2001):

- Verbalize relationships (links) among concepts by the GO.
- Provide opportunities for student input and questioning during your modeling and guided-practice experiences.
- Connect new knowledge to prior experiences.
- Develop "need-to-know" questions that relate to upcoming readings and further research.

NOTE-TAKING STRATEGIES

Purpose

There are many different systems for teaching students how to take notes as they listen (Cooter & Flynt, 1996; Lapp, Flood, & Farnan, 2004). Among the note-taking systems that have been proposed are the Cornell System (Pauk, 2000) and the REST system (Morgan, Meeks, Schollaert, & Paul, 1986). Recommendations about how notes should initially be recorded, the need for subsequent reorganization and expansion of the notes, and a strong recommendation for frequent review exemplify the common threads of these systems.

Materials

Students will need a notebook that can be used exclusively for learning note taking.

Procedure

Before discussing each of the components of effective note taking, we would first like to suggest a couple of general guidelines derived from the work of Cooter and Flynt (1996). First, students should be asked to obtain a single notebook specifically for use in learning note-taking skills. Dedicating a notebook for this purpose will help students keep the notes organized and will make it easier for you to collect and examine the notes. Second, if note taking is important to you, then some type of credit should be given to students who do a good job of recording and organizing their notes. Finally, adapt the amount and style of lecturing to your students' ability level. If you have an advanced class, more sophisticated lectures may be warranted. On the other hand, if your class has little experience with note taking and effective listening techniques, you may want to begin slowly and use a lot of visuals or perhaps a listening outline to assist students in determining and writing important information.

Two traditional note-taking systems are the Cornell System (Pauk, 2000) and *A Note-Taking System for Learning* (Palmatier, 1973). These systems share several features that we recommend for use in training students how to listen and take notes on lecture information.

First, students should divide their notebook paper into two columns. The left column should be about 2 or 3 inches wide, or one-third of the paper width. The remaining two-thirds of the page is used for recording the notes.

Second, students should write information in a modified outline form on the right side of the page. Students should indent subtopics and minor ideas using letters and numbers. They should be encouraged to use abbreviations to minimize time spent in writing down information. Heavily emphasized points should be marked with asterisks or stars.

Third, students should organize and expand their notes as soon as possible. Early in the school year, considerate teachers provide in-class time for this task. At this time, the students literally rewrite their notes on similarly lined paper. The purpose is for the students to write all abbreviations, expand phrases, and make sure that the information is sequentially organized. This is obviously a form of practice.

Fourth, students fill in the left margin for aid in study and review. As they reread their notes, students identify topics, key terms, and questions that may assist them in remembering the lecture information recorded on the right side of the paper.

Fifth, students use their notes for study and review. Students can now cover up the right-hand side of the paper and use the memory triggers they have recorded on the left-hand side for review. As they move down the left-hand side of the page, students use the headings, key terms, and questions as a means of assessing their ability to remember and paraphrase what they have recorded.

SQ3R

All effective reading or study strategies are metacognitive in nature because they cause readers to establish purposes for study, to determine whether they have been successful in satisfying their purposes, and to adjust their tactics if they have failed or fallen short in achieving their purposes for studying. Reading or study strategies require the students to actively attend to text information, respond to the text in some way (taking notes, underlining, answering questions), spend more time on task, and review the material for long-term retention. If one examines a reading or study "how-to" book, one often finds a plethora of reading or study strategies that are touted as either effective or tailor made for specific subject matter areas. They are usually presented by an acronym that reflects the various steps of the strategy. The most time-honored of all these reading or study strategies is SQ3R. Originally developed by Francis Robinson (1946) as a technique to help soldiers study manuals during World War II (Stahl & Henk, 1986), SQ3R has been used widely in schools as a way of providing students with a specific, albeit intense, method for independent study. SQ3R has spawned many other similar-looking reading or study strategies; however, since most of the other reading or study strategies reflect much of what SQ3R recommends, we confine this discussion to SQ3R. First, we present the steps of SQ3R and then discuss the strategy's relative usefulness in content reading and study.

Survey. Begin a new unit of study by quickly reading all chapter headings, subheadings, marginal notes, words printed in bold, pictures and their captions, and charts or diagrams. This will draw one's attention to some of the major topics to be learned.

Question. Based on your "survey," write several questions that pertain to the headings, subheadings, words in bold, and marginal notes you discovered. This will alert you to some of the key information while reading. (*Note:* We recommend that teachers model for students how to write questions on different levels of complexity, such as literal, inferential, and evaluative levels. Many students need a great deal of practice with higher-order thinking skills.)

Read. Read the chapter. As you do so, try to pay careful attention to information that answers the questions you created in the previous step. After reading, go back and answer each question in writing, being sure to note specific details from the chapter.

Recite. After you have answered all questions in detail, give yourself a quiz over those same questions and try to write your responses from memory. Any questions that gave you difficulty should be practiced by rereading the questions and answers aloud. Continue this practice until all questions and answers can be rewritten from memory.

Review. Once information has been learned and can be recited from memory, it should be reviewed daily so that it becomes permanent. The amount of time spent for review each day will depend on the complexity of the unit of study, but about 20 minutes per day is generally a good rule of thumb.

As you can see, SQ3R may require a great deal of effort on the part of the student and the teacher. Estimates suggest that a minimum of 10 hours of teacher-led instruction are required for low-achieving students to utilize SQ3R effectively (Orlando, 1986). In addition, the overall benefit of SQ3R on student achievement is not clear (Caverly & Orlando, 1991). We feel that teachers should stress only those components of SQ3R that can best serve students with a particular assignment.

VENN DIAGRAM HULA HOOPS

Purpose

Venn diagrams have been used for many years to help students understand similarities, differences, and common features of information gleaned from reading assignments. Venn diagrams are simply two overlapping circles used to graphically display three kinds of information. With *Venn Diagram Hula Hoops* (Cooter & Thomas, 1998), this concept is applied for students (elementary through high school) using the hula hoops first popularized in the 1950s.

Materials

You will need to purchase at least two hula hoops for each group of children (usually four students to a group) to be involved in this activity. For each group, sentence strips or tagboard and watercolor markers are needed for use in writing information from the readings.

Procedure

With a simple passage, begin by modeling for the class how Venn diagrams are used. You can use a dry-erase board, chart, chalkboard, or overhead projector for your modeling. For younger children—and perhaps for older ones, too—an easy-to-use comparison is a traditional telling of *The Three Little Pigs* contrasted to *The True Story of the Three Little Pigs* by A. Wolf. Another version of the story we enjoy using is "The Old Sow and the Three Shoats" found in Richard Chase's classic *Grandfather Tales* (1948). In Figure 12.4, we display how similarities, differences, and commonalities could be portrayed in the teacher's modeling exercise using Chase's version and the traditional story.

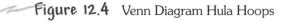

Figure 12.4　Venn Diagram Hula Hoops

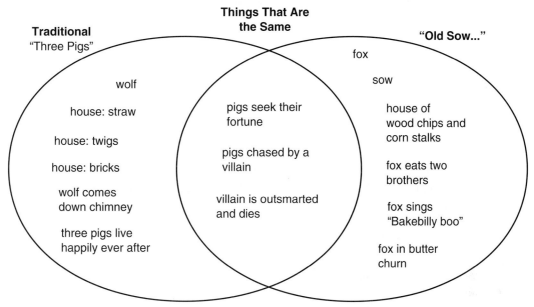

Source: Cooter, K. S., & Thomas M. (1998). *Venn diagram hula hoops.* Unpublished manuscript, Texas Christian University, Fort Worth, TX. Comparisons using the traditional telling of "The Three Little Pigs" and Richard Chase's (1948) "The Old Sow and the Three Shoats" from *Grandfather Tales* (Houghton Mifflin).

Once students seem to grasp the Venn diagram concept, repeat the modeling exercise in a large open space using the hula hoops. Simply ask the children to gather around in a circle where they can see the hula hoops laid across each other to form the familiar Venn diagram configuration. Be sure to print on sentence strips the appropriate name or title for each circle, and place the labels above the corresponding circle or center section (i.e., "Traditional Three Pigs Story," "Old Sow and the Three Shoats," "Both Stories"). Using the very same descriptors that you suggested in the modeling activity and wrote on sentence strips or tagboard strips (in this case, using the "Three Pigs" story descriptors), lay the sentence strips where appropriate within the diagram. Ask a volunteer if he or she can explain what each descriptor means in each circle or in the overlapping section.

Once students have demonstrated an understanding of how to use Venn diagram hula hoops, broaden the experience using nonfiction expository reading selections. Be sure to model first, then ask the students to do the task in small groups.

K-W-L-S Strategy Chart

Purpose

The K-W-L strategy is effective in improving reading comprehension by causing students to activate, think about, and organize their prior knowledge as an aid to reading comprehension. Ogle (1986), originator of K-W-L, asserts that this strategy is best suited for use with expository text. Sinatra (1997) found success using K-W-L with informational texts when adding one additional step—asking students what they *still* want to know (S) after the K-W-L routine has been completed. This addition to Ogle's original strategy helps create continuing interest in the topic under study, encourages a degree of metacognitive thinking (i.e., helping students realize what they know and do not yet know, and helps teachers assess student learning). We have adapted Sinatra's K-W-L-S Strategy Chart somewhat for use as a research tool.

Materials

Students will need a copy of the K-W-L-S Strategy Chart such as the one shown in Figure 12.5.

Procedure

As with a standard K-W-L activity, this version is intended as a metacognitive exercise to help guide students' learning. Begin by displaying an enlarged version of the K-W-L-S Strategy Chart at the front of the group, using either large tablet paper or transparencies and an overhead projector. Define and explain what each letter in the K-W-L-S Strategy Chart means and how an awareness of what one knows or does not know can help guide one efficiently through a research experience. This latter timesaving point can be motivational for most of us who hope to keep library search time to a minimum.

Next, use the enlarged chart to "walk through" the K-W-L-S procedure once using a combination of read-aloud and group participation. For example, say you have chosen a passage from a health textbook pertaining to heart disease to illustrate how the K-W-L-S Strategy Chart can be used as an aid in health research.

Say to the students: "Before we try out the K-W-L-S Strategy Chart on our own, let us try it out once together. A topic we will be learning about next has to do with the human heart and ways to prevent heart disease. The first step in using a K-W-L-S Strategy Chart is to think about what we know about the topic. That is what the *K* represents on the chart. Let us list some of the things we already know about the heart. Any volunteers?"

Begin to list things that are known in the first column. Note that we have included at the bottom of that column a question that pertains to reference tools that help students know what they already know about a subject. This helps students immediately think about tools they have used in some manner in the past or, in other columns, tools they could use as they progress in their research.

The next step is to complete the *W* column by answering the question, "What information about the human heart and its diseases would I want to know (or need to know)?" Once the *W* column has been completed, use student participation up to this point as a springboard to discuss in some detail the library or media center tools that can be helpful for locating information. Next, using one of the library or media center tools, instruct your students to listen as you read aloud a passage you have selected pertaining to your question (in this case, a passage on heart disease may be chosen). Once you have completed the reading, go back to the K-W-L-S Strategy Chart and complete the *L* section describing the additional information you learned from listening to the passage.

At this point in a standard K-W-L activity, the students would be finished. However, as Sinatra (1997) observed, there are usually many more facts yet to be learned and questions left unanswered—hence, the addition of the *S* stage, which essentially asks, "What do I still need to know about this subject?" Unanswered questions from the *W* stage of the activity, as well as any new questions emerging from the read-aloud activity, should be listed in this column. This final category sends some very important

Figure 12.5   K-W-L-S Strategy Chart

| Name: _____ | | Date: _____ | |
| Topic: _____ | | | |
"K" What I "Know" . . .	"W" What I "Want" to Know . . .	"L" What I "Learned" . . .	"S" What I Am "Still" Needing to Know . . .
Reference tools that helped me know what I know:	**Reference tools** I will need to find out more:	**Reference tools** that helped me:	**Reference tools** I will need to find out more:

messages to students: (a) there are always some unanswered questions in almost every research project; (b) as you learn more information, that information often spawns new questions, (c) there are sources of information in the library or media center to help me find answers to my questions; and (d) my teacher will help me to learn how to use these resources effectively.

K-W-W-L

Purpose

Another variation of the K-W-L (Ogle, 1986) strategy is K-W-W-L (Bryan, 1998). Much like Sinatra's (1997) K-W-L-S Strategy Chart, this activity helps students to identify starting points for their research.

Materials

Reproduce worksheets like the one shown in Figure 12.6 for each student, as well as an enlarged version with which you can model the activity.

Procedure

Follow the same process as described for the K-W-L-S Strategy Chart; however, use the K-W-W-L figure instead. We have included a partially completed K-W-W-L chart in Figure 12.7 or use in your modeling exercise.

SELECTED MAPS AND GRAPHIC ORGANIZERS FOR USE WITH INFORMATIONAL TEXT

Purpose

As noted earlier in the chapter, semantic maps and other graphic organizers (GOs) can help teachers assess what students know or do not know about a topic. They can also be used as a research and study tool to help students chart important knowledge they are acquiring, understand steps in a process or sequence, classify or categorize information, compare and contrast two or more features, determine causal patterns, and prepare and defend thesis statements concerning an area of study. In short, maps are a form of outlining that helps students determine which areas they must research.

Materials

Figure 12.8 through Figure 12.13 display each map as described in the next section.

Procedure

Sinatra, Gemake, Wielan, and Sinatra (1998) have identified several map forms and their usefulness with informational text. We offer an abbreviated summary of their research targeting maps that we wish to emphasize.

Figure 12.6   K-W-W-L Chart

Topic:

I "know" . . .	I "want" to learn . . .	"Where" I can learn this . . .	I have "learned" . . .
1.			
2.			
3.			
4.			
5.			
6.			
7.			
8.			

Figure 12.7   K-W-W-L Chart Example

Topic: "Oceans"

I know . . .	I want to learn . . .	Where I can learn this . . .	I have learned . . .
1. Oceans have salt water.	What makes the ocean salty?	• encyclopedia • Internet search • ask a scientist	
2. Salt water burns your eyes.	Is salt water harmful to your eyes?	• ask a doctor • look for a book in the library on this subject	
3. There are many kinds of sharks.	Are all sharks "man eaters"?	• ask a marine biologist • check the Internet	
4. Oceans have waves and tides.	What causes the tides?	• look for a book in the library on oceans • ask a scientist at the university • call the TV station weather personnel	
5. Many kinds of fish live in the ocean.	What kinds of sea creatures live in the deep waters?	• look for a library book on fish • ask a scientist • check the encyclopedia • try an Internet search	
6. There are other forms of sea life found in the ocean.	What are some of the main kinds of sea life?	• same as #5	
7. Songs have been written about the sea.	How would I go about getting a list of songs about the sea?	• check with the music teacher • try a search on the Internet with <Amazon.com> for songs	
8.			

Notes:

~~Figure 12.8~~ Steps-in-a-Process Map

Topic/Subject _____
_____
_____

| Event #1 Idea | _____ |

| Event #2 Idea | _____ |

| Event #3 Idea | _____ |

| Event #4 Idea | _____ |

Finally...

Student/Researcher _____

Date Submitted _____

Figure 12.9 Comparison/Contrast Map

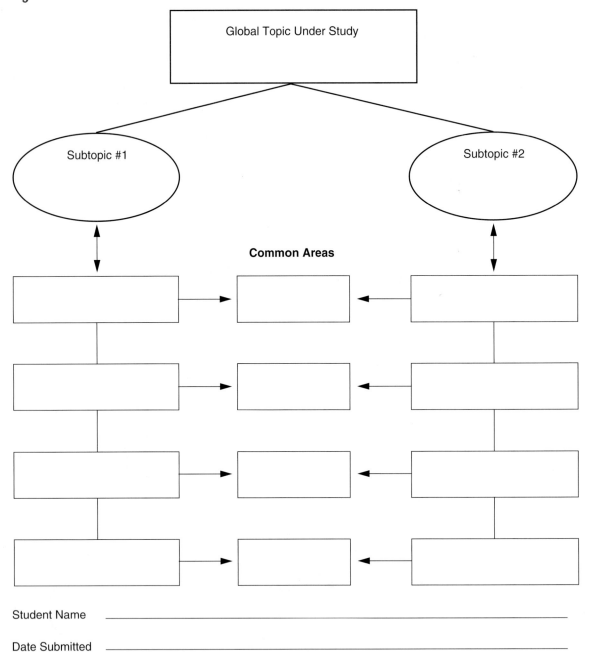

Student Name   _____

Date Submitted   _____

Figure 12.10 Same/Different Map

Topic or Main Idea _____

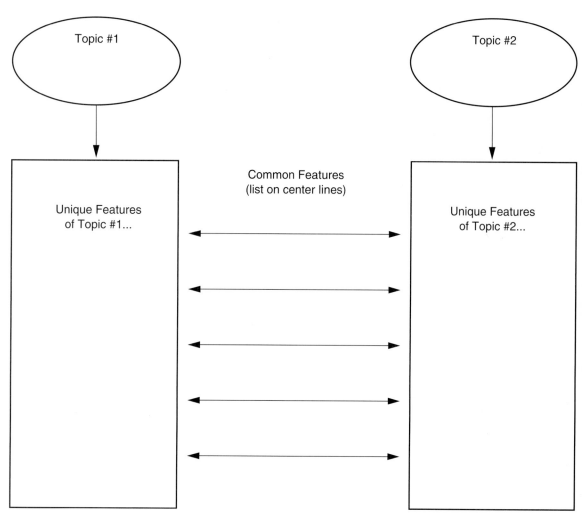

Student Name _____

Figure 12.11 Cause/Effect Map

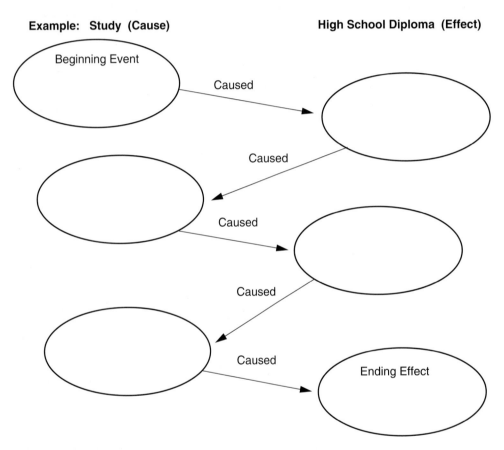

Example: Study (Cause)   High School Diploma (Effect)

Beginning Event

Caused

Caused

Caused

Caused

Caused

Ending Effect

Topic/Title Name _____

Student Name _____

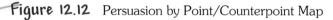 **Figure 12.12** Persuasion by Point/Counterpoint Map

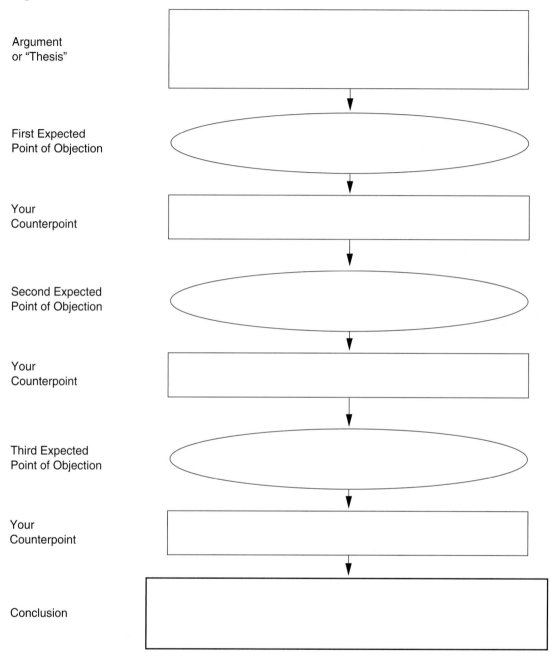

Argument
or "Thesis"

First Expected
Point of Objection

Your
Counterpoint

Second Expected
Point of Objection

Your
Counterpoint

Third Expected
Point of Objection

Your
Counterpoint

Conclusion

Figure 12.13   Turning-Point Map

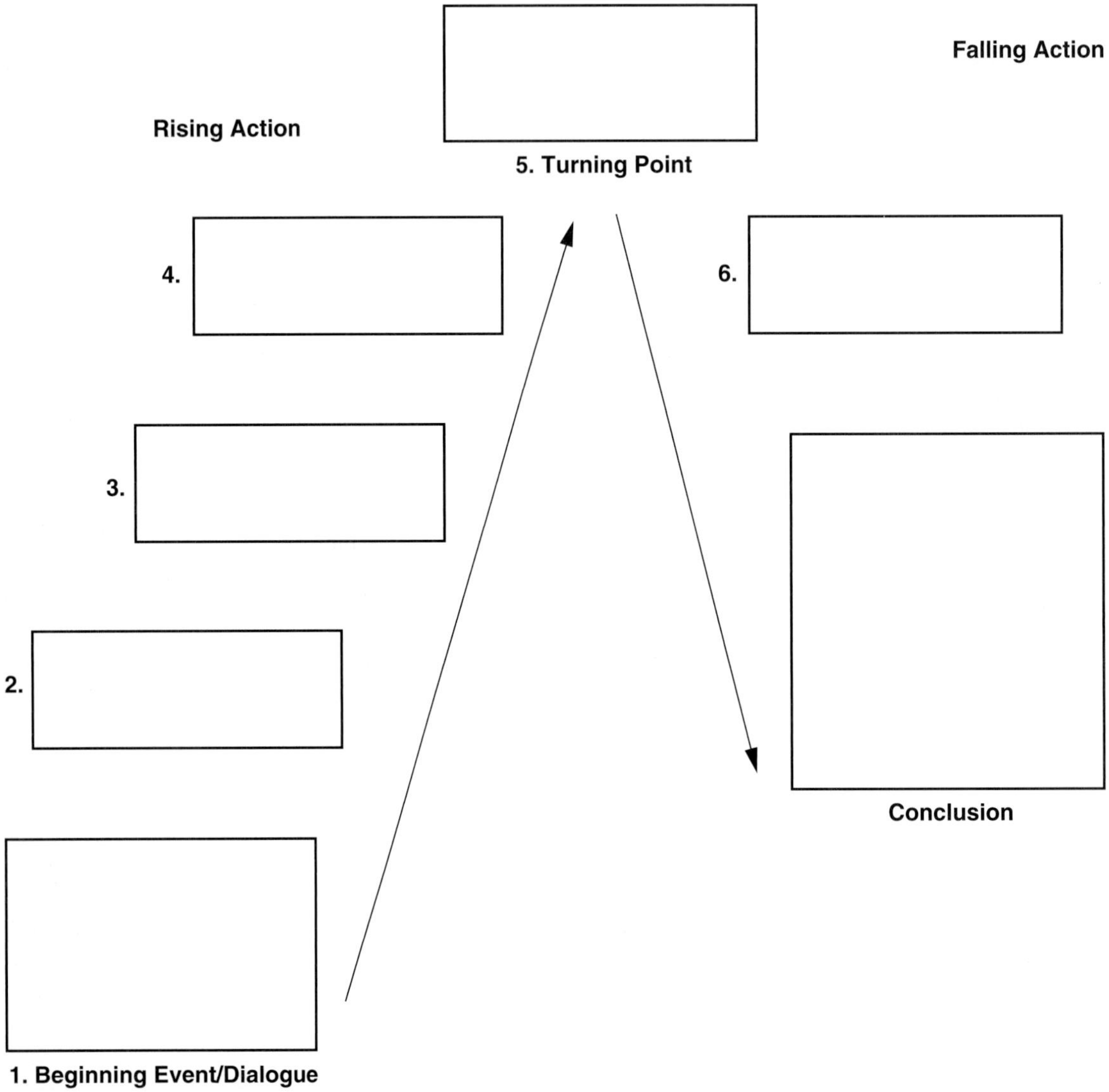

Falling Action

Rising Action

5. Turning Point

4.

6.

3.

2.

Conclusion

1. Beginning Event/Dialogue

Student Name _____   Date _____

Type of Map	Type of Text Structure	Type of Higher-Order Thinking
Steps in a Process	Time-related events with multiple episodes and/or a sequence of events, as with many science process steps or social studies events.	Students must be able to select and sequence events, describing processes in order. All are based on students' ability to locate appropriate information sources.
Compare/Contrast and Same/Different	Comparison information structures found in many expository texts, particularly in the sciences, literature, social studies, health, and mathematics.	Often inferential or implied in texts, comparison requires students to identify qualities of sameness and differences. Thus, this activity provides a logical framework for identifying and using library/media resources.
Chain of Events	Causal patterns found in the text descriptions, most often the sciences, literature, and social studies.	Identification of causal events that trigger an (often predictable) outcome.
Persuasion by Point/Counterpoint	Derived typically from literature, social studies, and studies of the arts.	Identification of problems or issues, location of information to support a thesis/belief/judgment, charting opposing views, and formulating counterarguments in support of the thesis.
Turning Point	Useful primarily with literature and history texts.	Students are required to detect important events in sequence that contribute to a final outcome.

Note that students may be helped or "coached" by teachers to locate additional research materials or databases to complete the map(s). In the end, it may be concluded that the construction of maps can indeed help students construct their own comprehension of the topic under study. Sinatra et al. (1998) urge teachers, as a next step, to challenge students to develop their own maps to represent new units of study, then present them to the class or group.

SELECTED REFERENCES

Bryan, J. (1998). K-W-W-L: Questioning the known. *The Reading Teacher, 51*(7), 1998.

Caverly, D. C., & Orlando, V. P. (1991). Textbook strategies. In R. F. Filippo & D. C. Caverly (Eds.), *Teaching reading and study strategies at the college level* (pp. 86–165). Newark, DE: International Reading Association.

Chase, R. (1948). *Grandfather tales.* Boston: Houghton Mifflin.

Cooter, K. S., & Thomas, M. (1998). *Venn diagram hula hoops.* Unpublished manuscript, Texas Christian University, Fort Worth.

Cooter, R. B., & Flynt, E. S. (1996). *Teaching reading in the content areas: Developing content literacy for all students.* New York: John Wiley.

De la Paz, S. (1999). Self-regulated strategy instruction in regular education settings: Improving outcomes for students with and without learning disabilities. *Learning Disabilities Research & Practice, 14*(2), 92–106.

Ediger, M. (2000). Writing, the pupil, and the social studies. *College Student Journal, 34*(1), 59–68.

Langer, J. (1981). From theory to practice: A prereading plan. *Journal of Reading, 25,* 152–156.

Lapp, D., Flood, J., & Farnan, N. (2004). *Content area reading and learning instructional strategies.* Mahwah: NJ: Lawrence Erlbaum.

Merkley, D. M., & Jeffries, D. (2001). Guidelines for implementing graphic organizers. *The Reading Teacher, 54*(4), 350–357.

Morgan, R. F., Meeks, J., Schollaert, A., & Paul, J. (1986). *Critical reading/thinking skills for the college student.* Dubuque, IA: Kendall/Hunt.

Ogle, D. (1986). K-W-L: A teaching model that develops active reading of expository text. *The Reading Teacher, 39*(6), 564–570.

Orlando, V. P. (1986). Training students to use a modified version of SQ3R: An instructional strategy. *Reading World, 20,* 65–70.

Palmatier, R. A. (1973). A note-taking system for learning. *Journal of Reading, 17,* 36–39.

Pauk, W. (2000). *How to study in college.* Boston: Houghton Mifflin.

Readence, J. E., Bean, T. W., & Baldwin, R. S. (2000). *Content area reading: An integrated approach.* Dubuque, IA: Kendall/Hunt.

Robinson, F. P. (1946). *Effective study.* New York: Harper Brothers.

Scieszka, J. (1989). *The true story of the 3 little pigs: (By A. Wolf)* New York: Viking Kestrel.

Sinatra, R. (1997). *Inner-city games CAMP-US: Literacy training manual.* St. John's University.

Sinatra, R., Gemake, J., Wielan, O. P., & Sinatra, C. (1998, March). *Teaching learners to think, read, and write more effectively.* The 1998 ASCD Annual Conference, San Antonio, TX.

Stahl, N. A., & Henk, W. A. (1986). Tracing the roots of textbook study systems: An extended historical perspective. In J. A. Niles & R. V. Lalik (Eds.), *Solving problems in literacy: Learners, teachers, and researchers. Thirty-fifth yearbook of the National Reading Conference* (pp. 336–374). Rochester, NY: National Reading Conference.

Swanson, P. N., & De la Paz, S. (1998). Teaching effective comprehension strategies to students. *Intervention in School & Clinic, 33*(4), 209–218.

Chapter 13

Writing and Reading

Ms. Kathy, as her fourth graders know her, has begun teaching her students strategies for comparing and contrasting two stories. She has already done a considerable amount of modeling for the students, as well as several days of guided practice with the students working in pairs. Ms. Kathy is convinced that her students are ready to move into some individual practice sessions (with her waiting "in the wings" to help when necessary). She showed the students how to use a comparison grid to chart out similarities and differences, then use the grid to write a brief summary comparing and contrasting the two narratives. In other words, she has been gradually releasing responsibility to her young charges and is pleased with their progress.

"Girls and boys, we are now ready to practice our new compare-and-contrast skills on our own so that I can see how each of you is progressing individually. Here is what I want you to do. First, complete this blank comparison grid I am distributing for the two movies we have just seen together: *Shrek* and *The Grinch Who Stole Christmas*. We will, as we have done before, compare and contrast the two stories in terms of main character, setting, the character's main problem, ways he tries to solve the problem, and the resolution of each story. This should be fun!

"After you finish your grid, please come see me for a miniconference before you begin writing your summary, just in case I have any questions. Is everyone with me? Okay, let's rock 'n' roll."

Reading and writing are two sides of the same coin, or, put another way, they are *reflections* of the same language process (Squire, 1983). Reading is a *receptive* language process in that the reader *receives* the message of a writer for mental processing. Writing, on the other hand, is a *productive* language process such that the author is *producing* a message to be interpreted later by a reader. Reading and writing are even more closely linked than one may think initially, however. This point is further examined later in this chapter in a discussion on teacher knowledge base. In addition, this chapter focuses on specific ways of measuring writing development. Further, it includes suggestions for activities that help foster the strengthening of reading and writing processes simultaneously.

BACKGROUND BRIEFING FOR TEACHERS: WRITING CONNECTIONS TO READING

Reading and writing are reciprocal processes (Shanahan, 1984): when teachers build students' skills in one process, the other tends to be strengthened as well. For example, when students act in the role of writer, they also act as readers because writers read and reread during writing. Similarly, when students read, they often notice and learn aspects of writing from the author, such as writing styles, interesting phrases, ways to write dialogue, new vocabulary, and methods of punctuation. Lucy Calkins (1994) has stated that one of the great benefits of writing process instruction for students is that it helps them feel like "insiders" or peers with their favorite authors. Tompkins (1999), in summarizing research pertaining to reading-writing connections, concludes that reading and writing are both meaning-making processes and experience with one process provides a scaffold or framework to support the learning of the other. Frank Smith (1983) reminds us that, in order for students to be writers, they must read like writers (p. 2).

ASSESSING WRITING DEVELOPMENT

At least two writing assessment perspectives are commonly thought of when analyzing student compositions: qualitative (also known as descriptive) and quantitative (also known as numerical). Each is briefly described, along with other ideas and an instrument useful in writing assessment.

QUALITATIVE ASSESSMENT

Purpose

Qualitative assessments use written summaries rather than numbers in assessing student work samples. Descriptive assessment is anecdotal in nature, meaning that teachers make "field notes" on a student's work during classroom writing activities, which are later placed into the student's portfolio. Additionally, teachers summarize their impressions of student writing samples gathered during learning experiences. By accumulating informal classroom observations and analyses of writing samples over time, teachers develop a more complete picture of students' development in writing.

Teachers compile written observations and interpretations of student accomplishments in writing that may be used in conjunction with other pieces of assessment evidence (i.e., quantitative measures) to form a more complete understanding of students' writing development.

Materials

Materials needed are a legal pad for note taking by the teacher and student work samples.

Procedure

It is very difficult to describe in specific terms how best to carry out this form of assessment; nevertheless, we do have a few suggestions to offer based on our own experiences. Qualitative assessments are based on a thorough understanding of writing development coupled with classroom experience. Many teachers accustomed to performing qualitative writing assessments in their classrooms try to identify two students per day whom they will observe during writing activities (do not alert these students that they are the ones being studied). This permits most teachers to observe each student about once every 2 weeks or so. At the end of the day, the teacher reviews the classroom observations, along with work samples collected by students in their writing folders, and attempts to draw some conclusions as to students' development.

Writing development may be said to encompass several broad abilities, including the capacity to transmit messages effectively and an understanding of the basic mechanics of writing. In the first aspect of writing development, students gain an understanding of the writing process: prewriting, drafting, revising, editing, and sharing or publishing. The mechanics of writing involve such aspects as spelling, punctuation, and appropriate use of reference materials. Of course, students' relative ability in each of these areas varies a great deal and is, by definition, developmental (one gets better at these skills with practice). The best advice we can offer is for teachers to read extensively about the writing process, then meet with colleagues to develop a kind of writing development checklist or checklists to help in monitoring student progress. We find that Gail Tompkins' (2004) book titled *Teaching Writing: Balancing Process and Product* is an excellent resource for gaining basic information about the writing process and for developing writing observation checklists.

QUANTITATIVE ASSESSMENT: HOLISTIC SCORING

Quantitative assessments use numbers rather than words to describe student development and performance in writing. There are at least two forms of quantitative assessment: *holistic* and *analytic*. These two forms are closely related, with the chief difference being that holistic scoring seems to work best with a single criterion, while analytic scoring is intended for multiple criteria. In all instances, students should understand the assessment criteria for which they are being held accountable.

Purpose

Holistic quantitative assessment is used to develop relatively objective measures of writing products using a numerical system.

Materials

You will need an assessment form that includes a numerical scale for each criterion, such as that shown in Figure 13.1, and student work samples.

Procedure

Probably the most convenient way to conduct a quantitative assessment is for teachers to first construct an assessment instrument. This makes the process much more time efficient when trying to review more than one work sample. Because only one criterion is being assessed, all that is required is a place for the student's name, date, the criterion specified, and a numerical scale (usually 1 to 5) to rate student performance using the writing skill. *In group settings*, we recommend that teachers read all of the student compositions once without grading to get a feel for the range of development in the class before assigning numerical values to each paper.

Figure 13.1 shows an example of an assessment form for emergent writers in a first-grade classroom focusing on students' use of temporary spellings (also called *invented spellings*) with at least beginning and ending sounds.

Figure 13.1　Sample Holistic Scoring Form for Writing: Single Criterion

| Student name: _____ |
| Date: _____ |
| |
| **Criterion:** |

	Not used				Used a great deal
Temporary (invented) spellings: Beginning and ending sounds	1	2	3	4	5

Comments/observations:

QUANTITATIVE ASSESSMENT: ANALYTIC SCORING

As already mentioned, analytic scoring methods are essentially holistic scoring systems for *multiple* criteria. Analytic scoring systems add a "weight" dimension for each criterion being measured, because the criteria tend to be of unequal value. For example, let us say a fifth-grade teacher has been teaching minilessons on using commas correctly, developing characters more fully in student-created stories, and completing a *prewriting outline* or *web* before writing a first draft. Let us also assume that, in this instance, the teacher feels that correct usage of commas is not quite as important (or as challenging) as is developing characters more fully. Further, if the teacher feels that developing characters more fully is more important than completing a prewriting outline or web (perhaps because her students have been creating webs and outlines since second grade and the focus on characters is a newly introduced skill), then the weighting used in scoring a work sample will reflect that priority as well. In any event, it is easy to see that the teacher feels that certain writing skills are somewhat more important or challenging than others.

When multiple criteria are being used in writing assessment, the teacher usually assigns a weighted value of *1* to the least important skill, *2* for the more important skill, and *3* for the next most important skill. As mentioned previously, the numerical scale frequently ranges from a low rate of 1 to a high rate of 5. Thus, for our example, the following assigned weights would apply:

Writing Skill/Criteria	Relative Weight or Value
Using commas correctly	1
Developing characters more fully	3
Prewriting outline or web	2

These teacher-determined weights are to be multiplied by the holistic scoring value (1–5) arrived at in the same way as described in the previous section on holistic scoring for a single criterion (i.e., a score of 1 to 5 is given based on the quality of the student's work on that criterion, say, using commas correctly). Figure 13.2 presents an assessment form based on the preceding example. (*Note:* The figure for "Total possible points" (30) is arrived at by first multiplying the maximum possible score of 5 for each skill by the weighted value, then adding the total possible scores [5 + 15 + 10 = 30]).

Figure 13.2 Analytic Writing Assessment Form Using Three Criteria

Student name: _____

Criteria

	Not used				Used a great deal		Weighted value		Total points
Using commas correctly	1	2	3	4	5	×	1	=	_____
Developing characters more fully	1	2	3	4	5	×	3	=	_____
Prewriting outline or web	1	2	3	4	5	×	2	=	_____

A. Total points for assignment   _____

B. Total possible points   30

C. Percentage of points achieved (A divided by B)   _____

Comments/observations:

Other Activities for Assessing Reading-Writing Connections

In addition to the quantitative and qualitative strategies mentioned previously, the following activities have value as both assessment and writing activities. These activities remind us that good assessment is frequently synonymous with good teaching.

Story Pyramids

Purpose

An activity popularized by teachers in the Rio Grande Valley area of south Texas is the *story pyramid*. It combines the use of story grammars as a means for assessing reading comprehension in narrative passages with writing (vocabulary knowledge) assessment. Story pyramids are interesting and simple to use, yet powerful in their assessment potential.

The assessment purpose of story pyramids is twofold. First, they require students to recall key information from stories using a modified story grammar scheme (main character, setting, problem, attempts to solve the problem, and solution). Next, students are asked to survey their vocabulary knowledge to find just the right word or words to report the story grammar information in the pyramid.

Materials

The materials needed include paper and pen or pencil, one sheet of poster board, and a narrative book recently read by the student.

Procedure

Teachers usually create a poster or bulletin board depicting a pyramid, such as the one shown in the photograph. It should show the required information needed in a story pyramid and an example based on a book shared during a read-aloud experience. The following information and pattern for writing are used in the story pyramid:

Line 1. One word for whom the story is about (main character)

Line 2. Two words describing the main character

Line 3. Three words describing the setting

Line 4. Four words stating the problem

Line 5. Five words describing an event in the story

Line 6. Six words describing an event in the story

Line 7. Seven words describing an event in the story

Line 8. Eight words describing the final solution

This activity not only assesses reading comprehension and vocabulary knowledge but also encourages economy of language when students compose.

FLIP MOVIES

Purpose

Flip movies is an activity suggested for assessing students' understanding of a book by having them illustrate and bind a series of scenes together from a story. Flipping through the scenes quickly simulates the action (Pike, Compain, & Mumper, 1997). In our version of this activity, students create a series of pictures and captions that summarize a key story event. Flipping through the book quickly simulates scrolling text that retells part of the story. Flip movies assess students' ability to retell key events in a story using written captions matched to illustrations.

Materials

The student will need a book that he or she read recently. In addition, you will need to collect the following art materials in order for students to make flip movies:

- Index cards (5" × 8")
- Writing and illustrating materials
- Drawing paper cut to a rectangular pattern of about 3" × 8"
- Access to a photocopier machine
- Book-binding tape or a heavy-duty stapler

Procedure

Students begin by choosing a key event in a story that they read recently. Next, they create a single illustration of the setting and characters depicting this key event. The illustration should not be colored in at first but created to look much like an uncolored coloring book page on a single sheet of 3" × 8" paper. On a separate sheet of paper (this can be a "messy copy"), the student should write a caption that describes the key event. For example, a student who read *The Polar Express* (Van Allsburg, 1985) may draw an illustration depicting the child in the story receiving a bell from Santa's sleigh at the North Pole. Perhaps the caption reads "Santa handed the sleigh bell to me!" Next, take the single uncolored illustration and make the same number of photocopies of the illustration as there are words in the caption. (In our example, the teacher would make seven copies of the student's illustration, because there are seven words in the caption). The copies of the illustration are then given to the student so that the final phase can be completed.

Next, students carefully trim each photocopy of the illustration to match the size of the original (3" × 8") and color each one as desired, making sure to use the same color scheme on each photocopy to produce identical copies. Next, glue each illustration to the upper portion of 5" × 8" index cards so that the student now has multiple identical copies of the illustration mounted on index cards. On the first card, the student writes only the *first* word in the caption. He or she writes the first *two words* of the caption on the second card, the first *three words* of the caption on the third card, and so on. After this process is complete and the cards have been bound together using binding tape or heavy-duty staples, the pages in the flip book can be slowly thumbed through so that the text appears to scroll out across the bottom of the page word by word until the full sentence has appeared. Older students may want to alter this activity, slightly changing the illustrations so that the flipping action simulates movement in the illustration.

Coat-Hanger Mobiles

Purpose

Coat-hanger mobiles are easy to construct and are an inventive way to combine reader response with writing. Students create illustrations and captions depicting important bits of information from a book they have read. Then, as a form of "publishing," these information bits are displayed on a common coat hanger that is hung from the ceiling as a mobile in the classroom. Coat-hanger mobiles work well with both narrative and expository texts. This activity is useful as a quick assessment of key ideas understood by the student after reading and as an indirect assessment of descriptive vocabulary in writing (likewise, the acquisition of technical vocabulary in expository books).

Materials

A coat-hanger mobile can be constructed using a wire coat hanger (preferably one that has been coated in colored plastic), string or dark thread, a sheet of poster board or tagboard, assorted color markers for illustrating and writing captions, and a book that the child has recently read.

Procedure

Using the poster board, ask the student to create at least five illustrations and captions representing key ideas or events found in the book he or she has recently completed. Students often like to make the illustrations in the shapes of characters, settings, or objects that pertain to the book. Remind them that they will need to illustrate both sides of each shape so that, as the mobile turns, the illustration can be read from any direction. Have students attach each illustration or caption to their coat hanger using thread or string as shown in Figure 13.3. Once it is completed, hang the mobile from the ceiling or from a light fixture.

Figure 13.3   A Coat-Hanger Mobile

A CHECKLIST FOR MIDDLE SCHOOL WRITING PROGRAMS

Purpose

Checklists help teachers maximize the efficiency of their contact time with students because of checklists' built-in organization and structure. You should be aware, however, that, while checklists may be useful in many situations, they are certainly no panacea in writing assessment. In fact, they have somewhat limited use; but, Gail Tompkins (2004), in her book *Teaching Writing: Balancing Process and Product*, offers a number of checklists that we believe teachers find useful. In this section, we offer an adaptation of a Tompkins checklist that can be of general use in the middle school. This activity is intended for the assessment of student compositions in order to review students' understanding of stages of the writing process.

Materials

A copy of the writing process checklist shown in Figure 13.4 is needed.

Procedure

As the teacher reviews samples kept in students' writing folders, he or she notes on the checklist evidence of the various writing process activities. Many teachers also note dates when different writing process activities were done. The result is that teachers can determine which writing process activities are being used by class members and which are not. Thus, the teacher can identify the writing skills that may be needed by some or all of the class members. Figure 13.4 offers a general form for this purpose.

In other chapters we offered a *Summary Matrix of Assessments* for procedures and instruments presented for a particular area of reading instruction. Because the topic of this chapter does not, strictly speaking, align with federally mandated areas of reading instruction, nor do the types of assessments presented lend themselves to rigorous reliability or validity studies, we have elected not to include a *Summary Matrix of Assessments* for this chapter.

Figure 13.4 Writing Process Checklist Form

Writing Process Checklist: Middle School

Name: _____

Date of writing folder review: _____

Title(s) of compositions: _____

Writing Process Stages and Activities

PREWRITING

1. Student develops a list of possible topics that are of high interest to him.

   _____

2. An organizational web or outline is constructed.

   _____

3. Student conducts research to gather necessary facts and information.

   _____

DRAFTING

4. Student produces one or more drafts before the final version.

   _____

5. Drafts are double- or triple-spaced to allow for editorial comments.

   _____

6. Evidence demonstrates that the student is more interested in ideas and content, rather than mechanics at this stage.

   _____

REVISING

7. Student shares the composition with others to obtain useful suggestions.

   _____

8. A new draft of the paper is generated incorporating suggestions offered by peers.

   _____

EDITING

9. Student again reviews composition, looking for ways to improve the mechanics of the piece (e.g., spelling, punctuation, etc.).

   _____

10. After improvements have been made mechanically, the student meets with the teacher for a writing conference.

    _____

SHARING

11. Student produces a final copy suitable for sharing.

    _____

12. An appropriate way of sharing the piece is chosen and carried out (e.g., author's chair, publication area in classroom or library, publishing in the school newspaper, others as appropriate).

    _____

Source: Adapted from *Teaching Writing: Balancing Process and Product* by G. E. Tompkins, 2004, Upper Saddle River, NJ: Merrill/Prentice Hall.

CONNECTING ASSESSMENT FINDINGS TO TEACHING STRATEGIES

Before moving on to specific research strategies, we have constructed an *if/then chart* connecting assessment findings to teaching strategies. It is our intention to help you select the most appropriate instructional interventions and strategies to meet your students' needs based on assessment data. Teaching strategies described in the next section are listed across the top of the grid in the figure. Potential instructional areas are listed vertically in the left-hand column.

TEACHING STRATEGIES

We begin this part of the chapter with a presentation of ideas that could be called **interactive writing** (Gipe, 2006). The idea is for the teacher to demonstrate new ideas about writing for learners in their zones of proximal development, that is, ideas that bridge the reading and writing processes and help students grow in each language area. We begin with a very flexible method of writing instruction known as "Writing Aloud, Writing To," followed by activities that fit nicely into this paradigm. Later, we describe other activities that make writing connections with books and other texts for students followed by bookmaking ideas.

WRITING ALOUD, WRITING TO: A WAY OF STRUCTURING YOUR TEACHING

In *read-aloud* activities, teachers share books orally with students and use read-aloud sessions as opportunities to model such reading essentials as comprehension strategies and decoding skills. "Writing Aloud, Writing To" (Cooter, 2002; Gunning, 2006) is an adaptation of Routman's (1995) technique for getting students' attention and demonstrating various aspects of the writing process. "Writing Aloud, Writing To" has been used with great success in the Dallas Reading Plan, a massive teacher education project in Texas, which has resulted in significant improvement in student writing and reading achievement levels. The "Writing To" part of "Writing Aloud, Writing To" comes from the notion of Writing *To, With,* and *By*; in a balanced writing program of instruction, teachers should engage daily in writing *to* students (demonstrations and minilessons), writing *with* students (guided practice sessions in which students implement new writing skills with the help of the teacher or a more skilled peer), and writing *by* students (independent writing sessions in which they practice their newly acquired skills).

The materials you will use depend greatly on the kinds of writing strategies you plan to model. In general, we like to use an overhead projector, transparencies, screen, and dry-erase markers for writing demonstrations with groups, or a large tablet on an easel. If it is a demonstration involving the computer, then it is usually best to do "Writing Aloud, Writing To" sessions in small groups, unless you have access to a computer projection system.

As with materials, the strategies you will employ will be based on the writing or reading connections you will emphasize. Routman (1995) and Cooter (2002) do, however, provide us with some useful tips to remember for "Writing Aloud, Writing To."

- In "Writing Aloud, Writing To," the teacher thinks aloud while writing in front of the students.
- Students watch the teacher as he or she writes, and they sometimes read aloud with the teacher as the teacher says explicitly what he or she is doing. This may include the

If-Then Strategy Guide for Writing Connections

"If" the student is ready to learn ↓ / "Then" try these teaching strategies →	Morning Message	Daily News	T-Shirts and Tapestries	Travels of Class Mascot	Sell-a-Bration	Movie Reviews	Capsulization Guide	Illustrator's Craft	Classroom Character	Writing Fairy Tales	Writing a Feature Story	Written Response to Picture Books	Pop-Up Books	Accordion Books	Innovation Books
Emergent Writer	+	+	−	*	*	−	−	*	*	*	*	+	+	+	*
Written Correspondence	+	+	−	+	−	−	−	*	*	*	−	−	−	−	*
Spelling	+	+	*	+	*	+	*	−	+	*	+	*	+	+	+
Decoding	*	*	*	*	*	*	−	*	*	*	+	*	*	*	+
Comprehension—Narrative	−	−	−	−	−	*	+	−	+	+	−	+	+	+	+
Comprehension—Expository	−	*	−	*	*	−	+	*	−	−	+	+	+	+	+
Motivation	+	+	+	+	+	+	+	+	+	+	+	+	+	+	+

Key: + Excellent Strategy
      * Adaptable Strategy
      − Unsuitable Strategy

389

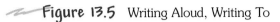 **Figure 13.5** Writing Aloud, Writing To

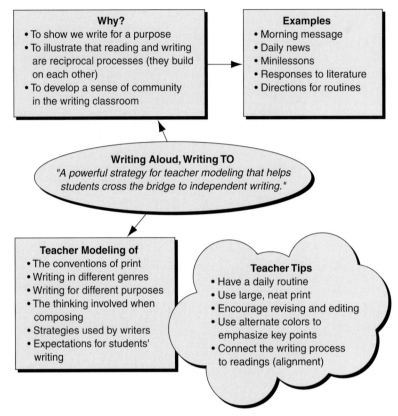

writer's thinking processes, format that has been chosen and why, layout of the piece, spacing, handwriting, spelling, punctuation, and discussion of vocabulary.

- Teachers help students relate the spoken word to the written word at all times.
- The teacher often asks questions that relate to the conventions of writing or features of text.

A graphic was prepared for the Dallas Reading Academy (Cooter, 2002) that summarizes key elements of "Writing Aloud, Writing To" based on the work of Regie Routman (1995). It is shown in Figure 13.5.

MORNING MESSAGE

Purpose

Another *writing to* activity that is basic to reading and writing instruction is the "Morning Message" (Cooter, 2002). The teacher writes about what will be happening that day in terms of schedule or activities or about what will be happening in the teacher's or students' lives. "Morning Message" is inherently motivational and provides an excellent opportunity for students to learn new reading skills. The whole activity only takes from 5 to 7 minutes and is a great way to reinforce skill lessons, such as spelling conventions, punctuation tips,

Figure 13.6 Morning Message

Monday, January 15, 200_

Dear Second Grade,

Today will be an exciting day at Robert Spencer Elementary School. At 10 o'clock Easy Reader will come to our school and tell stories. He will come on his motorcycle and bring his favorite books!

Yesterday, we learned that Toby Benson's mother is going to have a baby in August. He is very excited that he will soon have a baby brother or sister.

Let's make this a great day.

Your friend,

grammar rules, capitalization, and any parts of the writing process you may want to emphasize (Routman, 1995). An example is provided in Figure 13.6.

Materials

"Morning Message" is usually done at a reserved section of the chalkboard or on large chart paper and easel. If using chart paper, we recommend picking up some highlighter tape and various colored markers.

Procedure

The teacher does the following during "Morning Message":

1. Think aloud while writing the message. Students observe the writing procedures and may be invited to read aloud along with the teacher.

2. If you are working with emergent readers, compose the messages orally before writing. Demonstrate rereading to confirm that you have written what you intended (sometimes make deliberate errors to create "teachable moments"). This is also an opportune time to demonstrate strategies like "word rubber banding"—stretching out the sounds of a spoken word to hear phonemes and match appropriate letters. Students can also be helped to attend to conventions of print, such as leaving spaces, and rereading with finger pointing to illustrate a one-to-one match.

3. Teachers should be aware of group needs and model something noticed recently in the writing of students. For example, if students are struggling with the use of some homonyms (i.e., there, their), include these words in the "Morning Message" and mention in passing how you knew which word to use.

4. After the message is written and read together, take a few minutes to ask questions and familiarize students with the conventions of writing you have used. Ask students to explain the reasons for the conventions used, such as

Why did I capitalize _____?   *What do you notice about _____?*
Why did I use a comma here?   *Why did I begin a new paragraph here?*

5. After emergent readers "read" the "Morning Message" together, have students locate certain letters and words. Highlighter tape is great to use for this exercise when chart paper is used for the "Morning Message."

INNOVATIONS ON THE MORNING MESSAGE

Morning message innovation 1: skill messages

- Create a "planned" *Skill Message* to highlight a particular word structure or phonics element. The bottom of the chart can be used as a kind of minilesson. Do Skill Messages on chart paper so that you can post them around the classroom as reminders (see example in Figure 13.7).

Morning message innovation 2: modified cloze messages

- Modify the Morning Message using a kind of cloze technique that suits your instructional purpose. For example, you can modify a message to emphasize endings (-ed, -s, -ing), beginning sounds, ending sounds, and so forth. See Figure 13.8 for an example.

Morning message innovation 3: the mystery message

- As a variation of Innovation 2, have students complete and submit in writing a summary of a story the children have just read or heard. See who is a good detective! (See Figure 13.9.)

Figure 13.7   Morning Message Innovation: A Skill Message

September 1, 200_

Dear Students,

Yesterday I had to shovel snow from my driveway for three hours. Then I conk**ed** out!

look**ed**	crash**ed**
help**ed**	walk**ed**
stack**ed**	play**ed**

Figure 13.8   Modified Cloze Morning Message (Endings)

Directions: Look for words needing the following endings: -s, -es, -ed, -ing.

October 3, 200_

Dear Girl_and Boy_,

I am excit__ about go___ to the zoo on Friday. It will be a little frighten___when we see the lion_, tiger_, and snake_!

We must all remember to bring our lunch__ so we can have a picnic at the zoo.

See you on Friday!

Figure 13.9   The Mystery Message

> Ja__ kept climb___ th_ _ean st___ and t_king things fr__ __e gi__t. He g_t a sing___
>
> h__p, and a__n th__ l__s gold__ e_g_.

DAILY NEWS STORY

Purpose

The "Daily News Story" provides an opportunity for the class to discuss what is news to them and then record the information in a newspaper format. Some teachers like to glue a real newspaper front page header (i.e., *The Los Angeles Times, The Dallas Morning News, The Chicago Tribune*, etc.) to the chart paper used for writing the story.

Materials

Chart paper on an easel, newspaper front page headers from your local newspaper, and markers are all you will need.

Procedure

Introduce the activity by showing a newspaper and talking about how a newspaper tells us what is happening in our world. Give examples of what is news such as someone's birthday, a visiting relative, guest speakers for the class, holiday activities, and so forth. Share some of your own special "news" as a model for the class.

The class may want to begin by talking about an event the students have shared together or by using the activity as a way to share personal news. After students have shared ideas for a while, the teacher should choose one or two topics that have been shared and begin writing sentences on the chart paper saying each word as he or she writes. The teacher should "think aloud" as he or she writes to emphasize important new skills such as capitalizing the first letter of a person's name, matching letters to phonemes, and punctuation. Just do not overdo thinking aloud or the purpose of writing (constructing meaningful sentences in a fluid manner) will be lost.

We like to ask two students to illustrate the "Daily News Story" during center time. The requirements are that the illustration must match the message and fill up the space allotted. Display the story for students to read during the week as an ongoing vocabulary review. Also, you may want to type up the news stories at your computer and print copies of the text for students to take home each Friday for home review and practice. See Figure 13.10 for an example of the "Daily News Story."

T-SHIRTS AND TAPESTRIES

Purpose

Students love to make their own T-shirts and tapestries that display something of interest to the student (Pike et al., 1997). T-shirts and tapestries are easy to construct and can relate to such things as a student's soccer team, club memberships, favorite book characters, musical groups, or family members. Also, they are great for students who enjoy creating illustrations to accent their writing. Because the text that can appear on either a T-shirt or

Figure 13.10   Daily News Story

The Nashville Tennessean		
Volume 1, No. 35	November 30, 200_	Free

Today is Thursday and we learned that Arnot's family got a new car. It is a station wagon, and it is blue. Arnot likes to ride in the very back and look out the rear window.

(illustration here)

a tapestry is limited by space, students must work with teachers to discover just the right words and thus develop brevity in written communications.

Making T-shirts or tapestries that include illustrations and captions helps students develop brevity in written communications. This activity may also be linked to the usage of such writing tools as the dictionary and thesaurus.

Materials

The materials needed include a plain white T-shirt in the student's size or a sheet of cloth suitable for a tapestry, as well as fabric crayons or paints or liquid embroidery.

Procedure

It is best to begin by having students develop a diagram of their T-shirt or tapestry on paper. The usual steps in the writing process are quite helpful (prewriting, drafting, revising, editing). If this activity is used in a classroom setting, students should be encouraged to take part in peer conferences to share and refine their ideas.

Once the idea has been finalized and approved by the teacher, walk through the steps in creating T-shirt designs or tapestries. If a family member is available who has artistic expertise, by all means put him or her to work teaching the students art skills! Finally, students use the liquid embroidery or fabric crayons or paints to create their final products, as shown in Figure 13.11. "Publishing" is accomplished as students wear their T-shirts or display their tapestries in a place of honor.

TRAVELS OF YOUR FAVORITE STUFFED ANIMAL OR CLASS MASCOT

Purpose

A popular idea with early elementary students, this activity encourages students to write a story about the adventures (usually the students' own experiences that day) of their favorite stuffed animal through the school day or of a class mascot on an imaginary adventure (Wiseman, 1992). The idea is to encourage students to write a creative composition about an imaginary journey or adventure taken by a stuffed animal.

Materials

In order to create an example for students to see, we recommend that you obtain a copy of the book *The Velveteen Rabbit* (Williams, 1922/1958) and a stuffed animal—preferably one that is showing signs of wear—or a class mascot in the form of a stuffed animal.

Figure 13.11 Student-Made T-Shirt

Additional materials needed include the usual writing materials favored by students (markers and crayons), as well as magazine pictures, word cards, picture dictionary, index cards, lined and unlined paper, tape, stapler, paper clips, rubber bands, and scissors.

Procedure

Begin by reading and discussing *The Velveteen Rabbit* with students. Talk about how stuffed animals often seem real to us and how it is fun to fantasize about how our stuffed friends may have real adventures. Bring in a stuffed toy to serve as a class mascot (Wiseman, 1992), such as a teddy bear, and talk about how students could write stories about him—either real-life situations that may take place at school or fictitious adventures we may choose to create, like the author of *The Velveteen Rabbit* did. You may wish to choose a stuffed friend that is in some disrepair. For example, if an eye is missing, ask the children to create a story about how that could have happened.

Using a large tablet on an easel, begin an outline of the story the children are helping to generate, which will then be fashioned into a story following a kind of language experience format. Next, ask the children to bring in stuffed animals of their own on the following day to write about and share with the class. If a child does not have a stuffed animal, then let him or her use the class mascot. Completed stories, along with the associated stuffed animal friends, can be displayed in the classroom or school library as part of the publishing process.

SELL-A-BRATION

Purpose

This activity helps students develop an understanding of persuasive writing (propaganda) strategies used by advertisers through reading and reviewing commercials in print and other media forms, then constructing their own advertising campaigns using the writing process. The activity teaches students about persuasive writing while also inspiring interest in reading books, magazines, and other text forms they have not previously considered.

Materials

Materials needed include a variety of magazines and newspapers, video clips recorded on VHS/VCR tape from television commercials for popular products, radio commercials recorded on cassette tape, a videocassette recorder/player and television, and a cassette tape player/recorder.

Procedure

Prepare a minilesson about how persuasive writing strategies are used to sell necessities (such as soap, food products, clothing) and nonnecessities (such as computer games, sodas, and designer clothes). Conduct a classroom discussion about specific strategies used in advertising and the common features of each. A comparison grid such as the one shown in Figure 13.12 may be helpful for compare-and-contrast discussions.

Depending on the age group, you may need to talk about what would or would not be appropriate ways to sell things in your classroom. Some teachers appoint an advertising review committee made up of students who decide whether material is appropriate.

Have students review materials and make notes about the types of advertising strategies used. One strategy sometimes used in persuasive writing involves the use of humor (for instance, television commercials for the fruit juice Tropicana Twisters and many of the local commercials for automobile dealerships).

Finally, have students use the writing process to write their own commercials for real or created products. They may also write commercials for their favorite books read during self-selected reading (SSR) periods. The commercials should be presented or performed for the class as a publishing and sharing experience.

Figure 13.12   Comparison Grid: Persuasive Writing/Propaganda Types and Examples

Prop.type/ Example	Cigarette ads	Sports car ads	Political ads	Student's choice
Image makers	Cowboys; athletic-looking people	Racing image; sexy, etc.	Fight-for-right image	
Bandwagon	"Liberated women do it!"	"Join the 'new generation'"	"Come along with us and elect _____."	
Testimonial	(No longer used)	Famous NASCAR racers	Person-on-the-street testimonials	
Plain folks	Farmers, cowboys, soldiers	Not appropriate to image desired	"I'm just a country lawyer...."	
Name comparisons	"If you *like* Marlboro, then you'll *love*...."	"Audi outperforms Porsche and BMW...."	"Like Lincoln, our candidate stands for...."	

Movie Reviews

Purpose

One fun way for students to practice analytical reading skills and persuasive writing abilities is through *movie reviews*. In this activity, students read movie reviews and learn about writing styles used by critics, then construct reviews of movies they have recently seen. Movie reviews enable students to practice analytical reading skills, summarization abilities, and persuasive writing skills.

Materials

Collect several copies of past movie reviews, usual writing process materials, and blank comparison grids for compare and contrast.

Procedure

Conduct a minilesson series reviewing a current or popular movie that most students are aware of and for which reviews can be found. In your minilesson, begin by first reviewing and summarizing the story line through discussions with the students. Next, produce several (three or four) authentic movie reviews of the selected film that can be read with the class, either using overhead transparencies or photocopies for students. Organize the differing points of view by completing a blank comparison grid on the chalkboard or on an overhead transparency, then discuss different perspectives and writing styles that different critics seem to use. Next, construct a prewriting outline from information contained on the grid. Finally, draft a new movie review of your own, mimicking the style of your favorite critic. At the conclusion of the minilessons, have each student write a review of a film that he or she has recently seen. The reviews can be displayed on a bulletin board dedicated to the cinema or compiled in a special edition class newspaper.

Capsulization Guides (Summarization)

Purpose

In this activity, students create their own stories from brief, teacher-created summaries of short books called *capsulization guides* (Gauthier, 1989). Students then read the actual stories and compare. Using capsulization guides helps students learn and practice summarization and writing process skills.

Materials

Writing process materials, short books that the class has not heard before, and teacher- or student-generated capsulization guides are the essential materials for this activity.

Procedure

Step 1: *Choose a story or other form of text and write a summary or "capsulization guide."* Select a relatively short story or other text type (such as a nonfiction piece pertaining to science or social studies) and write a brief summary (also known as a *capsulization guide*) about the piece. For example, for the story *Gila Monsters Meet You at the Airport* (Sharmat, 1980), your capsulization guide may read: "A boy from New York City is moving to the West with his family. He talks about all the bad things he has imagined about the West and why he will not like living there." The capsulization guide may either be written by the teacher or, better yet, by another student from a different class or grade level. Once you have done this activity with students, you will begin to build a library of capsulization guides.

Step 2:   *Share the capsulization guide with your students and ask them to write a composition.* After reading the capsulization guide with your students, ask them to write their own stories by expanding the information provided in the capsulization guide. Students should be expected to use writing process skills appropriate to their levels.

Step 3:   *Have students share their compositions with peers.* Once compositions are completed, ask students to share their works with a group of students in an "author's chair" format or in pairs.

Step 4:   *Share the original story or nonfiction text.* Now, read the full text of the original story or nonfiction text to the students. Compare and contrast the compositions that students constructed to the original version and discuss similarities and differences. For stories (narratives), it may be helpful to use a story grammar comparison grid such as the one shown in Figure 13.13.

Step 5:   *Have students write their own capsulization guides.* As a final activity, have students select short books or passages of their own and write capsulization guides. Acting as the teacher, they are then paired with a peer and repeat the preceding cycle using their own capsulization guides.

Figure 13.13   Story Grammar Comparison Table

	Original story	Your story
Setting		
Characters		
Problem(s)		
Attempts to solve problems		
Conclusion/Resolution		
Theme/Moral		

WRITING CONNECTIONS WITH BOOKS: DRAWING STUDENTS CLOSER

We know that reading and writing are reciprocal processes and tend to strengthen each other the more the student engages texts, whether as a writer or reader. How can we do more to actually structure learning experiences that capitalize on this reciprocity? In this section, we share some strategies that do just that.

THE ILLUSTRATOR'S CRAFT

Purpose

The *illustrator's craft* encourages students to read and learn all that they can about a favorite illustrator, to create a composition reporting what they have learned, and then to share their report with the illustrator (optional). The illustrator's craft activity is intended to cause students to read, use the writing process as a summary tool for the investigation, and then share results with peers. Communications with illustrators may also help students see the importance and purposes of letter-writing skills.

Materials

Materials needed include several books with the same illustrator; writing materials; addresses of the illustrators (optional); and materials such as markers, paints, and colored pencils for making a diary or journal.

Procedure

Spend time with your students discussing different illustrators and looking at some of their work. Tell an interesting fact about each illustrator you have chosen for these activities in order to show something of the human side and motivations of the illustrators. For example, Rachel Isadora wrote and illustrated a Caldecott Honor book called *Opening Night* (1984), a story that grew out of her experience as a professional ballerina.

After students select an illustrator whom they would like to learn more about, have them design a portfolio of the illustrator's best work from favorite books. The portfolio may include discussions from the student's perspective as to why this is the illustrator's best work. Students could be creative in their presentation by adding captions to the illustrations or by writing a diary of the illustrator. Students should do some research into the illustrators, exploring how they create their illustrations, settings in which they like to work, and/or what was happening in the world at the time that might have influenced their work. After the portfolio is finished, have students make a copy and send it, along with a letter, to the illustrator.

An alternate version of this activity may be to have students review artwork by older high-school students, to find one person's work they like, and then to interview that person. They could also construct a portfolio of the high-school student's work and present it to the class.

CLASSROOM CHARACTER

Purpose

Classroom character (Adams, 1991) is a great activity for making writing connections with books and other texts by having students correspond with a book character whom they are getting to know during a daily read-aloud activity conducted by the teacher. Letters written to the character are mailed using a classroom mailbox; then the character's response comes back at the next class meeting either in the form of a letter or through cartoonlike "bubble" responses appearing on a special bulletin board depicting the character. The classroom character activity is intended to interest students in writing and reading through interaction with a classroom character, providing a perceived audience for writing.

Materials

Many teachers use a character-for-the-month who appears in a book the student or class has read, letters and stories from the character to the students (provided secretly by older buddy students or the teacher), a bulletin board featuring an illustration of the character, speech "bubbles" with comments from the character to the students to be displayed each day on a bulletin board depicting the character, and writing materials for the students.

Procedure

Select a character—either from a book just read aloud to the class or a book used in a core book unit (Reutzel & Cooter, 2004)—who will interact with the students each day. Sometimes you may decide to use a character associated with a seasonal or classroom theme, but we prefer to use characters from read-aloud or self-selected books (Keiser, 1991). The character should be displayed on a bulletin board or area on the classroom wall throughout the life of this activity. Students are encouraged to write to the character to find out more about him or her, to leave the character books to read, and to respond to letters or captions on the bulletin board each day "written by the character."

WRITING FAIRY TALES

Purpose

After careful study of common story grammar patterns found in favorite fairy tales, students write their own fairy tales using these same common patterns. It is an interesting introduction to "formula story writing" that offers students yet another way of making writing connections with books and other texts. Writing a fairy tale helps students to develop an understanding of ways an author creates tales and to apply this knowledge in the construction of one's own tales.

Materials

Materials needed include fairy tales with traditional endings; pictures of a mixing bowl, wooden spoon or spatula, old boxes of baking soda, and bags of flour or other ingredients used in baking; writing and illustrating materials; a baker's hat; and an artist's beret.

Procedure

Read aloud two or three fairy tales and discuss their common ingredients. For example, tales usually begin with "Once upon a time . . ." or "Long, long ago . . . ." Fairy tales also generally have good and bad characters; many contain a commandment or rule, as well as a punishment for breaking the commandment. Sometimes a key incident occurs three times in fairy tales (Three Pigs have their homes threatened by the wolf three times). Also, there is often some kind of magic, and most end with a "happily ever after" situation.

Set up a writing center with a picture depicting a mixing bowl and spoons, along with ingredient boxes labeled *Beginning, Good Character(s), Bad Character(s), Three Times, Magic,* and *Ending.* An office tray may be placed at the center with an organizational prewriting form using the same labels. Students visiting the center create their own fairy tales (and can wear a baker's hat, if desired). One could also have an illustrator's center, where the author wears an artist's hat or beret and illustrates compositions on an easel.

WRITING A FEATURE STORY ABOUT A CENTRAL CHARACTER

Purpose

This activity begins by reading several sensationalized "news" accounts of celebrities and other famous people as portrayed in tabloid publications (such as *The National Inquirer*). Students then choose from their free reading a book character and write newspaper articles (feature stories) about the character (based on Smith & Elliot, 1986). The stories are crafted onto a newspaper front page, complete with illustrations created by the student (or several students working in a group), for a fun and motivating writing experience. In writing a feature story, students construct a literature or expository text response in which a character or person from a self-selected book is described using a newspaper or feature story style (who, what, when, where, why, and how).

Materials

Materials needed include newspaper accounts of local or national personalities, a student self-selected book or other text(s) (may be fiction or nonfiction), writing and illustrating materials, and a sheet of poster board to serve as the "newspaper front page."

Procedure

Begin by showing and discussing actual newspaper articles about local or national figures. These may be legitimate press reports, but sometimes it is quite stimulating and fun for students when the teacher uses tabloid or "yellow" journalism. For example, one tabloid story we have used with students proclaims that a "Titanic Survivor Lived 20 Years on Iceberg" and, in the same issue (*Sun*, August 4, 1992), "Head of Goliath Found in Desert." Prepare a minilesson about the typical questions news reporters are interested in learning answers to: who, what, when, where, why, and how. In your minilesson, choose a character from a well-known book that both the students and you have read, then write a feature story about the character. You may prefer to choose a real person or event to write about from a nonfiction selection.

As you work through your minilesson, ask students to choose a character from a book they have read and construct their own feature story. The students should write several stories about different events in the books, complete with titles that suggest the main ideas of those events. It may be helpful to show the students the front cover of the book *The True Story of the Three Little Pigs! By A. Wolf* (Scieszka, 1989) as an example.

WRITTEN RESPONSE TO PICTURE BOOKS FOR OLDER STUDENTS

Purpose

Upper-grade students write in response to picture books about sensitive subjects (Miletta, 1992). The forms of writing vary a great deal based on the subject being studied and the types of response that seem appropriate. Written responses may take the form of poems, songs, letters, essays, debates, one-act plays, video productions, and many more. The key to these writing activities is finding an emotional connection between the theme and the student. In writing in response to picture books about sensitive subjects, students write passionate compositions.

Materials

Materials needed include picture books relating to important and possibly controversial themes and writing supplies.

Procedure

Introduce picture books (those that rely heavily on illustrations to help get ideas across to readers) that portray emotionally powerful themes. Possible themes include war and peace issues, peer pressures, family relationships across generations (such as between grandparents and grandchildren), and health issues (abortion, AIDS, etc.). Try to select books that show different perspectives of the same issue in order to encourage debate. For example, for a theme related to "War and Peace," one may choose *Hiroshima No Pika* by T. Maruki (1982), *The Butter Battle Book* by Dr. Seuss (Geisel, 1984), *The Wall* by Edith Bunting (1992), or *The Flame of Peace: A Tale of the Aztecs* by Deborah Nourse Lattimore (1991). For a theme pertaining to "Relationships Between Generations," one may choose *Wilfred Gordon McDonald Partridge* by Mem Fox (1985).

Written responses may take many forms. For controversial issues of the day, students may choose to debate positions and tactics or write letters to congressional leaders or platform positions for political parties. Issues that relate more to personal relationships could take the form of diary entries, letters, or discussions in one-act-play format.

It is important, however, to note that these books sometimes contain deep and emotional themes (child abuse and divorce, for instance). They are often controversial and, thus, should always be previewed in order to make judgments about the appropriateness of the material.

BOOK MAKING AND PUBLISHING ACTIVITIES

This section presents several highly interesting ways that students can publish their compositions by turning them into books. In each of these activities, teachers stimulate reading and writing in students by showing them easy ways to publish their compositions. Other benefits to book making include promoting creativity and problem-solving and decision-making abilities. Some of the following ideas have been adapted primarily from ideas by Routman (1995) and Yopp and Yopp (2000).

POP-UP BOOKS

Purpose

In this activity, children produce their own *pop-up books*—a fun and easy activity that stimulates students' interest in writing. An additional benefit is that pop-up books present parents with an impressive product documenting their child's literacy growth.

Materials

Materials needed include construction paper, glue, tape, scissors, and pictures to be used.

Procedure

Begin by sharing several pop-up books that have been commercially produced, as well as a sample the teacher or another student has produced. Next, have students illustrate the background for each page of their story and write in text. This step makes the finished product appear more professional and is less likely to frustrate young authors. It is possible to have one or more pop-up figures on a page by following these simple directions:

Step 1: Fold a sheet of construction paper in half and make two cuts an inch deep each and about an inch apart in the creased part of the paper.

Step 2: Open the paper about halfway, and push through the cut section carefully, and fold it inward.

Step 3: Glue the picture to be used to the protruding cut section.

Step 4: Fold each completed page in the closed position and stack the pages in order. The stack may be either glued or stitched together to complete the process. Remember to include an outside cover page.

ACCORDION BOOKS

Purpose

Accordion books are easy-to-construct books made of folded tagboard that are displayed in special areas in the classroom. This activity has been suggested for group situations not only as a type of problem solving but also as a means of putting together a composition in a sequence that makes sense.

Materials

Materials needed include multiple sheets of tagboard, tape, and crayons or other colored markers for writing and illustrating.

Procedure

After the teacher shows an example of an accordion book, each group of students selects a composition that it wishes to retell in this format: Groups first decide which student will summarize each of the parts of the selection. Students then write a summary statement and draw an illustration on the tagboard. Once group members have completed their assignments, the tagboard or transparencies are taped together in sequence. The finished accordion book is then placed on a table in the classroom for other students to read.

INNOVATION BOOKS

Purpose

Many of the early reading books students encounter have memorable patterns, repeating verses, or other literary devices that make them highly predictable. Dr. Seuss (Geisel, 1960)—*Green Eggs and Ham*—and Bill Martin (1983)—*Brown Bear, Brown Bear, What Do You See?*—are two authors who have created many such books familiar to most English-speaking children. *Innovation books* are adaptations of popular predictable books using the same basic themes as the original books. They may be created by individual students as literature-response projects using the writing process or generated in small-group settings with the assistance of the teacher.

Materials

Materials needed include regular 8 ½″ × 11″ sheets of paper or construction paper, laminating materials, writing and illustrating materials, a hole punch, and metal clasps or rings.

Figure 13.14 Innovation Book *White Skeleton, White Skeleton*

White skeleton, white skeleton
what do you see?

I see a black bat looking at me!

Procedure

Choose a popular book that has a clear pattern. Two popular books that have been used for innovations in the primary grades are *Brown Bear, Brown Bear, What Do You See?* (Martin, 1983) and *If You Give a Mouse a Cookie* (Numeroff, 1985). For example, Miss Tims's first-grade class in Kansas took the *Brown Bear, Brown Bear, What Do You See?* pattern and used it to create a Halloween version using scary words, titled *White Skeleton, White Skeleton* (see Figure 13.14 for a sample page from the book). Innovation books also can be written by older students for younger ones, thus encouraging the older students to practice writing skills and to enjoy a new form of publishing.

The procedure can be followed in either small-group or whole-class formats. First, read aloud a book, song (such as "On Top of Old Smokey"), poem, rap, or chant that has the desired pattern. Next, challenge the student or group to brainstorm possible new verses. Record them on chart paper, the chalkboard, or on an overhead projector/transparency. Once the new text has been written, each student then writes and illustrates an assigned page that will be laminated upon completion. Assemble all the pages in the desired order, punch three holes along the binding edge of the aligned pages, then bind them with chrome rings or clasps. The innovation book is now ready to be shared.

SELECTED REFERENCES

Adams, T. (1991). Classroom characters. *The Reading Teacher, 45*, 73–74.

Brown, M. K. (1992). *Sally's room.* New York: Scholastic.

Bunting, E. (1992). *The wall.* Boston: Houghton Mifflin.

Calkins, L. M. (1994). *The art of teaching writing* (new ed.). Portsmouth, NH: Heinemann Educational Books.

Cooter, R. B. (2002). *The Reading Academy instructor's guide.* Memphis, TN: Unpublished manuscript.

Ediger, M. (2000). Writing, the pupil, and the social studies. *College Student Journal, 34*(1), 59–68.

Flickenger, G. (1991). Pen pals and collaborative books. *The Reading Teacher, 45*, 72–73.

Fox, M. (1985). *Wilfred Gordon McDonald Partridge.* La Jolla, CA: Kane/Miller.

Gauthier, L. R. (1989). Using capsulization guides. *The Reading Teacher, 42*, 553–554.

Geisel, T. (Dr. Seuss). (1984). *The butter battle book.* New York: Random House.

Geisel, T. (Dr. Seuss). (1960). *Green eggs and ham.* New York: Random House.

Gipe, J. P. (2006). *Multiple paths to literacy: Assessment and differentiated instruction for diverse learners, K–12*. Upper Saddle River, NJ: Merrill/Prentice Hall.

Gunning, T. G. (2006). *Assessing and correcting reading and writing difficulties* (3rd ed.). Boston: Allyn & Bacon.

Isadora, R. (1984). *Opening night*. New York: Green Willow Books.

Keiser, B. (1991). Creating authentic conditions for writing. *The Reading Teacher, 45*, 249–250.

Lattimore, D. N. (1991). *The flame of peace: A tale of the Aztecs*. New York: HarperCollins.

Martin, B. (1983). *Brown bear, brown bear, what do you see?* New York: Henry Holt.

Maruki, T. (1982). *Hiroshuma no pika*. New York: William Morrow.

Miletta, M. M. (1992). Picture books for older children: Reading and writing connections. *The Reading Teacher, 45*, 555–556.

Miller-Rodriguez, K. (1992). Home writing activities: The writing briefcase and the traveling suitcase. *The Reading Teacher, 45*, 160–161.

Myers, W. D. (1975). *Fast Sam, Cool Clyde, and stuff.* New York: Puffin Books.

Numeroff, L. J. (1985). *If you give a mouse a cookie*. New York: Scholastic.

Pike, K., Compain, R., & Mumper, J. (1997). *New connections: An integrated approach to literacy*. New York: Addison-Wesley.

Reutzel, D. R., & Cooter, R. B. (2004). *Teaching children to read: Putting the pieces together* (4th ed.). New York: Merrill/Prentice Hall.

Routman, R. (1995). *Invitations*. Portsmouth, NH: Heinemann Educational Books.

Scieszka, J. (1989). *The true story of the three little pigs!* New York: Viking.

Shanahan, T. (1984). Nature of the reading-writing relation: An exploratory multivariate analysis. *Journal of Educational Psychology, 76*, 466–477.

Sharmat, M. W. (1980). *Gila monsters meet you at the airport*. New York: Aladdin Books, Macmillan.

Smith, F. (1983). *Essays into literacy*. Portsmouth, NH: Heinemann Educational Books.

Smith, C. B., & Elliot, P. G. (1986). *Reading activities for middle and secondary schools*. New York: Teachers College Press.

Squire, J. R. (1983). Composing and comprehending: Two sides of the same basic process. *Language Arts, 60*(5), 581–589.

Tompkins, G. E. (1992). Assessing the processes students use as writers. *Journal of Reading, 36*(3), 244–246.

Tompkins, G. E. (2004). *Teaching writing: Balancing process and product*. New York: Merrill/Prentice Hall.

Van Allsburg, C. (1985). *The polar express*. Boston: Houghton Mifflin.

Williams, Margery. (1958). *The velveteen rabbit: Or how toys become real*. New York: Doubleday. (Original work published 1922)

Wiseman, D. L. (1992). *Learning to read with literature*. Needham Heights, MA: Allyn & Bacon.

Yopp, R. H., & Yopp, H. K. (2000). *Literature-based reading activities*. Boston: Allyn & Bacon.

Chapter 14

Reading Fluency

Mikhal, a third grader, walked reluctantly toward the chair placed next to his teacher, Mrs. Smith. He carried a tattered copy of his favorite book. He had practiced reading several pages in preparation for his regularly scheduled individual reading conference. "Mikhal, I am glad to spend some time today listening to you read. Are you ready?" queried Mrs. Smith. "Yah, I think so," answered Mikhal.

"So, what story are you going to read for me today?"

"I have a book called *The Boy Who Owned the School* for today."

"Great! I have your audiocassette tape here. I need to load it into the recorder, and then we can begin," remarked Mrs. Smith. "OK, I'm ready for you to read now, Mikhal. Where are you going to start reading?"

"I'm going to start on page 7, chapter 2. It's called *The Joys of Home Life.*"

"OK then, start when you are ready."

Mrs. Smith pushed the record button on the cassette tape recorder. Mikhal began reading. "His father was a mechanical engineer who designed or invented a new drill bit for oil drilling, a self-cleaning, self-sharpening bit."

When Mikhal finished his reading, Mrs. Smith praised how well he had done. "Mikhal, you are reading very fluently. You sound just like you are speaking!"

Mikhal beamed with pride. "Thanks," he said quietly.

"Can you tell me what you remember from the pages you read?"

"I think so," responded Mikhal.

Mrs. Smith turned the recorder back on. When Mikhal finished, Mrs. Smith praised him one more time. "Would you like to hear what you said and add anything to it?" she questioned.

"Uh, huh."

Mrs. Smith played the tape for Mikhal, and he added one more detail he had remembered as he listened to his oral retelling of his own reading.

That afternoon, Mrs. Smith looked at the record she had made from Mikhal's earlier oral reading. He had read the text with 97% accuracy, so she knew that decoding this text was not a problem for Mikhal. Next, she timed his reading and figured out Mikhal's reading rate in words read correctly per minute and compared this against a chart showing expected reading rate ranges by grade level. Mikhal was on the upper end of the range for his grade level. Next, Mrs. Smith listened to Mikhal's reading tape recording again, noting any problems with expression, pacing, smoothness, and phrasing. Again, Mikhal had performed well. Finally, Mrs. Smith listened to Mikhal's oral retelling of the pages he had read aloud. He had remembered the major ideas and a good number of the details, evidencing his comprehension of the text. There was no doubt in Mrs. Smith's mind; Mikhal was progressing well toward the goal of becoming a fluent reader!

BACKGROUND BRIEFING FOR TEACHERS

For many years, reading fluency, the ability to read aloud smoothly at a reasonable rate and with expression, had been acknowledged as an important goal in becoming a proficient and strategic reader (Allington, 1983, 1984, 2001; Blevins, 2001; Dowhower, 1991; Klenk & Kibby, 2000; National Institute of Child Health and Human Development, 2000; Optiz & Rasinski, 1998; Osborn, Lehr, & Hiebert, 2002; Pikulski & Chard, 2005; Prescott-Griffin & Witherell, 2004; Rasinski, 2000, 2003; Rasinski, Blachowicz, & Lems, in press; Rasinkski & Padak, 1996; Reutzel, 1996; Reutzel & Cooter, 2004; Reutzel, Hollingsworth, & Eldredge, 1994; Stahl, 2004). However, with a shift in emphasis away from proficient oral reading in the early 1900s and toward silent reading for private and personal purposes in the 1930s, the goal of developing fluent oral readers all but disappeared from the reading curriculum (Rasinski, 2003; Reutzel et al., 1994; Kameenui & Simmons, 2001). This was so much the case that it prompted Allington (1983, 1984) to declare reading fluency to be a neglected goal of reading instruction.

Many reading methods textbooks and core reading program teachers' manuals today still provide little or no guidance for developing fluency as an important part of a comprehensive reading instruction program. A visit to many elementary school classrooms prior to 2001 would have likewise revealed little attention to reading fluency during daily reading instruction. However, since the publication of the *Report of the National Reading Panel* in 2000 (National Institute of Child Health and Human Development), there has been a marked increase in current attention given to teaching, practicing, and assessing reading fluency in the elementary school grades.

How can teachers assess and assist all students in becoming fluent readers? First, they must understand how children develop fluency in reading. Second, they must be able to assess fluency to determine which elements of fluent reading require instruction and practice. Finally, teachers should know about successful and proven ways to provide fluency instruction as well as fluency practice to assist all children to develop fluent reading behaviors. This chapter is intended to develop teacher knowledge in the area of reading fluency, describe fluency assessment strategies, and connect assessment results to selected fluency instruction and practice interventions to help all students develop fluent reading.

WHAT IS FLUENCY?

What makes up the ability to read fluently? Although teachers and reading researchers have yet to agree on every minor element of reading fluency, significant consensus has been achieved in recent years as to the major components of reading fluency (Allington, 2001; National Institute of Child Health and Human Development, 2000; Pikulski & Chard, 2005; Richards, 2000). Typically, fluency is described as (a) accuracy and ease of decoding (automaticity); (b) an age- or grade-level appropriate reading speed or rate; (c) appropriate use of volume, pitch, juncture, and stress (prosodic features) in one's voice; and (d) appropriate text phrasing or "chunking." Thus, a fluent reader can decode the words in the text accurately and effortlessly and also read with correct volume, phrasing, and appropriate intonation and at a reasonably rapid rate so as to facilitate comprehension of the text. In 1995, Harris and Hodges characterized reading fluency as reading smoothly, without hesitation, and with comprehension. Rasinski (1989) and Reutzel and Hollingsworth (1993), as well as others, have found that reading fluency contributes quite directly to improved reading comprehension.

How do readers achieve fluency in oral reading? This is a subject of contemporary focus and research (Jenkins, Fuchs, Van den Broek, Espin, & Deno, 2003; Kameenui & Simons, 2001; National Institute of Child Health and Human Development, 2000; Snow, Burns, & Griffin, 1998; Stahl, 2004; Wolf & Katzir-Cohen, 2001). We offer seven insights into how readers develop fluent oral reading over time with teacher instruction and support, as well as copious amounts of reading practice.

1. *Modeling*—Exposure to rich and varied models of fluent oral reading helps *some* children. For other students, modeling of nonfluent oral reading *seems* to alert attention to the specific characteristics of fluent reading that are sometimes transparent or taken for granted when teachers only model fluent oral reading. In other words, some students need to know what fluency is and is not to achieve clarity on the concept of fluency and its attendant characteristics (Reutzel, in press). In this case, parents, teachers, or siblings spend significant amounts of time reading aloud to children while modeling fluent oral reading. Through this process of modeling fluent (and sometimes nonfluent) oral reading, children learn the behaviors of fluent readers as well as the elements of fluent oral reading. Many researchers have documented the significant impact of "modeling" upon the acquisition of fluent reading (Rasinski, 2003; Rasinski, Padak, McKeon, Wilfong, Friedauer, & Heim, 2005; Stahl, 2004).

2. *Quality of instruction*—For fluency instruction to be effective and of high quality, elementary students need explicit instruction about what constitutes fluent reading and how to self-regulate and improve their own fluency (Rasinski, Blachowicz, & Lems, in press; Reutzel, in press; Worthy & Broaddus, 2002).

3. *Reading practice*—Good readers are given more opportunities to read connected text and for longer periods of time than are students having reading problems. This dilemma led Allington (1977) to muse, "If they don't read much, how they ever gonna get good?" The National Reading Panel (National Institute of Child Health and Human Development, 2000) has emphasized the need for children to experience regular, daily reading practice.

4. *Access to appropriately challenging reading materials*—Proficient readers spend more time reading appropriately challenging texts than students having reading problems (Gambrell, Wilson, & Gnatt, 1981). Reading appropriately challenging books with instruction and feedback may help proficient readers make the transition from word-by-word reading to fluent reading, whereas poorer readers often spend more time in reading materials that are relatively difficult. Doing so denies those students who are having reading problems access to reading materials that could help them develop fluent reading abilities. For the most part, children need to be reading in instructional-level texts with instruction, modeling, support, monitoring, and feedback (Bryan, Fawson, & Reutzel, 2003; Kuhn, 2005; Kuhn & Stahl, 2002; Stahl, 2004).

5. *Oral and silent reading*—The *Report of the National Reading Panel* (National Institute of Child Health and Human Development, 2000) indicated there was ample scientific evidence to support reading practice for fluency that included the following elements: (a) oral reading, (b) repeated reading of the same text, and (c) feedback and guidance during and after the reading of a text. On the other hand, silent reading of self-chosen books without monitoring or feedback did not have substantial scientific evidence to support its near exclusive use across the grades of the elementary school without regard to the reading fluency developmental levels of students. Recent experimental research suggests that silent, wide reading (across genre or text types, e.g., stories, poems, information books) with monitoring seemed to pro-

duce equivalent or better fluency gains in second- and third-grade students (Pikulski & Chard, 2005; Stahl, 2004; Reutzel, in preparation). There is mounting evidence that the old practice of SSR, in which the teacher read as a model for children, is giving way to a new model of using silent reading practice, one that incorporates book selection instruction, student monitoring and accountability, and reading widely (Bryan, Fawson, & Reutzel, 2003, Kuhn, 2005; Marzano, 2004; Reutzel, in preparation; Stahl, 2004).

6. *Monitoring and accountability are key*—For many years, teachers thought that sitting and reading a book silently were modeling sufficient to promote students' desires and abilities to read. This, of course, has never been proven to be the case. In recent years, Bryan et al. (2003) have reported that monitoring disengaged readers with quick stop-in visits to listen to oral reading and discuss a piece of literature during silent reading has a salutary effect on their engagement during silent reading. Furthermore, asking that children account for their fluency practice time by reading onto a tape or for a teacher has positive impact upon their fluency engagement and growth (Reutzel, in press).

7. *Wide and repeated reading*—There is considerable evidence that repeated readings of the same text lead to automaticity—fast, accurate, effortless word recognition (Dowhower, 1991; National Institute of Child Health and Human Development, 2000). However, once automaticity is achieved, reading widely seems to provide the necessary ingredients to move a student's fluency from automaticity to comprehension. Thus, it is important that at the point a student has achieved grade-level automaticity this student receive encouragement to read widely as well as repeatedly to develop connected text comprehension (Pikulski & Chard, 2005; Reutzel, in press; Stahl, 2004). From the currently available evidence, this occurs in second grade or third grade for some children while others may need to continue to read texts repeatedly until they achieve automaticity at grade level into the intermediate years.

An awareness of these seven insights into fluency development can help teachers create optimal conditions for students to become fluent readers.

Rasinski (1989); Rasinski and Padak (1996); Richards (2000); and Worthy and Broaddus (2002) described six effective instructional principles to guide teachers in providing effective fluency instruction: (a) repetition, (b) modeling, (c) explicit instruction and feedback, (d) support or assistance, (e) phrasing practice, and (f) appropriately challenging materials. When students practice a single text repeatedly, the oral reading becomes increasingly automatic. Observing, listening to, and imitating fluent reading models help students learn how to become fluent readers themselves. Modeling fluent reading for students and pointing out specific behaviors as texts are read aloud, as well as providing informative feedback, can also help students become fluent. Teaching children explicitly what constitutes the chief characteristics of fluent reading, coupled with instruction on how to detect and fix up fluency problems, is also critical in helping students become self-regulating readers. Supporting students using strategies like choral reading, buddy or dyad reading, and tape or computer-assisted reading can be most effective in a well-conceived reading fluency program. Finally, providing readers with appropriately challenging reading materials for oral reading is essential for developing fluency. Understanding the nature, quantity, and quality of teacher feedback during oral reading is a crucial part of helping students become fluent readers (Shake, 1986). Self-assessment questions for teachers are provided in Figure 14.1 to assist in this process.

Figure 14.1 Teacher Verbal Feedback Think Questions

1. Am I more often telling the word than providing a clue?
2. What is the average self-correction rate of my students?
3. Do I assist poor readers with unknown words more often than good readers? If so, why?
4. Am I correcting miscues even when they do not alter the meaning of the text? If so, why?
5. Does one reader group tend to engage in more self-correction than other groups? If so, why?
6. Does one reading group have more miscues that go unaddressed than other groups?
7. What types of cues for oral reading errors do I provide and why?
8. What is *my* ultimate goal in reading instruction?
9. How do I handle interruptions from other students during oral reading? Do I practice what I preach?
10. How does my feedback influence the self-correction behavior of students?
11. Does my feedback differ across reader groups? If so, *how* and *why?*
12. Would students benefit more from a form of feedback different from that which I normally offer?
13. Am I allowing students time to self-correct (3–5 seconds)?
14. Am I further confusing students with my feedback?
15. Do I digress into "minilessons" midsentence when students make a mistake? If so, why?
16. Do I analyze miscues to gain information about the reading strategies students employ?
17. Does the feedback I offer aid students in becoming independent, self-monitoring readers? If so, how?
18. Do I encourage students to ask themselves, "Did that make sense?" when they are reading both orally and silently? If not, why not?
19. Do students need the kind of feedback I am offering them?

Source: Adapted from "Teacher Interruptions During Oral Reading Instruction: Self-Monitoring As an Impetus for Change in Corrective Feedback," by M. Shake, 1986, *Remedial and Special Education, 7* (5), 18–24.

Armed with an understanding of the problems, obstacles, and possibilities for helping students become fluent readers, we now turn our attention toward assessing students' reading fluency to inform and direct our selection of instructional strategies.

ASSESSING CHILDREN'S READING FLUENCY

Assessing fluency has for many years focused somewhat exclusively upon how quickly students could read a given text. This is known as "reading rate" or reading speed. Reading teachers have historically used words per minute (wpm) to indicate reading rate. Although wpm is one indicator of fluent oral reading, it is only one. To adequately assess fluent oral reading, one should consider at least four different components: (a) accurate decoding of text; (b) reading rate or speed; (c) use of volume, stress, pitch, and juncture (prosodic markers); and (d) mature phrasing or chunking of text.

Educators have in recent years begun to discuss how one may more efficiently and authentically assess the ability to read fluently (Kuhn & Stahl, 2000). Most teachers feel that paper-and-pencil assessment tools appear to be inadequate or at least incomplete measures of fluency. One issue for many teachers today is accessing valid and reliable estimates of reading rates appropriate for children of differing ages and grades. In 1990, Harris and Sipay (see Figure 14.2) presented information about reading rates associated with several norm-referenced or standardized reading rate measures in the past.

Figure 14.2   Harris and Sipay (1990) Reading Rate Chart

Reading Rates by Grade Levels Expressed as Ranges of Words per Minute (WPM)

Grades	WPM
1	60–90
2	85–120
3	115–140
4	140–170
5	170–195
6	195–220
7	215–245
8	235–270
9	250–270
12	250–300

We offer a word of caution in strictly applying these ranges as the only assessment of fluency because other factors such as decoding accuracy, expression, and phrasing are also important. Furthermore, we do not believe that words per minute (wpm) is the best measure of reading rate as we shall explain later in this section on fluency assessment. Several approaches to assessing readers' fluency are described in this section. None of these approaches is sufficient alone; but, taken together, they offer a fairly complete picture of the fluency assessment.

ONE-MINUTE READING SAMPLE (AGE/GRADE APPROPRIATE: GRADES 1.5 AND UP)

Purpose

One of the simplest and most useful means of collecting fluency data is the one-minute reading sample (Rasinski, 2003). A one-minute reading sample is typical of that used in the Oral Reading Fluency (ORF) test drawn from the Dynamic Indicators of Basic Early Literacy Skills (DIBELS®) battery (Good & Kaminski, 2002). The passages and procedures in the DIBELS® ORF measure are based on the research and development of Curriculum-Based Measurement (CMB) of reading by Stan Deno and his colleagues at the University of Minnesota and use procedures described by Shinn (1989). Reading rate norms using CBM procedures have been established by Hasbrouck and Tindal (2005).

According to the DIBELS® Administration and Scoring Guide (Good & Kaminski, 2002), evidence of technical adequacy (reliability and validity) of this measure is drawn from a series of studies based on the CBM reading procedures in general. "Test-retest reliabilities for elementary students ranged from .92 to .97; alternate-form reliability of different reading passages drawn from the same level ranged from .89 to .94" (Tindal, Marston, & Deno, 1983). In addition, "criterion-related validity studied in eight separate studies in the past two decades ranged from .52 to .91" (Good & Jefferson, 1988; Good, Simmons, & Kameenui, 2001).

Materials

You will need the following materials for this assessment:

- One blank audiocassette tape per student (120-minute length strongly suggested)
- A portable audiocassette recorder with an internal microphone
- An audiocassette tape storage case for the class set
- DIBELS® grade level passage
- DIBELS® administration and scoring directions
- One-minute cooking timer (This should count down backward from 60 seconds to zero with an alarm sounding at zero.)
- Pencil for marking the DIBELS® passage

Procedure

To administer the ORF measure, children are asked to read aloud three passages (one passage only for progress-monitoring purposes) that are at their grade level for one minute. Words omitted, words substituted, or hesitations of more than 3 seconds are scored as errors. Words self-corrected within 3 seconds are scored as accurate. The number of words read *correctly* in one minute is the reading rate. By using this metric words correct per minute (wcpm), reading rate is corrected for the accuracy of the reading. If a student is unable to read correctly any of the words in the first line of print of the grade-level passage or if the student reads less than 10 words correctly in a passage, the student ORF test is discontinued. Full directions for using the ORF measurement can be obtained by going to the DIBELS® web site, registering as a user (This is free!), and downloading the grade-level passages and the administration and scoring procedures. The DIBELS® web site address is http://dibels.uoregon.edu/.

To minimize time spent by the teacher monitoring progress using DIBELS® grade-level passages, many teachers have found the use of an audiocassette recording tape for each child to be quite handy. The grade-level DIBELS® passage to be read, with a line for the student's name at the top, is made available in a quiet section of the classroom where each student's personal audiocassette tape is stored and the tape recorder is placed on a table or desk along with the cooking timer and a pencil for marking on the copy of the DIBELS® passage where the student finishes reading at the end of one minute. Students go to this area by assignment of the teacher on a regularly scheduled basis, roughly three or four students per day. They put their personal audiocassette tape into the recorder, set the time for one minute, turn on the record button, and start the cooking timer. At this point they begin reading the DIBELS® passage into the recorder and record on their personal audiocassette tape the one-minute reading sample (DIBELS® passage). When the one-minute timer rings, the student rewinds his or her personal audiocassette tape and marks the point where he or she stopped reading onto the DIBELS® passage using the pencil. This paper copy of the DIBELS® passage and the audiocassette tape is turned into the teacher for analysis and feedback. The teacher's job is to listen to four taped one-minute samples per day making note of each student's wcpm rate and accuracy rates. Feedback from this analysis by the teacher can be given to students in written form when they are in the intermediate grades and orally during a very brief individual reading conference for the primary-grade students. Teachers who have done this find the requirements of monitoring oral reading fluency growth to be much easier and a normal part of the daily routine in a classroom.

CURRICULUM-BASED ORAL READING FLUENCY NORMS (AGE/GRADE APPROPRIATE: GRADES 1-8)

One of the most common measures of oral reading fluency is that of reading rate or reading speed. A words correct per minute (wcpm) measure has been used extensively to research a new set of Oral Reading Fluency Curriculum-Based Norms for Grades 1–8 (Hasbrouck & Tindal, 2005. Hasbrouck and Tindal compiled their new ORF norms from a far larger number of scores, ranging from a low of 3,496 in the winter assessment period of eighth graders to a high of 20,128 scores in the spring assessment of second graders. They collected data from schools and districts in 23 states and were able to compile more detailed norms, reporting percentiles from the 90th through the 10th percentile levels. To ensure that these new norms represented reasonably current student performance, they used only ORF data collected between the fall of 2000 through the 2004 school year. (A more complete summary of the data files used to compile the norms table in this article is available at the web site of Behavioral Research and Teaching at the University of Oregon: http://brt.uoregon.edu/techreports/TR_33_NCORF_DescStats.pdf [Hasbrouck & Tindal, 2005].) The new ORF norms align closely with those published in 1992 and also closely match the widely used DIBELS® norms (http://dibels.uoregon.edu/) and those developed by Edformation with their AIMSweb® system (http://www.edformation.com/).

Purpose

The purposes for assessing oral reading fluency are varied. Some reasons include the following:

- Screening students for special program eligibility
- Setting instructional goals and objectives
- Assigning students to specific groups for instruction
- Monitoring academic progress toward established goals
- Diagnosing special needs for assistance or instruction

Materials

You will need the following materials for this assessment:

- A teacher-selected passage of 200 to 300 words
- Curriculum-based measurement procedures for assessing and scoring oral reading fluency
- Cassette tape player/recorder with blank tape
- Curriculum-Based Norms in Oral Reading Fluency for Grades 1–8 as shown in Figure 14.3.

Procedure

A student reads aloud for one minute from an unpracticed DIBELS® passage. For screening decisions, the DIBELS® passage is at the student's grade level. For diagnostic or progress-monitoring decisions, the difficulty level of the passage may need to be at either the student's instructional or goal levels. As the student reads, the teacher records errors as follows:

- A word that is mispronounced or substituted for another word or an omitted word is counted as an error.
- Words transposed in a phrase count as two errors (reading "jumped and ran" instead of "ran and jumped").

Figure 14.3   Oral Reading Fluency Norms, Grades 1–8, 2005

		Fall	Winter	Spring
Grade	Percentile	WCPM	WCPM	WCPM
1	90	XX	81	111
	75	XX	47	82
	50	XX	23	56
	25	XX	12	28
	10	XX	6	15
2	90	106	125	142
	75	79	100	117
	50	51	72	89
	25	25	42	61
	10	11	18	31
3	90	128	146	162
	75	99	120	137
	50	71	92	107
	25	44	62	78
	10	21	36	48
4	90	145	166	180
	75	119	139	152
	50	94	112	123
	25	68	87	98
	10	45	61	72
5	90	166	182	194
	75	139	156	168
	50	110	127	139
	25	85	99	109
	10	61	74	83
6	90	177	195	204
	75	153	167	177
	50	127	140	150
	25	98	111	122
	10	68	82	93
7	90	180	192	202
	75	156	165	177
	50	128	136	150
	25	102	109	123
	10	79	88	98
8	90	185	199	199
	75	161	173	177
	50	133	146	151
	25	106	115	124
	10	77	84	97

Source: Compiled by Jan Hasbrouck, Ph.D, & Gerald Tindal, Ph.D. From Hasbrouck, Jan. (2006, April). Oral Reading Fluency Norms: A valuable assessment tool for reading teachers. *The Reading Teacher, 59* (7), 636–644. Used with permission of the International Reading Association.
Count 5546 3496 5335
WCPM: Words correct per minute

- A word read incorrectly more than once is counted as an error each time.
- Words read correctly repeated more than once, errors self-corrected by the student, and words mispronounced due to dialect or speech impairments are not counted as errors.
- An inserted word (one that does not appear in the text) is not counted as an error because the final score is an indication of the number of words that were in the text that were read correctly by the student within the one-minute time period.

After one minute, the student stops reading. The teacher subtracts the total number of errors from the number of words read by the student to obtain a score of "words correct per minute" (wcpm). Using more than one passage to assess fluency rates helps to control for any text-based or genre-type differences or variations. If standardized passages are used such as those from published sources of CBM materials (e.g., *DIBELS®*, *Reading Fluency Monitor, AIMS Web*), a score from a single passage can be used (Hintze & Christ, 2004). The final wcpm score can then be compared to the ORF norms for making screening, diagnostic, or progress-monitoring decisions.

MULTIDIMENSIONAL FLUENCY SCALE (AGE/GRADE APPROPRIATE: GRADES 1.5 AND UP)

Purpose

The purpose of Rasinski's (2003) Multidimensional Fluency Scale (MFS) is to provide a practical measurement of students' oral reading fluency that provides clear and valid information about four components of fluent reading: (a) volume and expression, (b) phrasing, (c) smoothness, and (d) pace. Rasinski's (2003) recent revision of the original Zutell and Rasinski's 1991 Multidimensional Fluency Scale (MFS) adds assessment of a student's reading volume and expression. In the 1991 version of the Multidimensional Fluency Scale (MFS) by Zutell and Rasinski, the MFS was comprised of three subscales: (a) phrasing, (b) smoothness, and (c) pace. In the revised version, Rasinski has added a fourth and fifth subscale: (d) accuracy and (e) volume and expression. Zutell and Rasinski (1991) report a .99 test-retest reliability coefficient for the original MFS. Although no audio recording is necessary to use this instrument, it is highly recommended for accurate documentation.

Materials

You will need the following materials for this assessment:

- A teacher-selected grade-level or instructional-level passage for a one-minute sample (depending on decision-making purpose, i.e., diagnosis, screening, or progress monitoring)
- A paper copy of the Multidimensional Fluency Scale (MFS) as provided in Figure 14.4
- Cassette tape player/recorder with blank tape

Procedure

We recommend that students read a one-minute sample passage (see previous discussion of the one-minute sample in this chapter) using the Multidimensional Fluency Scale (MFS) shown in Figure 14.4 to assess each student's reading fluency. Teachers can rate student's fluency using the MFS either immediately following a student's reading or rate the

Figure 14.4   Multidimensional Fluency Scale

Use the following scale to rate reader fluency on the five dimensions of accuracy, volume and expression, phrasing, smoothness, and pace.

A. Accuracy

1. Word recognition accuracy is poor: generally below 85%. Reader clearly struggles in decoding words. Makes multiple decoding attempts for many words, usually without success.
2. Word recognition accuracy is marginal: 86%–90%. Reader struggles on many words. Many unsuccessful attempts at self-correction.
3. Word recognition accuracy is good: 91%–95%. Self-corrects successfully.
4. Word recognition accuracy is excellent: 96%–100%. Self-corrections are few but successful as nearly all words are read correctly on initial attempt.

B. Volume and Expression

1. Reads with little expression or enthusiasm in voice. Reads words as if simply to get them out. Little sense of trying to make text sound like natural language. Tends to read in a quiet voice.
2. Some expression. Begins to use voice to make text sound like natural language in some areas of the text but not others. Focus remains largely on saying the words. Still reads in a voice that is quiet.
3. Sounds like natural language throughout the better part of the passage. Occasionally slips into expressionless reading. Voice volume is generally appropriate throughout the text.
4. Reads with good expression and enthusiasm throughout the text. Sounds like natural language. Reader is able to vary expression and volume to match his or her interpretation of the passage.

C. Phrasing

1. Monotonic with little sense of phrase boundaries, frequent word-by-word reading.
2. Frequent two-and three-word phrases giving the impression of choppy reading; improper stress and intonation that fails to mark ends of sentences and clauses.
3. Mixture of run-ons, mid-sentence pauses for breath, and possibly some choppiness; reasonable stress/intonation.
4. Generally well-phrased, mostly in clause and sentence units, with adequate attention to expression.

D. Smoothness

1. Frequent extended pauses, hesitations, false starts, sound-outs, repetitions, and/or multiple attempts.
2. Several "rough spots" in text where extended pauses, hesitations, and soon are more frequent and disruptive.
3. Occasional breaks in smoothness caused by difficulties with specific words and/or structures.
4. Generally smooth reading with some breaks, but word and structure difficulties are resolved quickly, usually through self-correction.

E. Pace (During Sections of Minimal Disruption)

1. Slow and laborious.
2. Moderately slow.
3. Uneven mixture of fast and slow reading.
4. Consistently conversational.

Source: From *The Fluent Reader: Oral Reading Strategies for Building Word Recognition, Fluency, and Comprehension* by T. Rasinski. Copyright 2003 by Timothy V. Rasinski. Reprinted by permission of Scholastic Inc.

student's fluency later if the one-minute sample reading has been recorded on an audio-cassette tape. The MFS can also be used to rate group performances such as plays, reader's theater, and radio readings (Reutzel & Cooter, 2004). For radio readings, students can also prepare a text for reading and recording on a cassette tape player, complete with sound effects if they wish! After taping, the teacher can analyze the performance of individual students and provide helpful modeling and feedback for future improvement.

In Figure 14.5, we summarize the fluency assessment procedures and instruments we have discussed thus far and provide summary information about federally related assessment purposes (i.e., *screening, diagnosis, progress-monitoring,* or *outcomes* assessment), as well as type of test or procedure and psychometric evidence of test or procedure scores including reliability and/or validity evidence.

CONNECTING ASSESSMENT FINDINGS TO TEACHING STRATEGIES

Before discussing fluency intervention strategies, we have constructed a guide connecting assessment to intervention and/or strategy choices. It is our intention to help you, the teacher, select the most appropriate instructional interventions and strategies to meet your students' fluency development needs based on assessment data.

Once you have determined who in your class may need fluency development, as well as the areas of fluent reading to be developed, then you should select appropriate instructional and practice strategies. Most fluency development activities tend to fall into differing types of practice strategies. In the "If-Then Intervention Strategy Guide for Reading Fluency Development" we have listed the teaching strategies that appear in the next section and have linked them to key areas of need that your fluency assessments are likely to reveal.

In the next part of this chapter, we offer strategies for intervention based on the foregoing fluency assessment procedures and assessment instruments.

DEVELOPING READING FLUENCY FOR ALL CHILDREN

After a careful assessment of a student's reading fluency as outlined previously, one or more of the following fluency development strategies or integrated fluency lesson frameworks may be appropriately applied. Perhaps the most important thing to remember is that children with poorly developed fluency must receive regular opportunities to read and reread for authentic and motivating reasons, such as to gather information, to present a dramatization, or simply to reread a favorite story. The strategies described in this section offer effective and varied means for teachers to help learners become more fluent readers in authentic, effective, and motivating ways!

ORAL RECITATION LESSON

Purpose

Hoffman (1987) used a lesson format drawn from the one-room schoolhouse period of American education. During these early years of American education, teachers modeled reading aloud; students were assigned all or part of the text for practice; and, later, students were asked to read aloud to the class using a practice called "recitation." The oral recitation

Figure 14.5 Summary Matrix of Fluency Assessment Procedures or Tests

Name of Assessment Tool	Screening Assessment Purpose	Diagnostic Assessment Purpose	Progress-Monitoring Assessment Purpose	Outcomes Assessment Purpose	Norm-Referenced Test	Criterion-Referenced Test	Reliability Evidence	Validity Evidence
One-Minute Reading Sample (Oral Reading Fluency—ORF)	+	+	+	–	+	–	Test-retest reliabilities for elementary students ranged from .92 to 97; alternate-form reliability of different reading passages drawn from the same level ranged from .89 to .94	Criterion-related validity studied in eight separate studies in the past two decades ranged from .51 to .91
Oral Reading Fluency Norms CBM Scoring Procedures	+	+	+	–	+	–	Not Applicable	Not Applicable
Multidimensional Fluency Scale (MFS)	+	–	+	–	–	+	MFS has a 99 test-retest stability coefficient according to the MFS's authors	Criterion validity with the definition of fluency components

If-Then Intervention Strategy Guide for Reading Fluency Development

"If" the student is ready to learn → / "Then" try these teaching strategies ↑	Oral Recitation Lesson (ORL)	Fluency-Oriented Reading Instruction (FORI)	Repeated Readings	Assisted Reading	Choral Reading	Reader's Theater	Radio Reading	Explicit Fluency Instruction	Closed Caption Television	Neurological Impress Method (NIM)
Accuracy of Decoding	+	+	+	+	*	+	+	+	*	+
Reading Rate or Speed	+	+	+	+	+	+	+	+	+	+
Expressive Reading	+	+	+	+	+	+	+	+	*	+
Appropriate Volume	+	+	+	*	*	+	+	+	*	+
Smoothness of Reading	+	+	+	+	+	+	+	+	+	+
Phrasing of the Text	+	+	+	*	+	+	+	+	+	+
Monitoring and Self-Regulation of Fluency	*	*	*	*	–	*	–	+	*	*

Key: + Excellent Strategy
  * Adaptable Strategy
  – Unsuitable Strategy

lesson (ORL) shares many important theoretical and practical characteristics with the shared book approach strategy described in chapter 3. According to Rasinski (1990a), the shared book approach and the oral recitation lesson are similar in respect to teacher modeling, repeated readings of text, independent reading, and the use of predictable and meaningful materials. Thus, the shared book approach may be seen in many respects as a less formalized approach to developing fluency with children (Nelson & Morris, 1986). However, for some readers (and teachers), the oral recitation lesson (ORL) offers a degree of security through providing a predictable lesson structure for planning.

Materials

Student self-selected books appropriate for reading aloud are used.

Procedure

The oral recitation lesson incorporates two basic components, with each made up of several subroutines outlined here:

I. DIRECT INSTRUCTION

    A. Three Subroutines
        1. Comprehension
        2. Practice
        3. Performance

II. INDIRECT INSTRUCTION

    B. Two Subroutines
        1. Fluency Practice
        2. Demonstrate Expert Reading

Direct instruction consists of three subroutines: a comprehension phase, a practice phase, and a performance phase. When beginning an oral recitation lesson, the teacher reads a story aloud and leads the students through an analysis of the story's content by constructing a story grammar map and discussing the major elements of the story such as setting, characters, goals, plans, events, and resolution. Students are asked to tell what they remember about these parts of the story, and the teacher records their responses on the story grammar map. At the conclusion of this discussion, the story grammar map is used as an outline for students to write a story summary.

During the second subroutine, practice, the teacher works with students to improve their oral reading expression. The teacher models fluent reading aloud with parts of the text, then the students individually or chorally practice imitating the teacher's oral expressions. Choral readings of texts can be accomplished in a number of ways (see Wood 4-way oral reading described in the section "Choral Reading"). Text segments modeled by the teacher during the practice phase may begin with only one or two sentences and gradually move toward modeling and practicing whole pages of text.

The third subroutine is the performance phase. Students select and perform a part of the text for others in the group. Then, listeners are encouraged to comment positively on the performance. We begin this activity by asking students to state what they liked about the oral reading by their peers. Next we ask questions about parts of the reading they liked less. Teacher modeling is very important with this latter activity. For instance, the teacher may model a question about a strange rendition of the Big Bad Wolf in the Three Pigs story by saying, "I noticed that your voice had a nice and friendly tone when you read the Big Bad Wolf's part. I'm curious. Why did you choose to read his part that way when so many other readers choose to use a mean-sounding voice for that character?"

Many times the student has a perfectly logical reason for irregular intonation or other anomalies. Sometimes it is simply a matter of not enough practice time. If so, this regular format helps students be aware that there is some accountability to these lessons.

The second major component of the Oral Recitation Lesson is an indirect instruction phase. During this part of the lesson, students practice a single story until they become expert readers. Hoffman (1987) defined an *expert reader* as one who reads with 98% accuracy and 75-words-per-minute fluency. For 10 minutes each day, students practice reading a story or text segment in a soft or mumble reading fashion. Teachers use this time to check students individually—what we term "house calls"—for story mastery before moving on to another story. The direct instruction component creates a pool of stories from which the students can select a story for expert reading activities in the indirect instruction phase. In summary, the ORL provides teachers with a workable strategy to break away from the traditional practice of round-robin oral reading.

FLUENCY-ORIENTED READING INSTRUCTION

Purpose

Fluency-Oriented Reading Instruction (FORI), based on repeated reading research, is an integrated lesson framework for providing comprehensive instruction and practice in fluency in the elementary school (Stahl, Heubach, & Cramond, 1997; Stahl, 2004). FORI consists of three interlocking aspects, according to its authors: (a) a redesigned basal or core reading program lesson, (b) a free-reading period at school, and (c) a home reading program. Recent research on the effects of FORI showed that children receiving FORI instruction significantly outperformed a control group comparison (Stahl, Bradley, Smith, Kuhn, Schwanenflugel, Meisinger, et al., 2003).

Materials

You will need the following materials:

- Core reading or basal reading program text
- Richly appointed classroom library for free reading at school and home
- Extension activities drawn from the core or basal reading program text
- Teacher-prepared graphic organizer of the text in the core or basal program
- Teacher-prepared audio tape for tape-assisted reading practice

Procedure

On the first day of a FORI lesson, the teacher begins the week by reading the core reading program story or text aloud to the class. Following the reading by the teacher, the students and teacher interactively discuss the text to place reading comprehension up-front as an important goal to be achieved in reading any text. Following this discussion, the teacher teaches vocabulary words and uses graphic organizers and other comprehension activities focused around the story or text the teacher has read aloud.

On the second day of a FORI lesson, teachers can choose to have children echo read the core reading program text with the teacher *or* have children read only a part of the story repeatedly for practice with a partner or with the teacher. Following this practice session on the second day, the core reading program story is sent home for the child to read with his or her parents, with other older siblings, or with other caregivers.

On the third and fourth days of a FORI lesson, children receive additional practice as well as participate in vocabulary and comprehension exercises around the story read in the core reading program. On these two days, children are also given decoding instruction on difficult words in the core reading story or text. Finally, on the fifth and final day of the FORI lesson, children are asked to give a written response to the story to cement their comprehension of the text.

In addition to the basal or core reading program instruction to develop fluency found in the FORI framework, the teachers provide additional in-school free reading practice with easy books that are read alone or with a partner for between 15 and 30 minutes per day. At the beginning of the year, the time allocated to this portion of a FORI lesson is closer to 15 minutes; the time increases throughout the year to 30 minutes. As a part of their homework assignment in the FORI framework, children are expected to read at home 15 minutes a day at least 4 days per week. This outside reading is monitored through the use of reading logs (Stahl, 2004).

REPEATED READINGS

Purpose

Repeated readings engage students in reading short (100- to 200-word) passages orally over and over again. The essential purpose (and benefit) of repeated readings is to enhance students' reading automaticity—rate and accuracy (Rasinski et al., 2005; Dowhower, 1989; Rasinski, 2003; Samuels, 1979). Although it may seem that reading a text again and again could lead to boredom, it can actually have just the opposite effect, especially for younger readers.

Materials

In the beginning, texts selected for repeated readings should be short, predictable, and easy. Examples of poetry we recommend for repeated readings with at-risk readers include those authored by Shel Silverstein and Jack Prelutsky. Stories by Bill Martin, such as *Brown Bear, Brown Bear*, or Eric Carle's *The Very Hungry Caterpillar* are also wonderful places to start this activity. When students attain adequate speed and accuracy with easy texts, the length and difficulty of the stories and poems can gradually be increased.

Procedure

In this exercise, each reading is timed and recorded on a chart or graph. Students compete with themselves, trying to better their own reading rate and cut down on errors with each successive attempt. Also, with each attempt, students' comprehension and prosody or vocal inflections improve (Dowhower, 1987; Reutzel & Hollingsworth, 1993). Students with reading problems find it reinforcing to see visible evidence of improvement. Figure 14.6 illustrates a tracking graph of student progress in repeated readings. To increase reading rate, all students must learn to recognize words without having to sound them out. In Figure 14.6, both the amount of time it took to read the selection and the number of oral reading errors that occurred during each trial day have been graphed.

Repeated readings help students by expanding the total number of words they can recognize instantaneously and, as previously mentioned, help improve students' comprehension and oral elocution (performance) with each succeeding attempt. Improved performance quickly leads students to improved confidence regarding reading aloud and positive attitudes toward the act of reading. Additionally, because high-frequency words (*the, and, but, was,* and so on) occur in literally all reading situations, the increase in automatic sight word knowledge developed through repeated readings transfers far beyond the practiced texts.

Figure 14.6   Rate and Accuracy Tracking Graphs

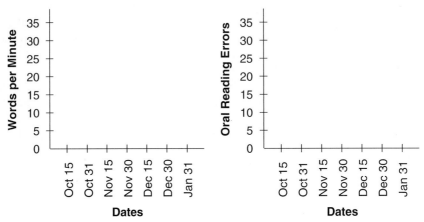

One way of supporting readers during repeated readings is to use a tape-recorded version of the story or poem. Students can read along with an audiocassette tape to develop fluency similar to the model on the tape. Also, students can tape record their oral reading performance as a source of immediate feedback. If two audiocassette tape players/recorders are available, ask students to listen and read along with the taped version of the text using headphones. At the same time, use the second recorder for recording the student's oral reading. The child can then either replay his or her version simultaneously with the teacher-recorded version to compare or simply listen to his or her own rendition alone. Either way, the feedback can be both instant and effective.

You may use taped recordings of repeated readings for further analysis of each reader's improvement in fluency and comprehension. Also, using a tape recorder frees the teacher to work with other students, thereby conserving precious instructional time and leaving behind an audit trail of student readings for later assessment and documentation. On occasion, teachers should listen to the tape with the reader present. During this time, the teacher and student can discuss effective ways of reducing word-recognition errors and increasing reading rate.

ASSISTED AND PARTNER READING

Purpose

Assisted reading can be accomplished in one of two ways: (a) with human support or (b) with technology support. When human support is provided, this is usually called *partner reading* (also called *buddy, dyad, peer,* or *paired reading*). Partner reading involves two students reading the same text aloud in unison for mutual support or one listening and one reading for informative feedback and guidance (Eldredge & Quinn, 1988; Greene 1970; Lefever-Davis & Pearman, 2005; Osborn et al, 2002; Topping, 1987; Topping & Ehly, 1998). When technology support is provided this is usually called *tape- or computer-assisted reading*. Tape-assisted reading involves students listening to an audiocassette recording of a passage or book multiple times for practice. Computer-assisted reading can be complex or simple depending upon the software employed. In most cases, computer-assisted reading is much like tape-assisted reading with the exception that the text is presented on the computer screen. As children read the words, the computer program often backlights or highlights the words with a color. If students do not know a word after a predetermined period of time, the computer will say the word. Some more expensive and complex computer-assisted programs even have voice-recognition software and maintain an individual student record of each student's fluency development over multiple rereadings. Two excellent but somewhat expensive computer-assisted programs are *Read Naturally* (Ihnot, 1997) and *Insights: Reading Fluency* (Adams, 2002). You can learn more about these two programs by going to the following web sites: (a) http://www.readnaturally.com and (b) http://www.charlesbridge-fluency.com.

Materials

Initial partner reading sessions should be structured so that the materials used are equally familiar and motivating for both students. Practice passages should be appropriately challenging, typically on the student's instructional level.

Procedure

Students are paired according to their general reading level; but, just as important, they should be paired according to their ability to work well with one another. A spirit of teamwork and cooperation must be present so that when one reader stumbles, the other lends assistance. The partner reading practice sessions can be tape recorded and played back for the students and teachers to evaluate. Discussions of taped replays should center not just on word recognition accuracy but also on reading rate, pausing, volume, intonation, expressive oral interpretation, and comprehension of the text.

CHORAL READING

Purpose

In many classrooms, special-needs students are asked to read aloud in a solo, barbershop, or round-robin fashion. Round-robin oral reading carries with it significant instructional, emotional, and psychological risks for all children but most especially for special-needs readers (Eldredge, Reutzel, & Hollingsworth, 1996; Opitz & Rasinski, 1998). Homan, Klesius, and Hite (1993) found that choral reading forms of fluency practice such as echoic and unison readings yielded excellent gains in fluency and comprehension for all children. Karen Wood (1983) suggested an approach for reading a story orally in a group called 4-way oral reading. Choral readings of this type alleviate some of the identified weaknesses of oral round-robin reading while adding variety to repeated readings.

Materials

One copy of a short and interesting story, poem, song, article, text, or script is needed.

Procedure

In 4-way oral reading, the oral reading of a text should be varied by using four different types of oral reading: (a) unison choral reading, (b) echoic or imitative reading, (c) paired reading, and (d) mumble reading (Wood, 1983). All of these approaches to oral reading, except mumble reading, are described elsewhere in this chapter. Mumble reading, or reading quietly aloud, is typically heard among young readers as they are initially told to read silently. These young readers tend to "mumble" as they attempt to read silently. Teachers should model this approach to oral reading before asking students to mumble read.

To use 4-way oral reading, Wood (1983) suggested that the teacher introduce the story content and the varied methods to be used in reading it. The teacher should pause briefly during the oral reading of the story to help students reflect on the story and predict ahead of themselves to focus and improve comprehension. During 4-way oral reading, students are called upon in random order to read but none of them will be put on the spot because none of the 4-way oral reading strategies require that students read solo. Because of this, all students participate repeatedly throughout the oral reading of the story, thus helping them remain actively involved and keep their place in the story. Also, students read together, often providing many minutes of reading aloud for pleasure and practice to support special-needs readers in becoming more fluent.

Reader's Theater

Purpose

Reader's theater is a strategy whereby students practice reading from a script, then share their oral reading with classmates and selected audiences (Allington, 2001; Opitz & Rasinski, 1998; Sloyer, 1982). Unlike a play, students do not memorize lines or use elaborate stage sets to make their presentation. Emphasis is placed on presenting an interpretation of literature read in a dramatic style for an audience who imagines setting and actions. Reader's theater has been widely used, and reports indicate that it is an effective practice strategy for increasing students' reading fluency at a variety of ages (Martinez, Roser, & Strecker, 1999; Griffith & Rasinski, 2004; Flynn, 2005).

Materials

We strongly recommend that scripts obtained for reader's theater be drawn from tales originating from the oral tradition, poetry, or quality picture books designed to be read aloud by children. Selections should be packed with action; have an element of suspense; and comprise an entire, meaningful story or episode. Also, texts selected for use in reader's theater should contain sufficient dialogue to make reading and preparing the text a challenge, as well as involving several children as characters. A few examples of such texts include Martin and Archambault's *Knots on a Counting Rope* (1987), Viorst's *Alexander and the Terrible, Horrible, No Good, Very Bad Day* (1972), and Barbara Robinson's *The Best Christmas Pageant Ever* (1972). Minimal props are often used in Reader's Theater, such as masks, hats, or simple costumes. Several excellent web sites make many excellent reader's theater scripts readily available to classroom teachers: http://www.aaronshep.com/rt/index.html, http://readinglady.com, http://readers-theatre.com, and http://geocities.com/Enchanted Forest/Tower3235. Commercially published reader's theater scripts are now available for the same script at differing levels of difficulty allowing all children to participate in a reader's theater performance at their level. Sundance Publishing Company is one group that began the publication of leveled reader's theater scripts (Martinez et al., 1999; Griffith & Rasinski, 2004; Flynn, 2005).

Procedure

If a story is selected for reading, students are assigned to read characters' parts. If poems are selected for a reader's theater, students may read alternating lines or groups of lines. Reader's theater in the round, in which readers stand around the perimeter of the room and the audience is in the center surrounded by the readers, is a fun and interesting variation for both the performers and audience. Students often benefit from a discussion prior to reading a reader's theater script. The purpose of this discussion is to help students make connections between their own background experiences and the text to be read. Also, struggling students benefit from listening to a previously recorded performance of the text as a model prior to the initial reading of the script.

Hennings (1974) described a simplified procedure for preparing reader's theater scripts for classroom performance. First, the text to be performed is read silently by the individual students. Second, the text is read again orally, sometimes using choral reading in a group. After the second reading, children choose their parts or the teacher assigns parts to the children. We suggest that students be allowed to select their three most desired parts, that they write these choices on a slip of paper to submit to the teacher, and that teachers do everything possible to assign one of these three choices to the requesting student. The third reading is also an oral reading with students reading their parts with scripts in hand. There may be several rehearsal readings as students prepare for the final reading or performance in front of the class or a selected audience.

Reader's theater offers students a unique opportunity to participate in reading along with other, perhaps more skilled readers. Participating in the mainstream classroom with better readers helps students having reading problems feel a part of their peer group; provides them with ready models of good reading; and demonstrates how good readers, through practice, become even better readers. Working together with other readers fosters a sense of teamwork, support, and pride in personal and group accomplishment.

RADIO READING

Purpose

Radio reading (Greene, 1979; Opitz & Rasinski, 1998; Rasinski, 2003; Searfoss, 1975) is a variation on repeated reading and reader's theater. This procedure for developing oral reading fluency in a group setting was intended to provide an alternative to the old and now discredited approach to oral reading called "round robin," in which students were assigned by the teacher to take turns reading aloud while all of the other students in the circle or small group listened and presumably followed along in the text (Eldredge et al., 1996). We have found radio reading to be most effectively used with short selections from information texts threaded together to make a news broadcast performance.

Materials

In radio reading, each student is given a "script" to read aloud. Selections can be drawn from any print media, such as newspapers, magazines, or any print source that can be converted into a news story such as short selections from articles or sections in information books.

Procedure

One student acts as a news anchor broadcaster, and other students act in the roles of various reporters reporting on the weather, sports, breaking news, and so on. Only the radio readers and the teacher have copies of the scripts. Because other students have no script to follow, minor word recognition errors will go unnoticed if the text is well presented. Struggling students enjoy radio reading from *Know Your World*® *Extra*. This publication is well suited for use in radio reading activities because the content and level of difficulty make it possible for older readers with fluency problems to read with ease and enjoyment. Short selections from information books on weather, volcanoes, spiders, sports figures, and so on can be presented as short reports by various reporters during the news broadcast.

A script for the anchor may need to be written by the children with help from the teacher to thread the various news reports together in a cohesive fashion.

Before performing a radio reading for an audience, students should rehearse the selections repeated with a partner or the teacher until they gain confidence and can read the script with proper volume, accuracy, rate, phrasing, and expression. Emphasis is first placed on the meaning of the text segments so that the students can paraphrase any difficult portions of the text if needed during the presentation. Students are encouraged to keep the ideas flowing in the same way as a reporter or anchor news broadcaster.

EXPLICIT FLUENCY INSTRUCTION

Purpose

The primary purposes of explicit fluency instruction are twofold: (a) to teach students to clearly understand what is meant by *fluency* and (b) to teach students how to self-monitor, evaluate, self-regulate, and otherwise "fix up" their own fluency problems over time. "Some students struggle with reading because they lack information about what they are trying to do and how to do it. They look around at their fellow students who are learning to read [fluently and well] and say to themselves, 'How are they doing that?' In short they are mystified about how to do what other students seem to do with ease" (Duffy, 2004, p. 9).

It is typically very difficult for teachers to provide explicit explanations for how to read fluently. To do so, they must become aware of the processes they use to read fluently. However, because teachers are already fluent readers, they do not think deeply about the processes they use to read text fluently (Duffy, 2004; Reutzel, in press; Reutzel, in preparation).

Materials

Materials for explicit fluency instruction should be selected from among several sources that represent at least the genres of information, story, and poem. Segments for practice should be limited to 100 to 300 words and should be at grade level for whole-class lessons and practice. Teachers will need means to enlarge text using the board, charts, computer projector, or overhead projector.

Procedure

To teach an explicit fluency lesson, a framework and template lesson plan is needed. Reutzel (in press) has developed an explicit lesson framework called **EMS**—explanation, model, scaffold. This framework expects that teachers will explicitly explain what fluency is composed of—accuracy, rate, and expression—as well as what each of these three concepts entails. Explicit fluency lessons are taught on accurate reading; reading at the proper rate; and expression that includes smoothness, volume, expression, and phrasing. Explanations include what is to be learned, where and when it is to be used, and why it is important. Modeling demonstrates how an aspect of fluency, like expression, is to be done (and for some students *not* done!). Finally, teachers gradually release through a series of guided practice experiences the reading of the class text to individual application through a process we call *You* (teacher model), *You and Me* (teacher and student share fluency reading in whole class and with partners), *and Me* (student reads independently). A template explicit fluency lesson is found in Figure 14.7 to demonstrate each of the parts of the EMS explicit fluency lesson.

Finally, students are also taught how to monitor, assess, and "fix up" their fluency through the use of a simple assessment rubric of the elements of oral reading fluency found in Figure 14.8 and through explicit fluency lessons on using the fluency fix-up strategies found in Figure 14.9.

Figure 14.7 Explicit Fluency Lesson Plan Template

Objective: *Children will pay attention to punctuation to help them read expressively.*

Supplies

- Book—*In a Tree* pp. 18–19
- Overhead transparency
- Overhead projector
- Three colored pens (overhead)
- Text Types: Narrative ( ) Information Books (x) Poetry ( )

Explain

- **What**

  Today, boys and girls, we are going to be learning about how to read expressively. Important parts of reading expressively are pausing, stopping, or raising or lowering our pitch as we read. Pitch is how high or low the sounds are that we make with our voices (demonstrate high and low pitch). Stopping means we quit reading for a moment like this. . . . Pausing means we take a breath and keep reading. Marks on the page called punctuation marks (point to) help us to know when we need to pause, stop, or raise or lower our pitch.

- **Why**

  We need to read expressively with pauses or stops so that we can show that we understand what we are reading. Punctuation tells us what we need to know about how to express the words, phrases, and sentences with the right pauses, stops, and pitch.

- **When/Where**

  Whenever we read, we should pay attention to the punctuation so that we know where to pause, stop, and raise or lower our pitch.

Modeling

- **Example**

  First, I am going to read this page with good expression paying attention to what the punctuation tells me to do, such as pause, stop, or raise or lower my pitch. Please look at the page on the overhead. Notice that I have colored each punctuation mark with a different color to help you see them more clearly. Follow what I read with your eyes. Listen very carefully to see if I stop, pause, or change my pitch where I should.

- **Non-Example**

  Next, I am going to read this page with poor expression paying no or little attention to what the punctuation tells me to do. I won't pause, stop, or raise or lower my pitch. Please look at the page on the overhead. Notice that I have colored each punctuation mark with a different color to help you see them more clearly. Follow what I read with your eyes. Listen very carefully to see where I should have changed my reading to stop, pause, or raise or lower my pitch.

Scaffolding: (Me, You and Me, You)

- **Whole Group (Me and You)**

  Now that I have shown you how and how not to read this page, let's practice it together! We will begin reading this page all together. (Point) Watch my pen so that we can all stay together. Next, we will read this again using echo reading. How many of you have ever heard an echo? So if I say, *Hello*, the echo will say *Hello*. So now I will read and you will echo me. Let's begin.

- **Small Group/Partners/Teams (Me and You)**

  Now turn to your neighbor. One person will read and the other will echo.

- **Individual (You)**

  Next, take fluency phone and read this again to yourself listening carefully to see where you are stopping, pausing, or raising or lowering your pitch.

Now, take your fluency phone and read this again to yourself listening carefully to see where you are stopping, pausing, or raising or lowering your pitch.

continued

Figure 14.7 continued

Assess
- Rubric for assessment
- Set personal goals
- Graph progress

Reflect
- What went well?
- How would you change the lesson?

Figure 14.8 Assessment Rubric of the Elements of Oral Reading Fluency

Accurate Reading

Speed or Rate

Expression

Figure 14.9 Fluency Fix-Up Strategies for Major Fluency Elements

Accuracy
1. Slow your reading speed down.
2. Look carefully at the words and the letters in the words you didn't read correctly on the page.
3. Think about if you know this word or parts of this word. Try saying the word or word parts.
4. Make the sound of each letter from left to right and blend the sounds together quickly to say the word.
5. Listen carefully to see if the word you said makes sense.
6. Try reading the word in the sentence again.
7. After saying the word, you may use pictures to help you make sure you have the right word.
8. If the word still doesn't make sense, then ask someone to help you.

Rate
1. Adjust your reading speed to go slower when the text is difficult or unfamiliar or if you need to read to get detailed information.
2. Adjust your reading speed to go faster when the text is easy, familiar, or you are reading to just enjoy this book.

Expression
1. Try to read three or more words together before pausing, stopping, or taking a breath.
2. Take a big breath and try to read to the comma or end punctuation without stopping for another breath.
3. Be sure to raise or lower your pitch when you see punctuation marks at the end of sentences.

Additional Strategies for English-Language Learners

Closed-Caption Television

Purpose

Several researchers (Koskinen, Wilson, & Jensema, 1985; Neuman & Koskinen, 1992) have found that closed-caption television is a particularly effective tool for motivating students who are learning English as a second language to improve fluency and comprehension. Closed-caption television, which uses written subtitles, provides students with meaningful and motivating reading material.

Materials

Teachers should carefully select high-interest television programs, record and preview programs before making final selections, then introduce the programs to students with attention to vocabulary and prior knowledge factors (Koskinen et al., 1985).

Procedure

Three elements should be considered in a successful closed-caption lesson. First, watch a part of the captioned television program together as a group (5 to 10 minutes). Stop the recorded tape and ask students to predict what will happen next in the program. Then, continue showing the program so that students can check their predictions. Second, watch a segment of the program that has examples of certain kinds of phonics patterns, word uses, or punctuation. For example, students can be alerted to the use of quotation marks and the fact that these marks signal dialogue. Students can then watch the remainder of the tape to identify the dialogue using their knowledge of quotation marks. Third, after watching a closed-caption television program, students can practice reading aloud along with the captions. If necessary, both the auditory portion and the closed captioning can be played simultaneously to provide students with fluency problems support through their initial attempts to read. At some later point, students can be allowed to practice reading the captioning without the auditory portion of the program. Koskinen et al. (1985) added that they "do not recommend that the sound be turned off if this, in effect, turns off the children. The major advantage of captioned television is the multisensory stimulation of viewing the drama, hearing the sound, and seeing the captions" (p. 6).

Including All Students

Neurological Impress

Purpose

The neurological impress method (NIM) involves the student and the teacher in reading the same text aloud simultaneously (Heckleman, 1966, 1969; Hollingsworth, 1970, 1978). The use of multiple sensory systems associated with using NIM is thought to "impress" upon the student the fluid reading patterns of the teacher through direct modeling. It is assumed that exposing students to numerous examples of texts (read in a more sophisticated way than the at-risk students could achieve on their own) will enable them to learn the patterns of letter-sound correspondence in the language more naturally. This assumption stands to reason when viewed in light of well-established advances in learning theory, especially those espoused by Vygotsky (1978).

Materials

Each NIM session is aimed at reading as much material as is possible in 10 minutes. As mentioned previously, the reading material selected for the first few sessions should be easy and predictable and make sense for the reader. However, other more challenging materials can be used rather quickly.

Procedure

To use the NIM, the student sits slightly in front of and to one side of the teacher as they hold the text. The teacher moves his or her finger beneath the words as they are spoken in near-unison fashion. Both try to maintain a comfortably brisk, continuous rate of oral reading. The teacher's role is to keep the pace when the student starts to slow down. Pausing for analyzing unknown words is not permitted. The teacher's voice is directed at the student's ear so that the words are seen, heard, and said simultaneously. In the first few NIM sessions, students should become acquainted with the process by practicing on short, familiar texts. Because most students with reading problems have not read at an accelerated pace before, their first efforts often have a mumblelike quality. Most students with reading problems typically take some time to adjust to the NIM; however, within a few sessions they start to feel at ease. Many students with reading problems say they enjoy the NIM because it allows them to read more challenging and interesting material like "good readers."

At first, the teacher's voice will dominate the oral reading, but in later sessions it should be reduced gradually. This will eventually allow the student to assume the vocal lead naturally. Usually three sessions per week are sufficient to obtain noticeable results. This routine should be followed for a minimum of 10 consecutive weeks (Henk, 1983).

The NIM can also be adapted for group use (Hollingsworth, 1970, 1978). The teacher tape records 10 minutes of his or her own oral reading in advance. Individual students can read along with the tape while following the text independently, or the tape can be used in a listening center to permit the teacher to spend individual time with each student as others participate in reading with the tape. Despite the advantages of the prerecorded tape format, teachers' one-to-one interactions with individual students result in a better instructional experience.

Selected References

Adams, M. J. (2002). *Insights: Reading Fluency*. Watertown, MA: Charlesbridge.

Allington, R. L. (1977). If they don't read much, how they ever gonna get good? *Journal of Reading, 21,* 57–61.

Allington, R. L. (1983). Fluency: The neglected reading goal. *The Reading Teacher, 36*(6), 556–561.

Allington, R. L. (1984). Oral reading. In R. Barr, M. Kamil, & P. Mosenthal (Eds.), *Handbook of reading research.* New York: Longman.

Allington, R. L. (2001). *What really matters for struggling readers: Designing research-based programs.* New York: Addison-Wesley/Longman.

Amarel, M, Bussis, A., & Chittenden, E. A. (1977). *An approach to the study of beginning reading: Longitudinal case studies.* Paper presented at the National Reading Conference, New Orleans, LA.

Blevins, W. (2001). *Building fluency: Lessons and strategies for reading success.* New York: Scholastic.

Bryan, G., Fawson, P. C., & Reutzel, D. R. (2003). Sustained silent reading: Exploring the value of literature discussion with three non-engaged readers. *Reading Research and Instruction, 43*(1), 47–73.

Carle, E. (1981). *The very hungry caterpillar.* New York: Scholastic, Inc.

Dowhower, S. (1987). Effects of repeated readings on second-grade transitional readers' fluency and comprehension. *Reading Research Quarterly, 22,* 389–406.

Dowhower, S. (1989). Repeated reading: Research into practice. *The Reading Teacher, 42*(7), 502–507.

Dowhower, S. (1991). Speaking of prosody: Fluency's unattended bedfellow. *Theory into Practice, 30*(3), 158–164.

Duffy, G. G. (2004). *Explaining reading: A resource for teaching concepts, skills, and strategies.* New York: Guilford Press.

Eldredge, J. L., & Quinn, D. W. (1988). Increasing reading performance of low-achieving second graders with dyad reading groups. *Journal of Educational Research, 82,* 40–46.

Eldredge, J. L., Reutzel, D. R., & Hollingsworth, P. M. (1996). Comparing the effectiveness of two oral reading practices: Round-robin reading and the shared book experience. *Journal of Literacy Research, 28*(2), 201–225.

Flynn, R. M. (2005). Curriculum-based readers theatre: Setting the stage for reading and retention. *The Reading Teacher, 58*(4), 360–365.

Gambrell, L. B., Wilson, R. M., & Gnatt, W. N. (1981). Classroom observations of task-attending behaviors of good and poor readers. *Journal of Educational Research, 74,* 400–404.

Good, R. H., & Jefferson, G. (1988). Contemporary perspectives on curriculum-based measurement validity. In M. R. Shinn (Ed.), *Advanced applications of curriculum-based measurement* (pp. 61–88). New York: Guilford Press.

Good, R. H., & Kamiski, R. A. (Eds.). (2002). *Dynamic indicators of basic early literacy skills* (6th ed.). Eugene, OR: Institute for the Development of Educational Achievement. Available: http://dibels.uoregon.edu/.

Good, R. H., Simmons, D. C., & Kameenui, E. J. (2001). The importance and decision-making utility of a continuum of fluency-based indicators of foundational reading skills for third-grade high-stakes outcomes. *Scientific Studies of Reading, 5*(3), 257–288.

Greene, F. P. (1970). *Paired reading.* Unpublished manuscript, Syracuse University, New York.

Greene, F. (1979). Radio reading. In C. Pennock (Ed.), *Reading comprehension at four linguistic levels,* p. 104–107. Newark, DE: International Reading Association.

Griffith, L. W., & Rasinski, T. V. (2004). A focus on fluency: How one teacher incorporated fluency with her reading curriculum. *The Reading Teacher, 58*(2), 126–137.

Harris, T. L., & Hodges, R. E. (Eds.). (1995). *The literacy dictionary: The vocabulary of reading and writing.* Newark, DE: International Reading Association.

Harris, T. L., & Sipay, E. R. (1990). *How to increase reading ability* (9th ed.). New York: Longman.

Hasbrouck, J. E., & Tindal, G. (2005). Oral Reading Fluency Norms: A valuable tool for reading teachers. *The Reading Teacher* (in submission); and *90 years of assessment* (BRT Technical Report No. 33), Eugene, OR. Data available at: http://brt.uoregon.edu/ TECHNICAL REPORTS.

Heckleman, R. G. (1966). Using the neurological impress remedial reading technique. *Academic Therapy, 1,* 235–239, 250.

Heckleman, R. G. (1969). A neurological impress method of remedial reading instruction. *Academic Therapy, 4,* 277, 282.

Henk, W. A. (1983). Adapting the NIM to improve comprehension. *Academic Therapy, 19,* 97–101.

Hennings, K. (1974). Drama reading, an ongoing classroom activity at the elementary school level. *Elementary English, 51,* 48–51.

Hintze, J. M., & Christ, T. J. (2004). An examination of variability as a function of passage variance in CBM progress monitoring. *School Psychology Review, 33*(2), 204–217.

Hoffman, J. V. (1987). Rethinking the role of oral reading in basal instruction. *The Elementary School Journal, 87*(3), 367–374.

Hollingsworth, P. M. (1970). An experiment with the impress method of teaching reading. *The Reading Teacher, 24,* 112–114.

Hollingsworth, P. M. (1978). An experimental approach to the impress method of teaching reading. *The Reading Teacher, 31,* 624–626.

Homan, S. P., Klesius, J. P., & Hite, C. (1993). Effects of repeated readings and nonrepetitive strategies on students' fluency and comprehension. *The Journal of Educational Research, 87*(2), 94–99.

Ihnot, C. (1997). *Read Naturally.* St. Paul, Minnesota: Reading Naturally: The Fluency Company.

Jenkins, J. R., Fuchs, L. S., Van den Broek, P., Espin, C., & Deno. S. L. (2003). Accuracy and fluency in list and context reading of skilled and RD groups: Absolute and relative performance levels. *Learning Disabilities Research and Practice, 18*(4), 237–245.

Kameenui, E. J., & Simmons, D. C. (2001). The DNA of reading fluency. *Scientific Studies of Reading, 5*(3), 203–210.

Klenk, L., & Kibby, M. W. (2000). Re-mediating reading difficulties: Appraising the past, reconciling the present, constructing the future. In M. L. Kamil, P. B. Mosenthal, P. D. Pearson, & R. Barr (Eds.), *Handbook of reading research* (Vol. 3). Mahwah, NJ: Lawrence Erlbaum Associates.

Know Your World® Extra. Weekly Reader Magazines. New York: Scholastic, Inc.

Koskinen, P., Wilson, R., & Jensema, C. (1985). Closed-captioned television: A new tool for reading instruction. *Reading World, 24,* 1–7.

Kuhn, M. (2005). Helping students become accurate, expressive readers: Fluency instruction for small groups. *The Reading Teacher, 58*(4), 338–345.

Kuhn, M. R., & Stahl, S. A. (2000). *Fluency: A review of developmental and remedial practices.* Ann Arbor,

MI: Center for the Improvement of Early Reading Achievement.

Lefever-Davis, S., & Pearman, C. (2005). Early Readers and Electronic Texts: CD-ROM Storybook Features That Influence Reading Behavior. *The Reading Teacher, 58*(5), p 446–454. Feb 2005.

Martin, B., & Archambault, J. (1987). *Knots on a counting rope.* New York: Henry Holt.

Martin, B. (1990). *Brown Bear, Brown Bear, What do you see?* New York: Henry Holt.

Martinez, M., Roser, N., & Strecker, S. (1999). "I never thought I could be a star": A Reader's Theatre ticket to reading fluency. *The Reading Teacher, 52,* 326–334.

Marzano, R. J. (2004). *Building background knowledge for academic achievement: Research on what works in schools.* Alexandria, Virginia: Association for Supervision and Curriculum Development.

National Assessment of Educational Progress. (2000). The nation's report card: Reading 2000. Washington, DC: Department of Education.

National Institute of Child Health and Human Development. (2000). *Report of the National Reading Panel: Teaching children to read.* Washington, DC: U.S. Government Printing Office.

Nelson, L., & Morris, D. (1986). *Supported oral reading: A year-long intervention study in two inner-city primary grade classrooms.* Paper presented at the annual meeting of the National Reading Conference, Austin, TX.

Neuman, S. B., & Koskinen, P. (1992). Captioned television as comprehensible input: Effects of incidental word learning from context for language minority students. *Reading Research Quarterly, 27*(1), 94–106.

Opitz, M. F., & Rasinski, T. V. (1998). *Good-bye round robin: 25 effective oral reading strategies.* Portsmouth, NH: Heinemann Educational Books.

Osborn, J., Lehr, F., & Hiebert, E. H. (2002). *A focus on fluency: Research-based practices in early reading series.* Honolulu, HI: Pacific Resources for Education and Learning (PREL). Available: http://www.prel.org.

Pikulski, J. J., & Chard, D. J. (2005). Fluency: Bridge between decoding and reading comprehension. *The Reading Teacher, 58*(6), 510–519.

Prelutsky, J. (1996). *A pizza the size of the sun.* New York: Greenwillow Books.

Prescott-Griffin, M. L., & Witherell, N. L. (2004). *Fluency in focus: Comprehension strategies for all young readers.* Portsmouth, NH: Heinemann Educational Books.

Rasinski, T. (1989). Fluency for everyone: Incorporating fluency instruction in the classroom. *The Reading Teacher, 42*(9), 690–693.

Rasinski, T. (1990a). Effects of repeated reading and listening-while-reading on reading fluency. *The Journal of Educational Research, 83*(3), 147–150.

Rasinski, T. (1990b). Investigating measure of reading fluency. *Educational Research Quarterly, 14*(3), 37–44.

Rasinski, T. (2000). Speed does matter. *The Reading Teacher, 54*(2), 146–151.

Rasinski, T. V. (2003). *The fluent reader: Oral reading strategies for building word recognition, fluency, and comprehension.* New York: Scholastic.

Rasinski, T. V., Blachowicz, C., & Lems, K. (in press). *Teaching reading fluency.* New York: Guilford Press.

Rasinski, T. V., & Padak, N. (1996). Five lessons to increase reading fluency. In L. R. Putnam (Ed.), *How to become a better reading teacher: Strategies for assessment and intervention.* Columbus, OH: Merrill/Prentice Hall.

Rasinski, T. V., Padak, N., Linek, W., & Sturtevant, E. (1994). Effects of fluency development on urban second-grade readers. *The Journal of Educational Research, 87*(3), 158–165.

Rasinski, T. V., Padak, N. D., McKeon, C. A., Wilfong, L. G., Friedauer, J. A., & Heim, P. (2005). Is reading fluency a key for successful high school reading? *Journal of Adolescent and Adult Literacy, 49*(1), 22–27.

Reutzel, D. R. (1996). Developing special needs readers' oral reading fluency. In L. R. Putnam (Ed.), *How to become a better reading teacher: Strategies for assessment and intervention.* Columbus, OH: Merrill/Prentice Hall.

Reutzel, D. R. (2006). "Hey, teacher when you say 'fluency' what do you mean?": Developing fluency in elementary classrooms. In T. Rasinski, C. Blachowicz, and K. Lems (Eds.), *Fluency instruction: Research-based best practices,* 62–85. New York: Guilford Press.

Reutzel, D. R. (in preparation). *Practicing reading for fluency: The effects of silent and oral reading on third-grade students' fluency and comprehension.* Logan, UT: Emma Eccles Jones Center for Early Childhood Education.

Reutzel, D. R., & Cooter, R. B. (2004). *Teaching children to read: Putting the pieces together* (4th ed.). Upper Saddle River, NJ: Merrill/Prentice Hall.

Reutzel, D. R., & Hollingsworth, P. M. (1993). Effects of fluency training on second grade students' reading comprehension. *The Journal of Educational Research, 86*(6), 325–331.

Reutzel, D. R., Hollingsworth, P. M., & Eldredge, J. L. (1994). Oral reading instruction: The impact on student reading development. *Reading Research Quarterly, 29*(1), 40–62.

Richards, M. (2000). Be a good detective: Solve the case of oral reading fluency. *The Reading Teacher, 53*(7), 534–539.

Robinson, B. (1972). *The best Christmas pageant ever.* New York: Harper & Row.

Samuels, J. (1979). The method of repeated reading. *The Reading Teacher, 32,* 403–408.

Searfoss, L. W. (1975). Radio reading. *The Reading Teacher, 29,* 295–296.

Shake, M. (1986). Teacher interruptions during oral reading instruction: Self-monitoring as an impetus for change in corrective feedback. *Remedial and Special Education, 7*(5), 18–24.

Shinn, M. R. (Ed.). (1989). *Curriculum-based measurement: Assessing special children.* New York: Guilford Press.

Silverstein, S. (1974). *Where the sidewalk ends.* New York: HarperCollins.

Sloyer, S. (1982). *Reader's theater: Story dramatization in the classroom.* Urbana, IL: National Council of Teachers of English.

Snow, C. E., Burns, M. N., & Griffin, P. (1998). *Preventing reading difficulties in young children.* Washington, DC: National Academy Press.

Stahl, S. (2004). What do we know about fluency? In P. McCardle & V. Chhabra (Eds.), *The voice of evidence in reading research,* pp. 187–211. Baltimore, MD: Paul H. Brookes.

Stahl, S. A., Bradley, B., Smith, C. H., Kuhn, M. R., Schwanenflugel, P., Meisinger, E., et al. (2003). *Teaching children to become fluent and automatic readers.* Paper presented at the annual meeting of the American Educational Research Association, Chicago.

Stahl, S. A., Heuback, K., & Cramond, B. (1997). *Fluency-oriented reading instruction.* Athens, GA, and Washington, DC: National Reading Research Center and U.S. Department of Education, Office of Educational Research and Improvement, Educational Resources Information Center.

Tindal, G., Marston, D., & Deno, S. L. (1983). *The reliability of direct and repeated measurement* (Research Rep. No. 109). Minneapolis: University of Minnesota Institute for Research on Learning Disabilities.

Topping, K. (1987). Peer tutored paired reading: Outcome data from ten projects. *Educational Psychology, 7,* 604–614.

Topping, K., & Ehly, S. (1998). *Peer-assisted learning.* Mahwah, NJ: Lawrence Erlbaum Associates.

Viorst, J. (1972). *Alexander and the terrible, horrible, no good, very bad day.* New York: Atheneum.

Vygotsky, L. S. (1978). *Mind in society.* Cambridge, MA: Harvard University Press.

Wolf, M., & Katzir-Cohen, T. (2001). Reading fluency and its intervention. *Scientific Studies of Reading, 5*(3), 211–229.

Wood, K. D. (1983). A variation on an old theme: 4-way oral reading. *The Reading Teacher, 37*(1), 38–41.

Worthy, J., & Broaddus, K. (2002). Fluency beyond the primary grades: From group performance to silent, independent reading. *The Reading Teacher, 55*(4), 334–343.

Zutell, J., & Rasinski, T. (1991). Training teachers to attend to their students' oral reading fluency. *Theory into Practice, 30*(3), 211–217.

Chapter 15

Engaging in Literature Response

"Boys and girls, I'd like to share several books with you today. Listen carefully as I tell you about each so that you can vote on which literature circle group you would like to join." Mr. Jackson shared three book titles, *Tuck Everlasting, Fog Magic,* and *The Great Gilly Hopkins,* with his third-grade class by giving a brief "book talk" about each. Children were handed a ballot containing the titles of the three books to rank in order from their first choice to their last choice. After voting, Mr. Jackson collected the ballots. He tallied the votes to form three literature circle groups with 8 to 10 students each. Students, wherever possible, were given their first choice literature circle selection. Next, Mr. Jackson met with each of the three groups for about 5 minutes to decide how many pages in the books each group will read before the next literature circle meeting and how students will respond to their reading. After the meeting of the second group, Mr. Jackson overhears a conversation between two children.

"Wow, this is going to be fun. We get to read books we choose. We get to talk about the books and do projects of all kinds. I think I'm going to like this."

"Me too," intones the other student.

The teacher in this class realizes the multiple benefits of "marinating" children in books and talk about text.

BACKGROUND BRIEFING FOR TEACHERS

Basal readers or core reading programs have dominated reading instruction in the United States for many years. More and more teachers in America's classrooms are using children's literature as a primary vehicle for teaching literacy skills (Morrow & Gambrell, 2000). Several researchers have documented a 20% increase in the use of literature as the primary means for providing reading instruction over a period of the past two decades (Gambrell, 1992; Strickland, Walmsley, Bronk, & Weiss, 1994). This trend is also evident in current basal reading series or core reading programs that contain many reprinted excerpts of award-winning literature (Hoffman, McCarthey, Abbott, Christian, Corman, Curry, et al., 1994; Reutzel & Larsen, 1995). One of the leading basal publishers, in fact, paid well over $50 million in royalties to children's book authors to cover the cost of reprinting their stories!

One of the most exciting changes in today's literacy instruction is a movement away from the traditional assumption that each text holds only one correct meaning or interpretation (Beach, 1997; Galda, Ash, & Cullinan, 2000; Marshall, 2000, Rogers, 1997). For both the child and the teacher, this assumption transforms the act of understanding a text and reading instruction itself from a pursuit to discover an author's (or, very often, the teacher's) single correct message or theme to discovering meaning based, at least in part, on one's own life experiences.

This alternative assumption about reading and the reading instructional process has resulted in what some call *reader or literature response*. Reader or literature response paradigms present a much more active role for students and teachers in constructing meaning from and with text (Bleich, 1978; Galda, et al., 2000; Marshall, 2000; Rosenblatt, 1978, 1989). Reader response advocates suggest that there are many possible meanings that can be constructed from or using a text, depending upon the reader's background and reaction to the text. Instruction guided by a reader response model or paradigm seeks to balance the influence of a reader's background experiences, beliefs, and purposes for reading with the author's style and intended meaning. The role of the teacher is to assist children to develop a creative product—usually a written or some other means of response—that explains their understandings of the author's message in the text.

Literature-based instruction is characterized by four major elements: (a) a knowledgeable teacher who guides children enthusiastically through the literature, (b) a classroom environment and teaching practices that encourage talk about the literature, (c) a teacher who encourages students to make choices about books, and (d) time and access to materials to read and respond (Galda, Cullinan, & Strickland, 1993; Galda, et al., 2000; Turner & Paris, 1995). Literature-based reading instruction, coupled with reader response activities, seems to hold great promise for all readers (Marshall, 2000; Morrow, 1992; Morrow, Pressley, Smith, & Smith, 1997; Reutzel & Cooter, 1990; Reutzel, Oda, & Moore, 1989). Increasing numbers of teachers who work with struggling readers are catching the spirit and excitement of using children's literature and response activities to spark reading among reluctant readers. Excellent results are reported from around the nation in which students with reading problems are discovering anew the joy of reading and writing with real books rather than struggling to learn to read with the often sterile, controlled readers used in the past (Goatley, 1996; Goatley, Brock, & Raphael, 1995; Goatley & Raphael, 1992; Morrow & Gambrell, 2000; Tunnell & Jacobs, 1989).

READER RESPONSE THEORY

Many teachers were reared with the tenets of *critical formalism* or *new criticism* in their elementary, secondary, and postsecondary literature study experiences. As undergraduate and graduate students, many of us were taught to admire and practice the close and critical reading of poetry and prose. As we read, the text was considered an isolated object that we should objectively and dispassionately prepare to discuss and analyze. Literature study from this perspective was like examining a glass prism by carefully turning it about in space to consider it from all possible points of view. If we merely turned it and handled it, we would not alter the work's integrity. Hence, literature was to be processed as an object separate from its social, political, or historical context. This approach to literature study occurred without the influence of the reader or the writer transacting with one another as in a conversation. It was a rather sterile analysis of the text with attention directed toward genre and structure, as well as to such stylistic devices as mood, imagery, and metaphor. Christenbury (1992) captured the feeling of this approach when he wrote, "What for us was a celebration of the intricate art of literature for our students became a repugnant dissection of an already difficult text, robbing it of joy, making it a task, not a connection to life" (p. 34).

Out of an increasing sense of dissatisfaction with the *new criticism* approach to literature study, Norman Holland (1975) and David Bleich (1978) proposed a more subjective position, called *subjective criticism,* stating that the reader was of greater importance than the literature selection itself. This position, however, became as equally untenable as the former position in that it emphasized the singular importance of the reader.

Rosenblatt's (1978) transactional theory declared reading and literature study to be a carefully orchestrated relationship or transaction between reader and text. Reader response evolved, in part, out of the work of Rosenblatt (Kelly, 1990). A transaction suggests a special type of relationship between the reader and the text—an act that causes the reader to be motivated to construct a personal meaning for a particular text. Situational conditions, such as time, mood, pressures, reason, intents, and purposes for reading, influence a reader's stance, or attitude, toward a piece of literature. Rosenblatt described two stances—efferent and aesthetic—in discussing how readers may choose to focus their attention during reading.

Efferent Stance

When readers focus their attention on information to be remembered from reading a text, they are taking an efferent stance. For example, reading the driver's license manual in preparation for an upcoming driving examination exemplifies an efferent stance toward reading a text. Similarly, reading a novel for the purpose of writing a book report that summarizes the plot is another example of taking an efferent stance toward reading text. Thus, when readers assume an efferent stance toward a novel, the focus of their attention is riveted upon memorizing or gleaning information from the text to pass a test rather than upon enjoying and learning from the experience. Obviously then, there is a need for another type of reader stance or motivation for reading a text—an aesthetic stance.

Aesthetic Stance

When adopting an aesthetic stance, the reader draws on past experiences and connects these experiences to the text; often savors the beauty of the literary art form; and becomes an integral participant in the unfolding events of the text. When reading John Scieszka's *The True Story of the Three Little Pigs* to students—even college students—they seldom if ever remark how the text follows accepted narrative form or contains three major repetitive plot episodes! Instead, they connect the zany perspective of the wolf's account and their own past experiences with the original tale of *The Three Little Pigs.* Arising from the bizarre twist of perspectives represented between the two stories, the humor of these perspectives often produces gales of laughter among students as they see the story through the eyes of the character "A. Wolf." Assuming an aesthetic stance toward a text leads readers to make personal connections; report feelings and images; and form ideas about how the elements of the story may occur in our their lives.

The quality or validity of readers' responses is often a concern for teachers who have been schooled in the "single correct" interpretation of *new criticism.* "How can we determine if a response to a text is valid?" is an oft-asked question. Karolides (1992) explained that the validity of a response depends on the degree to which an individual response

- includes the various features of the text and the nuances of language,
- includes aspects that do not reflect the text, and
- leads the reader to create a coherent reaction.

In discussions of texts as a whole class or when sharing responses in small groups called *literature circles,* students are often led into *grand conversations* about literature (Daniels, 1994; Peterson & Eeds, 1990; Tompkins, 2001). During these grand conversations, students are exposed to a range of possible personal responses to a text. Such grand conversations can *motivate* students to extend, clarify, and understand their own reactions to the text (Dahl & Freppon, 1995; Gerla, 1996; Turner & Paris, 1995). Further, research has shown that when children compare their responses to those of peers, this process can help them recognize that there may be more than one valid interpretation of a text (Galda et al., 2000; King, 2001; Martinez-Roldan & Lopez-Robertson, 2000; Morrow & Gambrell, 2000; Wood, Roser, & Martinez, 2001).

So far, this chapter has provided teachers with necessary information to understand the shift away from a *new criticism,* text-centered, literature-as-object-of-instruction paradigm toward a contemporary view of using text to stimulate discussion and interactions that lead to socially constructed interpretations of text paradigms in which quality texts and active readers are brought together. In the next section of this chapter, we discuss several informal assessment tools that can help teachers determine where students are in their reading development and understanding of text. Following our discussion of literature response assessment tools, we offer evidence-based or classroom-experience-based strategies for helping students to respond to written text in ways that greatly enhance their vocabulary, comprehension, and composition and develop personal tools and strategies for engaging in productive interactions with others around a variety of literature selections.

ASSESSING READERS' RESPONSES TO LITERATURE

Assessing children's responses to literature focuses on several different dimensions. First, responding to literature is intended to ensure that children deepen and broaden their comprehension of the materials they read. A second dimension of assessing participation in literature response groups or literature circles focuses on individual and group preparation for and participation in literature response groups or literature circles. Third, literature response participation is expected to positively influence children's attitudes toward reading. So then, assessing attitude is an important part of examining the impact of literature response participation on students' engagement and motivation. A fourth dimension of assessing students' participations in literature circles or response groups centers on carefully observing students' interactions around the selections during literature discussion and during independent reading time. Finally, we provide a tool for assessing student cooperation, collaboration, and teamwork during literature response group meetings. By using the combination of these assessment tools, teachers can gain a comprehensive understanding of their students' engagement with literature, the quality of the literature discussions, and the resultant understandings constructed around text.

LITERATURE RESPONSE READING COMPREHENSION ASSESSMENT

Purpose

Teachers building balanced reading programs using trade books quickly find that they must construct minilessons and assessment strategies to account for reading skills to be taught. Angeletti (1991) developed a way to engage children in a blend of reading, writing, and talking about books that yielded the necessary skill-based accountability demanded today in many schools, districts, states, and basal readers as a result of the No Child Left Behind Act (2001). Although originally conceived of as a teaching strategy, Angeletti's approach to questioning during literature circles is quite effective as an outcomes assessment procedure for measuring students' text understandings.

Materials

For this activity, you will need standard-size (8½" × 11") white letter paper, 11" × 14" colored construction paper, and a marker. If available, a computer with a word processing program and printer with large font or type size should be used for best results. Question cards should be produced similar to those shown in Figure 15.1.

Procedure

Begin by printing the question cards on white paper and mounting each question card on a colored construction paper backing. Next, pick a type of questioning you wish to emphasize. During shared reading or literature circle study, ask children questions of this chosen type for several days. After this, show the children the question card you have selected for emphasis. Model with a book how the question could be answered. Follow the modeling with whole-class practice using a shared book approach. Finally, practice in small groups and individually. Encourage students to select a question card to guide the construction of their responses in a literature log. Each of these responses to question cards can be judged against the type of "comprehension skill" represented by the question for documenting skill acquisition and instruction.

LITERATURE STUDY PREPARATION AND PARTICIPATION EVALUATION RECORD

Purpose

Although many teachers recognize the value of literature study groups (also called literature study circles), they often feel a need to satisfy the political realities of documenting student progress and growth as a result of their teaching. One means for doing this is to develop a checklist outlining the expectations for those who participate in literature study groups. Such a checklist can be used to assess student readiness or preparation prior to participation in the literature study group as well as to yield qualitative information about each student's participation during the literature study group (Peterson & Eeds, 1990).

Materials

The "Literature Study Preparation and Participation Evaluation Record" shown in Figure 15.2 is the main item needed for this activity.

Procedure

One form should be duplicated for each student in the literature study group. We recommend that the "Preparation" section be completed prior to participation and reevaluated at the conclusion of the literature study session. The "Participation" section should then be completed at the end of the literature study to evaluate each participant. Other items may be added to Figure 15.2 to tailor its use to individual classroom needs.

GROUP LITERATURE DISCUSSION CHECKLIST

Purpose

Although many teachers are coming to recognize the value of literature-based reading instruction, they also feel a need to satisfy the political realities of documenting student progress as a result of using literature to teach children to read (Hoyt, 1999). One means for doing this is to use a group checklist that outlines the qualities of young children's

Figure 15.1 Question Cards

Comparison and contrast card 1
Choose two characters from one story. Do the characters look alike? How are they alike? How are they different? What problems do the two characters have that are the same? How are the feelings of the characters different?

Comparison and contrast card 2
Choose two stories. How were the places where the stories took place alike or different? How were the stories the same? How were they different? How were the story endings different? Which story did you like better? Why? Which character did you like better? Why?

Opinions
What did you like about the main character? What did the character do that made you like him or her? What did you think about the ending? Was anything surprising to you in the story? What was it? Why were you surprised?

Inference
Look at the pictures and at the title. What do you know about the story before you begin to read it? Read the story. Think about the ending. If the story had continued, what might have happened? Why?

Drawing conclusions
Draw a picture of your favorite character. Tell as much as you can about what kind of person your character is. Tell things he or she did in the story. Is this a nice person? Why or why not? Would you like to have this person for a friend? Why or why not?

Characters
As you read a story, you learn about the characters by what they say and do. Choose a character from your story. What kind of person is your character? Do you like him or her? Why? How would he or she act if you were with him or her?

Author's style
Every writer has his or her own way of writing, called *style*. When we learn the author's style, we know what to expect from that writer. We often know whether books written by a particular author will be easy picture books or chapter books. We know what kind of characters are typical of the writer—animals that talk, or people like us. We might know whether there will be a happy ending. We know whether we would enjoy reading another book by the same author. Choose an author whose style you know and tell what you know about the author's style of writing. Give examples from books you have read by that author.

Author's purpose
Sometimes authors write a story to teach you something. Sometimes they tell a story about something that happened to them. Sometimes they just want to entertain you. Or, they may have another reason for writing. Tell in one sentence why you think the author wrote the story you read. Then tell how you knew the author's reason for writing the story.

Type of literature
Tell what kind of book you are reading. Look for clues that let you know. If it is *fantasy*, or *fiction*, for example, there may be animals that talk, or magic things may happen. If it is *realistic fiction*, there may be real people in the story and the story could have happened, but the author made it up, perhaps using ideas from his or her own life. If you find rhyming words, short lines, and writing that makes every word count, you are reading *poetry*. Or, you may be reading facts from a book like an encyclopedia. If so, the book is *factual*. Think about what section of the library you would go to in order to find the book. Then put your book into one group and tell what clues let you know which type of book it is.

Source: Adapted from "Encouraging Students to Think About What They Read" by S. R. Angeletti, 1991, *The Reading Teacher, 45*(4), 288–296. Copyright 1991 by the International Reading Association.

Figure 15.2   Literature Study Preparation and Participation Evaluation Record

Record of Preparation for and Participation in Literature Study*

Name: _____   Date: _____

Author: _____   Title: _____

Preparation for Literature Study

Brought book to group	Yes _____	No _____
Contributed to developing a group reading plan	Yes _____	No _____
Worked according to group reading plan	Yes _____	No _____
Read the book	Yes _____	No _____
Took note of places to share (ones of interest, ones that were puzzling, etc.)	Yes _____	No _____
Did nightly assignments as they arose from the day's discussion	Yes _____	No _____

Participation in Literature Study

Overall participation in the dialogue	Weak _____	Good _____	Excellent _____
Overall quality of responses	Weak _____	Good _____	Excellent _____
Referred to text to support ideas and to clarify	Weak _____	Good _____	Excellent _____
Listened to others and modified responses where appropriate	Weak _____	Good _____	Excellent _____
_____ **	Weak _____	Good _____	Excellent _____
_____ **	Weak _____	Good _____	Excellent _____
_____ **	Weak _____	Good _____	Excellent _____

*We suggest using this form at the end of each literature study to evaluate each participant.

**The rest of the items are intended to tailor this evaluation to your individual students. Choose appropriate items to complete the form from those listed in the Response to Literature Checklist in Figure 15.4 or add those you think are most appropriate.

Source: From *Grand Conversations: Literature Groups in Action,* by R. Peterson and M. Eeds, 1990, New York: Scholastic.

participation in quality literature discussions before, during, or after interactive read-aloud or shared reading sessions. Such a checklist is used to assess overall student participation in the literature discussion as well as to yield qualitative information about each student's participation (Peterson & Eeds, 1990; Vogt, 1996).

Materials

The "Group Literature Discussion Checklist" shown in Figure 15.3 is the main item needed for this activity.

Procedure

One form should be duplicated for each student in the literature study group. We recommend that each participant complete the form at the conclusion of the literature study session. After reviewing the completed forms, the teacher should lead a discussion of the group's evaluation of the session and point out areas where improvement can be made in the future.

Figure 15.3 Group Literature Discussion Checklist

Title of Book Discussed _____ Author _____

Date _____

Put an "X" on the face that tells what you feel.

Everyone was prepared to discuss the book.	☺	😐	☹
Everyone contributed to the discussion.	☺	😐	☹
We kept our talk focused on the book.	☺	😐	☹
We asked good questions that helped us all think.	☺	😐	☹
We used the book to support our opinions and ideas.	☺	😐	☹
We were respectful of others having a turn to talk.	☺	😐	☹
We invited our peers to talk and express their ideas.	☺	😐	☹
We talked about how the author had structured the writing.	☺	😐	☹
We talked about how the author used words and language.	☺	😐	☹

STUDENT RESPONSE TO LITERATURE CHECKLIST

Purpose

Teachers want to know if children are making personal connections between their own lives and experiences and those recorded in the books they are reading. Some teachers may want to assess whether students are interpreting and making meaning or are gaining insights in a story as they read. Peterson and Eeds (1990) developed a "Student Response to Literature Checklist" that we have found particularly helpful in providing documentation of the way in which children respond to particular stories or books within that programmatic framework.

Materials

Copies of the "Student Response to Literature Checklist" in Figure 15.4 are needed for each student for this activity.

Procedure

A copy of the checklist should be made for each student. We recommend that the teacher not try to evaluate all students in every area of the checklist daily. Instead, select one or two students each day to observe (preferably without their knowledge). For example, you may decide to observe two students as they select and read books during silent sustained reading (SSR) time while they are at their seats or in a reading nook. Then, for each of these students, you could complete Section I of the checklist: Enjoyment/Involvement. Another example of applying the checklist may include reading a student's reading log entry. You could determine whether the student was making sense of the reading or making personal connections. In this case, Section II, Making Personal Connections, and Section III, Interpretation/Making Meaning, would be used to assess the student's response to literature. Thus, the checklist should be used flexibly; teachers should not feel obligated to complete the checklist for every child during every observation. Instead, observations should be focused and selective.

ELEMENTARY READING ATTITUDE SURVEY

Purpose

Developing positive attitudes toward reading and writing is the primary instructional goal for teachers of children. This is particularly true for teachers who work with readers having learning problems. Assessing the impact of using real books on their students' reading and writing attitudes, however, can be challenging.

Over the years, several informal attitude measures have been developed and validated for classroom use. Heathington and Alexander (1978) developed a primary and intermediate scale of reading attitude assessment. More recently, McKenna and Kear (1990) developed and validated an instrument that is simple and effective for measuring reading attitudes. They incorporated into this instrument the Garfield cartoon character, but other characters—or figures ranging from smiling faces to frowning faces—may be substituted. The Elementary Reading Attitude Survey (ERAS) has been developed with and used in studies with virtually tens of thousands of children to investigate attitudes toward reading, literature-based instruction versus basal instruction, comprehension strategy instruction, and other reading reforms (McKenna, Kear, & Ellsworth, 1995; McKenna, Stratton, Grindler, & Jenkins, 1995; Reutzel, Smith, & Fawson, in press).

McKenna and Kear (1990) report Cronbach's alpha, internal consistency coefficients ranging from .74 to .89 for the two subscales (academic and recreational reading) of the ERAS instrument. Construct validity for the ERAS instrument was established by studying the recreational reading subscale scores of library card holders versus non–library card

Figure 15.4 Student Response to Literature Checklist

I. Enjoyment/Involvement

_____ Is aware of a variety of reading materials and can select those he enjoys reading
_____ Enjoys looking at pictures in picture story books
_____ Responds with emotion to text: laughs, cries, smiles
_____ Can get "lost" in a book
_____ Chooses to read during free time
_____ Wants to go on reading when time is up
_____ Shares reading experiences with classmates
_____ Has books on hand to read
_____ Chooses books in different genres

II. Making Personal Connections

_____ Seeks meaning in both pictures and the text in picture story books
_____ Can identify the works of authors that he enjoys
_____ Sees literature as a way of knowing about the world
_____ Draws on personal experiences in constructing meaning
_____ Draws on earlier reading experiences in making meaning from a text

III. Interpretation/Making Meaning

_____ Gets beyond "I like" in talking about story
_____ Makes comparisons between the works of individual authors and among the works of different authors
_____ Appreciates the value of pictures in picture story books and uses them to interpret story meaning
_____ Asks questions and seeks the help of others to clarify meaning
_____ Makes reasonable predictions about what will happen in a story
_____ Can disagree without disrupting the dialogue
_____ Can follow information important to getting to the meaning of the story
_____ Attends to multiple levels of meaning
_____ Is willing to think about and search out alternative points of view
_____ Values other perspectives as a means for increasing interpretative possibilities
_____ Turns to text to verify and clarify ideas
_____ Can modify interpretations in light of "new evidence"
_____ Can make implied relationships not stated in the text
_____ Can make statements about an author's intent drawn from the total work
_____ Is secure enough to put forward half-baked ideas to benefit from others' response

IV. Insight Into Story Elements

_____ Is growing in awareness of how elements function in story
_____ Can talk meaningfully about
　　　characters
　　　setting
　　　mood
　　　incident
　　　structure
　　　symbol
　　　time
　　　tensions
_____ Draws on elements when interpreting text/constructing meaning with others
_____ Uses elements of literature in working to improve upon personal writing
_____ Is intrigued by how authors work
_____ Makes use of elements in making comparisons

Source: From _Grand Conversations: Literature Groups in Action,_ by R. Peterson and M. Eeds, 1990, New York: Scholastic.

holders. ERAS recreational reading scores for the library card holders were significantly different from non–library card holders. Similarly, ERAS recreational reading subscale scores were compared between those students who reported watching one hour of television per night versus those who reported watching 2 or more hours of television per night. Once again there was a significant difference between these two groups. Correlations between the two subscales of the ERAS (academic and recreational) accounted for about 41% of the variance between academic and recreational reading with a correlation coefficient of .64. Finally, factor analyses were conducted demonstrating that the questions on the ERAS survey loaded heavily upon two factors supporting the recreational and academic reading subscales.

Materials

For each student, materials needed include one copy of the Elementary Reading Attitude Survey shown in Figure 15.5 and one copy of the Elementary Reading Attitude Survey Scoring Sheet shown in Figure 15.6.

Procedure

Attitude Survey Directions for the instrument (Figure 15.7) are those described by McKenna and Kear (1990). We suggest that you follow these instructions carefully so that the interpretive information found in Figure 15.8 can then be used.

DAILY READING RECORD

Purpose

Simple and easy-to-keep records of daily reading can give teachers an idea about how well students are progressing in developing positive reading habits. By using a version of the daily reading record shown in Figure 15.9, students also develop a greater sense of their own reading habits. Thus, these records provide documentation of how well students use their time for reading as well as inducing in students a sense of pride in what they are accomplishing.

A daily reading record should have a place to list the author(s) and title of the book as well as the date, time, and pages read. In addition, a brief written response may be encouraged but is not usually required on the daily reading record.

Materials

For each child, one copy of the Daily Reading Record form found in Figure 15.9 is needed.

Procedure

A time at the end of each day's literature study period should be allocated for student record keeping. During this brief period of 2 to 4 minutes, students should log into their daily reading records the information required and be encouraged to write a brief response if they desire. The teacher should review students' daily reading record forms at least weekly. We encourage teachers to avoid giving undue emphasis to the numbers of books read, recognizing instead the quality of the reading experience. Remember that "savoring" a good book takes time, just as fine food should be relished with appreciation.

Figure 15.5   Elementary Reading Attitude Survey

School: _____   Grade: _____   Name: _____

1. How do you feel when you read a book on a rainy Saturday?

2. How do you feel when you read a book in school during free time?

3. How do you feel about reading for fun at home?

Note: GARFIELD © PAWS

continued

Figure 15.5 Continued

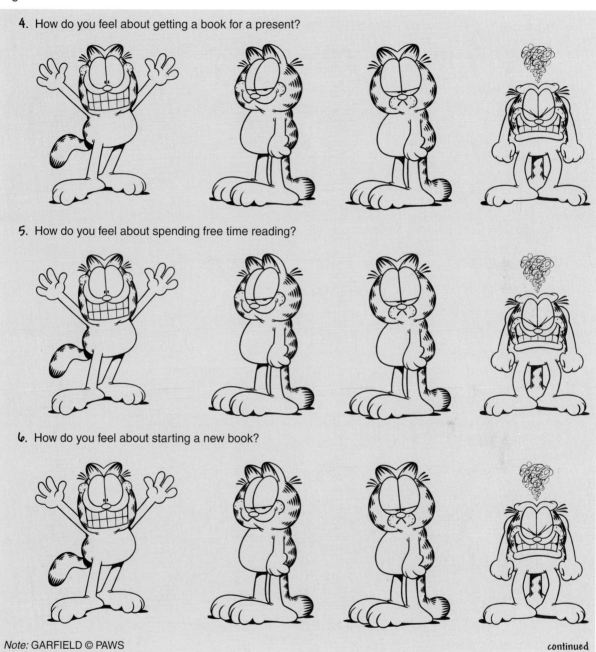

4. How do you feel about getting a book for a present?

5. How do you feel about spending free time reading?

6. How do you feel about starting a new book?

Note: GARFIELD © PAWS

continued

Figure 15.5   Continued

7. How do you feel about reading during summer vacation?

8. How do you feel about reading instead of playing?

9. How do you feel about going to a bookstore?

Note: GARFIELD © PAWS

continued

Figure 15.5 Continued

10. How do you feel about reading different kinds of books?

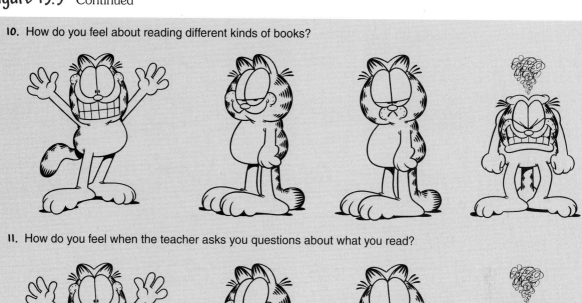

11. How do you feel when the teacher asks you questions about what you read?

12. How do you feel about doing reading workbook pages and worksheets?

Note: GARFIELD © PAWS

continued

Figure 15.5   Continued

13. How do you feel about reading in school?

14. How do you feel about reading your schoolbooks?

15. How do you feel about learning from a book?

Note: GARFIELD © PAWS

continued

Figure 15.5 Continued

16. How do you feel when it's time for reading class?

17. How do you feel about the stories you read in reading class?

18. How do you feel when you read aloud in class?

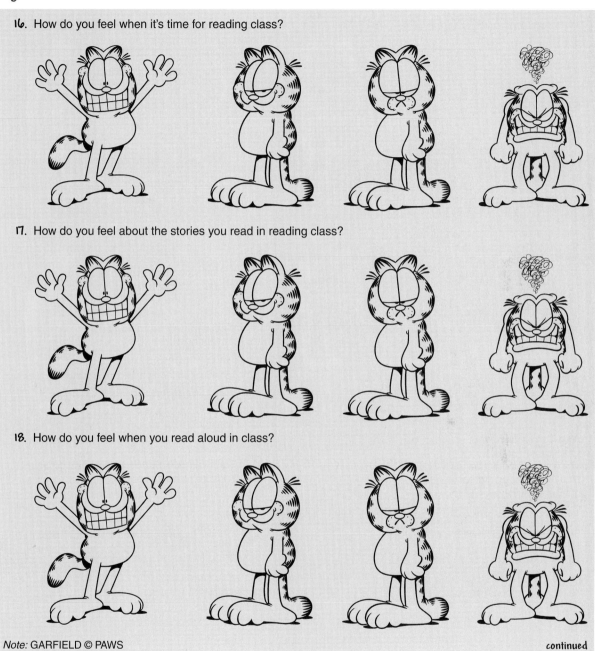

Note: GARFIELD © PAWS

continued

Figure 15.5   Continued

19. How do you feel about using a dictionary?

20. How do you feel about taking a reading class?

Note: GARFIELD © PAWS

Source: Elementary Reading Attitude Survey, by Michael C. McKenna, and Dennis J. Kear, 1990, May. Measuring attitude toward reading: A new tool for teachers. *The Reading Teacher 43*(9), 626–639. Copyright © 1990 by Michael C. McKenna and the International Reading Association. All rights reserved.

Observing Student Interactions With Books Checklist

Purpose

Teachers often observe the frequency and types of books students choose to read, but many do not keep records about when children choose to read, how frequently they read, and what types of books they select. To monitor and assist children in their book selections, we provide the Observing Student Interactions With Books Checklist. This checklist can be used to determine if children are selecting books that present them with an appropriate level of challenge as well as linking to their interests (see chapter 10 for a student interest survey). Teachers can, by using this assessment tool, observe how children use books as models for writing and as support for discussion in literature circles (Daniels, 1994; Hoyt, 1999; Spiegel, 1998; Wood et al., 2001).

Figure 15.6   Elementary Reading Attitude Survey Scoring Sheet

Student name: _____

Teacher: _____

Grade: _____   Administration date: _____

	Scoring guide	
4 points	Happiest Garfield
3 points	Slightly smiling Garfield
2 points	Mildly upset Garfield
1 point	Very upset Garfield

Recreational reading

1. _____
2. _____
3. _____
4. _____
5. _____
6. _____
7. _____
8. _____
9. _____
10. _____

Academic reading

11. _____
12. _____
13. _____
14. _____
15. _____
16. _____
17. _____
18. _____
19. _____
20. _____

Raw score: _____   Raw score: _____

Full scale raw score (Recreational + Academic): _____

Percentile ranks   Recreational

Academic

Full scale

Figure 15.7   Attitude Survey Directions

Directions for Use of Elementary Reading Attitude Survey

The *Elementary Reading Attitude Survey* provides a quick indication of student attitudes toward reading. It consists of 20 items and can be administered to an entire classroom in about 10 minutes. Each item presents a brief, simply worded statement about reading, followed by four pictures of Garfield. Each pose is designed to depict a different emotional state, ranging from very positive to very negative.

Administration

Begin by telling students that you wish to find out how they feel about reading. Emphasize that this is not a test and that there are no "right" answers. Encourage sincerity.

Distribute the survey forms and, if you wish to monitor the attitudes of specific students, ask them to write their names in the space at the top. Hold up a copy of the survey so that the students can see the first page. Point to the picture of Garfield at the far left of the first item. Ask the students to look at this same picture on their own survey forms. Discuss with them the mood Garfield seems to be in (very happy). Then move to the next picture and again discuss Garfield's mood (this time, a little happy). In the same way, move to the third and fourth pictures and talk about Garfield's moods—a little upset and very upset. It is helpful to point out the position of Garfield's mouth, especially in the middle two figures.

Explain that together you will read some statements about reading and that the students should think about how they feel about each statement. They should then circle the picture of Garfield that is closest to their own feelings. (Emphasize that the students should respond according to their own feelings, not as Garfield might respond!) Read each item aloud slowly and distinctly; then read it a second time while students are thinking. Be sure to read the item number and to remind students of page numbers when new pages are reached.

Scoring

To score the survey, count four points for each leftmost (happiest) Garfield circled, three for each slightly smiling Garfield, two for each mildly upset Garfield, and one point for each very upset (right-most) Garfield. Three scores for each student can be obtained: the total for the first 10 items, the total for the second 10, and a composite total. The first half of the survey relates to attitude toward recreational reading; the second half relates to attitude toward academic aspects of reading.

Interpretation

You can interpret scores in two ways. One is to note informally where the score falls in regard to the four nodes of the scale. A total score of 50, for example, would fall about midway on the scale, between the slightly happy and slightly upset figures, therefore indicating a relatively indifferent overall attitude toward reading. The other approach is more formal. It involves converting the raw scores into percentile ranks by means of Figure 15.8. Be sure to use the norms for the right grade level and to note the column headings (*Rec* = recreational reading, *Aca* = academic reading, *Tot* = total raw score). If you wish to determine the average percentile rank for your class, average the raw scores first; then use the figure to locate the percentile rank corresponding to the raw score mean. Percentile ranks cannot be averaged directly.

Source: From Elementary Reading Attitude Survey, by Michael C. McKenna, and Dennis J. Kear, 1990, May. Measuring attitude toward reading: A new tool for teachers. *The Reading Teacher, 43*(9), 626–639. Copyright © 1990 by Michael C. McKenna and the International Reading Association. All rights reserved.

Figure 15.8 Interpretive Information for Survey.

Midyear Percentile Ranks by Grade and Scale

Raw Scr	Grade 1 Rec Aca Tot	Grade 2 Rec Aca Tot	Grade 3 Rec Aca Tot	Grade 4 Rec Aca Tot	Grade 5 Rec Aca Tot	Grade 6 Rec Aca Tot
80	99	99	99	99	99	99
79	95	96	98	99	99	99
78	93	95	97	98	99	99
77	92	94	97	98	99	99
76	90	93	96	97	98	99
75	88	92	95	96	98	99
74	86	90	94	95	97	99
73	84	88	92	94	97	98
72	82	86	91	93	96	98
71	80	84	89	91	95	97
70	78	81	86	89	94	96
69	75	79	84	88	92	95
68	72	77	81	86	91	93
67	69	74	79	83	89	92
66	66	71	76	80	87	90
65	62	69	73	78	84	88
64	59	66	70	75	82	86
63	55	63	67	72	79	84
62	52	60	64	69	76	82
61	49	57	61	66	73	79
60	46	54	58	62	70	76
59	43	51	55	59	67	73
58	40	47	51	56	64	69
57	37	45	48	53	61	66
56	34	41	44	48	57	62
55	31	38	41	45	53	58
54	28	35	38	41	50	55
53	25	32	34	38	46	52
52	22	29	31	35	42	48
51	20	26	28	32	39	44
50	18	23	25	28	36	40
49	15	20	23	26	33	37
48	13	18	20	23	29	33
47	12	15	17	20	26	30
46	10	13	15	18	23	27

continued

Figure 15.8 Continued

Midyear Percentile Ranks by Grade and Scale

Raw Scr	Grade 1 Rec	Aca	Tot	Grade 2 Rec	Aca	Tot	Grade 3 Rec	Aca	Tot	Grade 4 Rec	Aca	Tot	Grade 5 Rec	Aca	Tot	Grade 6 Rec	Aca	Tot
45			8			11			13			16			20			25
44			7			9			11			13			17			22
43			6			8			9			12			15			20
42			5			7			8			10			13			17
41			5			6			7			9			12			15
40	99	99	4	99	99	5	99	99	6	99	99	7	99	99	10	99	99	13
39	92	91	3	94	94	4	96	97	5	97	98	6	98	99	9	99	99	12
38	89	88	3	92	92	3	94	95	4	95	97	5	96	98	8	97	99	10
37	86	85	2	88	89	2	90	93	3	92	95	4	94	98	7	96	99	8
36	81	79	2	84	85	2	87	91	2	88	93	3	91	96	6	92	98	7
35	77	75	1	79	81	1	81	88	2	84	90	3	87	95	4	88	97	6
34	72	69	1	75	78	1	75	83	2	78	87	2	82	93	4	83	95	5
33	65	63	1	68	73	1	69	79	1	72	83	2	77	90	3	79	93	4
32	58	58	1	62	67	1	63	74	1	66	79	1	71	86	3	74	91	3
31	82	53	1	56	62	1	57	69	0	60	75	1	65	82	2	69	87	2
30	44	49	1	50	57	0	51	63	0	54	70	1	59	77	1	63	82	2
29	38	44	0	44	51	0	45	58	0	47	64	1	53	71	1	58	78	1
28	32	39	0	37	46	0	38	52	0	41	58	1	48	66	1	51	73	1
27	26	34	0	31	41	0	33	47	0	35	52	1	42	60	1	46	67	1
26	21	30	0	25	37	0	26	41	0	29	46	0	36	54	0	39	60	1
25	17	25	0	20	32	0	21	36	0	23	40	0	30	49	0	34	54	0
24	12	21	0	15	27	0	17	31	0	19	35	0	25	42	0	29	49	0
23	9	18	0	11	23	0	13	26	0	14	29	0	20	37	0	24	42	0
22	7	14	0	8	18	0	9	22	0	11	25	0	16	31	0	19	36	0
21	5	11	0	6	15	0	6	18	0	99	20	0	13	26	0	15	30	0
20	4	9	0	4	11	0	5	14	0	6	16	0	10	21	0	12	24	0
19	2	7		2	8		3	11		5	13		7	17		10	20	
18	2	5		2	6		2	8		3	9		6	13		8	15	
17	1	4		1	5		1	5		2	7		4	9		6	11	
16	1	3		1	3		1	4		2	5		3	6		4	8	
15	0	2		0	2		0	3		1	3		2	4		3	6	
14	0	2		0	1		0	1		1	2		1	2		1	3	
13	0	1		0	1		0	1		0	1		1	2		1	2	
12	0	1		0	0		0	0		0	1		0	1		0	1	
11	0	0		0	0		0	0		0	0		0	0		0	0	
10	0	0		0	0		0	0		0	0		0	0		0	0	

Figure 15.9 Daily Reading Record

Student Reading Record Sheet

My Reading Record   Name: _____

Date	Pages Read	Title	Author	Time Spent Reading

Figure 15.10 Observing Student Interactions With Books Checklist

Student's Name _____ Date of Observation _____

1. Child chooses to read when finished with assignments.

   Often   Sometimes   Seldom

2. Child selects books that are appropriate and interesting.

   Often   Sometimes   Seldom

3. Child talks about the books selected with others.

   Often   Sometimes   Seldom

4. Child explains why he likes or dislikes a book.

   Often   Sometimes   Seldom

5. Child listens to other children talk about books.

   Often   Sometimes   Seldom

6. Child responds to reading books in a variety of ways.

   Often   Sometimes   Seldom

7. Child talks about the author's writing.

   Often   Sometimes   Seldom

8. Child explains how the book is organized.

   Often   Sometimes   Seldom

9. Child can retell the major points of the book.

   Often   Sometimes   Seldom

10. Child connects to his own experience when discussing a book.

    Often   Sometimes   Seldom

Materials

One copy of the Observing Student Interactions With Books Checklist (Figure 15.10) for each child in the classroom is needed.

Procedures

Observe children at least twice each reporting period (9 weeks) using the Observing Student Interactions With Books Checklist. Make note of the areas in which children are progressing and those in which students need assistance, instruction, or encouragement. This checklist is also useful as a part of individual reading conferences held as a part of the reading workshop.

GROUP FEEDBACK ON LITERATURE DISCUSSIONS

Purpose

Sometimes it is important for students to see their own learning and participation through the eyes of their peers. For some students, such a process is not only a reality check but also an opportunity to interact in positive ways and to extend support to individuals within the group. By engaging in peer feedback and accountability, literature discussion groups and the individuals within these groups create and maintain a spirit of healthy interdependence (Johnson & Johnson, 1995; Slavin, 1999).

Materials

An example of a teammate individual feedback form is shown in Figure 15.11. This or a modified version can be duplicated and distributed to teams to be completed at the conclusion of daily cooperative group activities.

Procedure

The Group Feedback on Literature Discussions form shown in Figure 15.11 is given on a periodic (usually weekly) basis to students within a group or partnership to be filled out on another individual. Next, partners or teammates share their comments and rating with the individual they evaluated. Encouragement in weak areas should be given and praise should be offered for the many and varied contributions the partner or teammate makes to the successful completion of group goals and tasks. Teachers should first model the types of responses and verbal feedback to be offered during discussions.

In Figure 15.12, we summarize the literature response assessment procedures and instruments we have discussed thus far and provide summary information about federally

Figure 15.11 Group Feedback on Literature Discussions

Student Peer Name _____

Evaluator Name _____

1. My friend offers facts, opinions, or ideas to help the group discussion.

    Usually   Frequently   Seldom   Never

2. My friend expresses a willingness to cooperate with other group members.

    Usually   Frequently   Seldom   Never

3. My friend supports group members who are struggling to participate in the group.

    Usually   Frequently   Seldom   Never

4. My friend listens carefully and respectfully to others in the group when they express themselves.

    Usually   Frequently   Seldom   Never

5. My friend evaluates the contributions of other group members in terms of usefulness and correctness.

    Usually   Frequently   Seldom   Never

6. My friend takes risks to express new ideas and feelings during a group discussion.

    Usually   Frequently   Seldom   Never

7. My friend expresses awareness of and appreciation for the gifts, talents, abilities, and skills of other group members.

    Usually   Frequently   Seldom   Never

8. My friend offers support and help to other team members.

    Usually   Frequently   Seldom   Never

9. My friend shares materials, books, resources, or information with others to help in the completion of tasks or solving problems.

    Usually   Frequently   Seldom   Never

10. My friend is open and willing to share and participate in the group.

    Usually   Frequently   Seldom   Never

Figure 15.12   Summary Matrix of Engaging in Literature Response Assessments

Name of Assessment Tool	Screening Assessment Purpose	Diagnostic Assessment Purpose	Progress-Monitoring Assessment Purpose	Outcomes Assessment Purpose	Norm-Referenced Test	Criterion-Referenced Test	Reliability Evidence	Validity Evidence
Literature Response Reading Comprehension Assessment	–	–	+	–	–	+	Not Available	Not Available
Literature Study Preparation and Participation Evaluation Record	–	–	+	–	–	+	Not Available	Not Available
Group Literature Discussion Assessment	–	–	+	–	–	+	Not Available	Not Available
Student Response to Literature Checklist	–	–	+	–	–	+	Not Available	Not Available
Elementary Reading Attitude Survey (ERAS)	+	+	–	+	+	–	Cronbach's alpha coefficients ranging from .74 to .89 for the two subscales	Construct validity evidence from outside predictor variable studies and factor analyses
Daily Reading Record	–	–	+	–	–	+	Not Available	Not Available
Observing Student Interactions With Books Checklist	–	–	+	–	–	+	Not Available	Not Available

related assessment purposes (i.e., *screening, diagnosis, progress-monitoring,* or *outcomes assessment*), as well as type of test or procedure and psychometric evidence of test or procedure scores including reliability and/or validity evidence.

CONNECTING ASSESSMENT FINDINGS TO TEACHING STRATEGIES

Before discussing an array of reading and literature response instructional strategies, we have constructed a guide connecting assessment findings to intervention and/or strategy choices. It is our intention to help you, the teacher, select the most appropriate instructional interventions and strategies to meet your students' needs based on assessment data. In the next part of this chapter, we offer strategies for intervention based on the foregoing assessments.

RESPONDING TO READING FOR ALL CHILDREN

After a careful assessment of each student's or each group's reading responses, text comprehension, work habits, interactions and discussions around text, and attitudes as outlined previously, one or more of the following literature or reading response instructional strategies or lesson frameworks may be appropriately applied. Perhaps the most important thing to remember is that children who do not respond or who respond poorly must receive regular opportunities to talk about books, stories, and texts for authentic and motivating reasons, such as to gather information, to present a dramatization, or simply to discuss a favorite story. The strategies described in this section offer effective and varied means for teachers to help children respond to reading in authentic, effective, and motivating ways!

IMAGERY: MAKING MENTAL MOVIES OF TEXT

Purpose

When students make visual images about what they read, the mental "movies" provide an effective framework for organizing, remembering, and constructing meaning from text (Sadoski & Quast, 1990; Wilson & Gambrell, 1988). Unfortunately, some readers with learning problems do not spontaneously create mental movies as they read and thus miss out on the comprehension-monitoring boost that mental movies can give them (Gambrell & Bales, 1986). Wilson and Gambrell (1988) indicated that specific instruction in how and when to apply imagery as a comprehension tool can be extremely helpful for students.

Materials

Activities and materials proposed by Wilson and Gambrell (1988) are summarized in Figure 15.13.

Procedure

Because research on visual imagery tells us that some students do not spontaneously use visual imagery but can when directed to do so, teachers need to provide guidance and

If-Then Strategy Guide for Engaging in Literature Response

"Then" try these teaching strategies. → / "If" the student is ready to learn ↓	Imagery	Literature Circles	Response Journals and Logs	Sketch to Sketch	Multiple Texts and Making Connections	Cooperative Group Rotation	Collaborative Reasoning Discussions	Book Clubs	Author Studies	Drama As Literature Response	Storytelling	Motivating
Story Comprehension	+	*	+	+	*	−	+	*	*	+		*
Enjoyment	*	+	*	+	*	+	*	+	*	+	+	+
Unprepared to Participate	*	+	+	+	+	+	+	+	+	+	+	*
Making Connections	*	*	*	*	*	*	*	*	*	*	*	*
Poor Attitudes	*	*	−	*	−	*	*	*	*	+	+	*
Accountability	+	*	+	*	+	*	*	*	*	*	*	+
Student Participation	*	+	*	*	*	+	+	+	*	*	*	*

Key: + Excellent Strategy
     * Adaptable Strategy
     − Unsuitable Strategy

<u>Figure 15.13</u> Imagery Hints

Hints on Imaging

1. Inform students that making pictures in their minds can help them understand what a story or passage is about. Specific directions, depending upon whether the text is narrative or expository, may be helpful. For example, "Make pictures in your mind of the interesting characters in this story." "Make pictures in your mind about the things that happened in this story." "Make a picture in your mind of our solar system." Using visual imagery in this manner encourages students to integrate information across the text as they engage in constructive processing.

2. Inform students that, when something is difficult to understand, it sometimes helps to try to make a picture in their minds. Using visual imagery can help students clarify meaning, and it encourages them to think about whether they are comprehending.

3. Encourage students to make visual images about stories or information they want to remember. Tell them that making pictures in their minds can help them remember. As a follow-up to story time or the silent reading of basal stories, have students think about the visual images they made and encourage them to use their images to help them retell the story to a partner (or, as homework, to retell the story to a parent or sibling). This activity will help students realize the value of using visual imagery to enhance memory.

practice in the use of imagery. Wilson and Gambrell (1988) recommended the following considerations when selecting materials to be used to encourage visual imagery:

1. For modeling and teacher-guided practice activities, select brief passages of about paragraph length.

2. Choose passages that have strong potential for creating "mental movies" (i.e., those that typically contain rich descriptions of events and objects).

3. Point out that not all text material is easy to visualize—especially when the material is about unfamiliar and abstract concepts. Tell students that in those instances they should select another strategy that would be easier to use and more helpful (be prepared with suggestions that better fit some of the text types they are likely to encounter). With minimal guidance and practice, students can learn and enjoy using visual imagery to enhance their reading experiences.

LITERATURE RESPONSE GROUPS (LITERATURE STUDY CIRCLES)

Purpose

The purpose of literature response groups (also known as literature study circles) is to emphasize the importance of reading and discussing children's literature or trade books (Daniels, 1994; Eeds & Wells, 1989; Peterson & Eeds, 1990; Reutzel & Cooter, 2000; Samway, Whang, Cade, Gamil, Lubandina, & Phommanchanh, 1991; Short, Harste, & Burke, 1988). Samway et al. (1991) reported that many students who participate in literature response groups often go through dramatic changes in just one year.

We noticed that in literature study circles the students naturally and spontaneously compared books and authors, initiated and sustained discussion topics as they arose, built their literary repertoires, and made associations between events and characters in books and their own lives (Reutzel & Cooter, 2000, p. 205). Additionally, our own experiences with literature response groups/study circles have caused us to become great believers in this teaching and learning option.

Figure 15.14   Choice Ballots

Literature Response Groups Choice Ballot

Name: _____

1st choice: _____

2nd choice: _____

3rd choice: _____

Materials

You will need six to eight copies of four or five books that will interest students and duplicated choice ballots as shown in Figure 15.14. You will also need to prepare a book talk on each of the four or five books selected.

Procedure

To initiate literature response groups, begin by selecting four or five books that will engender interest and discussion among students. Next, give a book talk on each of the four or five titles selected, enthusiastically presenting and describing each book to the students. Then, ask students to individually select their top three book choices they want to read. After the student ballots have been collected, make an assignment sheet for each book title. Give each student his or her first choice. If too many students want the same title, go to each student's second choice as you compile the assignments list. This system works well, because students always know that they get to read a book of their own choosing. After books are distributed the next day, give the students a large block of uninterrupted reading time in class. At the beginning of the year, students can read about 20 minutes without undue restlessness. However, later in the year, children can often sustain free reading for up to one full hour.

As students complete several hours of independent reading, each literature response group (comprising those students reading the same title and, thus, interest based) meets on a rotating basis for about 20 minutes with the teacher. Group members discuss and share their initial reactions to the book. We have found that meeting with one literature response group per day—with a maximum of 3 days of independent reading between meetings—works quite well.

Based on the group discussion, an assignment is given to the group to extend the discussion of the book into other interpretive media (i.e., writing, art, drama, and so on). Each member of the literature response group works on this assignment before returning to the group for a second meeting. This sequence of reading and working on an extension response assignment repeats until the entire book is completed. We recommend that the first extension assignment focus on personal responses and connections with the book. Subsequent assignments can focus on understanding literary elements (i.e., characterization, point of view, story elements, role of the narrator, and so on). At the conclusion of the book, the literature study circle meets to determine a culminating project (Reutzel & Cooter, 2000; Zarillo, 1989). This project captures the group's interpretation and feelings about the entire book as demonstrated in a mural, story map, diorama, character-wanted posters, and so on.

RESPONSE JOURNALS AND LOGS

Purpose

Children grow as readers as they learn to use their knowledge, experiences, and feelings to construct a personal response text. Response journals and logs offer students "an active and concrete means of participating in the text" (Tashlik, 1987, p. 177). When personal responses are encouraged, students feel an innate need to share their ideas, feelings, and questions (Parsons, 1990; Stillman, 1987). Journal writing results in more complete and elaborate responses to literature than questions provoke and, most important, facilitates students' growth, confidence, and motivation to read (Wollman-Bonilla, 1991a).

Materials

Collect reading materials (a) of high interest to students, (b) of high-quality literary merit, (c) within the reading abilities of the students, and (d) with text that helps integrate language arts within discipline-based content learning areas. Each student will also need a response journal. This can consist of almost any type of bound, lined, or unlined paper (e.g., loose-leaf paper, spiral notebook, composition notebook, stenographer's notebook, and so on).

Procedure

Using an overhead projector, begin by showing students several sample journal or log entries that reflect a range of possible responses. Text selections already familiar to students work best. Be sure to include honest feelings, questions, and reflections. Consider the following suggestions based on Wollman-Bonilla (1991b, p. 22) to guide responses:

1. What you liked or disliked and why
2. What you wish had happened
3. What you wish the author had included
4. Your opinion of the characters
5. Your opinion of the illustrations, tables, and figures
6. What the text reminds you of
7. What you felt as you read
8. What you noticed about how you read
9. Questions you have after reading

Once students begin using journals or logs, teachers need to find time to respond to students' responses. This sends a clear message that journal responses are not simply a required exercise but that someone cares about how the students feel about reading.

Perhaps the most important reason for replying to students' journal entries is to teach and support students. Finding time to do so is relatively easy. Do not feel that you must respond to each student every day, but simply respond on a rotating basis. As you do so, consider the following ideas:

- Share your own ideas and feelings about the book.
- Provide additional information where needed.
- Develop students' awareness of reading strategies and literary techniques.
- Model elaborated responses.
- Challenge students' thinking.
- Offer alternative perspectives on the student's observations from a book.

Journals and logs provide students with important evidence of their own growth in reading as well as substantial assessment data for teachers. Students can be brought to higher levels of thinking, greater strategic use of reading strategies, deeper understanding of literature, and improved skill in communicating their ideas through journal and log responses to literature. But the most important frequent outcome of journaling is an increase in the desire to read!

SKETCH TO STRETCH

Purpose

"Sketch to stretch" (Short, Harste, & Burke, 1996; Siegel, 1983; Whitin, 2002) offers a wonderful opportunity for students to draw pictures illustrating "what this story meant to me or my favorite part of the story." Drawing helps students understand that there are ways to respond to their reading, such as through music, art, drama, writing, and movement (Whitin, 2002). Siegel (1983) claimed that by translating and expressing what we know and feel from one communication system (written language, for example) into another (say, music, dance, or art), new knowledge and understanding are created. This process of "recasting" knowledge or feeling into another form of expression is called *transmediation*.

Materials

Artistic media of all varieties (e.g., paints, markers, brushes, easels, paper, pencils, chalk, crayons, cloth, and so on) are the materials needed for this activity.

Procedure

The procedure for using sketch to stretch begins by placing children in groups of about four or five with multiple copies of the same story (either basal story or trade book). After the children have read the story, each child independently reflects on the meaning of the story. Then, they draw their own interpretations of the story. Plenty of time should be given for students to complete their sketches. Remember that the emphasis is on meaning, not artistic ability. Next, each student shares his or her sketch (without comment) and allows the other group members to speculate on its meaning as related to the book. Once the questions and comments of the other children are concluded, the artist has the final word. After each child in the group has shared his or her sketch, the group may wish to pick one sketch to share with the class. The sketch chosen by the group usually offers a good synopsis of the book or story.

Sketch to stretch offers teachers an opportunity to discuss with students why each reader may have different interpretations of a story even though the gist is recognized by all. Sketch to stretch also helps encourage a spirit of risk taking among students as they see that there is no single "correct" response to stories and books but that interpretations depend on a reader's background knowledge and interests.

Sketch to stretch has many follow-up possibilities. Sketches may be collected as part of the teacher's ongoing assessment portfolio, bound together into a group or class book, displayed on bulletin boards, or used as a metacognitive strategy to help students monitor their own comprehension of a story. Another possibility is that sketches may be collected and combined to create a kind of story map to depict major events in a story. Thus, sketch to stretch may

- Provide a lead into students' engagement in literature discussions.
- Aid students' story comprehension.
- Serve as rehearsal for students' engaging in the writing process.

EXPLORING MULTIPLE TEXTS AND MAKING CONNECTIONS

Purpose

For students to become lifelong readers, they need to regularly enjoy rich and satisfying experiences with great books. It is sometimes difficult, however, to help students find books that offer positive experiences for every class member. Consequently, it is important to offer as many choices for students as possible (Poe, 1992), especially for comprehension instruction.

Reading comprehension instruction has often been viewed traditionally in terms of having individual students recount the story line or the main idea of the passage (Hartman, 1992; Hartman & Allison, 1996). This concept of comprehension instruction is actually contrary to what better readers do, namely, comprehending text along a somewhat zigzag path. When reading is understood as a complex, layered process that cuts across the boundaries of single passages, stories, or texts, then using multiple texts to intensify readers' transactions takes on increasing importance. Hence, using multiple texts on a single topic or theme not only helps readers to develop and appreciate individual responses to books but also helps to develop their capacity to make intertextual links between different books.

Materials

Once a theme is chosen, you will need a selection of related texts to support that topic or theme. You will also need to develop a procedural minilesson on using multiple texts for literature study, as discussed in the "Procedure" section.

Procedure

To begin, invite students to write in their journals about the selected theme (e.g., grandparents). Students should express in their journals their feelings, thoughts, and associations concerning this concept. These prewriting entries can be used at the end of a literature study to compare their pre- and postreading thoughts and knowledge levels. Next, select three or four novels on the theme of grandparents, such as *Grandparents: A Special Kind of Love; Childtimes: A Three-Generation Memoir; Grandmother Came From Dworitz;* and *Grandpa, Me, and the Wishing Star.* Introduce the three or four novels about grandparents by giving a brief book talk on each. Tell the children they will be reading these books to explore their own response.

During the weeks in which students are reading the novels, they should discuss them periodically in small literature discussion groups. Each group should comprise a mix of students who are reading the given book based on choice. In other words, their grouping should not be based on assumed ability levels. Students should decide, as a group, which days will be reading days and which will be discussion days. In these groups, students should share and expand upon their responses, developing understanding about why they and others in their group reacted as they did. Teachers should sit in on these discussions regularly to evaluate students' participation in this important aspect of the unit. As students finish their books, they should write their response to the work as a whole. Whole-book responses give students an opportunity to synthesize their thoughts and feelings about the book, reflect on their experiences with it, and self-evaluate what they gained from reading it.

After writing whole-book responses, groups gather for a class discussion and presentation. Students in each group lead a panel discussion of each person's responses to their group's book. When all groups have finished their presentations, students are invited to make comments that connect the commonalities among the three or four books read by

Figure 15.15 Comparison Grid for the Grandparents Theme

	Grandparents: A Special Kind of Love	Childtimes: A Three-Generation Memoir	Grandmother Came from Dworitz	Grandpa, Me and the Wishing Star
Grandparent				
Significant other				
Problem				
Resolution				
Theme/Moral				

members of the class. A comparison grid is often helpful for making these comparisons (Reutzel & Cooter, 2000). One example of a comparison grid is shown in Figure 15.15.

Finally, individual students usually engage in personal response projects intended to strengthen their connections to the text read. They often create a project that appropriately expresses their responses to an aspect of the book they read. Students share their projects with the class by explaining the relationship between their project, the book, and their feelings or thoughts about the book.

COOPERATIVE GROUP ROTATION

Purpose

By using cooperative group rotation (Mermelstein, 1994), students have access to a variety of quality literature books and to nonfiction trade books in small-group settings. Children collaboratively participate in actively gathering and using information to create projects that demonstrate the lessons learned from reading literature (Wood et al., 2001).

Materials

You may want to design a poster that describes the expectations and processes of the cooperative group rotation, such as the one shown in Figure 15.16. Also needed are topic, subject, or theme-related trade books sufficient in number for each group.

Procedure

Begin the process by dividing the students into groups of four or five. Next, the group assigns the major roles at the beginning of each day's sessions: reader, note taker, and leader. Next, select at least enough books on a selected subject, topic, or theme for each group to have one book per group. The student selected for the role of the reader reads the book aloud to the rest of the group, stopping at the end of each page. The student who is selected as the leader reminds the reader to stop at the end of each page and also asks the group members to answer the question, "What do you think was important on the page?" After this, the student selected to fill the role of the note taker writes down the group's answers to the question. When the group has finished reading the book, each student selects

Figure 15.16 Cooperative Group Rotation

Cooperative Group Rotation
1. Get together with your assigned group or team.
2. Decide who will fill the roles of reader, note taker, and leader for today. *(Remember this should change each day.)*
3. The "reader" should get the book for the day and read it aloud to the rest of the group.
4. The "leader" reminds the reader to stop at the end of each page and ask the group members to answer the question, "What do you think was important on the page?"
5. The "note taker" writes down the group's answers to the question, "What do you think was important on the page?"
6. Select a project from the following list for today's book:
   • Composing different kinds of poetry
   • Drawing a picture showing the topic or subject
   • Writing a paragraph about the subject
   • Creating an adjective word web
   • Writing a creative story about the subject
   • Making a puppet
   • Creating a diorama
7. Choose your favorite project to display when the group has finished reading the book.

a project about the topic using the book and the note taker's list as resources. For the next day's sessions, the remaining books are rotated around the groups, so that all of the groups will have an opportunity to read the books. After the group reads all the books, the students complete their individual projects for each book. Finally, each student selects his or her favorite project to be displayed in a class portfolio, display area, or bulletin board.

COLLABORATIVE REASONING DISCUSSIONS

Purpose

"Collaborative reasoning (CR) is an approach to literature discussion intended to stimulate critical reading, thinking and is intended to be personally engaging" (Chinn, Anderson, & Waggonner, 2001, p. 383). During CR discussions, children take a position on a central question raised by a story. Then they present reasons and evidence for and against their positions. Using a collaborative reasoning (CR) discussion has been shown to increase student engagement in reading and in discussion. It has also been shown to induce students to use higher-level cognitive processes than other forms of discussion (Chinn et al., 2001).

Materials

A list of possible central questions about the story or text, around which different positions may be taken, is needed.

Procedure

A CR discussion begins with the students reading a story or text silently at their seats. After reading, students and teacher gather as a group. The teacher begins the discussion with a single, central story question about a significant issue related to the story or text. It is possible to write more than one question about a significant issue related to the text or story. For example, *The Paper Bag Princess* (Munsch & Munsch, 1988) is a story about a princess who has fallen in love with a prince who is kidnapped by a fire-breathing dragon. Elizabeth, the princess, takes off on a long quest to find her prince charming in a paper bag because her clothes were burned up when the dragon carried off her prince. At the end, the princess looks a mess but rescues her prince from the clutches of the dragon. When the prince sees her, he tells her to come back when she looks more like a princess. The question for this story may be, "Should Elizabeth marry the prince anyway?" After the question is asked, children raise their hands to share their positions. They may adopt a "yes" or "no" position, or they may say, "The prince needs to apologize and then the princess should forgive him." Some children may suggest that the princess date someone else for a while to make the prince jealous. Other students may support these positions or take their own. When disagreements come up, they challenge one another with counterarguments and present text-based evidence. During the CR discussion, the teacher says little or nothing during long stretches of time. When teachers do enter the discussion, they should ask students to clarify their ideas, prompt students to present evidence, and model clear arguments and counterarguments. During this time, students speak without raising their hands in an open participatory structure. In the end, the interpretative authority for the story rests with the students. Books on how people work in collaborative settings may be a good prerequisite for using CR discussions (See Wood et al., 2001).

Book Clubs

Purpose

Book clubs provide teachers a structure for providing groups of students engaging experiences with books, opportunities to talk about books as a community of learners, time to teach specific strategies and skills, and a way to foster an enjoyment of and appreciation for reading. During book club (BC) meetings, students read, write, respond, and participate in instruction. Book clubs not only enable children to develop their literacy abilities but also encourage a desire to read and an appreciation of texts because children have extended opportunities to read, write, and discuss their stories and texts (McMahon & Raphael, 1997).

Materials

Select a quality book recommended by others, with a reputable author, and on a topic of interest to the students and the teacher. Use a focused, short writing assignment (see Figure 15.17).

Procedure

A book club meeting begins with the selection of a quality text or book for discussion. To be effective, book club books must be quality literature, reflect character diversity (ethnicity, gender, class, and race), and meet curricular needs. To meet curricular needs, book club books must meet the needs of students and address the skills and strategies included in the district curriculum guide. Once a quality book is chosen, the book club begins with reading the book. During the book club time, teachers and students read books aloud to model fluent reading. The teacher may begin reading a part of the book to set the example and the tone for reading. Frequently, following the teacher, students read silently. In some cases, students read in pairs, taking turns. Students are also encouraged to keep their book club books handy for reading when they have free time, at recess, and at lunch. Students must complete the same amount of reading to participate in discussions. So, if book club time is insufficient to complete the amount of reading needed to participate in the discussion, then students must plan their reading to include additional time out of school or during the day.

Figure 15.17   Problem-Solution Think Sheet Showing a Problem-Solution Chain of Events

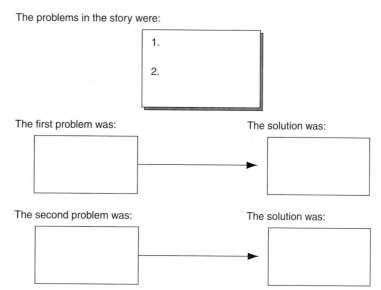

During book club reading, students are given the choice of where they read. They can read their books anywhere in the room or in the adjacent hallway, as long as they read. They can sit on the floor, lie under a table, or stand in a corner, so long as they are comfortable and are reading. Students who struggle with reading are provided additional support during the book club reading time. Some are given additional time to read. Some are given individual or small-group instruction with the teacher focusing on particular needs.

Once the reading assignment is completed, students engage in a reading-writing connection. Writing within the book club takes two primary forms: (a) short, focused writing and (b) extended writing projects. Short, focused writing could be done in the student's "Reading Log" or using a "Think Sheet" focusing on a particular writing procedure using prompts. Extended writing projects typically take the form of theme essays, stories within the genre of the book club book, and informational writing (i.e., articles or reports).

Having read and written about the reading assignment, all students are ready to discuss the assigned portion of the book club book. During discussions, the teacher focuses students' conversations around literary elements such as characters, sequence of the story, or text elements, making intertextual links between the book being read and others read previously. Daily writing assignments may be focused on helping students consolidate their understanding of story/text characters, story elements, and connections with other books after the discussion concludes. A new book or portion of a book is to be read by the next meeting date. In many ways, the book club structure parallels the reading workshop described in chapter 4.

Author Studies

Purpose

Author studies involve learning about the author as a person and a writer and becoming acquainted with his or her published works (Kotch & Zackman, 1995). Studying an author and sharing books written by an author can bond every member of the class into a community of learners. Sharing an author's techniques and strategies helps students gain insights into the author's craft as a writer. Choosing authors whose works span various genres facilitates curriculum integration across subject fields.

Materials

Select three or four books published by a single author.

Procedure

When selecting an author, students' interests, reading and writing needs, and attitudes need to be considered. Once the author has been identified, information about that author can be obtained from publishers, Internet sites, books, and tapes. Some of these resources are listed here:

- *Meet the Authors and Illustrators, Vols. I & II.* Deborah & James Preller. (1991, 1993). Scholastic.
- *Meet the Authors, Vols. 1–5.* Rozanne Williams. (1993). Creative Teaching Press.
- *Scholastic Authors on Tape,* Scholastic.

Roser, Hoffman, and Farest (1990) offered the use of a Language to Literacy Chart to compare authors' works along the lines of genre, themes, illustrations, special effects, characters, settings, episodes, and resolutions. Language to Literacy charts are constructed from large pieces of butcher paper ruled into a lattice or matrix with headings that help to focus children on relations among various books read in a unit or in various response groups. In Figure 15.18, the chart includes headings on title, characters, the goals or purposes of the characters, and how the author makes each of his or her books special or

Figure 15.18   Example of a Language Chart for a Literacy Unit

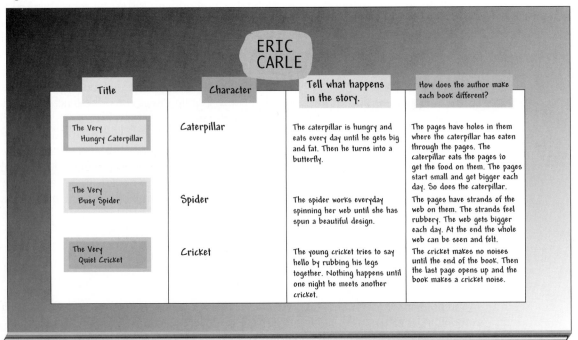

Title	Character	Tell what happens in the story.	How does the author make each book different?
The Very Hungry Caterpillar	Caterpillar	The caterpillar is hungry and eats every day until he gets big and fat. Then he turns into a butterfly.	The pages have holes in them where the caterpillar has eaten through the pages. The caterpillar eats the pages to get the food on them. The pages start small and get bigger each day. So does the caterpillar.
The Very Busy Spider	Spider	The spider works everyday spinning her web until she has spun a beautiful design.	The pages have strands of the web on them. The strands feel rubbery. The web gets bigger each day. At the end the whole web can be seen and felt.
The Very Quiet Cricket	Cricket	The young cricket tries to say hello by rubbing his legs together. Nothing happens until one night he meets another cricket.	The cricket makes no noises until the end of the book. Then the last page opens up and the book makes a cricket noise.

ERIC CARLE

different. Children are invited to respond to each of Eric Carle's books separately under the first three headings. Under the final heading, children respond to the books by comparing the techniques the author used to make each book distinctive. One way to minimize the risk of language charts limiting the range of responses is to begin by simply recording students' initial, unorganized responses to literature in a collection language chart. Then, another more focused language chart with specific categories drawn from the collection language chart could be used to organize a chart as shown in Figure 15.18.

ADDITIONAL STRATEGIES FOR ENGLISH-LANGUAGE LEARNERS

DRAMA AS LITERATURE RESPONSE

Purpose

McCaslin (1990) asserted that creative drama is an art, a socializing activity, and a way of learning. Drama as an art form to satisfy human needs and to foster the development and learning of children has been recognized by leading educators for many years (Rhodes & Dudley-Marling, 1988; Siks, 1983). As an oral and interpretive response to literature, Lynch-Brown and Tomlinson (1993) strongly recommended creative drama for use with children of all ages and abilities. McCaslin (1990) specifically recommended creative drama activities for students with learning problems. Creative drama is the act of informal play making comprised of several distinct techniques:

- Plays
- Movement and rhythms
- Pantomime
- Improvisation
- Puppetry and mask making
- Reader's and chamber theater

Creative drama offers teachers and children a wide array of possibilities for responding to literature through dramatic interpretation. McCaslin (1990) recommended that teachers bear in mind the following as they use creative drama for interpretive responses to literature:

1. Creative drama activities should be based on literature.
2. Authors create the dialogue, and scripts are not prepared or memorized.
3. Improvisation is a critical feature of creative drama.
4. Acting is primarily through improvisation and movement; there is minimal use of props.
5. Creative drama is for the benefit of the performers, not for the approval of an audience.
6. No one dramatic interpretation of a story is correct. Several interpretations are to be encouraged.

Materials

Materials needed for dramatic interpretations include a good story, chapter, or literature book and perhaps an assortment of props such as hats, glasses, puppets, clothes, and so on (optional).

Procedure

Creative drama is an enjoyable literature response alternative that makes use of children's imagination and oral language. Some educators have said, "Drama comes in the door of the school with every child" (Siks, 1983, p. 3). Literature-based drama may reenact a single scene from a chapter, a short picture book, or a brief story. It is best to begin with simple, short stories with two to six characters and a great deal of action. Folktales and fairy tales tend to fit this description well. When using creative drama to interpret literature responses, the following steps should be kept in mind:

1. Students listen to or read the story selected.
2. Students determine if this is a story they would like to act out. If so, they then read or listen to the story again, paying particular attention to the characters, action, and sequence of the story episode.
3. Students list the events on the board or on chart paper to review their sequence.
4. Students cast the play.
5. Actors use the list of sequenced events to plan actions, dialogue, and props suitable for the dramatization.
6. The cast of actors takes a few minutes to decide how the play will be presented and then rehearses it.
7. After the first performance, other students or groups can be invited to evaluate the success of the first performance. Actors in the performance can also self-evaluate their performance.

Based on McCaslin (1990), we suggest the following questions to guide the evaluation of dramatic interpretations of books and stories:

- Did the performance tell the story?
- What did you like about the opening scene?
- Did the characters show they were excited and interesting?
- When we play it again, can you think of anything that would improve the performance?
- Was anything important left out?

INCLUDING ALL STUDENTS

STORYTELLING AS LITERATURE RESPONSE

Purpose

Storytelling is first and foremost an art form (Sawyer, 1970). Cooter (1991) explained that storytelling—an ancient art form—is enjoying renewed attention nationally in language arts classrooms. Goodlad (1984), in his book, *A Place Called School,* punctuated the need for breaking the emotional neutrality of most American classrooms. Storytelling appears to offer a solution to this problem. Although teachers may enjoy storytelling as an exciting teaching strategy, children can also find increased joy in responding to their reading through storytelling. We say this for at least two major reasons. First, children can learn more about the richness of our language through storytelling. And second, they can reach out to their environment and other persons through storytelling (Ross, 1980). Teaching students how to select and tell stories well is an important means of dramatically responding to literature and exploring new modes of self-expression.

Figure 15.19   Storytelling Poster

Steps to Becoming a Storyteller
- Find a story that is just right for *you.*
- Prepare the story for telling.
- Use books, props, and voices.
- Get the audience involved.

Materials

Construct a poster showing the four steps to becoming a storyteller, as described in Figure 15.19.

Procedure

Tell children that a storytelling response to a story begins by selecting a story that suits their personality and preferences. The storyteller and the story must become emotionally linked to be believable. Therefore, children should not select storytelling as a reader response unless the story truly interests them. Next, encourage each child to prepare to tell the story by "picturing" the events, characters, setting, and episodes in the story in his or her mind's eye. The child should read the story repeatedly until the story line is fully committed to memory—like a "mental movie." If a story has a specific sequence or linguistic dialect, children should learn the language of the story verbatim. Tell each child that practicing the storytelling alone in his or her bedroom or in front of a mirror allows for seeing himself or herself as he or she is seen.

After rehearsing, some storytellers enjoy selecting props such as eyeglasses, hats, makeup, or puppets. Children storytellers can be invited to consider various simple props for telling their story. In addition, using different voices to tell a story is very effective. Varying the pitch of one's voice, adjusting the speed of speech, or using dialects or foreign accents establishes story characters as real and believable. However, subtlety is an important key, because extreme variations of one's voice can also detract from the story.

Finally, arrange a legitimate audience for children storytellers. Groups of classroom peers or younger children are the most readily available audiences for child storytellers. For some children, a performance at home with their families may be a sufficient audience. Encourage young storytellers to get their audiences involved in parts of the story. This can be accomplished by copying a repeated phrase in the text onto a large cue card for the audience members to read at various points in the storytelling. For example, in *The Gingerbread Man,* the cue card may read, "Run, run as fast as you can. You can't catch me, I'm the Gingerbread Man."

To bring a storytelling event to closure, teachers may wish to ask a child storyteller to construct a storytelling map modeled after a story grammar map (see chapter 10) in order to review the parts and plot of the story in a visual graphic form for display in the classroom.

MOTIVATING LITERATURE RESPONSE

Purpose

Turner and Paris (1995) have studied the conditions for fostering student engagement in and motivation for completing a variety of literacy tasks including responding to, discussing, and interacting around texts. Turner (1995) found six instructional and contextual strategies that have been shown in research to support and increase student motivation in responding to literature and in completing open-end literacy tasks. Many of these same conditions also have been found to increase students' comprehension of text as reported by the National Reading Panel (National Institute of Child Health and Human Development, 2000). We offer these six strategies coupled with open-end literature response activities such as those previously described in this chapter to teachers as an additional means for addressing the diverse needs of students within a classroom to successfully engage in literature response and discussions.

Materials

Construct a poster showing the six *C*s for supporting motivation in literacy tasks in the classroom, as shown in Figure 15.20.

Procedure

Place the poster in Figure 15.20 on an easel in the classroom where all the children can see it. Explain that you have been studying ways to help everyone in the classroom enjoy reading, writing, and talking about literature more. Tell them about each of the six *C*s in the chart.

Choice. Past research has shown that *choice* is a powerful motivator (Schiefele, 1991). As a teacher, you need to provide authentic, sometimes bounded or limited choices and purposes for engaging in reading and talking or writing about literature. Connecting the reading of literature to the completion of authentic responses such as writing a "thank you card" to the main character in a story, drawing a wanted poster of the villain in a story, or making a map of the travels of the main character in a story offers students a variety of authentic choices for responding to the characters in a story. When speaking of literature response tasks, do not refer to these as work to be completed but rather discuss them in terms of their functions, that is, expressing gratitude for solving a problem in the story, advertising to capture the villain, or tracking the movements of a character while reading a literature selection (Turner & Paris, 1995).

Challenge. Some teachers have thought that assigning tasks that children can easily complete is motivating because children can succeed, thus building their confidence. Turner's (1995) research found that children who were the most engaged in completing literacy tasks associated with reading and discussing literature were engaged in moderately challenging tasks. Moderately challenging tasks led children to discover new insights and to restructure their understanding of story events. Allowing students to effect minor modifications of tasks that increase the level of difficulty slightly will lead to greater levels of interest and will address the multiple needs and abilities of children in the classroom. Provide several ways of completing a task and provide successful models of completion—such as different ways to show that they

Figure 15.20 Six Cs of Motivating Literature Response

- Choice
- Challenge
- Control
- Collaboration
- Construct Meaning
- Consequences

have learned vocabulary words in a given story (i.e., fill in the blank, matching word to definitions, multiple choice, etc.).

Control. One of the primary goals of literature circles and discussion is to support learners' independence and flexibility as readers and writers. When teachers share control with students, they learn to make crucial decisions independently. Ryan and Grolnick (1986) reported that children in shared-control classrooms were more interested in their schoolwork and perceived themselves to be more competent than those children in teacher-only-controlled classrooms. Teaching children how and when to self-monitor their understanding of texts and their appropriate participation in literature response groups is a critical part of guiding students' development of independence in literacy.

Collaboration. When teachers view their role as "apprenticing" children into the world of literature discussions and appreciation, they foster collaboration in their classrooms. Scaffolding and guiding students' talk, thinking, and independence are best accomplished in a social setting that requires substantial interaction and collaboration. One of the eight effective comprehension strategies for which there was significant available scientific support as reported by the National Reading Panel (National Institute of Child Health and Human Development, 2000) was the use of "cooperative or collaborative" discussions and interactions around texts. This means that activities are designed so that students have many opportunities to work together with peers to complete assigned literature responses and to engage in significant literature discussions with peers and the teacher.

Constructing Meaning. Constructing meaning promotes engagement in literature response activities by helping children to connect to their own experiences and the experiences of others, resulting in making greater sense of their own learning (Paris & Byrnes, 1989). Also, constructing meaning implies that students must be taught a repertoire of comprehension and meaning-making strategies in order to respond effectively and flexibly in reading and writing (see chapter 10 and chapter 11).

Consequences. Students need to be taught how to judge their work differently from the perspective of accuracy—"right or wrong." In the literature response tasks you assign as a teacher, encourage student self-evaluation. Such self-evaluation may focus on participation in or preparation for literature response groups. It may also focus on the completion of group-assigned literature response tasks. In any case, when asked to perform self-evaluations, students should focus on such qualities as (a) the effort they expended, (b) the enjoyment they experienced, and (c) the personal meaningfulness of the activity for them. From this, students derive feelings of ownership, self-efficacy, responsibility, self-regulation, and achievement.

SELECTED REFERENCES

Angeletti, S. R. (1991). Encouraging students to think about what they read. *The Reading Teacher, 45*(4), 288–296.

Beach, R. (1997). Students' resistance to engagement with multicultural literature. In T. Rogers & A. Soter (Eds.), *Reading across cultures* (pp. 69–96). New York: Teachers' College Press.

Bleich, D. (1978). *Subjective criticism.* Baltimore, MD: Johns Hopkins University Press.

Chinn, C. A., Anderson, R. C., & Waggonner, M. A. (2001). Patterns of discourse in two kinds of literature discussion. *Reading Research Quarterly, 36*(4), 378–411.

Christenbury, L. (1992). The guy who wrote this poem seems to have the same feelings as you have: Reader response methodology. In N.J. Karolides (Ed.), *Reader response in the classroom: Evoking and interpreting meaning in literature.* New York: Longman.

Cooter, R. B. (1991). Storytelling in the language arts classroom. *Reading Research and Instruction, 30*(2), 71–76.

Dahl, K. L., & Freppon, P. A. (1995). A comparison of inner-city children's interpretation of reading and writing instruction in the early grades in skills-based and whole language classrooms. *Reading Research Quarterly, 29,* 104–122.

Daniels, H. (1994). *Literature circles: Voice and choice in the student-centered classroom.* York, ME: Stenhouse.

Eeds, M., & Wells, D. (1989). Grand conversations: An exploration of meaning construction in literature study groups. *Research in the Teaching of English, 23,* 4–29.

Galda, L., Ash, G. E., & Cullinan, B. (2000). Children's literature. In M. L. Kamil, P. B. Mosenthal, P. D. Pearson, & R. Barr (Eds.), *Handbook of reading research, Volume III* (pp. 361–379). Mahwah, NJ: Lawrence Erlbaum Associates.

Galda, L., Cullinan, B. E., & Strickland, D. S. (1993). *Language, literacy and the child.* New York: Harcourt Brace.

Gambrell, L. B. (1992). Elementary school literacy instruction: Changes and challenges. In M. J. Dreher & W. H. Slater (Eds.), *Elementary school literacy: Critical issues* (pp. 227–239). Norwood, MA: Christopher-Gordon.

Gambrell, L., & Bales, R. J. (1986). Mental imagery and the comprehension-monitoring performance of fourth- and fifth-grade poor readers. *Reading Research Quarterly, 21*(4), 454–464.

Gerla, J. P. (1996). Response-based instruction: At-risk students engaging in literature. *Reading and Writing Quarterly: Overcoming Learning Difficulties, 12*(2), 149–169.

Goatley, V. J. (1996). The participation of a student identified as learning disabled in a regular education book club: The case of Stark. *Reading and Writing Quarterly: Overcoming Learning Difficulties, 12*(2), 195–214.

Goatley, V. J., Brock, C. H., & Raphael, T. E. (1995). Diverse learners participating in regular education "book clubs." *Reading Research Quarterly, 30*(3), 352–380.

Goatley, V. J., & Raphael, T. E. (1992). *Non-traditional learners' written and dialogic response to literature: Fortieth yearbook of the National Reading Conference* (pp. 313–322). Chicago: National Reading Conference.

Goodlad, J. I. (1984). *A place called school: Prospects for the future.* New York: McGraw-Hill.

Hartman, D. K. (1992). Eight readers reading: The intertextual links of able readers using multiple passages. *Reading Research Quarterly, 27*(2), 122–123.

Hartman, D. K. & Allison, J. (1996). Promoting inquiry-oriented discussions using multiple texts. In L. B. Gambrell & J. F. Almasi (Eds.), *Lively discussions: Fostering engaged reading* (pp. 106–133). Newark, DE: International Reading Association.

Heathington, B. S., & Alexander, J. E. (1978). A child-based observation checklist to assess attitudes toward reading. *Reading Teacher, 31*(7), 769–771.

Hoffman, J. V., McCarthey, S. J., Abbott, J., Christian, C., Corman, L., Curry, C., et al. (1994). So what's new in the new basals? A focus on first grade. *Journal of Reading Behavior, 26*(1), 47–73.

Holland, N. N. (1975). *5 readers reading.* New Haven, CT: Yale University Press.

Hoyt, L. (1999). *Revisit, reflect, retell: Strategies for improving reading comprehension.* Portsmouth, NH: Heinemann Educational Books.

Johnson, D. W., & Johnson, R. T. (1995). *Learning together and alone: Cooperative, competitive, and individualistic learning* (5th ed.). Boston: Allyn & Bacon.

Karolides, N. J. (1992). *Reader response in the classroom: Evoking and interpreting meaning in literature.* New York: Longman.

Kelly, P. R. (1990). Guiding young students' response to literature. *The Reading Teacher, 43*(7), 464–471.

King, C. (2001). "I like group reading because we can share ideas:" The role of talk within the literature circle. *Reading, 7,* 32–36.

Kotch, L., & Zackman, L. (1995). *The author studies handbook: Helping students build powerful connections to literature.* New York: Scholastic.

Lynch-Brown, C., & Tomlinson, C. M. (1993). *Essentials of children's literature.* Boston: Allyn & Bacon.

Marshall, J. (2000). Research on response to literature. In M. L. Kamil, P. B. Mosenthal, P. D. Pearson, & R. Barr (Eds.), *Handbook of reading research, Volume III* (pp. 381–402). Mahwah, NJ: Lawrence Erlbaum Associates.

Martinez-Roldan, C. M., & Lopez-Robertson, J. M. (2000). Initiating literature circles in a first-grade bilingual classroom. *The Reading Teacher, 53*(4), 270–281.

McCaslin, N. (1990). *Creative drama in the classroom.* New York: Longman.

McKenna, M. C., & Kear, D. J. (1990). Measuring attitude toward reading: A new tool for teachers. *The Reading Teacher, 43*(9), 626–639.

McKenna, M. C., Kear, D. J., & Ellsworth, R. A. (1995). Children's attitudes toward reading: A national survey. *Reading Research Quarterly, 30*(4), 934–955.

McKenna, M. C., Stratton, B. D., Grindler, M. C., & Jenkins, S. J. (1995). Differential effects of whole language and traditional instruction on reading attitudes. *Journal of Reading Behavior, 27*(1), 19–44.

McMahon, S. I., & Raphael, T. E. (1997). *The book club connection: Literacy learning and classroom talk.* New York: Teachers' College Press.

Mermelstein, B. (1994). Cooperative group rotation. *The Reading Teacher, 48*(3), 281–282.

Morrow, L. M. (1992). The impact of a literature-based program on literacy achievement, use of literature, and attitudes of children from minority backgrounds. *Reading Research Quarterly, 27*(3), 251–275.

Morrow, L. M., & Gambrell, L. B. (2000). Literature-based reading instruction. In M. L. Kamil, P. B. Mosenthal, P. D. Pearson, & R. Barr (Eds.), *Handbook of reading research* (Vol. 3, pp. 563–586). Mahwah, NJ: Lawrence Erlbaum Associates.

Morrow, L. M., Pressley, M., Smith, J. K., & Smith, J. (1997). The effect of a literature-based program integrated into literacy and science instruction with children from diverse backgrounds. *Reading Research Quarterly, 32*(1), 54–76.

Munsch, R. N., & Munsch, M. (1988). *The paper bag princess.* Toronto: Annick Press.

National Institute of Child Health and Human Development. (2000). *Report of the National Reading Panel: Teaching children to read.* Washington, DC: U. S. Government Printing Office.

Paris, S. G., & Byrnes, J. P. (1989). The constructivist approach to self-regulation. In B. J. Zimmerman & D. H. Schunk (Eds.), *Self-regulated learning and academic achievement* (pp. 169–200). New York: Springer-Verlag.

Parsons, L. (1990). *Response journals.* Portsmouth, NH: Heinemann Educational Books.

Peterson, R., & Eeds, M. (1990). *Grand conversations: Literature groups in action.* New York: Scholastic.

Poe, E. A. (1992). Intensifying transactions through multiple text exploration. In N. J. Karolides (Ed.), *Reader response in the classroom: Evoking and interpreting meaning in literature.* New York: Longman.

Reutzel, D. R., & Cooter, R. B. (1990). Whole language: Comparative effects on first-grade reading achievement. *Journal of Educational Research, 83*(5), 252–257.

Reutzel, D. R., & Cooter, R. B. (2000). *Teaching children to read: Putting the pieces together* (3rd ed.). Upper Saddle River, NJ: Merrill/Prentice Hall.

Reutzel, D. R. & Larsen, N. S. (1995). Look what they've done to real children's books in the new basal readers! *Language Arts, 72*(7), 495–507.

Reutzel, D. R., Oda, L. K., & Moore, B. H. (1989). Developing print awareness: The effect of three instructional approaches on kindergartners; print awareness, reading readiness, and word reading. *Journal of Reading Behavior, 21*(3), 197–217.

Reutzel, D. R., Smith, J. A., & Fawson, P. C. (2005). An evaluation of two approaches for teaching reading comprehension strategies in the primary years using science information texts. *Early Childhood Research Quarterly, 20*(3), 276–305.

Rhodes, L. K., & Dudley-Marling, C. (1988). *Readers and writers with a difference.* Portsmouth, NH: Heinemann Educational Books.

Rogers, T. (1997). No imagined peaceful place: A story of community, texts, and cultural conversations in one urban high school English classroom. In T. Rogers & A. Soter (Eds.), *Reading across cultures* (pp. 95–115). New York: Teachers' College Press.

Rosenblatt, L. M. (1978). *The reader, the text, and the poem.* Carbondale, IL: Southern Illinois University Press.

Rosenblatt, L. M. (1989). Writing and reading: The transactional theory. In J. M. Mason (Ed.), *Reading and writing connections.* Boston: Allyn & Bacon.

Roser, N. L., Hoffman, J. V., & Farest, C. (1990). Language, literature, and at-risk children. *The Reading Teacher, 43*(8), 554–561.

Ross, R. (1980). *Storyteller.* Columbus, OH: Charles E. Merrill.

Ryan, R. M., & Grolnick, W. S. (1986). Origins and pawns in the classroom: Self-report and projective assessment of individual differences in children's perceptions. *Journal of Personality and Social Psychology, 50*, 550–558.

Sadoski, M., & Quast, Z. (1990). Reader response and long-term recall for journalistic text: The roles of imagery, affect, and importance. *Reading Research Quarterly, 24*(4), 256–272.

Samway, K. D., Whang, G., Cade, C., Gamil, M., Lubandina, M. A., & Phommanchanh, K. (1991). Reading the skeleton, the heart, and the brains of a book: Students' perspectives on literature study circles. *The Reading Teacher, 45*(3), 196–205.

Sawyer, R. (1970). *The way of the storyteller.* New York: Penguin Books.

Schiefele, U. (1991). Interest, learning, and motivation. *Educational Psychologist, 26*, 299–323.

Scieszka, J. (1989). *The true story of the three little pigs!* New York: Viking.

Short, K., Harste, J., & Burke, C. (1988). *Creating classrooms for authors.* Portsmouth, NH: Heinemann Educational Books.

Short, K. G., Harste, J. C., & Burke, C. (1996). *Creating classrooms for authors and inquirers.* Portsmouth, NH: Heinemann Educational Books.

Siegel, M. (1983). *Reading as signification.* Unpublished doctoral dissertation, Indiana University.

Siks, G. B. (1983). *Drama with children.* New York: Harper & Row.

Salvin, R. E. (1999). *Cooperative learning: Theory, research, and practice* (2nd ed.). Boston: Allyn & Bacon.

Spiegel, D. L. (1998). Reader response approaches and the growth of readers. *Language Arts, 76*(1), 41–48.

Stillman, P. (1987). Of myself, for myself. In T. Fulwiler (Ed.), *The journal book* (pp. 77–86). Portsmouth, NH: Heinemann Educational Books.

Strickland, D. S., Walmsley, S., Bronk, G., & Weiss, K. (1994). *School book clubs and literacy development: A descriptive study* (Rep. No. 2.22). Albany, NY: State University of New York, National Research Center on Literature Teaching and Learning.

Tashlik, P. (1987). I hear voices: The text, the journal and me. In T. Fulwiler (Ed.), *The journal book* (pp. 171–178). Portsmouth, NH: Heinemann Educational Books.

Tompkins, G. E. (2001). *Literacy for the 21st century: A balanced approach.* Upper Saddle River, NJ: Merrill/Prentice Hall.

Tunnell, M. O., & Jacobs, J. S. (1989). Using "real" books: Research findings on literature based reading instruction. *The Reading Teacher, 42,* 470–477.

Turner, J. C. (1995). The influence of classroom contexts on young children's motivation for literacy. *Reading Research Quarterly, 30,* 410–441.

Turner, J., & Paris, S. G. (1995). How literacy tasks influence children's motivation for literacy. *The Reading Teacher, 48*(3), 662–673.

Vogt, M. E. (1996). Creating a response-centered curriculum with literature discussion groups. In L. B. Gambrell & J. F. Almasi (Eds.), *Lively discussions: Fostering engaged reading* (pp. 181–193). Newark, DE: International Reading Association.

Whitin, P. (2002). Leading into literature circles through the sketch-to-stretch strategy. *The Reading Teacher, 55*(5), 444–451.

Wilson, R. M., & Gambrell, L. B. (1988). *Reading comprehension in the elementary school.* Boston: Allyn & Bacon.

Wollman-Bonilla, J. E. (1991a). Reading journals: Invitations to participate in literature. *The Reading Teacher, 43*(2), 112–113.

Wollman-Bonilla, J. E. (1991b). *Response journals.* New York: Scholastic.

Wood, K. D., Roser, N. L., & Martinez, M. (2001). Collaborative literacy: Lessons learned from literature. *The Reading Teacher, 55*(2), 102–111.

Zarillo, J. (1989). Teachers' interpretations of literature-based reading. *The Reading Teacher, 43*(1), 22–29.

Chapter 16

Getting Families Involved: Helping Parents to Help Their Children

"M. J." is Ruth Adams's mother and has come in for a parent-teacher conference.

"I want to help Ruth become a better reader, but there's one big problem," said M. J. rather sheepishly, "I don't read so well myself. Y'know, I never finished high school."

"Oh, M. J., that's quite alright. There are lots of things you can do to help Ruth become a better reader and writer," I began. "For one thing, children *love* to read out loud to their mom. All you have to do is be a good listener and ask a few questions. And that's just the beginning. Let's talk about some of the other things you can do for Ruth that will really make a difference!"

M. J.'s face lit up as we talked about three powerful ways she could help Ruth at home.

Later, I said, "M. J., we're trying to organize a community reading program and I need some help. Would you be interested?" I could tell by her expression that I had a new "recruit"!

Families, in sending their children to our schools each day, send us the best and most precious gifts they have. When we are able to offer them quality suggestions of ways they can help their children succeed, they deeply appreciate the assistance: they are the bedrock of support for their children.

Parent and community involvement is essential for student success in reading (R. Cooter, 2004). Between birth and the age of 19, children spend just 9% of their lives in school, and 91% elsewhere. Paul Barton (1992, 1994) of the Educational Testing Service estimated that 90% of the differences among students and their schools across the United States could be explained by five factors: number of days absent from school, number of hours spent watching television, number of pages read for homework, quantity and quality of reading materials in the home, and the presence of two parents in the home. That fifth factor is supremely important because it is apt to decisively influence the other four (Will, 2002). Barton concluded that school success is heavily dependent on the platform of readiness and support of learning created in the home.

If we are to maximize the learning potential of every child, we must enlist the aid of family members. We cannot afford to overlook the needs, strengths, contributions, and perspectives that family members can bring to school programs (Handel, 1999, p. 127). Recognition of adult family members as a valuable resource is evident nowadays in such federal legislation as the 1998 Reading Excellence Act, the Workforce Investment Act, and the No Child Left Behind Act (NCLB).

In this chapter, we share several ideas that have been shown to be effective in getting families involved in their children's literacy development. Because this chapter is quite *unlike* our others (there is no real diagnosis of reading problems to be done), we simply summarize key research briefly, then share some great ideas used by highly effective teachers. We do, however, include an "If-Then" chart that explains which ideas are appropriate for each age group.

Background Briefing for Teachers

Sara Williams (2001), in an extensive review of the research concerning family involvement in children's education, offers us some valuable insights. First, it is important that we understand that many families are rather passive in their children's education—not necessarily because of a lack of interest in their children's future but often due to a lack of knowing just *what* to do. Sadly, one study (Garshelis & McConnell, 1993) concluded that families having the greatest needs (i.e., poverty issues, children with severe handicaps, etc.) are less likely to feel they have input in their child's education. Williams's second research finding was that "professionals [teachers] should serve a more facilitative and empowering role for families" (p. 10). Given that so many family members lack either the knowledge or financial resources to provide books and reading opportunities in the home, it is incumbent on the teacher to help bring resources and information to the primary caregiver. Finally, Williams concluded that there is a need for further training and education for teachers in this area. Few teachers were prepared to take charge of family involvement programs, but the need is clear. Therefore, teachers should receive extensive professional development, support, and necessary materials to encourage family involvement.

When Mama Can't Read

In our opening vignette, we looked in on a situation that is quite common in many urban and rural classrooms—the parent wants to help her child succeed as a reader but has limited literacy abilities. Kathleen Cooter (2006) summarized important research into this growing phenomenon in an article titled "When Mama Can't Read: Counteracting Intergenerational Illiteracy." Though many parents may lack even functional literacy skills, this researcher concluded that there is much a proactive teacher can do to help these parents help their children become successful readers. Indeed, in one study done by Miller (1978), parents were given direct instruction in methods designed to increase their young child's speech and language skills to improve reading achievement. The parents became avid partners and used and maintained the methodologies taught over time to enhance their child's language skills.

Based on her research, Cooter (2006) recommended a number of strategies that can be used by nonreading parents to help their children. Since these ideas can be used by *any* parents to help their children, we include them throughout this chapter. She also made 12 specific suggestions for teachers when working with parents having limited reading ability; they are summarized in Figure 16.1. Strategies mentioned in this figure, such as *dialogic reading*, are described later in this chapter.

In the next section, we take a look at other important research findings that relate to family involvement.

Figure 16.1   When Momma Can't Read: Suggestions for Teachers

1. Value what she knows, how she lives, and the uniqueness of her family.
2. Teach her to use books to make up stories for her children.
3. Urge her to have her own "show and tell" times at home.
4. Teach her to use dialogic reading techniques with her children.
5. Teach her to choose books that engage and can be manipulated with her child.
6. Teach her that speaking in long sentences models strong language for her child.
7. Teach her to be responsive to her child's speech and language—to spend time in language activities.
8. Teach her how to combine language and play.
9. Teach her to use complex or uncommon words when she talks to her child.
10. Urge Mom to tell her child family stories, songs, and rituals.
11. Have Mom point as she talks with her child about objects in the environment.
12. Teach her that just by talking and listening she can help her child to be a reader.

Source: K. S. Cooter (2006). "When Mama Can't Read: Counteracting Intergenerational Illiteracy," *The Reading Teacher.*

INCREASING ORAL LANGUAGE IN EARLY AND EMERGENT READERS

It is widely conceded by researchers that the size of a child's vocabulary is a strong predictor of school success (*Harvard Education Letter,* November–December 2005). Similarly, when parents set aside time to talk to their children, there can be a long-term positive impact on academic literacy development. Other researchers studying low-income parents at play with their children found that supportive play by both mothers and fathers increased positive language gains in their children (Tamis-Lemonda, Shannon, Cabrera, & Lamb, 2004).

Mean Length of Utterance

When studying children at an early age, the mother's **mean length of utterance (MLU),** the average number of words spoken together, is predictive of her child's later language development (Murray, 1990; K. Cooter, 2006). When parents speak in longer word chains—sentences that are longer and more complex, children tend to imitate and create longer sentences as well. Vocabulary becomes more complex and expressive as well. Sometimes just adding gestures is a valuable hint.

Research on increasing a child's mean length of utterance provides some valuable insights for teachers who are coaching semiliterate or illiterate parents (K. Cooter, 2006).

- Parents who speak or question using complete sentences are more likely to have children who respond in longer word chains, longer utterances (Peterson, Carta, & Greenwood, 2005).

- Parents who read books or talk through books that are both narrative and manipulative—children can touch, pull or handle the book—can increase their children's questions and length and number of utterances (Kaderavek & Justice, 2005).

- Simply giving children models and opportunities of lengthening and elaborating their sentences significantly increases their oral language ability (Remaly, 1990; Farrar, 1985).

MORE ACCESS LEADS TO MORE READING

In his book *The Literacy Crisis: False Claims, Real Solutions,* Jeff McQuillan (1998) makes a powerful case for increasing student access to books in the home. In summarizing a number of rigorous research studies on the topic of access, McQuillan came to the following conclusions:

- More access to reading materials leads to more reading and, subsequently, higher reading achievement.
- In a study of parental attitudes among a group of African American families in which such variables as speaking to children about certain topics, telling children how to pronounce words correctly, teaching names of countries and states, and so forth were discussed, the *only* behavior that correlated significantly with reading scores was the number of books in the home. Thus, providing reading materials to low-income African American families, concludes this study, may be one of the most important things schools can do.
- In a study of middle school reluctant readers, the primary reason for students' infrequent reading was not a dislike of reading necessarily but was because they did not have access at home to the kinds of reading materials that interested them (e.g., comics, magazines, books on relevant topics). In another study, reading performance was improved at elementary and junior high schools when students were given two free subscriptions to magazines of their choice.

THE NEED FOR COMMUNITY INVOLVEMENT

Families can be approached either directly or indirectly. For example, an indirect way of getting the attention of adult family members is through communitywide efforts. R. Cooter, Mills-House, Marrin, Mathews, and Campbell (1999) report success in gaining community involvement in reading through a number of strategies, which we highlight later in this chapter. Here is a brief summary of the types of activities they found helpful:

- *Summer Food and Reading Programs.* Efforts involving community religious organizations provide food to children of poverty and also nourish their minds with books. Volunteers work with children in motivational read alouds, DEAR (Drop Everything and Read) time, and discussion groups.
- *Public Access Television.* School districts in metropolitan areas are allotted free public access airtime on television, time that often goes unused. A "Reading Channel" can be put together inexpensively that brings reading ideas into the living rooms of families.
- *Web Pages.* The Internet is rapidly becoming a commonplace tool in many homes and businesses. Sponsorship of a community web page by such groups as the Rotary, chambers of commerce, and local corporations can be quite effective.
- *Citywide DEAR Time.* Imagine a day each month when the entire city stops at an appointed time just to pull out a book and read as a sign of solidarity and recognition of the necessity of reading. Citywide Drop Everything and Read (DEAR) accomplishes just that.

FAMILY INVOLVEMENT AND ENGLISH-LANGUAGE LEARNERS

A rapidly growing segment of the school population is the English-language learners (ELLs): students who are learning English as their second language. Indeed, in many southwestern school districts in the United States, ELLs are the majority. The question then arises, *How can we assist the family members of ELL children in reading development?* This can be quite a challenge for teachers who are not bilingual themselves.

One avenue that shows a great deal of promise relates to adult education as part of family involvement with children. It is a well-known and accepted research finding that the mother's level of education correlates positively with the school achievement of her children (McQuillan, 1998). Many mothers of ELL children in urban areas, however, have low levels of education and often cannot speak English themselves. Therefore, there is a double challenge: helping mothers increase their own literacy levels while also teaching them ways to assist their children in reading. Yarosz and Barnett (2001) concluded from their research that parent education programs targeting those with the least education may be especially valuable in trying to improve the literacy levels of children.

A successful research project known as the *Harvest America's Family Reading Program* (Lanteigne & Schwarzer, 1997) provides us with a splendid prototype that can work in many communities. Adult English classes are held in a local library having an extensive collection of adult education and ESL materials. Each week, six children's books are selected that would interest both adults and children. The books are read aloud and discussed as part of the adult class. The focus is on ways of reading aloud to *children* and strategies for discussing the content, new vocabulary, and reactions to the stories. Test results confirmed that the reading proficiency levels of both children *and* adults in the program (many men participate as well as moms) improved dramatically.

Be Proactive

Williams (2001) concluded that teachers must be proactive in seeking family involvement using an *enablement model* (quoting Dunst et al., 1994). Teachers, she said, should

1. *Offer supportive assistance* to adult family members rather than wait for a problem in students' reading to emerge.
2. *Help families set reading goals* such as turning off the television at a designated time each night for family reading.
3. *Suggest materials and activities that will not be an uncomfortable burden* for the family in terms of time or financial resources. You do not want costs to become an obstacle.
4. *Offer aid that can be reciprocated,* if desired. Some families, particularly those from poverty, are more likely to respond if they can "give something back" to the school for what they have received. Even illiterate adults as parent volunteers can be good listeners for children reading aloud, for example.
5. *Try not to interfere with the family's natural supports.* School efforts should not supplant or interfere with a family's own ability to provide reading resources.

In other chapters we offered a *Summary Matrix of Assessments* for procedures and instruments presented for a particular area of reading instruction. Because the topic of this chapter does not, strictly speaking, align with federally mandated areas of reading instruction, nor do the types of assessments presented lend themselves to rigorous reliability or validity studies, we have elected not to include a *Summary Matrix of Assessments* for this chapter.

Activities for Family and Community Involvement

Following is an If-Then chart of family outreach activities found in the remainder of the chapter matched to appropriate grade levels for your convenience. Note that many can be adapted for different levels.

If-Then Strategy Guide for Family and Community Involvement

"Then" try these teaching strategies. ↑ / "If" the student is ready to learn (By Grade Levels) ↘	Dialogic Reading	Make-Believe Alouds	Magazines, Comics, Catalogs	Refrigerator Reading	Family Projects	Voice Mail	Reading Backpacks	Class-books	Writing Briefcase	Buddy Journals	D.E.A.R. City	Ed. Major Pen Pals	Summer Food/Read	Reading Channel	Internet Homepage
K–2	+	+	+	+	+	*	+	+	+	+	+	+	+	+	+
3–4	+	+	+	+	+	+	+	+	+	+	+	+	+	+	+
5–8	–	–	+	*	*	+	*	*	*	+	+	+	+	*	+

Key: + Excellent Strategy
* Adaptable Strategy
– Unsuitable Strategy

PART I: PROVIDING STRATEGIES FOR PARENTS

START OUT RIGHT: CONTACT THE FAMILY

Harry Wong has a superb book that we highly recommend to teachers titled *The First Days of School* (Wong & Wong, 1998) in which he explains how to get your school year off on the right foot. One of his ideas is to send home a letter that [italics added for emphasis]

- Tells parent that you are looking forward to having their child in your class
- Asks parents to put the dates of the school's open house on their calendar and explains that it is important for them to attend as you will be explaining homework, grading, discipline, classroom procedures, and *what they can do at home to help their child succeed*
- Includes a list of materials the child will need at school *and at home*

At the first open house, use that time to "train" your parents on strategies they can use at home that will help their children grow in reading and writing abilities. In this section are strategies and tools you may consider for parent involvement.

PARENTS WITH LIMITED ENGLISH AND/OR READING ABILITY

Given that some of your parents may have limited reading and/or English knowledge, we recommend that your "note" to parents be offered on a VCR tape with you as the speaker. Most families regardless of socioeconomic status have access to a VCR and television. For non-English speakers, you will need to record or have recorded your message in the second language.

DIALOGIC READING

Purpose

One of the most powerful and promising strategies for parents to use is called **dialogic reading** (K. Cooter, 2006). Often thought of as simple picture book reading, dialogic reading has a much different face. It transfers the book's linguistic responsibility to the child who leads the dialogue with his or her parent around the pictures he or she chooses. Some of the original dialogic reading research was done by Whitehurst, Falco, and Lonigan (1988) and was replicated many times in the ensuing years—each time with results that are educationally, linguistically, and statistically significant (Scarborough & Dobrich, 1994; Whitehurst, Arnold, & Epstein, 1994; Huebner, 2001; Huebner & Meltzoff, 2005).

Materials

Any picture book may be used that has illustrations that effectively tell the story. Examples we often use to demonstrate this strategy are *Flossie and the Fox* (McKissack, 1986) and *Chicken Sunday* (Polacco, 1992). Either fiction or nonfiction books may be used, but we favor a heavy diet of nonfiction books for improving language and vocabulary.

Procedure

It is recommended that the text be read first to the child, but that is not the critical element in dialogic reading. The child directs and leads in the conversation around the pictures of the book; the parent is open to the child talk, uses "what" questions, and rephrases and extends the child's utterances but remains at all times the follower in the dialogue. As one child put it, "I talk the book." The parent can be helped to learn how to engage the child in this child-led dialogue as well. The American Library Association, for instance, hosts parent trainings and can help teachers locate trainers throughout the nation in their Every Child Ready to Read @ Your Library program (for more information, see their http://www.ala.org web site).

Picture book "dialogic reading" seems to have the best result of improving the length of children's sentences (Whitehurst et al., 1988; K. Cooter, 2006). Vocabulary becomes more complex and expressive as well. Sometimes just adding gestures is a valuable hint. Mothers who point as they talk establish joint attention and help children learn object names.

Huebner (2000) found that parents must be *taught* to use a book in this language-rich manner. Parents without training typically resort to the more traditional page turning and labeling of story time with their children. This can lead to parents who are increasing their efforts to read to their children at home, but the quality or nature of the reading has not changed.

Parents with limited English literacy skills can easily partner with their child in dialogic reading in that the book itself is a tool in the parent-child dialogue.

MAKE-BELIEVE ALOUDS

Purpose

Reading aloud to children is one of the most common recommendations made by literacy experts and agencies across the nation as a preparation for academic success. But if mama can't read . . ., consider reframing read alouds as simple **make-believe alouds** (K. Cooter, 2006). This is an alternative to read alouds in which parents use picture books to construct their own stories as a means for interacting with their child and the reverse of dialogic reading in which the child constructs the make-believe story.

Materials

As with dialogic reading, picture books rich in illustrations that "tell the story" work best. Either fiction or nonfiction books may be used, but we favor a heavy diet of nonfiction books for improving language and vocabulary. Magazines, comics, and catalogs are also recommended as a low-cost change of pace (K. Cooter, 2006).

Procedure

A parent does not have to know the words on the page to construct a fanciful story about the pictures, nor does storytelling about a picture book story have to be exactly the same for each retelling. A teacher or parent literacy guide can easily demonstrate a variety of ways that any book can be shared without having any knowledge of the words included.

Demonstrate to parents how to move through a book page by page, and create a wildly imaginative tale for fiction selections or rich descriptions and questions that coincide with the pictures and illustrations. Morgan and Goldstein (2004) found that teaching low socioeconomic status (SES) mothers how to use a story book in a fanciful and imaginative manner with their young children increased the type and quality of language in child-parent interactions.

USING MAGAZINES, COMICS, AND CATALOGS

When books are not readily available in the home, many families have access to magazines, comics, or catalogs. Simply engaging the child in conversations using this variety of texts and pictures can stimulate language, vocabulary, and storytelling. One mother we know plays the "Million Dollars" game with her children using assorted catalogs. "If we win a million dollars, we will buy . . . ." A kindergarten teacher borrowed this idea from the family and brought catalogs to create a catalog center in her classroom. She believes it is the most talkative, noisy, and engaging center in her classroom.

REFRIGERATOR READING

Purpose

Whether engaging in a major reading initiative in a large urban center or in a single classroom, communication with families is critical. Many times adults will say to our teachers, "I would love to help my child become a better reader . . . I just don't know what to do. Can you help me?" Cooter et al. (1999) found that monthly newsletters for families are a great vehicle for communicating easy-to-do activities to primary caregivers. Theirs is called *Refrigerator Reading,* a reference to the age-old practice of putting important school papers on the refrigerator for everyone to see.

Materials

Refrigerator Reading newsletters are typically put together on a computer, then photocopied for each child to take home. Thus, you will need access to a computer, printer, and photocopier.

Procedure

The idea is to send home tips for parents on ways they can help their child develop in reading and writing in both Spanish and English, if necessary. You may choose to include such areas as helping your child self-select high-interest books using "rule-of-thumb" method, how to do read alouds, how to encourage recreational writing, being a good listener when your child reads, conducting retellings, questioning after reading, study tips, ways to become involved in your child's classroom as a volunteer, and humorous tales about school life (like one principal's "No whining" rule).

Reports from Cooter et al. (1999) are that some parents collect *Refrigerator Reading* newsletters and mail copies to grandmas and new moms, confirming the usefulness of this easy-to-do medium.

FAMILY PROJECTS

Purpose

Andrea Burkhart (2000), a teacher at a school on the south side of Chicago, asked parents to help her come up with ideas for family-school projects. They responded with many great ideas that she incorporated into her curriculum as *family projects* that get adults at home actively involved.

Materials

Plan on constructing a monthly newsletter with a full description of the family project assignment and "deliverables" (products you would like for the students to bring in to school when the project is done). Sometimes parents are willing to come in with their child to present their product!

Procedure

In Figure 16.2 is an outline of the topics Burkhart (2000) developed for her class. You will want to adapt and expand the descriptions to suit your needs and fit grade-level expectations.

Figure 16.2 Family Projects Curriculum

September: Family Tree
Parents and students work together to trace their family roots. They should create a visual display and present an object that reflects their family history, such as an antique picture, clothing, food, music, or literature.

October: Weather
Parents and students predict weather patterns for the next month. They will watch weather reports to compare their predictions and keep track of their work in a journal.

November: Family Reading Month
Parents and students read to or with each other daily. The books read and the amount of time spent reading will be recorded in a daily log and turned in at the end of November.

December: Biographies
Students learn about biographies and how they are constructed in class. They then create interview questions and interview a parent or primary caregiver. Students write a biography of that person and share it with their family.

January: Measurement
Parents and students predict the measurement (length, width, area, etc.) of an object or distance two or three times each week. After actually measuring each object, a journal entry is completed, showing the predicted measurement and the actual measurement.

February: Poetry Month
A book of family poetry is created. Students are responsible for educating their families about poetry, collecting the poems, and compiling them into a book.

March: Plants
Each student will take home two plants in milk cartons. The student will care for one, and an adult family member the other. One plant will be given light and the other plant will not. The progress of each plant will be tracked by the child and adult together and their progress recorded in a journal entry regularly.

April: Decisions
Two or three times per week students will take home a proposed (hypothetical) question that requires a decision. Topics might include issues related to drugs, gangs, honesty, or others proposed by parents. The parent and child will discuss options together and create a written response.

May: Simple Machines
After learning about simple machines in class, students will construct a simple machine with the guidance of a parent.

Source: From "Breaking the Parental Barrier" by A. L. Burkhart, in T. V. Rasinksi and N. D. Padak, et al. (Eds.), 2000, *Motivating Recreational Reading and Promoting Home-School Connections* (pp. 110–113), Newark, DE: International Reading Association.

VOICE MAIL

Purpose

Many teachers have access to their school district's voice mail system and usually have their own account or number. Willman (2000), a remedial reading teacher, uses voice mail during the summer break to keep contact with her students. They report back to her verbally about books they have chosen to read, and parents are often involved. We feel this strategy could be used throughout the school, as well as during summers for developing readers.

Materials

The primary tools needed for this activity are books for self-selection by students, a touch-tone phone, a voice mail account, and writing materials. For summer use, the students will need three books apiece: two fiction, one nonfiction (Willman, 2000).

Procedure

Begin by creating a letter to the parents explaining how the assignment will work, how to access the voice mail system, and what your expectations include. If you will be using this activity during the school year (as opposed to summer only), plan on conducting this briefing in person at the first open house.

In Willman's (2000) model, she asked students to call in to the voice mail and read aloud for 3 minutes or summarize a chapter from the book they are reading. It is also recommended that you have specific questions for each book for student response. They can answer these questions when they call in to read.

Another adaptation is for students to call in to the school's homework hotline to hear the teacher read aloud portions of the book. This provides a fluent reading model for students. However, a better idea is for parents to read aloud a portion of the book regularly for their child.

Willman (2000) reported that the summer voice mail program succeeded in its inaugural year in preventing all remedial readers from losing ground (26), and one student actually increased his reading level by a half year!

READING BACKPACKS

Purpose

One of the challenges is getting high-quality books into the hands of children at home. Many families are economically disadvantaged and simply do not have books for their children to read. The "reading backpacks" strategy (Cooter et al., 1999) gets books of appropriate interest and reading levels into each child's home at least once per week.

Materials

You will need five backpacks per classroom (with the school logo or mascot, if possible), leveled books that can be sent home, writing materials, card stock, and markers.

Procedure

Based on the *Traveling Tales* backpacks concept (Reutzel & Fawson, 1990; Reutzel & Cooter, 2000) for promoting writing, reading backpacks contain a supply of trade books on varying topics and readability levels (often in both English and Spanish); easy activities for parents to do with their children on printed card stock adapted from Mooney's (1990)

Reading To, With, and *By* strategies; and materials for written responses (markers, colored paper, scissors, etc.). Also included is a simple Family Report Form for adults to note which books were read by the child and to whom, as well any reader response activities they were able to do at home. In this way teachers were able to track student interests and, to a degree, outside reading habits.

Reading backpacks are regarded as a wonderful success in many schools and are treasured by young readers.

CLASSBOOKS

Purpose

Laura Lee Scott (2000), a second-grade teacher, recommends the construction of *classbooks* by students to send home for reading and sharing with parents. Contributions for the classbook are made by each student using the writing process or by the class as a whole using the language experience approach.

Materials

You will need writing materials for individual students to use in the writing process or an easel, markers, and chart paper for use during a language experience with the class. Photocopies of the final classbook for each child will also be needed.

Procedure

Each student composes a contribution (i.e., story, poem, expository passage about a topic of interest, song, etc.) for the classbook independently, or the class writes together using a language experience approach. After working through the revising and editing process, copies of the classbook are taken home by students to share with adult family members. The book can be read *by* students to adults or *to* students by the adult.

Some classbooks have emphasized academic subjects like science and social studies, as well as other topics of personal interest. Titles of student contributions included *If I Could Be a Dinosaur, My Mom,* and *When I Grow Up.* Classbooks constructed by the whole class in a language experience format have included *Halloween Stories* and *Christmas Memories.*

Scott (2000) reports a great success using classbooks, including an increase of parent volunteers during her writing workshop period!

THE WRITING BRIEFCASE

Purpose

The *writing briefcase* (Miller-Rodriguez, 1992) is a brilliant idea that helps parents become more involved with their child's literacy learning. In our interpretation of this activity, students periodically take home a briefcase containing materials helpful in the creation of new compositions. We see the writing briefcase as especially useful for emergent writers and readers in the early grades and as a tool for involving parents in their child's literacy learning at home.

Materials

You will need an old briefcase (a backpack works just as well), stickers and other decorations for the outside of the briefcase, a laminated letter to the family member, markers, crayons, magazine pictures, word cards, picture dictionary, index cards, lined and unlined paper, tape, stapler, paper clips, rubber bands, scissors, and any other writing and illustrating materials of your choice, as well as easy-to-read books of various kinds that may inspire different text types (e.g., poetry, songs, stories, etc.).

Procedure

A different child takes home the briefcase each night and writes (or completes, in some cases) a story and illustrates it. He or she also reads his or her story, as well as the other books enclosed, to family members. A letter included in the briefcase is directed to family members explaining the activity and the importance of their involvement. This letter ideally serves as a follow-up refresher course on the writing and other literacy-learning processes previously described by the teacher at the beginning of the school year in a parent meeting expressly held for that purpose. Figure 16.3 is a sample letter to family members.

Finally, students may wish to have their own writing briefcase or backpack that they can use throughout the year in which to take their compositions and writing materials home. Some students like to emulate adults by "taking work home from the office."

BUDDY JOURNALS

Purpose

Buddy journals (Klobukowski, 2000) are a version of reading logs that have students and parents read the same book together, silently or orally (whatever works best), then respond to each other in a journal. Parents often make superb models of fluent reading and respond well to this activity.

Figure 16.3   Sample Letter for the Writing Briefcase

Sarah Cannon School
711 Opry Place
Nashville, TN 37211

Dear Family Member:

Children in our class are becoming more and more interested and excited about their abilities as writers and readers. I am interested in helping them realize that writing and reading are not just school activities, but are also skills they can use and enjoy at home and in other places.

This writing briefcase allows your child to experience writing at home using the different tools enclosed. I'd like for you to encourage your child to create a story, poem, song, recipe, rap, or any other composition. You might want to encourage your child to take the briefcase and write outside, perhaps in a favorite hiding place.

Please allow your child to try out the enclosed materials. It would be especially helpful if you would take time to listen to your child's finished products. The product may not look like a story or other composition, but you will find that your child can read and understand it. Please have your child return the written composition, along with the writing briefcase, tomorrow.

Sincerely,

Materials

Two copies of the book that will be sent home with the child are needed, as well as two spiral notebooks to serve as buddy logs.

Procedure

The procedure is simple. The adult family member and the child each read the book or portions of the book, then respond in their journals. Then, the adult and child swap journals, read the entry, and respond to the entry. Here are some further suggestions from Klobukowski (2000):

- Encourage parents to reread portions of the text orally, if they are not already reading the book aloud, so that the child can have a reading role model.
- When parents are making entries in their buddy journal, ask them to relate what happened to book characters, to themselves, and to their family and help their child understand these connections.
- Encourage both parents and students to identify the feelings of the characters and share in their journals what they think the characters should do.
- Ask parents to help their children find information in the text and clarify for them any misunderstandings they detect in the buddy journal entries.
- Urge parents to give their children lots of positive reinforcement and praise for what they can do, and avoid negative criticism.
- Parents should try to include humor in their responses.
- Let parents know that this activity will work best if there is an appointed time to complete the task at home. This avoids last-minute rushes to complete a "homework" assignment.

PART II: COMMUNITY INVOLVEMENT

D.E.A.R. "City"!

Purpose

Research indicates that young children average reading only about 7 to 8 minutes during the school day (Anderson, Hiebert, Scott, & Wilkinson, 1985, p. 76). Yet we know that the development of fluent reading requires massive amounts of practice in order to satisfy student interest, build fluency, increase vocabulary, and improve comprehension. Clearly, some sort of sustained silent reading on a daily basis is needed. _D.E.A.R. your city's name here_ (Cooter et al., 1999) sets up a designated day and time, usually by a mayoral proclamation, in which every business, school, and corporation stop for 5 minutes to pull out a book and read as a sign of their unified commitment to the importance of reading.

Materials

This project requires political support, newspaper coverage (an "Op-Ed" piece), media coverage, and a lot of volunteer workers to spread the word.

Procedure

The goal of _D.E.A.R. "City"!_ (modeled after the _Drop Everything And Read_ classroom strategy) is to get everyone in the city to join local schools in making a dramatic statement in support of reading. The original vision in Dallas Public Schools (Cooter et al., 1999) was that citizens would stop whatever they were doing for just 10 minutes at an assigned time (10:00 to 10:10 a.m. on March 6) and read a book, newspaper, or magazine just for fun. Publicity was arranged in cooperation with local newspapers, television and radio stations, and with the city buses that would travel about the city brandishing large advertising banners (see Figure 16.4) to help spread the word.

Who joined the original _D.E.A.R. Dallas_ citywide effort? Nearly everyone. The mayor proclaimed March 6 as "D.E.A.R. Dallas Day" and joined in by reading with all teachers and children of Dallas in grades K–12. The police chief, also a strong supporter of children and education in Dallas, joined in along with downtown businesses and corporate offices as an act of solidarity. Then Governor George W. Bush, seeing _D.E.A.R. Dallas!_ as consonant with his statewide reading initiative, issued a statement praising the effort and reiterating how we must all encourage our children to read everyday for fun and to strengthen their literacy skills for improved life choices.

Getting DEAR time started at the classroom or school level is really quite simple. It begins with an understanding that time set aside for pleasure reading is not a frill but a necessity in a balanced reading program. Teachers should set aside about 20 minutes per day for students to self-select and read books. We teach students to self-select books using the "rule-of-thumb method (Reutzel & Cooter, 2000): After choosing a book of interest, open the book to any page with a lot of words and count the number of words you do not know. If you use all five fingers to count unknown words on one page, the book is too difficult; put it back and choose another you like just as well. Schoolwide DEAR time can be achieved with the principal's support. Simply set aside a time daily in which everyone drops everything to read. It is a truly powerful tool that can have magnificent results so long as everyone participates.

Figure 16.4   D.E.A.R. Dallas Poster

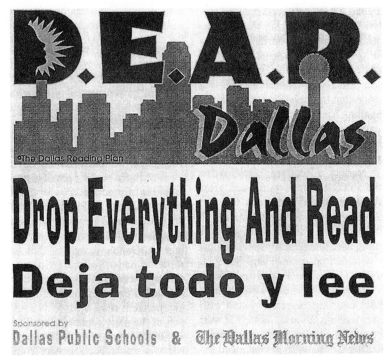

Education Major Pen Pals

Purpose

Education major pen pals (Flickenger, 1991) is a slight variation on the pen pals theme that has met with great success in many areas. Its only substantive difference is that, instead of pairing students with other students or peers, education major pen pals matches students (usually elementary level) with young adults majoring in education at a local college or university. A final book project based on the elementary student is completed jointly between the youngster and the university student.

In addition to providing an audience and reason for writing, this form of pen pals gives students other motivational reasons for reading: the anticipation and receiving of letters, personalized books, or other compositions from the student teachers. Education students are likewise given opportunities as new professionals to connect with students in a way that offers valuable insights.

Materials

Begin by obtaining a list of education majors interested in working with your students. This may be obtained from a local college or university professor (usually specializing in reading, literacy, and/or language arts education) interested in such a project. Materials needed include writing center materials for final drafts of letters, such as writing paper, envelopes, pens, and stamps; bookmaking materials, such as laminating materials, stiff cardboard for book covers, and art materials for illustrations; first draft (messy copy) writing materials (paper and pencils) for the elementary students; transparency-making equipment and materials for the construction of overhead projector examples of each of the writing process stages as they pertain to the composition of letters; and, if possible, a word processor/computer (such as Macintosh, IBM, etc.) on which students can type letters and other compositions.

Procedure

This activity is essentially the same as with the standard pen pals activity, except that students correspond with student teachers attending education classes at the local college or university. Students in early elementary grades are encouraged to use invented (we prefer the term *temporary*) spellings. Elementary students are encouraged to talk and/or draw about families, interests, friends, and special events taking place in their lives at school and at home.

One expectation, which takes the form of a book project, is that university students write books (text only) for their pen pals using what they have learned about their pen pals' interests. The university students bind the nearly finished books but leave room on each page for illustrations. Then, the elementary students illustrate their personalized books and send them back to the university students. After making one or more copies of the finished books, the university students return the original books to their pen pals.

An additional teacher-education benefit is that university students are able to use the letters and other compositions written by their pen pals for analysis of writing development and discovery of children's learning.

SUMMER FOOD AND READING PROGRAM

Purpose

One of the great concerns of urban communities is the welfare of children during the summer months. When schools are out, for example, many children regress in their literacy development. Another worry is that some of the children may not have access to the kind of nutritious meals available to them during the school year. To respond to both of these needs, one community developed a *Summer Food and Reading Program* (Cooter et al., 1999). Community members discovered that a city with numerous, bored, 5- to 12-year-olds; comfortable space available at local churches; a pool of enthusiastic volunteers; and thousands of "gently used" donated books can provide all the ingredients needed for a successful summer "reading and feeding" program.

Materials and Resources

This project requires at least five books per child to be served, volunteer workers, and co-ordination by a local community group.

Procedure

Many have selected the *Reading To, With,* and *By* model (Mooney, 1990) to train volunteers and involve the more reluctant readers. Several teachers usually design and deliver interactive training for the volunteers in effective balanced reading instruction. Making reading *fun* is one of the basic tenets of the training model for the volunteer tutors. Volunteers are taught ways to read aloud favorite poems and stories, encourage buddy reading using big books, make big books, and to use supportive strategies for encouraging children's oral reading. Volunteers are also taught how to establish a print-rich environment using primarily children's work.

To start your own summer reading and nutrition program, we suggest contacting local church leaders, social support agencies, and youth organizations (boys and girls clubs, the local Y, etc.). Urban centers have a number of such agencies looking to leverage their resources through partnering. Business-oriented clubs, such as Rotary International and Kiwanis, can also be helpful in recruiting volunteers and securing funding.

THE READING CHANNEL

Purpose

The purpose of this project is to use a public access television channel available to a school district as an outreach tool for reading development in the home.

Materials and Resources

This primarily requires official contacts and negotiations between the local PBS network provider and the local school district leadership. At least one full-time equivalent teacher will be needed to organize the Reading Channel and serve as liaison with the television station personnel.

Procedure

One of the tools many large urban school districts have at their disposal is one or more "public access" cable television channels from the local providers. The *Reading Channel* (Cooter et al., 1999) can be organized as a support for families in raising literate children. One way this is accomplished is to air each evening during prime time (6 to 9 p.m.) alternative television offerings oriented toward positive literacy habits. As part of the Public Broadcasting System (PBS) and cable television charters, school districts having a public access channel can rerun at no charge any PBS program from the prior year. Thus, such programs as *Reading Rainbow, Mr. Rogers, Sesame Street,* and *Wishbone* can be aired on a new Reading Channel. A regular slate of offerings can be planned so that the Reading Channel can become a welcomed friend to families in the region.

School districts interested in taking advantage of public access channels should do several key things. First, check with the central office administrator in your school district responsible for communications and distance learning initiatives. This person is a valuable resource who will know the details for public access initiatives in your district and the procedures to get things started. If your district is new to this kind of enterprise, then contact the cable television provider in your area directly and inquire as to the public access provisions in its charter. Finally, if you are interested in rebroadcasting PBS television programs like the ones mentioned, get in touch with your area Public Broadcasting affiliate to learn about how you can partner with it to make your plan a reality.

READING INTERNET HOME PAGE

Purpose

As computers in the home, public libraries, workplace, and schools have become increasingly commonplace, many organizations are establishing an Internet home page. The purpose of the *Reading Internet Home Page* is to create another tool for your students that is tailor-made to your curriculum.

Materials

If your school district has a technology department, ask for assistance in setting up an Internet web page of your own. If not, most large business equipment retailers carry software packages for creating web pages.

Procedure

We prefer to persuade a talented "web master" (a techie already on the district payroll) to help us design a new home page as a distance learning tool for parents, teachers, college researchers, foundations, business leaders, and others frequently asking for more information on reading. The web page enables people from literally around the world to access at any time information on upcoming learning events, how to contact teachers and resource professionals, support materials for assisting children in becoming literate in the home, links to other related Internet web sites, and many other options.

The home page is a living document that is constantly under construction and revision (pardon our dust!) and is a terrific tool for serving all stakeholders in the balanced literacy reform effort. (*Note:* If you would like to see one of our home pages, go to http://www.literacyacademy.org.)

SELECTED REFERENCES

Anderson, R. C., Hiebert, E. F., Scott, J. A., & Wilkinson, I. A. G. (1985). *Becoming a nation of readers: The report of the Commission on Reading.* Washington, DC: The National Institute of Education.

Barton, P. (1992). *America's smallest school: The family.* Princeton, NJ: Educational Testing Service.

Barton, P. (1994). *Becoming literate about literacy.* Princeton, NJ: Educational Testing Service.

Burkhart, A. L. (2000). Breaking the parental barrier. In T. V. Rasinski, N. D. Padak, et al. (Eds.), *Motivating recreational reading and promoting home-school connections* (pp. 110–113). Newark, DE: International Reading Association.

Cooter, K. S. (2006). When Mama can't read: Counteracting intergenerational illiteracy. *The Reading Teacher, 59*(7), 698–702.

Cooter, R. B. (Ed.). (2004). *Perspectives on rescuing urban literacy education: Spies, saboteurs, and saints.* Mahwah, NJ: Lawrence Erlbaum.

Cooter, R. B., Mills-House, E., Marrin, P., Mathews, B., & Campbell, S. (May, 1999). Family and community involvement: The bedrock of reading success. *The Reading Teacher, 52*(8), 891–896.

Dunst, C., Trivette, C.M., & Deal, A.G. (Eds.) (1994). *Supporting and strengthening families: Methods, strategies and practices.* Cambridge, MA: Brookline Books.

Farrar, E. B. (1985). *Accelerating the oral language of children of low socio-economic status.* Belle Glade, FL: Unpublished Dissertation. (ERIC Document Reproduction Service No. ED 262 913).

Flickenger, G. (1991). Pen pals and collaborative books. *The Reading Teacher, 45*(1), 72–73.

Garshelis, J., & McConnell, S. (1993). Comparison of family needs assessed by mothers, individual professionals, and interdisciplinary teams. *Journal of Early Intervention, 17,* 36–49.

Handel, R. D. (1999). The multiple meanings of family literacy. *Education & Urban Society, 32*(1), 127–144.

Harvard Education Letter. (2005). Playing with words. *Harvard Education Letter, 21*(6), 7.

Huebner, C. E. (2000). Promoting toddlers' language development: A randomized trial of a community-based intervention. *Journal of Applied Developmental Psychology, 21,* 513–535.

Huebner, C. E. (2001). *Hear and say reading with toddlers.* Bainbridge Island, WA: Bainbridge Island Rotary (instructional video).

Huebner, C. E., & Meltzoff, A. N. (2005). Intervention to change parent-child reading style: A comparison of instructional methods. *Applied Developmental Psychology, 26,* 296–313.

Kaderavek, J. N., & Justice, L. M. (2005). The effect of book genre in repeated readings of mothers and their children with language impairment: a pilot investigation. *Child Language Teaching and Therapy, 21*(1), 75–92.

Klobukowski, P. (2000). Parents, buddy journals, and teacher response. In T. V. Rasinski, N. D. Padak, et al. (Eds.), *Motivating recreational reading and promoting home-school connections* (pp. 74–78). Newark, DE: International Reading Association.

Lanteigne, B., & Schwarzer, D. (1997). The progress of Rafael in English and family reading: A case study. *Journal of Adolescent and Adult Literacy, 4*(1), 36–45.

McKissack, P. (1986). *Flossie and the fox.* New York: Dial.

McQuillan, J. (1998). *The literacy crisis: False claims, real solutions.* Portsmouth, NH: Heinemann Educational Books.

Miller, P. (1978). *Direct instruction in language and speaking: A study of mother-child discourse in a working class community.* Rockville, MD: National Institute of Mental Health. (ERIC Document Reproduction Service No. ED 178 203)

Miller-Rodriguez, K. (1992). Home Writing Activities: The writing briefcase and the traveling suitcase. *The Reading Teacher, 45,* 160–161.

Mooney, M. E. (1990). *Reading to, with, and by children.* Katonah, NY: Richard Owen.

Morgan, L., & Goldstein, H. (2004). Teaching mothers of low socioeconomic status to use decontextualized language during storybook reading. *Journal of Early Intervention, 26*(4), 235–252.

Murray, A. D. (1990). Fine-tuning of utterance length to preverbal infants: Effects on later language development. *Journal of Child Language, 17*(3), 511–525.

Peterson, P., Carta, J, & Greenwood, C. (2005). Teaching milieu language skills to parents in multiple risk families. *Journal of Early Intervention, 27,* 94–109.

Polacco, P. (1992). *Chicken Sunday.* New York: Philomel.

Remaly, B. K. (1990). *Strategies for increasing the expressive vocabulary of kindergarten children.* Fort Lauderdale, FL: Nova University. (ERIC Document Reproduction Service No. ED 332 234)

Reutzel, D. R., & Cooter, R. B. (2000). *Teaching children to read: Putting the pieces together.* Upper Saddle River, NJ: Merrill/Prentice Hall.

Reutzel, D. R., & Fawson, P. C. (1990). Traveling tales: Connecting parents and children in writing. *The Reading Teacher, 44,* 222–227.

Scarborough, H. S., & Dobrich, W. (1994). On the efficacy of reading to preschoolers. *Developmental Review, 14,* 245–302.

Scott, L. L. (2000). Classbooks: Linking the classroom to the home. In T. V. Rasinski, N. D. Padak, et al. (Eds.), *Motivating recreational reading and promoting home-school connections* (pp. 93–94). Newark, DE: International Reading Association.

Tamis-LeMonda, C. S., Shannon, J. D., Cabrera, N. J., & Lamb, M. E. (2004). Fathers and mothers at play with their 2 and 3 year olds: Contributions to language and cognitive development. *Child Development, 75,* 1806–1820.

Whitehurst, G. J., Arnold, D. S., & Epstein, J. N. (1994). A picture book reading intervention in day care and home for children from low income families. *Developmental Psychology, 30,* 679–689.

Whitehurst, G. J., Falco, F. L., & Lonigan, C. J. (1988). Accelerating language development through picture book reading. *Developmental Psychology, 24,* 552–559.

Will, G. (2002, January 6). Mom and dad mean more than Miss Wormwood. *Fort Worth Star-Telegram,* p. 4E.

Williams, S. G. (2001). *Participation of families in interventions.* Unpublished manuscript, George Peabody College of Vanderbilt University, Nashville, TN.

Willman, A. T. (2000). "Hello, Mrs. Willman, it's me!": Keep kids reading over the summer by using voice mail. In T. V. Rasinski, N. D. Padak, et al. (Eds.), *Motivating recreational reading and promoting home-school connections* (pp. 51–52). Newark, DE: International Reading Association.

Wong, H. K., & Wong, R. T. (1998). *The first days of school.* Mountain View, CA: Harry Wong.

Yarosz, D. J., & Barnett, W. S. (2001). Who reads to young children?: Identifying predictors of family reading activities. *Reading Psychology, 22*(1).

Appendix

Directions for Responding to the CLEP

Purpose of the CLEP

The CLEP is an instrument that can be used by teachers, administrators, and researchers to assess the "print richness" of kindergarten and elementary school classrooms (K–6).

General Directions

This instrument may be used with or without the teacher and students present in the classroom. No feedback is needed from anyone to respond to the items. All judgments are made based on the observable literacy tools, materials, arrangements in the classroom.

Time schedule

30 min.– Completing rating scale in classroom

10 min.– Scoring rating scale and interpreting score

40 min.– Total time required

Directions for Responding to the Rating Scale

The descriptors for each item evidence increased implementation of a "print rich" classroom environment. A rating of 1 is the lowest level of implementation and 7 represents the highest. Therefore, it is imperative to read all descriptors for each item progressing from 1 through 7 before selecting a rating.

Descriptors at 1, 3, 5, and 7 on the rating scale are explicitly stated. Circle one of these numbers if the description accurately matches the environment. If 1, 3, 5, or 7 is not a match, then select 2, 4, or 6 which are implied descriptors indicating degrees of implementation between two descriptors. Circle the selected number above the rating scale.

For example, to select a rating for item # 4, you might follow these thought processes. If about 200 books are present, circle a rating of 3. If about 75 books are present, circle a rating of 2. If about 275 books are present, circle a rating of 4.

Definition of Terms

Literacy Event

A communicative act in which reading, writing, speaking, and/or listening are integral to the participants' interactions and interpretive processes.

LITERACY PRODUCTS

A concrete object or a demonstratable event that occurs as the result of interaction with literacy tools.

LITERACY TOOLS

Physical objects present in the environment which support the acquisition of literacy (e.g., paper, pencils, professionally published books and magazines, adult- and child-authored materials, computers, and bookshelves).

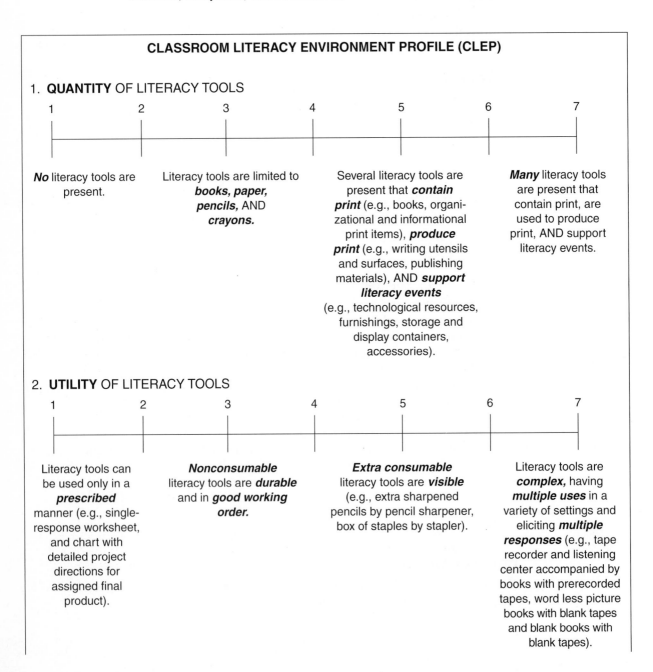

CLASSROOM LITERACY ENVIRONMENT PROFILE (CLEP)

1. QUANTITY OF LITERACY TOOLS

1   2   3   4   5   6   7

No literacy tools are present.

Literacy tools are limited to **books, paper, pencils,** AND **crayons.**

Several literacy tools are present that **contain print** (e.g., books, organizational and informational print items), **produce print** (e.g., writing utensils and surfaces, publishing materials), AND **support literacy events** (e.g., technological resources, furnishings, storage and display containers, accessories).

Many literacy tools are present that contain print, are used to produce print, AND support literacy events.

2. UTILITY OF LITERACY TOOLS

1   2   3   4   5   6   7

Literacy tools can be used only in a **prescribed** manner (e.g., single-response worksheet, and chart with detailed project directions for assigned final product).

Nonconsumable literacy tools are **durable** and in **good working order.**

Extra consumable literacy tools are **visible** (e.g., extra sharpened pencils by pencil sharpener, box of staples by stapler).

Literacy tools are **complex,** having **multiple uses** in a variety of settings and eliciting **multiple responses** (e.g., tape recorder and listening center accompanied by books with prerecorded tapes, word less picture books with blank tapes and blank books with blank tapes).

3. **APPROPRIATENESS** OF LITERACY TOOLS

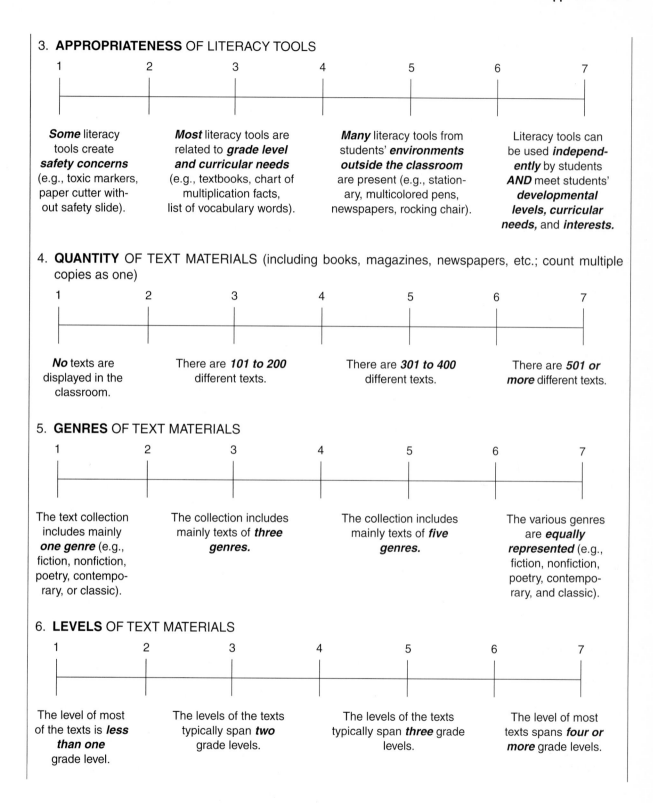

1	2	3	4	5	6	7

Some literacy tools create *safety concerns* (e.g., toxic markers, paper cutter without safety slide).

Most literacy tools are related to *grade level and curricular needs* (e.g., textbooks, chart of multiplication facts, list of vocabulary words).

Many literacy tools from students' *environments outside the classroom* are present (e.g., stationary, multicolored pens, newspapers, rocking chair).

Literacy tools can be used *independently* by students *AND* meet students' *developmental levels, curricular needs,* and *interests.*

4. **QUANTITY** OF TEXT MATERIALS (including books, magazines, newspapers, etc.; count multiple copies as one)

1	2	3	4	5	6	7

No texts are displayed in the classroom.

There are *101 to 200* different texts.

There are *301 to 400* different texts.

There are *501 or more* different texts.

5. **GENRES** OF TEXT MATERIALS

1	2	3	4	5	6	7

The text collection includes mainly *one genre* (e.g., fiction, nonfiction, poetry, contemporary, or classic).

The collection includes mainly texts of *three genres.*

The collection includes mainly texts of *five genres.*

The various genres are *equally represented* (e.g., fiction, nonfiction, poetry, contemporary, and classic).

6. **LEVELS** OF TEXT MATERIALS

1	2	3	4	5	6	7

The level of most of the texts is *less than one* grade level.

The levels of the texts typically span *two* grade levels.

The levels of the texts typically span *three* grade levels.

The level of most texts spans *four or more* grade levels.

7. **FORMAT** AND **CONTENT** OF TEXT MATERIALS

| 1 | 2 | 3 | 4 | 5 | 6 | 7 |

Only textbooks are present.

A few of the text materials include ***varying formats*** (e.g., newspapers, magazines, paperback books, hardcover books, big books, catalogues, directories) AND ***content*** (e.g., plays, joke and riddle books, books about movies or television shows, books reflecting cultural and ethnic diversity, picture books, wordless books, student-authored).

Many of the text materials include ***varying formats*** AND ***content.***

The collection of text materials includes a ***wide assortment*** of formats AND content.

8. PRINT USED FOR CLASSROOM **ORGANIZATION**

| 1 | 2 | 3 | 4 | 5 | 6 | 7 |

No printed directions, schedules, OR labels are visible.

Some displayed print is used for ***organizational*** (e.g., class rules and expectations; daily, weekly or monthly assignments; school lunch menus) AND ***labeling*** (e.g., contents of shelves and storage containers) purposes.

Some displayed print is ***associated with literacy tools and events*** (e.g., timetables for use of materials and areas, project guidelines, sign-up sheets for reading/writing conferences).

A wide assortment of print in the form of directions, schedules, AND labels is clearly visible.

9. CLASSROOM **LITERACY PRODUCT** DISPLAYS

| 1 | 2 | 3 | 4 | 5 | 6 | 7 |

No displays of student or class activities ***include print.***

Several of the displays of student or class activities ***include print*** AND ***most*** of the print is ***teacher-produced.***

Many displays of student or class activities ***include print*** AND ***most*** of the print is ***student-produced.***

Both teacher- and student-produced print is included in displays of student or class activities with the ***majority*** of the print being ***student-produced.***

10. REFERENCE MATERIALS

1	2	3	4	5	6	7

No reference materials are present.

Several reference materials of **frequently used information** are present (e.g., students' names, calendar, alphabet, maps, globe, student dictionaries, a set of encyclopedias, almanac, atlas).

Several reference materials provide **literacy guidelines** (e.g., editing markings, writing format models, frequently misspelled words).

Numerous reference materials of frequently used information and literacy guidelines are **present** with **several** designed to support the creation of **open-ended literacy products** (e.g., rhyming word book, thesaurus, spelling dictionary, address file, word bank).

11. WRITTEN COMMUNICATIONS

1	2	3	4	5	6	7

No written communications are present.

Most written communications are **commercial published** (e.g., books, posters, charts).

Some adult-authored (e.g., school or classroom announcements, teacher-written directions on chalkboard) AND **student-authored** (e.g., books, notes, bulletin board titles) written communications are present.

There are **about equal numbers** of **commercially published** AND **adult- and student-authored** written communications.

12. WRITING UTENSILS

1	2	3	4	5	6	7

No writing utensils are **present**.

Writing utensils are **limited** to **crayons, #2 lead pencils, white or yellow chalk,** AND **dry erase pens.**

Writing utensils include **several** different types of **pens and pencils** AND a **computer with a word processing program.**

A variety of **many** difference **types, sizes, shapes, and colors** of writing utensils are present (e.g., lettering stencils, alphabet stamps with assorted colors of inkpads).

13. WRITING **SURFACES**

1	2	3	4	5	6	7

No writing surfaces are present.

Writing surfaces are limited to ***wall-mounted chalk or marker boards*** AND ***lined writing paper.***

Writing surfaces include ***individual chalk or marker boards*** AND ***different types of paper*** (e.g., chart, story, unlined, butcher, newsprint, construction).

A variety of different **types, sizes, shapes, AND *colors*** of writing surfaces are present (e.g., a computer printer, stationery, graph paper, post-it notes, postcards, blank books).

14. **PUBLISHING MATERIALS**

1	2	3	4	5	6	7

No literacy tools to use in publishing literacy products are available.

Several literacy tools are available to ***edit*** (e.g., revised draft, date rubber stamps and stamp pads; correction tape and erasers; paper clips), ***assemble*** (e.g., tape, glue, stapler, brads, plastic covers, stencils, stickers), OR ***decorate*** (e.g., fabric, ribbon, yarn, lace, buttons, pictures) literacy products.

Many literacy tools are available to ***edit, assemble,*** AND ***decorate*** literacy products.

About an ***equal number*** of a ***wide variety*** of literacy tools are available to ***edit, assemble*** AND ***decorate.***

15. **TECHNOLOGICAL RESOURCES** TO SUPPORT LITERACY EVENTS

1	2	3	4	5	6	7

No technological resources to support literacy learning are present.

Several technological resources are available for ***teachers' use*** in supporting literacy events (e.g., overhead projector, laser pointer, computer with printer) AND for ***prescribed student interactions*** in literacy events (e.g., listening center with phonograph, cassette or CD player and books with text recorded on records, tapes, or CDs; television and VCR with recorded stories on video tapes; computer with literacy-learning programs).

Several technological resources support ***students' open-ended interactions*** in literacy events (e.g., video camera and blank videotapes; cassette recorder and blank cassette tapes; photographic camera with film; computer printer, and word processing program).

A ***variety*** of technological resources are available for ***teacher and student use*** in both a ***prescribed and open-ended manner.***

16. **FURNISHINGS** TO SUPPORT LITERACY EVENTS

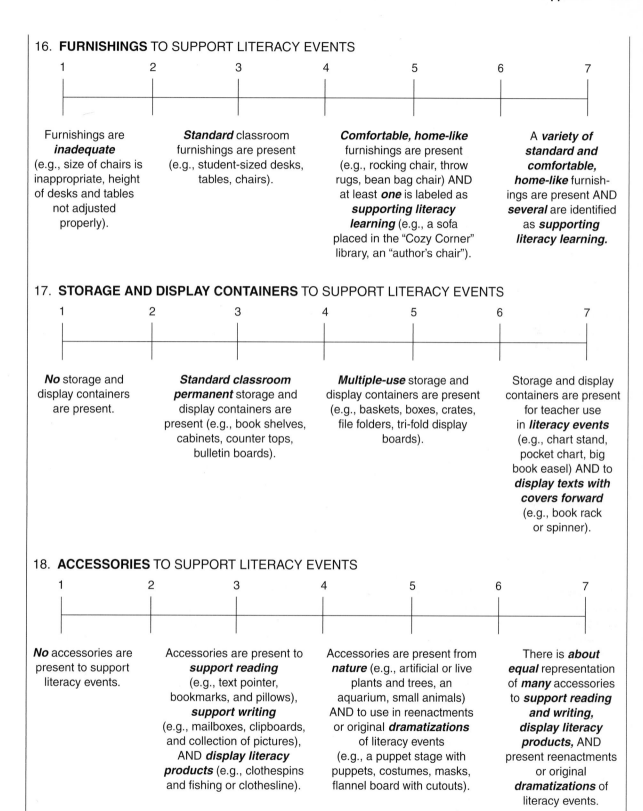

1   2   3   4   5   6   7

Furnishings are **inadequate** (e.g., size of chairs is inappropriate, height of desks and tables not adjusted properly).

Standard classroom furnishings are present (e.g., student-sized desks, tables, chairs).

Comfortable, home-like furnishings are present (e.g., rocking chair, throw rugs, bean bag chair) AND at least **one** is labeled as **supporting literacy learning** (e.g., a sofa placed in the "Cozy Corner" library, an "author's chair").

A **variety of standard and comfortable, home-like** furnishings are present AND **several** are identified as **supporting literacy learning.**

17. **STORAGE AND DISPLAY CONTAINERS** TO SUPPORT LITERACY EVENTS

1   2   3   4   5   6   7

No storage and display containers are present.

Standard classroom permanent storage and display containers are present (e.g., book shelves, cabinets, counter tops, bulletin boards).

Multiple-use storage and display containers are present (e.g., baskets, boxes, crates, file folders, tri-fold display boards).

Storage and display containers are present for teacher use in **literacy events** (e.g., chart stand, pocket chart, big book easel) AND to **display texts with covers forward** (e.g., book rack or spinner).

18. **ACCESSORIES** TO SUPPORT LITERACY EVENTS

1   2   3   4   5   6   7

No accessories are present to support literacy events.

Accessories are present to **support reading** (e.g., text pointer, bookmarks, and pillows), **support writing** (e.g., mailboxes, clipboards, and collection of pictures), AND **display literacy products** (e.g., clothespins and fishing or clothesline).

Accessories are present from **nature** (e.g., artificial or live plants and trees, an aquarium, small animals) AND to use in reenactments or original **dramatizations** of literacy events (e.g., a puppet stage with puppets, costumes, masks, flannel board with cutouts).

There is **about equal** representation of **many** accessories to **support reading and writing, display literacy products,** AND present reenactments or original **dramatizations** of literacy events.

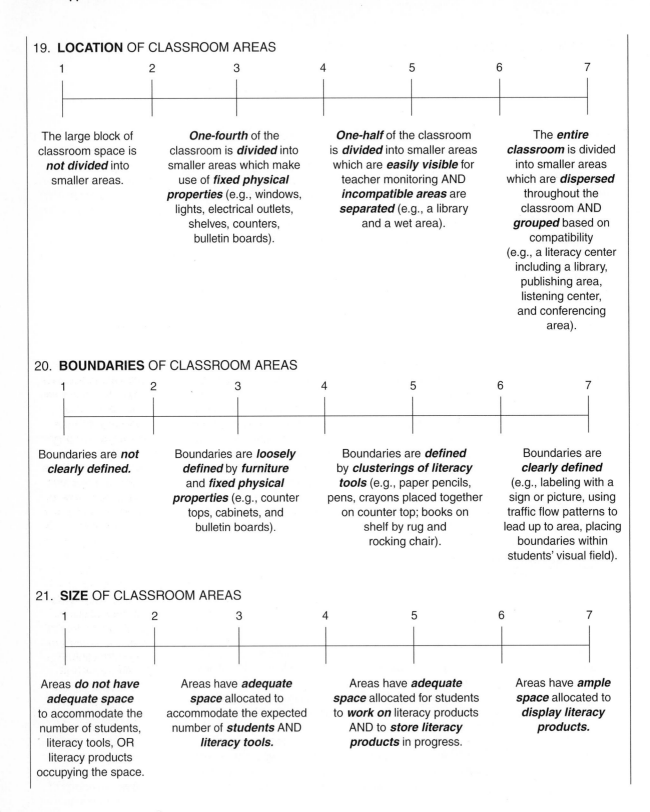

19. **LOCATION** OF CLASSROOM AREAS

| 1 | 2 | 3 | 4 | 5 | 6 | 7 |

The large block of classroom space is **not divided** into smaller areas.

One-fourth of the classroom is **divided** into smaller areas which make use of **fixed physical properties** (e.g., windows, lights, electrical outlets, shelves, counters, bulletin boards).

One-half of the classroom is **divided** into smaller areas which are **easily visible** for teacher monitoring AND **incompatible areas** are **separated** (e.g., a library and a wet area).

The **entire classroom** is divided into smaller areas which are **dispersed** throughout the classroom AND **grouped** based on compatibility (e.g., a literacy center including a library, publishing area, listening center, and conferencing area).

20. **BOUNDARIES** OF CLASSROOM AREAS

| 1 | 2 | 3 | 4 | 5 | 6 | 7 |

Boundaries are **not clearly defined.**

Boundaries are **loosely defined** by **furniture** and **fixed physical properties** (e.g., counter tops, cabinets, and bulletin boards).

Boundaries are **defined** by **clusterings of literacy tools** (e.g., paper pencils, pens, crayons placed together on counter top; books on shelf by rug and rocking chair).

Boundaries are **clearly defined** (e.g., labeling with a sign or picture, using traffic flow patterns to lead up to area, placing boundaries within students' visual field).

21. **SIZE** OF CLASSROOM AREAS

| 1 | 2 | 3 | 4 | 5 | 6 | 7 |

Areas **do not have adequate space** to accommodate the number of students, literacy tools, OR literacy products occupying the space.

Areas have **adequate space** allocated to accommodate the expected number of **students** AND **literacy tools.**

Areas have **adequate space** allocated for students to **work on** literacy products AND to **store literacy products** in progress.

Areas have **ample space** allocated to **display literacy products.**

22. **TYPES** OF CLASSROOM AREAS

No literacy purposes are associated with any classroom areas.

There are areas for **small group** AND **whole class literacy instruction** (e.g., thematic or curriculum studies, writing and publishing, silent reading).

There are areas for **individual literacy instruction** (e.g., reading or writing conferencing) AND a **classroom library** is present.

Every classroom area has one or more recognizable **literacy purposes** associated with it.

23. **CLASSROOM LIBRARY**

No part of the classroom functions as a library.

A **small collection of books** is placed at one location.

A **clearly identifiable** area is **labeled** as the library. Bookshelves or furniture are used to establish **boundaries** and create **privacy.** The library is located in a **quiet** area outside the general traffic pattern and accommodates at least **5-6 students.**

The library is **highly visible** and occupies up to 25% of the wall space. It contains **literacy-oriented displays and props** which encourage reading and participation in extension activities. **Books** are displayed both **spine and cover forward** and include a variety of **genres and reading levels.** The book collection includes **duplicate copies** of favorite books and a total of **5–6 books per student.** The library is furnished with **comfortable seating** and is **well lighted.**

24. GROUPING OF LITERACY TOOLS

1   2   3   4   5   6   7

No groupings of literacy tools are evident.

A few literacy tools are neatly arranged in several areas.

Many literacy tools are **organized thematically** in **several areas** (e.g., by science, math, or social studies topics).

A **variety** of **many** literacy tools, **including boxes of leveled books,** are grouped in **all areas** of the classroom.

25. ACCESSIBILITY OF LITERACY TOOLS

1   2   3   4   5   6   7

Literacy tools are **not readily accessible.**

Many literacy tools are at **eye level or below, easy to reach,** AND **clearly visible.**

Many literacy tools are clearly **labeled** AND **organized** by type and use.

Most literacy tools are **readily accessible.**

26. PARTICIPATION IN LITERACY EVENTS IS ENCOURAGED

1   2   3   4   5   6   7

There is **no written or artistic evidence** to **encourage reading and writing** OR identify them as **pleasurable activities.**

Several commercially- and **teacher-produced** print items encourage reading and writing AND identify them as **pleasurable activities** (e.g., posters, signs, book covers).

Book recommendations by students AND teachers are displayed.

The **classroom is filled** with students' **written and artistic responses** which encourage reading and writing and suggest that reading and writing are pleasurable activities.

27. PARTICIPATION IN LITERACY EVENTS IS INVITING

1   2   3   4   5   6   7

Literacy tools are **not prominently displayed.**

Literacy tools, **especially books,** are **prominently displayed.**

Displays of literacy tools are enhanced with **natural features** (e.g., plants, shells, lighting, an aquarium).

Displays of literacy tools that include **varying textures, colors,** AND **objects** to create an attractive and comfortable museum-like atmosphere

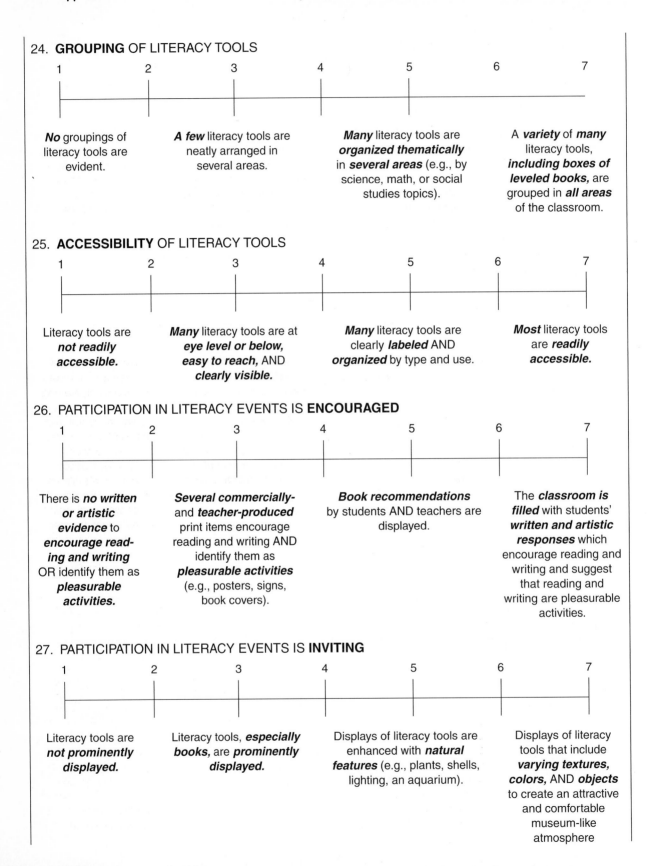

28. AUTHENTIC LITERACY **SETTINGS**

| 1 | 2 | 3 | 4 | 5 | 6 | 7 |

There is **no evidence** of attempts to connect reading and writing with **authentic settings.**

A few authentic literacy tools are present (e.g., a couch and lamp in the classroom library, newspapers and magazines, a calendar, recipes).

Several displayed literacy tools and products replicate **authentic settings** (e.g., book clubs, puppet theater, mailboxes, library, editing and publishing area resembling an office).

Most areas are enriched with **several authentic literacy tools** creating a **realistic atmosphere.**

29. AUTHENTIC LITERACY **EVENTS**

| 1 | 2 | 3 | 4 | 5 | 6 | 7 |

There is **no evidence** of attempts to connect reading and writing with **authentic events.**

Several displays of written texts indicate that reading and writing are included in **daily routines** (e.g., student completed assignment sheets, sign-up sheets for equipment use, written schedules of classroom activities).

Several displays of written texts indicate that reading and writing are related to **events outside the classroom** (e.g., intramural schedules, school lunch menus, public library programs, weather reports, current events).

Many displays of written texts indicate students use reading and writing for their **own purposes and interest** (e.g., recording field trip experiences, science experiments, library check-outs; responding with thank you cards, letters, notes on message board).

30. **INTERACTIONS** WITH LITERACY TOOLS

| 1 | 2 | 3 | 4 | 5 | 6 | 7 |

Literacy tools are only used in a **prescribed** manner (e.g., project directions with an example of the expected final product, chart with behavior expectations).

A few classroom areas give **options** for interactions with literacy tools (e.g., a classroom library that includes many books, magazines, and newspapers; a listening center with assorted books and accompanying cassettes; floor pillows, a rocking chair, and a tent).

Several classroom areas extend the **freedom** to use literacy tools as needed (e.g., extra consumable supplies are visible; a range of literacy tools are gathered in the areas).

A variety of **many** literacy tools is available to use in an **open-ended** manner in **each classroom area** (e.g., a tape recorder with blank tapes, bulletin board with areas designated for each student to display literacy products).

31. **RECORD KEEPING** OF LITERACY INTERACTIONS

1	2	3	4	5	6	7

There is *no* visible record keeping of *class* OR *individual* students' participation in literacy events.

There are a few visible records of *class* participation in literacy events (e.g., a list of books read aloud in class, a tally of time spent by the class reading outside of school, a display of correspondence from authors).

One record of *individual* students' participation in literacy events is visible (e.g., record of books read or time spent reading, portfolio of writing samples, journal of daily reflections on readings).

Several records of *individual* students' participation in literacy events are visible.

32. **VARIETY** OF LITERACY PRODUCTS

1	2	3	4	5	6	7

Displayed literacy products follow the *same format* (e.g., worksheets with identical responses in each blank).

Most literacy products are **curriculum related; long term,** taking more than one school day to complete; AND in *a formal format* (e.g., final copy, published).

Several short term (e.g., completed in one school day) AND *informal* (e.g., personal messages, homework lists) literacy products are present.

There is a *balance* between *many short term/long term* AND *formal/informal* literacy products. Literacy products include students' *original content* in both *creative* (e.g., story extensions, dioramas, poems) AND *functional forms* (e.g., thank you notes, letters, school/class newspapers).

33. **SHARING** LITERACY PRODUCTS

1	2	3	4	5	6	7

No students' literacy products are displayed.

Students' literacy products are displayed in *different forums* (e.g., bulletin board with designated areas for each student's literacy products, author's chair).

Students' literacy products are displayed in *clearly designated areas* (e.g., student-authored books on labeled shelf, students' informal notes on message board).

Many literacy products are displayed AND have been *completed within the last two weeks* (e.g., products are dated or are clearly related to current topics of study).

CLEP Scoring Guide

1. Enter each rating in the spaces below and total Subscale 1 and Subscale 2.

Subscale 1

1. _____
2. _____
3. _____
4. _____
5. _____
6. _____
7. _____
8. _____
9. _____
10. _____
11. _____
12. _____
13. _____
14. _____
15. _____
16. _____
17. _____

_____ **Total: Subscale 1**

Subscale 2

18. _____
19. _____
20. _____
21. _____
22. _____
23. _____
24. _____
25. _____
26. _____
27. _____
28. _____
29. _____
30. _____
31. _____
32. _____
33. _____

_____ **Total: Subscale 2**

2. Complete each equation for Subscale 1 and Subscale 2.

Subscale 1

_____   divided by   18 =

Subscale 1 Total   divided by   18 = **Subscale 1 Score**

Subscale 2

_____   divided by   15 =

Subscale 2 Total   divided by   15 = **Subscale 2 Score**

3. Enter the score for each Subscale on the scale below.

Subscale 1

1   2   3   4   5   6   7

Subscale 2

1   2   3   4   5   6   7

Interpretive Descriptions

Subscale 1: Provisioning the classroom with literacy tools

1.0-2.4 = Impoverished

> An unacceptably small number of a few different types of literacy tools are present. Some of the literacy tools are of low utility being damaged, outdated, or undersupplied.

2.5-3.9 = Minimal

> Several different types of literacy tools are present in moderate amounts. There are enough literacy tools to support the number of students in the classroom.

4.0-5.4 = Satisfactory

> An acceptable number of literacy tools of all types are present. The literacy tools are in good working order.

5.5-7.0 = Enriched

> The classroom is abundantly supplied with all types of literacy tools. The literacy tools are complex, elicit multiple responses in varied settings, and are developmentally appropriate.

Subscale 2: Arranging classroom space and literacy tools, gaining students' interest in literacy events, and sustaining students' interactions with literacy tools

1.0-2.4 = Impoverished

> The physical environment provides little support to literacy acquisition. There is a bleak or stark quality in the classroom atmosphere due to the random placement of only a few literacy tools. Literacy tools or products are not featured. Literacy is not identified as a valued goal.

2.5-3.9 = Minimal

> The physical environment provides some support to literacy acquisition. The classroom atmosphere has a neutral feeling and does not capture the observer's interest. A narrow range of literacy tools and products are present but not featured. Literacy is not identified as a valued goal.

4.0-5.4 = Satisfactory

> The physical environment provides an acceptable level of support to literacy acquisition. A comfortable classroom atmosphere is created by the presence of many literacy tools of varying types and the display of some literacy products. Literacy is identified as one of several curricular goals.

5.5-7.0 = Enriched

> The physical environment provides optimum effectiveness in support of literacy acquisition. A museum-like quality and pleasing ambience is created by prominently featured literacy tools and products. Literacy is easily identified as a valued, life-long goal.

Chart on p p. 504–514, material on pp. 515–516 from "Directions for Responding to the CLEP and Appendix D from Wolfersberger, M., Reutzel, D. F., Sudweeks, R. & Fawson, P. F. (2004). Developing and Validating the Classroom Literacy Environmental PRofile (CLEP): A Tool for Examining the "Print Richness" of Elementary Classrooms. *Journal of Literary Research, 36*(2), 211–272.

Name Index

Subject Index